W9-BKG-442

MODERN RHETORIC

Cleanth Brooks

Robert Penn Warren

MODERN

RHETORIC

SECOND EDITION

HARCOURT, BRACE & WORLD, INC.

NEW YORK / BURLINGAME

COPYRIGHT, 1949, © 1958, BY HARCOURT, BRACE & WORLD, INC.

All rights reserved. No part of this book may be reproduced in any form by mimeograph or any other means, without permission in writing from the publisher.

[f · 6 · 61]

PRINTED IN THE UNITED STATES OF AMERICA

to David M. Clay

PREFACE

With this revision of *Modern Rhetoric* we have not changed our notion of what such a book should be. This revision is, rather, an attempt to realize our original notion more clearly and vigorously. We are convinced that good writing is not merely a matter of rules or tricks but a natural expression of necessary modes of thought. Good writing cannot be learned — or cannot readily be learned — by a process of blind absorption, trial and error, or automatic conditioning. It is learned as the student becomes aware of the underlying principles. If, in the practical, day-to-day business of writing, the student can be made constantly aware of the principles underlying what he is trying to do, then he comes to a deeper realization of the workings of his own mind and feelings and, through that realization, to a greater skill in expressing himself.

The first thing we have tried to do is to make the theory that informs the book more readily accessible to the ordinary student. To this end we have eliminated certain distinctions, omitted some theoretical niceties that might blur more fundamental matters, and have relegated some of the specialized discussions to the appendixes.

Our second aim has been to make the book itself more practical for classroom use. With this in mind, we have included a large number of student themes, not merely to provide models to be imitated or examples of what is to be avoided, but also, in some instances, to illustrate the actual process of composition and, in all instances, to counterpoint the literary selections to which the student's attention is constantly called. We have also rewritten the exercises in order to provide the student with more specific and attractive invitations to develop his own skill. With this end in view, we have tried to make references to the Readings more systematic and fruitful. In the Readings themselves, we would point out, we have increased the number of selections, with the idea of furnishing greater variety in subject matter and tone.

One of the changes aimed at making *Modern Rhetoric* more useful is the addition of a handbook of grammar and usage. Since our book, as the title indicates, is primarily a rhetoric, the handbook is concise and is designed chiefly for reference, with a great deal of space devoted to the highly practical matter of " Exceptions and Problems." In our approach to grammar, though we have included some of the more useful formulations of the functional grammarians, we have attempted no radical innovations.

One further consideration: A book about writing should, alas, be well written. We hope that, with time and tears, we have refined our own style.

Whatever improvement appears in this revision of *Modern Rhetoric* is largely due to the criticisms and suggestions of friends of the book. Though these friends are many and all merit our deep gratitude, we wish to make special mention of Mr. Lloyd Bruno of Sacramento Junior College, Mr. Henry Cassady of Hartnell College, Mr. Sanford Kahrmann of Columbia University, Mr. Daniel A. Lindley, Jr., the Reverend Dennis B. McCarthy, O.P., of Providence College, Mr. Ernest Nagel of Columbia University, Mr. George B. Rodman of the University of Wisconsin, Mr. Gerald A. Smith of the University of Rochester, Mr. Richard M. Weaver of the University of Chicago, Mr. Rulon Wells of Yale University, Mr. Harold Whitehall of Indiana University, and particularly Mr. Donald A. Sears of Upsala College, who kindly provided us with very valuable material.

C. B.

R. P. W.

CONTENTS

THE
ESSENTIALS
OF
RHETORIC

PART 4 THE RESEARCH PAPER

A

BOOK

OF

READINGS

HANDBOOK OF GRAMMAR, PUNCTUATION, AND MECHANICS

MODERN RHETORIC

THE
ESSENTIALS
OF
RHETORIC

CHAPTER ONE

Language, Thinking, and Rhetoric

What is this course all about? Is it primarily concerned with commas and figures of speech and participial phrases? Does it have to do with outlining themes, constructing topic sentences, and working to achieve unity, coherence, and emphasis? These questions obviously have to be answered with a *yes;* but there is a larger sense in which the proper answer has to be *no,* for the essential purpose of this course goes far beyond the mere technicalities of grammar and rhetoric. Ultimately, this course engages your deepest needs and interests, your thinking, your feelings, your relationships with other people. These last assertions will not seem too sweeping when you realize that language is an indispensable instrument in the functioning of the human mind and personality and that rhetoric is the art of using language effectively.

If you doubt what has just been said, consider for a moment the college career before you. No matter what major interest you are to pursue in college, most of the instruction will be in language and you will be required to respond in language. If you do not understand language well and cannot use it effectively, the chances are that you will not do very well in college. When you leave this course, you will not, then, be through with the subject of language. You will be just beginning it. The analysis of city planning assigned for Government 11 and the textbook used in Astronomy 6 present complicated ideas through language, ideas more complicated than any you will commonly encounter here. The term paper you must write in Economics 114 and the essay questions in the Biology 63 examination will make greater demands on your use of language than any theme you will have to write in this course.

The Need To Use Language Well

Nor are you through with the need to use language well when you leave college. In most occupations there are letters and reports to be written, conferences to be held, policies to be drawn up and debated, many forms of communication which require skill in language. But language is not only necessary for communication; it is tied fundamentally to thinking. Lacking competence in language, you will spend much of your life fumbling in a kind of twilight world in which facts and ideas are perceived only dimly and often in distorted shapes.

How important language is to the whole business of thinking, the way in which it gives definition and outline to our world, is dramatically put by Helen Keller's account of learning her first word when she was seven years old. She had been blind and deaf almost from birth and had never learned to speak. Then a wise teacher began her education:

We walked down the path to the well-house, attracted by the fragrance of the honeysuckle with which it was covered. Someone was drawing water and my teacher placed my hand under the spout. As the cool stream gushed over one hand she spelled into the other the word *water*, first slowly and then rapidly. I stood still, my whole attention fixed upon the motions of her fingers. Suddenly I felt a misty consciousness as of something forgotten — a thrill of returning thought; and somehow the mystery of language was revealed to me. I knew then that "w-a-t-e-r" meant the wonderful cool something that was flowing over my hand. That living word awakened my soul, gave it light, hope, joy, set it free! There were barriers still, it is true, but barriers that could in time be swept away.

I left the well-house eager to learn. Everything had a name, and each name gave birth to a new thought. As we returned to the house every object which I touched seemed to quiver with life. That was because I saw everything with the strange, new sight that had come to me.

— HELEN KELLER: *The Story of My Life.*

To the arguments advanced so far you may retort, "I intend to be a physicist, and physics has its own special mathematical language." Or: "I intend to be a businessman. Look at Mr. Horton. Why, he made a million dollars and he can scarcely write his name. He has his secretary compose his letters." Or: "I intend to be a painter, and a painter understands the world and expresses himself by line and color, not by words."

The first thing to be said in reply to such remarks is not by way of rebuttal but of agreement. The physicist *does* make use of a special mathematical "language." The businessman *does* manipulate his world of business through considerations of supply and demand, business organization, profit and loss, and the ledger. The painter *does* define his world through line and color. But these various ways of understanding the world are not brainless and automatic activities. They are "languages" of a special sort. As such, they are manifestations of intelligence and serve to develop and extend intelligence.

Of course, there are some people with special aptitudes, talent, or genius, whose thinking seems to be nonverbal — the born physicist, the born businessman, the born soldier, the born painter. Such people may be able to by-pass much of the conscious discipline that most of us have to go through in order to develop our capacities.

Yet even the person who has a very special aptitude does not live his whole life in the exercise of that aptitude. The physicist in the laboratory may seem very far away from the demands of everyday life, but a few years back we had a startling demonstration that he is not far away at all. With the development of the atomic bomb, physicists suddenly saw that physics had to be thought of in relation to the whole society, in relation to the survival of the race. Some physicists took the position that they would do no research directed toward military use; some took the opposite stand; but both groups were forced into thinking about their relation to the world outside physics, and many of them felt compelled to express their thoughts in letters and articles.

Or take a businessman. More and more, the businessman, big or little, sees that business is not a mere matter of supply and demand, profit and loss. It has enormously complicated relations to the whole of the society in which it is exercised — from the management of the Community Chest to the conduct of national foreign policy. And in dealing with the relation of business to society in general, the businessman who is businessman and nothing more, who happens to have an aptitude for making money or building up a great organization, may be a baby, even a dangerous and destructive baby.

A prominent businessman,[1] one-time chairman of the board of a great steel company, has recently said that for years he has made a policy of hiring half the new men for his company from among those who have majored in the humanities. In his words:

---

[1] Clarence Randall, in an address at Colby College, May, 1956.

I always chose in each group half that were trained in the technical disciplines and half in the Liberal Arts, feeling that in business we need both
those disciplines, and that in no man's life is there time for him to achieve,
in the early years, both. So I looked to the Liberal Arts boys to catch their
metallurgy on the fly, and I looked to the technically trained to do their
best to make up in general education. . . . Now what did I ask for as I
interviewed young men? I wanted, first of all, intellectual superiority — let
there be no nonsense about that. I had no patience with the theory that a
man who wastes his time in college is apt to embrace his opportunities the
minute he enters business. I leave that to the others to find out. I want
those who have proven that they understand opportunity when they see it
and know how to make the most of it. I wanted then evidence that a man
could master a subject and lick it. I didn't care what the subject was. When
a man came into the steel industry, it didn't make any difference to me
what he had studied. We do not employ young men for what they know.
That may be a shock to some of you boys, but that's a fact. We employ you
for your capacity to learn. I wanted first to know that he could lick a subject. I wanted secondly to know whether he had sufficient intellectual flexibility to be willing to tackle a job for which he was not trained. It is un-
thinkable that you will find in industry the task for which you are adequately prepared, and your capacity to prepare yourself thereafter is the
test. I have always believed that the educated man must learn to walk with
confidence upon unfamiliar grounds. Moreover, I wanted the young man
I hired to be able to communicate ideas. I wanted him to be able to speak
and write the English language with persuasion and conviction. And therein
lies the weakness of technical education. When a young engineer comes to
my desk to present a matter, he always reaches for a pad and a pencil to
draw a sketch. And I never let him have it. I say, " Sit there now and tell me
without the pencil."

But the most important use of language, no matter how specialized the user's occupation, is in his personal life. A man lives with
a family, with friends, with neighbors, with fellow church members,
with people on civic or political committees, with the stranger on
the street. He needs to understand these people, to express himself
to them, and to think about his relation to them. So here we are
back to language as, first, a means of communication and, second,
a means of thinking. We are once again talking about language as
one way of learning how to live.

How Language Shapes Thought

There is the joke about the old lady who, when asked to say what
she meant, replied, " How can I know what I mean till I say it? " Was
the old lady a scatter-brained rattletrap, or was she talking sense?

She was talking sense. Her retort is just one way of expressing an idea that, from our own experience, we all know to be true. How often have we felt that we knew our own minds perfectly on something or knew all about something, only to find, when we started to put what we knew into words — to tell about it or to write about it — that we didn't know our own minds at all or didn't know what we were talking about? We don't, generally, have an idea or a body of information all clear in our heads, thoroughly worked out and organized, and then set about reporting it in words. No, more usually, in order to get the idea clear or the body of information logically organized, we have to try to put it into words. When we try to frame even the simplest sentence, we are forced to establish a set of meaningful relations; that is, we are forced to think more clearly. We instinctively know this, and we imply as much when we say, " I must talk this out."

" Writing things out," which will be the main business of this course, is simply a more rigorous way of talking things out. It is a way of training the mind in logical thought. For one thing, in writing we must understand the structure of language, what the parts of speech do, how words relate to one another, what individual words mean, the rules of grammar and punctuation. For another thing, we must understand the principles of organizing a discourse; that is, how to go about explaining something, how to argue a point, how to tell about an event. Once we start putting into words an explanation — or an argument or an account of an event — we have to organize the material in a way that will be readily understood by others.

We must constantly remember, however, that neither the structure of language nor the organization of discourse is a matter of doing tricks with words. Both are patterns that express the normal workings of the mind.

Language and Feeling

A human being isn't, of course, merely a machine for logical thought. Thought shades off into feeling, and feeling shades off into thought. We cannot exclude feeling from our experience, nor do we wish to do so, but we do want our life of feeling and our life of thought to be consistent with each other, to make some kind of total sense. A person whose desires run counter to his judgment is bound for considerable unhappiness. This is not to say that his judgment is necessarily good and his desires necessarily bad. It may very well be the other way around. But if the desire and the judgment are not more or less consistent, that person will be constantly jangled and disorganized. We all want some degree of unity in ourselves, some harmony.

To gain this unity, this harmony, we need not only to be able to think straight but also to be able to understand our own feelings and to see how they are related to each other, to our own general experience, and to the world around us. A considerable part of our use of language involves an attempt to clarify our feelings, to come to grips with them. We say, " Now that I've talked about it, I feel better." In other words, the talking-out process not only helps us make up our minds but helps us " make up our feelings," too.

As an instrument for expressing emotion, language necessarily undertakes to discriminate shades of feeling. The poet's metaphor and the schoolboy's bit of slang have this purpose in common — and the bit of slang may sometimes serve the purpose better than the metaphor. At this point we cannot go into a discussion of the various means which language employs to make these discriminations — means such as figurative language, rhythm, tone, and so on, which we shall deal with later — but we can emphasize the fact that in discriminating shades of feeling, language helps us to understand our emotions and to understand ourselves.

We have been talking about language and feeling in relation to the individual. But the individual must constantly deal with the feelings of other people and constantly make his own feelings understood by others. He may be writing a letter of condolence to a bereaved friend, or trying to collect a bill or sell an insurance policy, or making an after-dinner speech at a club. In these and a thousand other situations of ordinary life a person needs to understand the feelings of others. Such occasions involve what we shall call problems of tone and attitude. To manipulate language so as to convey the proper attitude in a given situation, will be a part of our study here. True skill in the use of language can scarcely be had apart from a knowledge of how words affect our fellow human beings. And a real command of the language is a powerful means for improving our relations with other people. Of course, we may be able to get along without skill in language. But why go through life under a handicap when there is a good opportunity, here and now, to overcome it?

What You Bring to This Course

We have been saying that language is at the very center of the life of thought and the life of feeling for both the individual himself and the individual as a member of society. We have said this in order to indicate the final business of this course. Naturally, in this short space, we have not been able to explain fully why this idea is true. In fact, to explain it fully and finally would require not one book but a library of books.

These remarks may sound very grand and impressive — perhaps too grand and impressive — and may seem to cast an awesome shadow over the day-to-day business of studying exposition or description, of writing themes or exercises. They may sound so impressive, in fact, that you may feel somewhat shy of beginning.

But you should remember that you are not beginning at the beginning. You have behind you many years of effort which can be made to apply to the writing you now do. You are already the beneficiary of a long training.

This training has not been wholly, or even in large part, in writing, in the study of grammar and the writing of weekly themes. Those things have been part of your training, and a very important part, but it cannot be said that they are the most important part of the training on which you can now draw as you come to this course.

PAST EXPERIENCE WITH LANGUAGE

In the first place, your sense of your language was not acquired primarily from books. You began the process of learning language when you were an infant, and the process has continued ever since. Books have helped you, and they will help you even more, toward an effective use of your language. They will broaden your vocabulary and give you a sense of the subtleties and shadings of words. But you, like any normal person of your age, are already the master of enormous resources in your native tongue.

A CAPACITY FOR STRAIGHT THINKING

In the second place, your experience has given you a great range of subjects and a capacity for thinking logically about them. Almost any event of your day, any sport or craft which you understand, any skill or technique which you possess, any scene which you have witnessed, any book or article which you have read, any person whom you know — all these are potential subjects. And any one of them can become interesting in so far as it is actually important to you and in so far as you can think straight about it.

A BROAD SOCIAL EXPERIENCE

In the third place, all your experiences with other people in the past have provided a training that will help you adjust yourself to your intended reader. Your social experience, from your early child-hood, has given you a training in tact, in grasping the truth about a human relationship, in adjusting your manner to the mood or prejudice of another person in order to convince, persuade, enter-tain, or instruct him. Every child is aware that when he wants some-thing from his mother or father, there is a right way to go about asking for it and a wrong way. And he knows that what is the right way for asking his mother may very well be the wrong way for asking his father. No doubt, the child never explains his actions to himself in these terms, but he acts on the truth behind them.

The discussion in this section comes to this: You already possess a great deal more of the equipment of the writer than you realize. All of your experience in the past can be said, without too much wrenching of fact, to have been a training for the writing which you will now do. Your problem is, in part, to learn to use the resources which you already possess in order to improve your sense of lan-guage.

• Applications •

The exercises given here are to suggest to you some of the questions in-volved in writing. The first group will have to do with the meanings of individual words. The second group will have to do with the meanings of passages. Consider the questions carefully, and try to analyze your re-sponses to the word or passage involved. In explaining your responses you will be using words. Are you saying what you mean? Did you know what you meant before you tried to put it into words?

I. Here you are to match words for meaning. Choose the word in the right-hand column that comes closest in your opinion to giving the mean-ing of the word to the left. Some of the words, of course, are not closely synonymous. Often even the closest synonym has some important shade of difference in meaning. Can you state whatever difference in meaning you find between the word on the left and the word you choose as closest to it? (When you have completed the exercise, check in the dic-tionary to see which words it regards as synonyms.)

1. success	result	2. spite	irritability
	achievement		rancor
	luck		unforgivingness
	money		hate
	fame		mercilessness
	happiness		
	respect		

3. subversion	craftiness	4. hopelessness	despair
	treason		desperation
	substitution		stoicism
	defalcation		failure
	dishonesty		timidity
	overthrow		
	innocuousness		

II. Here follow two pairs of passages. One member of each pair represents the original form of the passage.[2] The other member has been rewritten to garble the vocabulary or to blur the meaning in some other way. Choose the " good " passage in each case, and write a brief statement explaining your choice:

A—1. A few months before Muggs died, he got to " seeing things." He would rise slowly from the floor, growling low, and stalk stiff-legged and menacing toward nothing at all. Sometimes the Thing would be just a little to the right or left of a visitor. Once a Fuller Brush salesman got hysterics. Muggs came wandering into the room like Hamlet following his father's ghost. His eyes were fixed on a spot just to the left of the Fuller Brush man, who stood it until Muggs was about three slow, creeping paces from him. Then he shouted. Muggs wavered on past him into the hallway, grumbling to himself, but the Fuller man went on shouting. I think mother had to throw a pan of cold water on him before he stopped. That was the way she used to stop us boys when we got into fights.

Muggs died quite suddenly one night. Mother wanted to bury him in the family lot under a marble stone, with some such inscription as " Flights of angels sing thee to thy rest," but we persuaded her it was against the law. In the end we just put up a smooth board above his grave along a lonely road. On the board I wrote with an indelible pencil, " Cave Canem." Mother was quite pleased with the simple classic dignity of the old Latin epitaph.

A—2. A few months before our dog died, he had hallucinations. He would rise and, with low growls, move slowly toward the thing that he thought he saw. Sometimes this apparition seemed to be somewhere behind a visitor. Once a Fuller Brush salesman became hysterical. Muggs came into the room with eyes fixed as though he were viewing a ghost and appeared to locate the ghost to the left side of the salesman. When the dog advanced to within three paces of the salesman, he called out. The dog walked past him, but the salesman continued to call out. My mother, I believe, threw cold water upon him to bring him out of his fit. She frequently used cold water to end fights between her sons.

The dog died suddenly one night. Though my mother wished to bury him in the family plot beneath a stone inscribed with some appropriate quotation, she was persuaded that we should not do so. We buried the dog beside a lonely road and used a board for a headstone. I wrote on the board the Latin words " Cave Canem," and my mother was pleased with this Latin epitaph.

B—1. James Bowie was not the man he had once been — the half-legendary figure whose evanescent exploits were a tradition from St. Louis to Mexico City.

---

[2] Selection A is from " The Dog That Bit People " by James Thurber, in *My Life and Hard Times*. Selection B is from " Siege of the Alamo " by Marquis James, in *They Had Their Hour*.

In the old days Bowie was a power in Northern Mexico. He had married the daughter of a grandee and, turning his energies to less spectacular pursuits, accumulated a large income, and his family lived like royalty. Just when his wild days seemed behind him, a plague swept Bowie's beautiful wife and their children into the grave, and the magnanimous Jim almost perished of grief. Nothing mattered after that. Life became a quest for activity to turn his mind from his loss. Abandoning his property, he threw himself into the Texas contest and supported Houston in the contest that had spoiled the Texas army. With little left but blind zest and a name at which enemies still trembled, Jim Bowie then decided to stand by the wreck. His enormous form was gaunt and worn, his blue eyes especially bright from the fever of tuberculosis. Whipping up his exuberant forces with whisky, Jim Bowie had drifted into Bexar, wistfully yearning to sell his life dearly. He could not have come to a better place.

B–2. James Bowie was not the man he had once been — the half-legendary figure whose tremendous exploits were a tradition from St. Louis to Mexico City. In the old days Bowie was a power in Northern Mexico. He had married the daughter of a grandee and, turning his abilities to less spectacular pursuits, accumulated a fortune, and his family lived like royalty. Just when his wild days seemed behind him, a plague swept Bowie's beautiful wife and their children into the grave, and the lion-hearted Jim almost died of grief. Nothing mattered after that. Life became a quest for activity to turn his mind from his loss. Abandoning his property, he threw himself into the Texas struggle and supported Houston in the contest that had demoralized the Texas army. With little left but blind courage and a name at which enemies still trembled, Jim Bowie then decided to stand by the wreck. His enormous form was gaunt and worn, his blue eyes unnaturally bright from the fever of tuberculosis. Whipping up his flagging forces with whisky, Jim Bowie had plunged into Bexar, determined to sell his life dearly. He could not have come to a better place.

CHAPTER TWO

The Problem of Making a Beginning

In the preceding chapter we answered the question: "What is the ultimate purpose of the study of writing?" The next question, then, is: "Where should the study of writing begin?" Should it begin with the medium — that is, with a study of words? With the subject — that is, with the ideas that one wishes to express? Or with the occasion — that is, the situation in which the writer finds himself with respect to a particular audience? [1] It is impossible to say that any one of these considerations is more important than the two others, and it is also impossible to say that one of the three should logically precede the others, since they are all intimately related.

We might argue, if we liked, that we should begin with the medium, with the study of words, and then move by easy stages from diction through the next larger units, the sentence and the paragraph, and then on to the general problems of organization to be met in the whole theme.

But we could counter this argument by pointing out that when we choose words, we choose them in relation to other words, in relation to the general subject about which we mean to write, and in relation to our attitude toward our reader (that is, in relation to the occasion). In the same way, we could argue that the study of the sentence, important as it is, should not necessarily precede the study of problems of general organization. For it is the pattern of sentences, the relation of sentences to one another, that defines the progression of our ideas. In writing, we are first concerned — just as we are finally concerned — with our complete utterance, our over-all idea, our main purpose. There is something to be said, therefore, for

---

[1] With regard to this matter of the audience we shall have a good deal to say later in this book. Chapter 12 in particular deals with the audience and with the whole problem of attitude toward the audience and toward the material to be discussed.

our beginning, as we do here, with problems of general organization. Those problems usually first take specific form in the writer's attempt to come to grips with his subject.

Finding a True Subject

Your constant practical task as a student, not only in this course but in many other courses, will be to write compositions, essays, and reports. In any kind of writing your first problem is to establish a clearly defined subject. In other words, you have to know exactly *what* you are writing about. Unless you can do this, you cannot handle the second problem, which is to develop that idea clearly and forcefully. You must think before you write; and you must think as you write.

First, what is a truly usable subject? The answer depends in part upon the scope of your composition. Your subject must be so limited as to allow you to say all that has to be said about it in the number of words that you have allotted yourself. Similarly, it must be sufficiently unrestricted to provide matter, without padding, for the allotted words. The more usual problem for the student, however, is the former, that of too broad a subject. Often the student chooses a subject that turns out to be too vague, too inclusive. In trying to deal with it, he feels as though he were attempting to grasp a handful of fog. " George Washington," for instance, may sound like a subject that one could write on. But is it? Obviously, it would require several fat volumes to say everything that could be said about the topic of George Washington. So the topic must be narrowed, and the direction of the narrowing will depend in great part upon our interests. Are we interested in saying something about " George Washington as a Colonial Planter," or " George Washington's Development as a Leader," or " What the Frontier Taught George Washington," or " George Washington as a Statesman," or " The Influence of George Washington on American Political Thought," or " Myths about George Washington," or " The Courtship of George Washington," or " George Washington as a Military Strategist "? These titles indicate only a few of the various kinds of interest in Washington; and because they constitute focusing of interest, they are (or at least tend to be) true subjects. A **true subject** is a topic brought to focus.

• **Application** • See pg. 22

Below is a list of topics. No one of them is a true subject, because they are all too general. Select five topics from the list and frame three true subjects for each.

Divorce	Reading
The United Nations	Communism
Alcoholic Beverages	A Church
Public Education	The Postal Service
The Jury System	The American Indian
Robert E. Lee	The Revolver
Abraham Lincoln	Patriotism
The Income Tax	River Traffic
Amateurism in Sport	Shakespeare's Plays
Military Training	Thrift

Main Divisions of a Discourse

Once you have found your true subject, one that you can really write about, you must consider the general organization into which your writing will fall. You know that there will be an **introduction,** a **body of discussion,** and a **conclusion.** Very probably in trying to settle on your true subject you have already struck on some of the main points, perhaps all of the main points, which will be presented in the discussion. You may also have organized these points into an outline. But how do you get to the discussion? How do you write the first sentence? The first paragraph?

INTRODUCTION

The introduction must really introduce. But introduce what? And introduce to whom? The answer to the first question seems easy. The reader is entitled to know as soon as possible what business is in hand. Your title probably tells him something, but the introduction usually must limit and fix the subject somewhat more precisely. The introductory paragraph (or paragraphs) must define and limit the subject more precisely than the title has done; it must suggest to the reader what the central idea is and how the writer intends to present it. Here is the first paragraph of a theme with the title " Sam Houston as a Youth ":

Sam Houston grew up in a world that was very different from the one in which most boys now live. His world, so filled with adventure, has always interested me, as it would interest anyone of my age who has a taste for the outdoors and exciting action. But long ago I became interested also in the effect that the world of Sam Houston's youth had upon him. Houston became a great man, a frontiersman, a politician, a soldier who conquered Santa Anna and gained Texas independence, and the first president of the Republic of Texas. It is interesting to see how a person's youth helps determine the kind of man he becomes.

The writer has given us our bearings. We know that there will be some contrast, stated or suggested, between the world of the young Houston and our world. We are told who Houston was and given some notion of his achievements. We are told the line the writer will follow: He intends not merely to give a list of events, however interesting in themselves, but to indicate how those events affected Houston's character and achievements, the central idea of the theme. We are thus well prepared for the body of the theme.

A theme about the youth of Houston is, however, longer and more ambitious than any that you will soon be called upon to write. It is the kind of research paper, or long essay, that will come later in the course. Here is the introduction of a much simpler theme, with the title " Why I Am Glad I Went to a Country School ":

Not long ago I saw a newspaper advertisement which cast some slurs on the old-fashioned " little red school house " because it did not have modern conveniences and a school cafeteria and a gymnasium. I did not go to a little *red* school house, but the color of the paint, what paint there was left on my school, was the only difference. Then for a year I went to a big county consolidated school. So I feel qualified to have an opinion. I want to write of some of the things I think more important than running water, cafeterias, and gymnasiums.

We do not yet know what things the writer thinks more important than running water, cafeterias, and gymnasiums, but we are ready for what he has to say about them. We know what has moved him to write the theme, and we know the personal experience that qualifies him to have an opinion. A reference to one's personal experience with the subject under discussion can be a useful method for constructing an introductory paragraph.

Here is an even simpler, but nevertheless adequate, introduction:

Everyone knows the importance of jet propulsion today, but not everyone knows the history of how it was developed. That history is a good example of how important and complicated inventions can be worked out from the simplest of ideas. We can start by stating the simple idea behind jet propulsion.

Here the method used may be described as a statement of the writer's purpose. By stating it, he has let us know his subject and the central idea that he is going to follow.

Here is an introductory paragraph from a story in *Newsweek*

(Nov. 12, 1956). The story occurs in the "Press" section and is entitled "Troop Movement."

For the first time since the frantic rush to the Korean war front on a late June day six years ago, the U.S. typewriter brigade mobilized and got on the move last week. Trench coats patched and portables oiled, reporters plunged through transportation and accreditation muddles toward the Middle East and Red satellite Europe. They were badly needed where the action was.

The story goes on to discuss the details of the rush of newspaper correspondents to the trouble spots, mentioning the names of some of the more prominent correspondents and describing typical problems encountered by them on the way to the embattled regions and typical adventures experienced at the fighting fronts. The introductory paragraph has as its principal device the use of details likely to catch the reader's interest. In view of the kind of story that it introduces, this device is probably a good choice. The mention of the patched trench coats and oiled portables helps us visualize the "frantic rush," and the mention of transportation and accreditation muddles prefigures the difficulties ahead.

So far we have been concerned with our first question: "Introduce what?" When we turn to the second question: "Introduce to whom?" we are concerned with what we have called the *occasion,* the kind of reader we are writing for, his attitude toward us and what we are writing about, and our attitude toward him. Before you begin to write, it is wise to ask yourself some questions about the occasion, questions that will serve as a guide primarily for the introduction but also, to some extent, for the development of the theme as well.

1. Does the reader have any interest in my subject, or must I try to attract his attention?

2. If I have to attract his attention, how do I go about it?

3. How ignorant is he of my subject? How much do I have to explain to him to give a background for my discussion?

If we assume that the reader is already more or less interested in our subject, then the introduction itself may be properly concerned with presenting what background we think necessary for the discussion. We have moved on to question 3. All we need to do is simply to state our subject and fix its limits. For example, here is the beginning of a student theme called "Backcourt Strategy in Tennis":

Anyone who plays tennis knows what I mean by backcourt strategy, and anyone who does not play tennis would never know what I meant no matter how many words I used. You may have split-second coordination and a good wrist and a quick foot, but none of these assets is any good to you if you can't outthink your opponent.

The device used here is that of a definition of the reader for whom the student is writing as well as of the subject about which he is writing. The writer has put his cards on the table. He is writing strictly for tennis players, that is, for a special reader who is keenly interested in the subject and who needs no general instruction in the game. This writer can thus move quickly into the development of his subject. He has warned off duffers and general readers.

With the general reader who is already interested but who does not have the background information, the problem is different. He must be given his bearings as quickly and simply and systematically as possible. Here is the beginning of a theme called " Jet Pilots Are Human ":

As new planes fly higher and faster every day, we begin to feel that there is no limit to what the designers and engineers can do. But we tend to forget one thing. There are no new designs for the human body and there are no new models being built in the hush-hush atmosphere of the experimental shop. The pilot is the old model, and we have to think of what speed and altitude do to his " liver and lights " and how much sloshing around he can stand.

What has the writer done in this paragraph? He has corrected a misconception that the general reader may well have — the idea that design and engineering are the only important factors in the future of aviation. And he has given a preliminary, general statement of the problem of the body in flight, which is his central idea. He has built his introductory paragraph around an important fact, a fact that we are likely to forget but must not be allowed to forget.

In discussing our typical introductory paragraphs we have mentioned a number of basic devices that may be used in constructing them. The following example may be said to present certain aspects of the general subject to be discussed, in this case Wordsworth's attitude toward nature. The title is " Wordsworth in the Tropics."

In the neighbourhood of latitude fifty north, and for the last hundred years or thereabouts, it has been an axiom that Nature is divine and morally uplifting. For good Wordsworthians — and most serious-minded people are now Wordsworthians, either by direct inspiration or at second hand — a walk in the country is the equivalent of going to church, a tour through Westmorland is as good as a pilgrimage to Jerusalem. To commune with the fields and waters, the woodlands and the hills, is to commune, according to our modern and northern ideas, with the visible manifestations of the " Wisdom and Spirit of the Universe."

— ALDOUS HUXLEY: *Do What You Will.*

This opening paragraph warns off the uninformed reader, for it assumes that the reader is familiar with the poetry of William Wordsworth and that he knows what a "good Wordsworthian" is and may quite possibly be one himself. But for the informed reader, the first sentence is immediately provocative; its opening mention of latitude develops the implications of the word *tropics* in the title and looks ahead to "modern *and northern* ideas" about communion with nature in the last sentence. Certain aspects of nature worship, which the reader may have taken for granted or overlooked, are described, and the reader is led to begin thinking about the central idea to be explored in the essay.

There is no certain formula for the beginning paragraph. How to start it is largely a matter of common sense. Try to put yourself in the reader's place, and ask yourself what preliminary information you would need to follow the discussion intelligently; then state that information as simply and economically as you can. But here is a caution. You may find that your introduction is running away with you, that it is becoming a theme in itself. If so, you probably have not limited your subject closely enough. Perhaps the introductory material contains the real subject you should treat.

Up to this point we have been assuming a willing and interested reader. But suppose that he is not interested and that you must catch his attention. How do you go about that? In the sample paragraphs already discussed we have more than hinted at some ways of solving this problem. On many occasions you yourself have been the uninterested reader who, idly thumbing through a magazine or newspaper feature section, has been caught by the first few sentences of an article and has gone on to read the whole piece. In his opening sentences, the skillful writer has shown that something previously uninteresting to you bears on your welfare, your health, your ambitions and aspirations, your pocketbook, your prejudices, your patriotism, your religion, your education. Or he may simply have shown the general human interest in a subject that you had thought abstract and dull.

The author of the following paragraph is making a bid for the reader's attention by showing how his subject, "The Alaskan Islands," might affect the personal life of his reader:

There was a time when I thought that geography was the boring subject that happened in the first period after the noon recess or that it was the pictures in the old *National Geographic* magazines in the dentist's office which you thumbed through while you were waiting for a new filling. But now I know that what the Arabs eat in Mecca or the Burmese gets as take-home pay affects our national security and our tax bill. This fact was brought home to me last summer when I went to Alaska and had the good fortune to be asked to go on a ten-day cruise through the Aleutian Islands in a private boat. Those islands are steppingstones between America and Asia, and you know that you can go two ways on steppingstones.

Having challenged the reader to accept his point of view about geography, the writer concludes his paragraph with what will become the chief point to be made in his theme: the military importance of the Aleutians.

Another writer, the author of a research theme on the history of the Post Office, in his first paragraph makes a different kind of attempt to catch the reader's attention; he makes a novel assertion:

Many people today argue about how much the government should mix into business, and most of us tend to think that government in business is something new. But the United States government has been in one business a long time, and if we look at how it got into this business and how successful it has been, we may have some background for our present debate. I am referring, of course, to the mail-carrying business.

Here is the introduction of a theme on coal mining in Kentucky, with an attempt to make ordinary human interest the bait for the reader:

To a man who works in the mines, coal isn't just a dirty black substance that you shovel into the furnace. It is life itself — and sometimes it is death. Like most people, I had never understood the real meaning of coal until I spent two summers in eastern Kentucky. Then I met old Thad Holloway, and I learned about his life in the mines (and out, when there wasn't any work), and I heard the tales he told in his dry, mountaineer way. If you knew Thad, you knew about coal.

Again, it must be conceded that there is no formula for catching the reader's interest in an introduction. The best advice is to put yourself in the place of your imaginary reader. What would catch your attention? You are as good an example of the general reader as anyone.

We have taken a good deal of space in discussing the introduction. But the introduction is extremely important. For the reader, it is the first impression, and first impressions tend to color subsequent impressions. And for you, the writer, the introduction is equally important; a good notion of how to write an introduction tends to diminish what the great novelist Joseph Conrad called " the terror of the blank page." When you can write a first paragraph, you have taken a long step toward the end of your theme.

We shall now make a suggestion, however, that may seem to contradict what has just been said. Sometimes the way to write a good introduction is not to begin the actual process of writing with the introduction. It may be a good idea to plunge straight into the body of the theme and follow through to the end. Then ask yourself what you have accomplished, what needs to be said in the introduction to give the reader his bearings for what you have already put down. As we saw earlier on pages 6–7, it often occurs that we know what we want to say only after we have tried to express it in words.

This introduction-in-reverse process should not be used regularly, but it may help give you a better sense of the relation between the introduction and the body of the theme. When the introduction is written *before* the rest of the theme, it may be well to reconsider it after the body of the theme has been completed. In the light of the completed theme, you may be able to make very useful revisions.

THE BODY OF THE DISCUSSION AND THE CONCLUSION

For the present, we shall take very little space to discuss the body of the discourse and the conclusion. There is a good reason for this, for everything we shall be doing in this course from this point on will be a way of studying how to develop the main body of the discussion. Suffice it to say here that the body of the discussion should not betray the promise of the introduction. You have promised the reader to develop a fixed and limited subject along a certain line. Having made this promise, keep it.

About the conclusion there are one or two things that ought to be said. A short theme often does not need a formal conclusion. The paragraph making the last important point, or the climactic point, may constitute a thoroughly adequate conclusion, provided always that the theme has a sound general organization.

But whether your concluding paragraph is elaborate or simple, it occupies one of the two naturally emphatic positions in the composition. Moreover, it constitutes your last chance at your reader. Failure at this point may well mean failure for the whole piece of writing. You must avoid two things: blurred effect, that is, a mere trailing off or vague generalities, and repetitious summaries. The conclusion must really " conclude " the discussion; the theme should not simply stop as if you had suddenly become tired or run out of ink. A summary is one way of making a genuine conclusion; but if a theme is short and well organized, the reader should have the thing as a whole pretty clearly in mind, and there is no need to go back over all the ground. Put your finger on your main point, on what you want to bring to focus. Then write your conclusion on that point.

• Applications •

I. Read the introductions to the essays on pages 463, 469, 497, 551, and 700 in the Readings. Which particularly caught your interest? Try to analyze the reason. Then read through one of the pieces that attracted you. Did the body of discussion fulfill the promise of the introduction? Examine the conclusion. Does the writer use a summary? If so, is he justified? What last effect does he try to make on the reader? What kind of reader is he writing for?

II. Bring to class a good example of an interest-catching introduction from some magazine or newspaper feature article. What appeal does it make? What kind of conclusion does the article have?

III. Go back to the Application in this chapter (page 15) in which you were asked to frame several true subjects from a list of general topics. Select one of the true subjects you have framed, and write a brief introductory paragraph, say 75 to 100 words, for an interested but uninformed reader. Select another subject and write an introduction which must attract an uninterested reader.

IV. Examine the introductory paragraphs of " The American Civilization Puzzle " (Readings, page 666). What appeals to interest does the author try to make? Does he really convince you that his subject is " important "? Even if you think it important, has he given adequate reasons for its importance?

CHAPTER THREE

Organizing the Composition

The division into introduction, body, conclusion, or, if you like, into beginning, middle, and end, is the natural sequential division of a piece of writing. It is the mode of organizing that naturally occurs to anyone who is getting down to the actual business of writing, whatever the topic. But there is another threefold set of terms that is also fundamental to any process of composition. They are **unity, coherence,** and **emphasis.**

Any sound piece of writing will exemplify these three principles, and a study of them is our first step toward understanding how to develop the main body of the discussion in a discourse and how to relate that discussion to the introduction and the conclusion.

Unity

Any good piece of writing has unity. The fundamental interest, which determines the writer's subject, must permeate the whole composition. The composition must be *one* thing — not a hodge-podge. We have already encountered the demands made by unity in our discussion of the matter of finding a true subject. " George Washington," we said, was too vague to be a true subject; it included too many things. It lacked the unity that such a limited topic as " What the Frontier Taught George Washington " possessed.

Unity is not an arbitrary thing, a limitation imposed from the outside. It is simply an indication that the writer's mind can work systematically and can, therefore, arrive at a meaning. A unified composition indicates that the writer's ideas about his subject are unified, that he is not scatterbrained. But unity is not always easily achieved.

Suppose that you are given " Preparing for a Career " as a topic

23

for a theme. After turning it over in your mind a few times, you realize that this topic includes too many possibilities to constitute a true subject. Therefore, your first step toward gaining unity is to limit and fix the subject. You bring your own interest to bear upon the topic. For example, you are a college freshman, and you are beginning to prepare for a career as a civil engineer. You decide, therefore, to call your theme: " Why I Wish To Be an Engineer." This title is more limited than the more general " Preparing for a Career," and it has the merit of drawing upon subject matter with regard to which you rightfully believe that you have some competence — the state of your own mind.

The essay is to be short. You do not plan an elaborate introduction or conclusion. The introduction will simply make reference to your own experience with the subject (see page 16). The conclusion can be a sentence or two in which you will reaffirm your main point, your choice of a career. Following is a theme such as you might write:

WHY I WISH TO BE AN ENGINEER

Choosing one's life work is about the most important decision that a person ever has to make. Many of my friends are still undecided about what they want to be. But my choice has been an easy one. For nearly as long as I can remember I have wanted to be an engineer.

I suppose that one reason why I want to be an engineer and have made my college plans in that direction is that my father is an engineer. He was a student here at the State University back in 1909–1914. He began his college career with the intention of being a doctor, but he soon changed his mind. He finished his course in 1914 and worked as a draftsman for two years in Chicago in an engineering firm. But World War I got him into the army, and he wound up a major in the Engineering Corps. His war experience was valuable to him in more ways than one, for he says it taught him how to deal with men of all kinds and to get work done under pressure. Also, it meant that he acquired a taste for action and adventure. After the war, he went to Mexico and worked on building a railroad in the mountains. He had many difficult construction problems to solve there. I was born in Mexico, and I was raised in a family where engineering was discussed all the time, for my mother was interested in my father's work.

There is a great future for an engineer in this country. It is true that during the depression many engineers were out of work, but that was true of many occupations and professions. Besides, many of the engineers out of work were not well trained to begin with. If you are really well trained and are willing to put out your best efforts, you can almost always get along. Engineering is especially important today, for we are in the midst of a great technological revolution which will mean the rebuilding of much of the industrial plant and the development of new transport facilities. There are also opportunities in land reclamation, the expansion of public works, and other long-range programs. This country is an engineer's paradise, for we are the most mechanical-minded people in the world. They say that industry is the great talent of America, and I see nothing to be ashamed of in that. Engineers make the world easier to live in for everyone. Think of the great bridges and dams, the highways and airports. What would we do without them?

I like a life of action, and that is another reason why I plan to be an engineer. My father had a very interesting life in Mexico. After five years there he went to Argentina. He had learned Spanish in Mexico and had made a name for himself there. So he got a good offer in Argentina. He sent my mother and me back to the United States until I grew up a little, but he came to see us at the end of the first year and took us back to Argentina with him. We lived there four years. Then he went to India and supervised the building of some bridges there. But he did not take us to India with him. He understood that the climate was too bad. And he was right, because he almost died there of dysentery. He never left America again, but his talk about his adventures gave me a desire for an active life, and he has never discouraged me.

I make my best marks in mathematics, which is the basis of engineering, and I think that a man should follow his best talent. I like other subjects, too — history, for instance, and I read a good many novels and stories. But I cannot see myself making a profession of any of these fields. Business would be too confining for me. I have an uncle who is a lawyer, and it seems to me that he never gets out of his office except to come home at night.

Taking everything together, I think that engineering is the right profession for me.

This theme has the unity of a true subject, but lacks the larger unity of good writing. When we examine the theme carefully, we can dig out the reasons for the student's choice of a career: family, the opportunity to make a good living, the appetite for action, and the aptitude for mathematics. These four reasons should give him the outline for his theme.

But he is constantly bringing in material which does not bear directly on the subject or which is developed without reference to the main line of interest. For instance, he is so much impressed with his father's life that he devotes far too much attention to it: most of the second and fourth paragraphs. For his purpose he needs to tell us only the barest facts about his father's career. The last part of the second paragraph, too, is not relevant. The writer may have two points here: that an engineer feels himself characteristically American and that the engineer has the sense of being a useful member of society. But he does not state these points, and they are lost in his general remarks. If we get them at all, we get them by implication only. In the fourth paragraph, too, we find some irrelevant material: the reference to the writer's interest in history and fiction and the remark about his uncle's occupation. The writer has a main idea, but he does not stick to it.

Coherence

An effective discourse must have unity. It must also have coherence; that is, the elements of the discourse must stick together. This last comment may seem to be simply another way of saying that a discourse must have unity. Indeed, the failure of the student theme just discussed might be stated as a failure in coherence quite as accurately as a failure in unity; we have in effect pointed out how one part does not lead to the next, how the writer fails to develop needed linkages, and how he has pointlessly introduced items that he does not need and that do not tie in to anything else. Unity and coherence are indeed ultimately related; and yet it is worth making a distinction between them. That distinction may be stated thus: When we speak of unity, we refer primarily to the relation of the materials to the subject. When we speak of coherence, we refer primarily to the organization of the materials so as to give a continuous *development* to the subject. A discourse that lacks coherence will, of course, seem to lack unity; for even though the individual parts are actually related to the subject, the incoherent author will have failed to demonstrate how they relate to each other and that they thus make up *one* discourse.

COHERENCE THROUGH OVER-ALL ORGANIZATION

There is no one principle by which the materials of a discourse are to be organized. Obviously, a principle of organization that is good for describing a woman's face would not be good for telling the story of a baseball game or a battle, or for arguing in favor of the abolition of Greek-letter fraternities, or for explaining the causes of the Russian Revolution. Different intentions demand different principles of organization. The basic intentions and some of the characteristic methods of organization, we shall study in subsequent chapters. Here we can content ourselves with the common-sense principle that one thing should lead to another.

Let us suppose that the student who wrote the essay entitled " Why I Wish To Be an Engineer " sets out to write another theme and, in writing it, undertakes to pay special attention to the principles of unity and coherence. The topic "Interesting People" has been assigned to him, and, after some thought, he brings it down to a more limited and specific subject, something nearer to his special interests and experience and something nearer to a true subject. He decides to write about a member of the family that he knows intimately; his central idea will be to define his special admiration for that person. He will call his theme "The Person I Admire Most: Uncle Conroy."

But before starting to write the theme, the student does something else. He is determined to overcome his tendency to be scatterbrained; so he now jots down some of the points that he wants to make and tries to arrange them into a kind of sketch or outline. His outline looks something like this.

STATEMENT OF THE SUBJECT   Why I admire my Uncle Conroy

INTRODUCTION
  I. My uncle as he now appears — apparent failure and real success

BODY
  II. The background of my uncle's achievement
      A. His worldly success and ruin
      B. His illness and despair
  III. The nature of my uncle's achievements
      A. His practical achievements
          1. Help with the children
          2. Help with my father's business
          3. Help with my mother's illness
      B. His achievement in self-control
          1. Naturalness of his actions
          2. Cheerfulness in the face of pain
      C. His greatest achievement, an example to others — the summary of his other achievements

CONCLUSION
  IV. My uncle as a type of success and my admiration for him

The outline has narrowed the true subject to the uncle's success in life. The title of the theme thus could be, "Success and Uncle Conroy." Although the outline is relatively simple, it should be adequate for the preliminary study of such a subject. But a student who has trouble in organizing his material may do well to consult the Appendix on outlining (page 818). A little practice in making sentence outlines may increase his power to deal with a body of material. But there is no virtue in outlining for its own sake. It is a means to an end, a help to straight thinking and well-organized writing; it is not an end in itself.

Though not an end in itself, an outline is a help in the actual writing of a theme. It helps especially in solving the problem of unity and coherence, in making all the parts relate to the subject and hang together properly. An outline, however, need not be followed slavishly. In the process of writing, new thoughts may come, and new material may be suggested. The writer should always be ready to take advantage of these. He may have to stop writing and go back to make a new outline, or he may be able to incorporate the new thoughts or new material directly into the body of the theme. In any event, it is a good idea to check the finished theme against the original outline after the writing is completed and, if necessary, make a new outline. By means of an outline the bare bones are laid out, so that the writer can criticize the organization of his work.

Actually, the student did not follow his outline slavishly in writing his theme about Uncle Conroy. Some of the ways in which he departed from it we shall discuss a little later. First, let us look at his theme. (Note that he has taken some care to make the introduction engage our interest in what is to come.)

SUCCESS AND UNCLE CONROY

(1) I suppose that my Uncle Conroy is the person I admire most in the world. This statement would probably seem strange to anyone who happened to visit our home and see the old man sitting, hunched over and shabbily dressed, at a corner of the hearth, not saying much. He looks like the complete failure, and by ordinary standards he is. He has no money. He has no children. He is old and sick. But he has made his own kind of success, and I think he is happy.

(2) At one time in his life he was a success by ordinary standards. He was the son of a poor Methodist minister (my mother's father), but he ran away from home in Illinois to Oklahoma, back in the days when things were beginning to boom out there. He had a fine house in Oklahoma City and a ranch. He was hail-fellow-well-met, and men and women liked him. He was a sportsman, kept good horses, and took long hunting trips to Mexico and Canada. Then one day, on his own ranch, his horse stumbled in a gopher hole and threw him. He was badly hurt and was in the hospital for many months. While he was still in the hospital, the Depression came on. If he had been well and able to take care of his affairs, he might have saved some of his money from the crash. As it was, he lost everything. So he came back to Illinois, and my mother and father took him in.

(3) It must have been an awful come-down for a man like that to be living on charity. But the worst was yet to happen, for he developed arthritis in a very painful form. I remember the first year or so, even though I was a very small child. He even tried to commit suicide with gas from the stove. But my mother saved him, and after that he began to change.

(4) The first thing was that he began to take an interest in us children. He would read to us and talk to us. He helped us with our lessons. That relieved mother a great deal and made her life easier. My father was an insurance man and had a lot of paper work to do. It got so that my uncle took an interest in that, and before long he was helping my father by doing reports and writing letters. He helped my father tide over the bad time of the Depression. Then when my mother was ill for a long time, he learned to do some of the housework, as much as his strength would permit, and even dressed the two smaller children.

(5) What he did was important, but more important was the way he did things. He was so natural about it. You never got the impression he was making any effort or sacrifice. We all got so we didn't notice what he did, and I am sure that that was what he wanted.

(6) As I look back now, or when I go home and see Uncle Conroy, the biggest achievement, however, seems to be the kind of example he gave us all. He was often in pain, but he was always cheerful. If he felt too bad, he simply hid away from the family for a while in his room — what he called his "mope-room." He even made a joke out of that. And he didn't act like a man who had failed. He acted like a man who had found what he could do and was a success at it. And I think that he is a success. We all admire success, and that is why I admire my Uncle Conroy.

This theme is coherent. We can see how each section of it fits into the general pattern. The main business of the writer is to tell why he admires his uncle, but he does not immediately set up the reasons. First, by way of introduction, he gives a brief sketch of the man as he now appears — the man who is to be interpreted. The appearance of failure in contrast to the reality of success gives dramatic interest and excites the reader's curiosity.

In the second paragraph the writer tells of his uncle's days of outward success. This topic does not get into the theme merely because the uncle, as a matter of fact, had such success. Many things that happened to him are certainly omitted here. Instead, it gets in because the taste of worldly success makes more impressive the uncle's achievement in being able to shift his values in the face of adversity.

The third paragraph presents the despair of the uncle — a normal response to bankruptcy and illness. This topic has a place in the general organization, for it states the thing that the uncle must fight against.

The fourth, fifth, and sixth paragraphs define the nature of the uncle's achievement. The order here is one of ascending importance, toward a climax — the special practical things he did, the attitude he took toward the doing, the long-range effect of his example on others. (There is one small defect in the organization here. The reference to the uncle's cheerfulness in the sixth paragraph probably should go back into the fifth paragraph, for it really belongs under the heading of the uncle's attitude.) The sixth paragraph not only states the uncle's most important achievement but serves as a kind of summary of the preceding material.

In discussing the relation of part to part in the foregoing theme, it may be well also to review briefly the relation of the theme to the student's preliminary outline. Paragraph 1 corresponds to I (Introduction) ; paragraph 2, to II:A; paragraph 3, to II:B; paragraph 4, to III; paragraph 5, to III:B:1; and paragraph 6, to III:B:2, III: C, and IV.

Topic III:B:2, now in paragraph 6, should probably be in paragraph 5; and the writer of the theme should probably have made topic IV into a separate paragraph. This new separate paragraph would give a statement of the writer's definition of success and the application of the definition to his uncle's case. Nevertheless, the student has written a theme which is fundamentally systematic. The theme builds continuously toward a climax, and the outline has helped define the stages of that progression.

COHERENCE THROUGH LOCAL TRANSITIONS

Thus far, we have been talking about what is involved in the over-all organization of a piece of writing. But the question of local transitions within the discourse is also extremely important. How do we get from one section to another, one paragraph to another, one sentence to another?

Obviously there must be an intrinsic continuity: What one section, paragraph, or sentence presents must bear some relation to the whole subject and to what has just preceded. But even when there is this intrinsic continuity, we may have to help the reader by using certain devices of connection and transition, by giving him links or signposts.

We can begin a section, paragraph, or sentence with some reference to what has gone before. The repetition or rephrasing of something in the preceding element will provide a link. For example, let us look at the link that ties together the first and second paragraphs of the theme:

. . . He is old and sick. But he has made *his own kind of success,* and I think he is happy.

At one time of his life he was *a success by ordinary standards.* He was. . . .

The repetition of the word *success* (which points up the antithesis between " his own kind " and that according to " ordinary standards ") provides the link between the two paragraphs. But pronouns and other words of reference (such as *such, similar, that, these,* and so forth) may serve the same purpose. Notice, for example, how paragraphs 4 and 5 of the theme are linked.

. . . he *learned to do some of the housework* . . . and even *dressed* the two smaller children.
What he did was important, but more important was the way he did things. . . .

Furthermore, there are words, though none are used in this theme, the function of which is to indicate specific relations: conjunctions, conjunctive adverbs, and some adverbs. These words say what they mean. *And, or, nor* establish a coordinate connection. *But, however, nevertheless* establish a contrast. *So, therefore, consequently* establish a result. *Moreover* and *furthermore* indicate additions or elaborations. *First, second, next, last,* and so forth, indicate items in a series.

Another way to establish continuity is found in a large group of more or less conventional phrases. Such phrases are also self-explanatory: *in addition, as has been said, that is to say, that is, by consequence, for example, for instance, as a result, on the contrary.*

None of these lists is complete. They are merely suggestive. But they may serve to indicate the function of such words and phrases so that the student can by his reading build up his own resources.

We must not use such transitional words and phrases unless they are necessary. They are not ornaments, and they impede the reader rather than help him if the sense is clear without them. Overuse of such expressions may, in fact, indicate a breakdown in the coherence of the composition.

Emphasis

A piece of writing may be unified and coherent and still not be effective if it does not observe the principle of **emphasis.** When this principle is properly observed, the intended scale of importance of elements in the discourse is clear to the reader. All cats are black in the dark, but all things should not look alike in the light of a reasonable writer's interest in his subject. To change our metaphor, there is a foreground and a background of interest, and the writer should be careful to place each item in its proper location. Like unity and coherence, emphasis is a principle of organization.

EMPHASIS BY FLAT STATEMENT

How do we emphasize an element in a piece of writing?

The first and most obvious way is for the writer to state quite flatly his own view on the importance of a matter. If we turn back to the theme " The Person I Admire Most," we find that paragraphs 4, 5, and 6 represent a scale of importance.

(4) The first thing was that he began to take an interest in us children. . . .

(5) What he did was important, but *more important* was the way he did things. . . .

(6) As I look back now, or when I go home and see Uncle Conroy, the *biggest achievement,* however, seems to be the kind of example he gave us all. . . .

In depending on his own statement for emphasis the writer should remember that the actual content must justify the statement. Before he makes the statement, he must think through the subject and be sure that he really believes in his own statement.

EMPHASIS BY POSITION

A second way to emphasize is by position. "First or last" is a fairly sound rule for emphasis by position. This rule corresponds to two general methods for treating a subject. The main idea can be presented and then discussed or proved, or discussion or proof can lead up to the main idea. Ordinarily the second method is better, and the end is the most emphatic position, for the last impression on a reader is what counts most. But some rather conventionalized forms of writing, such as news stories, put the most important material first. In any case, the middle is the least emphatic position.

EMPHASIS BY PROPORTION

Proportion in itself is a means of emphasis. The most important topic in a discussion reasonably receives fullest treatment. This principle, however, is more flexible than the preceding statement would indicate. In some writings the last and most important topic may have been so well prepared for by the foregoing discussion that it does not require elaborate treatment. The writer must decide each case on its own merits and be sure that he is not indulging in elaboration merely for the sake of elaboration.

OTHER DEVICES OF EMPHASIS

Flat statement, order of importance, proportion, and style (to be discussed in Chapter 12) are major means of expressing emphasis, but there are certain minor ones. For instance, repetition of an idea can give it prominence. The danger here is that the repetition may become merely mechanical and therefore dull. To be effective, repetition must be combined with some variety and some progression in the treatment of the subject. Then there is the device of the short, isolated paragraph. The idea set off by itself strikes the eye. But not all short paragraphs are in themselves emphatic. The content and the phrasing of the short paragraph must make it appear worthy of the special presentation. Obviously if many paragraphs are short, all emphasis disappears.

FAULTY DEVICES OF EMPHASIS

Certain frequently occurring devices of emphasis are worse than useless. Irresponsible exaggeration always repels the reader. Catchwords and hackneyed phrases, such as *awfully, terribly, tremendously, the most wonderful thing I ever saw, you never saw anything like it, I can't begin to tell you,* make a claim on the reader's attention that he is rarely prepared to grant. Random underlining and italicizing and the use of capitals and exclamation points usually defeat their own purpose. Writers use these devices when they are not sure that what they have to say will stand on its own merits. To insist that what you have to say is important does not prove the point. As the writer, you must prove it.

In applying any of the means of emphasis the writer must first of all be sure that the thing emphasized is worth emphasizing. Common sense must help him here. Nothing else can.

• Application •

You will now write your first theme, a theme of 750 words or more about yourself. Remember that you have a particular audience, the instructor. That person is almost a stranger to you, but he is friendly and interested. He wants to know you better. For one thing, he wants to know the basic facts of your life. These facts are bound to be part of your story. But he wants to know a good deal more, something of the inside "you," your character, your training, your ambitions, your view of yourself.

But "yourself" is a big topic. Begin by thinking about it, by exploring it. Try to answer honestly, in your own mind, such questions as the following:

1. What kind of family do I have?
2. What kind of intellectual and moral training have I received?
3. What would I criticize about that training?
4. What people have had the greatest influence on me?

5. Has that influence been for good or bad?
6. What important experiences have I had? Why were they important to me?
7. What have I done that I am most proud of?
8. Have I made the most of my opportunities?
9. What is my own character like?
10. What are my strong points? Weak points?
11. What do I enjoy most?
12. What do I dislike most?
13. Did I get good training in high school?
14. Who were my good teachers? Why were they good for me?
15. Why did I come to college?
16. Did I drift to this college or have I some reason for being here?
17. What is my ambition?
18. What is my best talent? How does it relate to the career I plan?
19. What other questions should I answer to arrive at some estimate of myself?
20. Have I answered these questions thoughtfully and honestly?

You now have a large body of material laid out for your theme. You will not be able to use it all. In the first place, your theme will not be long enough. In the second place, if you try to use it all, you will end with a lot of unorganized facts and remarks. But attempting to answer these questions about yourself may have given you some perspective on yourself, the lead to some line of interest which will serve as the central idea of your theme and the spine for its organization. Or at least you may now see how various facts and ideas may be connected.

In trying to see how you can relate various facts and ideas to one another, you may find certain further general questions helpful. For instance:

1. To what extent have circumstances (heredity, family situation, certain persons, and experience) made me what I am?
2. To what extent do I feel myself responsible for what I am?
3. How do I assess myself and my possibilities at this moment?

Having pondered these questions, you may come up with such thematic statements as: "I am of a decayed New England stock," "My grandparents arrived in America stony broke," "I have to live down my father's fame," or "I am that monster, the completely average person." Or perhaps the three questions produce nothing that is helpful. In that case, you may be able to frame others much more important and fruitful for your purposes.

Below you will find a student's theme in autobiography. Although you should not take it as a model, it may give you some useful ideas. Note, first, that the student assumes a sympathetic and interested reader, as for such a theme he has a right to do. In his introduction he says that he has a single main idea for his theme. He does not tell what it is, though he might very well have done so, but prefers to move toward it through a piece of narrative. Note, too, how many details of the writer's life get into the theme, even though it is all directed toward a main idea. Do you feel that you have a fairly good notion of his character? Do you feel that you understand the father's character? Note how the theme concludes. How does the writer gain emphasis? He does make a straight statement of what he has learned, but he does not say straight out how this learning came from the experiences of the past. Does he need to? Can you frame a statement that shows how what he learned came from his experience?

Here is the theme itself:

LEARNING THE HARD WAY

I don't know how I could tell all about myself, but at least I can tell what seems to me now the most important thing I have yet learned about myself. To tell it I shall have to tell what led up to my learning it.

My home is in Illinois, in the southern part of the state that is known as Egypt. My family lives on a farm (it is good farming country), but my father practices law in ———, which is a county seat. My mother has been dead some years, and we have a housekeeper to run our household. The county high school where I went is not very good, and since my father used to help me a lot with my studies, I made a fine scholastic record and had time to spare for the basketball team and plenty of fun. I thought I was pretty good, if I must confess the truth. Then if I had had any lingering doubts about my abilities, they were demolished when I got a scholarship to go East to ——— Hall, which is a good prep school. I was ready to conquer the world, single-handed.

It didn't work out quite that way. The boys at ——— Hall had had much better training than I had and were used to tougher competition. They could breeze through lessons that broke my back. Besides, I hadn't realized before how much I had relied on my father's help at home. He was always around if I got stuck with Cicero or solid geometry. I hadn't realized either how much I had depended on getting a pat on the head from those old-maid school teachers at County High or on getting a cheer when I sneaked a fast one into the basket in the last two minutes of play on the basketball court.

Now things were different, and I simply could not bear the thought of defeat. Yet it looked as though that was what I was in for. To make matters worse, I was now up against boys with plenty of money, who took trips to Europe and Canada and had expensive hobbies. I had never thought about such things before. Now I began to get self-conscious about my lack of money, and this did not help my work. And I didn't make the basketball team. I didn't even make substitute. I had miserable grades in January and was on the verge of being busted out.

I don't know why my father came to see me. He told me that he had had to go on to New York City on a business trip, but now I suppose that he was lying. Perhaps one of the teachers had written him. He did not hang around the school much after he had met my teachers and seen the place and eaten one meal in the big hall. After dinner that night I broke down and showed him my marks. He looked at them and just burst out laughing. "Heck, son," he said, "that's just fine. I wish they were worse!"

I must have looked surprised. He laughed again and slapped me on the shoulder. "You sure thought you were a rooster, didn't you?" he said. I grinned in what must have been a sickly way.

Then he said for me to forget it. He said we were going to pack up and go to the city and paint the town. I cut classes for twc days. We had a fine time, going to shows and seeing the sights. When he put me on the train to go back to school, he said, as he shook hands good-by: "You know, Jack, maybe you are as much of a rooster as any guy ought to be." He left me with that to chew on.

I don't mean to suggest that I went back to ——— Hall and conquered the world the rest of the year. But things were different. I slept and ate better, and studies seemed to come easier. I began to make some friends and went home with one of the guys for Easter. In the spring I had a good deal of tennis and began to improve my game, for there is a good coach at ——— Hall. I passed my work. I wasn't sensational, but I made it under the wire for college. And now that I'm here, I think I know better how to go about things than if I had come a year ago. I know better how to depend on myself and roll with the punch. And I know that it is the last punch that counts.

As we said above, do not consider this theme as a model, but try to imitate it in one respect: Take some leading idea about yourself for your true subject (see pages 14–15 and 23–24) and try to relate all details to that. To do so will give you some control over your material. Furthermore, to gain more control after you have settled on the leading idea, but before you begin to write, make an outline for your projected theme. But do not feel bound by the outline. When you actually begin composition, keep an open mind. If new ideas come, as they almost certainly will, think them over on their merits, even if this means a change in your plan.

After you have finished the first draft of your theme, check it by the outline. If the theme seems good and systematic but does not match the outline, revise the outline to conform to the theme. But if the theme does not seem satisfactory and the outline does, revise the theme to conform to the outline. Attach the outline to the theme before you hand it in.

CHAPTER FOUR

The Main Intention

Thus far we have been talking about some of the fundamentals of writing. We have discussed briefly the basic parts of any piece of composition: the introduction, the body of the work, and the conclusion; and we have discussed the three interrelated principles that undergird even the humblest piece of writing: unity, coherence, and emphasis. But up to this point we have not discussed the writer's main intention, as such, and the ways in which it determines the kind of writing that he does. We have dealt with that intention only as a concrete and special thing. In the student themes previously discussed, one student meant to make plain to us why he wanted to be an engineer, another to explain to us why his Uncle Conroy was the person that he most admired, and another to present a significant event in his own life. In order to carry out his intention, each writer has told us a little of the story of his life; he has set forth explanations, has implied a certain argument, and has even attempted very tentatively to describe people and scenes. That is, within these themes we can distinguish, in various combinations, four kinds of intention.

The Four Kinds of Discourse

The four kinds of intention correspond to the four basic kinds of discourse: **exposition, argument, description,** and **narration.**

In the first of these, exposition, the intention is to explain something, to make clear to the reader some idea, to analyze a character or situation, to define a term, to give directions. The intention, in short, is to inform.

In argument, the intention is to make somebody change his mind, his attitude, his point of view, or his feelings. Whatever change is aimed at is to be achieved primarily by an appeal to the powers of logic.

In description, the intention is to make the reader see or hear something as vividly as the writer himself has seen or heard it (or imagined it), to make him get the feel of the thing described, the quality of a direct experience. The thing described may be anything which we can grasp through the senses, a natural scene, a city street, a cat or a race horse, the face of a person, the sound of a voice, the texture of bark, the odor of an attic, a piece of music.

In narration, the intention is to present an event to the reader — what happened and how it happened. The event itself may be grand or trivial, a battle or a ball game, a presidential campaign or a picnic; but whatever it is, the intention of the writer is to give the impression of movement in time, to give some immediate impression of the event, the sense of witnessing it.

Mixture of the Kinds of Discourse and the Main Intention

We have just listed the four kinds of discourse as traditionally described in their pure form. But we do not, of course, regularly encounter them in a pure form. We began this discussion, in fact, by pointing out that the kinds of discourse were mixed in the student themes we had been examining. In more elaborate pieces of writing the forms may be even more intricately intertwined. A magazine article on international affairs may very well employ narrative, as in an illustrative anecdote, or description, as in presenting the statesmen on whose decision the settlement of affairs may rest. Argument and exposition may be intertwined in a most complicated fashion. For example, the writer must make clear to the reader an existing state of affairs and thus will use exposition; but the writer may also have in mind some conviction that he wishes to pass on to his reader, some course of action that he wishes to recommend, and will therefore use argument.

At this point the student may well ask: " What becomes of the notion of a kind of discourse as the main intention if the kinds are so mixed up in ordinary practice? " This is a reasonable question, and the answer to it is fundamental. *In a good piece of writing the mixing of the kinds of discourse is never irresponsible. There is always a main intention, a fundamental purpose.* The class report will always be, by its very nature, a piece of exposition. The novel, no matter how much exposition, description, or argument it may contain, will always be primarily an example of narration. Certain instances may not be as clear-cut as these. Our example of the magazine article on international affairs may be primarily expository, with argument as a sort of aside, or it may aim, in the end, to convince the reader of the desirability of a certain policy and thus be primarily an argument. But always, in any piece of writing, the writer should know what his main intention is, whether he wants chiefly to explain, persuade, describe, or narrate.

Though most writing does involve a mixture of the kinds of discourse, we can best study them in isolation, one by one, as we shall do in the four succeeding chapters. This method of study will mean the systematic analysis of relatively pure examples in order to observe the types of organization appropriate to any one kind. It is only after one understands the kinds of discourse in pure form that one can make them work together in unity in a larger composition.

• Application •

Thumb through the section of Readings. Find a paragraph with exposition as the main intention; with argument; with description; with narration. What other kinds of discourse do you find mixed in each? What mixtures, for example, do you find in " Mother Sea: The Gray Beginnings " (page 469), " Dawn over Zero " (page 490), " The Hour of Letdown " (page 601), or " Saturday's Smells " (page 611)?

CHAPTER FIVE

The Methods of Exposition

Exposition is the kind of discourse that explains or clarifies a subject. The word *exposition* quite literally means to set forth a subject. It appeals to the understanding. Argument also appeals to the understanding, but it does so, not to explain something, but to convince the reader of the truth or desirability of something. Description and narration may, of course, lead to understanding, but their special appeal is to the imagination, to the reader's capacity for recreating in his mind the immediate qualities of an object or event.

Exposition is the most common kind of writing, for it is applicable to any task that challenges the understanding — the definition of a word, the way to a street address, the structure of a plant, the mechanism of a watch, the meaning of a historical event, the motive of an act, the meaning of a philosophy.

Exposition thus challenges the understanding, and when we study the methods of exposition, we are studying some of the ways in which our minds naturally work, some of the ways in which we observe and reason about things. We need to think things through, to try to understand them. We need to try to communicate with people, to make ourselves understood, in either speech or writing, and to try to understand what other people say or write. Now, as we study exposition, we are simply doing something systematically which ordinary living, in its hit-or-miss, unsystematic way, has been forcing on us, quite naturally, all the time.

Interest

A piece of exposition may be regarded as the answer to a question. If a specific question has been asked — " Why are you majoring in chemistry? " or " What were the causes of the American Revolution? " — it is rather easy to frame an answer that does not waver too badly from the point. But if we set out to write a piece of exposition simply because we feel that a subject is engrossing or important, we are very likely to give a confused account. Our vague feeling will not be enough to guide us. We must decide what specific question is our concern. We must decide this, because the question embodies the **interest** that the subject holds for us and that we want to appeal to in our readers.

An informal list may suggest the kind of interests to which exposition appeals:

1. What is it?
2. What does it mean?
3. How is it put together?
4. How does it work?
5. What was it intended for?
6. How did it come to be this way?
7. When did it occur or exist?
8. What is it worth?
9. What is its importance?
10. How well does it fulfill its intended function?

We can ask other questions, of course, about a subject, but these are among the most usual.

Naturally, not all of these questions would be appropriate for the same subject. If we are trying to explain the nature of a triangle, we would scarcely ask when it occurred, since the nature of a triangle — what makes a figure a triangle and not something else — has no reference to time at all. Or if we are discussing a railroad wreck, we would scarcely ask how well it fulfilled its intended function. It would be appropriate, however, to ask about its causes.

In Chapter 2, we discussed the problem of locating the real subject in a general topic, the concern that gives unity to a composition. The problem here is the same. The interest we wish to appeal to determines the line we follow in our discussion and gives that discussion its unity.

Let us take an example. A student who is fond of dogs and has had many around his home decides to write a theme about dogs. But that subject is too general. He must find some way to narrow it, to locate his true subject, to specify an interest. If he starts with the question: " What is it? " he might place the dog in its zoological classification and give an account of its evolution. Or the question: " What was it intended for? " might lead to a discussion of how certain breeds have been developed for special purposes. Or the question: " What is it worth? " might suggest the process of judging in a dog show. Or the question: " How does it work? " might lead to an explanation of how to train a dog. Any one of these topics would be a true subject, would appeal to a specific interest.

Here is the actual theme in which the student has narrowed his subject to the training of dogs, his special interest.

TRAINING A DOG

I have always liked dogs. I come by this naturally, for my father is crazy about them too, not only his hunting dogs, but other kinds as well. We always had a half dozen or so around the house, and my father and I like nothing better than talking about dogs, or reading about them, or going to dog shows. Dogs are a fascinating subject to us. One of the most fascinating things is to raise and train a dog. You really feel, then, that it is yours.

For the best results you have to start to train a dog young. I always feel, as a matter of fact, that you ought to start when the dog is only a puppy. It is true that the puppy can't learn, but you set up some kind of confidence, and he gets to recognize and like you. This makes things easier later.

To train a dog you need several qualities. You must be patient. You must put yourself in the dog's place. You must be consistent. You must be fair.

A dog can learn only by constant repetition. It is boring for a human being to go over and over the same simple thing, but you have to realize that this boredom is the price you pay for a good dog. You have to be patient and never let your boredom show. And you must never lose your temper.

This leads to the second thing, putting yourself in the dog's place. You have to sympathize with him. If you do, you will not be irritated. You will feel how hard it is for the animal to understand your wishes and how dependent he is on you.

It is obvious why you have to be consistent. The dog understands you only when your word or signal is always exactly the same as before. If you are inconsistent, he gets confused. For the same reason you must never change your mind. Once you give an order stick to it, even if it was a bad order. Your word must be law or you are wasting your breath.

Fairness is important always, but especially in training. You have to show the dog that you appreciate him, and once he gets this point, he wants nothing more than to please you. There is no use bribing a dog to obey. You have to make him want to please you, and the only way is by fairness. As for punishment, there is no use in punishing the dog if he doesn't know why he is being punished. You should punish immediately after the misbehavior, and you should always use the same punishment for the same kind of misbehavior. But don't lose your temper.

Training brings out the best in a dog and is worth all the time it takes. But my father says something else in addition. He says that when you train a dog you are training yourself, too. You teach yourself more than you teach the dog. My father says that you can't learn enough patience and sympathy, consistency and fair play, and so you ought always to be training a dog just to learn to control yourself.

In his introduction the writer gives some hint of the difficulty he had in selecting his true subject. He indicates that he had various kinds of interests competing in his mind — a number of " fascinating things," as he puts it — and that he realized the necessity for a choice. Once he has made the choice, he tells us when to start the training, but he does not actually give us a method for training. He perhaps assumes that common sense will tell us this, and he wants to put his emphasis on the qualities the trainer must possess. The listing of the qualities and the explanation of why they are important give him the body of the theme. The conclusion stems naturally out of the body of the theme, for the writer justifies the training, not merely by the desire for an obedient dog, but by the development of the character of the trainer.

The theme is not perfect, certainly. There is some repetitiousness, the phrasing is occasionally vague, and the organization in the next to last paragraph is a little fuzzy. But the writer has intelligently located his true subject, which gives his theme unity; he has a clear system of organization for the main body (the listing and discussion of the qualities of the trainer), which gives his theme coherence; and he has a sensible conclusion, which carries a little agreeable surprise with it (not the dog but the man learns most from the training process).

The author of this theme located and followed through one interest in his theme about dogs. This *main interest* gave him his subject. A writer may, however, appeal to more than one interest in the same composition, and in any extended discussion he is almost certain to do so. But in so doing he must be careful to keep the interests distinct. He must develop each interest at a different stage in his over-all treatment. And he must be sure that all the interests to which he appeals are related to the main interest of the composition. To say this in another way, he must be careful to maintain coherence and unity.

Here is another student theme, this time one which appeals to several kinds of interest:

1. From the title we know that the main interest is the importance of Boone, but in this paragraph the interest lies in the question : " *What is importance* — being or doing? " In other words, this is an example of our first question in the list.

2. Here the author discusses the first of the two kinds of importance of Boone as a man who accomplished things : opening the land.

3. Here he discusses the second example of the importance of accomplishment.

If someone had asked me when I was twelve years old what was the importance of Daniel Boone, I would have thought that person was crazy. I would have said, " Any idiot can see he is important just because he is Daniel Boone! " I had read a lot of boys' books about my hero, and one or two adult books, too; and I thought that being able to live in the woods alone and not be lonesome, or being able to know all the animals so well and their ways, or being able to endure hardship were the finest qualities a man could have. But now I am told that what counts is not just being something but accomplishing something. So I have to ask myself what Daniel Boone accomplished.

One of the books I have read about Boone makes the point that to understand his importance you must understand the life of the border settlements, how the people were land-hungry and had the urge to push on and better themselves. Boone, more than anybody else, opened up the new country to them. He gave them a place to go. It is true that he was hired as a sort of guide by the big rich land speculators who had bought a chunk of Kentucky from the Indians. Some credit is also due those men even if their motive was just to make money. But it was Boone who took the personal risk, and it was to Boone that the settlers looked for guidance.

The other important thing Boone did was to lead the settlers against the Indians at the time of the Revolution. The British were using the Indians against the settlers, and if the Indians had managed to win a victory in Kentucky, they might have gone on and caused real damage farther east and hurt seriously the cause of American Independence. It was Boone who inspired the settlers in Kentucky to fight and who showed them how. In that way he made a real contribution to our independence.

We can't say that Daniel Boone intended to accomplish these things. When he started out, all he wanted was to get a big land grant from the company he worked for, the Transylvania Company, and it was only bad luck and not knowing how to stake claims that prevented him. And when the country was settled, he moved on to Missouri, which was then part of Spanish territory. That action may not seem very patriotic, even taking into account the facts that he had gone broke in Kentucky and that nobody appreciated him. Also he felt cramped as Kentucky became settled and the game thinned out. You might say he was thinking more about good hunting than about helping the country.

4. The author here discusses the question : "*What was it intended for?*" He applies it, of course, to Boone's accomplishment.

5. In this paragraph the author gives a summary of the two kinds of important accomplishments of Boone, but he also goes back to the question : "*What is importance anyway?*"

But he did help the country anyway, in the two things he accomplished, whether he intended to or not — opening the land and helping to achieve independence. Those things are enough, in my mind, to make anybody a hero. There is one question, however, I would like to ask. Don't we remember Boone more for what he was than for what he accomplished? Maybe I am not yet grown up enough, but I can't help thinking more about him just walking through the wilderness by himself and being perfectly at home than I do about his accomplishments. It makes me feel happy and free just to think of him that way. To give that feeling may be a kind of importance, too.

Our marginal notes indicate the kinds of interest appealed to in the different paragraphs. We can see by the notes, too, how one interest leads to another. To summarize:

1. If the author is to discuss the importance of Boone, he must settle what importance is — *being* or *doing*. He accepts the common notion of *doing*.

2. Now, in two paragraphs he gives examples of what Boone accomplished, what he *did* for the country.

3. In the fourth paragraph he admits that Boone did not originally *intend* these accomplishments for the good of the country, but he says that the accomplishments are there anyway. (As a matter of fact, this last statement is in the fifth paragraph; the writer should have put it back into the fourth paragraph, for it is the end of his discussion of Boone's intention.)

4. In the last paragraph, the author comes back to the importance of Boone as a certain kind of individual. He won't give up that idea and tries to explain why. We are back to our first interest, but with a different answer to the question.

In other words, we have a large, main interest: " What is it? " — " What is the importance of Daniel Boone? " Then we have another, smaller interest in the first paragraph, again, " What is it? " — " What constitutes importance? " Then we have two examples of importance, answers to the question: " What did he do? " Then we have the answer to the question: " What was intended? " In the last paragraph, we go back to the first interest: " What constitutes importance? " But the whole essay has centered around the importance of Boone.

• **Applications** •

I. In the Readings, study " The Colors That Animals Can See " (page 478), " The Seven Deadly Fallacies " (page 551), or " The American Civilization Puzzle " (page 666). What is the main interest? What other interests are appealed to?

II. Below is a list of general subjects. Select three that interest you, and for each state five interests that might be used as true subjects. For instance, the general subject " Jet Propulsion " might provide several true subjects: (1) the history of its development, (2) the engineering principles involved, (3) the comparison of jet propulsion with other methods of propulsion, (4) the effect of jet planes on tactics in air warfare, (5) the effect on military strategy, (6) the effect on design of aircraft.

Baseball	Photography
The Eighteenth Amendment	The Battle of Gettysburg
Capital Punishment	Military Discipline
Socialism	Nationalism
Laissez-faire Economics	Charity
The Potato	Walt Whitman
Marriage	Symphonic Music
The Horse	Saint Paul
My Church	Nazism
Jazz	Going Steady

Heroism	*Hamlet*
Blind Dates	Propaganda
Postal Service	The Kibitzer
Prejudice	Good Manners
The Diesel Engine	Flower Gardening

III. Take one of the lists of true subjects you have prepared and try to develop several interests which might be related to one another in a discussion. Return to the section on outlining in Chapter 3 (and if your instructor suggests it, to Chapter 13, pages 391–93, and the Appendix on outlining, page 818), and prepare a topic outline of the discussion.

The Methods of Exposition

We shall now study the methods of exposition: identification, definition, comparison and contrast, illustration, classification, process analysis, and causal analysis. These are the ways in which we go about answering questions that demand exposition. This statement does not mean that there is a method to correspond to each question on our list. Some methods may be used in answering more than one question, and the answer to a single question may sometimes be made by a combination of methods.

Any discourse — for example, an editorial, an essay, a theme, a chapter in a textbook — will probably use more than one expository method. As a matter of fact, we rarely find a method in its pure state. But here, where we are trying to understand the nature of each method, we shall be concerned with relatively pure examples.

The First Method: Identification

Identification, one of the simplest methods of exposition, is a way of answering the question: " What is it? " It is a kind of pointing by means of language. " Who is Mrs. Bertrand Smith? " somebody asks, and the answer is, " Oh, she is the blond woman in the black dress, sitting to the right of the white-haired old man." The reply has in effect pointed a finger at Mrs. Smith. But perhaps Mrs. Smith is not there to be pointed at so easily. So the answer may be, " She is the woman who won the city golf tournament last year and then married the son of old Jason Smith, the banker." In either case the answer places the subject, Mrs. Smith, in such a context that she can be identified.

We constantly use such casual forms of identification in conversation. But we can use the same method in writing. For example, we can begin an article on the Carmel Mission by writing: " The Carmel Mission stands just outside the village of Monterey, California. It was founded by Padre Junipero Serra, who had come up from San Diego in the year 1770." We have thus identified the subject.

If identification becomes elaborate, it tends to move into other expository methods; it begins, for example, to overlap with definition or to use analysis, comparison, or contrast: and it may become lost in other more interesting methods. Even so, the method of identification is a useful and simple way of locating, of placing, of making possible the recognition of a subject.

The Second Method: Definition

Like identification, **definition** tries to answer the question: " What is it? " Before we can well discuss how a definition is made, however, we must settle on what the *it* is that is being defined. Strictly speaking, we can say that a definition is not of a thing but of a word. If we define *cat,* we are telling how to use the word *cat.* A definition sets the limits or bounds within which a term can be used, as the derivation of the word *definition* implies (it comes from two Latin words: *de,* meaning " with relation to," and *finis,* meaning " limit ") . This idea of definition as the limiting of a word is illustrated by the demand, which we are likely to make during an argument: " Define your terms." We do not usually make this demand about a word such as *cat,* but we frequently require a definition of a word such as *democracy, religion, honesty,* or *goodness,* which has several possible — and often slippery — meanings. We have the right to know how such a term is being used, and so we ask for the definition. By *term* we mean any word, or group of words, that constitutes a unit of meaning, that refers to one thing or idea.

The process of making a definition is not a mere game of words. It is clear that we cannot make a useful definition without knowledge of the thing (that is, the object, event, idea) to which the term refers. So the process of making a definition involves knowledge, and it may not only enlarge the understanding of the person who receives the definition but, more importantly, may even lead the maker of the definition to clarify his own thoughts on the subject involved.

Parts of a Definition: Convertibility

A definition is an equation. If we are asked to define term *A*, we say, " *A* is *B* " — or is *X*, *Y*, or *Z*. The equation has two terms, the *to-be-defined* and the *definer*, which quite literally equal each other. That is, in any statement you can substitute one term for the other without changing the sense of the statement in any respect. The terms are **convertible**.

For example, let us define *slave* as a human being who is the legal property of another and then set up this definition as an equation:

Slave	is	human being who is legal property of another
The *to-be-defined*	=	the *definer*

If we make a statement using the word which is the *to-be-defined*, we may substitute the *definer* for that word without any change of sense. The statement " To be a slave is worse than death " has exactly the same meaning as the statement " To be the legal property of another is worse than death." To repeat, the terms are convertible.

Let us take another proposition: " A slave is a man." This statement is, clearly, true. But is it a definition? Let us consider the question by thinking of two classes, or groups — the class *slave* and the class *man*. The class *man* is, clearly, a bigger group than the class *slave;* that is, there are men who are not slaves. Our original proposition, " A slave is a man," is true because the big class *man* includes the smaller class *slave.*

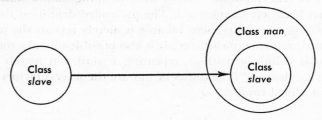

It is obvious that any statement we make about man as a class (that is, any statement that is true of *all* men) will necessarily be true of slaves, for the class *slave* is included in the class *man*. But no statement about slaves is *necessarily* true of all men. It *may* be true (as when we say, " Slaves have two legs "), but there are many reasonable statements about slaves (such as our statement above, " To be a slave is worse than death ") which are not applicable to all men (for we can scarcely substitute *man* for *slave* in our last statement and say, " To be a man is worse than death "). In other words, our proposition, " A slave is a man," does not have convertible terms. The *definer* is larger than the *to-be-defined* and includes it.

We can also go wrong in the other direction. We can have a *definer* that is smaller than the *to-be-defined*. We make that error, for instance, if we say that a table is a piece of furniture on which we serve meals. The *definer* (" a piece of furniture on which we serve meals ") is too small, because it will not cover many kinds of tables – study tables, bedside tables, sewing tables, etc.

To sum up, the *to-be-defined* and the *definer* must, if we think of them graphically as one superimposed on the other, be the same size; they must be coterminous.

Definer   To-be-defined   Definition

A Caution: Circular Definition

We cannot define a thing by itself. If, for example, we define the word *statistician* by saying that it means anybody who makes a profession of compiling and studying statistics, we have committed this error. The real question: " What kind of thing does a statistician do? " has been left unanswered. The pretended definition does not enlarge anybody's knowledge, because it merely repeats the term to be defined: *statistics, statistician*. It is also possible to make the error of **circular definition** without repeating a word, but merely by repeating an idea, as, " The causes of war are the several factors which result in armed conflict."

• Application •

Some of the following statements are correct definitions, and some are not; that is, some are real equations, and some are not. Distinguish those that are correct, and explain why. If you lack the information necessary to judge some of the definitions, use a dictionary or some other reference book, such as an encyclopedia. For example, statement 12 uses the word *anthropology*. If you do not know what anthropology is, try to find out. If anthropology studies more than morality, then statement 12 is not a correct definition.

1. A *soirée* means a social function which does not take place in the afternoon.
2. The French word *cheval* means horse.
3. A collar is the thing a man wears around his neck.
4. A protuberance is a thing that protrudes.
5. A man is a featherless biped.
6. A collie is the Scotch shepherd dog.
7. A collie is a long-haired dog.
8. A hero is a man who is useful to society.
9. Interment is the act or ceremony of putting a dead body in the earth.
10. Patriotism is a holy sentiment.
11. Patriotism is the last refuge of the scoundrel.
12. The science of anthropology is the science which studies morality.
13. Faith is the substance of things hoped for, the evidence of things not seen.
14. The word *poet* means a man interested in poetry.

Process of Definition

Identification answers the question: " What is it? " by pointing to its subject in space and time. Definition, too, is a kind of pointing, but it locates its subject, not in space and time, but according to another kind of scheme. A definition indicates the class into which a thing may be put and then points out how it differs from other things in that general class. The process of definition is not arbitrary; it is the natural way the mind works. We make definitions constantly, without thinking about how we make them. Let us examine a very simple example of this natural process.

A small child who has never seen a cat receives one as a pet. The father tells the child that the animal is a cat — a kitty. The proud parent now assumes that the child knows what the word *cat* means, but he may be surprised one day to find the child pointing to a Pekingese and calling, " Kitty, kitty." It is obvious that the child is using the word to mean any small, furry animal. When the father takes him to the park, the child is very likely to call a squirrel a kitty, too.

The father now undertakes to give the child a definition of *cat*. To do so, he must instruct the child in the differences between a cat, a Pekingese, and a squirrel. In other words, he undertakes to break up the class, or group, that the child has made (all small, furry animals) into certain subgroups (cats, Pekingese, squirrels) by focusing attention upon the differences, the differentiae.

If the child understands his father, he can then give a questioner a definition of the word *cat* — an inadequate definition, of course, but nevertheless a definition:

QUESTIONER: What does *cat* mean?

CHILD: It's a little animal, and it's got fur.

QUESTIONER: But dogs have fur, too, and dogs aren't cats.

CHILD: Yes, but dogs bark. Cats don't bark. Cats meow. And cats climb trees.

QUESTIONER: But squirrels have fur, and they climb trees and are little.

CHILD: Yes, but squirrels don't just *climb* trees like cats. They live in trees. And they don't meow like cats.

The child has put *cat* into a class, or group (small, furry animals), and then has distinguished the subgroup of cats from the other subgroups, Pekingese and squirrels.

If we chart the child's reasoning, we get a diagram like this:

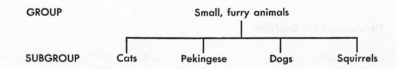

Whenever we make a definition, we go through the same process as the child trying to tell what a kitty is. We locate the *to-be-defined* as a **species** in relation to a group (**genus**) that includes several different species and then try to say what quality or qualities (**differentia** or **differentiae**) distinguish the *to-be-defined* from the other species in the genus. So we get the formula:

$$\text{Definition of species} = genus + differentiae$$
$$\text{The } to\text{-}be\text{-}defined = \text{the } definer$$

The pattern of the child's attempt to define *cat* is the usual pattern of definition, but the definition that the child gives will not serve us in our adult world. It will not serve us, because the genus and differentiae which the child adopts are not significantly distinguished. For instance, smallness and furriness are not traits that significantly mark off a genus, and meowing and climbing trees are not traits that significantly mark off the species cat from the other subgroups adopted by the child.

A zoologist would go about the business very differently. He might begin by saying: " A cat — *Felis domestica,* we call it — is a digitigrade, carnivorous mammal of the genus *Felis,* which includes the species tiger (*Felis tigris*), the species ocelot (*Felis pardalis*), the species lion (*Felis leo*), the species cougar (*Felis concolor*), and several other species. All the species of the genus *Felis* have lithe, graceful, long bodies, relatively short legs, with soft, padded feet, strong claws, which are retracted into sheaths when not in use, powerful jaws with sharp teeth, and soft, beautifully marked fur. The cat is the smallest of the genus, usually measuring so-and-so. It is the only species easily domesticated. . . ."

Like the child, the zoologist has set up a group, which he calls a *genus*, and has given the characteristics of the group. Then he has broken up the group into several subgroups, each of which he calls a species. Last, he has set about pointing out the differences between the species *cat* and the other species of the same genus.

Diagramed, his thinking has this form:

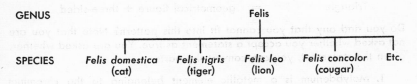

The form used by the zoologist is, we see, the same as that used by the child. The difference is that the zoologist thinks in *significant* classes. We should note that the zoologist uses the words *genus* and *species* with somewhat different meanings from ours. For him the word *genus* means not only a group including smaller groups called species, but also a group of species closely related structurally and by origin; and the word *species* means a subgroup whose members possess numerous characteristics in common and interbreed to preserve those characteristics. In other words, the zoologist has a specialized significance for the words *genus* and *species,* a significance dictated by the materials he is dealing with — living forms. Despite this specialized significance, he uses the words in his pattern of definition just as we do, for instance, in setting up the formal scheme for the definition of *bungalow:*

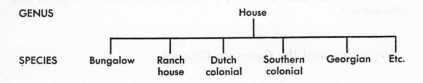

Though genus and species are part of all definition, we do not ordinarily use technical language in giving a definition. For *bungalow* we are apt to say: " Oh, it's a kind of house. It differs from

Dutch colonial, Southern colonial, Georgian, and some other styles in that it has only one story. The best way to distinguish the bungalow from other one-story houses is by the floor plan. For instance, if we compare it with a ranch house, we find . . . etc."

• **Applications** •

I. From the following group of statements sort out those that are equations. Then take each equation and set it up in the formal pattern of the to-be-defined equaling genus plus differentiae. For example, the statement " A triangle is a three-sided geometrical figure " would be analyzed as follows:

The *to-be-defined* = *genus* + *differentiae*
Triangle = geometrical figure + three-sided

Do you find any that you cannot fit into this pattern? Note that you are not asked whether you accept a statement as true. You are asked whether, given the statement, you can convert the parts.

1. Molybdenum is a metallic element belonging to the chromium group, whitish in color, and resembling iron in its malleability and difficult fusibility.
2. Beauty is truth, truth beauty.
3. A line is what is described by a moving point.
4. A straight line is the shortest path between two points.
5. To be good is to be happy.
6. Nationalism means to love your country.
7. Nationalism is that attitude which would put the aggrandizement of country above all other considerations whatsoever.
8. Propaganda is an effort to dominate public opinion.
9. Advertising is an effort to dominate public opinion.
10. Propaganda is the corruption of the judgment of the public.
11. Advertising is a means of public service.
12. To be cultured is to love music, art, and poetry.

II. Look back at the statements which you have rejected as not being proper equations. Can you fit any of them into the pattern of genus plus differentiae?

Definition and the Common Ground

Suppose, language and history permitting, that we should try to give our definition of a bungalow to an American Indian of the old days. He probably would not let us get beyond the first sentence, " Oh, it's a kind of house," for he would immediately want to know what a house is. In other words, if we give a definition, we assume that our audience knows the genus we are going to work in. If the audience does not know the genus, we must go back to a more inclusive group, a group including our genus as a subgroup, and try again, hoping now to have a common ground. So, if our Indian does not understand what a house is, we may try again and begin by saying, " It's a kind of shelter — but a shelter you make, etc." Our Indian knows what a shelter is, and he can get a notion of man-made shelter, for he has a tepee or lodge or hogan.

What we have developed by implication is a scheme something like this:

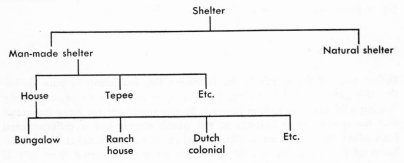

The Indian has pushed us back a couple of stages, and we now have a common ground and can define *house*. It is not likely that we'll get down to *bungalow*, for the Indian probably will not understand our necessary differentiae under the now-established genus *house*.

Not only with our poor Indian but with everyone, a common ground is necessary for an effective definition. This principle of the common ground is very important, for it implies that a definition is not only *of some term* but is *for somebody*. The giver of the definition can define only by reference to what his particular audience already knows or is willing to learn for the purpose at hand.

This necessary knowledge must be of two kinds: of words and of things. It must be of words, for a definition is in words. The giver of the definition must use words that his audience can understand or can readily become acquainted with. For instance, when the zoologist refers to the cat as a " digitigrade mammal," and so on, he is using words that most of us would not know. For the general reader, the zoologist would need to explain further that *digitigrade* means " walking on the toes," as a cat does, as opposed to " walking on the whole foot " (*plantigrade*) , as a man does. In this way the zoologist would provide the common ground.

The knowledge must also be of things, for if the audience does not know the things a definition refers to, the definition will not work. For instance, there is no use in trying to define the color beige to a man blind from birth. If you say that beige is a light, brownish color, the natural color of wool, you have really said nothing to him, for he has had no experience of color. If you go on and give the physicist's definition of color, referring to wave lengths of light, you run into the same difficulty. He can grasp the notion of wave length, but he has no basis for knowing what light is. You run into a defect in his experience, in his knowledge. There is always the possibility of running into some defects in our audience's knowledge, and, in so far as possible, we must work with what is known.

• Application •

Define each of the words in the following list, indicating in your definition the genus and differentiae. For example: *river* — a large, constantly flowing (differentiae) stream (genus). By our statement we have indicated that the species *river* belongs to the genus *stream* but is differentiated from other streams (brooks, rills, branches, runs, and creeks) by its size. Some of the problems will, however, be more complicated than this. If you do not have enough information to make a definition that satisfies you, use a dictionary or some reference work, such as an encyclopedia. Do not hesitate to copy a definition from a dictionary. But if you do, indicate the genus and differentiae in the dictionary definition. Perhaps even the dictionary will not help much with a word like *democracy*. You may feel that the dictionary definition does not express what you think to be the really important qualities of the word. In that case, do not hesitate to risk your own judgment.

pond	battalion	liberty	experiment
house	personality	tennis	yellow
lassitude	noun	fence	charity
anger	corporal	essay	automobile
horse	color	democracy	conscience
psychiatrist	depth	capitalism	book
morality	love		

Extended Definition

While words like *house* or *pond* may be defined rather easily, other words — for instance, *morality, liberty,* or *conscience* — may lead us into very complicated discussions (as you have probably discovered). A simple definition will not serve. We need to extend our definition and try to think through the meaning (or, more likely, the meanings) of the term. Often such a definition requires an essay, or even a book.

The attempt to define *wealth* given below is not a full essay, but it is considerably more extended than any definition we have yet encountered:

There is a certain desirable thing which is and must be the subject of political economy. Whether avowed or not, a definite conception is, in reality, under discussion in every treatise on this science. For this conception the term *wealth,* if used in accordance with history and etymology, is an accurate designation. The Saxon *weal* indicated a condition of relative well-being, the state of having one's wants well supplied as compared with a prevailing standard. No possession common to all men can constitute such relative well-being. The limitless gifts of nature do not produce it, since they are indiscriminate in their ministrations; air and sunlight make no differences among men and, though creating absolute well-being, cannot create that social condition indicated by the term wealth. This relative condition can be produced only by that which, besides satisfying wants, is capable of appropriation.

It is by a transfer of meaning that the term which primarily designated a condition of life has been applied to the things which produce the condition. But not all causes of comparative happiness are included in the meaning of the word. Wealth, as historically used, signified the well-being resulting from outward rather than inward causes. Health and contentment may make a shepherd happier than the owner of flocks; yet the owner only is " well off." Reserving a broader term to designate well-being in general, usage has employed the word *wealth* to signify, first, the comparative welfare resulting from material possession and, second, and by a transfer, the possessions themselves.

Wealth then consists in the relative weal-constituting elements in man's material environment. It is objective to the user, material, useful, and appropriable. . . . — JOHN B. CLARK: *The Philosophy of Wealth.*

We can see that what the author has done is to start with the derivation of the word and show how the meaning has become specialized by the addition of differentiae. Then he gives the differentiae that distinguish wealth from other kinds of weal, or well-being. Since the differentiae are complicated, he does not simply list them, but explains each one.

Here is another, somewhat more elaborate definition of *wealth,* in which the author uses a different approach to definition. Whereas Clark builds his definition by *including* the differentiae properly belonging to the term, Hilaire Belloc, the author of the definition to follow, begins by *excluding* the *differentiae* that do not properly belong.

The economic definition of Wealth is subtle and difficult to appreciate. . . . First, we must be clear as to what Wealth is *not*.

Wealth is never properly defined, for the purpose of economic study, by any one of the answers a person would naturally give off-hand. For instance, most people would say that a man's wealth was the money he was worth. But that, of course, is nonsense; for even if there were no money used, his possessions would still be there, and if he had a house and cattle and horses, the mere fact that money was not being used where he lived would not make him any worse off.

Another and better, but still wrong, answer is: "Wealth is what a man possesses." For instance, in the case of this farmer, his house and his stock and his furniture and implements are what we call his "wealth." In ordinary talk that answer will do well enough. But it will not do for the strict science of Economics, for it is not accurate.

For consider a particular case. Part of this man's wealth is, you say, a certain gray horse. But if you look closely at your definition and make it rigidly accurate, you will find that *it is not the horse itself which constitutes his wealth, but something attaching to the horse,* some quality or circumstance which affects the horse and gives the horse what is called its *value.* It is this *value* which is wealth, not the horse. To see how true this is consider how the value changes while the horse remains the same.

On such and such a date any neighbor would have given the owner of the horse from 20 to 25 sacks of wheat for it, or, say, 10 sheep, or 50 loads of cut wood. But suppose there comes a great mortality among horses, so that very few are left. There is an eager desire to get hold of those that survive in order that the work may be done on the farms. Then the neighbors will be willing to give the owner of the horse much more than 20 to 25 sacks of wheat for it. They may offer as much as 50 sacks, or 20 sheep, or 100 loads of wood. Yet the horse is exactly the same horse it was before. The wealth of the master has increased. His horse, as we say, is "worth more." *It is this **Worth**, that is, this ability to get other wealth in exchange, which constitutes true Economic Wealth.*

I have told you that the idea is very difficult to seize, and that you will find the hardest part of the study here at the beginning. There is no way to make it plainer. One has no choice but to master the idea and make oneself familiar with it, difficult as it is. *Wealth does not reside in the objects we possess, but in the economic values attaching to those objects.*

We talk of a man's wealth or a nation's wealth, or the wealth of the whole world, and we think at once, of course, of a lot of material things: houses and ships, and pictures and furniture, and food and all the rest of it. But the economic wealth which it is our business to study is not identical with those *things.* Wealth is the sum total of the *values* attaching to those things.

That is the first and most important point.

Here is the second: Wealth, for the purposes of economic study, *is confined to those values attaching to material objects through the action of man, which values can be exchanged for other values.*

I will explain what that sentence means.

Here is a mountain country where there are few people and plenty of water everywhere. That water does not form part of the *Economic Wealth* of anyone living there. Everyone is the better off for the water, but no one has *wealth* in it. The water they have is absolutely necessary to life, but no man will give anything for it because any man can get it for himself. It has no *value in exchange*. But in a town to which water has to be brought at great expense of effort, and where the amount is limited, it acquires a value in exchange, that is, people cannot get it without offering something for it. That is why we say that in a modern town water forms part of *Economic Wealth*, while in the country it usually does not.

We must carefully note that wealth thus defined is *not* the same thing as well-being. The mixing up of these two separate things — well-being and economic wealth — has given rise to half the errors in economic science. People confuse the word " wealth " with the idea of well-being. They say: " Surely a man is better off with plenty of water than with little, and therefore conditions under which he can get plenty of water for nothing are conditions under which he has *more wealth* than when he has to pay for it. He has more wealth when he gets the water free than he has when he has to pay for it."

It is not so. Economic wealth is a separate thing from well-being. Economic wealth may well be increasing though the general well-being of the people is going down. It may increase though the general well-being of the people around it is stationary.

The science of Economics does not deal with true happiness nor even with well-being in material things. It deals with a strictly limited field of what is called " Economic Wealth," and if it goes outside its own boundaries it goes wrong. Making people as happy as possible is much more than Economics can pretend to. Economics cannot even tell you how to make people well-to-do in material things. But it can tell you how exchangeable Wealth is produced and what happens to it; and as it can tell you this, it is a useful servant.

That is the second difficulty at the very beginning of our study. *Economic Wealth consists in* **exchangeable** *values, and nothing else.* . . .

Let us sum up this first, elementary, part of our subject, and put it in the shortest terms we can find — what are called " Formulae," which means short and exact definitions, such as can be learnt by heart and retained permanently.

We write down, then, two Formulae:

1. Wealth is made up, not of things, but of economic values attaching to things.

2. Wealth, for the purpose of economic study, means *only* exchange values: that is, values against which other values will be given in exchange. — HILAIRE BELLOC: *Economics for Young People.*

The maker of this definition of *wealth* starts by ruling out certain common misconceptions. Wealth is not money. Wealth is not what a man possesses. But merely to rule out these errors requires discussion and illustration, through which we arrive at the notion that the "ability to get other wealth in exchange" is the key to the definition, that wealth resides not "in the objects we possess, but in the economic values attaching to those objects."

This statement gives us, of course, a genus (value) and differentiae (summed up under the term *economic*). We have a notion what the genus *value* means, but the differentiae are not clear to us. The writer, then, sets about explaining that economic value is exchange value, "values attaching to material objects through the action of man, which can be exchanged for other values." He discusses this idea by illustration, the illustration of water in the country and water in the town. This discussion leads him to make a sharp distinction between wealth and well-being, thus making a definition exactly opposite that of the previous writer. Having completed his explanation, Belloc is prepared to set up what he calls his formulas, which embody both his definition of wealth as economic value and a summary of his explanation of economic value, which amounts to another definition. So here, to understand one definition we have to have another.

Here is a student theme in definition:

AMERICAN DEMOCRACY

Everybody knows that there are always differences between the idea of a thing and the way a thing works out in practice, and it is no different in American democracy. There are sometimes injustices in it. Furthermore, the way it has worked out has been different from one time to another, from 1790 to 1954. I do not mean by this just injustices and break-downs in the system, but different kinds of general practice. In the early days there was, for instance, a property qualification for voting, and there was legal acceptance of slavery. I do not want to discuss the abuses, and I do not want to discuss the development through history of American democracy. I want to try to define it as the basic idea, and, you might say, ideal, of our country.

The first thing I think of is equality, for that is the way the Declaration of Independence starts. I do not mean the nonsensical notion that everybody is exactly like everybody else. I mean that everybody has certain equal rights, what the Declaration calls the rights to life, liberty, and the pursuit of happiness. Anybody but a fool knows that you have this kind of right only so long as it does not interfere with the similar right of other people. The fact that sticking up filling stations is what makes you happy does not mean that you have the right to that particular kind of happiness.

The next thing I think about is that if people have these rights, then a government has as its main business to see that these rights are maintained.

Everything it does ought to bear on that purpose, either directly or indirectly. Every act, say even a law about truck loads on highways or a tariff or an ordinance about muzzling dogs or a declaration of war, is supposed to promote these rights and nothing else. A government does not exist for itself, or to get privileges for a small outfit, or to gain power, or even to make people be good.

The third important characteristic of our country is the organization of the government to insure equal rights. It is organized by majority rule. If you look up the derivation of the word *democracy* in a dictionary, you will find that it comes from two Greek words, *demos,* meaning " people," and *crateo,* meaning " rule." A democracy is a government by the people. But right here you ask about the people who are in the minority. By this principle, can't the majority just kick a minority around worse than any king or aristocracy ever did? You can point out that Hitler and Stalin got mighty big majorities in elections and ask if that was not democracy. We all know that it was not democracy, American or any other kind. It was not, because my notion of democracy means that the majority cannot do anything that is against the rights of the minority. When Hitler got his big majority, where were the rights of the Jews? By the same line of reasoning, the minority cannot pick up pistols and start trouble just because they lose an election. They have to stick to the rules of the game and try to win the next round.

I have been thinking mostly about rights, but the next thing I think of is what a man in a democracy is supposed to do to have these rights. He is supposed to take some responsibility to see that democracy works.

But there is another thing he ought to do. Earlier I said that government does not exist even to *make* people good. A democracy takes it for granted that people, if you give them their rights, will appreciate them enough to behave decently. It is true that the government makes people do certain things — send children to school and not dump garbage in the street. But these are things too closely tied to everybody's good to be left to individuals to decide.

It is not only a question of being good. A democracy assumes that people, with the opportunity, will work and have ambition and contribute something, and that the right kind of liberty makes people pursue their happiness in a constructive way. This sounds sort of prissy and Sunday School-ish, but that is the way it strikes me. If we don't assume this, how would the country operate for even a week?

I will sum up my definition. American democracy is not just a system of government. It is an attitude toward the way to live which assumes equal rights for everybody. This attitude leads to a system of government based on majority rule, but the majority must avoid breaking the rights of the minority. Under this system it is taken for granted that people will take some responsibility for government and will be decent and constructive and contribute something. That is, at the bottom of democracy is the assumption about human nature that the right kind of liberty encourages a man to be decent and constructive.

Let us glance at the defects of this theme, for a moment. It is written rather dully. The formula which introduces most of the paragraphs (" The first thing I think of . . ." " The next thing I think
about . . ." etc.) gets very monotonous. The writer could use much
better devices of transition, devices that would really indicate how
his thought progresses. Furthermore, his sentence structure tends to
be monotonous. And the organization of the theme leaves something
to be desired, a defect which we shall discuss in a moment. But, by
and large, the writer has made a sound attempt to think through his
subject.

In the first paragraph the writer undertakes to say what is to be
defined, not the actual practice of democracy but the idea of democracy. He even indicates that the idea is in a constant process
of development in our history, but he doesn't elaborate this point.

With the second paragraph, in the discussion of equality and
rights, he begins to line up differentiae. But — and here is the cause
of the blurring of the organization — we aren't quite sure what the
genus is. Is it to be *government?* We begin to suspect that it is not,
for by the fourth paragraph he is referring to government as something set up to accomplish democracy. Then a few sentences on, he
says that democracy is a " government by the people." Perhaps at
this point the writer has not really decided what the genus is. In
any case, he now describes a kind of government. After doing this,
however, he comes back to what obligations we assume citizens to
have and what kind of behavior we can expect under such a government.

When we get to the last paragraph, we do find out what the genus
is — to use his language, " an attitude toward the way to live." Having stated this genus, the writer sums up the theme. Here again he
could be more systematic. Not that he would have to use words like
genus and *differentia,* but he should indicate a little more clearly
the relation among the elements.

Let us, however, set up his definition in a formal scheme to see
what it looks like:

TO-BE-DEFINED	=	DEFINER	
American idea of democracy	is	" an attitude toward the way to live "	(*genus;* i.e., a way of life)
		1. based on assumption of	(*differentiae*)
		a. equality among men in sense of equal rights to life, lib-erty, pursuit of happiness, and	

       b. willingness of people to accept constructive responsibility with liberty, and
2. taking political form of a government
       a. devoted to the purpose of maintaining the rights of individual citizens, and
       b. operating by majority rule

METHOD OF EXTENDED DEFINITION

There are many ways to compose an extended definition. We see that in the former of the two definitions given above the writer takes as his key the derivation of the word *wealth* from the Anglo-Saxon *weal*. In the other definition, the author begins by excluding certain things from his definition, by dealing, that is, with what he thinks are misconceptions. Here is the first paragraph of Cardinal Newman's famous essay, " What Is a University," which indicates yet a third way:

If I were asked to describe as briefly and popularly as I could, what a University was, I should draw my answer from its ancient designation of a *Studium Generale,* or " School of Universal Learning." This description implies the assemblage of strangers from all parts in one spot; — *from all parts;* else, how will you find professors and students for every department of knowledge? and *in one spot;* else, how can there be any school at all? Accordingly, in its simple and rudimental form, it is a school of knowledge of every kind, consisting of teachers and learners from every quarter. Many things are requisite to complete and satisfy the idea embodied in this description; but such as this a University seems to be in essence, a place for the communication and circulation of thought, by means of personal intercourse, through a wide extent of country.

How does this differ from the method used by J. B. Clark in defining *wealth?* They start in much the same way, it is true. Clark takes the word *weal* and uses it as a guide in developing the economic concept *wealth.* Newman takes the old term *studium generale* and tells us how it was applied in the Middle Ages. Then he says that, despite changes with time, this old term is still a good description of a modern university. In fact, the body of his essay is the attempt to apply the implications of the old term to the modern situation. Clark, then, uses the root meaning of a key word as a guide in developing a modern definition; Newman applies an old definition to a new form.

Turn to the essay " True Americanism," by Louis D. Brandeis (Readings, page 587). Notice how Justice Brandeis uses the motto of the United States, *E pluribus unum,* as a starting point for his definition. On the way toward the definition, he finds it necessary to discuss American ideals, the American standard of living, and various other topics; but all these concerns are, in the end, related to his making of a definition. Observe that the motto is *not* the definition: it is a point of reference for making the definition, and the definition could perfectly well be made without the use of the motto.

We can readily see that an extended definition usually involves other methods of exposition, such as classification and comparison, and may involve other types of discourse, such as description and narration. In fact, an extended definition may simply be the beginning of an essay which moves from an extended definition to a discussion of the topic in question.

Let us now examine a student theme which has the purpose of making and explaining a definition:

A TRUE PATRIOT

I. *Introduction:*
Definition not yet begun; statement of need for a definition

In these times when our country is going through dangers, everyone claims to be a patriot, and many people attack their opponents by impugning their patriotism. It seems to me that we would do well to define patriotism, to determine what we really mean by the word.

II. *Body of Discussion:*
1. Basic definition

The *Shorter Oxford Dictionary* says that the word *patriot* comes from the late Latin *patriota,* meaning "fellow-countryman." If my memory of Latin is correct, *patriota* derives from *patria,* or "fatherland." The dictionary definition of *patriot* most applicable to our present discussion is "One who exerts himself to promote the well-being of his country." *Patriotism* thus means "the love or zealous devotion" to the well-being of one's country.

2. Reason why basic definition is not adequate

But this definition, although it appears adequate, is not really satisfactory; for everyone, as I have said, claims to have love and devotion and to be promoting the well-being of the country. We must then decide first what *well-being* is and how one can best contribute to it, for a man who claims he is a patriot and perhaps really does love his country might

3. First differentia: a man must understand well-being

still do more harm than good if he is promoting a cause detrimental to the general well-being. In other words, a man has to have good judgment before he can be a good patriot.

4. Various kinds of contributions to well-being

What exactly constitutes the well-being of a country? Well-being is no single thing but a composite of many things essential to the life of a country: a country has to have industry, business, agriculture, and mining. It has to have educational institutions. It has to have civil service. It has to have writers and journalists, and artists and musicians. It has to have scientists and soldiers. It even has to have politicians. Whatever strengthens and improves any of these institutions, whatever gives us better writers, scientists, and politicians, contributes to the well-being of the country. Thus there are many ways of contributing. Perhaps the basic way is to do your job well, whatever it is.

5. Second differentia: risk discussed as step toward determining 2nd differentia: unselfishness

Ordinarily, however, when we think of a patriot, or patriotism, we think of a spectacular deed, of Teddy Roosevelt leading a cavalry charge or of those men who let themselves be experimented on to discover the cause of yellow fever. What is the common quality in these spectacular deeds that makes them examples of patriotism? I think it is this: all these people are taking some kind of risk for their country.

6. But risk itself not enough; must be unselfish risk

You may say that any soldier takes a risk but that all soldiers are not outstanding patriots. There is a further qualification: the risk must be unselfish. If a man is drafted, and then gets into battle just because he cannot escape the watchful eye of the sergeant, and finally is shot, you cannot consider him much of a patriot. He was simply trapped. He didn't take the risk; the risk took him. We have to say, then, that the patriot takes risks, unselfishly and in a spirit of self-sacrifice. It follows, too, that if someone makes a contribution to his country, such as in-

7. — as it must be an unselfish contribution

8. Third differentia : actual achievement not essential ; essential thing is willingness to make sacrifice, to do duty no matter how simple

9. Contrast with great achievement undertaken for selfish reason

III. *Conclusion:*
Summary of defended definition

venting a useful machine or practicing medicine, he isn't necessarily a patriot — his motives may be those of self-interest and the desire to make as much money as possible.

We think of the spectacular patriot because he illustrates the willingness to demonstrate " zealous devotion " for his country. But can a man be a patriot *unless* he takes a big risk? Isn't a man a patriot if he simply has the *willingness* to make a sacrifice, that is, do his duty as it happens to come along? Can't he exert himself just when the occasion arises? I think so. In fact, I'm inclined to admire more a man who has a quiet willingness to serve than those people who want to show off their patriotism, even if they are willing to take big risks in showing it off. One can never be sure whether they are taking risks for the country unselfishly or are taking risks just to feel important.

To summarize my feelings, I should say that a patriot is a man who makes an intelligent contribution to the well-being of his country, who is willing to take risks or make a self-sacrifice in so doing, even if his contribution isn't spectacular. Finally, the willingness must be genuinely for the sake of the country and not for the sake of showing off. Perhaps all these ideas and more are implicit in the words " love and devotion " in the dictionary definition, but I feel that they need expansion and clarification if we are really to understand the meaning of patriotism.

We can see from the marginal notes what the writer's outline — if he actually made one — may have been. If he did not make one, he was taking a risk, for in writing a definition it is very important to be systematic, to know where you are going before you start. In addition to the outline, let us try another device to see how carefully the writer has thought through his ideas. Here is the scheme of genus and species for the definition:

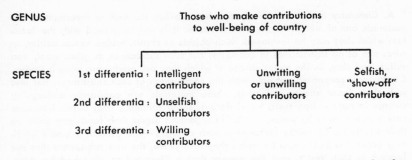

GENUS — Those who make contributions to well-being of country

SPECIES
- 1st differentia : Intelligent contributors
- 2nd differentia : Unselfish contributors
- 3rd differentia : Willing contributors

Unwitting or unwilling contributors

Selfish, "show-off" contributors

So we have our old formula again. Much of the discussion in the theme was to explain distinctions needed to make the formula clear. The writer had, for instance, to explain the nature and variety of possible contributions to the country's well-being (II:4). He had to discuss why we think of risk first (because it is the most obvious form of unselfishness, or self-sacrifice — II:5,6); and then he had to apply the differentia of unselfishness to contributors in general (II:7). The formula has been fleshed out by discussion.

Before we turn to Applications and the writing of a theme of extended definition, it should be emphasized once again that there is no single correct way to develop a definition. It is not even necessary that the definition be of the genus + differentia type. We define " 2 " as " 1 + 1," and this is a proper definition, though it is not of the genus + differentia type. But most of the definitions that the student will encounter in his own writing are of that type, and his main problem will usually be to get his central conception right — that is, to see what the genus in question is and what the proper differentiae are. If he does that, then with common sense, he should have little difficulty with his organization, with the explanation and illustration of the differentiae.

• Applications •

I. Criticize the student theme above for

1. Sentence structure
2. Punctuation
3. Paragraph structure

Refer to the Handbook sections on syntax (p. 770) and punctuation (p. 783) for rules on 1 and 2. Do you think you could improve the general organization? What grade would you give it?

II. Below are two examples of extended definition. What are the genus and differentiae in each? How is each definition developed?

A. Chemistry is that branch of science which has the task of investigating the materials out of which the universe is made. It is not concerned with the forms into which they may be fashioned. Such objects as chairs, tables, vases, bottles, or wires are of no significance in chemistry; but such substances as glass, wool, iron sulfur, and clay, as the materials out of which they are made, are what it studies. Chemistry is concerned not only with the composition of such substances, but also with their inner structure. Further, these materials are constantly undergoing change in nature: iron rusts, wood decays, sugar ferments, coal burns, limestone rock is eaten away by water, and living organisms digest their foods and build up their structures. Chemistry investigates such changes — the conditions under which they occur, the mechanism by which they take place, the new substances that are formed as their result, and the energy that is liberated or absorbed by them. Chemistry also studies the way in which these and similar changes can be carried out in the laboratory or on a larger scale in the chemical plant. As a result of investigations along these lines, chemistry has found how metals can be extracted from their ores; how impoverished fields can be made fertile again; and how the materials that are found in nature can be converted into thousands of new substances to help feed the race, to cure the sick, and to provide such comfort and even luxury for the common man as was not enjoyed by the wealthy of an earlier generation. — John Arrend Timm: *General Chemistry*.

B. At first, then, instead of asking what religion is, I should prefer to ask what characterizes the aspirations of a person who gives me the impression of being religious: a person who is religiously enlightened appears to me to be one who has, to the best of his ability, liberated himself from the fetters of his selfish desires and is preoccupied with thoughts, feelings, and aspirations to which he clings because of their super-personal value.

It seems to me that what is important is the force of this super-personal content and the depth of the conviction concerning its overpowering meaningfulness, regardless of whether any attempt is made to unite this content with a Divine Being, for otherwise it would not be possible to count Buddha and Spinoza as religious personalities.

Accordingly, a religious person is devout in the sense that he has no doubt of the significance and loftiness of those super-personal objects and goals which neither require nor are capable of rational foundation. They exist with the same necessity and matter-of-factness as he himself. In this sense religion is the age-old endeavor of mankind to become clearly and completely conscious of these values and goals and constantly to strengthen and extend their effects. — Albert Einstein: " Science and Religion," *Science News Letter*.

III. Here are some statements about religion. Which are definitions? In any which does not have the form of definition, can you see what definition may lie behind the statement? What genus and differentiae are involved in each definition?

A. " Religion, after trying to see as best I could what various religions and religious people had in common, I felt impelled to define as the reaction of the personality as a whole to its experience of the Universe as a whole." — J. S. Huxley.

B. Religion is " morality tinged with emotion." — Matthew Arnold.

C. Religion is the " belief in spiritual beings." — E. B. Tylor.

D. Religion is " that voice of the deepest human experience." — Matthew Arnold.

E. Religion is the " opium of the people." — Karl Marx.

F. Religion is " a propitiation or conciliation of powers superior to man which are believed to direct or control the course of nature and of human life." — Sir James Frazer.

G. " Pure religion and undefiled before God is this, to visit the fatherless and widows in their affliction, and to keep himself unspotted from the world." — St. James.

IV. Write an extended definition (600 words or more) of one of the words listed below, or on some word approved by your instructor, using the following pattern of discussion insofar as it will apply in the particular case:

1. Derivation of the word — does the origin enlighten us?
2. History of the application of the word — do earlier applications differ from the present application?
3. Genus and differentiae in present application — how can the species be distinguished from other significant species?
4. Analysis of species — does it have any " subspecies," and if so, how are they to be distinguished from one another?
5. Application of the definition to individual instances — does the definition really meet this test, and does it enlighten us about the individual instances?

republic	empire	contemplate
cynicism	imagination	radical
fascism	theology	democracy
culture	cathedral	

(Note: For the derivation of a word, any large dictionary can be consulted. For the history of its applications, the *Oxford English Dictionary* provides the best source of information. For other sources of special information required in extending the definition, the instructor can provide suggestions. Most of the work for this theme will be in the reading and thinking before you begin to write. Study your subject. Be sure that you have something to say. Then prepare an outline before you actually begin o write. Turn in the outline with your theme.)

The Third Method: Classification

In studying definition, we found that we were distinguishing one species from all other species under a particular genus (pages 51–53). In other words, we had to sort out various species under the general group or class — the genus. When we discussed the common ground of definition, we found that sometimes we had to concern ourselves not with just one group, or genus, and its subdivisions, but with a series of groups in descending order (page 54). We have, in fact, in our study of definition, been using the method of classification.

Classification is a way of thinking in terms of a system of classes.

By a *class* we mean a group whose members have significant characteristics in common. What constitutes a significant characteristic may vary according to the interest involved. For example, a maker of cosmetics may think of women in groups determined by complexion, and the secretary of a Y.W.C.A. may think in groups determined by religious affiliations. What is significant for one is not significant for the other. Similarly, the registrar of a college may group students according to grades, and the gymnasium instructor, according to athletic ability. The registrar and the gymnasium instructor have different interests in classifying the same body of students.

By a *system* we mean a set of classes ranging from the most inclusive down through the least inclusive. Let us set up a simple example of such a system:

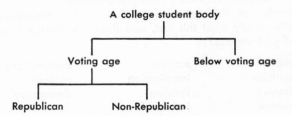

Here the group *student body* is the most inclusive class. Under it we find classes less and less inclusive.

This system, we observe, indicates only two classes at any one stage: *voting age* and *below voting age, Republican* and *non-Republican*. Such a system, which has an *X* and *non-X* for each stage, is called **simple**. But we can readily see that we might find it useful to have more than this simple pairing at any one stage.

For instance, let us imagine that our books have been in storage and are delivered to us in a great mixed-up heap in the middle of the library floor. We know that it would be almost useless to arrange our library merely in terms of, say, literature and nonliterature. If we lumped the nonliterature together on the shelves, we should have a bad time finding anything in a hurry. We need some other classes *at the same stage* as the class of literature. For example, history, philosophy, and mathematics. Then, if we have many books, we may need to carry our classification down another stage or two. We would get a scheme — a **complex** one — something like the following:

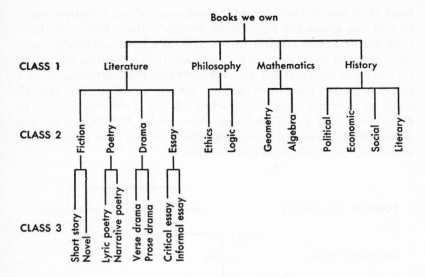

This scheme indicates the classification of the books in this particular collection. Of course, the collection does not include examples of all kinds of books. For example, in class 1 we do not have science or theology. In class 2 under philosophy we have only ethics and logic, and under mathematics, only geometry and algebra. In class 3 under poetry, we have only lyric and narrative poetry, and under the essay, only critical and informal essays. So we find many classes missing in our particular scheme, classes which would appear in the scheme for the classification of books for a great general library, such as a university library. The method of classification for our little collection and that for the great library are, however, the same. The complex scheme recognizes at each stage all the classes available — all the books, say, in our personal library, or all in a university library, or all in a publishing catalogue.

Requirements of Classification

To be useful a scheme of classification must fulfill certain requirements:

1. There can be only one principle applied at each stage.
2. The subclasses under any class must account for all the members of the class.

We can best understand what is at stake in Rule 1 by taking an example. Sometimes we want to work a classification in reference to more than one interest. Suppose some political organization wants to find out about the Republican co-eds in the college who have been in the armed services in wartime. We have, obviously, three interests to be considered in a classification: (1) political affiliation, (2) service in war, and (3) sex. We can't mix these interests up in a single stage. We have to work them out one at a time. We have already in Scheme I (page 70) worked out the classification down to *Republican* and *non-Republican*. Now under *Republican* we can distinguish *veteran* and *nonveteran;* then, having done that, we can, under *veteran,* distinguish *male* and *female*.

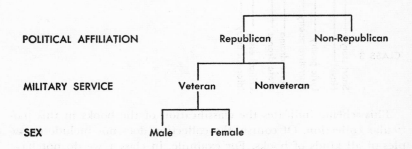

POLITICAL AFFILIATION   Republican   Non-Republican

MILITARY SERVICE   Veteran   Nonveteran

SEX   Male   Female

In other words, when a new interest enters, we really start a new classification and hang it onto the appropriate subclass of the classification we have just completed. This method can be applied to a complex classification as well as to a simple one such as we have given above.

The problem involved in Rule 2 does not arise in simple classification. Obviously, such a classification as *Republican* and *non-Republican,* for example, must exhaust the members of the student body. But if we are making a complex classification and set up subclasses for Democrats and Socialists, we had better be sure that there are no stray Prohibitionists wandering about, or Liberal party members from New York State. We have to be certain that our sorting is complete.

The Use of Classification

We may ask ourselves what the making of such schemes of classifications has to do with writing exposition. The answer is simple: The scheme, we may say, is simply a way of sorting out things, tying them up in bunches, labeling the bunches, and indicating the relations among the bunches. It is one way of organizing a hodgepodge of things or ideas; and the particular system we use is dictated, we remember, by some interest we bring to bear on the original hodge-podge. What we do in making a classification is comparable to what we do in the process of finding a true subject (see Chapter 2, page 14). In classification the process is carried down to the subdivisions of the topic. For instance, if we are interested in religion, we classify the student body by religious affiliation; if in politics, we classify it by political affiliation. Classification is, then, simply one way of thinking about the material of our piece of exposition to give order to it.

A scheme of classification provides a kind of outline, an outline that needs to be expanded. Just as the short definition can be expanded into an essay, so the scheme of classification may be developed at considerable length, as we explore the implications of our original scheme.

In the following example — an essay from a college magazine — we can easily detect the scheme underlying the discussion and, at the same time, see that without the discussion the scheme would not be very interesting.

FOR WOMEN MOSTLY

With all the controversy about the relative uselessness of Penn men and Penn women, there seems to be a need for a certain amount of field work in the subject. Apparently each side is judged by the most objectionable of its kind, so — girls — here is submitted a carefully compiled report on Penn Men You Need to Avoid. If referred to before you accept dates, it may save you a lot of bitterness and gnashing of teeth.

Type 1. The Party-Boy. This one simply isn't himself until he gets outside of a little alcohol. Then he manages to be so much himself that you are bored to death. His conversation is either quiet or loud; when quiet, it consists of long accounts of drinking bouts, in which he took part; and when loud, it is usually carried on with his buddy across the room who wants everybody to sing the "Whiffenpoof Song," while our joyboy favors " Roll Me Over in the Clover." For these occasions he is conveniently equipped with a foghorn voice that makes everybody turn around and look. If you happen to be sitting next to him you cringe and wilt and feel about two inches high. You gaze up at him with a sick smile that you hope will make everybody think you're having as much fun as he is.

There may be occasions in the course of the evening when he feels like dancing. Dancing, to him, consists of zooming around ricocheting off walls, other couples, moose heads, etc. They ought to jail him for flying low.

Then the fire-eater creeps up on him and he commences to be morose. In the life of every party-boy there is an unrequited love; and furthermore given even less than half a chance, he will tell you all about it. It sounds vaguely like *True Confessions*. But because you have nothing better to do at the moment, you listen, and sympathize — outwardly, with him; inwardly, with the girl.

Finally he quietly passes out, wrapped comfortably around a chandelier or something, and one of his less enthusiastic brothers takes you home. All this is very interesting, provided you can hold him up long enough to get through the party. And he really isn't useless; he always makes a good bar rag.

Type 2. The Lover. He is a ball of fire with the women — the sultry, slow-burning kind, of course. He overwhelms you with attentions. He leans so close to you when you talk that you get the impression he is concerned about the condition of your wisdom teeth. He has a special hungry sick-dog look which he uses for gazing deeply into eyes. When you go away and talk to somebody else, he sulks. He may even follow you and turn you around to face him, and look silently at you. He is hurt. You have crushed him. You are ashamed. You monster.

An evening with him is like a nice quiet session with a boa constrictor. No amount of hinting around that, as far as he's concerned, you are of the let's-just-be-friends school of thought, will do; you have to pick up a bottle or something and slug him before he gets the idea. Then, kid, you're washed up. Your name is mud. Not only are you nasty, ungrateful, and a terrible date — but to top it all off, you're an icebox — and this is the sin unforgivable.

Type 3. The Great Mind. You have to prepare ahead of time for a date with one of these. If you're not read up on your Nietzsche and Schopenhauer, you've got two strikes against you before you start. You and Junior will sit down together, cozy-like, in a corner and solve world problems. Then for the sake of variety you might go on to metaphysics. You toss Absolutes and Causes and Effects back and forth for a whole evening. I won't say any more on this subject. There's nothing more to say.

Type 4. The Bohemian. This one's theme song is " I Don't Care." He dreams of a garret for two on the Left Bank and a Jug of Wine, a Loaf of Bread — and Thou; and if Thou isn't crazy about the idea, Thou is inhibited, repressed, suppressed, a slave to convention, a conformist, and a louse. The boy knows he's a genius, but just because he dyes his hair pale green and wears a purple satin shoestring for a necktie, people don't appreciate him.

He has moods. Blue moods, black moods, red moods — all kinds. If he's having mood number 157E, keep away from him. Keep away from him anyway. Unless you've reserved a bunk at Byberry, that is.

Type 5. The Dud. He gives you a fleeting impression of a horrible, sticky, gray nothingness. He doesn't smoke, drink, dance, drive, stay out late, or raise his voice. He isn't funny — he isn't interesting — he isn't clever. You talk into a vacuum. He is probably very good to his mother, but every time he comes out with that slightly hysterical giggle you feel like slapping him. He sits there like a rock in mid-stream and the party eddies around him. He has a wonderful time. You go home and get a nice big ax and go hunting for the person who got you the date.

Watch the aftereffects of this. He'll call you up, sure as next week. He'll call you again. He'll call you nine or ten times more. If you happen to be wandering around on campus with somebody whom you'd like to impress, he'll pop up out of his hole in the lawn and greet you like a long-lost sister. He's the world's best argument for mercy killing.

Type 6. The Missing Link. Not that we object to muscles, but there is a type that has too much of a good thing. He has an amazing supply of every kind of matter but gray. He looks like something out of the Old Stone Age — and talks surprisingly like it, too. His knuckles drag on the ground. He grunts occasionally to show he's alive. You expect him to stand up and hammer on his chest at any minute. He majors in-duh-phys ed, and takes Advanced Pencil Sharpening on the side.

He's a charming date if you're taking anthropology. Or if you have to write a criticism of *The Man with the Hoe* or *Of Mice and Men*. You couldn't find a better case study.

Of course you have to watch these creatures. If he gets playful you're liable to end up mashed into dog food. It's best to take along a whip and a light metal chair and be able to say " Back, Sultan," in an authoritative voice. Once your nerve fails, you're done.

Well, there they are. Now the object of the game is to go out and find one that doesn't fall into one of these categories. Then, if it's got blood and skin and if it moves around, you're set. Hang onto it. It must be a man.

— BARBARA JONES.[1]

Here is a student theme, again based on a classification:

TEACHERS I HAVE KNOWN

STAGE I

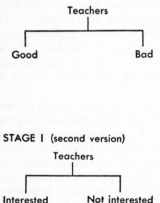

STAGE I (second version)

In my thirteen and a half years at school, I have, of course, known many teachers; I have made rather a hobby of studying my teachers because I hope one day to become a teacher myself. There are many kinds of teachers, but they can all be classified under one of two headings — good and bad. Fortunately for students there are many more teachers under the first heading than under the second.

Actually, it does not mean much to say that teachers are good or bad — the same can be said of people in any profession. A better way of separating the teachers that really teach from those that just stand up in front of a class is to ask how they got to be teachers in the first place: Did they

[1] From *Penn Pics*, a Franklin Society publication of the University of Pennsylvania.

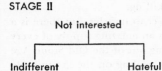

STAGE II

Not interested

Indifferent   Hateful

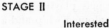

STAGE II

Interested

In subject

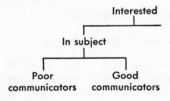

STAGE III

Interested

In subject

Poor   Good
communicators   communicators

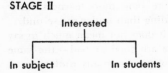

STAGE II

Interested

In subject   In students

become teachers because they were really interested in their subject and in young people, or did they just drift into the profession through indifference or necessity?

I should like to dispose of the second category first. There is little need to say much about such teachers; every student has known a few of them. Either they are indifferent toward their job, in which case the class is terribly boring, and the students fool around; or they actively hate teaching. Then watch out! The best thing to do in a class like that is to keep quiet and do just as much work as necessary to avoid the teacher's notice.

The other teachers are much more interesting, and there are many more kinds of them. Some become teachers because of an intense interest in their subject. They may be great teachers or well-known researchers; particularly in college, they may be outstanding men in their field. Some of them do not have the ghost of a notion how to put their subject across; they may not even try particularly, for students simply don't exist for them. All that matters is the subject. Even so, the student can get a lot out of their courses *if* he puts some effort into understanding them. Other teachers in this category do have a gift for organizing and communicating their subject. Their classes are a constant challenge — the teacher is not likely to make his subject easy! — and a delight.

Another variety of teacher with a purpose is the kind who is interested in his students. He is not a scholar; his main motivation is to help students. That is his mission in life. At the college level you probably find fewer of these teachers than in elementary or high school. I remember particularly my seventh-grade arithmetic teacher. It was a bad year for me; more than once I got into trouble with the school authorities. But this teacher was so decent to me that I became ashamed of myself; I started to behave better, and I even learned some arithmetic. Miss Jones may not have been a great mathematician, but she did me more good and taught me more than many other teachers I have had.

I should mention one other kind of interested teacher, a kind to be careful of. That is the teacher who wants to indoctrinate his students. He believes fanatically that all automobile engines should be limited to 60 horsepower, and he wants you to believe this, too. He is likely to spend lots of class time preaching about this *idée fixe,* and that time will be largely wasted for you. But otherwise he may be an excellent teacher. You should be tolerant and remember that the teacher is just a person, too.

STAGE II

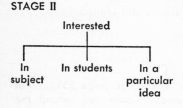

This theme, it is clear, is based on a classification, as we have indicated along the left margin. If we assemble the notes on the margin, we find a scheme like this:

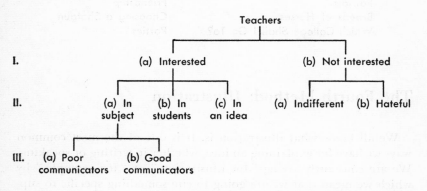

The theme has some faults. There is some lack of consistency in the way the classification is worked out. Only one item is taken to Stage III, and the author never does get around to giving his idea of the best kind of teacher, the kind he wants to be. Perhaps this classification does exhaust his experience, just as the scheme on page 71 might exhaust the books in our personal library; but if the writer means to be logically complete, he would need some more classes. In any case, he would do well to let us know whether his scheme of classification covers absolutely all the teachers he has known; that

is, whether his classification is exhaustive within the limits he proposes. He occasionally suggests that it is not, but he never makes the point really clear. And while we are on the theme, we might point out that it just stops, that it has no proper conclusion.

Despite these limitations, the author does have a pretty clear notion of how to use classification to organize a subject. And he does attempt to fill out the scheme by illustrations and comparisons.

• Applications •

I. Look at " The Seven Deadly Fallacies " (Readings, page 551). What scheme of classification lies behind this essay? Could you extend the scheme upward or downward?

II. What other expository methods can you recognize in the development of the discussion? How, in other words, has the author filled out the scheme?

III. Write a theme of some 400 words based on a scheme of classification. The following list may be helpful, but do not feel limited to it:

Liars I Have Known	Mother Love
Trout Flies	Philanthropy
Patriots	Friendship
Breeds of Horses	Choosing a Shotgun
Which College Shall I Go To?	Parties

The Fourth Method: Illustration

We all know what illustration is. It is one of the most common ways we have for explaining an idea, whether in writing or speaking. We are constantly saying " for illustration " or " for example," by which we mean that we are going to cite something specific to support or clarify a general point. Here is an example of the method of illustration:

If anyone wants to exemplify the meaning of the word " fish," he cannot choose a better animal than a herring. The body, tapering to each end, is covered with thin, flexible scales, which are very easily rubbed off. The taper head, with its underhung jaw, is smooth and scaleless on the top; the large eye is partly covered by two folds of transparent skin, like eyelids — only immovable and with the slit between them vertical instead of norizontal; the cleft behind the gill-cover is very wide, and, when the cover

is raised, the large red gills which lie underneath it are freely exposed. The rounded back bears the single moderately long dorsal fin about its middle.
— THOMAS HENRY HUXLEY: " The Herring."

We may indicate by a diagram what Huxley has done:

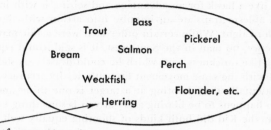

to exemplify the meaning of the word fish, he cannot choose a better animal than a herring"

Illustration, like definition and classification, is a way of thinking in terms of classes. In definition we seek to understand the particular by placing it in relation to a class. In classification we arrange particulars in terms of a class, or classes, as we indicate in the pictures on pages 70 and 71. In illustration we use a particular to explain a class, to help us grasp it better — herring to explain fish. The class which is explained by the particular, the illustration, may be a type or thing or person, a type of method, a general idea, a general condition, and so on. The illustration must truly represent the chief qualities of the class. At the same time it may have individual characteristics which enhance its interest to the reader.

When Huxley chose the herring to exemplify fish in general, he was not choosing an individual fish. He was choosing a species, and any herring would have done. Below, however, we see an individual, not a genus, used for illustration. The very first sentence tells us that the outlaw Billy the Kid, an individual, is going to be described as the representative, almost the perfect representative, of the desperado type of the Old West. Mixed in with some of his merely individual traits — his build, his love of dancing — we find the qualities that mark the type.

The secret of Billy the Kid's greatness as a desperado — and by connoisseurs in such matters he was rated as an approach to the ideal desperado type — lay in a marvellous coordination between mind and body. He had not only the will but the skill to kill. Daring, coolness, and quick thinking would not have served unless they had been combined with physical quickness and a marksmanship which enable him to pink a man neatly between the eyes with a bullet at, say, thirty paces. He was not pitted against six-shooter amateurs but against experienced fighters themselves adept in the handling of weapons. The men he killed would have killed him if he had not been their master in a swifter deadliness. In times of danger, his mind was not only calm but singularly clear and nimble, watching like a hawk for an advantage and seizing it with incredible celerity. He was able to translate an impulse into action with the suave rapidity of a flash of light. While certain other men were a fair match for him in target practice, no man in the Southwest, it is said, could equal him in the lightning-like quickness with which he could draw a six-shooter from its holster and with the same movement fire with deadly accuracy. It may be remarked incidentally that shooting at a target is one thing and shooting at a man who happens to be blazing away at you is something entirely different; and Billy the Kid did both kinds of shooting equally well.

His appearance was not unprepossessing. He had youth, health, good nature, and a smile — a combination which usually results in a certain sort of good looks. His face was long and colorless except for the deep tan with which it had been tinted by sun, wind, and weather and was of an asymmetry that was not unattractive. His hair was light brown, worn usually rather long and inclined to waviness. His eyes were gray, clear, and steady. His upper front teeth were large and slightly prominent and to an extent disfigured the expression of a well-formed mouth. His hands and feet were remarkably small. He was five feet eight inches tall, slender and well proportioned. He was unusually strong for his inches, having for a small man quite powerful arms and shoulders. He weighed, in condition, one hundred and forty pounds. When out on the range, he was as rough looking as any other cowboy. In towns, among the quality folk of the frontier, he dressed neatly and took not a little care in making himself personable. Many persons, especially women, thought him handsome. He was a great beau at fandangos and was considered a good dancer.

He had an air of easy, unstudied, devil-may-care insouciance which gave no hint of his dynamic energy. His movements were ordinarily deliberate and unhurried. But there was a certain element of calculation in everything he did. Like a billiardist who " plays a position," he figured on what he might possibly have to do next. This foresightedness and forehandedness even in inconsequential matters provided him with a sort of subconscious mail armor. He was forearmed even when not forewarned; forever on guard.

Like all the noted killers of the West, Billy the Kid was of the blond type. Wild Bill Hickok, Ben Thompson, King Fisher, Henry Plummer, Clay Allison, Wyatt Earp, Doc Holliday, Frank and Jesse James, the Youngers, the Daltons — the list of others is long — were all blond. There was not a pair of brown eyes among them. It was the gray and blue eye that flashed death in the days when the six-shooter ruled the frontier. This blondness of desperados is a curious fact, contrary to popular imagination and the traditions of art and the stage. The theater immemorially has portrayed its unpleasant characters as black-haired and black-eyed. The popular mind associates swarthiness with villainy. Blue eyes and golden hair are, in the artistic canon, a sort of heavenly hallmark. No artist has yet been so daring as to paint a winged cherub with raven tresses, and a search of the world's canvases would discover no brown-eyed angel. It may be remarked further, as a matter of incidental interest, that the West's bad men were never heavy, stolid, lowering brutes. Most of them were good-looking, some remarkably so. Wild Bill Hickok, beau ideal of desperadoes, was considered the handsomest man of his day on the frontier, and with his blue eyes and yellow hair falling on his shoulders, he moved through his life of tragedies with something of the beauty of a Greek god. So much for fact versus fancy. Cold deadliness in Western history seems to have run to frosty coloring in eyes, hair, and complexion.

— WALTER NOBLE BURNS: *The Saga of Billy the Kid*.[2]

If we make a scheme for this discussion of Billy the Kid, we have something like that for Huxley's description of the herring as an illustration of fish.

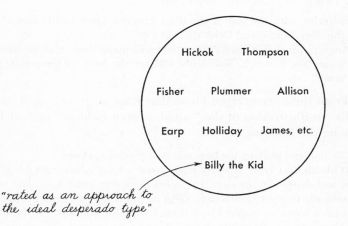

In the passage just given, description is used for illustration. Narration can be used for the same purpose. For instance, the episode below is used to explain a class, in this case a class of events, the process used among Eskimos to hunt bear. In other words, the narrative is not given to tell about a special, unique event — how Anarvik and Ernenek, two individuals, killed a particular bear. It is given to explain the method generally used. If we draw a picture of it, we have something like this:

---

2 From *The Saga of Billy the Kid* by Walter Noble Burns. Copyright 1925, 1926 by Doubleday and Company, Inc.

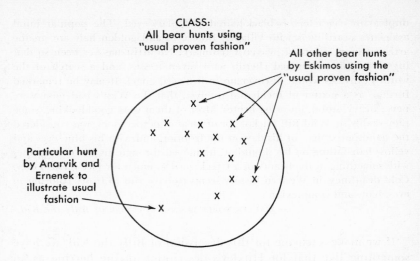

CLASS:
All bear hunts using
"usual proven fashion"

All other bear hunts
by Eskimos using the
"usual proven fashion"

Particular hunt
by Anarvik and
Ernenek to
illustrate usual
fashion

We see this readily enough if we look at the conversation between the two hunters before they begin:

Shivering with the lust of the hunt Ernenek knelt beside him. " Let us set the dogs on him and finish quickly."

Anarvik shook his head. " He might kill many dogs, and we have none to spare. No, Ernenek. Somebody will get the bear in the usual, proven fashion."

From these remarks we know that what is to come will be, basically, an illustration of the " usual, proven fashion " of bear killing among the Eskimos.

Circling and sniffing, the bear was slowly moving closer.

With his flint knife Anarvik had carved a long splint from his whalerib bow and sharpened the ends. He coiled the splint in his hand and released it suddenly to test its resilience. Then he pulled out a chunk of blubber he had been warming within his clothes, against his stomach. He kneaded the blubber into a ball, swiftly, before it could freeze, and pressed the tightly coiled whalebone splint into it. The blubber ball hardened instantly on the ice.

He began moving forward on all fours and the bear withdrew growling, with little jumps, throwing up his shaggy hindquarters and leering over his shoulder. Anarvik stopped and called to him with motions and cooing sounds, and the bear returned tentatively, in a half-circle. Anarvik's sparse mustache quivered as he rolled the spring bait forcefully over the thin blanket of snow.

The yellow ball came to a halt a few paces from the bear. Puzzled, he approached cautiously, stretching out his nose forward and whimpering a little in uncertainty. Hunger told him to eat; another instinct, deeper and more mysterious, told him to distrust whatever came from those little beings, so frighteningly purposeful.

Anarvik waited flat and motionless, arms and legs spread out. Behind him Ernenek breathlessly watched the bear put out a long blue tongue and lick the bait, retire, lick again, and staunchly retire again. But it was impossible to resist temptation forever. Bear are only human. With a billowy movement, his snout suddenly shot forward and engulfed the bait, dropping it into the bottomless pit of his belly.

Simultaneously, Anarvik and Ernenek leaped to their feet with cheers and laughter, for the bear was theirs.

Almost.

At the men's sudden outburst the bear backed up. Mystified, he began to circle, then sat down on his haunches and studied them for a while. Finally, he began closing in.

The men were preparing to retreat when suddenly he jumped up and gave a long anguished moan that ran unchecked over the great sea, silencing the dogs, then bucked about and growled savagely.

" In his stomach the blubber has melted," cried Anarvik triumphantly. " And the blade has sprung open! "

All at once the bear turned on his heels and shuffled off yammering.

Dusk was dimming already, for day was short as yet, lighting the roof of the world for but a few hours with each turn of the sun. Without a word Anarvik and Ernenek gripped their spears and started after their quarry, glancing at each other and laughing, just laughing with the glee of the hunt, everything else forgotten.

Stumbling and wailing the bear drifted coastward, as the men moved to cut off his retreat toward the sea fields, his element and abode. After reaching the first foothills of the land he began to stop frequently and look over his shoulder to see if the chase was still on, threads of spittle dangling on his chest. His lair must be nearby, but he wouldn't lead the hunters there. Reluctantly he moved on, up the frozen hillsides.

The soles of his feet, covered with close-set hair, enabled him to walk securely on the ice, while the men's boots had a poor grip on the slippery slopes. And they had to take heed not to work themselves into a sweat, which meant freezing to death. But the bear's course was wayward and erratic and the men could keep up with him covering only half as much ground.

It grew colder on the heights, fifty or sixty below, and the beloved gale blew, and Anarvik and Ernenek were happy because they hunted. Never for an instant did they worry about the forsaken provisions, and the dogs and the woman. They were not hungry at the moment; the dogs were always hungry anyhow, whether they were fed or not; and the woman would manage somehow as women always did. This was the Hunt — the very essence of life.

They ate nothing but the bear's droppings that were streaked with blood, and after the beast was gutted of everything but fear and pain, and hunger came knocking at the walls of their stomachs, Ernenek said:

"Somebody is hungry." These were the first words spoken since the chase had started.

Anarvik nodded his agreement.

But never for a moment did they consider turning back.

When day had once more risen tentatively, a gale pouring in from the Glacial Ocean churned up the shallow snow, turning the pallid heaven a murky gray, and for a space they lost sight of their quarry in the blinding blizzard and plunged forth in sudden alarm.

They were led back to the bear by his laments and almost crashed into him, and both men contrived to give him a good poke in the ribs with their horn-tipped spears to let him know he wasn't dreaming. A snarl of rage rose from the huge shadow fumbling upright in the snow swirl and drowned off in the wind, and from there on they stuck so close to their quarry that they could smell it — smell the bitter odor of fear emanating from its pelt.

A few times the bear wheeled about in rage and charged; they then waddled off in a hurry, whining in terror, stumbling and slipping downhill, until the bear sat down on his haunches, wagging his head; and the instant danger was past, the men laughed.

The second night was the worst. The blizzard thickened, forcing them to follow the bear too close at the heels for comfort, and the pangs of hunger hammered with mounting intensity, weakening their knees and increasing the danger of perspiration, while the bear, that seemed to have a hundred lives, kept trekking his furious trek up and down the forbidding slopes. . . .

Once they came within a brief march of one of the meat caches which they kept scattered on land and sea.

"Maybe he goes off that way," Anarvik said. "Then one of us can get provisions."

They tried to drive the bear in the right direction, without success. He knew nothing about the cache. . . .

By this time the bear was very sick. In his lumbering fashion he jogged on laboriously, dragging on the ground a head that had grown too heavy. Sometimes slipping and stumbling to their knees the men followed stonily, their laughter gone, the lines of strain marking their greased faces, their eyes red and rimmed with rime. Hunger had departed. Stomachs had gone to sleep. They did not even scoop up handfuls of snow any longer. Their mouths were set, their bellies forgotten, and in their very minds all thoughts and memories had perished. Between skin and flesh, fat had been burning away incessantly, unreplaced, their motion no longer warmed them and they shivered a little, the cold knifing noticeably down their throats with every breath.

And still, could there be anything greater than this — chasing the white bear over the top of the world?

The end came suddenly. All at once the bear gave up. As though he had decided that if he had to die he might as well die with dignity, he squatted on his hindquarters, put his forepaws in his lap, and waited. Round his neck was a pink napkin of frozen froth. He held his ears flat and his teeth bared as in a sneer. No longer did he cry. Only the white clouds of respiration came fast and raspy and his little bloodshot eyes moved helplessly.

The two men closed in slowly, Ernenek from the front and Anarvik from the side, ready to jump if he pawed. The bear grabbed Anarvik's spear and broke it like a straw the instant Ernenek speared him clean through the top of the throat, below the jaw, where the pelt was thinnest. . . .

— HANS RUESCH: Top of the World.[3]

In the following selection particular instances are used not to explain a method, but to explain an idea — in this case, that of neighborliness:

A good neighbor, as the term was understood in the days when as a little girl I lived on a farm in Southern Michigan, meant all that nowadays is combined in corner store, telephone, daily newspaper, and radio. But your neighbor was also your conscience. You had to behave yourself on account of what the neighbors would think.

A good neighbor knew everything there was to know about you — and liked you anyway. He never let you down — as long as you deserved his good opinion. Even when you failed in that, if you were in trouble he would come to your rescue. If one of the family was taken sick in the night, you ran over to the neighbor's to get someone to sit up until the doctor arrived. Only instead of sending for the doctor, you went for him. Or one of the neighbors did.

The Bouldrys were that kind of neighbors. Lem Bouldry was a good farmer and a good provider. Mis' Bouldry kept a hired girl and Lem had two men the year round. They even had a piano while the most the other neighbors boasted was an organ or a melodeon. Mis' Bouldry changed her dress every afternoon (my mother did too; she said she thought more of herself when she did) , and they kept the front yard mowed.

But the Covells were just the opposite — the most shiftless family the Lord ever let set foot on land. How they got along my father said he didn't know, unless it was by the grace of God. Covell himself was ten years younger than my father, yet everybody called him " Old Covell." His face and hands were like sole leather and if his hair had ever been washed, it was only when he got caught in a rainstorm. Father said Old Covell would borrow the shirt off your back, then bring it around to have it mended; Mother said, well, one thing certain, he wouldn't bring it around to be washed.

Yet the time Mis' Covell almost died with her last baby — and the baby did die — Mis' Bouldry took care of her; took care of the rest of the children too — four of them. She stayed right there in the Covell house, just going home to catch a little sleep now and then. She had to do that, for there wasn't so much as an extra sheet in the house, much less an extra

---

[3] From Top of the World by Hans Ruesch. Copyright 1944, 1946, 1947, 1950 by Hans Ruesch. Reprinted by permission of Harper & Brothers.

bed. And Mis' Bouldry wasn't afraid to use her hands even if she did keep a hired girl — she did all the Covells' washing herself.

But even Old Covell, despite his shiftlessness, was a good neighbor in one way: he was a master hand at laying out the dead. Of course, he wasn't worth a cent to sit up with the sick, for if it was Summer he'd go outside to smoke his pipe and sleep; and if it was Winter he'd go into the kitchen and stick his feet in the oven to warm them and go to sleep there. But a dead man seemed to rouse some kind of pride and responsibility in him. There was no real undertaker nearer than ten miles, and often the roads were impassable. Folks sent for my mother when a child or woman died, but Old Covell handled all the men. Though he never wore a necktie himself, he kept on hand a supply of celluloid collars and little black bow ties for the dead. When he had a body to lay out, he'd call for the deceased's best pants and object strenuously if he found a hole in the socks. Next, he'd polish the boots and put on a white shirt, and fasten one of his black ties to the collar button. All in all, he would do a masterly job.

Of course, nobody paid Old Covell for this. Nobody ever thought of paying for just being neighborly. If anybody had offered to, they'd have been snubbed for fair. It was just the way everybody did in those half-forgotten times.　　　　DELLA T. LUTES: " Are Neighbors Necessary? "

The four selections above are expository, but (with the exception of the description of the herring) the way of illustrating is not expository. If illustration is to be effective, it must usually have something of the vividness and individuality that are characteristic of description and narration. Nevertheless, that vividness and individuality must be used with reference to the expository intention which gives unity to the composition. The quaint habit of Old Covell, in the last selection, of keeping a supply of celluloid collars and the little black bow ties for the dead he laid out, is a vivid, individualizing trait, but this is only his individual way of expressing the general notion of neighborliness. The good illustration, no matter how vivid and individual it may be, always makes us see more sharply than before the outline of the type or group or idea being illustrated.

• Application •

Write a theme of some 300 words using the method of illustration. Remember that you have two obligations: the first, to make your particular example interesting in itself, and, the second, to make it truly represent its group, type, class, or idea.

In fulfilling the first requirement, you want to be specific in identifying the chosen example and use details that catch our attention: the scales

4 From " Are Neighbors Necessary? " by Della T. Lutes. Reprinted by permission of the *American Mercury* and Mrs. Cecily I. Dodd.

of the herring, Billy the Kid's teeth, the pink napkin of foam around the neck of the dying polar bear, the little black ties kept on hand by Old Covell.

In fulfilling the second requirement, you must be sure that you know what really are the essential qualities of the type (or idea) that you wish to illustrate, as contrasted with merely individual qualities of your example, and you must be sure that your example possesses those qualities, plus whatever individualizing ones you may use. If the qualities of the type are fairly numerous and complicated, be sure that you are systematic in establishing the connection between your example and those qualities. You may organize your theme by giving a generalized description of your subject, say a good officer, and then presenting your example. Or you may present your example, say an individual officer, and indicate in the course of your presentation the qualities of the type embodied in the individual. But be sure you find some way to give your theme a shape. Go back to the examples we have had in this section and try to see what method of organizing has been used, what way of shaping the whole theme.

If none of the following topics interests you, use one of your own.

What Makes a Good Officer?	Something Will Turn Up
The Campus Go-getter	A Typical Ranch
True Courtesy	Laziness Pays
The Fraternity Man	Citizenship
Family Happiness	A Mother
A Balanced Life	The Importance of Money
Cowardice	Child of the Slum
Hope Springs Eternal	The American Town
A Good Novel	A Good Movie

The Fifth Method: Comparison and Contrast

In comparison, as a method of exposition, we clarify a subject by indicating similarities between two or more things; in contrast, by indicating differences. We constantly and instinctively use comparison and contrast, but not always for expository purposes. For example, a poet making a comparison in a poem or a painter making a contrast of two forms in planning the composition of a picture may not be doing so for an expository purpose. The poet or the painter is acting with an appreciative or artistic motivation, as contrasted with an expository or scientific one, and all of us, even though we may not write poems or paint pictures, sometimes make comparisons and contrasts out of a similar motivation to gain vividness, to appeal to the imagination.

We also use comparison constantly and instinctively for expository purposes. A child asks, " What is a zebra? " And we may reply, " Oh, a zebra — it's an animal sort of like a mule, but it's not as big as a mule. And it has stripes like a tiger, black and white stripes all over. But you remember that a tiger's stripes are black and orange." Here we have used both comparison and contrast. We have compared the shape of the zebra to that of the mule, but have contrasted the two animals in size. And we have compared the stripes of the zebra to the stripes of a tiger, but have contrasted them in color. If the child knows what mules and tigers are like, he now has a pretty good idea of a zebra. Our informal application of comparison and contrast can be made more useful if we are systematic.

Area of Interest

To be systematic means, for one thing, to realize that mere similarities and differences are not very instructive. If we happen to observe that a passing cloud is shaped like a camel or that a spot on the wall looks like a snail, the observation is merely casual. By the resemblance we learn nothing about clouds or camels, wall damp or snails.

The significant comparison or contrast is between two or more items within a special area of interest, two members, that is, of a group or class which is defined by a special interest brought to the material. A zoologist, for example, may profitably compare and contrast a hawk and a garter snake, for his interest in them as living creatures stemming from a common remote ancestor would embrace them both and make his study significant. An aeronautical engineer might compare the hawk and an airplane, but it isn't likely that he would find much profit in putting an airplane and a garter snake together.

As we have just seen, the hawk may appear in more than one area of interest. Anything, in fact, can be thought of in different ways and can be put in different areas of interest. A farmer looks at a field and thinks of the quality of the soil, of drainage, of the exposure, and so on. He puts the field in the class of *arable land* and compares or contrasts this field with other tracts of his acquaintance. But suppose that an infantry officer comes along and looks at the same field. He may well think of how defensible a position might be found here. He would, that is, put the field in the class *defensible position* and compare or contrast it with other spots. What we are saying is that we set up the area of interest for comparison or contrast, and then we draw the two or more particular items out of the class to provide the basis of comparison and contrast.

We bring our interest to bear on a situation, but our interests, of course, are not unchangeable. The military man may also be a farmer, and one moment he may regard the field as in the class *defensible position,* and the next, as in the class *arable land.* Or he may also be interested in painting, and at a particular moment he may think neither of crops nor of machine-gun emplacement, but of the color relations of the landscape.

Kinds of Purpose

To be systematic means, we have just seen, to understand the area of interest for comparison and contrast. But to be systematic also means to understand the purpose for which the items are put up against one another for inspection.

We may distinguish three types of purpose. According to the first purpose, we may wish to present information about one item and may do so by relating it to another item with which our audience is familiar. For example, if we wish to explain the British Parliament to a fellow American, we may do so by comparing it with our Congress, which our fellow American does know about.

According to the second purpose, we may wish to inform about both items of the comparison or contrast, but to do so by treating them in relation to some general principle which would apply to both and with which our audience is presumed to be familiar. For example, if we are reviewing two novels, with neither of which our audience is acquainted, we may compare and contrast them by reference to what we assume our audience knows about the principles of fiction.

According to the third purpose, we may compare and contrast items with which the audience is familiar for the purpose of informing about some general principle or idea. For instance, if we want to arrive at a notion of what religion is, we may compare and contrast several kinds, say Protestantism, Catholicism, Buddhism, and the religion of the Aztecs, to show what elements they have in common. In this process, we are, of course, using comparison and contrast as a way to move back from our examples, or illustrations, to a general description of the class to which the particulars belong. (See pages 167–71, under Argument.)

To sum up: to be systematic in making a comparison or contrast means (1) that we have to know from what area of interest the things being treated are drawn, (2) that we have to know what points of those items being treated are relevant to the dominant idea of the area of interest, and (3) that we have to know what purpose dictates the comparison or contrast.

• Applications •

I. Describe one area of interest (or more) for each of the following sets of items, and give a few points of comparison or contrast for each set.

> Chess, bridge, and poker
> Mussolini and Julius Caesar
> Carpentry and writing verse
> Andrew Jackson, U. S. Grant, and Dwight Eisenhower
> The postal system and socialized medicine
> New Orleans and San Francisco
> New York and ancient Rome
> The Nile and the Mississippi
> An athlete and a musician
> The poet and the advertising man
> Napoleon and Robert E. Lee
> Abraham Lincoln and Thomas Jefferson

II. Give five different sets of items for comparison or contrast, and state your reason for putting each set of items together.

III. Read "Motes, Beams, and Foreigners" (Readings, page 555). This is a discussion of the mistakes one may make in comparing and contrasting different nationalities, but the analysis Dorothy Canfield makes could be applied to comparison and contrast in any area. Give some examples of false comparison and contrast drawn from some other area. For instance, would it be fair for a reviewer to attack a book by Ellery Queen because it did not resemble the work of Dickens? If *not*, why not? Here the general area of interest would be "novels." Work out a little graph of the sort Dorothy Canfield uses as applied to this or some other, similar situation.

Ways of Organizing Comparison and Contrast

When we come to apply comparison and contrast in extended form, we find that there are two general ways of organizing the material. We may fully present one item and then fully present the other, or, we may present a part of one item and then a part of the other, until we have touched on all the parts relevant to our comparison or contrast.

Each of these ways of organization has its utility. The first method is, generally speaking, appropriate when the points of comparison and contrast are fairly broad and obvious. But when a great many details are involved, the second method is more apt to be useful. It is possible, too, to use a compromise between the two methods. One can present the first of the items in full and then, in presenting the second, refer the reader, point by point, to the earlier treatment.

Here is an example of the first type of organization in a student's theme:

MY CHILDHOOD

My father died when I was a small child, and I do not even remember him. I was raised by my mother and my maternal grandfather, in whose home we lived until I came to college. My mother loved her father, and I have no reason to think he did not love her, but they were so different that I was aware from the first of a conflict between them. Or, if it was not a direct conflict between them, it was a conflict between what they stood for. And both of them exerted a strong influence over me. Therefore, as I grow up, I think more and more about their contrasting personalities and values and try to detect in myself the traces of each of them. I do this because I am trying to understand myself.

My grandfather, whose name was Carruthers McKenzie, was of Scotch-Irish blood and belonged to the Presbyterian Church. He had a long, bony face, sunken cheeks, and a straggly beard. He was a man with an iron will if I ever saw one, and all of his way of life was one long discipline for himself and everybody about him. But it was a discipline chiefly for himself. He never spent a day in bed in his life until his last illness, and yet he was probably ill a good part of his life. After he died — and he died of a cancer of the stomach — the doctor told us that he could not understand how any man could keep on his feet so long without giving in to the pain.

There was discipline enough left over for my mother and me and the two Negroes who worked about the place. We had morning prayers and evening prayers. I had to read the Bible an hour a day and learn long passages by heart. My grandfather was a prosperous man, but I never had a nickel to spend which I had not earned, and his rates of payment for my chores were not generous. From the time I was eight, I had to study three hours in the afternoon and at least two hours at night, except for week ends. My grandfather never uttered a word of praise to me except now and then the statement, "You have done your duty." As one could guess, my grandfather never told jokes, was scrupulous about all kind of obligations, never touched an alcoholic beverage or even soft drinks, and wore sober black, winter and summer.

My mother must have taken after her own mother, who was of South-German parentage and a Catholic by training. My mother's mother had given up her religion to marry my grandfather and had taken on his way of life, but she died very young. My mother was rather short in stature and had a rather full but graceful figure, the kind they call " partridge-y." She had round, pink cheeks and a complexion like a child's. She had blue eyes, very large. She loved to laugh and joke and spent a great deal of time in the kitchen with Sally, the Negro cook. They laughed and talked together a great deal. My mother was a good mother, as the phrase goes; she loved me and she was careful of all my wants. But she also liked idleness. She would sit on the veranda half the afternoon and look across the yard, just rocking in her chair and enjoying the sunshine. And she went to bridge parties and even took an occasional glass of wine or, as I imagine, a high-ball.

She was made for a good time and noise and people, and when my grandfather was out of the house, she used to romp and play with me or take me on long walks in the country back of our place. After my father's death when I was six, I am sure that she would have got married very soon if she had not felt it best to keep me in my grandfather's home with the advantages which his prosperity would give me. When I was eighteen and went off to college, she got married.

She married the kind of man you would expect her to pick. He is big and strong-looking, with a heavy, black mustache with a little gray in it. He smokes cigars and he likes fine whisky. He has a Packard agency in the city, and he keeps a little plane out at the airport. He loves sports and a good time. My mother has married exactly the man for her, I think, and I am enough like my mother to think he is fine, too. But as I look back on my grandfather — he died three years ago, when I was seventeen — I have a great admiration for him and a sneaking affection.

Here, in an excerpt from a discussion of English and American sportsmanship, is an example of the second method, which proceeds by a series of contrasts on different points of the items under discussion:

Thanks to this universality of athletic sports, English training is briefer and less severe. The American makes, and is forced to make, a long and tedious business of getting fit, whereas an Englishman had merely to exercise and sleep a trifle more than usual, and this only for a brief period. Our oarsmen work daily from January to July, about six months, or did so before Mr. Lehmann brought English ideas among us; the English varsity crews row together nine or ten weeks. Our football players slog daily for six or seven weeks; English teams seldom or never " practice " and play at most two matches a week. Our track athletes are in training at frequent intervals throughout the college year and are often at the training table six weeks; in England six weeks is the maximum period of training, and the men as a rule are given only three days a week on the cinder track. To an American training is an abnormal condition; to an Englishman it is the consummation of the normal.   — JOHN CORBIN: *An American at Oxford.*

The third way of organizing comparison and contrast — the mixture — is shown in the following selection. First, one item of the comparison, General Grant, is given in full. Then Grant is compared, point by point, with General Lee.

Grant was, judged by modern standards, the greatest general of the Civil War. He was head and shoulders above any general on either side as an over-all strategist, as a master of what in later wars would be called global strategy. His Operation Crusher plan, the product of a mind which had received little formal instruction in the higher art of war, would have done credit to the most finished student of a series of modern staff and command schools. He was a brilliant theater strategist, as evidenced by the Vicksburg campaign, which was a classic field and siege operation. He was a better than average tactician, although, like even the best generals of both sides, he did not appreciate the destruction that the increasing firepower of modern armies could visit on troops advancing across open spaces.

Lee is usually ranked as the greatest Civil War general, but this evaluation has been made without placing Lee and Grant in the perspective of military developments since the war. Lee was interested hardly at all in " global " strategy, and what few suggestions he did make to his government about operations in other theaters than his own indicate that he had little aptitude for grand planning. As a theater strategist, Lee often demonstrated more brilliance and apparent originality than Grant, but his most audacious plans were as much the product of the Confederacy's inferior military position as of his own fine mind. In war, the weaker side has to improvise brilliantly. It must strike quickly, daringly, and include a dangerous element of risk in its plans. Had Lee been a Northern general with Northern resources behind him, he would have improvised less and seemed less bold. Had Grant been a Southern general, he would have fought as Lee did.

Fundamentally Grant was superior to Lee because in a modern total war he had a modern mind, and Lee did not. Lee looked to the past in war as the Confederacy did in spirit. The staffs of the two men illustrate their outlooks. It would not be accurate to say that Lee's general staff were glorified clerks, but the statement would not be too wide of the mark. Certainly his staff was not, in the modern sense, a planning staff, which was why Lee was often a tired general. He performed labors that no general can do in a big modern army — work that should have fallen to his staff, but that Lee did because it was traditional for the commanding general to do it in older armies. Most of Lee's staff officers were lieutenant-colonels. Some of the men on Grant's general staff, as well as on the staffs of other Northern generals, were major and brigadier generals, officers who were capable of leading corps. Grant's staff was an organization of experts in the various phases of strategic planning. The modernity of Grant's mind was most apparent in his grasp of the concept that war was becoming total and that the destruction of the enemy's economic resources was as effective and legitimate a form of warfare as the destruction of his armies. What was realism to Grant was barbarism to Lee. Lee thought of war in the old way as a conflict between armies and refused to view it for what it had become — a struggle between societies. To him, economic war was needless cruelty to civilians. Lee was the last of the great old-fashioned generals; Grant, the first of the great moderns. — T. HARRY WILLIAMS: *Lincoln and His Generals.*[5]

Here is another example of the mixed method of organization, in an extended contrast between two types into which the author would divide humanity, the " Red-bloods " and the " Mollycoddles." In the first paragraph he devotes his attention to setting up a picture of the " Red-blood," with, however, a few incidental contrasts with the " Mollycoddle," but in the second paragraph he uses the method of a series of individual contrasts, point by point, between the two types. This method, we see, leads readily to a series of balanced sentences (see Chapter 9, pages 285–86) , each treating a single point of contrast. How is the third paragraph organized? Would you say that the third paragraph is a good example of clear organization?

We have divided men into Red-bloods and Mollycoddles. " A Red-blood man " is a phrase which explains itself; " Mollycoddle " is its opposite. We have adopted it from a famous speech by Mr. Roosevelt [Theodore Roosevelt], and redeemed it — perverted it, if you will — to other uses. A few examples will make the notion clear. Shakespeare's Henry V is a typical Red-blood; so was Bismarck; so was Palmerston; so is almost any businessman. On the other hand, typical Mollycoddles were Socrates, Voltaire, and Shelley. The terms, you will observe, are comprehensive and the types very broad. Generally speaking, men of action are Red-bloods. Not but what the Mollycoddles may act, and act efficiently. But, if so, the Mollycoddle acts from principle, not from the instinct for action. The Red-blood, on the other hand, acts as the stone falls, and does indiscriminately anything that comes to hand. It is thus that he carries on the business of the world. He steps without reflection into the first place offered him and goes to work like a machine. The ideals and standards of his family, his class, his city, his country, his age, he swallows as naturally as he swallows food and drink. He is therefore always " in the swim "; and he is bound to " arrive," because he has set before him the attainable. You will find him everywhere in all the prominent positions. In a military age he is a soldier, in a commercial age a businessman. He hates his enemies, and he may love his friends; but he does not require friends to love. A wife and children he does require, for the instinct to propagate the race is as strong in him as all other instincts. His domestic life, however, is not always happy; for he can seldom understand his wife. This is part of his general incapacity to understand any point of view but his own. He is incapable of an idea and contemptuous of a principle. He is the Samson, the blind force, dearest to

5 From *Lincoln and His Generals* by T. Harry Williams. Copyright, 1952, by Alfred A. Knopf, Inc.

Nature of her children. He neither looks back nor looks ahead. He lives in present action. And when he can no longer act, he loses his reasons for existence. The Red-blood is happiest if he dies in the prime of life; otherwise, he may easily end with suicide. For he has no inner life; and when the outer life fails, he dies too. Nature, who has blown through him, blows elsewhere. His steps are numb; he is dead wood on the shore.

The Mollycoddle, on the other hand, is all inner life. He may indeed act, as I said, but he acts, so to speak, by accident; just as the Red-blood may reflect, but reflects by accident. The Mollycoddle in action is the Crank; it is he who accomplishes reforms; who abolished slavery, for example, and revolutionized prisons and lunatic asylums. Still, primarily, the Mollycoddle is a critic, not a man of action. He challenges all standards and all facts. If an institution is established, that is a reason why he will not accept it; if an idea is current, that is a reason why he should repudiate it. He questions everything, including life and the universe. And for that reason Nature hates him. On the Red-blood she heaps her favors; she gives him a good digestion, a clear complexion, and sound nerves. But to the Mollycoddle she apportions dyspepsia and black bile. In the universe and in society the Mollycoddle is " out of it " as inevitably as the Red-blood is " in it." At school, he is a " smug " or a " swat," while the Red-blood is captain of the Eleven. At college, he is an " intellectual," while the Red-blood is in the " best set." In the world, he courts failure while the Red-blood achieves success. The Red-blood sees nothing; but the Mollycoddle sees through everything. The Red-blood joins societies; the Mollycoddle is a non-joiner. Individualist of individualists, he can stand alone, while the Red-blood requires the support of a crowd. The Mollycoddle engenders ideas, and the Red-blood invents. The whole structure of civilization rests on foundations laid by Mollycoddles; but all the building is done by Red-bloods. The Red-blood despises the Mollycoddle, but, in the long run, he does what the Mollycoddle tells him. The Mollycoddle also despises the Red-blood, but he cannot do without him. Each thinks he is master of the other, and, in a sense, each is right. In his lifetime the Mollycoddle may be the slave of the Red-blood; but after his death, he is his master, though the Red-blood may know it not.

Nations, like men, may be classified roughly as Red-blood and Mollycoddle. To the latter class belong clearly the ancient Greeks, the Italians, the French and probably the Russians; to the former the Romans, the Germans, and the English. But the Red-blood nation *par excellence* is the American; so that in comparison with them, Europe as a whole might almost be called Mollycoddle. This characteristic of Americans is reflected in the predominant physical type — the great jaw and chin, the huge teeth, the predatory mouth; in their speech, where beauty and distinction are sacrificed to force; in their need to live and feel and act in masses. To be born a Mollycoddle in America is to be born to a hard fate. You must either emigrate or succumb. This, at least hitherto, has been the alternative practiced. Whether a Mollycoddle will ever be produced strong enough to breathe the American atmosphere and live, is a crucial question for the future. It is the question whether America will ever be civilized. For civilization, you will have perceived, depends on a just balance of Red-bloods and Mollycoddles. Without the Red-blood there would be no life at all, no stuff, so to speak, for the Mollycoddle to work upon; without the Mollycoddle, the stuff would remain shapeless and chaotic. The Red-blood is the matter, the Mollycoddle the form; the Red-blood the dough, the Mollycoddle the yeast. On these two poles turns the orb of human society. And if, at this point, you choose to say that the poles are points and have no dimensions, that strictly neither the Mollycoddle nor the Red-blood exists, and that real men contain elements of both mixed in different proportions, I have no quarrel with you except such as one has with the man who states the obvious. I am satisfied to have distinguished the ideal extremes between which the Actual vibrates. The detailed application of the conception I must leave to more patient researchers.

— G. LOWES DICKINSON: " Red-bloods and Mollycoddles," *Appearances*.[6]

• Applications •

I. Read " The Marxian Philosophy of History " (Readings, page 524). Has the contrast been fully developed?

II. Work out in outline form the points of comparison or contrast for two or three of the following topics:

1. A country childhood and a city childhood
2. Military life and civilian life
3. Education in high school and education in college
4. George Washington and Abraham Lincoln
5. Catholicism and Protestantism
6. College football and professional football
7. The value of a liberal education and the value of a scientific education
8. Life on a farm and life on a ranch
9. Two novels
10. Two people you know
11. The construction of land-based fighter planes and the construction of carrier-based fighter planes
12. Poor relations and rich relations
13. The American temperament and some other national temperament
14. General Eisenhower and General MacArthur
15. General Rommel and General Montgomery

III. Write a theme of about 500 words on one of the above topics.

---

[6] From *Appearances* by G. Lowes Dickinson. Copyright 1914 by G. Lowes Dickinson. Reprinted by permission of Doubleday & Company, Inc.

The Sixth Method: Analysis

In studying the methods of exposition thus far we have been much concerned with the relation of the particular to the general, of the individual item to the class. This relation applies even in comparison and contrast, for, as we have seen, we compare the individual items in the light of some general principle, some area of interest. Now, when we turn to the method of **analysis** we treat the individual item, whatever it may be, not in relation to something more general or inclusive, but in relation to something in the item itself, in relation to its own parts.

Analysis is the method of dividing into component parts. (The word *analysis* actually means "loosening into parts.") It can be applied to anything that can be thought of as having parts. We can analyze an object, such as a dog, a house, a tree, a picture. We can analyze an organization, such as a church or a corporation. We can analyze a process such as baking bread, or an event, such as the French Revolution.

Analysis, Classification, and Structure

One may ask how analysis differs from classification, which we have already studied. A class includes the individual items in that class, and the act of classifying means sorting out the individual items of the class. But here is the difference from analysis. A class has no *structure,* and the individual items of the class are not *parts* of the class. An object or idea is an analyzable structure when its components are organized and have a mutually supporting function in determining the nature of the structure. A brick wall is a structure, for the individual bricks supporting one another are necessary to one another and to the wall. The human body is a structure, for the parts are mutually necessary and necessary to the whole. A class does not have these characteristics. A class exists as the *idea* of the qualities shared by a number of individual items. But no one item or set of items belonging to the class is necessary for the existence of the class. We can destroy one individual book, or a million, and the class of *book,* the idea of what constitutes a book, is not impaired. But we cannot knock many bricks from a wall or do much cutting on a human body. Nor can we omit a logical step from an argument, unless we can assume the hearer knows it already, nor omit an act from a play. The individual books have, as far as the class is concerned, no relation to one another except the sharing of those qualities necessary to define *book,* while the other things — the bricks or the act of the play — are necessarily related to the whole of which they are a part.

In a structure there is some principle that determines the relation among the parts, and we must understand that principle to know what is significant in an analysis. If we are analyzing the ignition system of an automobile, we need to know enough about the principles of electricity to understand the significance of the spark plugs, the timer, and the generator. And we need to understand what qualities are *not* significant. We know, for example, that the color of the insulation of an automobile wiring system is not significant.

Analysis, Method, and Interest

An analysis cannot take place, we have said, except in accordance with the structure of the thing analyzed. A baby beating on an alarm clock is not analyzing the mechanism, no matter how many fragments he makes of it. Nor can an analysis take place by accident or at random. It represents an intention, an interest on the part of the person making the analysis. The baby beating on the alarm clock does not want to know how the clock works. He would beat just as happily on a tin pail.

Analysis requires method, and the method of an analysis depends on the structure of the thing analyzed and the interest prompting the analysis. Though an interest must dictate an analysis, different interests can dictate different analyses of the same thing. According to our different interests, we may regard the same thing as having various kinds of structure. For example, the botanist would regard an apple as a botanical structure and therefore would analyze it into stem, skin, flesh, seeds, and so forth; whereas a chemist would regard it as a chemical structure and would analyze it into certain elements, or a painter would regard is as an aesthetic structure and would analyze it into a pattern of color. Each man would perform his analysis in terms of a particular interest, and the interest prompting his analysis would decide the kind of structure which he took the object to be. The kind of structure would in turn determine what might be regarded as the parts of the structure.

In illustrating the fact that an object may be regarded as having different kinds of structure, we have used an example having physical existence, an apple. But what we said may also apply to something with no physical existence, say a short story. We may regard it as a grammatical structure, for it is made up of words. Or we may regard it as a fictional structure, that is, as being composed of plot, of characters, of theme — elements which we can think of and discuss separately. Or an institution may be regarded as having different kinds of structure. For instance, we may regard the family as an educational structure, or as an economic structure, or as a moral structure. Each of these structures implies different relationships among the members of a family.

Analysis and Technical (or Expository) Description

Analysis may be regarded as the description of a thing by distinguishing its parts. This kind of description, which we shall presently contrast with ordinary description, is called technical (or expository) description.

We can contrast technical description and ordinary description by considering the different types of occasion from which they arise. Technical description arises from the demand for *information about* the thing described; ordinary description, from the demand for an immediate sense impression of the thing described. The first kind of description is expository in that it attempts to enlarge the understanding. The second kind, ordinary description, aims to give us an experience of the object through imagination. (See Chapter 7, pages 196–202 for a fuller discussion.) We shall call it suggestive description.

Let us take two examples and contrast them:

TECHNICAL

FOR QUICK SALE

Attractive Cape Cod cottage, lge. liv. rm., 13 x 25, knotty pine, stone fireplace; din. rm., sunny, 12 x 14; small den or libr., fireplace; kitchen, modern, elec. stove, lge. gas refrig., dishwasher, all practically new; med.-size, concrete basement, gas furn., ht. watr.; 2 bedrms., 14 x 16, 15 x 18; 2 baths, lge. and small; roof white oak shingle. Lot well planted, landscaped, brook, 2 acres; heated garage, 2 cars; small greenhouse. Built by owner, 1936. Excellent condition. Take reasonable offer. Call: BE–1632.

SUGGESTIVE

Dear Mother:

We have found a place at last, and we love it, Jack just as much as I. I must tell you about it, so you can have some notion before you come to see us here. Well, you don't see it from the highway, for there is a high hedge with just a little gap that lets you into the lane, a winding lane among a grove of white oaks, like a lane going down to a pasture on somebody's farm, a million miles away from town. When you pass the oaks you see a dip down to a brook, lined with willows, and a stone bridge, and just beyond the bridge the house on a slight rise. The house is white and trim, two stories, but rather low, just seeming to crop out of the ground. You have the feeling that once you cross that bridge and enter that door you'll be safe and sound and the world will never come to bother you.

When you do enter, you know that your feeling is right. There is a long room with a big fireplace, and windows to the east for the morning sun. It is a perfect room for the furniture which Grandmother left me, just the sort of room she would have loved, peaceful and old-fashioned. The instant you come in, you think of a fire crackling on the hearth, and a kettle humming to heat water for tea, and you see the copper glinting on the andirons. . . .

The motives behind the two pieces of description are very different. The seller of the house wants to give information about the house. The buyer of the house, writing to her mother, wants to give the feel, the atmosphere, of the house. (Note that we are here using the method of contrast, with illustrations, to drive home the difference between the two kinds of descriptions.)

The advertisement is an instance of technical description which is an analysis of the house. Except in so far as we know the general type of Cape Cod cottage, we have no basis for visualizing the actual house. The writer of the advertisement has not been concerned that we should get an impression of the house; the only attempt in this direction is his use of the word *sunny* about the dining room. But if the writer has not been concerned to give us the picture and atmosphere of his house, he has been greatly concerned to give us a systematic and complete body of information about the house considered from a technical point of view as a shelter and a mechanism for living.

We should find the same motive behind a naturalist's description of a species of bird, a mechanic's description of the ignition system of an automobile, or a physiologist's description of the structure of the human brain. In none of these examples would there be any attempt to make us perceive the thing described except in so far as that attempt would enlarge our understanding of the object's structure.

In the excerpt from the letter above, however, the situation is reversed. The writer is concerned to make an appeal to her reader's senses, to establish the impression of the house, its quietness and isolation, its old-fashioned charm. The details she has selected for comment all contribute to this impression. The suggestive description does not, as does the technical, give a systematic and relatively complete body of information concerning the object; it does not analyze the subject. Instead, it simply presents the details that support the sensory and emotional effect the writer wishes to communicate. The technical description *tends* to be enumerative; the suggestive description *tends* to be selective and impressionistic.

There is another and very important distinction between the technical and the suggestive description. In the strictly technical description there is no place for interpretation by the writer. The description is concerned only with the facts about the object, facts that can be observed by anyone. For example, when the writer of the advertisement of the Cape Cod cottage lists six rooms, or says that the living room is of knotty pine, he is stating a fact, something objective and beyond dispute. He is being strictly technical. But when he says that the cottage is " attractive," he is not being strictly technical. He is interpreting the situation according to his own idea of what constitutes attractiveness. Likewise when the buyer writes her letter and says that the house is peaceful and charming, she is interpreting. To another person with different tastes the place might seem depressing rather than peaceful.

In the above technical description a specific house is described. Sometimes, however, technical description analyzes the characteristics of a *type* and not a specific thing.

GENERALIZED DESCRIPTION

Chestnut oak is the big tough-looking tree with bark in heavy ridges. At the bottom of the furrows between ridges, bark is cinnamon-red. Chestnut oak has largest acorns known on oaks — 1½ or even 2 inches. This is the acorn to roast and eat. It's the sweetest of all the northern oaks. Look for orange-brown twigs that are not round but angled in an interesting way. Name comes from resemblance to chestnut leaves — large ovals with wavy edges; one of the most beautiful of oak leaves.

— RUTHERFORD PLATT: *A Pocket Guide to the Trees.*

This description is aimed at giving the characteristics of a species of oak. Note how different it is from an ordinary description of a particular tree one has known — the tree at the corner of the yard, shading childhood play, or the tree on the ridge blasted by lightning to a peculiar shape, weird in the moonlight.

The Developed [7] *Analysis*

The two examples of technical description, the advertisement for the Cape Cod cottage and the description of the species of oak, are very brief. They are little more than unsystematic listings of parts. For their special purposes they may serve well enough, but many occasions for analysis demand more development and more system. For one thing, we want to indicate the relation among the parts, to give an over-all concept of the thing analyzed. Let us look at a paragraph from a book on fly-fishing, which begins an analysis of that sport:

Fly-fishing has three elements: equipment, knowledge of stream life, and presentation. The equipment centers on the artificial fly; the knowledge of stream life encompasses insects and trout; presentation is skill, acquired and magical, in presenting the fly to the trout. Fly-fishing argument, which is fabulous, revolves around the comparative value of these elements.

— JOHN McDONALD: Introduction to *The Complete Fly Fisherman, The Notes and Letters of Theodore Gordon.*

This example differs from the two previous examples, we can readily see, by indicating systematically the relation among the elements. Though the excerpt does not develop this relation, it is nevertheless recognized, and that is the start of a good analysis. It is the relation among the parts which establishes the thing analyzed as a structure.

Not only should we establish the relation among the parts, but to make understanding easier for our reader or listener, we should settle on some single governing idea by reference to which, for the purpose of the description, the parts can be charted. In the following exposition of the tryworks (the great kettles in which whale blubber was cooked down) of an old whaler, we notice how our understanding of the parts is governed by the strange image of a brick kiln set on the deck of a ship:

Besides her hoisted boats, an American whaler is outwardly distinguished by her try-works. She presents the curious anomaly of the most solid masonry joining with oak and hemp in constituting the completed ship. It is as if from the open field a brick-kiln were transported to her planks.

The try-works are planted between the foremast and mainmast, the most roomy part of the deck. The timbers beneath are of a peculiar strength, fitted to sustain the weight of an almost solid mass of brick and mortar, some ten feet by eight square, and five in height. The foundation does not penetrate the deck, but the masonry is firmly secured to the surface by

---

[7] By " developed " we do not necessarily imply longer or more detailed.

ponderous knees of iron bracing it on all sides, and screwing it down to the timbers. On the flanks it is cased with wood, and at top completely covered by a large, sloping, battened hatchway. Removing this hatch we expose the great try-pots, two in number, and each of several barrels' capacity. When not in use, they are kept remarkably clean. Sometimes they are polished with soapstone and sand, till they shine within like silver punch-bowls. — HERMAN MELVILLE: *Moby-Dick.*

In the following passage the comparison of the heart to a pump gives us the basis for understanding the relation among the parts:

The heart is a complicated mechanism. Essentially it is a muscular pump composed of four chambers and their incoming and outgoing blood vessels. The action of these chambers is coordinated and controlled by an intricate nervous mechanism. The chambers are paired into a right half and a left half. The upper chamber on each side is called the auricle; the lower, the ventricle. Each auricle is separated from its ventricle by a muscular valve which permits the flow of blood downward but prevents the leakage of blood backward. — LOUIS I. DUBLIN: *The Problem of Heart Disease.*

Functional Analysis

The kind of analysis we have been discussing thus far answers the question: " How is it put together? " A tree, we say, is composed of trunk, roots, branches, and leaves, attached to each other in a certain way. A radar set is composed of a modulator, a radio-frequency oscillator, an antenna with scanning mechanism, a receiver, and an indicator. But with the tree or the radar set (or almost anything else) , as soon as we begin to explore the idea of the relation among parts, we come to another question: " How does it work? " It is not merely the parts, but the function of the parts in relation to a characteristic function of the whole thing that now concerns us. Explaining how the parts of anything relate to one another in action we may call **functional analysis.**

In the passage about the heart the use of the comparison with a pump makes us think of the parts in action. If we continue the paragraph we see that the writer has moved from analysis of parts into functional analysis: What does the pump do?

Venous blood arriving from all parts of the body in the right auricle passes from the auricle through the valve into the right ventricle. It is then pumped through the pulmonary arteries to the lung where it is aerated. The blood then returns to the left auricle, passes down through the valve on that side into the left ventricle, whence it is pumped out through the aorta to be distributed to all parts of the body.

We might list and describe all the parts of a radar set, and this would give us a certain amount of information about radar. But to make a thorough analysis, we must say what function the parts perform. So the analysis goes something like this:

While the physical form of each of these components may vary widely from one kind of radar set to another, each radar must have the following complement of parts in order to function:

1. The *modulator* is a device for taking power from the primary source (which may be the commercial power line, a special engine or motor-driven generator, or storage batteries) and forming suitable voltage pulses to drive the radio-frequency oscillator in its bursts of radio-frequency oscillations. In other words, it is the modulator which turns on the radio-frequency oscillator to oscillate violently for a millionth of a second or so, turns it off sharply, and keeps it in repose until time for the next burst.

2. The *radio-frequency oscillator* is a vacuum tube of suitable design, or a group of such tubes, which will oscillate at the desired radio frequency and give the desired bursts of radio-frequency power when connected to the modulator. . . .

And so on, through all the components, with an explanation at each stage of the function of the part in the operation of the whole apparatus.

Here is a student theme analyzing the parts of an apparatus in relation to function:

HI-FI

Your hi-fi phonograph has to do three different and distinct things: It has to get the electric impulse off the record; to amplify that impulse, or signal; and to turn it into sound.

For the first operation you need a turntable and an arm — a tone arm it is called — which swings over the record on the turntable. This arm has at the end a pick-up cartridge, which presses the needle, or stylus, into the track on the record.

The most important requirement for a turntable is that it run at an exact speed for each type of record — 78.26, or 45, or 33⅓ rpm — without any variation. If there is variation, you get changes in pitch, "wowing" or "fluttering," as the experts say.

The tone arm has to be balanced so that exactly the right pressure is always on the grooves of the disc, and the cartridge should always point directly down at the disc. Also the arm must swing without any friction. And it must move at an even rate.

Of the four types of cartridge, I prefer the magnetic type. It is called magnetic because the stylus is set in the end of a cantilever spring fastened at one end to a permanent magnet. I use the General Electric cartridge, which I have found perfectly satisfactory.

When it comes to the stylus, or needle, the most economical type to buy is the most expensive. Many styli will cut your records in a few playings. In the long run you will save money, and records, if you get a diamond stylus. It will cost you around twenty dollars, but it will play five hundred to a thousand hours before it wears. It is about ten times better than a sapphire stylus.

For the second distinct operation of your rig you need an amplifier. The kind you get is determined by the answer to two questions: (1) How much power do you need? (2) How good is your other equipment? The power you need is based on the size of your room and the kind of speaker you have. If you haven't got enough power your music will be too soft, or if it gets loud the sound will be harsh and fuzzed. In other words, you won't have music. For ordinary purposes you should be safe with a thirty-watt amplifier.

Last are the speaker and box. The center of every ordinary speaker is a magnet and coil of wire. A current flows in through the coil and sets up an electromagnetic field, and this fluctuating field pulls across the steady magnetic field from the magnet, just as a bow pulls across the fiddle strings. Hence your music bounces out into the air. I use a Bozak speaker, but I have friends who get good results from several other kinds. If you are a real hi-fi enthusiast, you can pay nearly a thousand dollars for this part of the rig.

You can buy some fancy housing for the speaker, too. But you can save a lot by building it yourself, and you will find the results equally good. In building mine, I discovered that the main thing is to get the enclosure big enough and firm enough. My enclosure is five feet long and two feet high and over a foot deep. It is glued and screwed together, with no nails (never use nails), and for added firmness it is fastened with long, heavy screws into the studs of the wall. I used fiber-glass stuffing for the box.

Do you like music? If you do, you had better leave hi-fi alone, because you will become so interested in the technical side that you will never listen to music any more. Like me, you will just listen to hi-fi.

This theme wavers somewhat in its intention. It is clear enough in distinguishing the parts and indicating their function, but it is not consistent in explaining the way the parts work. It does explain how the speaker works (the two magnetic fields, one like a bow the other like the fiddle strings), but it gives no explanation, for instance, of the operation of the cartridge. The result is that we do not get a clear notion of the over-all process involved.

Here is a much more systematic piece of functional analysis, the description of a city government:

While the importance of good personnel certainly cannot be minimized, personnel of any kind is capable of doing its best work only under competent, carefully designed systems of administrative organization. This organization may be divided, for purposes of rapid analysis, into three prime elements — line agencies, staff agencies, and auxiliary agencies.

Line Agencies

A *line agency,* as the term is used by specialists in administration, is a unit of government that serves the public directly. A department that sells water, at the meter, to householders and industrial and commercial concerns is a line agency; so is a department of sanitation which cleans the streets and removes wastes.

Line agencies make wholesale use of the principle of the *division of labor;* that is, the work of the city is divided among many kinds of specialists. One group of employees, for example, may merely repair streets, while another maintains the fire-alarm telegraph system and a third confines itself to detecting criminals. By concentrating on and learning about a special field of activity, employees may perform their tasks with maximum success.

Where sound principles of administration are in force, a *chain of command* is established in order to tie together all such specialized groups. The purpose of the chain of command is to insure that orders and ideas coming from the highest officials are obeyed by their subordinates, down to the lowest-ranking employee. Only in this way can confusion be avoided and responsibility for the execution of the laws be firmly established. It is because this chain of command may be so short, at the municipal level, that cities can sometimes get things done with so much more facility than the National Government.

Ordinarily, the chain of command follows functional lines. As chief executive, for instance, a city manager may issue orders to a series of immediate subordinates, known as department chiefs, each in charge of one of the five to fifteen or more departments of the city. An effort is usually made to see that each department has only one broad function to perform. Thus the health department deals primarily with births, disease, and death, while the fire department seeks to prevent and to fight fires and the police department engages in various law enforcement operations.

In a carefully organized administration, the subdivisions of a department are similarly established along functional lines. Directly responsible to the chief of police in charge of the police department, for example, there is the head of the detective bureau which traces clues to apprehend criminals. The detective bureau is in its turn subdivided according to duties, with an officer in charge of each. By dividing and subdividing as far as is necessary, on a functional basis, several grades of officials may be established which will allow orders to pass from the city manager downward to the lowest rank of employees. The result is a clear chain of command.

The chain of command may have a geographical rather than a functional basis. The administration of a fire department is a case in point. The success of a fire-fighting unit in the discharge of its duties often depends upon the speed with which it arrives at a danger spot after a fire alarm has rung;

and speed in turn depends, in a large measure, upon the size of the geographical district that an engine company must cover. In large cities, therefore, the whole metropolitan area is laid out into districts, each with its own company, firemen, and captain. Over all the companies is the fire chief whose responsibility it is to supervise and control fire-fighting in all districts of the city.

Another principle of municipal administration usually applied is that the *span of control* of a high official should be reasonably restricted. If an officer has too many immediate and equal subordinates to superintend, he cannot keep close watch over all their performances. On the other hand, when he has a small number of chief subordinates he can readily keep in touch with them and thus discharge his managerial duties.

The span-of-control principle may be illustrated by reference to a fire department. A large city must, of necessity, have so many fire-fighting companies that it is impossible for the fire chief to deal with all of them individually and directly. Consequently the companies may be grouped in a few large districts, each under the care of a battalion chief. When this is done, the fire chief merely supervises and issues orders to a few battalion chiefs who on their part assume responsibility for relaying orders to the captains and forces of the several companies.

Although the major portion of the city's administration is conducted by line agencies headed by chief administrators, other branches are often placed in the care of boards or commissions, composed of several persons elected separately by the voters or appointed by the mayor. This principle is commonly applied in creating agencies that have charge of matters likely to be highly controversial or that are invested with power to make rules and regulations deeply affecting life and property. In this class fall functions pertaining to education, public health, and housing.

In such instances, the voters of the city are apt to feel that granting full control to a single official may put the function in question at the mercy of whatever political or other biases he cherishes. It is to escape this danger that boards are used. The theory of this practice is that on a board various interests may be represented and that at board meetings the interplay of divergent ideas will lead to moderation and compromises more acceptable to the community than the decisions of a single administrator. On this principle, the city usually has one or more boards, each endowed with power to make rules and often to appoint its subordinates. Frequently, however, the board has a single executive officer to execute its judgments and decisions.

Formerly boards were more extensively used in municipal administration than at the present time. Often even the management of the police force was given to a commission. But it has been found by experience that boards can display serious weaknesses. The wrangling at board meetings may easily lead to confusion, hesitancy, and deadlocks. If gross negligence occurs, it is hard for the public to discover who among the members are responsible, whereas with regard to every agency directed by a single official the blame for misdeeds cannot be hidden. It was after many bitter lessons had been learned from the operation of boards that cities began to abolish them and, except in a few special cases, to substitute departments.

Auxiliary Agencies of Administration

Unlike line agencies, auxiliary agencies do not serve the public directly. Auxiliary agencies are set up primarily to assist the city government as a whole and the administrative departments in particular. All branches of the government need money, supplies, equipment, and competent employees, and in the larger cities special divisions are established to meet these demands.

Every city has one or more auxiliary agencies to handle its finances. These agencies assess property for taxation, collect the municipal revenues, safeguard the public money, pay bills on proper orders, and audit the accounts of all officials. In the large municipalities there is usually a department of finance, with perhaps a separate auditor or comptroller in charge of checking receipts and expenditures.

A second type of auxiliary agency buys supplies and equipment for many departments, bureaus, and offices in the city government. The reasons for the establishment of such an agency are grounded in practical experience. If each department bought its own supplies in small quantities, it might have to pay for them at correspondingly high retail rates. On the other hand, if requests from all the departments for such common items as ink and typewriters are pooled and buying them is turned over to a single central office, items may be secured at substantially lower wholesale rates.

Moreover, the business of buying supplies in an individual department may not be large enough to justify the appointment of even one really skilled full-time purchasing agent, whereas in the aggregate the buying for a whole city may warrant employing a well-trained staff. With such a staff, it is practicable to install a testing laboratory to check the quality of supplies delivered under city contracts and to maintain warehouses for storage of supplies — a practice which individual departments, perhaps, could not very well afford. In brief, turning over departmental buying to a centralized purchasing bureau offers opportunities for substantial improvements in the character of supplies, assurance of delivery, and the saving of time and money.

A third major type of auxiliary agency deals with personnel problems. It has been found that when the heads of line agencies freely appoint their own employees, they may reward loyal party workers with jobs for which they are poorly suited. The result is the so-called " spoils system," based on the theory that to the victor at the polls belong all the jobs in the city government. At a time when the wide range of technological operations carried on by cities calls for the possession of a high degree of specialized skill on the part of many municipal employees, this program is worse than wasteful; it may be positively dangerous to the public.

To prevent the spoils system from overloading city offices with incompetents, many municipalities have created civil service commissions as auxiliary services, and charged them with supplying to the line agencies employees trained in the various kinds of work undertaken by the city. The typical commission advertises openings, holds competitive examinations for them at which applicants may demonstrate their mental and manual ability, grades the results, and makes up lists of satisfactory eligibles. When an appointing official has occasion to fill a particular vacancy in the city service, he must usually choose one of the three persons having the highest scores on the appropriate list supplied by the commission.

Staff Agencies

Boards and single executives, when engaged in administering large line organizations, frequently encounter problems that they cannot solve until someone else takes the time to furnish them with detailed reports on the law and facts in question. Hence there have come into being units charged with the sole task of investigating special problems, making surveys, and giving advice to line officers. Where these exploratory agencies issue no commands and render no direct services to the people, but only conduct inquiries and offer suggestions, they are known as staff agencies. New York City, for example, established some advisory planning boards to aid its city planning commission.

— WILLIAM BEARD: *Government and Liberty, the American System.*[8]

• Application •

Write a theme of 500 words analyzing a mechanism, institution, or idea. In doing so, you should consider the following points:

1. Identify or define the structure to be analyzed.
2. Specify what principle of structure is to be considered.
3. Indicate the parts.
4. State what relations exist among the parts in reference to the principle of structure you have chosen.

The list of topics below may suggest a subject for your theme:

A Regiment of Infantry	A Church
A University	A Business Organization
Nationalism	A Football Team
Morality	American Sectionalism
The Internal-Combustion Engine	A Poem
A Newspaper	A Picture
A Political Party	True Charity
A Television Set	A Hospital

FUNCTIONAL ANALYSIS AND PROCESS

Thus far we have been putting the emphasis on the parts of a structure as explained by their characteristic function. That is, we

---

[8] From *Government and Liberty, the American System* by William Beard, Garden City Publishing Co., 1947. Reprinted by permission of the author.

have been concerned, by and large, with mechanism. But we may switch the emphasis to the analysis of a process. A process may involve a mechanism — the human heart or a legislature — but our chief concern will be with the stages of the process and not with the parts of the mechanism. The parts are interesting only in so far as they help explain the stages.

Functional analysis, then, is the method by which we distinguish the stages in a process which may be regarded as having a characteristic function or purpose.[9]

EXPOSITORY NARRATION

Once we are concerned with the stage of a process, we are dealing with a sequence of events in time. That is, we have narration, but narration used for an expository purpose.

As we can make a distinction between technical (or expository) description and ordinary description (page 99), so can we make one between **expository narration** and ordinary narration. Ordinary narration, as we shall see when we come to discuss it as a basic kind of discourse (in Chapter 8), is concerned with presenting an action. It aims to give the sense of the event as experienced, and it involves an appeal to the imagination. But narration may be employed merely to give information, to enlarge the understanding. If we give directions as to how to build a boat or make a cake, we are treating a sequence of events in time, and we are forced to use a form of narration. If we tell how radar works, we are again using a kind of narration. An instructor in military history lecturing on the First Battle of the Marne in World War I is concerned to make his class understand the stages of the event and the problems of tactics, but he is not necessarily concerned to bring the event into the imagination of his audience. So he, too, is using expository narration.

By analogy with generalized description, we can see that when expository narration deals with a type of process or type of event, instead of a unique and particular event, we call it **generalized narra-**

---

[9] Though we use the word functional to describe the particular kind of analysis, we may distinguish between function and purpose. If we are discussing a university, we can treat the subject in terms of purpose, for it is an institution created by men to gain certain ends. But if we are discussing the circulation of the blood, we can treat the subject only in terms of a characteristic function. We cannot say that purpose is involved. Or, to take another contrasted pair of examples, if we give directions for making an apple pie, we are treating our subject in terms of purpose, but if we discuss the stages of development of an apple, we are treating the subject in terms of function. In both instances we can, of course, observe a regular pattern, but in one case we interpret the pattern as representing purpose and in the other as representing function.

What is the significance of the distinction for purposes of exposition? In making this distinction we define our subject; we determine the sort of structure we are dealing with.

tion. For example, we may narrate the basic steps in baking an apple pie, or we may give the steps that we went through in baking our first pie.

Let us glance at one of the simplest forms in which expository narration may be used, the giving of directions for a process. The following is a section from a handbook on repairing antique furniture:

GLUING FELT TO WOOD

You may occasionally wish to glue thin felt to wood, as when replacing it in an old desk top. Other occasions are applying felt to a lamp base or to the bottom of legs of heavy furniture so that floors will not be scratched.

Thin felt for such purposes may usually be purchased in a variety of colors at department stores. The most popular colors are green and brown. Measure the size needed and buy a piece larger than required, as it may shrink somewhat when applied and the glue dries.

Use either the " Synthetic Resin Waterproof Glue " mixed a bit thick or " Old Fashioned Glue " as it comes from the container.

Proceed as follows:

1 — When the surface is prepared, by removing any old glue, scratch or roughen it with coarse abrasive paper and clean off. Then apply a generous and even coat of the glue. Allow this to dry until it becomes very sticky and is not too liquid. Otherwise, it might soak through the felt.

2 — Apply an oversize piece of felt to the surface, starting on one side and laying it carefully in correct position with no wrinkles. The felt must overlap on all sides. The hands must be clean and free from dust.

3 — The felt must now be rolled or patted into the glue. This is best done with a photographer's roller. If a roller is not available, hold a lintless clean cloth around a small wood block and pat the entire surface. It is best not to rub it for fear of moving or stretching the felt.

4 — Allow to dry for 24 to 48 hours in a warm room.

5 — If the felt goes beyond the edges, trim off closely with sharp scissors. Should it be used on a piece such as a desk top which has a wood border around the surface to which it is applied, the excess felt material is best cut off with a safety razor blade against a straight edge as a guide. (A carpenter's large steel square is good for this purpose.)

— RALPH PARSONS KINNEY: *The Complete Book of Furniture Repair and Refinishing.*[10]

This is a very clear and systematic account of the process. It has a single point — to tell us how felt is glued — and it never wavers from that intention. It is complete; it tells us everything we can reasonably want to know, assuming nothing on our part, not even that

---

10 From *The Complete Book of Furniture Repair and Refinishing* by Ralph Parsons Kinney. By permission of Charles Scribner's Sons.

we know where to get the felt or what kind of glue is best. And it uses very simple language. Technical terms known only to expert cabinetmakers are not used; any amateur of furniture repairing can understand the directions given.

The organization is systematic. We note that the piece begins by stating the kind of situation that demands the process, then identifies the materials needed, and then, as the body of the passage, gives the process, stage by stage, in strict chronological order, except for occasional cautions or suggestions, for example, the caution to have the hands clean and free from dust.

We see that the directions are little more than an expanded outline, a skeleton which is to be fleshed out, not by words but by the actual doing. But often we are concerned with the explanation of a process, not in order to carry it out but merely to satisfy curiosity and to enlarge the understanding. In such instances the strict schematic method used above will scarcely satisfy us or our readers. Some filling out is needed.

Here is an account of the method of planting dark tobacco in Tennessee and Kentucky, written as part of an introduction to an American novel translated into French. The account is thus intended for a public that knows nothing of farming in those states and is expected to have only the casual interest provoked by the novel itself, certainly with no intention of going out and raising a crop.

The work begins in January, when winter breaks a little and the soil thaws. On the sunny side of a patch of woodland, where the soil is thick and rich, the farmer piles up some dry wood, mixed with a little green, on a space about twenty feet wide by fifty to a hundred feet long. At evening he sets fire to his big woodpile, and sometimes in a sort of ritual picnic all the family comes down to watch, for this is the beginning of a new year of work and hope. Next day the soil, mixed with the ashes of the bonfire, is turned up, pulverized and raked to prepare a bed for the little seeds of tobacco which the farmer then treads into the soil and ashes. Long ago the farmers used to place boughs over the bed to protect it, but in later times they stretch over the bed, on a frame, a cheap white cloth, very light, called canvas, light enough to allow sun and rain to come through. In this protected bed the fragile plant of tobacco develops until the time when it will be replanted in the open field.

The time of setting out the plants comes in May or June. The farmer has prepared his field. He has plowed and harrowed the soil to pulverize it as perfectly as possible, and he has laid it out in squares. When the rain comes and the soil is well soaked — that is to say, when the farmer gets what he calls a "season" — the tender plants are drawn from the bed. Now every available person turns out, women and children, to carry the plants in baskets across the field, letting one fall at the exact center of each square. Behind the "droppers," the women and children with the baskets of plants, come the men, the "setters," who with one hand pick up the plant and with the other drive a sharpened stake of wood, called a "dibble," into the earth to make a hole for the plant. The setter presses down the damp earth around the plant, and without straightening up, takes another step forward, to the next square and the nearest plant. This setting out process is a grinding work: in May or June, the sun of Kentucky is already powerful, and you can't interrupt yourself, even to straighten an aching back, for every moment is precious as long as the soil is damp enough to receive the plant.

Here the writer has tried to fill out the skeleton of the account with just enough material — the family coming down to watch the fire, the heat of the sun, the aching back, and so on — to make the French reader have some immediate sense of the process. In other words, there are certain elements in the passage that belong to suggestive narration or description. But the intention here is primarily expository — to analyze the process of tobacco setting for the French reader.

• **Applications** •

I. In the Readings, study "The American Civilization Puzzle" (page 666). What is the author's view of the process of the diffusion of ideas? Write a paragraph summarizing the process.

II. Below is a list of possible subjects for themes, some that may well be treated as directions, some more properly adapted to the account of a process to satisfy curiosity. Select one of the subjects that interests you (or think up one of your own). First decide whether your subject suggests a particular or generalized form of narration. The two examples given above are generalized; the directions for gluing felt are, of course, supposed to be applicable in general, as is the account of setting tobacco. But if you take the Battle of the Bulge, you will be explaining a specific event.

If you are giving a generalized treatment, you must remember that you are trying to present the essential pattern that never varies significantly from one instance to another. If you are giving the explanation of an event — for instance, the last football game — you are concerned with its particularity and must make clear why you won or lost under the *special* circumstances.

Having decided whether you are concerned with a particular or general treatment, make your outline, breaking the process or event down into its stages, in chronological order. Then write a short theme, say about 500 words, to develop the outline. Remember that you are supposed to be giving information to a person relatively ignorant of the subject, that you should leave nothing of consequence to his surmise, and remember, too, if you are writing directions, to include any appropriate cautions or suggestions. But always stick to your main point; do not let your cautions or suggestions lead you away from it.

The Curing of Tobacco	Baking an Apple Pie
Assault from the Sea	Registration Day
The Production Line	A Charity Drive
How To Use a Library	How the News Story Gets
Pigeon Raising	on the Front Page
How Wheat Is Marketed	How To Lay Out a Vegetable
A Chemical Experiment	Garden
The Battle of the Bulge	Organizing a Dance
Putting On a Student Play	A Beaver Dam
(or Putting On a Particular Play)	Last Saturday's Football Game
How I Shot My First Deer	

Causal Analysis

In dealing with some processes we often want to go beyond a mere account of the stages in time sequence. When we want to see what makes one stage lead to another, we make a **causal analysis**.

Causal analysis concerns two questions: " What caused this? " and " Given this set of circumstances, what effect will follow? " In answering the first question we must reason from effect back to cause, and in answering the second, from cause forward to effect. Causal analysis usually takes the form of expository narration. We are accustomed to think of cause and effect in a time sequence, as a chain of happenings.

CAUSE

We all have a rough-and-ready notion of what cause is. Some understanding of cause is necessary to manage our daily lives. The burnt child shuns the fire only after he has learned that a certain act, putting his finger in the flame, is followed by a certain unpleasant effect, a burn. He has made a connection between events.

Cause is a kind of connection between events that enables us to say, (1) without event A, event B would not have come about, and (2) whenever you have A you will have B.[11]

---

[11] The use of the word *event* here may be objected to. It may be said that the word *thing* is more appropriate, at least in some circumstances. For example, we can reason that a nail is the cause of the fact that a picture hangs on the wall. A nail is a thing, but it is not the nail as a *thing* that sustains the picture. It is

CONDITION

No event takes place in isolation. It always involves a complicated set of circumstances spreading in all directions. Tennyson, in the poem " Flower in the Crannied Wall," states the notion:

> Flower in the crannied wall,
> I pluck you out of the crannies,
> I hold you here, root and all, in my hand,
> Little flower — but *if* I could understand
> What you are, root and all, and all in all,
> I should know what God and man is.

Since in the world there is this almost infinite texture of relations, if the poet could know the complete " cause" of the flower, he would know the entire universe.

Clearly, we aren't concerned with the notion of cause in any such wide sense. We need a workaday, useful concept of cause. Let us look at a simple experiment. To a rod is attached a little bell. The rod, in turn, is attached to an electric mechanism which will make it sway back and forth when a button is pushed. The whole affair, except the control button, is rigged up in a hermetically sealed jar connected with a vacuum pump. Somebody pushes the button, the rod sways, the bell rings. We hear the sound of the bell. What is the cause of the sound?

One person says it is caused by the clapper striking the inside of the bell. Another says it is caused by the movement of the rod. Another says: " No, Jack pushed the button." And common sense tells us that everybody is right and everybody is wrong. In each case the person answering has fixed on some particular factor and assumed the other factors.

How much assumption is involved in our talk about cause we can see more clearly if we pump the air entirely out of the jar, and then push the button. The mechanism works, the bell clapper strikes metal, but there is no sound. We know why. For sound to exist, there must be a medium, in this instance air, in which the sound waves can travel.

The first three people who specified a cause for the sound forgot all about the necessity for a medium for the sound waves. But now a fourth person says: " Ah, it was the air that caused the sound." Again, he is both right and wrong, as common sense will tell us. All

---

the nail's state of being in the wall that causes the picture to be sustained, and being in the wall is an event. Things must exist, of course, for events to exist, but the event is what we are concerned with. The state of a thing is an event, in our meaning of the word.

the factors had to be there — the bell, the clapper striking it, the mechanism, the person pushing the button, the air for the waves.

Other circumstances are also present: the bell, for example, is brass, not steel; the electric wires have red insulation; and so on. But the particular kind of metal, or the color of insulation, has no *necessary* effect on the existence of the sound: steel would do for the bell, and the insulation might as well be blue. We are concerned with the principle of the mechanism, not its accidental features.

Any necessary factor, any factor that must be present for the event to take place, we shall call a **condition.**

IMMEDIATE CONNECTION

As Tennyson has pointed out, the world may be thought of as an enormously complex texture of conditions for any single event. We, however, are concerned with the more or less **immediate connection** between an event and its conditions. Certainly, the birth of a grandfather may be in the long range a condition of the death of a grandson, for without the old man's birth the boy would never have existed, and so forth. But that connection is not immediate enough to be very instructive to us.

CAUSE AND INTEREST

Among the conditions that have a more or less immediate connection with an event, how do we determine which is to be taken as a cause? In one way we must say that our special interest determines what condition is to be taken as cause.

Let us take the case of the death of the grandson. We have ruled out the condition of the birth of the grandfather because of its lack of immediate connection. But let us sort out some immediate conditions. When the little boy falls from the stepladder and is killed, a neighbor commenting on the event would probably be satisfied by the fact of the fall from the ladder as the cause. But the mother might take her own carelessness as the cause: She had left the stepladder standing on the edge of the back porch instead of putting it away in the closet where it belonged. Or a doctor might take a more scientific view of the cause and say that death was the result of a fracture of the skull.

In relation to the special interest brought to bear on the event, each of these statements may be true. It is important, however, to know what we are about when we select a particular line of interest to explain an event. From a group of conditions with more or less immediate connection with the event in question, we select the cause that is appropriate to our interest. But we must select it responsibly.

REASONING ABOUT CAUSE

We can deal responsibly with cause only if we are aware of certain principles. Let us look at a passage by Leo Tolstoy:

> Whenever I see the movement of a locomotive I hear the whistle and see the valves opening and wheels turning; but I have no right to conclude that the whistling and the turning of wheels are the cause of the movement of the engine.
>
> The peasants say that a cold wind blows in late spring because the oaks are budding, and really every spring cold winds do blow when the oak is budding. But I do not know what causes the cold winds to blow when the oak buds unfold, I cannot agree with the peasants that the unfolding of the oak buds is the cause of the cold wind, for the force of the wind is beyond the influence of the buds. I see only a coincidence of occurrences such as happens with all the phenomena of life, and I see that however much and however carefully I observe . . . the valves and wheels of the engine, and the oak, I shall not discover the cause of . . . the engine moving, or of the winds of spring. To do that I must entirely change my point of view and study the laws of the movement of steam . . . and of the wind.
> — LEO TOLSTOY: *War and Peace.*

The fact that something is merely associated with something else in time does not mean that it is to be regarded as either cause or effect. In fact, one of the most common failures in reasoning about cause and effect is the assumption that if something comes after something else it is to be regarded as the effect. The Russian peasants in Tolstoy's novel think the cold wind is the effect of the budding of the oak because it comes after it. To avoid such an error, we must try to find the essential characteristic in the situation that we are studying. The color of the insulation on the electric wire, we remember, is not relevant.

UNIFORMITY

Not only must we try to see what conditions are relevant; if we are to reason well about cause, we must also understand the principle of uniformity.

When we say that A is the cause of B, we are not merely referring to the particular case of a particular A and a particular B. We are also implying that a general principle exists, that under the same circumstances any A would cause a B. We imply a principle of uniformity behind the particular case. Let us take a simple instance:

TOM: Why did Jane speak so curtly at dinner last night?

JACK: Because she was angry with her husband.

TOM: How do you know?

JACK: That's the way she always behaves when she's angry with him.

TOM: You must have been around the family a lot.

JACK: Sure. I lived in the house for a year.

When Jack says that the cause of Jane's conduct was her anger with her husband, he is not merely commenting on the particular instance. And Tom's further question elicits the fact that a principle of uniformity is involved: Jane behaves this way *every* time she gets angry with her husband. The principle here may not be one on which we can depend with any great degree of certainty. On some future occasion she may not merely be short with her husband at dinner but may kick the cat, get a divorce, or shoot her husband. But past observation gives us some degree of probability that when Jane is angry with her husband, she merely behaves in a certain way at dinner, that a principle of uniformity is involved.

Uniformity is the principle involved in what we call a law of nature. A chemist says that when we ignite hydrogen in the presence of oxygen we will get water (H_2O). Under specified conditions the element hydrogen and the element oxygen always behave in the same way. At least, we believe that they will so behave because they have always behaved that way in the past. We appeal to experience and to a number of instances for our principle.

The principle of uniformity, we must remember, refers only to the essential characteristics of the situation. For instance, it does not matter whether the laboratory worker igniting hydrogen in the presence of oxygen is a Catholic or a Jew, a Republican or a Democrat, a Chinese or a Greek. The boy who, in Charles Lamb's essay, accidentally discovered how to roast a pig by burning down a house, had not isolated the essential characteristic of the situation: he had not learned that he did not need to burn down a house every time he wanted roast pig. He had not isolated the essential characteristic of fire by which to roast meat.

In the laboratory a scientist can control the circumstances of his experiments and repeat them over and over, without variation. But outside the laboratory it is difficult to control circumstances with any certainty, and many events that we want to explain — for instance, a political election — cannot be repeated at will and identically. When we want to understand the causes of an event which we cannot repeat, we must simply examine similar events, that is, the various political elections we know about, and try to make sense of them. We must try, in other words, to see what is uniform in them that can lead to the discovery of a cause. When we try to find the cause of a particular effect, we must look for uniformities beyond the particular situation.

COMPLEX CAUSE

Even in an ordinary, simple event — the bell ringing in the jar, say — we find, as we have pointed out, a number of conditions which may be taken to have causal relation to the event. Many events are, however, enormously more complicated than our experiment. In any situation, but especially in a complicated one, we must be sure that when we select one condition as a cause we are not taking that single condition to be a total cause. It may be something that we can talk about legitimately in the terms of our special interest as a cause, as, for instance, when the doctor says that the fracture of the skull, and not the mother's carelessness or the fall from the ladder, caused the boy's death. But we must be very careful not to treat such a cause as *the* explanation, *the* cause. If we are trying to determine, in so far as such a thing is possible, *the* cause of an event, we must try to see the relations among the various conditions which might be selected as causes. We must aim for a complete picture.

For instance, if a certain business firm failed in 1932, should we take as *the* explanation someone's statement that its failure was caused by the incompetence of the chairman of the board? Or are we willing to accept the idea that the firm was merely the victim of the depression? Or can the failure be blamed on the Republican party, then in power? Or can we say that technological advances made the failure inevitable?

Events involving human behavior are always difficult to treat as cause and effect, but many occupations and professions are concerned primarily with the effort to do so. Advertising men, politicians, teachers, parents, psychiatrists, poker players, novelists, historians, sociologists, all are concerned with cause and effect. The advertising man, for example, must study the causes of men's desire to buy in order to know what will appeal to prospective buyers of the product he is promoting. If he is selling a new stove, he may put a picture of a gray-haired housewife on a billboard. Why won't he do the same thing if he is selling an eight-thousand-dollar automobile? The historian needs to know the cause of human action in order to interpret the events of the past, not only the nature of individual leaders, but those common human traits that make for mass movements. And he needs to know, or to try to know, how differences in time and differences in culture cause changes in human nature. In fact, we are all concerned, instinctively, with trying to find causes in human behavior. If we do not understand the people we live with, and do not understand ourselves, we are apt to make a mess of our lives.

NEGATIVE TESTS

There are two handy, rule-of-thumb tests to apply when trying to determine cause:

1. A cannot be the cause of B if A is ever absent in any instance when B is present.
2. A cannot be the cause of B if B is ever absent in any instance when A is present.

A LAST CAUTION

In the foregoing discussion of cause many of the ideas have probably struck the student as familiar. He does know these ideas. He has been making judgments of cause and effect all his life — in fishing and hunting, in games, in gardening, in laboratory work, in crossing the street. Being acquainted with the ideas, however, is not quite enough. One must make a practice of applying them systematically to a situation. If the student can think straight about a problem of cause and effect, then it will be easy for him to write well about it. And to think straight, he must be systematic in applying ideas. (For further study, see the Appendix on causal analysis, page 813.)

• Applications •

I. Find two examples of reasoning about cause in "The American Civilization Puzzle" (Readings, page 666). Do you consider them good reasoning?

II. Read the following passage by a noted scientist, Robert A. Millikan:

When in 1825 my grandfather loaded into a covered wagon his young wife, his Lares and Penates, and all his worldly goods, and trekked west from Stockbridge, Massachusetts, first to the Western Reserve in Ohio, and again in 1838 to the banks of the Rock River in western Illinois, the conditions of that migration, the motives prompting it, the mode of travel of the immigrants, their various ways of meeting their needs and solving their problems, their whole outlook on life, were extraordinarily like those which existed four thousand years earlier when Abraham trekked westward from Ur of the Chaldees. In a word, the changes that have occurred within the past hundred years, not only in the external conditions under which the average man, at least in this Western world, passes his life on earth, but in his superstitions, such as the taboo on the number thirteen or on Friday sailings (why, my own grandmother carried a dried potato in her pocket to keep off rheumatism), in his fundamental belief, in his philosophy, in his concept of religion, in his whole world-outlook, are probably greater than those that occurred during the preceding four thousand years all put together. Life seems to remain static for thousands of years and then to shoot forward with amazing speed. The last century has been one of those periods of extraordinary change, the most amazing in human history.

If, then, you ask me to put into one sentence the cause of that recent, rapid, and enormous change and the prognosis for the achievement of human liberty, I should reply, *It is found in the discovery and utilization of the means by which heat energy can be made to do man's work for him.* The key to the whole development is found in the use of power machines, and it is a most significant statistical fact that the standard of living in the various countries of the world follows closely the order in which so-called labor saving devices have been most widely put to use. In other words, the average man has today more of goods and services to consume in about the proportion in which he has been able to produce more of goods and services through the aid of power machines which have been put into his hands. In this country there is now expended about 13.5 horsepower per day per capita — the equivalent of 100 human slaves for each of us; in England, the figure is 6.7, in Germany 6.0, in France 4.5, in Japan 1.8, in Russia 0.9, in China 0.5. In the last analysis, this use of power is why our most important social changes have come about. This is why we no longer drive our ships with human slaves chained to the oars, as did the Romans and the Greeks. This is why we no longer enslave whole peoples, as did the Pharaohs, for building our public structures and lash them to their tasks. This is why ten times as many boys and girls are in the high schools today in the United States as were there in 1890 — more than five million now, half a million then. This is why we have now an eight-hour day instead of, as then, a ten-, twelve-, or sometimes a fourteen-hour day. This is why we have on the average an automobile for every family in the country. This is why the lowest class of male labor, i.e., unskilled labor, gets nearly twice as much in real wages in the United States as in England, three times as much as in Germany or France, and thirteen times as much as in Russia, and this is why the most abused class of labor in the world, domestic service, is even better off relatively in this country, though completely unorganized, i.e., through the unhampered operation of economic laws, than is any other class of labor, skilled or unskilled, in other countries. — Robert A. Millikan: " Science, Freedom and the World of Tomorrow," in *Freedom: Its Meaning.*[12]

1. The author has here said that the discovery and utilization of means of developing power has caused the changes in modern life, but has not explained how this is so. What causes can you think of to support his view?

2. Even while Dr. Millikan wrote this essay, " whole peoples " were being enslaved by countries which possessed modern machines. What caused such enslavement in Germany or Russia? How deeply does this fact affect his general conclusion?

III. You are going to be asked to write a theme in causal analysis, but before you begin, here is an example of a student theme to consider. It is not complete; it is only the first part of a long research theme for late in the course. But the writer has chosen a subject involving causal analysis. (The footnotes proper to a research theme are here dropped out. We will take up the problems of the research paper in Chapters 13 and 14.)

[12] From *Freedom: Its Meaning*, edited by Ruth Nanda Anshen, copyright, 1940, by Harcourt, Brace and Company, Inc.

CAUSES OF THE TEXAS REVOLUTION

I was born and raised in Texas, and in fact never left the State until I came here to college. I suppose I have my share of Texas patriotism, but I don't take it out in wearing high-heel boots. Instead, I have a kind of hobby of reading Texas history. The Texas revolution, which made Texas into an independent nation, as Texans have a sneaking feeling Texas still is, was a very romantic thing. But I have read enough history to know that it was not only romantic. It was also very complicated. Here I am going to try to sort out the causes leading up to it.

In this paper, I intend to do three things: First, to list the causes of the Texas revolution and define each one. Second, to show how these causes combined to bring about the revolution. Third, to sort out the causes in some order of importance. It is all a little bit like trying to keep three Indian clubs in the air at one time. But since I can't do everything at once, I shall list and define the causes first, then try to tell the story, and then, by way of a conclusion, line them up in importance, or what to me seems to be their importance.

The first cause was simply the difference in civilization between the Mexicans who owned Texas and the Americans who came there. I don't mean in the amount of civilization; I mean in the kind of civilization they had. The Mexicans had a Spanish and Catholic civilization, and they believed in power and authority and tradition. The Americans believed in democracy and self-reliance. You might say that this difference was the thing underlying all the trouble that followed. But perhaps it would not have been enough of a thing to make the revolution if certain other things had not been the way they were.

The second cause was the fact that the Mexicans couldn't get rid of a fear of American adventurers coming in to seize Texas. There had been a lot of adventurers coming in to filibuster far back in the Spanish times, and the Mexicans didn't really trust the Americans that they themselves invited in and who took out citizenship and honestly tried to be good and loyal Mexicans.

The third cause is related to the second. There were a good many adventurers in Texas, and you might go so far as to say that some of the leaders, like Sam Houston, were adventurers and were seeking to take Texas from Mexico.

The fourth cause was bad Mexican policy and administration. After they had called in American settlers to develop the country they couldn't develop and fight off the Indians they hadn't been able to control, the Mexican government turned around and tried to block the prosperity of these people. They used heavy custom duties, passed laws to prevent further immigration, and failed to establish coastwise trade with Mexico proper.

The fifth cause was violation of civil rights when a dictatorship was set up, the sending in of troops to hold down the people, sometimes convict troops, and Santa Anna's flinging Austin into jail.

Another cause was the United States policy in trying to buy Texas. The United States government had very bad judgment in the choice of diplomats. A man like Butler tried to bribe high Mexican officials and wrote anonymous letters to stir up rebellion.

It was the big financial panic of 1819 that drove so many Americans to Texas, especially frontiersmen of Kentucky and Tennessee. The self-reliance of the frontiersman was . . .

This theme is written in a dull, pedantic style. The opening paragraph is a good example of how not to begin a composition. But the writer has tried to be systematic. His concern with being systematic makes this theme useful here. The student can see another writer wrestling with the problem of organization, and basically the way the writer of the theme solves his problem is sensible. The difficulty is merely that he is somewhat awkward in applying the solution.

For your own theme in causal analysis you may take some historical event that you already know something about or an event that you have observed or experienced. Suppose that you have heard about an automobile accident, which involved several friends coming home from a dance. One of the friends, whom you know very well, was driving. He had a quarrel with his date and was in a surly mood. To spite her, he had taken a few drinks. On the way home he drove very fast, and, in passing, he sideswiped another car and catapulted into a ditch. He and his date were seriously hurt. The others in the car suffered only slight injury. You make the following list: There was a wet road. The car being passed wavered a little. Your friend was exceeding the speed limit and common sense. He had been drinking, and he was not used to drinking. Your friend has a short temper, but ordinarily comes out of anger very quickly and apologetically. The girl had made him angry by teasing him. When he got angry, she didn't laugh it off. Your friend's father was a very short-tempered man who had never controlled himself around his children. When the father lost his temper, the mother made the situation worse by being sullen and resentful. The mother had spoiled your friend. And so on. You know many of the facts of the situation. Your job is to sort them out and try to find out where the responsibility lies.

The topics listed below may help you get a subject for your theme:

Why We Lost to State
Why I Failed Algebra
He Says He Had To Learn
    To Be a Good Father
A Triumph of Character
    over Circumstance
Why Benedict Arnold Became
    a Traitor
Was It Bad Luck or Good?

My Aunt's Character
What Caused the Great
    Depression?
The Automobile Changed American
    Life
The Battle of Midway: Five Minutes
    Is All You Need
Why Adlai Stevenson Lost
    the Election

CHAPTER SIX

Argument

College students, like everybody else, spend a good part of their time arguing. Every time you try to prove a point to a friend, or support an opinion in class, or decide with your friends what to do Saturday night, you are using argument. Argument appears in conversation, in public addresses, in a lawyer's presentation of his case, in feature articles in magazines, in textbooks, in essays, in poetry, in editorials, in drama, in fiction. The salesman trying to sell a car uses argument. The historian trying to prove that a certain event took place at a certain time uses argument. The congressman speaking on behalf of a bill uses argument.

Argument, like the other forms of discourse, does not always appear in a pure form. It is often mixed with other forms, especially exposition. Indeed, the mere exposition of facts will sometimes settle an argument. In this chapter, however, we shall study the methods that belong strictly to argument, and only incidentally notice how other forms of discourse may be used in conjunction with it.

How does argument differ from other forms of discourse? It differs in its initial motivation. An argument starts in conflict. People, in good humor or bad humor, disagree. If they try to settle the disagreement by words, an argument begins. We do not argue with a person who already agrees with us. We do not argue about a subject if only one position can possibly be taken in regard to it. The arguer presumably believes that his own position is the right one, but by the fact of arguing at all he recognizes that another position may be held, no matter how mistakenly.

The purpose of argument is to make another person " change his mind." It aims to resolve the conflict, the disagreement, in which the argument originates.

Argument and Reason

How may argument resolve the original disagreement? By an appeal to reason, for argument aims to show that one opinion is correct and that the opposing opinion is not. We ordinarily recognize this fact of the appeal to reason when we say of a speaker, " He didn't really have an argument; he merely carried the audience by appealing to their emotions." The speaker has persuaded, but he has not convinced. The advertiser who puts the picture of a sweet-faced, gray-haired housewife beside the picture of his refrigerator is not appealing to reason but to emotion. He may have a good sales argument in favor of his refrigerator on grounds of economy, efficiency, or convenience, but he is not presenting it. The political speaker who screams, " Every red-blooded American will vote for John Jones, the friend of the people! " is not offering an argument any more than the defense lawyer who points to the accused murderer and, with tears in his voice, demands of the jury, " This man before you, this simple man who loves his children, who prays for them every night — would you send him to the gallows? You fathers and mothers, would you make those poor babes fatherless? " The advertiser may actually sell the refrigerator, the politician may actually get the votes, the lawyer may actually get an acquittal for the accused by the appeal to the emotions, but in no case has an argument been offered.

The objection may be raised: " What does it matter if the advertiser or politician or lawyer didn't offer an argument? The refrigerator *was* good — or the politician *was* honest and able — or the accused *was* innocent." If the refrigerator was worth buying, then the question is merely a practical one: " Is the simple appeal to the emotions the best and safest way of achieving the good purpose? " Perhaps not; for if a person becomes aware that no real argument is being offered, that there is only an attempt to play on his emotions, he may feel that he is being treated like a child, that proper respect is not being paid to his powers of reason, that he is being duped and betrayed. So the appeal to the emotions may backfire, and regardless of the merits of the case there may be blind resentment instead of blind agreement.

But another objection may be raised: " Suppose that the advertiser or politician or lawyer did gain his purpose, no matter what the merit of the case. He won, didn't he? And isn't the object to win? " If the refrigerator was not good, the question now becomes a moral one: " Is a man entitled to practice a fraud merely because he has the ability to do so — in this instance, to sway people by the appeal to the emotions? " (The same question would apply if the man did not simply appeal to the emotions of his audience but offered them misleading arguments.) This question must be answered by each individual in accordance with his personal standards.

If argument appeals to reason, then what becomes of the appeal to the emotions which occurs in many arguments? Nothing becomes of it. It is still a very important consideration in argument. If we have a good case on logical grounds, we may still lose it because we present it untactfully, because we do not know how to make the most of the temperament and attitude of the audience. Frequently the problem may be to " persuade " the audience to give our logical case an examination. Persuasion is very important in the strategy of argument, and at the end of this chapter we shall discuss it. But for the present we shall consider questions arising from the consideration of argument as an appeal to reason.

Therefore, in this chapter we shall be concerned with the principles of reasoning. With many of these principles we are already acquainted, and in so far as we have been able to think straight up to now we have been thinking in accordance with them. The principles are not rules imposed on our minds. They are, in fact, the way our minds work naturally when they are working well. But if we study the principles systematically, we shall be able to use them more readily; that is, we shall be able to think more clearly, not only in argument but in all other ways.

Argument and the Common Ground

We have said that argument originates in conflict. We have also said that it appeals to reason, and this statement implies that the conflict will be settled by reason. We know, for instance, that now and then, when we aren't too stubborn or resentful, we change our minds in the middle of an argument. We may even pride ourselves on being fair-minded enough to submit to reason when reason is presented to us -- even when we have been in the wrong. And certainly, when we are thinking something over privately, are balancing off the *pro's* and the *con's* of a question, are " arguing with ourselves," we are trying to be reasonable. In other words, we assume that argument, to be significant, must take place among reasonable men; or if we are arguing with ourselves, that it must take place in the mind of a reasonable person. Argument, though it originates in disagreement, in a situation of conflict between persons, opinions, or possibilities, may, from this point of view, be considered not as a matter of antagonisms, but as an effort to find truth — or at least the "reasonable thing."

Thus, although there is disagreement at the beginning of argument, there is also implied agreement — the agreement to abide by reason. To convince someone means, then, to find a common ground in reason, to find a standard of reason.

Suppose that a Mr. Brown has strong anti-Semitic views and a Mr. Smith is arguing with him. Now the fact that they are arguing at all indicates, as we have said, that they accept, momentarily anyway, a common ground in reason. But clearly, in the conversation below, Mr. Smith is trying to find a more specific common ground, a starting point, to work from. Argument must have a starting point. If there is no starting point possible, argument is not possible. There remains only the resort to force if a question is to be resolved.

SMITH: Look here, I know how you feel, but I'm just curious to know how it squares with your other views. It just doesn't seem consistent with what I know about you.

BROWN: What do you mean?

SMITH: Well, just the way you manage your affairs, the way you treat people.

BROWN: What's that got to do with it?

SMITH: Well, nobody ever said you aren't a straight shooter, or don't believe in justice, or any of these things. Like that time when you —

BROWN: That hasn't got anything to do with it.

SMITH: You don't deny that you believe in people getting justice.

BROWN: Sure, I don't deny that, but —

Smith has tried to locate the more common ground in the notion of justice. He has made Brown admit that he has a notion of justice. Now he has the job of making Brown see what justice would mean in a given situation. That may be a hard job, but at least there is a starting point in the common agreement that justice is desirable. But suppose that Brown denies that he is interested in justice:

BROWN: Look here, I know justice is all right, by and large. But, buddy, this is a tough world, and a man's got to look out for himself. He's got to watch his interests.

SMITH: O.K., let's forget that justice stuff. A man's got to watch his own interests. That's right. It's a good practical point of view.

BROWN: I'm a practical man.

SMITH: Well, the question just boils down to what a man's interests are, doesn't it?

BROWN: Sure.

SMITH: Now on the Jewish question, maybe our interests aren't as simple as they sometimes seem —

Smith has here dropped the common ground of justice and accepted the common ground of practical self-interest. Now his job is to show that in the light of self-interest anti-Semitism may be a shortsighted policy in any society. Again, he may not convince his friend, but at least he has a starting point.

When we are sure about our common grounds, we can say to our readers or listeners: " We disagree about the question before us, but we really agree on a more important question than this one, on something that lies deeper. And since we do agree on that deeper question, I can show you that we ought reasonably to agree on the present question." We may not say this in so many words, but it is what we mean to convey.

What Is Argument About?

We can begin to answer the question of what argument is about by showing some things it *cannot* reasonably be about. To illustrate:

John comes upon a group obviously engaged in a heated argument and asks: " What are you arguing about? "

JACK: Football!

JOHN: What about football?

JACK: About who won the Army-Navy game in 1936.

JOHN (*laughs*) : You idiots, what are you wasting your breath for? Why don't you telephone the information bureau at the newspaper and find out?

John is right; they are idiots. When a fact can be readily established by investigation, there is no *need* for argument. Why argue about the length of a piece of string if there is a ruler handy?

Or, again, suppose that John asks his first question, and Jack replies, " Football."

JOHN: What about football?

JACK: Which is the better game, football or basketball?

JOHN (*laughs*) : For the Lord's sake, what are you wasting your breath for? You can't settle that. A guy just likes the game he likes. Take me, I like tennis better than either of them.

John is right again. An argument about a matter of mere taste is useless, and in so far as the word "better"[1] in the above conversation merely means what one happens to like, there is no proper matter for argument.

In other words, a matter of absolute taste is not a matter for argument, and only a matter of judgment is a matter for argument. We must remember, however, that there is no single sharp and fast line between matters of taste and matters of judgment. In between the obvious extremes is a vast body of questions about which it is difficult to be sure. Each such question must be examined on its own merits.

Let us take, for example, an argument about whether Wordsworth or Longfellow is the finer poet. Are we dealing with a matter of taste or a matter of judgment?

If one person says, " I don't care what other people think, I just like Longfellow better," he is treating the question as a matter of taste. He is making no appeal to reason. But if another person tries to set up a standard for poetic excellence in general and tests the poets by that standard, he is making an appeal to judgment. He might say, for instance, that Wordsworth has greater originality in subject matter, has more serious ideas, has had more influence on later poets, and uses fresher and more suggestive metaphors. He might not win agreement, but he is at least using the method of argument; he is trying to appeal to reason in terms of an objective standard.

If argument cannot reasonably be about a readily verifiable matter or a mere matter of taste, what can it be about?

But before answering this question, let us come back to our original illustrations. We note that in both instances when Jack says that he and his friends are arguing about football, John asks: " What about football? "

---

[1] In ordinary usage expressions such as " better," " more desirable," " to be preferred," " greater," " good," " acceptable," and so forth may indicate mere preference, an unarguable question of taste. When dealing with such an expression in an argument, one should ask questions which will determine whether or not the word has an objective content. Take the simple statement: " That is a good horse." We immediately have to ask, " Good for what? " For draying, for racing, for the bridle path, for the show ring, for the range? Or does the speaker merely mean that the horse is gentle, responsive, and affectionate, a sort of pet? By forcing the question we may discover the real meaning behind the original statement. Sometimes there is no meaning beyond the question of taste. Somebody says: " Jake is a good guy." If you force the question here and get the reply, " Oh, he's just regular. I like to be around him," you discover that the statement has no objective content. It tells you nothing about Jake. As the philosopher Spinoza would put it, Paul's opinion about Peter tells more about Paul than about Peter.

Useful forcing questions to apply to such expressions are: What is it good, desirable, useful for? What is it good in relation to? Is the standard invoked objective and therefore worth discussing?

John is bound to ask this question if he has any real curiosity about the argument.

JACK: Oh, about the Michigan-Purdue game last Saturday.

JOHN: Gosh, but you are thick-headed. What *about* the game?

JACK: About Randall and Bolewiensky.

JOHN: Well, I give up!

John is outdone by his friend's stupidity because he knows that one can't reasonably argue about something just in general — *about* the game, for instance, or *about* Randall and Bolewiensky. So John now says: "What about Randall and Bolewiensky?"

JACK: About which is the more useful player.

JOHN: Well it's sure time you were telling me.

John's thick-headed friend has finally managed to state what the argument is about. If there is an argument here, somebody holds that Randall is a more useful player than Bolewiensky and somebody denies it. In other words, the argument is about a **proposition**. And a proposition is the declaration of a judgment, what purports to be a reasonable judgment. It can be believed, doubted, or disbelieved.

The Statement of the Proposition

A proposition is, simply, the declaration of a judgment. A proposition is what an argument is about, and it is the only thing an argument can be about. We all know that in formal debates the proposition is given as a formal resolution. For instance: *Resolved,* That the United States should adopt free trade. Or: *Resolved,* That the language requirement for the B.A. degree should be abolished. In such circumstances the nature of the proposition is obvious.

But formal debates make up a very small fraction of all argument. Ordinarily the proposition underlying an argument is not formally stated or sometimes may not be stated at all. If we want to think straight, however, and want to be effective in argument, we ought to be able to state whatever proposition underlies our argument. We must know what is at stake, and the best way to know that is to frame the proposition, at least for ourselves.

When we come to writing a theme in argumentation, we shall find that the proposition provides our subject. If we don't know what the proposition is, we shall be floundering or wandering; the theme will lack point and unity; it will have poor organization. Even if argument is only a subordinate part of a theme that is primarily expository, descriptive, or narrative, we should make sure that we can state the proposition which constitutes the interest in that part of the theme.

The Proposition: Two Kinds

A proposition states one of two things. It states that something is a fact, or it states that something should be done. Of course, any proposition may be believed, doubted, or disbelieved, but here we are concerned with the types of propositions and not the truth or falsity of any particular one. Even if we state the proposition negatively and say that something is *not* a fact or that something should *not* be done, the basic types remain; we have only turned them upside down.

One type of proposition, we have just said, concerns the existence of a fact; the other, the desirability of an action. When a lawyer argues that his client has an alibi, he is dealing with a proposition of fact: the client was at a certain place at a certain time — or so the lawyer declares. When a bond salesman tries to sell a bond to an investor, he is dealing with a proposition of action: the investor would be wise to buy the bond — or so the salesman says. We should keep this distinction in mind; for, as we shall see, one kind of proposition demands a different method of arguing from the other. In a proposition of fact, you have only to establish the key fact in so far as possible. In the proposition of action, you have to work from the establishing of facts to the desirability of action.

• Application •

Which of the following propositions are of fact and which are of desirability of action?

1. You should vote in every election.
2. We need a new automobile.
3. The Mississippi River is the largest in the world.
4. Wealth corrupts morals.
5. If you are going to be an engineer, you don't need to study history.

The Clear Proposition

A proposition must clearly state the fact or action it proposes. It is not always easy to state matters clearly. For one thing, most words, as we ordinarily use them, do not have very precise limits. Even words which refer to an objective, physical situation may be vague. How " tall " is a tall man? Five feet eleven? Six feet? Six feet three? Any of these men is well above average height, but should all be considered " tall "? We may use " tallish," " tall," and " very tall " to indicate the scale; but even then we might hesitate about the choice of a word. Or take the word " bald." How much hair must be lacking before we can say that a man is bald? The word does not fix an objective standard, although it does refer to an objective situation.

The problem is even more complicated when we come to such words as " good," " cute," or " progressive," which do not refer to easily measurable attributes. If we hear, " Mr. Black is a progressive citizen," what are we to understand? That Black works hard, pays his taxes, treats his family decently, saves money, and stays out of jail? Or that he is interested in improving the local school, bringing new factories to town, and planting flowers in the park? Or that he has a certain political philosophy? The word seems to indicate some general approval on the part of the speaker, but we do not know exactly what, and the odds are that he does not know either. The word is vague.

Let us take another example of vagueness, the proposition, " Soviet Russia is more democratic than England." A person defending this proposition might argue that Russia is more democratic than England because in its system there are no hereditary titles, because great fortunes cannot be accumulated, and because the worker is glorified. A person attacking the proposition might argue that England is more democratic because actual political power is in the hands of leaders chosen by the majority of voters in free elections, because there is freedom of speech, and because a man can choose his occupation. Therefore the word " democratic " is vague; the two disputants are using it in different senses. They can have no argument on the original proposition until they have agreed on a definition of democracy. And this, of course, may mean that the argument will shift to a new proposition: " Democracy is so-and-so."

Many words, like " democracy," have no generally accepted meaning to which we can refer. Even the dictionary does not help us much with such a word. It can give us a generally accepted meaning for a word like " horse," since a horse is a horse wherever we find it. But for a word like " democracy," the dictionary may give us several more or less well-accepted senses and may start us on the way to a clear statement, but the dictionary definition can rarely be full enough to cover the meaning of the word as it will appear in an argument. In framing a proposition we should try to fix the definition (pages 48–67) of any significant word, to determine exactly what we mean by it. Then we should stick to that definition.

The Clear Proposition: History of the Question and Occasion of the Discussion

Thus far we have been discussing the clarity of a proposition by thinking of the meaning of the words that compose it. Sometimes, however, we need to go beyond this and try to see the meaning of the proposition in some general context. One of the best ways to do this is to investigate what handbooks of debating call the *history of the question*. To do this is to inform ourselves about the circumstances that brought the argument about. For example, if we are arguing that such-and-such a bill to raise tariffs should be passed, we cannot know what is at stake in the proposition unless we know something of how tariffs have affected our economy in the past and what situations, and motives, generally lead to the raising of tariffs. And it is equally important, of course, to investigate the particular situation behind the present bill — what we may call the *occasion of the discussion*.

• **Applications** •

I. Study the following propositions with these questions in mind:
   a. Which are propositions of fact and which are propositions of desirable action?
   b. Are any vague? If so, discuss the difficulty.
   c. Are any nonarguable — mere matters of taste, for instance?

      1. A good book is the best friend a man can have.
      2. No good Democrat will vote for a Republican.
      3. Mussolini was a great man.
      4. Square dancing is more interesting than ballroom dancing.
      5. Edison was a greater man than Napoleon.
      6. Good citizens of the United States ought to support the United Nations.
      7. Amateur athletics are more desirable than professional athletics.
      8. Capital punishment is no deterrent to crime.
      9. The atomic bomb is the most important invention since the steam engine.
      10. The atomic bomb is the most useful invention since the steam engine.

11. War is necessary to maintain the manhood of the race.
12. In our present situation high wages do not mean higher prices.
13. The Washington Monument is 490 feet high.
14. Man is a rational animal.
15. The Federal government should take over public education.
16. Installment selling has bad economic consequences.
17. Mary Pickford is the most attractive actress the screen has ever presented.
18. "There is a good deal of human nature in man." — Samuel Clemens

II. Frame (1) an unclear proposition and (2) a properly stated proposition for each of five of the following topics:

United Nations	Intoxicants
Hobbies	Tennis
Religion	Reading Habits
Motherhood	Profession of Medicine
War	Foreign Missions

The Single Proposition

An argument, like any theme, must have a main point if it is to make sense. That main point is what the proposition of the argument should state, and the proposition should state only the *main* point. In other words, the proposition behind an argument should be single.

Let us take an example. A college student named George is in a very depressed condition, is lacking energy, has headaches and poor digestion, and doesn't seem to be able to study. A friend says: "You should see a doctor."

There are many factors in the situation behind the proposition — George's depression, lack of energy, and so forth — but the proposition is single. It involves a single decision, a single act: to go or not to go to the doctor.

George does go to a doctor, who says: "You ought to take more exercise and study harder." This, clearly, is two propositions, and the fact that they occur in the same sentence doesn't make any difference. True, the reasons that make the doctor decide on more exercise and the reasons that make him decide on more study may be intimately related. They must be intimately related, for they have to do with George's total condition and the causes of that condition. But there are two independent propositions: (1) exercise more and (2) study harder.

We see this fact immediately if we think of George going to another doctor, who says that George should get a job on a pick-and-shovel gang to build up his strength and should, for the time being, forget study altogether. And another doctor may say: "Take no exercise at all, for your heart is very bad, but try to develop an interest in your studies."

We don't know anything about George and we don't know which doctor is right, but we do see, by common sense, that to accept one of the ideas, that about exercise, doesn't necessarily mean that we have to accept the other one, that about study. They are independent propositions; we may accept one and not the other. And if they are independent, then two arguments, not one, are involved.

Here is the first paragraph of a student theme which illustrates the looseness and poor organization one is likely to fall into when trying to argue a double proposition.

NATIONAL FRATERNITIES SHOULD BE ABOLISHED HERE IN FAVOR OF DINING CLUBS

One of the bad features about national fraternities is that there is a financial drain on the members for no good purpose. I have never been able to see where the money goes except to pay some fellow to be national secretary, and most likely he is somebody who hasn't grown up enough to quit being a fraternity man and campus big-shot all his life. My father was a member of the same fraternity I am a pledge of, but he says, "Son, when you get that old sheepskin on graduation day, you just lose that frat pin till your fiftieth class reunion." Dining clubs have certain good features of the same kind as fraternities. They can give fun and companionship and a place in which to hang out and argue and hold bull sessions. And there is no reason why they shouldn't have athletic teams for intramural games and give dances and parties. But the fact that fraternities are national gives a spirit of competition that isn't very healthy in some ways. I don't mean in games, which is all right, but in social showing off and feeling bigger than you have a right to. There is no reason why dining clubs shouldn't have their own libraries, too, and the same pride in their members who amount to something on the campus. [Etc.]

There are really two propositions to be argued here: (1) the desirability of abolishing national fraternities, and (2) the desirability of establishing dining clubs. These are quite separate notions, as we can readily see if we remember that dining clubs are not the only alternative to fraternities. Each proposition should be argued on its own merits.

A more systematic way of going about things would be to argue first the need for a change. What is wrong with the present system that makes the author dissatisfied with it? Then after establishing the need for a change, one might consider the dining club, as compared with other possibilities and with fraternities, asking perhaps the following questions: (1) " Would dining clubs avoid the defects of fraternities? " (2) " Would they introduce new defects of their own? " (3) " How do we weigh these considerations? " But each topic should be considered individually, in sequence.

What all this amounts to is this:

1. The fact that two ideas appear in one sentence does not mean that they are one proposition. They are still two.

2. The fact that two ideas relate to the same situation (such as George's health) does not mean that they are one proposition. They are still two.

3. If there are two propositions, each has to be argued individually.

The Main Proposition and Supporting Points

To say, as we have just been suggesting, that an argument must have a main point, a main proposition, to give it unity is not to say that more than one idea may not well appear in the course of an argument. In support of the main proposition the arguer may make a number of different individual points, and each point will, in itself, no matter how it is stated, represent the declaration of a judgment. It, too, will be a proposition and will have to be argued individually. Such supporting points, or minor propositions, should be subordinated to the main proposition, the real subject of the argument.

With this in mind, let us look at a short theme in defense of free trade.

WHY I BELIEVE IN FREE TRADE

1st MINOR PROPOSITION : Protective tariff was once needed.

There was a time when the United States needed tariffs to protect its infant industries. The manufacturers could not have competed with the low prices of goods from the more advanced industries of England. But today the picture is completely different. Giant industries, such as General Motors and General Electric and dozens of others, no longer require pro-

2nd MINOR PROPOSITION : Industries now are able to meet competition.

MAIN PROPOSITION : Free trade should be adopted (in a negative form).

Continuation of 2nd MINOR PROPOSITION : A man of experience speaks.

3rd MINOR PROPOSITION : Technology would enable us to compete.

4th MINOR PROPOSITION : Competition accelerates technological advances.

5th MINOR PROPOSITION : Technological advances increase prosperity.

6th MINOR PROPOSITION : Free trade would help merchant marine.

7th MINOR PROPOSITION : Subsidy of merchant marine for military purposes would be reduced.

8th MINOR PROPOSITION : Free trade would improve international relations.

tection. Today the United States has no reason for refusing to reinstitute free trade.

In spite of the fact that the United States has the biggest industries in the world, some people feel that American goods cannot compete even on the home market with goods made abroad at cheap wages. But in a recent article in the *Atlantic Monthly* an official of a large corporation took the opposite view, saying that in his own experience open competition without tariff was the best. He argued that constantly improving technology will enable United States industry to keep an edge in reducing prices even in competition with cheap foreign labor costs. Furthermore, he stated that without foreign competition American industry even on home ground would not progress technically at an optimum rate. To his conclusions may be added the theory that every reduction in prices increases the total prosperity through an increase in consumption.

Another reason for the restoration of free trade concerns the merchant marine. If free trade is instituted, the increase in the amount of ocean traffic will lead to the expansion of the merchant marine. Since the United States government must subsidize the maintenance of a large merchant marine for military purposes, free trade might reduce the taxpayer's bill somewhat.

Finally, a free trade policy by the United States would improve its relations with other countries. Opening our markets freely to other countries would be strong evidence of our good will and might help the allies of the United States improve their economic position, thus reducing world tensions. And any reduction in world tension will, of course, result in an economic advantage for the United States, through lowering the need for defense expenditures.

PROPOSITION AND SUPPORTING POINTS / 137

We have here eight minor propositions in addition to the main one. Each minor proposition, we can readily see, could be discussed independently. But — and here we are back to the principle of unity in a theme -- all the minor propositions are related to the main one. They are used as supporting points for the main proposition that free trade should be adopted.

An Issue

The main proposition in an argument may, as we have just seen in the theme defending free trade, raise various questions — minor propositions — for discussion and controversy. When one of the minor propositions *must* be proved in order to get the main proposition accepted, that is, to win the argument, that minor proposition is called an **issue.** To state the matter a little differently: An issue is a question on which the whole argument hangs. If you defeat the issue, you defeat the argument.

For an example let us look back in the theme on free trade. It is clear that the second minor proposition (our industries now can meet competition) is an issue. If that proposition is not true, then none of the other propositions matter. If our industries are destroyed and we are a bankrupt nation, what use would there be in talking about the merchant marine or foreign relations? If it is accepted that our industries can now survive, then the other minor propositions are relevant and may be used to support the argument.

But can more than one question, or minor proposition, be an issue? Let us look back at the theme. Even after we decide that our industries can meet competition, we may feel that in the world today international good will is necessary to our survival, and so that proposition, too, would become an issue in this argument. We now have two issues.

Let us take another example. The constitution of a certain college honor society, the Corinthians, specifies that to be eligible for membership a student must (1) have a scholastic average of B or above, (2) have won a letter in at least one college sport, (3) have made some substantial contribution to the general good of the college community, and (4) have conducted himself as a gentleman during the period of his college career. William Smith is proposed for election. His sponsor argues that Smith has made an A average, has won the state junior championship in swimming, has brought about a reform of the student council system by his editorials in the college paper, and is a person of high character and good manners. Smith seems certain of election until one Corinthian refers to the constitution and regretfully points out that Smith cannot fulfill requirement 2. " But he is an excellent athlete," the sponsor retorts. " He can outswim anybody in this school."

" That's not the point," the other Corinthian replies. " The constitution explicitly states that to be eligible a student must have won a letter in at least one sport. Our college has no swimming team and therefore does not give a letter for swimming."

If the constitution is taken seriously, Smith's eligibility must be denied. The proposition is that Smith is eligible for membership in the Corinthians, and the constitution is the source of authority for the requirements for eligibility.

Each of those requirements is essential. In the case of Smith's eligibility for membership, each is a minor proposition or issue, the acceptance of which is necessary if the argument is to be won. About three of the requirements there is no question; they are admitted by both sides and may therefore be termed _admitted_ issues. Only requirement 2 is questioned. It is on this _crucial_ issue, then, that the argument hinges.

In the case of another student, the situation, however, might well be different. John Jones has fine grades and a letter in football and has worked hard for certain good causes on the campus. These things are admitted. But in some of his private behavior he may fall short of being a gentleman. So his gentlemanliness, or lack of it, is here the crucial issue.

To return to the matter of Smith's eligibility for the Corinthians. Suppose that someone says: " Well, Smith ought to be elected, and if a man like Smith can't get in, what's the meaning of the Corinthians? "

This remark may be true and just — in a general sense. Smith may be the sort of man the college would willingly honor. But — and here is the rub — eligibility isn't based on a general notion of suitability, but on the constitution. Perhaps someone else then says, " The constitution of the Corinthians ought to be changed." Maybe it should, but this proposition would start a new argument and would raise another problem.

This situation is similar to that in certain cases at law in which one may feel that the letter of the law defeats justice. For example, a defending lawyer in a first-degree murder case may argue that his client had suffered intolerable provocation, that the victim had grievously slandered the defendant's wife, and that the defendant, a simple man, raised in rather primitive surroundings, had thought killing the slanderer to be the only course of honor and decency. The prosecution argues that these facts are not issues in the case, because the legal definition of murder is such-and-such and makes no recognition of the provocation of slander or of the personal background of the accused. The prosecution is, of course, right. The law defines the issues by which the proposition that the defendant is guilty of murder in the first degree must stand or fall. If the jury does acquit the defendant, it does so out of sentiment, prejudice, or some notion of justice which is inconsistent with the law.

In the case of William Smith and the Corinthians, or of the murderer, the issues are handed us on a silver platter: in the first case the constitution of the society defines eligibility; in the second, the law defines murder. But in many cases, we must locate the issues for ourselves. We do this by making an **analysis** of the proposition. Let us remember that in analyzing a proposition of fact and one of action we use quite different methods.

Analysis and Propositions of Fact

Let us take some propositions of fact and see how we should go about analyzing them to determine the issues.

We shall begin with a very simple instance, one in which there can be only a single issue. If two men in the wilderness wish to cross a stream, one of them may propose that they drop a tree across it. The other objects that the available tree is too short. They can establish the height of the tree but they cannot establish the width of the stream. Therefore the proposition (that the tree is long enough) is a matter of judgment and is subject to argument. Several arguments, good or bad, may be offered on either side, but there is only one issue: Is the tree long enough? In such cases of simple fact, the proposition itself establishes the issue. But in other cases the fact may not be simple, and there may be no prior definition of the issues (as by the constitution of the Corinthians).

Let us take such an example in the proposition: " John did right in leaving his fortune to the Ashford Medical Foundation."

First, is this a proposition of fact? It may look like a proposition of action, for John did perform an action. Certainly this would be a proposition of action if it were stated: " John will do right to. . . ." Or: " John should leave. . . ." But in its original form, the proposition concerns an action that has *already* taken place and concerns a judgment of the value of the event. This becomes clear if we translate the proposition into the standard form: " John's conduct in leaving his fortune to the Ashford Medical Foundation *is* (or *was*) right."

Second, how can we establish the issues? To do so, we must decide what we mean by the word " right " — a vague word in the predicate of the proposition. Suppose the opponents agree that a deed is ethically right *only* if it fulfills *all* of the following requirements: (1) the doer is responsible; (2) the doer undertakes the deed for a laudable motive; and (3) the consequences of the deed are beneficial. The issues then become:

1. Was John of sound mind when he made his will?
2. Was his motive laudable?
3. Was the money to be used for a beneficial activity?

The affirmative must establish all of these issues in order to win the argument. Suppose that there is no doubt of John's sanity and no doubt that the money will be used for a good purpose. Suppose that these facts or issues are admitted. The second issue then becomes crucial. If the negative establishes that John, in a fit of fury at his daughter for making a marriage without his consent, changed his will to leave his money to the foundation, his motive is a bad one, and the proposition is lost.

Where a fact is complex, as in the proposition above, the locating of the issues becomes a matter of analyzing the fact. In practice this may mean defining the key word (or words) in the proposition, as *right* was defined above.

• **Applications** •

I. In the Readings, study " The Marxian Philosophy of History " (page 524) and the excerpt from " The Abolition of Man " (page 545). State the main proposition, the minor propositions, and the issues in each of these selections.

II. Analyze several of the following propositions of fact into minor propositions and issues:

Big-time college football destroys sportsmanship.
Air travel is safer than automobile travel.
Christianity is the basis of American democracy.
The doctrine of state rights caused the defeat of the Confederacy.
Democracy makes for military inefficiency.
Preparedness prevents war.
The study of literature is useless for a man who plans to go into business.
Industry now attracts the best brains in the country.

Politics has ceased to be attractive to our best men.
Security is the basis of happiness.

ANALYSIS AND PROPOSITIONS OF ACTION

To analyze a proposition of action effectively, to be certain that
we understand all sides of an argument and can anticipate and
answer positions taken by possible opponents, or simply to clear our
own minds, we should systematically set up all the propositions we
can think of on each side of the main proposition. The minor
propositions will tend to go in pairs, one for and one against.

Then we should examine the propositions with these questions
in mind:

1. Are the propositions all significant?
2. Do they cover the subject?
3. Do they overlap one another?
4. Does any proposition really include more than one idea?

If a husband and wife are arguing about moving to town, the
husband may argue that his salary in town would be more than he
makes off the farm, but the wife may argue that in the country
they need less money; the husband may argue that the schools in
town are better, but the wife may counter by saying that schools
aren't all of education, that getting acquainted with nature and having to develop one's own resources in solitude are important; and so
on. But not every proposition in an argument will actually be attacked. One side may admit certain issues. The husband, for example, may say that the house in the country is not convenient,
and the wife may admit this. Or he may admit her proposition
that the whole family loves outdoor life.

The propositions might be stated as follows:

HUSBAND	WIFE
1. Better salary in town	1. Need less money in country for same living
2. Better schools in town	2. Schools not all of education, etc.
3. House in country not convenient	3. Admitted
4. Admitted	4. Both love outdoor life
5. No theater in country	5. Admitted
6. Impossibility of getting farm help	6. Buy more machines
7. Long course of dental work for Susie easier in town	7. Don't mind driving once a week to Smithville, where there is a good dentist

We do not know how the couple will decide this argument. We
do not know them well enough to know what issues will be taken

as crucial in their decision. But suppose that the husband finally confesses that his doctor has told him he has a bad heart and must drastically reduce his physical activity. The issue of the husband's health would become crucial, and the family would probably move to town.

Let us glance again at the student theme defending free trade. We have made the breakdown indicated in the left-hand column. We don't know whether or not the author worked out these issues before he began writing. He may, simply, have started writing and hoped his natural good sense would see him through, letting one proposition suggest another, as is the way in the rough-and-tumble argument of conversation. When time permits, however, it is much safer to be systematic and try to work out the problems beforehand. Here is the first stage in the analysis leading to a student theme. The proposition to be analyzed is: " The present system of required courses should be abolished." Or, as the student puts it in his title, " I Don't Like the System of Required Courses."

The first stage is a random jotting down of a number of possible propositions about the subject. Even though our student takes the affirmative side, that is, he wants to abolish the present system, he puts down the negative propositions, too. If he does not, he will not know where to begin, what to answer.

FOR	AGAINST
1. You get the best out of a professor who stimulates you and whose personality you like; in the present system you usually cannot get the professor you want and who is best for you.	The course, well and objectively taught, is the main thing.
2. People are different and should follow their interests and talents.	Everyone needs discipline in doing certain things he is not interested in.
3. For a person who has not yet settled on a plan for the future, the elective system is best, since it allows him to shop around according to what interests he already has.	The required courses give a good cross section and make his shopping around systematic.
4. For a person who wants to specialize, the broad requirements are a distraction. Specialization will naturally lead to diversity, but a diversity of related things.	Specialization ought to develop from a broad base.

5. Granted that requirements are needed for certain courses, say American history, reading, writing, and so on; but not in general, for everyone is different.

A common background is necessary if society is to be stable.

6. The more talent a man has, the more he tends to object to general requirements.

A person should not be allowed to warp his talent by idiosyncrasies in choosing courses.

7. Lazy students are still lazy in required courses, a situation which lowers standards.

Elective system encourages laziness and election of easy courses.

8. Elective courses for people who have their interests defined encourage thinking, not just cramming.

Required courses encourage thinking by showing broad relationships among different subjects.

9. The elective system permits a really systematic survey for the man with interests already set; discourages smattering.

No man can be systematic in everything. An acquaintance with a subject does not have to be a smattering, can be good as far as it goes, and give a useful background.

10. Elective system encourages individualism and responsibility — *my* mistakes, not the dean's.

The required system gives a basis for responsible judgment. Mistakes are no asset.

11. Your best relation to society is in good work in your chosen occupation.

The broad base of the present system gives a student a better, because more informed, relation to society.

12. The purposes of an education are to teach you to think and give you something to think about.

Granted; but see numbers 5 and 11.

If we look closely at this list, we see that the items are not in any consistent order. We can see no continuity among them; a theme following this list would lack coherence. So now the problem for the student is to put the various propositions in such order that some sort of transition is possible.

Here is the new ordering:

⑤ 1. Granted that requirements are needed for certain courses — say American history, reading, writing, and so on. But requirements are not necessary for all courses.

A common background is necessary if society is to be stable.

⑪ 2. Your best relation to society is in good work in your chosen occupation.

The broad base of the present system gives a student a better, because more informed, relation to society.

⑫ 3. The purposes of an education are to teach you to think and give you something to think about.

Granted; but see numbers 1 and 2.

② 4. People are different and should follow their interests and talents.

Everyone needs discipline in doing certain things he is not interested in.

③ 5. For a person who has not yet settled on a plan for the future, the elective system is best, since it allows him to shop around according to what interests he already has.

The required courses already give a good, because systematic, cross section and make his shopping easier and more fruitful.

④ 6. For a person who wants to specialize, the broad requirements are a distraction. Anyway, specialization will naturally lead to diversity, but a diversity of related things.

Specialization ought to develop from a broad base, for if it does not the student will never see the implications of his specialty.

⑧ 7. Elective courses for those who have their interests already defined encourage thinking, not just cramming, for the student comes with curiosity.

Required courses encourage thinking by showing broad relationships among different subjects.

⑨ 8. The elective system permits a really systematic survey for the man with interests already set; discourages smattering.

No man can be systematic and complete in everything. An acquaintance with a subject does not have to be a smattering, can be good as far as it goes, and give a useful background.

⑦ 9. Lazy students will still be lazy in required courses, a situation which lowers standards.

Elective system encourages laziness; people seek easy courses.

① 10. You get the best out of a professor who stimulates you and whose personality you like; in the present system you usually cannot get the professor you want and who is best for you.

The course, well and objectively taught, is the main thing.

11. Elective system encourages individualism and responsibility — *my* mistakes, not the dean's.

The required system gives a basis for responsible judgment later. Mistakes are no asset.

Here the circled numbers indicate the order of the first stage, the rough jottings. The other numbers indicate, of course, the present sequence of ideas after the writer has, presumably, thought things through. What has he done?

For one thing, he has cleared the ground by first admitting that certain required courses are necessary. This admission, we note, is in answer to the negative contention that a common background is necessary for a stable society. In the actual theme, as we shall see, he will give his reasons for making the admission. In number 2 he is answering the claims of those who want " core courses " as a way of giving the student a better sense of his relation to society. Now he has indicated answers to the general claims of the negative, those who want a fixed curriculum.

Now, having countered the two main contentions of the negative, he starts his own line of thought by stating what he regards as the purposes of education: to learn to think and to learn something to think about. His emphasis, we see, is on the individual, and with number 4 we come to a statement of this emphasis: the development of individual capacities rather than a general discipline. From that point on through number 10 he is dealing with the specific advantages that he thinks an elective system gives. But with number 11, he returns to a general proposition, the advantage of the elective system in building character, in developing a sense of individual responsibility. This proposition might have come early, along with the purposes of an education, and perhaps it would have been more systematic to put it there. But it can serve as a sort of conclusion, a general proposition, the result of the other propositions.

We see that the student has the main body of the argument fairly well lined up. But is he ready to write? Probably not; for to open with the development of proposition 1 would be abrupt and perhaps misleading. How would the reader get his bearings and see the main proposition? The next step would be to work out an introduction. The introduction should state the main proposition of the argument, that is, give the subject, and it should indicate why the argument is interesting or urgent for the writer and for the reader. (See Chapter 2.)

Some indication of the background of the question, even if

given in a most casual way, may be useful to catch the reader's interest and to help him orient himself.

Here is the theme, embodying the student's introduction:

I DON'T LIKE THE SYSTEM OF REQUIRED COURSES

Introduction

I have been in college nearly a year and I begin to see what I am up against in getting an education. I don't want to seem prissy about this, for getting an education is not all I think about. But I do have some sense of why I came here in the first place. If I forgot it, my father would remind me, and how! Besides, I put in three hours a day as bus boy in the cafeteria just to help pay for my education, and if anybody thinks those three hours are undiluted pleasure, he is mistaken. That pleasure is like the chicken soup and the Grade A milk — *diluted*. Every time I put on that white jacket I have to remind myself why I am here and not out selling insurance to an insurance-hungry public or making five dollars an hour at the Acme Machine Company. I don't mean to say either that I am a brilliant student. I make an occasional A, and more than an occasional C. I've been known to make an F. I expect an F in " Social Studies I " this term. It is a required course, by the way. I am opposed to the present system of required courses. They make it hard to get an education.

⑤   I.

I don't mean to say that there should be no required courses. Professional schools have to have certain prerequisites, such as biology for medical school. And I'll grant that everybody ought to be able to read and write reasonably well and ought to know some other things, for instance, American history, just so he won't fall for every politician's speech, if for no other reason. But what after that?

They say in the catalogue that what they call " required core courses " give the student a " common background to make for a stable society." They give a common background, all right. It is the common background of being bored. I am bored at one thing and the next man is bored at something else, and so the whole course is in an atmosphere of boredom. But seriously, if you are in this atmosphere of boredom, you don't learn enough to get a common background. That common background is just in the minds of the people who wrote the catalogue.

Ⓘ   **2.** Another thing they say in the catalogue is that these core courses give the student an intelligent relation to his society, which means, I guess, that he sees how he personally fits into the picture. Now it seems to me that a man fits into the picture well enough when he does decent, honest work at his chosen occupation. That is his best relation to society, and anybody but a simpleton knows what his job is in relation to society. Somebody has to roll pills and somebody has to drive trucks.

Ⓘ   **3.** As a starting point for my argument, I'll simply declare that the purpose of an education is twofold: to learn how to think, and to learn something to think about. The first, it seems to me, is more important than the second, for if you don't know how to think, putting information in your head is just like burying the gold at Fort Knox. It is there, but what good is it? But I think that both purposes are important, and if a college doesn't deliver them, then that college is on the wrong track. The question is, what is the right track?

②   **4.** I don't mean to imply that you spend a part of your time learning how to think and then the next year start getting something to think about. You have to do both at the same time, and that's the way a college curriculum ought to be set up. This college curriculum is not set up that way. It fails because it doesn't recognize a very important fact, the fact that everybody is different, and that what is good for one person isn't necessarily good for the next one and doesn't help him develop his best qualities. The dean says he knows what is best for everybody. But it seems to me that the dean, or whoever is responsible, ought to help the student find what is most interesting to *him,* to Joe Doaks, so he can put his heart into it and get somewhere. For example, I have to take a course next year called "Books That Have Made History." I have read a few already, just two or three, but enough to know that I'll like some and hate others. I looked into Newton, and I don't see why I have to read it. Apples are going to fall whether I do or not. But what I did read of the Frenchman Rousseau I liked. That is human interest. I don't mean that I am going to be a psychologist, but what is human, like history or fiction, interests me. What I am saying is that I want to be able to follow my own interests and be *me,* and not a serial number in

eight required courses of two thousand students each.
If I can find and develop my interests, maybe I can
find some sort of capacity for doing something in life.

I have said that people ought to follow their interests. You can divide beginning college students into
two groups: those who don't know what they want
and those who do. I think the elective system is better
for both groups.

As for the first group, everybody has some interests,
and even if the interests aren't very strong or haven't
settled into a definite plan, the elective system lets
him explore. You can say that the required courses
give a systematic exploration, a cross section of knowledge, but the very fact that the courses are required
kills off the sense of exploration, of being on your
own and trying to find out about yourself. The student is put through a mill and may or may not happen to find an interest. For one thing, he may be so
resentful at the pressure from upstairs that he wants
no part of the courses. And he won't do much thinking or learning either. Not his best, anyway.

As for the student who really knows what he wants,
the required courses are just a bother and a distraction. He comes to college to get to work, and these
courses begin to block him and kill interest. You
can argue that everybody needs discipline, but I
would argue back that the business of working up the
subject you are interested in is a discipline, too. You
aren't interested in every aspect of the subject, but
you drive yourself to fill out the picture of your big
interest. To me that is the useful kind of discipline.
They say you ought to have a " broad base " for specialization, but I don't see any reason for " diversity "
if the diversity isn't somehow related to what your
main interest is.

To prove my point I'll mention my cousin, who is
twelve years older than I am and who went to Cambridge, England, on a fellowship. He tells me that
there you specialize in one thing for your whole four
years. You really know a subject when you get
through, even if you aren't in the top of your class.
I asked him last summer if it didn't seem awful narrow, but he gave me something to think about when
he said that if you really, honestly specialize, you begin to see how a lot of things relate to your subject
and you want to find out about them on your own.
So specialization starts you to thinking on your own.

⑧ 7. It encourages you to branch out. My cousin said he never cared much for Shakespeare until he got to studying the reign of Queen Elizabeth (he specialized in English history) , but now he reads the plays all the time, for fun. Then he got interested in economics, for without understanding something about that he couldn't understand what was behind a lot of historical facts.

⑨ 8. What I am saying is that my cousin didn't get just a smattering here and a smattering there. He learned a lot about one thing and in a well thought-out and organized way. Then when he learned a little about economics it was more than a smattering. It wasn't equal to majoring in economics, but it had relevance to his interests and he remembered it.

⑦ 9. You may say that my cousin sounds like an egghead or a superman, but he isn't. He just has common sense, but he developed his interests. He was in a place where he was encouraged to develop them. But no system is going to do anything for a fellow who is dumb or lazy. He sits there in the required course and flunks or cribs notes or crams, and because the teacher has to work on a curve, the level of passing gets pretty low. And the fellow who is dumb in fiction (which I like) may be a genius over in the physics lab — year after next. Meanwhile, he is just suffering.

① 10 If one of the purposes of an education is to teach you to think, the present system fails. For one thing, the professor you like and respect is the one who best helps you to think; you get to follow his way of thinking and that gives you a kind of model. But now you rarely get more than one shot at such a teacher. For another thing in the big required courses, the professor has to dish it out of the can with ten minutes a week for questions. You are just being passed down the hopper.

⑩ 11. There is one more objection, and a big one. The present system violates my notion of individualism and character building. I know I need advice and help. I came to college for that. But I need advice on how to find out things for myself, how to develop my own interests. I want to be able to take or leave the advice. I want my own responsibility. I'll make mistakes, but they'll be *my* mistakes and not the dean's.

The body of the theme is fairly well worked out. But has the writer clearly indicated what the crucial issues in the argument are?

Probably not, but if we look closely we can see what they are. For one thing, this writer puts a very strong emphasis on the individual, and on individual interests and capacities, while the negative (as it is worked out in the analysis of the proposition) tends to put more emphasis on the relation of the individual to society and on the disciplining of the individual.

As for the actual course of the argument, the writer's notion of the purpose of education is clearly a manifestation of his bias toward individualism: to teach the individual to think and to give him something to think about. After stating this purpose, he is committed to stacking up the advantages and disadvantages, point by point.

To summarize, three issues are crucial for the writer: (1) he must gain acceptance of his notion of the value of the emphasis on the individual; (2) he must gain acceptance of his idea of the purposes of education which stem from this emphasis; and (3) he must assemble particular propositions indicating that the elective system better accomplished those purposes than the other system. If he does not get our acceptance on *any one* of these points, he has lost the argument. He has not convinced us. Naturally, in a short theme we can scarcely expect to find elaborate development of the first and second of these issues, but we might have expected a fuller awareness of their underlying importance than he has given us. A fuller awareness of these issues would have given the theme a better sense of unity and coherence.

(We should, in criticizing this theme, touch on another point or two of a different sort. In the first paragraph the " and how! " seems out of keeping with the rest of the theme. It is good to aim for naturalness and ease, but this is stridently slangy in a theme which at least attempts to be more sober and serious. In the same way, the joke about undiluted pleasure and the diluted chicken soup and Grade A milk seems out of keeping, perhaps a little too flippant and frivolous. But the joke in the third paragraph about boredom being the only common background given by the system of required courses is probably acceptable. At least, it is not forced, as the joke about the diluted chicken soup and milk seems to be.) [2]

• Applications •

I. Can you think of any additional propositions on either side? If so, state and develop them. Where might they fit into the student's analysis at the second stage without violating continuity? Perhaps there is no ap-

---

[2] For further discussion of diction, see Chapter 12.

propriate place. If so, how would you reorganize the list to accommodate them? Do you accept the conclusions of the theme? If not, explain your reasons.

II. Which of the following propositions are of fact and which are of action?

1. Television reporting of Congressional hearings should be prohibited by law.
2. All college football players should be paid a flat salary, the sum to be fixed by the conference.
3. All majors in science with an average of B should be exempt from military service.
4. Laws are the projections of the mind of the majority.
5. Military service makes for democracy.
6. Capital punishment should be abolished.
7. Big-time college football should be abolished.
8. Mr. Jones would do well to apologize to his brother.
9. The presence of the UN headquarters on our soil threatens our sovereignty.
10. The repeal of the Eighteenth Amendment was a mistake.
11. The modern girl should be trained for a profession, trade, or business.
12. Democracy means the worship of the mediocre.
13. All veterans' organizations represent a political menace.
14. All veterans' organizations must be disbanded.
15. Intercollegiate athletics have to be discontinued.
16. The profit motive causes our economic progress.
17. No businessman has ever been elected President.
18. The FBI should be given jurisdiction over all major crime.
19. The jury system is an anachronism.
20. The jury system retards justice.
21. The jury system should be abolished.
22. Fraternities are undemocratic.
23. Fraternities should be abolished.
24. Religious training should be part of the public school system.
25. Public ownership of power serves the social good.
26. Religion should be encouraged even by the unbeliever.

III. Make an analysis of two or three of the above propositions.

IV. In the Readings, study " The Marxian Philosophy of History " (page 524) or " The American Civilization Puzzle " (page 666). What propositions and issues has the author selected in his argument? Why? Can you think of other questions relevant to the argument? How has he indicated a " history of the question "? Has he indicated the " occasion of the question "?

V. You are now going to write a theme in which you argue for some conviction you hold. Think over your strong convictions, the things which are really important to you.

1. Select a conviction which you can put in the form of a proposition of action. (See page 131). The list in II above may give you some ideas.
2. Be sure that the proposition is *clear* and *single*.
3. Make an analysis of the proposition, first jotting down minor propositions for and against, as they happen to come into your head, then putting them in order.
4. Now that you have your propositions in order, develop them; that is, show how the propositions that you accept are stronger, more reasonable, than the objections that might be raised against them. This will give you a series of independent paragraphs, or independent groups of paragraphs, for each individual proposition you discuss.
5. Now, to make a rounded theme of your material, you need (a) to write an introduction, (b) to establish some kind of continuity and transition from one paragraph, or group of paragraphs, to the next in the body of your argument, and (c) to write a conclusion. (See Chapter 2.) The introduction may well say why you think the subject should be argued at all. What is the importance of the subject to you at this time or to society in general? Why is the subject interesting at all? In other words, if you expect your audience to follow your argument, you must catch their attention. As for the conclusion, that may well be a summary of your position.

Evidence

Once we have analyzed the proposition of an argument and know the issues, have arranged and outlined the order of the argument, and have decided on an introduction, we are ready to flesh out the discussion, to argue each supporting point of the main proposition. We have already read two student themes, one about free trade and one about the required curriculum, and have seen how the writers went about filling out their arguments. These themes are fairly well worked out, even though the writers had not yet studied some of the principles of reasoning which we are about to take up. As we have said before, the principles of argument as an appeal to reason are *not* something imposed upon the mind; they are, instead, simply a statement of the way the mind naturally works when we are thinking clearly.

When we analyze a proposition, we are, in a manner of speaking, putting our chips down. We are deciding what we are playing for. When we take the next step and assemble our evidence and reason from it to our conclusion, we are playing our cards. Here we shall win or lose.

Your opponent, when you get into an argument, will be from Missouri. He will say, " Seeing is believing," and what he wants to see is the evidence. Without evidence you can offer only your own unsupported views, which you already know your opponent will not accept, for if he did accept them, there would be no argument in the first place.

But what constitutes evidence? Either fact or opinions may constitute evidence, and both are applicable in support of propositions of fact or propositions of action. People constantly appeal to facts (or try to appeal to facts) to support argument. For example, we need facts to justify an action; we don't want to act ignorantly. " The facts of the case " are important as evidence, but they are not the only thing that can be used as evidence. Arguers also appeal to the opinions of other people who are supposed to have authority. " Expert testimony " is offered in the courtroom as evidence to support a case. A murder trial may bring out an alienist, a ballistics expert, a medical examiner, and any number of other experts whose opinions are to be considered by the jury. Presumably they base their testimony on facts, but what the jury is asked to accept is their *opinion,* their judgment of the facts. An expert may be wrong, and experts frequently disagree among themselves, but what they disagree about is ordinarily not the facts but their interpretation of the facts.

This so-called expert opinion is not the only kind that may appear as evidence. The law also recognizes what is called the " character witness," an ordinary person who offers his opinion as to the character of the defendant.

What tests can we apply to evidence to satisfy ourselves that it is worth admitting into an argument?

Facts as Evidence

A fact must be a fact. What is offered as a fact may on occasion turn out to be merely a mistaken opinion. We know this pattern well from detective stories. A " fact " points to the guilt of a certain character, who is arrested by the stupid police sergeant. The clever detective proves that the " fact " — that Miss Perkins was observed near the scene of the crime at a certain hour — is not a fact at all; the true criminal had taken Miss Perkins' hooded raincoat and worn it while committing his crime. Justice is done; Miss Perkins is exonerated and the criminal is arrested.

A fact must be (1) verified or (2) attested to by a reliable source.

VERIFICATION

Certain facts can be established by referring to some regularity in nature: that a certain type of cord will not support a certain weight, that potassium permanganate will explode under certain conditions, that the robin's egg is a certain shade of blue with brown markings, that a certain night of the year does not have a full moon, that *rigor mortis* sets in at a certain time after death. Each such fact belongs to a pattern in nature which is observable, and to test a particular fact we refer it to the pattern. We have an example in a story of one of Abraham Lincoln's law cases. A witness testified that he had observed a certain event. Lincoln asked him how, and he replied that he had seen it by moonlight. By producing an almanac, Lincoln showed that there had been no moon on the night in question. Lincoln tested the fact by referring it to a natural pattern. He produced testimony that could be and was verified.

FACT ESTABLISHED BY TESTIMONY

Suppose, however, that Lincoln had not been able to check the witness by an almanac. What questions could he have asked to determine the reliability of the evidence offered by the witness? Four questions are relevant in such a case:

1. Is there opportunity for the witness to observe the event?
2. Is the witness physically capable of observing the event?
3. Is the witness intellectually capable of understanding the event and reporting accurately?
4. Is the witness honest?

The first question is clear enough, but the others are a little more complicated. For instance, if a blind newsman attests that Bill Sims was present in a railway station at such a time, how good is his evidence? Was he capable of observing the event? If it can be demonstrated that the blind man is capable of recognizing a familiar step and is acquainted with the step of Bill Sims, who stopped at his newsstand every day to buy cigarettes, then it can be assumed that the newsman is capable of recognizing Bill Sims' presence. If, furthermore, it can be accepted that the blind newsman has common sense, is not given to delusions, flights of fancy, or exaggeration, and has a good memory, then it can be assumed that he is intellectually able to understand and report the event. What remains is the question of honesty. If the blind newsman has no connection with the case, if no malice, profit, or other special interest is involved, then it can be readily assumed that his report is an honest one. But if some motive which might make him color or falsify the report can be established, then this fact must be assessed in relation to what is known about the newsman's general character. If such a motive can be established, his report probably would not be readily accepted, especially by a hostile or indifferent audience.

The case we have given for reliability here — the blind newsman's testimony — is a relatively simple one, but it illustrates the kind of questions that must be raised in all situations involving testimony. A historian trying to determine the truth about an event long past, a Congressional committee conducting a hearing on an economic situation, a farmer shopping for a new tractor, all are engaged in assessing the reliability of testimony and must ask the same questions. And so must you, on occasion after occasion, in daily life as well as in your college reading and writing.

To sum up: Only facts that can be verified or reliably attested should be admitted into the argument.

Opinion as Evidence

We can set up a parallel set of tests for the admission of opinion into the argument. Corresponding to verifiability — the first requirement for the admission of a fact — we find the authority for an opinion. There is no use in introducing an opinion to support an argument if the opinion will carry little or no weight. For instance, no lawyer would want to introduce as expert a witness who had no reputation for competence in his particular field. The manufacturer of athletic supplies wants a champion, not a dud, to endorse his tennis racquet, and the manufacturer of cosmetics wants a lady of fashion or a famous actress to give a testimonial for his facial cream. We should be as sure as possible that any authority which we invoke in an argument is a real authority: a second-rate navy is no navy, and a second-rate authority is no authority, when the moment of combat comes.

TESTS OF AUTHORITY

How do we find out if an authority is real authority? "Ask the man who owns one," a famous automobile advertising slogan suggests; and the maker of a washing machine shows the picture of a happy housewife standing by her prized appliance. The advertisers here appeal to authority on the principle that the proof of the pudding is in the eating: ask the eater, for he is an authority. This is a kind of rough-and-ready authority based on experience, useful but very limited in the degree of conviction which it can carry. Very probably the automobile buyer has not used many different makes of cars, and the housewife has not used many different kinds of washing machines. The opinion of an impartial technical expert who had tested many makes of car or washing machine for efficiency, durability, and so forth, would carry much more authority. Here we appeal to experience, too, but to the experience of the expert.

Authority is very often based on an appeal to success. The rich man is supposed to know how to make money, the famous painter how to paint pictures, the heavyweight champion how to fight. Success carries prestige and predisposes us to accept the pronouncement of the successful man. But we should still scrutinize success as a criterion for authority. Perhaps the rich man got rich by luck — he *happened* to get into business at a time of expansion and rising markets. No doubt he himself attributes his success to his own sterling character, shrewdness, and indefatigable industry, but we may be more inclined to trust the evidence of the economic situation of his time. Or the famous painter may have been lucky enough to hit upon a popular fashion; history is littered with the carcasses of artists of all kinds whose success was the accident of the moment. The heavyweight gives us a better instance, for it is a simpler one — he merely had to square off with one man at one moment and slug it out. But perhaps a granite jaw, a fighting heart, and an explosive punch gave him the championship, and all that he has to say about training, footwork, and strategy may be wrong. He didn't succeed by luck, as did the businessman or the painter; he really did flatten the opponent by his own force — but he may give the wrong reasons for his success. The fact of success doesn't mean that the successful man really knows the conditions of his success. And he can speak with authority only if he does know. Many successful people are like the man who lived to be a hundred and revealed his secret for long life: " I never read less than one chapter of the Holy Writ a day or drink more than three slugs of likker a night."

Not infrequently we encounter an appeal to what, for lack of a better phrase, we may call authority by transference. Because a man is considered an authority in one field, it is assumed that he is an authority on anything. The famous musician is used as an authority on statesmanship, the great mathematician is appealed to as an authority on morality, and the great physicist on religion; the All-America fullback endorses a certain breakfast food, and a debutante prefers such-and-such a cigarette. This sort of reasoning is obviously nonsensical and pernicious, for it is simply a means of imposing on the gullibility of the audience.

Authority, too, has some relation to time. What was acceptable as authority at one time may not be acceptable at another. In any field where the body of knowledge is constantly being enlarged and revised, timeliness is very important. A book on chemistry or physics written ten years ago may now lack authority in certain respects, or a history of the American Civil War written in 1875 may now be considered very misleading. Should George Washington's views on foreign policy influence our own? We want the best authority of *our* time.

What tests, in the end, can we apply to determine authority? There are no ready-made tests. We must, in the end, use our own judgment to select the authority by which we wish to support our argument. This seems to leave us where we started; but that is not quite true. Finding the man who might know is, after all, different from finding out for ourselves what he knows. If we are dealing with authority presumably based on experience, we can ask about the nature of the experience (one washing machine or ten washing machines?) and the intelligence and training of the person who has had the experience. If we are dealing with authority based on success, we can inquire into the nature of the success (how much was luck?) and into the capacity of the successful person for analyzing the means to success. And we should not forget to ask if the authority of the successful man is being used as authority by transference. Furthermore, we have to ask if our authority is timely.

Let us suppose that we wish to find an authority on some point of American history. It will not do to go to the library and take down the first book on the subject. The mere fact of print bestows no authority, for every error is somewhere embalmed between boards. We have to find out something about the author. Is he of recent date? (That is, would he have available the latest research on the subject?) Does he have any special bias or prejudice which must be discounted? Does he occupy a responsible position or has he had other professional recognition? (That is, is he on the faculty of some important university, have his works been favorably reviewed, and so forth?) How do his views compare with the views of other historians of recognized importance? To answer these questions means that we have to find out something about American history, even though we are not capable of settling the particular point in question by our own investigation.

AUTHORITY AND THE AUDIENCE

One more thing must be considered. The authority we use must convince a particular audience. Effective authority is authority which is acceptable to the particular audience. The Mohammedan *Koran* carries no authority to a Catholic, the Pope carries no authority to a Methodist, and the first chapter of Genesis carries no authority to a geologist. If we can use an authority that our audience already knows and respects, we have an initial advantage. If this is not possible, then we must establish the prestige of the authority. We can sometimes do this merely by informing the audience, but sometimes we must resort to persuasion. As we have said, the discussion of persuasion will be taken up later in the chapter.

• Applications •

I. Analyze the evidence offered in one of the following selections in the Readings: "Mother Sea: The Gray Beginnings" (page 469) or "The Colors That Animals Can See" (page 478).

II. In "The American Civilization Puzzle" (Readings, page 666), George F. Carter attacks certain examples of "expert testimony"— views held by scientists whom he opposes. On what grounds does he do so?

III. Analyze and criticize the evidence offered in some advertisements of common commodities; for instance, a tooth paste, a breakfast food, an automobile or a truck, a cigarette, a face powder, a laundry soap.

IV. Analyze and criticize the evidence offered in a political editorial or article.

V. Study "Three Views of Mary Todd Lincoln" in the Readings (page 680). In comparing the different views expressed there, what problems of evidence do you encounter?

VI. Analyze the evidence you have offered in your last theme. Would you now care to revise your theme?

Reasoning

Once we have assembled our evidence and tested its acceptability, we need to find out for ourselves, and show to others, what the evidence means in relation to the argument, how the evidence will lead to our conclusion. This is not a new process for us. The whole business of living, from first to last, is a long education in the use of reason. Fire burns, cats scratch, pulling things off tables brings a frown or a spanking — we learn these great truths early. Later on we learn other truths — a stitch in time saves nine, honesty is the best policy, to be good is to be happy. We say we learn from experience (or from someone else's experience), but that is not quite true. Experience would teach us nothing if we could not reason about experience.

Reasoning, therefore, is not something which we learn from books. The race learned it the hard way over a long time: if your powers of reasoning failed you once too often, you were liquidated by a falling tree, a saber-toothed tiger, or a neighbor who had *reasoned* out that a sharp stone tied to the end of a stout stick gave him certain advantages in a dispute. But you can train your powers of reason by learning something about the reasoning process.

Reasoning is the process by which the mind moves from certain data (the evidence) to a conclusion. We can make this progress from data to conclusion because we recognize some regularity in our world. We are back, in other words, to the principle of uniformity, which we talked about in connection with cause (page 118; see also the Appendix on causal analysis, page 813).

How does the principle affect our reasoning? We put the particular case up against the general principle to see whether it fits. We know that green apples are sour; therefore we do not eat the green apple we find hanging so invitingly on the bough before us. We know that heavy drinkers tend to have unsteady hands; therefore we don't want Dr. Jebb to operate on our uncle.

Induction: Generalization

Let us examine two examples of the kind of reasoning called **induction**. A businessman has, at different times, hired five boys from the Hawkins School and has found them all honest, well mannered, and well educated. Therefore, when the sixth boy comes along for a job, the man will be inclined to hire him. In other words, the man has generalized from the five instances to the conclusion that all boys from Hawkins School are honest, well mannered, and well educated. The man has made a **generalization,** moving from a number of particular instances to the general conclusion that all instances of the type investigated will be of this same sort.

To take a second example of generalization: After long observation men have concluded that water always freezes at a certain temperature, 32 degrees Fahrenheit. We assume that the same kind of event in nature always happens in the same way under the same conditions — metal expands when heated; in a vacuum falling bodies, no matter what their mass, move at the same rate. Without this assumption of uniformity we could not accept the conclusion that we arrive at from examining the individual instances. And, in fact, all science is based upon this assumption.

The principle also applies in the reasoning about the boys from Hawkins School. We assume that certain intellectual standards are maintained, that certain manners are insisted upon, that honesty is inculcated, and that the stupid, idle, boorish, or dishonest boy is not graduated. It does not matter that the conclusions we reach in these two instances compel different degrees of assent. We scarcely doubt that the next pail of water we leave out will freeze at a certain temperature, but we do doubt that absolutely all graduates of Hawkins School are models of education, manners, and honesty. We recognize here that the principle of uniformity (Hawkins's standards) in human nature is scarcely as dependable as the principle of uniformity in nature.

THE INDUCTIVE LEAP

We recognize that the conclusion we reach about the boys from Hawkins School is only a probability, but students of logic tell us that from the strictly logical standpoint the conclusion that water always freezes at 32 degrees Fahrenheit is also a probability. This is true because no argument which moves from *some* to *all* can give more than a probability. Undoubtedly millions of instances of water freezing at that temperature have been observed, but *all* instances — past, present, and future — have not been observed. After examining a certain number of instances, we take the leap from the some to the all, the **inductive leap** — another word for the process of *generalization*. We cannot be sure about all possible instances. It does no good to appeal to the principle of uniformity in nature by saying that water is water and will always behave the same way, for that principle is itself simply derived from the inspection of a number of instances and itself represents a leap from some to all.

What tests can we apply to reduce the risk of error in making the inductive leap?

TESTS FOR GENERALIZATION

First, a fair number of instances must be investigated. One instance or two prove nothing. Somebody says: " All Chinese are short and slender. Why, I used to know one out in Wyoming, and he wasn't more than five feet tall and I bet he didn't weigh more than a hundred pounds." Or: " All boys from St. Joseph's College are snobs. There was a fellow from home. . . ." We all know this type of reasoning and can see that it proves nothing. A fair number of instances have not been examined. But there is no way to determine certainly what is a fair number of instances. We simply must use all the evidence available to us in the given circumstances and remember that only the untrained mind is rash enough to leap without looking.

Second, the instances investigated must be typical. In a laboratory the scientist may be able to test a substance to be sure it is typical of its kind. He can, for example, detect alcohol in a sample of water and therefore will not use that sample in an experiment to demonstrate the freezing point of water.

But sometimes we have to assume, without testing the fact, that the instances available are typical. For example, the businessman who has hired five boys from Hawkins School assumes that they are typical, that other boys from the school will be like them. At other times, however, when we are facing such a problem, we can choose from among a number of instances for our investigation; in such a situation we should be sure that the instances chosen are representative. Let us consider the problem of a sociologist who, for some purpose, wishes to give a description of life in the southern Appalachians. The sociologist picks three settlements, investigates the pattern of life there, and concludes that life (in general) in the southern Appalachians is such-and-such. But a rival sociologist may point out that the settlements chosen are not typical, that the people are of Swiss descent and maintain a good many Swiss customs. The first sociologist's generalization, then, may be worthless because his instances are not typical.

Third, if negative instances occur they must be explained. Obviously, any negative instance occurring among those which we are using as a basis for generalization will reduce the force of the generalization unless we can demonstrate that the negative instance is *not* typical and therefore need not be considered. For example, if the businessman who has hired five Hawkins boys and found them all honest, hires a sixth and finds that he is pilfering in the stock room, he may decide that he must give up the generalization that the Hawkins graduates are desirable employees. But he may discover that the boy who did the pilfering is a very special case, that he is really unbalanced, is a kleptomaniac, and consequently cannot be taken as typical. Therefore, the businessman returns to his generalization that Hawkins graduates are desirable employees.

To summarize, the tests for making a generalization are:

1. A fair number of instances must be investigated.
2. The instances investigated must be typical.
3. All negative instances must be explained.

Induction: Analogy

Another type of induction is by **analogy.** This type of reasoning is based on the idea that if two instances are alike in a number of important points, they will be alike in the point in question. For example, a board of directors might argue that Jim Brown would make a good corporation executive because he has been a colonel in the army. The analogy here is between the requirements for a good army officer and a good business executive. The points of similarity might be taken as the ability to deal with men, the ability to make and execute policy, the willingness to take responsibility. Then if Brown has been successful as a colonel, it is assumed that he will be successful as a business executive.

We can arrive at certain tests for analogy similar to those for generalization:

1. The two instances compared must be similar in important respects.

2. Differences between the two instances must be accounted for as being unimportant.

In addition to these tests, we must remember that increasing the number of similar instances tends to strengthen our argument. For example, if Brown, the man being considered for an executive position in the corporation, has been a successful division chief in a government bureau as well as a successful colonel, his case is strengthened in the eyes of the board. But with analogy, as with generalization, we can arrive only at probability.

• Applications •

I. Here is another student theme of argument. In a rather informal way it gives examples of induction, both by generalization and by analogy. Study it as a first step toward writing a theme of your own. The comments on the left margin may help you in seeing the general organization and the uses made of induction.

WHY I CHOSE ——— COLLEGE

The proposition, which is never fully stated but given informally, is: " I should go to ——— College." This is, of course, a proposition of action. The analysis, which is also given informally, involves the three ways in which ——— College could

Before I decided on coming here to ——— College, I had to do a lot of arguing with myself and with my family and some friends. But first, I had better say what the argument was about. All my family are doctors, all the men, that is — my father, two uncles, and a first cousin — and all of them are good at the business. When I was a kid, it just never

contribute to the student's medical preparation. These are the issues.

Here the writer is assembling facts as evidence for the college as a place for pre-med work. Here is an inductive argument, a generalization: Men from ———— College are well prepared for medical school. True, there are two negative cases, but one of those can be explained on grounds of poor health.

More evidence; in fact, another generalization: Many men from here have done well in medicine.

Here an argument by analogy comes in: The famous biologist is accessible in this small college and will provide an opportunity for observation similar to that the boy enjoys with his father and family. " Learning by osmosis " is another use of analogy. Look up *osmosis* and see how it provides an analogy.

Here again are facts used as evidence: Distance from home and the honors course will help the student gain a sense of responsibility.

crossed my mind to be a policeman or cowboy. It was doctor all the way, to use the language of the race track where my father takes me now and then when he gets any time off. He once said to me that it was just as well that being a doctor takes so much time, for otherwise he might be a tout.

My marks in school were good enough for me to have some choice in the college I could go to. Naturally the first thing I wanted to know about any college was whether you could get good pre-med work. Everybody knows that you can get good pre-med training at Harvard or the other big universities, and I am aiming at the Harvard Medical School, but a smaller college like this one has to be investigated. I did, and I found out that in the last ten years, 22 per cent of the graduates of ———— College have gone into medicine, and most of them have studied at medical schools in the top ten or so. Only two men failed to finish, and one of them had a physical breakdown. This record seems to settle the case for ———— College as a good place for pre-med. I knew, too, that a lot of older men from here had become very successful doctors.

On the faculty here, too, is one famous biologist. In a small place like this you can work pretty close to a big man and watch how he does things and thinks about problems. You see, I think I have learned a lot already, just hearing my father and the family talk about cases and medical problems, and I calculated that the same process of what you might call learning by osmosis (I had high school biology and know about osmosis) could continue for me in a smaller college better than in a big one.

This last paragraph sounds as if I were tied to my family and dependent on them. I admire them, but I don't want to be dependent. That is one reason I didn't go to college near home, or to Stanford, where my family all went and are well remembered for studies and athletics. I wanted to get far away and be on my own so that I would become grown-up. A doctor has to learn responsibility early, or he is no good. The senior honors course here at ———— also teaches responsibility, because it requires you to work out a big problem on your own.

The fact of a good English department will help in medical training. But this statement needs explaining. The explanation is made necessary by the cousin's objection.

The explanation in opposition to the cousin's view comes with some weight of authority in the opinion, for here another successful doctor speaks, the uncle. But the uncle uses analogy in presenting his argument. Or rather, he attacks the cousin's implied analogy: The body is like a machine. This analogy will not hold for general medicine.

More opinion as corroborative evidence, with weight of authority, for the father is a good doctor. The father is attacking the cousin's implied analogy, but he uses one of his own: The body isn't just a machine, but a machine *with* a driver.

Poker gives another analogy. How good an analogy is this?

The conclusion sets out to be a mere summary of the

There was another reason why I chose ————, in addition to its good pre-med record and the distance from home. It has a well-known English department. I don't mean this to sound like flattery, because everybody knows it is true. When I mentioned this reason to my cousin, Dr. Bob Mathews, he laughed at me and said I had better leave that English alone and get in some extra science. "Son," he said, "all the writing you will have to do if you are a good doctor is filling out prescriptions and signing your income tax return." I know that my cousin sort of laughs, too, at Uncle Bob, his father, in a friendly way and kids him for reading so much and writing a lot of articles, some of them not straight-through professional, but just for the layman.

I asked my uncle about Cousin Bob's point of view, and he said about Cousin Bob: "That's what you can expect from a surgeon. A surgeon is like a car mechanic. He just gets into the machine and patches it up. Except for what is wrong with the mechanism, every patient looks alike to him. That may be all right for a surgeon, but you plan to be a general practitioner. I'm one myself, and I wouldn't be anything else. It's the kind of medicine that has the human quality in the fullest way."

My father says, too, that in general practice human nature plays a big part. You have to understand the patient all the way through, not just the patient as a machine with a broken part. He says that you have to know who the driver of the machine is, and when he says that, he touches his forehead. "Lots of times it is bad driving that busts the axle, no fault in the steel."

My father agrees with my uncle and says that literature is one way of studying human nature — and a good way. But he winked at me, then, and said, "But don't forget poker. That's a pretty good way, too. Why do you think I strip all these lawyers around here in my biweekly game? Hell, they're being so logical about everything, and I'm just looking at their faces for symptoms." My father kids a lot, but he is supposed to be one of the best poker players in Santa Barbara, as well as one of the best doctors.

To sum up, I had to know that ———— is a good place for pre-med work, that it is a

three issues as resolved in the discussion, but the writer trails off rather unsystematically into an observation about his personal interest in literature and the use of a hobby for a doctor.

good place for me to try to be independent, and that it is a good place for me to study literature for the purpose I have in mind (though I mean to study it, too, because I like it, and a doctor needs some sort of relaxation, such as my father's racing and occasional poker).

II. Read "Freedom and the Control of Men" (Readings, page 536). What examples do you find here of generalization and analogy? Do you accept them?

III. Consider the following problems in the light of the principles of generalization and analogy:

1. You are in charge of hiring for a big industrial concern. You have to choose between a young engineering graduate with a college average of C and a young graduate who majored in mathematics with an average of A—. Which would you take? How would you defend your decision?
2. I am not going to marry a girl whose mother is always sick and complaining. Look at what happened to Jack Carton after he married Elizabeth.
3. That man has had three accidents. I won't ride in his car. He's jinxed.
4. Our last three wars were entered into while we had a Democratic president. That proves that the Democratic party is certainly the war party.
5. Dolores del Riovini, the movie star, smokes Whistler Cigarettes. Roger Armstrong, the heavyweight champ, smokes Whistler Cigarettes. Successful people smoke Whistler Cigarettes. You'll like them.

Bring to class further examples of fallacious reasoning which you have discovered in newspapers, magazines, and television or radio programs.

IV. Write a theme in argument (about 500 words), using in the course of your discussion both generalization and analogy. Indicate, however briefly, the "occasion of the question," and, if it seems necessary, the "history of the question." In other words, give an introductory setting for your argument. One of the following topics may suggest a subject to you:

There ought to be a required course in English composition (or in American history or some other subject).
Professional wrestling is faked.
College students should not have cars on campus.
Hemingway is a better novelist than Faulkner (or vice versa).
Despite modern appliances, housewives today are worse off than housewives of fifty years ago.
Comic books are a cause of juvenile delinquency.
Young people today are more conservative and more fearful than young people of twenty years ago.

The dead ball should be restored to baseball.
It's love that makes the world go round.
Human nature can be changed.

Deduction

In concluding our discussion of induction, we said that in both generalization and analogy we do not get certainty, only probability. This was not to say that generalization and analogy are not useful. In fact, they are necessary to us, for many of our most important questions have to be dealt with in terms of probability. But there is a type of reasoning which can be distinguished from induction on the basis of probability: **deduction** does not give probability; within its proper limits it gives certitude.

We are already familiar with the process of deduction from our study of geometry in high school. We remember that geometry starts with certain axioms. For instance: " Things that are equal to the same thing are equal to each other." Or: " If equals be added to equals, the wholes are equal." There is no attempt in the system of geometry to prove these axioms. They simply seem right to us, and we accept them as our first theorem. Then, having deduced that first theorem, we can prove the second — and deduce it — and so on through the whole system generated by the axioms. Once we have the axioms, the whole system of geometry must, *necessarily,* follow. It cannot be otherwise.

What we start with in geometry we call *axioms,* the things we accept without discussion or demand of proof. In general argument, when we are reasoning deductively, we also start from certain assumptions, which we call **premises.** Once certain premises are accepted, a certain conclusion *must* follow. We said above that " within its proper limits " deduction gives certitudes. Those " proper limits " are always what the particular premises will permit. Of course, if we accept bad premises, our conclusion may well be bad. *What we are concerned with here, however, is not the selection of premises, but the process of reasoning from them deductively to their necessary conclusion.*

DEDUCTION AND REASONING BY CLASSES

The word *deduction* comes from two Latin words, *de,* meaning " from," and *ducere,* meaning " to lead." To deduce is, then, to lead from something to a conclusion. What we lead from is, of course, the premise. What is the process by which we move deductively from premises? How do we think deductively?

Thinking deductively means thinking *by classes*. We already have made an acquaintance with this process in studying various types of exposition; for instance, definition. In studying definition, as in studying classification, we are concerned with seeing how larger classes include smaller classes, and so on, up and down a scale. In discussing the process of definition, we tried to explain by a chart of classes the notion of convertibility as a test of definition (pages 49–50).

For instance, we found that the statement, "A slave is a man," is not a definition. It is a true statement, but that does not make it a definition. In a definition we must be able to substitute either term for the other in any form of the statement. We accepted the definition that a slave is a person who is legally held as the property of another because we can substitute the term *person legally held as property of another* in any context where the term *slave* is acceptable. Take the statement, "To be a slave is worse than death." Here we can make the substitution — can *convert* the terms — and we get exactly the same sense: "To be a person legally held as the property of another is worse than death."

We cannot, however, convert the terms of the statement, "A slave is a man." If we try it in the statement above, we get, "To be a man is worse than death," a notion which will find few takers.

Why are the terms *man* and *slave* not convertible, since they are linked in a true statement? The answer is simple: The term *man* indicates a class more inclusive than the term *slave*. In fact, *slave* is just one of many subclasses under the class *man*. We can indicate this by drawing a circle:

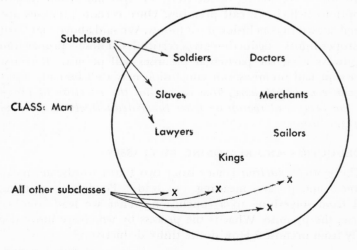

It is clear that much we might say about the class *slave* is not necessarily true about the class *man;* that is, about men in general. But it is also clear that whatever we can say about the class *man* is *necessarily* true about the class *slave,* for the class *slave* is included in the class *man.* And what we say about the class *man* would be applicable, too, to doctors, lawyers, soldiers, and all other kinds of men. For instance, once we say, " God loves all men," we can clearly say, " God loves slaves." We have stated a premise, " God loves all men," and the other statement, the conclusion, necessarily follows from it. It follows necessarily because we accept as another premise the notion that slaves are men.

If we put these premises into circles, we will have a little circle, the class *slave,* which is in a larger circle, the class *man,* which we now have in a still larger circle, the class *what God loves,* which, of course, includes more than men.

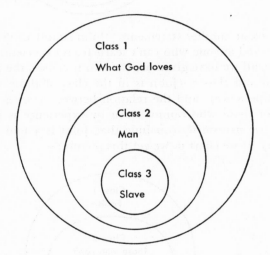

Behind the simple statement that God loves slaves, we have the reasoning indicated in our circles. This, then, is the process of deduction. There are two premises. The first, " God loves man," indicates the relation between class 1 and class 2. The second premise, " A slave is a man," indicates the relation between class 2 and class 3. From those two premises we **deduce** the conclusion, " God loves slaves." In other words, if class 3 is in class 2, and class 2 is in class 1, then class 3 is in class 1.

Let us take another example, the statement, " Even kings die." What is the reasoning behind it? We have the class *king* included in the class *man,* and the class *man* included in the larger class *things that die;* and so we can attach the meaning *(to die)* of the biggest class to the smallest class *(king)*, or to any member, to come down a stage, of that class. We can say, "No matter how proud King William is, he will die like the rest of us." In the picture it looks this way:

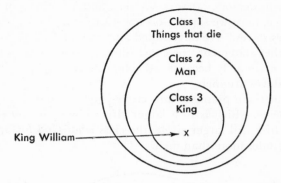

Let us look at another statement: "John simply can't learn from experience, and anyone who can't learn from experience is a fool." In this case, all we have given are the two premises, the relation between John and class 2 (John is in the class of those who cannot learn by experience), and the relation between class 2 and class 1 (the class of those who cannot learn by experience is in the class *fool*). But we *necessarily* conclude that John is a fool (that John is in class 1). If we chart it, we get this picture:

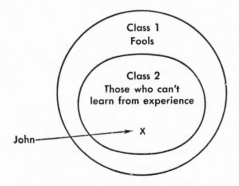

It does not matter whether we start with the conclusion (as in the statement, "King William will die like the rest of us") and have to work back to the chain of reasoning, or whether we start with the premises (as in the statement, "John simply can't learn from experience, and anybody who can't learn from experience is a fool"); the kind of picture we get is the same, a picture of the relation of classes, and in these two instances, of the relation of an individual to classes. The same is true if we are given the conclusion and one premise. For instance, suppose we say, " John is an awful fool. He can't learn from experience." Here we have the conclusion and one premise, but we immediately know that the other premise is, " People who can't learn from experience are fools." And again we have the picture above.

• **Application** •

For each of the following items, state whether we have given a conclusion and premise or two premises. Draw the picture for each item as a fully rendered piece of deductive reasoning. For a guide let us consider: " If you want to cut expenses, better buy an Acme typewriter." We have a general proposition, "You want to cut expenses," and a particular suggestion, " Buy an Acme typewriter." We can chart it by a circle with an X in it:

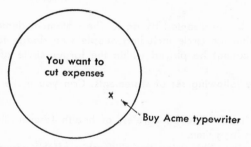

But on what grounds is the X placed in the circle? Obviously one premise is missing — which we may indicate by an intermediate circle that will be in the big one and will include the X. Of course, this circle would be, " Acme typewriters cut expenses." So we would have the picture:

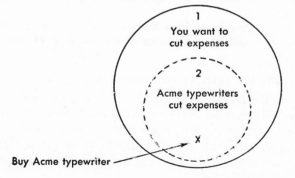

For another guiding illustration, consider: "Maybe people with lots of money can get by with dodging taxes, but you can't." If we diagram the reasoning here, clearly we must draw a large circle for the class of people who have lots of money and a smaller circle for those who are able to dodge taxes with impunity. Our statement declares that the smaller circle falls within the larger, thus:

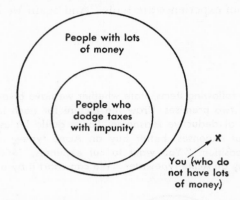

"You" would be represented by an X. The statement denies that X can be placed within the circle including people who dodge taxes with impunity, for it cannot be placed within the larger circle of people with lots of money.

Examine the following set of statements. Can you make diagrams for them?

1. One can't afford to be careless of health forever. Sam has been careless a long time.
2. Why do you, who enjoy the citizenship of this country, think you should be exempt from the draft?
3. At the Battle of Gettysburg, an old woman called out to a detachment of Federal troops who were retreating. "What are you afraid for? They're only men!"
4. "I am an aristocrat. I love justice and hate equality." — John Randolph.
5. "Fools say they learn from their own experience. I have always contrived to get my experience at the expense of others." — Bismarck.

A CAUTION: STATEMENT OF PREMISES

Sometimes the form of the statement of a premise is confusing. The most ordinary cause of such confusion is the use of a restrictive or exclusive element in the proposition, an expression such as *all but, all except, none but*. For example, the proposition, "None but the brave deserve the fair," seems at first glance to mean, "All the brave deserve the fair." But a little reflection shows that such is not the case, and that it really means, "All who deserve the fair are included in the class of the brave." That is, some of the brave do not deserve the fair. In the picture we clearly see that some of class 1 (the brave) are not in class 2 (those who deserve the fair).

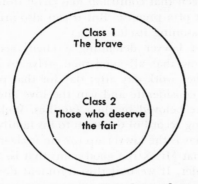

Or, to take another example: "Only students willing to work will pass this course." This does not mean, "All who work will pass this course." Rather, it means, "All who do pass this course will be in the class of those who are willing to work." So we have the picture:

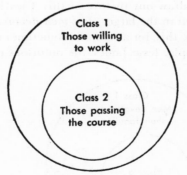

In other words, it is quite possible that some students who work very hard will fail, because they are, let us say, badly prepared or stupid or in poor health.

• Application •

Interpret and draw the picture for each of the following propositions:

1. None but a fool fails to learn from experience.
2. Only the brave deserve the fair.

3. Only women bear children.
4. Democracies alone can afford mistakes.
5. All but the foolish seek to know God's will.

SLIPS IN REASONING

We have just seen that confusion may arise from misunderstanding the statement of a premise. But it can also arise from a slip in the process of reasoning itself.

Suppose that a lawyer defending a client accused of murder argues: "We know that all good men strive to provide well for their families. They work day after day for that purpose. All good men strive to be considerate and win the love and esteem of their families. They are beloved by their families. Well, I point out to you this man's long record of devotion to his family, and their devotion to him." What is the lawyer up to? He is clearly trying to indicate to his jury that Mr. X is a good man; that is, a man who could not commit murder. If we boil this argument down, it comes out like this:

Good men are devoted to their families, etc.
Mr. X is devoted to his family.
Therefore, Mr. X is a good man, etc.

Let us start to draw our picture of this. Clearly, we get the class *good men* included in the larger class *men devoted to their families*. We can readily see this, for a criminal sometimes is a devoted family man, as, for example, Jesse James, the notorious outlaw.

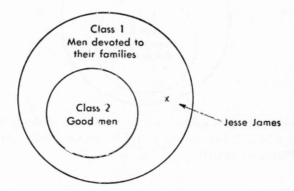

Now the lawyer wants us to put Mr. X inside the class *good men.* But we see that we do not have to. All we have to do, according to our second premise, is to put him inside the class *men devoted to their families.* Since that class is bigger than the class *good men,* we are able to put him there without putting him inside the class *good men* — that is, men who could not commit murder. There is no *necessity* to put him in the class *good men,* and the necessity is what counts, *not* the possibility. So we have the picture:

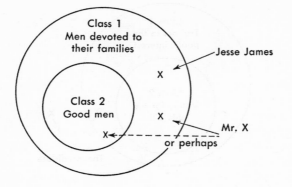

It is obvious that the chain of reasoning has slipped. In this case, we presume that the lawyer hoped the jury would not notice the slip and would vote for acquittal. But sometimes we slip without meaning to and deceive even ourselves.

Let us try another example. A political candidate says, " Every Congressman who voted for the Jones-Higgins Bill betrayed this state. But I did not vote for it. I am no traitor to your interests, but would fight to the death for them. . . ."

We do not have to be impressed. The candidate has not offered any convincing reasoning that he is not a traitor to the public interest. Voting for the Jones-Higgins Bill would not be the only way a Congressman could betray the public interest.

What the candidate *wants* his conclusion to look like is this picture:

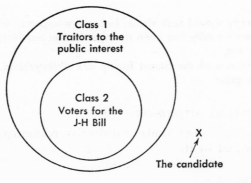

But all we are sure of is that the candidate belongs outside class 2 (voters of the J–H Bill). For all we know, he may still be inside class 1 (traitors to the public interest). So our figure should indicate that he may fall either in class 1 or outside it:

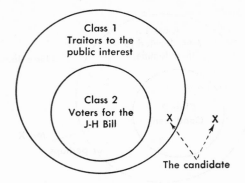

There are many ways to make a slip in reasoning. A good check on yourself or on the reasoning of other people is to try to look behind the words and see what is *necessarily* included in what. The *maybe* or *perhaps* does not count in this kind of reasoning. To be convincing, the conclusion *must* follow from the premises.

• Application •

Which of the following arguments would you accept and which not? Draw a picture to show why. Sometimes a premise or conclusion is not stated and you will have to supply it.

1. No member of this fraternity has ever been expelled from college. So, you see, no member has ever disgraced us.
2. We, like beasts, are the products of Nature. We are no better than beasts.
3. Everybody should seek virtue, because everybody wishes happiness.
4. The Stuart family has been distinguished in our history, and Joseph is a Stuart.
5. All members of the Stuart family are distinguished, and Joseph is no exception.

REASONING BY *EITHER–OR*

There are two other kinds of deductive reasoning, distinguished by **either-or** and by **if**.

Let us set up an example of reasoning by *either-or*. Upon going into the kitchen and finding the steak on the floor under the sink, we think that either the cat or the dog has pulled it down. Then we discover that the cat is locked in the barn to catch rats. Therefore the dog must have committed the crime. The formula is simple. We decide on two possibilities. We exclude one. Naturally the other becomes our conclusion.

To get a true conclusion, we must be sure, as with the usual process of deduction, that our starting point is dependable. The *either-or* premise must really cover the case. The alternatives must be exhaustive. In the example of the cat and dog, if the cat is locked in the barn and the dog is out chasing rabbits, the premise simply does not cover the case. We must investigate further to discover all the possibilities. We find that, after all, it was curly-headed little Willie who pulled the steak off the table and deserves the punishment.

In the example of *either-or* reasoning just given, the pattern of reasoning may be described as follows: A or B, not B, therefore A. (The cat or dog was the culprit; the cat was not the culprit; therefore it was the dog that took the steak.) Can we also reason through this pattern: A or B, B, therefore not A? The validity of such reasoning will depend upon what we mean by *either-or*. We may mean (1) A or B, but not both (i.e., *or* used exclusively), or (2) A or B, or both (i.e., *or* used inclusively). If we are using *or* in an exclusive sense, the pattern represented by A or B, B, therefore not A yields a valid conclusion. If the cat or the dog, but not both, could have got the steak, and if we can be sure that the dog did get it, then it is valid to conclude that the cat did not. But suppose that we are using *or* in an inclusive sense; then the pattern of reasoning involved in A or B, B, therefore not A may yield a nonsensical conclusion. For example: " The man who said that is either a fool or a liar. Now I know that he is a liar; therefore he is not a fool." The truth of the matter may be that the man is foolish as well as guilty of false statement. (It is unlikely that we mean he is a fool or a liar but *not both*.) In a case so simple as the last, there is not much danger of our getting into trouble, but in more complicated cases we may very well get into fallacies unless we check very carefully the sense in which we are using *or*. There is a real opportunity for equivocation. (See page 180.) But note that in the *negative* pattern of reasoning (A or B, *not* B, therefore A) it does not matter whether we are using *or* in an exclusive or inclusive sense. The negative pattern of reasoning is valid for both.

• Application •

Discuss the following instances of reasoning by *either-or*:

1. What is not animal must be vegetable or mineral.
   This is not animal.
   So this must be vegetable or mineral.

2. Bankruptcies are caused either by dishonesty or by idleness.
   John Sutter's bankruptcy was not caused by idleness.
   John Sutter must be dishonest.

3. If Williams told our plans, he is either a coward or a traitor.
   We know he is a coward.
   He is no traitor.

REASONING BY *IF*

Reasoning by *if* deals with a condition and a result. *If* the condition is fulfilled, the result necessarily follows.

We constantly use reasoning of this kind, as in the statement, " If you had banked the furnace, we might have had heat this morning." Fully stated, the argument would go like this:

If you do not bank the furnace, the fire will die.
You did not bank the furnace.
Therefore the fire died.

The reasoning above is correct. We have affirmed the *if,* the condition, and therefore the result necessarily follows. But the reasoning is also correct if we deny the consequence and affirm the condition, as in the following instance:

If you do not bank the furnace, the fire will die.
The fire has not died.
Therefore you did bank the furnace.

The following example does not, however, give us correct reasoning:

If you do not bank the furnace, the fire will die.
The fire died.
Therefore you did not bank the furnace.

The result here is not *necessarily* acceptable. The fire may have died because the furnace was not banked, but it also may have died from some other cause. For instance, there may not have been enough fuel. For the reasoning in this last example to be valid, the *if* would have to mean *only if*. Most errors in reasoning of the type of *if* come about because we incorrectly interpret an *if* as an *only if*.

Of course, there are instances where the *if* should legitimately be interpreted as *only if*. But this is a matter of the truth of the premise with which we start, and if we mean *only if* we should say so in the premise.

• Application •

Examine the pieces of reasoning below. Which are acceptable as they stand? Which could be accepted if the *if* were to be taken as *only if*?

1. If there is smoke, there must be fire.
   There is no smoke.
   Therefore there is no fire.

2. If you leave bounds, you will be expelled from school.
   You have not been expelled from school.
   Therefore you did not leave bounds.

3. If you leave bounds, you will be expelled from school.
   You have not left bounds.
   Therefore you will not be expelled from school.

4. If you leave bounds, you will be expelled from school.
   You have been expelled from school.
   Therefore you did leave bounds.

5. If you do not catch this car, you will be late.
   You did not catch this car.
   Therefore you will be late.

6. If you do not catch this car, you will be late.
   You are late.
   Therefore you did not catch this car.

PREMISE AND THE COMMON GROUND

When we first mentioned the word *premise* (page 167), we said that if we do not have sound premises, our reasoning will very likely give a wrong conclusion. If we adopt such premises as " All college graduates are honest," or " All well brought up children are intelligent," or " Man is either ambitious or happy," we shall get into trouble. Arguing from such premises, we may proceed very logically but still have error in the end. And we certainly cannot start a chain of reasoning to convince someone else unless that someone else will accept our premises. That "American policy is always disinterested " we may piously hope is true, but it is scarcely a premise to be used in argument with our allies. In other words, for any given piece of reasoning — even if it is just one little stage of reasoning in the course of an elaborate discussion — the premises must be accepted by all concerned. The premises are the common ground of a piece of reasoning, as the axioms are for geometry (page 167). Therefore, if we are to argue convincingly, we must start from premises generally acceptable. The most certain way to fail in an argument is to start from false premises.

Fallacies

But there are other ways in which argument may fail. We have already indicated a good many characteristic errors in developing a line of reasoning; for example, in induction a generalization based on too few instances (page 161) or an analogy based on instances different in important respects (page 163), or in deduction the failure to relate classes properly (page 174). Such an error we call a **fallacy**. There are other fallacies not yet touched on, at least not directly, which are all too common in argument. They are **equivocation, begging the question, ignoring the question,** and *non sequitur* (Latin for " It does not follow ").

EQUIVOCATION

Equivocation is the fallacy of using the same term with different meanings. Here is a well-known example:

Even scientists recognize a power beyond nature, for they speak of " natural law "; and if there is law, there must be a power to make the law; such a power beyond nature is called God; therefore scientists believe in God.

Here the word *law* is used equivocally, that is, in two meanings. In the sense in which scientists use it when they speak of " natural law," it means the recognition of regularity in natural process — the law of gravity, for example. Here the sense is descriptive. But in the second sense it means what is ordinarily meant in government, a command given by a superior authority. Here the sense is prescriptive. Since the whole argument is based on the word *law*, the argument does not make sense *as an argument* if the word shifts its meaning. It may be true that a number of scientists do believe in God, but that does not make this a good argument.

BEGGING THE QUESTION

Begging the question occurs when an arguer assumes something to be true which really needs proof. One way to beg the question is to smuggle into the original statement of the proposition, consciously or unconsciously, what is really supposed to be at stake in the argument. Suppose that someone offers the proposition, " The unsanitary condition of the slaughter pens is detrimental to health."

What we are supposed to argue, if there is to be an argument, is whether the condition of the slaughter pens is detrimental to health. But the word *unsanitary* means " detrimental to health," and that word has been put into the original proposition. The question that is supposed to be at stake has been begged. The argument is poisoned before it starts.

When we encounter such a proposition, we should restate it and then see exactly what is being argued.

The same principle appears on a larger scale whenever we argue in a circle. For example:

A: I admire Rembrandt's painting " The Night Watch."
B: Why?
A: Because it is a great painting.
B: How do you know?
A: All the best critics say it is.
B: How do you know who the best critics are?
A: Why, the best critics are those who recognize great painting.

Here speaker A gives a circle in the proof. He sets out to prove that the painting is great by appealing to the best critics and then identifies the best critics as those who recognize great painting. This instance is very simple, but sometimes the begging may be concealed in a very elaborate argument. We must always be on the watch for it, for such question-begging is an attempt to establish a thing *by itself*.

IGNORING THE QUESTION

An arguer ignores the question when he introduces any consideration that will distract from what is really at stake. There are numberless ways of doing this. A competing question may be set up so that argument is shifted to new ground, or an appeal may be made to some emotional attitude having nothing to do with the logic of the case. For instance, if a man arguing for a Republican candidate shifts the issue from the candidate's qualifications to the praise of Lincoln, the great hero of the party, he is ignoring the question. Or if a Democrat leaves a present question of party policy and begins to discuss the glorious achievements of Thomas Jefferson, he is ignoring the question. Or if a lawyer defending a man accused of murder does not deal with the question of guilt, but argues that the victim was a wicked man or that the family of the accused is worthy of pity, he is likewise ignoring the question.

One of the commonest forms of ignoring the question is to shift from the question to the character or personality of the opponent. For instance, a husband criticizes his wife, and she replies, "Well, you aren't so perfect yourself!" She has ignored the rights and wrongs of the question, her own burnt bread or bad arithmetic or overbid at bridge, and has begun to discuss his shortcomings. We find another instance when we argue that we cannot endorse a certain political measure because the Congressman who proposes it has been divorced or drinks whisky. We have shifted from the measure to the man.

NON SEQUITUR

Non sequitur, as we have said, means, " It does not follow." In one sense, of course, any fallacy is a *non sequitur,* because by the very nature of the case the conclusion does not follow from fallacious reasoning. But here we shall use the term to cover certain more special kinds of argument.

For instance, it may be argued: " William Brown doesn't drink or smoke, and so he ought to make a good husband." But it is obvious that a man who does not drink or smoke may still make a poor husband. He may gamble, or loaf, or beat his wife. To take another example, it may be argued: " Harry Thompson would make a good governor because he belongs to the upper class." We know, however, that belonging to a certain social class proves nothing about a man's ability or integrity. So the conclusion that Thompson would make a good governor does not follow. A connection has been asserted which does not exist.

A somewhat more complicated form of *non sequitur* appears in a piece of parental reasoning like this: " As soon as I increased Billie's allowance, his grades at school began to fall. Therefore we ought to reduce his allowance, since having extra money makes him idle." But Billie may have been suffering from eye strain, or may have fallen in love, or may now be beginning a subject for which he is badly prepared. Let us take another example: " Just after Herbert Hoover was elected President we had the greatest depression in history. How can you respect a man like that? "

In the argument about Billie and the argument about Hoover the same error occurs. It is argued that because A (an increase in Billie's allowance or the election of Hoover) precedes B (Billie's bad grades or the depression), A must necessarily be the cause of B. The arguer does not understand the nature of a cause (pages 114–20) or has not taken the trouble to analyze the situation. He simply assumes that if one thing precedes another, the first is the cause of the second.

FALLACIES AND REFUTATION

An understanding of fallacies is useful in helping us to reason straight, but it is also useful in helping us to locate defects in an opposing argument. If we can point out a fallacy in an opposing argument, we can **refute** that argument, and **refutation** is a powerful secondary weapon for maintaining our own position. Even when we are not engaged in a debate and must refute arguments made by an opponent, but are simply writing a piece of argument, we often find that we have to refute certain arguments — arguments that we can anticipate or that occur to us in turning a question over in our minds.

It is not necessary to memorize a list of fallacies to discover defects in reasoning or to reason straight. Many people who have never heard the word *fallacy* can reason straight or locate defects in the reasoning of another person. When we meet the example of a fallacy in cold type on the page of a textbook, we are inclined to say, " Nobody with common sense would commit such an error." That is true. But common sense is not, after all, so common, and sometimes we have to work for it.

• Applications •

I. The selection " How To Detect Propaganda " (Readings, page 518) is really an analysis of certain fallacies, but fallacies used quite deliberately to deceive the public. Which of the false appeals analyzed there correspond to fallacies which we have studied here under other names? Which are new?

II. Read " Love Is a Fallacy " (Readings, page 613). Which of the fallacies listed in this essay have we studied under other names?

III. Identify the unacceptable propositions or arguments among the following instances, and explain the fallacy, or fallacies, involved in each:

1. The holder of one hand in this poker game is bound to win. Jack holds one hand, and therefore is bound to win.
2. On the seacoast a dying man usually breathes his last just as the tide begins to ebb because the going out of the water takes his strength with it.
3. You should not read the poetry of Byron, because his private life was immoral.
4. Telegrams bring bad luck.
5. No man can live without faith. Faith is the mark of a good Christian. Therefore all men are inherently Christians.

6. I am strongly opposed to our participation in any European war, because Washington, the father of our beloved country, warned us against foreign entanglements.
7. The Irish love whisky, and so I am not going to hire Pat McGoon.
8. After taking several bottles of Lightfoot's Liver Syrup, Mrs. Jones felt much better. So Mrs. Smith immediately bought a bottle.
9. Nothing is better than peace of mind. But half a loaf is better than nothing. Therefore half a loaf is better than peace of mind.
10. This unjust tax should be repealed.

IV. Locate, if you can, any fallacious argument in editorials, advertisements, or articles that you have lately read. Copy them, and indicate the nature of the fallacies involved.

Deduction and Extended Argument

When we finished discussing inductive reasoning, it was relatively easy and natural to set up an extended discussion embodying what had been learned. But often deductive reasoning seems limited and niggling, not suited to a full discussion of a subject. It seems useful only for hacking away at some small point.

Throughout the last several pages we have been hacking away at small points. That is the only way to illustrate what is involved in deductive reasoning. But once we have assimilated the principles, we constantly use them, without self-consciousness, in the development of a discussion.

In much ordinary argumentative prose, we find a series of limited bits of argumentation simply absorbed and used, step by step. We have already seen (pages 170–71) how the full chain of reasoning may be indicated by, say, one premise and the conclusion, or the two premises with the conclusion left to the logical sense of the audience. In this way much argument proceeds, without taking time to develop each piece of reasoning in full. The basic lines of reason may be embedded in the midst of incidental evidence, examples, and other material. Here, for example, is a paragraph from an editorial:

Nobody denies that our tax situation is desperate and that we are facing a crisis, and nobody denies that there is great need for wise legislation in all matters affecting the business of the nation. We must scrutinize with redoubled attention every bill which comes before Congress and try to see what its effect will be in this sphere of activity. This is undoubtedly necessary with the present bill to lower taxes. If it is passed, it will have an inflationary effect. What attitude shall we take toward the present bill?

The main point here concerns a tax reduction bill. It is assumed as background that the present situation is desperate and that good legislation is needed. The argument to follow can be divided into two chains of reason linked together:

Tax reduction promotes inflation.
The present bill would reduce taxes.
Therefore the present bill would promote inflation.

The conclusion of this chain provides a premise for the next one, the link in the argument:

Whatever promotes inflation is bad.
The present bill would promote inflation.
Therefore the present bill is bad.

The editorial writer feels that his reader knows that inflation is bad, and he says only that the present bill is bad. Nor does he bother to state the conclusion that this bill is, therefore, bad. He feels that the conclusion will strike the reader more powerfully if the reader is forced to come to it himself. The reader will himself answer the question: "What attitude shall we take toward the present bill?"

Here is a student theme in argument. For the moment, ignore the marginal material and read it through.

CAREERS FOR GIRLS

Recently I read an article by a lady psychologist who argued that all women ought to have life-long careers just as men do. The article did not impress me particularly until one of my friends commented that she thought it the most inspiring article she had ever read. On the strength of what the psychologist said, she was going back to her ballet lessons, which she had dropped in her second year of boarding school. Anne is not built like any ballerina I ever saw, but that fact apparently has not discouraged her. Later I heard two girls in my English class excitedly discussing the article. They obviously had also been impressed.

I suppose that the article really had impressed me, perhaps subconsciously, for

(1) Ballerinas are built in a certain way.
My friend is not built that way.
Therefore she won't be a ballerina.

(2) If you listened, you must have been impressed.
I listened.
Therefore I must have been impressed.

(3) You are impressed, either consciously or unconsciously.

I was not impressed
consciously.
Therefore I must have been
impressed unconsciously.

when I went to visit my aunt last week end I asked her whether she had read it. "No," she said, "but I am sure that I know what it said." And she reeled off all the psychologist's main arguments, almost word for word.

Perhaps I should explain a little about my aunt. She was once the fashion editor of a large woman's magazine. She lived in New York, and she traveled two or three times a year to Europe. When I was a child, I thought that she was the most elegant, chic person I had ever seen. And when I was attending boarding school, her visits gave me tremendous prestige with the other girls.

(4) Fashion editors dress and
live in a certain way.
My aunt was a fashion editor.
Therefore I expected her to
dress and live in a certain
way. (And was surprised
when she did not.)

Last week end was the first time I had seen my aunt in four years, since she married and moved to Connecticut. I was surprised by the change. Her house is pleasant and comfortable in an old-fashioned way but not at all "smart." She is still pretty, she dresses well, and she has kept her figure, but she is by no means a fashion plate.

To go back to our conversation, I asked her how she knew what the psychologist had said. "Oh," she said, "those are the arguments they used to pump into us at ——— College, back before Methuselah and World War II. That line is strictly old hat."

"But," I said, "it's by a psychologist."

"That just makes it worse," she said. "It's worse to be an old-hat psychologist than any other kind of old hat." Then the baby began to cry, and she dashed off upstairs.

While I was waiting for her to come down, I began to think about what she had said. I realized that I also disagreed with the author of that article, and I tried to decide why.

(5) In a free country women may
follow whatever life they
prefer.
This is a free country.
Therefore women here may

To me the crucial point in the article is the author's proposition that *all* women *ought* to have careers. Of course, in our free country, a woman ought to be al-

follow whatever life they prefer.

(6) Whoever does not do what he ought is inferior.
Women ought to have careers.
Therefore women who do not have careers are inferior.

(7) The most important job is to be a human being (i.e., develop personality).
A career develops personality.
Therefore women ought to have careers (to develop personalities and be human beings).

(8) You must fulfill yourself.
A career fulfills you.
Therefore you must have a career.

lowed to do as she likes. If she has a special talent and cannot be content unless she expresses that talent, then she should have a career. For example, I know a woman doctor, who is married and has three children, but who has continued her career. She seems to manage all aspects of her life very successfully. (I am not concerned in this discussion with those women who have no choice but to work.) Nor do I oppose the idea that most girls should try their wings a little while and find out what the business world is like. What I object to is the idea that all women ought to have life-long careers, with all that this implies of drive, ambition, and the dedication of their major energies.

To say that every woman ought to have a career is the same as saying that the woman who marries and simply takes care of her family is inferior. She is not making her proper contribution to society. The author, in fact, makes this point pretty explicitly when she says that the woman who does not have a career is failing to do " the most important job of all — the job of being a human being." She is not " fulfilling herself as a person in the modern world," and she does not have a well-rounded personality. The woman without direct contact with the world finds her horizon increasingly constricted.

But can one rightly assume, as the author does, that there is one way only of achieving self-fulfillment? It seems to me that each woman must find her own way and stick to it, even if it does not meet the commonly accepted standards of success. Then, too, isn't the woman who tries to make her " self " over to conform to someone else's ideas likely to be unhappy? My aunt told me that half the women in her neighborhood are discontentedly trying to live up to a false notion of themselves that they acquired in college. Their

" careers " never really amounted to much — a clerical job in a publishing house or bit parts in a Greenwich Village theater — but they feel that they are " intellectual " and that marriage has robbed them of a chance to be another Katharine Cornell or Edna St. Vincent Millay. They are jealous of their husbands or of their classmates who did not marry, and they do not seem to realize that if they had kept on with their careers, they might still be clerks or bit players.

Another reason is advanced by the psychologist for advocating careers for women. She says that a career fills the gap in a woman's life when her children grow up and leave her. Middle-aged women frequently become neurotics, the author says, because they have no careers to fall back on. Here it seems to me that the author is confusing interests with a career. A middle-aged woman should have interests; that is true. She may garden, or work for the Republican party, or head a committee for the church bazaar, or brush up on her bookkeeping to help her husband in his business. She may even take up one of her husband's hobbies, such as hunting. My mother often goes hunting with my dad, and he says that she is a better shot than he is! All these interests are not the same as a career, but they have the same function: to fill up the gaps in a woman's life and to make her happy.

And that finally is what self-fulfillment amounts to — to be happy and contented with yourself, to understand and accept your strengths and weaknesses. My aunt, as I said, has spent a lot of time in Europe, and she told me that European women are often happier than American women because, she says, they do not feel themselves in competition with men. Although they may study and work hard to cultivate their minds and personalities, they do not intend thereby to make money or have a career. They cultivate their interests for enjoyment and for the pleasure of being the right kind of companion for a worthy man. Some women in Europe never make public appearances, but they have more to do with making policies than many American women who run for office. As my aunt, who likes to make jokes, says, " The hand that pounds the gavel doesn't always rule the roost." According to her, many of these European women feel themselves more a *part* of life than the women here who are always in the public eye.

Now, when I say that I do not believe all women ought to have careers, I am not being old-fashioned. I do not want to forbid women something just because they are women. To the contrary, I think it is the author of the article who is old-fashioned. She doesn't realize that to be the best possible wife and mother in today's world is the most challenging job a woman can have. She has to know not only the job of housekeeping, but she has to be an alert and informed citizen so that her family gets the best education and hospital care. She has to keep up with the interests of her sons and daughters; she has to be able to talk intelligently to her husband's boss when he comes to dinner. I do not consider a woman a very good wife if she is too stupid to know anything about her husband's business or if her daughter is ashamed to bring a Phi Beta Kappa boy friend home to meet the family.

How do all these fine arguments apply to me? I don't know exactly, for I am not sure exactly what kind of " self " I have to " fulfill." But I intend to find out before I finish college. Perhaps if my grades are right, I will go on to medical school after I get my B.A. Even if I do become a doctor, I will probably get married, too. Medicine will be subordinate to my family, for a while, at least. But that won't matter to me, because I intend to practice medicine only if I like it and not to have a big career and show the world how successful I am.

Now look at the marginal material. These items represent some of the pieces of reasoning lying behind the theme. As you will see, some of the reasoning is not fully developed in the text. In 1, for example, in the text we have the two premises but not the conclusion. We reach the conclusion ourselves from what the author says of her friend. In 4, the text of the theme does not give the first premise; it is merely assumed. And so on.

Again, some of the pieces of reasoning are drawn from the newspaper article that the student is commenting on and do not represent the student's views. For instance, in 6, the student does not accept the second premise of the reason, which is the one under debate. Furthermore, the student may admit the premises of 7 as individually stated but not accept the reasoning. The trouble here lies in the way the second premise is taken. If we take it, as the newspaper writer tries to sneak it in, that " *Only* a career develops personality," then the reasoning is correct. But the premise does not say that. It may be true as far as it goes; that is, a career does develop personality. But other things do too, and so there would be other ways to fulfill the accepted first premise and become a human being with a well-developed personality.

We have not indicated all the pieces of reasoning behind the theme, but enough to show, perhaps, something of the process.

• Applications •

I. In the theme, " Careers for Girls," why doesn't the student accept 8 as given by the newspaper writer? Draw a picture of it.

II. Find five more pieces of reasoning concealed in the theme. Do you accept them?

III. Let us forget for a little the deduction implied in the theme and turn to *induction*. The first premise of 1 is a generalization. Do you find any other premises in the eight pieces of deductive reasoning given here, or among the five you have drawn out, that are generalizations? If so, how acceptable do you find them?

IV. We may now glance at the theme as a whole. The student confronted another person's developed piece of argument and at first tended to agree with it. Then she found something wrong with it. She picked the issue on which she would start the disagreement. What was the issue? Did she find any other issues to disagree on? To go back a moment, why did the aunt's opinion make her switch her view of the whole argument and begin to gather her negative propositions? Does the importance of the aunt in the whole process tend to make us accept the very long introduction, the " history of the question " and the " occasion of the question "?

THE WEAKEST LINK

In this theme we can see how deeply embedded the individual pieces of reasoning are in the texture of an argument. But no matter how deeply embedded, each much be considered on its own merits. A chain is no stronger than its weakest link, and we must be careful, when we are arguing, not to insert weak links. The best insurance against weak links is to get the habit of inspecting each link individually, even links that will be concealed in our argument. We must cultivate, as a matter of discipline, the habit of stating the individual pieces of reasoning to ourselves, to see if they are convincing.

• **Applications** •

I. Turn back to the student theme arguing for elective courses (page 147), and see how many individual chains of deductive reasoning you can locate in it in support of the various propositions. Do they seem acceptable? If not, criticize them. In a similar spirit criticize your own last theme (page 166).

II. Read " Freedom and the Control of Men " (Readings, page 536). Locate three individual pieces of deductive reasoning embedded in the discussion. Do any issues depend on the support of these pieces of reasoning?

III. Make a list of the pieces of evidence that George F. Carter offers for his own views in " The American Civilization Puzzle " (Readings, page 666). Indicate how each piece is used, inductively or deductively, in his argument.

Persuasion

In the beginning of the chapter we said that although argument makes the appeal to reason and aims at convincing, the appeal to the emotions, which we call persuasion, may be very important in the strategy of presenting an argument. The appeal to reason and the appeal to the emotions can be distinguished, but both may appear in the same discourse.

The human being is a unit, after all, and his reason and his emotions are but different aspects of that unity. Even the most rigorously impersonal and logical mathematician, who may be considered the archetype of the rational man, is driven to his work by some *desire;* he feels that knowledge is good in itself, that using his faculties is good, that satisfying his curiosity is good. He is not thinking what his work is good *for,* merely that it is good.

Though all our reasoning is against the broad background of our emotional life and though in the end we want it to lead to satisfactions of the emotional life, emotions may locally, at a given moment, get in the way of the exercise of reason. Then we have a kind of short circuit, and the short-range satisfaction of the emotions will defeat the long-range satisfaction. So Tom Smith votes Republican (or Democratic) against his long-range interests, just because his grandfather fought under General Sherman (or General Lee). So Jack Brown hits the bottle to avoid a problem instead of facing the problem and trying to solve it. So Susie Perkins makes a joke at the expense of a friend just to please her own vanity in her wit and in doing so loses a friend.

Reason should serve to show us the way to long-run satisfaction; but sometimes, human nature being what it is, we have to appeal to short-range satisfactions in order to lead someone to see the long-range satisfaction. We have to make a person feel that the immediate effort is worth while. Our problem is to find the way to establish fruitful contact with him. That is the problem of persuasion in argument.

We cannot expect our ideas, no matter how good they are, to make their way readily if we do not know how to present them. Even the scientist is irritated and put off if he does not find clarity in the discussion he is attending to, no matter how valuable the ideas may be in that discussion. And when we get away from the cold, accurate language of mathematics and science into the warm and confused language of the ordinary world, the way of presenting an idea becomes even more important. The right way may make our audience willing to hear us out, to listen with sympathy, to give us the benefit of the doubt.

The Occasion and the " Right Way "

What is the " right way "? There is no single right way; for what is right for one subject and one audience may be wrong for another. But the right way always accomplishes one basic thing — it catches the attention of the audience by defining a common ground for the speaker, or writer, and his audience.

The good writer, or speaker, is aware of his occasion (pages 17–20), and the occasion involves (1) the speaker, (2) the subject, and (3) the audience. All three are interrelated, and we should ask several questions about them:

1. What is the audience's attitude toward the subject?
2. What is the speaker's attitude toward the subject?
3. What kinds of treatment will the subject permit?
4. What is the audience's attitude toward the speaker?
5. What is the speaker's attitude toward his audience?

As we learned in Chapter 2, if we are addressing an audience already especially interested in our subject, half the battle is won. The writer of an article in a scientific journal can assume that his reader is interested; he is addressing the specialist. The speaker addressing a mass meeting to protest a particular tax bill can depend on his audience. But the writer of an article on a scientific subject or on some theory of taxation in a popular magazine, such as the *Atlantic Monthly* or *Harper's,* has to capture his audience — and capture it quickly.

Once the audience's attention has been caught, the game is merely begun. Vividness remains important. The audience must be constantly made aware of what is going on, of what issues are at stake, of how the argument moves from one point to another. The audience must catch the sense of impending climax, the moment when the question will be settled. Without clarity of language and organization, this is not possible; we cannot hold the attention of the audience.

These considerations are relative to any given situation, to the answers we would have to give to our first three questions. We might, for instance, catch the attention of an audience which had a neutral attitude toward our subject, but then find that in doing so we had falsified our own attitude toward the subject. The anecdote that might be right for a political article might be wrong for the pulpit. And for some subjects, certain methods of treatment are inapplicable. Even clarity is relative; for what is clear to some people is not clear to others, and some subjects cannot be simplified beyond a certain point. The question is always, " Clear for whom and clear about what? "

We must, in other words, find a common ground in attitudes as well as in assumptions of reason. And this matter of attitudes we shall discuss more fully in the chapter on Tone.

• Applications •

I. Locate some of the devices for catching and holding attention in the following essays in Readings: " The Hickman Story " (page 496), " The Seven Deadly Fallacies " (page 551), and " A Lark's Flight " (page 570). Do you find any indications of fair-mindedness, tact, respect for the reader? Where? What is the common ground established between writer and reader in the one you like best?

II. You are about to write a long theme arguing for some conviction that you hold.

1. State the proposition for your theme.
2. Analyze the proposition. First, jot down points of conflict between your view and the opposing view. Second, think over your jottings and try to decide which points are the issues on which the argument should hinge. Third, arrange your jottings in an order to give unity and coherence to the theme.
3. As before (see page 153), write a paragraph, or more if necessary, on each point of conflict.
4. Now criticize what you have written to see whether (a) the evidence seems reliable and (b) the reasoning free of fallacies.
5. Try to establish transitions between the treatment of the various points, keeping in mind that your obligation is to refer each point to the main contention of your theme, the main proposition.
6. Now think of your introduction. What is the history of the question? What is the occasion of your theme? In other words, what makes this topic worth arguing about now? What kind of people are you writing for? Can you depend on an interested and sympathetic hearing, or must you gain attention? If you have to gain attention, how will you go about it? After you have thought about these matters and written a first draft of your introduction, do you think it necessary to go back and revise the discussion in the body of your theme to make it better adapted to your audience?
7. The conclusion is the last impression that you leave on your reader. Do you really return here to your key point, showing how your whole argument bears on it, supports it? Do you leave your reader with a sympathetic feeling toward your endeavor, even if you cannot be sure of having totally convinced him by reason?
8. Here are some subjects that may be useful as suggestions. But

don't take one unless you feel some interest in it and conviction about it. If nothing here appeals to you, you may find an article or an editorial that provokes you to reply. Sometimes this is a convenient provocation for a theme; for the issues the writer seems to hang his argument on may indicate the points that you should try to attack most strenuously. In other words, part of the analysis of the proposition has already been done for you by the adversary you select. But don't rely completely on his analysis. You may be better at the analysis than he, and he may have tried to conceal the weak points in his position.

One of the following propositions may suggest a topic for your theme:

American policy in the Near and Middle East has been shortsighted.

College football has exploited the student.

The trend toward conformity threatens to stifle intellectual vigor in this country.

Congress should abolish the custom of assigning committee chairmanships on the basis of seniority.

Our foreign policy depends too heavily upon our friendship with Western European countries.

A healthy regionalism would improve the culture of this country.

New York, as our needed cultural capital, exercises a healthful influence on the arts.

The Taft-Hartley Law (or any other Federal law) should be repealed.

Abolish the draft and build a first-rate professional army.

The adolescence of our young people is too prolonged.

CHAPTER SEVEN

Description

Description, as we shall understand the word here, is the kind of discourse concerned with the impression that the world makes on our senses. It is concerned with indicating the qualities of objects, persons, conditions, and actions. It aims to suggest to the imagination the thing as it comes immediately to an observer. We call this kind of description **suggestive** to distinguish it from technical description, which is really a form of exposition. We have already given (pages 99–101) some discussion of the difference between technical description and suggestive description, but let us return to it, with new and more elaborate examples.

TECHNICAL:

The West Indies stand in a warm sea, and the trade winds, warmed and moistened by this sea, blow across all of them. These are the two great primary geographic facts about this group of islands whose area is but little larger than that of Great Britain.

These trade winds, always warm, but nevertheless refreshing sea breezes, blow mostly from the east or northeast. Thus one side of every island is windward, and the other side is leeward. The third great geographical fact about these islands is that most of them are mountainous, giving to the windward sides much more rain than the leeward sides receive. This makes great differences in climate within short distances, a thing quite unknown in the eastern half of the United States, where our slowly whirling cyclonic winds blow in quick succession from all directions upon every spot of territory. Thus both sides of the Appalachian Mountains are nearly alike in their rainfall, forest growth, and productive possibilities. On the contrary, the West Indian mountains have different worlds on their different slopes. The eastern or windward side, cloud-bathed and eternally showered upon, is damp and dripping. There are jungles with velvety green ferns, and forests with huge trees. The rainbow is a prominent feature of the tropic landscape. On the windward side one receives a striking impression of lush vegetation. On the leeward side of the very same ridge and only a few miles distant there is another kind of world, the world of scanty rainfall, with all its devastating consequences to vegetation. A fourth great geographic fact is the division of these islands into two great arcs, an outer arc of limestone and an inner arc of volcanic islands. The limestone areas are low. The volcanic areas are from moderately high to very high. Some islands have both the limestone and the volcanic features.

    — J. RUSSELL SMITH and M. OGDEN PHILLIPS: *North America.*

SUGGESTIVE:

Take five-and-twenty heaps of cinders dumped here and there in an outside city lot; imagine some of them magnified into mountains, and the vacant lot the sea; and you will have a fit idea of the general aspect of the Encantadas, or Enchanted Isles. A group rather of extinct volcanoes than of isles; looking much as the world at large might, after a penal conflagration. . . .

It is to be doubted whether any spot on earth can, in desolation, furnish a parallel to this group. Abandoned cemeteries of long ago, old cities by piecemeal tumbling to their ruin, these are melancholy enough; but like all else which has once been associated with humanity they still awaken in us some thought of sympathy, however sad. Hence, even the Dead Sea, along with whatever other emotions it may at times inspire, does not fail to touch in the pilgrim some of his less unpleasurable feelings. . . .

In many places the coast is rock-bound, or more properly, clinker-bound; tumbled masses of blackish or greenish stuff like the dross of an iron furnace, forming dark clefts and caves here and there, into which a ceaseless sea pours a fury of foam; overhanging them with a swirl of grey, haggard mist, amidst which sail screaming flights of unearthly birds heightening the dismal din. However calm the sea without, there is no rest for these swells and those rocks, they lash and are lashed, even when the outer ocean is most at peace with itself. On the oppressive, clouded days such as are peculiar to this part of the watery Equator, the dark vitrified masses, many of which raise themselves among white whirlpools and breakers in detached and perilous places off the shore, present a most Plutonian sight. In no world but a fallen one could such lands exist.

    — HERMAN MELVILLE: " The Encantadas,
    or Enchanted Isles," *The Piazza Tales.*

The first of these passages, from a geography of North America, lists four " great geographic " facts and then indicates their influence upon climate, vegetation, and appearance of the landscape. There are occasional, and feeble, attempts to make the reader see the islands, as for instance in the phrases " cloud-bathed " and " velvety green ferns," but the tendency is to give generalized information.

For instance, concerning the rainbow, instead of giving us images which would stir our imaginations, the writers simply say, " The rainbow is a prominent feature of the tropic landscape." Or, instead of picturing for us the arid slopes of the leeward side of the mountains, the writers simply offer the phrase " all its devastating consequences to vegetation." The purpose of the description, then, is to present information; the chief structural features of the islands are identified, so that we may understand various other facts about the islands.

The second passage, like the first, is the description of a group of tropic islands. But Melville, the author, is not concerned to give us a list of the great geographic facts and their consequences. His description naturally involves some of these facts, but the passage is not organized about an enumeration of them. It is organized in such a way as to return the reader continually to the sense of loneliness, ruin, and desolation which characterizes the islands. He wants to give the reader an impression of the islands, a feeling for them, rather than a systematic analysis of their characteristics.

The passage begins with the comparison of heaps of cinders in a dumping ground, with the association of the used-up, the finished, the dreary. The first paragraph ends with the phrase " penal conflagration," which implies ideas not merely of ruin and waste but also of sin and punishment — sin and punishment on a universal scale. The next paragraph is based on the ideas of the unhuman desolation, the blankness. In the last paragraph appears again the image of the wasteland of cinders in the phrases " clinker-bound " and " like the dross of an iron furnace." And also in the constant tumult of the sea, in the phrase " lash and are lashed," appears the idea of punishment and suffering, which becomes explicit in the last sentence, " In no world but a fallen one could such lands exist."

In other words, the whole passage is based on two things: the image of the cinder heap and the idea of sin and punishment, which combine to give the notion of a world after the Judgment, the final desolation. And it is this notion that provides the organizing principle for the description. It is the key to the interpretation that Melville gives to his facts.

We do not expect to write like Melville, but if we examine some of the principles used by a great writer, we may be able to adapt them to our own more modest and ordinary needs. The principles of a good theme are the same as those Melville, or any of the other famous writers whom we shall look at, uses in his work. It is the principles we are concerned with, not mere imitation. Imitation is useful only if it makes us aware of principles.

Suggestive Description and the Senses

Suggestive description tells what impression the world makes on our senses. The apple is red, tweed is rough, lilies are fragrant. But these are crude and general bits of description and do not make us vividly aware of this apple or tweed or lily. A good writer would not be satisfied with this kind of description. He would want to make sharper discriminations. But to do so he would have to cultivate his power of observation. Even when he is writing of an imagined object rather than a real one, he will have to call on the store of impressions drawn from actual observation. Observation gives us our sense of the world.

Indeed, a person who wants to become a good writer should make some effort to train his powers of observation and to expand his vocabulary, especially in words that indicate differences in perception. He must tie his perceptions and his words together. The loud noise must cease to be loud noise for him and must become the crash, the bang, the thud, the clatter, the clash, the boom, the bong, the clang, the howl, the wail, the scream, or whatever most vividly presents the thing he has heard. And this applies equally to the other senses, for all the senses are important to the writer who wants to give a clear picture of the world.

Here are three bits of description, each one primarily concerned with impressions of a single sense. Note the discriminations made in each passage and the language used to record the observation.

To tell when the scythe is sharp enough this is the rule. First the stone clangs and grinds against the iron harshly; then it rings musically to one note; then, at last, it purrs as though the iron and stone were exactly suited. When you hear this, your scythe is sharp enough; and I, when I heard it that June dawn, with everything quite silent except the birds, let down the scythe and bent myself to mow.

— HILAIRE BELLOC: " The Mowing of a Field," *Hills and the Sea.*

The thing I chiefly remember about my grandfather's barn is the way it smelled. I reckon this is because when I was there I was often lying with my eyes closed, on the hay in the loft, with only the smell coming to me, or I was down in my little workshop and so preoccupied again that only the smells were there. Up in the loft, when I lay there on a rainy day, all I had to do was close my eyes, and there was the impression of a hayfield in summer, one of the days when I had had such a good time, the kind of dry, sweet smell you get from hay. When I was down in my workshop, there was the smell like ammonia from the stalls on one side, a clear, sharp sort of smell that makes your nose tingle. There was also the smell of good leather and saddle soap from the tack room. — From a theme.

When I think of hills, I think of the upward strength I tread upon. When water is the object of my thought, I feel the cool shock of the plunge and the quick yielding of the waves that crisp and curl and ripple about my body. The pleasing changes of rough and smooth, pliant and rigid, curved and straight in the bark and branches of a tree give the truth to my hand. The immovable rock, with its juts and warped surfaces, bends beneath my fingers into all manner of grooves and hollows. The bulge of a watermelon and the puffed-up rotundities of squashes that sprout, bud, and ripen in that strange garden planted somewhere behind my finger tips are the ludicrous in my tactual memory and imagination.

— HELEN KELLER: *The World I Live In.*

In the first of these selections the sense of hearing is dominant; in the second, the sense of smell; and in the third, the sense of touch. But in the third selection, which comes from a remarkable book written by a woman blind and deaf almost from birth, we also find temperature and pressure and strain: the coolness of water and the " upward strength " of the hill.

Ordinarily, however, we do not depend on one sense exclusively to give us our feeling of the world, because if we do, we tend to have one adjective tied to one noun, and the effect becomes mechanical and tiresome. It is tiresome because it is not letting the reader get a full sense of things. If we say, " The apple is red," we are not giving a very good impression of the apple. The apple is not only red; it is slick-looking and juicy-looking and fragrant. Our response to the apple is more massive than the response of one sense alone. If we say " slick-looking," we bring in another sense, touch. Or with " juicy-looking " we bring in taste. And sometimes with a single word we may evoke a whole series of different qualities, all at the same time — as, for example, if we say, " The ice is glassy," with the word *glassy* we evoke slickness, hardness, transparency, brightness. Or if we say " The clouds were cottony," the adjective evokes the texture as well as the appearance of cotton wool. Though description may occasionally confine itself to a single sense — and the sense of sight is the one we use most fully — description usually tries to give an impression of the fullness or massiveness of perception.

The use of description is not a trick we learn. It is our natural instinct to tell how things really are, how they really strike us. If we study description systematically, as we are now about to do, we are simply developing our natural instinct for observing the world around us and for communicating our observations to others.

• Application •

At the end of this chapter (pages 225–30) there is a group of examples of description. Read them carefully.

1. Do you find among them any examples of technical description? In examples that are prevailingly suggestive description, do you find any elements or sections that might appear in technical description?
2. Do you find any passages that are, for the most part, based on one sense?
3. Do you find any instances, say in a phrase or sentence, of the attempt to give the kind of massiveness of impression which we have been talking about?

Uses of Suggestive Description

In our study of exposition, we say (page 99) that technical description is concerned with providing information *about* things, and we distinguish it from suggestive description, which is not concerned with information *about* things but with the direct presentation *of* things. These two kinds of description correspond, we may say, to the two kinds of motives that may underlie our use of description.

We may think of this distinction as the fundamental distinction between the motive of the scientist and the motive of the artist. The scientist appeals to our interest *about* the world and to our interest in explanations *of* the world. He is concerned with the general laws of nature. The artist (of every kind — painter, poet, novelist, musician, and so on), on the other hand, appeals to our interest in the direct experience *of* the world. He is concerned with particulars as they strike him — particular experiences, particular objects. This is not to say that the artist may not be also concerned with generalizations — generalizations, for example, about human behavior. But the artist tends to approach even generalizations through the presentation of particulars. The novelist, for example, embodies his generalizations about human conduct in a particular story about a particular man, Sydney Carton or Silas Marner.

This distinction between the two kinds of motives means that we find technical description characteristically in scientific writing and suggestive description characteristically in the work of literary artists — poets or essayists or fiction writers. For instance, the geographers describing the West Indies in our first example are writing as scientists. They want to give *information about* the climate, vegetation, and so on, of the islands. Melville, describing his islands, is writing as an artist; he wants to give us the direct *impression of* the place and indicate to us how we might feel if we saw it.

Most of us are neither scientists nor artists, but we all have a little of the scientist and a little of the artist in us. We want to know about the world and we want to extend our experience of the world. These two kinds of interest lead us, in so far as we become well-developed human beings, to the use of the two kinds of description.

All of this does not mean that we find technical description only in scientific works and suggestive description only in artistic works. Technical description may occur in a letter, an essay, a guidebook, a history, an advertisement — wherever and whenever the impulse appears to give information about an object. By the same token, suggestive description may occur in any piece of writing at any point where the impulse for immediacy and vividness comes into play. Sometimes, both types appear in the same piece of writing.

• Application •

You have just read the description of the West Indies by the geographers and the description of the Encantadas by Melville. Turn back to the chapter on Exposition and read the realtor's advertisement of a house and the corresponding piece of suggestive description of the house in the letter (page 99). Also, glance again at the section on comparison and contrast in which we discussed how a thing may be regarded as belonging to different areas of interest — how, for example, a field may be regarded by a farmer, an infantry officer, and a painter (pages 88–89). Here, clearly, the farmer and infantry officer, if they had to write descriptions, would give us technical description. But the painter would be concerned with the appearance of the field, with the kind of description that might appear in a familiar letter or in a short story if the field were the setting of an episode.

Now select some object, such as the house, or some spot, such as the field, and write one paragraph — say 150 words — of technical description about it, in whatever area of interest you prefer. Then write a paragraph of suggestive description about the same thing.

Description and the Other Kinds of Discourse

Not infrequently we encounter pieces of technical description in isolation — an article for a specialist or a technician of some kind — and we often find technical description as an extended part of long works of exposition or argument. But suggestive description is not often used by itself in an extended passage. There are, of course, descriptive essays, but if they are even moderately long, they tend to bore us. They seem static. They " don't get anywhere."

Does this mean that description is a kind of discourse that we can lightly dismiss? No, for though it rarely stands alone and though it is usually brief, its effect is great. The vivid stroke of description, small in itself and apparently unimportant, may lend a needed touch of reality and stir the imagination.

Here is a piece of narrative which has been stripped of all its descriptive elements:

> The other waved the cigar, the other hand, in Horace's face. Horace shook it and freed his hand. " I thought I recognized you when you got on at Oxford," Snopes said, " but I — May I set down? " he said, already shoving at Horace's knee with his leg. He flung the overcoat on the seat and sat down as the train stopped. " Yes, sir, I'm always glad to see any of the boys, any time. . . ." He leaned across Horace and peered out the window at a station. " 'Course you ain't in my county no longer, but what I say a man's friends is his friends, whichever way they vote. Because a friend is a friend, and whether he can do anything for me or not. . . ." He leaned back, the cigar in his fingers.

Here is the passage in its original form, with the descriptive elements italicized. Note how they give the sense of reality, of the immediately observable world, to what otherwise would be a bare synopsis of events.

> The other waved the cigar, the other hand, *palm-up, the third finger discolored faintly at the base of a huge ring,* in Horace's face. Horace shook it and freed his hand. " I thought I recognized you when you got on at Oxford," Snopes said, " but I — May I set down? " he said, already shoving at Horace's knee with his leg. He flung the overcoat — *a shoddy blue garment with a greasy velvet collar* — on the seat and sat down as the train stopped. " Yes, sir, I'm always glad to see any of the boys, any time. . . ." He leaned across Horace and peered out the window at a *small dingy station with its cryptic bulletin board chalked over, an express truck bearing a wire chicken coop containing two forlorn fowls, at three or four men in overalls gone restfully against the wall, chewing.* " 'Course you ain't in my county no longer, but what I say a man's friends is his friends, whichever way they vote. Because a friend is a friend, and whether he can do anything for me or not. . . ." He leaned back, the *unlighted* cigar in his fingers.
>
> — WILLIAM FAULKNER: *Sanctuary.*

It is clear that in the passage above description is subordinate to narrative. As a matter of fact, description is usually subordinate when it appears mixed with some other kind of discourse. Nevertheless, without the resources of description most kinds of composition — fiction, poetry, letters, feature articles, reporting, history, essays, biography, speeches, and even certain kinds of philosophical writing — would be very bare and unconvincing. Description is far more important than its mere proportion in what we read would seem to indicate. And, furthermore, any attempt to understand its principles will sharpen our own perceptions and increase our pleasure in both our reading and the real world we live in.

The Dominant Impression

How often when we are trying to tell a friend how to recognize somebody we talk like this: " Just watch for that nose; it's the only nose like it in the state. Just think of W. C. Fields and his nose, and you won't miss Jack Purden." Or: " No, Susie isn't good looking, not if you look close. But you never look close, for she has those wonderful blue eyes. That's all you notice. They're so big and expressive."

When we talk like this, we are illustrating an important principle of description: the principle of the **dominant impression.**[1] Jack Purden's big, bulbous nose (probably with grog blossoms, too) and Susie's wonderful, expressive eyes are dominant features. We recognize the individual by the dominant impression he makes. But the same thing may be true of a place or of anything else as well as of a person. Here, for example, is a paragraph from a student theme in autobiography:

I was born and went to school in Cheyenne, Wyoming, but I never cared much about the town. What Easterners think romantic about it was just ordinary to me. What I cared about was the place we had for summers, not terribly far from Shoshone Falls. It is a valley with a river, and the valley and river suddenly widen out there with some alfalfa fields and trees and our place. But the big thing, the thing you always are conscious of, is the cliff on the west side. They call it Drum Mountain, because it looks like a drum, round-shaped, squat, and flat on top, an unusual shape for a mountain in that region. The first thing you look at in the morning is the sunlight hitting it and making the black rock glitter. It glitters then like it had fool's gold in it (iron pyrites, that is), but of course it hasn't. If it

---

[1] Something like this principle is used in caricature. The caricaturist sketches in the likeness with a few bold strokes and exaggerates certain expressive details. Any good political cartoonist will furnish a simple and effective example of the general method.

doesn't glitter, you think it won't be much of a day today, and the fishing will be rotten. Toward the middle of the afternoon, you suddenly know that the shadow of Old Drum is coming across everything. It makes a night down in the valley long before night comes, and it is peculiar to see bright sky off yonder, high up, when it is already getting dark in the valley. When there is going to be a full moon, the whole family will wait up to see when the moonlight first hits Drum Mountain. Then you go to bed, and I bet in some way Old Drum is always with you even when you are sound asleep.

Drum Mountain dominates the paragraph, provides the main impression, the unifying idea, even as it dominates the valley where the student goes for his summers.

A prominent thing catches the eye. But sometimes the mere prominence of an object is not what is important, is not what catches our interest. Some mood or feeling provoked by the object, even though we find it hard to pin it down to a particular detail, may strike us more strongly than any single, prominent physical feature. So when we describe something, we may be concerned not so much with making it merely recognizable, with indicating salient features, as with indicating how we feel about it, how we interpret it. Of course, since we are using description, we must present the object, but the dominant impression that we strive to give is a feeling provoked by the object — the mood, the atmosphere. So we use what elements in the object contribute to that dominant impression, and we may even comment on the impression itself.

We have already seen how Melville, in describing the Encantadas, keeps emphasizing the ruined, wasted, and tormented aspects in his impression of the islands, the aspects that point to his basic interpretation of the scene. True, the actual physical impression of the islands is strongly rendered. They are " clinker-bound," are like " the dross of an iron furnace." There are dark clefts and caves overhung by " a swirl of grey, haggard mist, amidst which sail screaming flights of unearthly birds." But this objective description is constantly moving over into an emphasis on Melville's own interpretation of the island as an image of ruin and punishment, as when, in the bit of quotation above, he calls the birds " unearthly," and as when, in the last sentence of the piece, he winds up with an explicit statement, " In no world but a fallen one could such lands exist."

We do not need to be as explicit as Melville, however, to convey very strongly a dominant mood for a thing described. Look at the following description by Dickens of a country estate in England:

The waters are out in Lincolnshire. An arch of the bridge in the park has been sapped and sopped away. The adjacent low-lying ground, for half a mile in breadth, is a stagnant river, with melancholy trees for islands in it, and a surface punctured all over, all day long, with falling rain. My Lady Dedlock's "place" has been extremely dreary. The weather, for many a day and night, has been so wet that the trees seem wet through, and the soft loppings and prunings of the woodsman's axe can make no crack or crackle as they fall. The deer, looking soaked, leave quagmires where they pass. The shot of a rifle loses its sharpness in the moist air, and its smoke moves in a tardy little cloud towards the green rise, coppice-topped, that makes a background for the falling rain. The view from my Lady Dedlock's own windows is alternately a lead-coloured view, and a view in Indian ink. The vases on the stone terrace in the foreground catch the rain all day; and the heavy drops fall, drip, drip, drip, upon the broad flagged pavement, called, from old time, the Ghost's Walk, all night. On Sundays, the little church in the park is mouldy; the oaken pulpit breaks out into a cold sweat; and there is a general smell and taste as of the ancient Dedlocks in their graves. — CHARLES DICKENS: *Bleak House.*

All the details are selected to reinforce the impression of dampness, depression, and gloom. The river is "stagnant," the blows of the ax make only "soft loppings," the report of the rifle "loses its sharpness in the moist air," the church is "mouldy," and the pulpit "breaks out into a cold sweat." Note how the phrase "breaks out into a cold sweat," though applied quite literally to the damp wood of the pulpit, actually serves to remind us of a situation that would make a human being do the same thing and leads us up to the "general taste and smell as of the ancient Dedlocks in their graves."

Items that might contradict the impression which Dickens wants dominant are left out. For example, if Dickens had presented the roaring fires on the hearths of the Dedlock mansion and the steaming roasts and puddings, he would have distracted from the impression he wished to make. Undoubtedly, as a matter of fact, the Dedlock family would have had roaring fires and steaming roasts, but that is beside the point.

Dickens, as we have seen, depends primarily on the piling up of details supporting the main impression. Only twice does he use a word that is explicit: *melancholy* (once) and *dreary* (once).

Let us turn to a piece of description within our own present range, a passage from a student autobiography:

You know, in the country, what the middle of an afternoon in summer can be. Maybe a rooster crows, far off, down back of the barn, and you hear it, but it seems as though it is lost in the stillness. As soon as the sound is gone, you don't believe it ever happened. That was the way it was, day after day, at my aunt's house, in summer. If I walked down the road toward the pike, just to see if anything might be passing, the dust was so thick in the lane I didn't make any more sound than a ghost, and if some bird or animal moved back in the brush by the field, it would scare me. This was of course, when I was little, say about eight. Maybe I would be down at the pike a half hour, and nothing would pass, and then I would come back to the house, an old-fashioned white farmhouse, and go in. It was always dim in the house, and for coolness I might go in the shut-up parlor and lie on the floor, where a little light came in under the blinds, and read. It was as quiet as being under water, and you thought no time could be passing anywhere. You thought it would be a big, important event if a leaf fell off the white oak outside the window.

In the above passage the author has, as we say, created a certain atmosphere. By atmosphere we mean the mood, the general feeling associated in the description with the scene, person, or event described. We have the atmosphere of gloom and dampness and decay in the description by Dickens and that of peace in the student theme.

We know, however, even as we use these words to define the atmosphere of this or that piece of description, that the labels we put on the passages are too vague and loose to define really the effect that they give. Our defining words do not really define the atmosphere; they merely give a kind of crude indication, a not very dependable clue, to the effect that we find in the actual description.

Our inability to define the atmosphere in general terms indicates the importance of the way the author himself goes about presenting it to us. He knows that he cannot create the desired mood or atmosphere simply by using the loose, general words which we have used above in trying to define the effect of the passages. Therefore, he undertakes to give us such concrete details, such aspects of his object as will stir our imaginations not only to grasp the appearance of the object (or the sound, the color, and so forth), but to adopt a certain feeling toward the object.

We have said earlier that suggestive description aims *not to tell* us about its object, but *to give* us the object. It also can be said that it aims *not to tell* us what feelings to have about the object and what attitudes to take toward it, but *to create* those feelings and attitudes within us. Vividness and immediacy, not only in regard to the physical qualities of the object, but in regard to the feelings and attitudes involved, are what the writer desires.

• **Applications** •

I. From the set of examples at the end of this chapter (pages 225–30), select two that give a dominant impression by emphasizing some prominent feature of the thing described. Then select two that seem successful in creating a dominant impression of mood. In these latter two examples, underscore the details that contribute to the dominant impression. Do you find any contradictory details?

II. Think of some place with which you are well acquainted that impresses you as having a very definite mood. Make an informal list of the items of the place that contribute to this dominant impression. Make another list of items that seem contradictory.

Selection

In discussing dominant impression, we made a distinction between features of an object that are impressive in themselves and features that are important because they contribute to the mood or atmosphere. We might say, then, that details in description are important for either vividness or significance, though we know all the while, of course, that vividness and significance tend to merge. But in any case, the vividness and significance of details is what makes us select them in a piece of description. The power of observation, as we have said, is essential, but we cannot merely accumulate details. We must choose the telling ones. Description works by **selection,** and when we are studying description, we ought to get the habit of asking ourselves, over and over again, " Why did he select this detail? " Or, " Why that one? " Or, " Why does this detail stir my imagination, and why does that one fail to do so? "

Let us look at a few examples in which the reasons for selecting details differ.

Here is the description of a town as approached from the sea. The most obvious quality of what is emphasized, the blinding brilliance of light, strikes the observer at the first moment.

But when at last we anchored in the outer harbor, off the white town hung between the blazing sky and its reflections in the mirage which swept and rolled over the wide lagoon, then the heat of Arabia came out like a drawn sword and struck us speechless. It was midday; and the noon sun in the East, like moonlight, put to sleep the colors. There were only lights and shadows, the white houses and black gaps of streets; in front, the pallid lustre of the haze shimmering upon the inner harbors; behind, the dazzle of league after league of featureless sand, running up to an edge of low hills, faintly suggested in the far away mist of heat.

— T. E. LAWRENCE: *Seven Pillars of Wisdom.*

Vividness, however, may be gained by indicating some detail which might escape ordinary observation. In such a case, it is the precision and subtlety of the description that makes the thing being described come alive for us. John Burroughs, the naturalist, in a passage on the art of observation, gives a list of details which would escape most observers but which sharply evoke a series of scenes and moments:

His [the naturalist's] senses are so delicate that in his evening walk he feels the warm and cool streaks in the air, his nose detects the most fugitive odors, his ears the most furtive sounds. As he stands musing in the April twilight, he hears that fine, elusive stir and rustle made by the angleworms reaching out from their holes for leaves and grasses; he hears the whistling wings of the woodcock as it goes swiftly by him in the dusk; he hears the call of the killdee come down out of the March sky; he hears far above him in the early morning the squeaking cackle of the arriving blackbirds pushing north; he hears the soft, prolonged, lulling call of the little owl in the cedars in the early spring twilight; he hears at night the roar of the distant waterfall, and the rumble of the train miles across country when the air is " hollow "; before a storm he notes how distant objects stand out and are brought near on those brilliant days that we call " weather-breeders." When the mercury is at zero or lower, he notes how the passing trains hiss and simmer as if the rails or wheels were red-hot.

— JOHN BURROUGHS: *Leaf and Tendril.*

The rustling of the angleworms gives a vivid and immediate sense of the stillness, more vivid and immediate than any number of the usual and easily observable details. Or take the squeaking cackle of the blackbirds; it is the absolutely right phrase to describe the sound, and because of the accuracy of the observation, our imagination fills the sky with the flock of birds passing over. Or think how striking are the *hiss* and *simmer* of the train on the rails!

The process of seizing on either the striking characteristic or the small, sharply perceived detail may lead to exaggeration and caricature. The detail, as it were, becomes the whole object. In the first of the following passages, Dickens takes the obvious oiliness of Mr. Chadband as the key to the description of his appearance and, finally, of his character:

Mr. Chadband is a large yellow man, with a fat smile, and a general appearance of having a good deal of train oil in his system. Mrs. Chadband is a stern, severe-looking, silent woman. Mr. Chadband moves softly and cumbrously, not unlike a bear who has been taught to walk upright. He is very much embarrassed about the arms, as if they were inconvenient to him, and he wanted to grovel; is very much in a perspiration about the head; and never speaks without first putting up his great hand, as delivering a token to his hearers that he is going to edify them.

— CHARLES DICKENS: *Bleak House.*

Dickens uses a striking detail and exaggerates it into the whole person, and in the following passage the writer uses caricature, the trivial detail of Miss Plimsoll's nose — and the little drop of moisture at its tip — as the main feature of the comic and pitiful portrait of the poor old maid.

Miss Plimsoll's nose was sharp and pointed like that of Voltaire. It was also extremely sensitive to cold. When the thermometer fell below 60° it turned scarlet; below 50° it assumed a blue tinge with a little white morbid circle at the end; and at 40° it became sniffly and bore a permanent though precarious drop below its pointed tip. I remember with what interest I watched that drop as we drove from the station at Sofia. My parents went in front in the first carriage and Miss Plimsoll and I followed in the brougham. The night was cold and we drove along an endless windswept boulevard punctuated by street lamps. With the approach of each successive lamp Miss Plimsoll's pinched little face beside me would first be illuminated frontways, and then as we came opposite the lamp, spring into a sharp little silhouette, at the point of which the drop flashed and trembled like a diamond.   — HAROLD NICOLSON: "Miss Plimsoll," *Some People*.

• **Applications** •

I. From examples of description already studied in this chapter and in the group of examples at the end (pages 225–30), indicate some details which are used because they are striking and some that are used because they are suggestive and provoke the imagination of the reader.

II. Locate an example, in the selections at the end of the chapter, of the method of caricature or exaggeration. (See page 204.)

III. Locate, in the examples at the end of the chapter, two instances in which description leads the reader to an understanding of the character of the person described. Try to define in general terms the character of the person presented. What evidence among the details of the portrait can you find for your interpretation?

IV. Write a brief description (from 250 to 300 words) of some character of your acquaintance. Use the method of caricature, if you wish.

Choice of Words [2]

Inexperienced writers tend to make adjectives bear the burden in description. An inexperienced writer tends to overload his descrip-

---

[2] The problem of diction, the choice of words, is naturally important for all writing and is discussed in detail elsewhere in this book; see especially pages 300–01.

tion with adjectives, with the idea of specifying all the qualities of the thing being presented. Such a writer forgets that suggestion is often better than enumeration and that the mere listing of qualities is not the best method of evoking an image in the reader's mind. Let us look at the following portrait:

The woman's face was fat and shapeless, so fat that it looked very soft, flabby, grayish, and unhealthy. The features were blurred because her face was fat. But her small, black, glistening eyes had a quick inquisitive motion as they moved from one face to another while the visitors stated their errand.

In that description the writer has piled up the adjectives, trying to specify each of the qualities of the woman's face and eyes. The result is a rather confused impression. Let us now take the passage as William Faulkner originally wrote it (before we tampered with it):

Her eyes, lost in the fatty ridges of her face, looked like two small pieces of coal pressed into a lump of dough as they moved from one face to another while the visitors stated their errand.

— WILLIAM FAULKNER: "A Rose for Emily."

Here the writer has managed to dispense with most of the adjectives, for the word *dough* implies *soft, flabby, grayish, shapeless, blurred,* and (when associated with flesh) *unhealthy,* and the word *coal* implies *black* and *glistening.* The use of a comparison of this kind will frequently enable the writer to dispense with adjectives. But when the writer does use adjectives, he should be sure that each adjective really adds something essential to the description. Rather than give the list of adjectives above, one could simply say that the face was " fat and doughy."

The discussion above really returns us to the question of selection. But here we are talking about diction — the selection of words rather than details. Although adjectives are an essential part of every writer's equipment, one can frequently get greater vividness by using nouns, adverbs, verbs, and verbals. (For verbals, see Handbook, page 767.) For instance, note the descriptive force of the italicized nouns in the following examples:

The very smoke coming out of their chimneys was poverty-stricken. Little *rags* and *shreds* of smoke, so unlike the great silvery *plumes* that uncurled from the Sheridans' chimneys.

— KATHERINE MANSFIELD: "The Garden Party."

They crept up the hill in the twilight and entered the cottage. It was built of *mud-walls,* the surface of which had been washed by many rains into *channels* and *depressions* that left none of the original flat *face* visible: while here and there in the thatch above a rafter showed like a *bone* protruding through the *skin*.   — THOMAS HARDY: " The Withered Arm."

And a wind blew there, tossing the withered tops of last year's grasses, and *mists* ran with the wind, and ragged *shadows* with the *mists,* and *mare's-tails* of clear *moonlight* among the *shadows,* so that now the boles of birches on the forest's edge beyond the fences were but opal *blurs* and now cut alabaster.   — WILBUR DANIEL STEELE: " How Beautiful with Shoes."

We can see that in these passages the nouns are of two kinds. First, there are those which simply point to some items in the thing described, such as *channels, depressions, mists, shadows, moonlight*. Second, there are those which involve comparisons, such as *rags, shreds, alabaster, bone,* and *skin*.

When we turn to the use of adverbs, we find that this part of speech sometimes enables a writer to get an effect with great economy by fusing the quality of a thing with its action. When Dickens writes, in describing Chadband, that he " moves softly and cumbrously, not unlike a bear who has been taught to walk upright," the adverbs *softly* and *cumbrously* give a much more vivid and immediate effect than would be possible if we broke up the description in the following fashion: " Mr. Chadband is soft, heavy, and awkward-looking. When he walks his motion is not unlike that of a bear which has been taught to walk upright." But adverbs, like other parts of speech, are subject to misuse. Vague, overworked " intensifiers " like *very, so,* and *really* often actually weaken the effect of a passage.

In the following description of a Mexican revolutionist who is (as we could know from the whole story from which the paragraph comes) both sentimental and cruel, energetic and self-indulgent, lazy and sinister, note how the details selected are expressive of that character:

Braggioni catches her glance *solidly* as if he had been waiting for it, leans forward, *balancing* his paunch between his spread knees, and sings with tremendous emphasis, *weighing* his words. He had, the song relates, no father and no mother, nor even a friend to console him; lonely as a wave of the sea he comes and goes, lonely as a wave. His mouth opens round and *yearns sideways,* his balloon cheeks grow oily with the labor of the song. He *bulges marvellously* in his expensive garments. Over his lavender collar, crushed upon a purple necktie, held by a diamond hoop; over his ammunition belt of tooled leather worked in silver, buckled *cruelly* around his gaping middle; over the tops of his glossy yellow shoes Braggioni *swells* with ominous ripeness, his mauve silk hose stretched taut, his ankles bound with the stout leather thongs of his shoes.

When he *stretches* his eyelids at Laura she notes again that his eyes are tawny yellow cat's eyes. — KATHERINE ANNE PORTER: " Flowering Judas."

We have italicized the adverbs, verbs, and verbals that seem expressive. Think how right and unexpected the word *solidly* is as applied to the way Braggioni catches the girl's glance — the sense of his massiveness and imperviousness and, perhaps, brutality, and the sense, too, as indicated in the clause, " as if he had been waiting for it," of his being braced in calculation. Or think of the sense of theatricality in the image of the fat man twisting his mouth sideways in his sentimental song, a song so unlike his real nature. If the writer had merely put down that he had opened his round mouth in song, we wouldn't have much to stir our imagination, the description would lack expressiveness. Or take *marvellously* and *cruelly,* and consider what they imply not only about the visual image but about the personality of the man.

In the use of verbs, the same concentration of effect is possible; for frequently the right verb can imply something about the nature of the thing or person performing an action as well as about the nature of the action. For instance, the verbs *yearns* and *bulges* are extremely important. *Yearns* implies the sentimental expression on the fat revolutionist's face, and *bulges* implies the brute heft of the man, in contrast to the sentimental song he sings. So the two verbs here really indicate the contrast in his nature as well as in his appearance. What is the significance of the other verbs?

In the following passage, which describes a herd of wild horses corralled in a barn lot, note how the variety and accuracy of the italicized verbs and verbals give the impression of furious, aimless motion and define the atmosphere of violence of the scene:

" Come on, grab a holt," the Texan said. Eck grasped the wire also. The horses *laid* back against it, the pink faces *tossing* above the *backsurging* mass. " Pull him up, pull him up," the Texan said sharply. " They couldn't get up here in the wagon even if they wanted to." The wagon moved gradually backward until the head of the first horse was *snubbed* up to the tail-gate. The Texan took a turn of wire quickly about one of the wagon stakes. " Keep the slack out of it," he said. He *vanished* and *reappeared,* almost in the same second, with a pair of heavy wire-cutters. " Hold them like that," he said, and *leaped.* He *vanished,* broad hat, *flapping* vest, wire-cutters and all, into a kaleidoscopic maelstrom of long teeth and wild eyes and *slashing* feet, from which presently the horses began to burst, one by one like partridges *flushing,* each wearing a necklace of barbed wire. The first one crossed the lot at top speed, on a straight line. It *galloped* into the fence without any diminution whatever. The wire *gave, recovered,* and *slammed* the horse to earth where it lay for a moment, *glaring,* its legs still *galloping* in air. It scrambled up without having ceased to gallop and crossed the lot and *galloped* into the opposite fence and was *slammed* again to earth. The others were now freed. They *whipped* and *whirled* about the lot like dizzy fish in a bowl. It had seemed like a big lot until now, but now the very idea that all that fury and motion should be transpiring inside any one fence was something to be repudiated with contempt like a mirror trick.   — WILLIAM FAULKNER: *The Hamlet*.

A good writer can make adjectives, nouns, adverbs, and verbs all serve his purpose. He can blend them to give his effect.

Now let us look at a student theme. This theme is, essentially, a piece of narrative; however, description, as we have said, may be importantly involved with any other form of discourse. So let us try to see what its importance is here; let us see, in other words, to what extent vividness of description might contribute to our acceptance of the narrated event.

GETTING ENGAGED

It had been such a lovely day, perfectly lovely. There was bright sun and the ocean as still as the ocean ever gets, with a slow swell and instead of waves just some ripples now and then. Joseph had taken me out in his little putt-putt to the island to fish and have a picnic. We fished from the boat, and then came ashore to eat lunch. We ate, then got in the shade of the rocks and sort of dozed off. At least, I did. I woke up with a start. Joseph had called me, I guess. It was easy to tell why. Off yonder, beyond where the sun was still shining, you could see the clouds piling up high. They were black and gray with some purple. It was like a cliff that somehow grew taller while you looked at it.

It fascinated you to watch it. I couldn't take my eyes off, and then I took a look at Joseph. He was looking at the clouds, too. It was a funny expression, sort of rapt and awe-struck, you might say. And suddenly he seemed so much younger than I had thought of him. It was like a little boy's face, with eyes wide while he looked at the clouds. There was some oil on his left cheek, toward me, and some sand was there in the oil.

He came out of his trance. "Gosh," he said, "gosh, did you ever!" He suddenly went toward the boat, fast as a basketball player catching the ball and turning toward the basket for a shot. (Joseph is a wonderful basketball player.) "Grab the stuff, girlie, and come on!" he said.

I got in, and he shoved off and climbed over the side. He began to pull the lanyard to start the motor. He was nervous, not under control. Then the lanyard broke. I looked into his face and knew what had happened. We were in trouble.

Then he grinned. He looked somewhat scared, but he grinned. "Girlie," he said, "Old Joe got you into this and I reckon he will get you out."

Then he stopped grinning. He picked up the oars and put them in the oarlocks, not in a hurry. His face was different from what I had ever seen it to be. It looked like a man's face now, and I knew the way he would look at forty or forty-five, or a thousand. I thought that that was a face I wouldn't mind looking at for a long time.

To make a long story short, we did manage to get in, but it was a tough trip. That evening I got engaged.

Here is the same theme as revised after discussion with the instructor. Some of the changes are, it is obvious, to improve paragraph and sentence structure, but by and large, the revision has been directed toward making the description of the scene and the actions more vivid.

GETTING ENGAGED

It had been such a lovely day, perfectly lovely, with bright sun and the ocean as still as the ocean ever gets, a slow swell like somebody breathing in an easy sleep, and instead of waves a lazy rippling now and then that made you think of a cat waking up and stretching in the sunshine, and then dozing off again. Joseph had taken me out in his little putt-putt to the island to fish and have a picnic. After we had fished and come ashore to eat our lunch, we lay in the shade of the rocks and sort of dozed off. At least, I did. I woke up with a start. Joseph had called me, I guess. It was easy to tell why.

Off yonder, beyond the glitter of the water where the sun still struck, you could see the clouds piling up like a cliff, black and slate-colored, streaked with purple. I said like a cliff, but it was like a cliff that somehow, momentarily, grew taller while you stared at it, looking awfully solid but somehow swelling and coiling upward at the same time.

It fascinated you to watch it. I couldn't take my eyes off it, and then I sneaked a look at Joseph. He was staring at it, too. He had a funny expression, sort of rapt and awe-struck. And suddenly he looked so much younger than I had thought of him. It was a little boy's face, round and tanned, with eyes brown and wide while he stared. There was a smudge of oil on the left cheek and some white sand had stuck untidily in the oil, against the brown skin.

He jerked out of his trance. " Gosh," he said, " gosh, did you ever! " He suddenly swung toward the boat, fast as a basketball forward snagging the ball and swinging toward the basket for a shot. (Joseph is a wonderful basketball player.) " Grab the stuff, girlie, and come on! " he yelled.

I got in, and he shoved off and piled over the side. He was jerking the lanyard to start the motor. It was a nervous motion, not steady and controlled, with the right pause, like a count between tries. Then the lanyard snapped, and Joseph was looking stupidly down at the piece in his hand. Then he looked up at me. I knew that that was that. One look at his face, and I knew we were in trouble.

Then he grinned. He grinned twistedly, with the lips tightening and a little white showing splotchily at the corners of the mouth, even under the tan. But it was a grin. " Girlie," he said, " Old Joe got you into this, and

I reckon he will have to get you out." All at once, like the edge of a knife blade coming down, the grin was cut off. He grabbed the oars, fast all right, but he set them competently into the oarlocks, without any jiggling.

His face was different from what I had ever seen before. And all at once I knew it was a man's face, and I knew the way he would look when he was forty years old, or forty-five, or a thousand. I thought that that was a face I wouldn't mind looking at for a long time.

To make a long story short, we did manage to get in, but it was a tough trip. That evening we got engaged.

• Applications •

I. In the passage by D. H. Lawrence (E, page 226) at the end of this chapter, locate some adjectives, nouns, adverbs, and verbs which you think are used with strong descriptive effect. (If you have any uncertainty as to the parts of speech, turn to page 729 of the Handbook.) In each case try to explain what makes the word effective. How would you characterize the atmosphere of the passage?

II. In the student theme above, make a detailed comparison of the two versions. Perhaps the best way would be to underscore all the changes in the revised version. Then, item by item, try to read the mind of the author in making the revisions. What, in each instance, is at stake?

Texture and Pattern in Description

Thus far in this chapter we have been concerned with the observation of details, the relation of such details to a dominant impression of the thing described, and the choice of words in giving description. We may call the combination of these three things the **texture** of description.

In so far as the details of description relate to the dominant impression, they have some principle of order, and in the last analysis the relation of details to the dominant impression is the most important single consideration. But we also must think of the way details are grouped in relation to the structure of the thing described — whatever that thing is, a landscape, an object, a human face. We cannot simply list details at random, even when they do contribute to a dominant impression. There must be some principle of **pattern**.

Pattern and Point of View

If one observes a person, an object, or a scene, one notes that each has its proper unity — in a flash we recognize a friend, a tree, a familiar room, a meadow with woods beyond. But if, when we set out to describe one of these things, we give a mere catalogue of unrelated details, a mere enumeration of this, that, and the other, the sense of vital unity is gone.

The reason is not far to seek. When we look at something, even though our attention is focused on some one aspect, we are constantly aware of the totality; it is all there before us at one time. In description, however, the details are presented to us one after another; instead of the simultaneous presentation which we find in fact, we now have presentation in sequence. Since simultaneous presentation is impossible in description, the writer must provide some pattern into which the reader can fit the details if he is to give them a proper unity.

When we are dealing with visual description, which is by far the most common kind, it helps to give an impression of unity if we think of whatever is being described as seen by an observer. We need not specify the observer literally in the description; we may merely imply such a presence by the way we give the details of the description. We simply ask how, under such-and-such conditions and from such-and-such a location, would an observer see the details?

The most obvious and simple pattern is to assume an observer at some fixed point from which he views the whole scene or object and then reads off the details from left to right, from foreground to background, from bottom to top, or in some such way. In other words, we simply take the details as they come in the object itself, starting from some arbitrary point. Here is an example from a theme:

When I went home from college for Christmas, I got in on the night train, and as soon as the excitement wore off, I went straight upstairs to bed in my old room, where I had been ever since my baby days. I was so sleepy I didn't see a thing. I just tumbled in. But I woke up early. I couldn't hear a sound in the house, and so I lay there idly just looking around. Suddenly I felt as though this were the first time I had ever been in that room, it was so strange.

Way at the left of my range of vision was the closet, with the door open, the way I must have left it the night before. Inside I could see my summer dresses hanging up in covers, all neat as a pin, and my shoes on racks. I remembered how untidy I had left things and thought that my mother must have done that for me. Next was my dressing table, almost bare, for I had taken a lot of things with me to college, but what was there was in order, laid out to the quarter of an inch on the glass top. Around the mirror were still stuck some invitations and things, keepsakes from my last year in high school. Then on the wall was a water color I had done in art class, and it was awful — a river too blue, I knew now, and a sunset like a fried egg with catsup.

Then I looked out the window, turning my head on the pillow just a little toward the wall opposite the bed, and I could see the blue patch of sky, no clouds at all, and the snow on the steep, jumbled-up roofs of the Madison place, which is very Victorian, with sharp roofs and little turrets, with lightning rods and weathervanes. You know the kind of place, for every town has a few left. I wondered about Jack Madison, for on the wall just to the right of the window was the Harvard pennant he had given me last summer because he was going to be a freshman at Harvard. I thought now that he was probably ashamed of that, as kid stuff.

Beyond the pennant was my high school picture, the ordinary kind, with the boys looking awful stiff and trying to be grown-up, and the girls all cocking their heads trying to look glamorous like movie queens. I sort of smiled, looking at them, they were so kid-looking and unsophisticated, you might say. Then, all at once I thought that I was in the picture, too, and the silliest one of the lot. I blushed to think how silly. Then suddenly I felt sad. It was as though I had died, that was why everything was so tidy in the room, and I was somebody else who happened to be sleeping in a strange room where somebody else used to live and had died.

The girl who writes the theme has a general idea, of course. She is now grown-up and away at college, and she wants to tell how she feels when she comes back home for the first time. This idea provides the dominant impression she is trying to give: the sense of strangeness and, also, the awareness of a kind of loss. But what we are concerned with at the moment is not the impression she wants to convey, but the way the details which produce the impression are put into order. The order she uses is almost the simplest possible: as she lies on her pillow her glance moves from left to right, and she simply lists the things she sees.

Here is another example, written not by a student this time, but by a famous writer. He is addressing an imaginary companion — the reader — who is supposed to stand by his side looking up at an English cathedral. But the author here, though his description is much more elaborate than that in the girl's theme, uses the same basic pattern, listing items in the simple order of observation, this time from bottom to top.

And so, taking care not to tread on the grass, we will go along the straight walk to the west front, and there stand for a time, looking up at its deep-pointed porches and the dark places between their pillars where there were statues once, and where fragments, here and there, of a stately figure are still left, which has in it the likeness of a king, perhaps indeed a king on earth, perhaps a saintly king long ago in heaven; and so higher and higher up to the great mouldering wall of rugged sculpture and confused arcades, shattered, and grey, and grisly with head of dragons and mocking fiends, worn by the rain and swirling winds into yet unseemlier shape, and coloured on their stony scales by the deep russet-orange lichen, melancholy gold; and so, higher still, to the bleak towers, so far above that the eye loses itself among the bosses of their traceries, though they are rude and strong, and only sees, like a drift of eddying black points, now closing, now scattering, and now settling suddenly into invisible places among the bosses and flowers, the crowd of restless birds that fill the whole square with that strange clangour of theirs, so harsh and yet so soothing, like the cries of birds on a solitary coast between the cliffs and sea.

— JOHN RUSKIN: *The Stones of Venice.*

The two pieces of description above have been given from a fixed point — the girl's pillow when she wakes up and the open space at the west front of a cathedral in England. But often we find it more useful to think of a moving observer — either a real one, quite literally specified, or an imaginary one, not specified. In the following example a real person is really climbing up a gorge in Arabia, over the pass, and down the other side. He reports things as he comes to them in his movement.

Our path took us between the Sakhara and the Sukhur by a narrow gorge with sandy floor and steep bare walls. Its head was rough. We had to scramble up shelves of coarse-faced stone, and along a great fault in the hill-side between two tilted red reefs of hard rock. The summit of the pass was a knife-edge, and from it we went down an encumbered gap, half-blocked by one fallen boulder which had been hammered over with the tribal marks of all the generations of men who had used this road. Afterwards there opened tree-grown spaces, collecting grounds in winter for the sheets of rain which poured off the glazed sides of the Sukhur. There were granite outcrops here and there, and a fine silver sand underfoot in the still damp water-channels. The drainage was towards Heiran.

— T. E. LAWRENCE: *Seven Pillars of Wisdom.*

In the following description of the main street of a little Middle-Western town, no observer is specified. The details are shown, one after another, not even put in complete sentences, merely listed, jotted down as they were. (This loose method, the use of jottings as a style of presentation, is called *impressionistic.*) The whole effect is as though a movie camera has simply swung over the street, picking up a detail here, a detail there.

From a second-story window the sign, "W. P. Kennicott, Phys. & Surgeon," gilt on black sand.

A small wooden motion-picture theater called "The Rosebud Movie Palace." Lithographs announcing a film called, "Fatty in Love."

Howland & Gould's Grocery. In the display window, black, overripe bananas and lettuce on which a cat was sleeping. Shelves lined with red crepe paper which was now faded and torn and concentrically spotted. Flat against the wall of the second story the signs of the lodges — the Knights of Pythias, the Maccabees, the Woodmen, the Masons.

Dahl & Oleson's Meat Market — a reek of blood.

— SINCLAIR LEWIS: Main Street.

This impressionistic method, the use of jottings as a style of presentation, seems easy, and therefore tempting — we don't have to bother with sentence structure or even with paragraph structure. But the very easiness is a danger. It is easy to be tedious, to accumulate too many details, to lose all sense of structure and of a dominant impression. To be effective in this method we have to be very careful that the details are telling, are sharp, and we must not pile up so many details that the sense of a whole is lost.

In any case, we must remember that the impressionistic method is not the only method to be used with the moving, unspecified point of view; there can be description with an unspecified observer and with a moving point of view that does *not* use the impressionistic method, as in the following passage from a theme:

The approach to ———— is anything but attractive, and it is made worse by the contrast with the nice hilly country the road has just passed through, where there are lots of woods and streams. The first thing one sees on the approach is a paper mill, where they convert the pulp. It is a big, sprawly, disorderly looking mass of buildings, two of them very high. They are drab colored. The smell is awful, and what they do to Techifaloo River is a caution, for the waste goes in there.

After the paper plant come the real Negro slums of the town. They are mostly shacks, but farther on are quite a few very nice houses, with good lawns and flowerbeds, for the position of the Negro is improving in ————. For one thing, beyond the nice section of Negro houses is the Negro hospital, a fine new brick building, modern in style. It is as nice as anything in town, or nicer, for my money. There are two fine Negro doctors in town, and one writes articles for medical journals and things.

The warehouse section begins not far beyond the hospital, for here is where the railroads from the east cross the Techifaloo. . . .

There is some incidental comment and opinion here, along with the description, but the description itself is patterned by the eye of an unspecified observer assumed to be entering the town by the highway.

Pattern by Interest

So far we have talked of unifying a description by assuming an observer who actually sees the details of the object in some physical order — say from left to right, or as he comes to them in moving. But let us assume an observer who is less passive, who brings some strong interest to the thing described. This interest then gives us the unity for describing the object. Here is a soldier inspecting a bridge he is about to dynamite. The structure of the bridge and the location of the enemy defenses give focus to the description.

The late afternoon sun that still came over the brown shoulder of the mountain showed the bridge dark against the steep emptiness of the gorge. It was a steel bridge of a single span and there was a sentry box at each end. It was wide enough for two motor cars to pass and it spanned, in solid-flung metal grace, a deep gorge at the bottom of which, far below, a brook leaped in white water through rocks and boulders down to the main stream of the pass.

The sun was in Robert Jordan's eyes and the bridge showed only in outline. Then the sun lessened and was gone and looking up through the trees at the brown, rounded height that it had gone behind, he saw, now that he no longer looked into the glare, that the mountain slope was a delicate new green and that there were patches of old snow under the crest.

Then he was looking at the bridge again in the sudden short trueness of the little light that would be left, and studying its construction. The problem of its demolition was not difficult. As he watched he took out a notebook from his breast pocket and made several quick line sketches. As he made the drawings he did not figure the charges. He would do that later. Now he was noting the points where the explosive should be placed in order to cut the support of the span and drop a section of it back into the gorge. It could be done unhurriedly, scientifically and correctly with a half dozen charges laid and braced to explode simultaneously; or it could be done roughly with two big ones. They would need to be very big ones, on opposite sides and should go at the same time.

— ERNEST HEMINGWAY: *For Whom the Bell Tolls.*[3]

Here the dynamiter's interest in the bridge holds the passage together. In the passage below, the comparison which Huckleberry Finn draws between houses in town and the house of the Grangerford plantation provides the unifying interest.

It was a mighty nice family, and a mighty nice house, too. I hadn't seen no house out in the country before that was so nice and had so much style.

[3] From *For Whom the Bell Tolls* by Ernest Hemingway. Copyright 1940 by Charles Scribner's Sons.

It didn't have an iron latch on the front door, nor a wooden one with a buckskin string, but a brass knob to turn, the same as houses in a town. There warn't no bed in the parlor, nor a sign of a bed; but heaps of parlors in town has beds in them. There was a big fireplace that was bricked on the bottom, and the bricks was kept clean and red by pouring water on them and scrubbing them with another brick; sometimes they washed them over with red water-paint that they call Spanish-brown, same as they do in town. They had big brass dog-irons that could hold up a saw-log. There was a clock on the middle of the mantel piece, with a picture of a town painted on the bottom half of the glass front, and a round place in the middle of it for the sun, and you could see the pendulum swinging behind it.

— SAMUEL CLEMENS: *The Adventures of Huckleberry Finn.*

And let us remember that, sometimes, the mood itself may serve as the device for unifying a description, as for instance in Dickens' description of the Dedlock estate.

Frame Image

So far we have been concerned with unifying description by reference to an observer, specified or unspecified, but the use of an observer is not the only possibility. For instance, a writer may compare the rather complicated object he is describing with something simpler and more easily visualized, and this simpler object is then imagined as providing a kind of **frame image** into which we can fit the details of the original thing to be described. Here is the image of an arm used to give unity to an impression of Cape Cod:

Cape Cod is the bared and bended arm of Massachusetts; the shoulder is Buzzard's Bay; the elbow, or crazy-bone, at Cape Mallebarre; the wrist at Truro; and the sand fist at Provincetown, — behind which the state stands on her guard, with her back to the Green Mountains, and her feet planted on the floor of the ocean, like an athlete protecting her Bay, — boxing with northeast storms, and, ever and anon, heaving up her Atlantic adversary from the lap of earth, — ready to thrust forward her other fist, which keeps guard while upon her breast at Cape Ann.

— HENRY DAVID THOREAU: *Cape Cod.*

In this example, the writer has begun by providing the frame image and then giving the details which are to be set in the frame. But sometimes the writer will reverse the process; that is, he will first give the details, perhaps a swarm of them, which stimulate and baffle the reader's imagination, and then give the frame image which will suddenly reduce all to order. Here is a very simple example of the method in a student theme:

My roommate is very fat and sort of bleared-looking. His eyes are large and round. They are the palest blue you ever saw, and they tend to be watery and blinking. His nose is shapeless, just a kind of aimless blob of putty stuck on his face, and his lips are so thick and sort of loose that his small mouth looks as though he is about to whistle or has just tasted a dill pickle and didn't like it too well. His hair is pale blond, almost albino but not quite, and it never lies in place. It isn't thick, but it is always scruffed up in all directions. He is the sort of person who is always sleepy, and when I wake him up in the morning and he lifts his head off the pillow, with that bleared look and his face so round, I always think of a moon coming up in a watery haze that blurs its shape and makes it lose outline.

It is clear what the writer has done. He has given the details — eyes, nose, mouth, hair — and then absorbed them into one image, the round rising moon blurred in a watery haze. Of course, the image of the watery moon does contribute something to the dominant impression, the blurred, slow, confused appearance of the roommate, but it also gives a frame for putting the details in place; it pulls them together.

Mixed Patterns

We have been trying to distinguish several typical ways of unifying description and have given examples of relatively simple and unmixed methods. But the methods can be mixed, and sometimes the most effective description does combine the methods.

About four in the morning, as the captain and Herrick sat together on the rail, there arose from the midst of the night, in front of them, the voice of the breakers. Each sprang to his feet and stared and listened. The sound was continuous, like the passing of a train; no rise or fall could be distinguished; minute by minute the ocean heaved with an equal potency against the invisible isle; and as time passed, and Herrick waited in vain for any vicissitude in the volume of that roaring, a sense of the eternal weighed upon his mind. To the expert eye, the isle itself was to be inferred from a certain string of blots along the starry heaven. And the schooner was laid to and anxiously observed till daylight.

There was little or no morning bank. A brightening came in the east; then a wash of some ineffable, faint, nameless hue between crimson and silver; and then coals of fire. These glimmered awhile on the sealine, and seemed to brighten and darken and spread out; and still the night and the stars reigned undisturbed. It was as though a spark should catch and glow and creep along the foot of some heavy and almost incombustible wall-hanging, and the room itself be scarcely menaced. Yet a little after, and the whole east glowed with gold and scarlet, and the hollow of heaven was filled with the daylight.

The isle — the undiscovered, the scarce believed in — now lay before them and close aboard; and Herrick thought that never in his dreams had he beheld anything more strange and delicate. The beach was excellently white, the continuous barrier of trees inimitably green; the land perhaps ten feet high, the trees thirty more. Every here and there, as the schooner coasted northward, the wood was intermitted; and he could see clear over the inconsiderable strip of land (as a man looks over a wall) to the lagoon within; and clear over that, again, to where the far side of the atoll prolonged its pencilling of trees against the morning sky. He tortured himself to find analogies. The isle was like the rim of a great vessel sunken in the waters; it was like the embankment of an annular railway grown upon with wood. So slender it seemed amidst the outrageous breakers, so frail and pretty, he would scarce have wondered to see it sink and disappear without a sound, and the waves close smoothly over its descent.

— ROBERT LOUIS STEVENSON: *The Ebb Tide.*[4]

In the passage it is clear that we have a location and an observer specified. At one time, in the course of the description (the view across the atoll), we find the method of simple spatial ordering used, the method of the fixed point of view. At another time, the principle of sequence comes into play, the method of the moving point of view. In fact, it comes into play in two different ways. First, we have the principle of sequence in time (in the coming of dawn), and then we have it in space as the schooner coasts northward along the island. But we also find the frame image used to give us a clearer notion of the island: Herrick, the observer, "tortured himself to find analogies," and to describe the atoll we find the frame images of the " rim of a great vessel sunken in the waters " and of the " embankment of an annular railway grown upon with wood." We may note that there is an organization in terms of climax, for only at the end of the passage as given here do we get the full statement of the frame image and of the basic mood, Herrick's response to the fragile and dreamlike beauty of the island, which is the dominant impression.

The use of a mixed method, certainly of a mixed method which employs as many individual methods as the above passage, offers certain difficulties to the inexperienced writer. By and large, it is better for the inexperienced writer to try the simpler approaches to his material, at least until he is confident that he understands the principles involved in the various methods and has acquired some skill in adapting them. But in reading it is useful to be aware of what more experienced writers have done. Intelligent observation is the basis of all our learning.

---

[4] From *The Ebb Tide* by Robert Louis Stevenson. Copyright 1905 by Charles Scribner's Sons.

• Applications •

I. In the earlier part of this chapter and in the selections at the end there are a number of descriptive passages. List the different types of pattern that are illustrated in them.

II. Description, as we have said, rarely appears in an extended form. Here are three exercises for description in a limited, incidental form:

1. You are now sitting in a room. Look at your extreme left, then turn your eyes slowly from left to right. What do you see? Describe what you see, nothing more, nothing less, in order, in perhaps 100 to 150 words. What impression, what mood if any, seems dominant as you read your paragraph? What mood or impression strikes you as you look about you again? Revise what you have written with this in mind.
2. Think of your home town, your home block, or some familiar spot. Imagine that you are approaching it. What do you see, item by item, and in what order? What feelings and ideas suggest themselves as you imagine approaching the scene? Write a paragraph or two of description, with the objects and your feelings in mind.
3. You have some special interest. You hunt, you fish, you play baseball, you collect postage stamps, you watch birds, you watch people. Think of some scene or occasion in which your special interest was appealed to. Then write a description of that, using your interest as the device for giving the whole thing unity.

III. This exercise comes much later, a day or a week. You now have your grade on the work requested above. Read over what you have written, and at the same time try to remember your imagined subject and your feelings about your subject. Would the words now before you give you an impression of that subject and of your feelings about the subject? Be honest with yourself. If you are dissatisfied with what you have written, how would you now improve it?

Examples

On the following pages are a number of examples of description. These have already been referred to under Applications, and your instructor may frame new problems for investigation. For review, however, the following suggestions may be helpful:

1. Locate instances of appeals to different senses. What words, phrases, and comparisons make such appeals?
2. Find instances of several types of pattern.
3. Are there any instances of caricature?
4. In instances where description is used to suggest a character, an

atmosphere, or a state of feeling, try to state in your own words what the character, atmosphere, or state of feeling is. What details contribute to your impression?

5. Locate a number of comparisons. Which are used for vividness? Which are used for interpretation? Are there any that seem too strained to be effective? Are there any that seem stale?

A. A knot of country boys, gabbling at one another like starlings, shrilled a cheer as we came rattling over a stone bridge beneath which a stream shallowly washed its bank of osiers.

— WALTER DE LA MARE: *Memoirs of a Midget.*

B. Charmian is a hatchet faced, terra cotta colored little goblin, swift in her movements, and neatly finished at the hands and feet.

— GEORGE BERNARD SHAW: *Caesar and Cleopatra.*

C. Without being robust, her health was perfect, her needlework exquisite, her temper equable and calm; she loved and was loved by her girlfriends, she read romantic verses and select novels; above all, she danced. That was the greatest pleasure in life for her; not for the sake of her partners — those were surely only round dances, and the partners didn't count; what counted was the joy of motion, the sense of treading lightly, in perfect time, a sylph in spotless muslin, enriched with a ribbon or flower, playing discreetly with her fan, and sailing through the air with feet that seemed scarcely to touch the ground.

— GEORGE SANTAYANA: *Persons and Places.*

D. Leaning over the parapet, he enjoyed, once more, the strangely intimate companionship of the sea. He glanced down into the water, whose uneven floor was diapered with long weedy patches, fragments of fallen rock, and brighter patches of sand; he inhaled the pungent odor of seawrack and listened to the breathings of the waves. They lapped softly against the rounded boulders which strewed the shore like a flock of nodding Behemoths. He remembered his visits at daybreak to the beach — those unspoken confidences with the sunlit element to whose friendly caresses he had abandoned his body. How calm it was, too, in this evening light. Near at hand, somewhere, lay a sounding cave; it sang a melody of moist content. Shadows lengthened; fishing boats, moving outward for the night-work, steered darkly across the luminous river at his feet. Those jewel-like morning tints of blue and green had faded from the water; the southern cliff-scenery, projections of it, caught a fiery glare. Bastions of flame. . . .

The air seemed to have become unusually cool and bracing.

— NORMAN DOUGLAS: *South Wind.*

E. So the day has taken place, all the visionary business of the day. The young cattle stand in the straw of the stack yard, the sun gleams on their white fleece, the eyes of Io, and the man with the side-whiskers carries more yellow straw into the compound. The sun comes in all down one side, and above, in the sky, all the gables and grey stone chimney-stacks are floating in pure dreams.

There is threshed wheat smouldering in the great barn, the fire of life: and the sound of the threshing machine, running, drumming.

The threshing machine, running, drumming, waving its steam in a corner of a great field, the rapid nucleus of darkness beside the yellow ricks: and the rich plough-land comes up, ripples up in endless grape-colored ripples, like a tide of procreant desire: the machine sighs and drums, wind blows the chaff in little eddies, blows the clothes of the men on the ricks close against their limbs: the men on the stacks in the wind against a bare blue heaven, their limbs blown clean in contour naked shapely animated fragments of earth active in heaven.

Coming home, by the purple and crimson hedges, red with berries, up hill over the heavy ground to the stone, old three-pointed house with its raised chimney-stacks, the old manor lifting its fair, pure stone amid trees and foliage, rising from the lawn, we pass the pond where white ducks hastily launch upon the lustrous dark grey waters.

So up the steps to the porch, through the doorway, and into the interior, fragrant with all the memories of old age, and of bygone, remembered lustiness. — D. H. LAWRENCE: *Letters*. [5]

F. When I say they [the gondoliers of Venice] are associated with its [the city's] silence, I should immediately add that they are associated also with its sound. Among themselves they are extraordinarily talkative company. They chatter at the *traghetti* [landings], where they always have some sharp point under discussion; they bawl across the canals; they bespeak your commands as you approach; they defy each other from afar. If you happen to have a *traghetto* under your window, you are well aware that they are a vocal race. I should even go farther than I went just now, and say that the voice of the gondolier is, in fact, the voice of Venice. There is scarcely any other, and that, indeed, is part of the interest of the place. There is no noise there save distinctly human noise; no rumbling, no vague uproar, no rattle of wheels and hoofs. It is all articulate, personal sound. One may say, indeed, that Venice is, emphatically, the city of conversation; people talk all over the place, because there is nothing to interfere with their being heard. Among the populace it is a kind of family party. The still water carries the voice, and good Venetians exchange confidences at a distance of half a mile. It saves a world of trouble, and they don't like trouble. Their delightful garrulous language helps them to make Venetian life a long *conversazione*. This language, with its soft elisions, its odd transpositions, its kindly contempt for consonants and other disagreeables, has in it something peculiarly human and accommodating.
— HENRY JAMES: " Venice," *Portraits of Places*.

5 From *The Letters of D. H. Lawrence*, edited by Aldous Huxley. Copyright 1932 by the Estate of D. H. Lawrence. Reprinted by permission of The Viking Press, Inc., New York.

G. The dress of the rider and the accouterments of his horse, were peculiarly unfit for the traveller in such a country. A coat of linked mail, with long sleeves, plated gauntlets, and a steel breastplate, had not been esteemed sufficient weight of armor; there was also his triangular shield suspended round his neck, and his barred helmet of steel, over which he had a hood and collar of mail, which was drawn around the warrior's shoulders and throat, and filled up the vacancy between the hauberk and the head-piece. His lower limbs were sheathed, like his body, in flexible mail, securing the legs and thighs, while the feet rested in plated shoes, which corresponded with the gauntlets. A long, broad, straight-shaped, double-edged falchion, with a handle formed like a cross, corresponded with a stout poniard on the other side. The Knight also bore, secured to his saddle, with one end resting on his stirrup, the long steel-headed lance, his own proper weapon, which, as he rode, projected backwards, and displayed its little pennoncelle, to dally with the faint breeze, or drop in the dead calm.

— WALTER SCOTT: *The Talisman.*

H. Say that I had walked and wandered by unknown roads, and suddenly, after climbing a gentle hill, had seen before me for the first time the valley of Usk, just above Newbridge. I think it was on one of those strange days in summer when the sky is at once so grey and luminous that I achieved this adventure. There are no clouds in the upper air, the sky is simply covered with a veil which is, as I say, both grey and luminous, and there is no breath of wind, and every leaf is still.

But now and again as the day goes on the veil will brighten, and the sun almost appear; and then here and there in the woods it is as if white moons were descending. On such a day, then, I saw that wonderful and most lovely valley; the Usk, here purged of its muddy tidal waters, now like the sky, grey and silvery and luminous, winding in mystic esses, and the dense forest bending down to it, and the grey stone bridge crossing it. Down the valley in the distance was Caerleon-on-Usk; over the hill, somewhere in the lower slopes of the forest, Caerwent, also a Roman city, was buried in the earth, and gave up now and again strange relics — fragments of the temple of "Nodens, god of the depths." I saw the lonely house between the dark forest and the silver river, and years after I wrote "The Great God Pan," an endeavor to pass on the vague, indefinable sense of awe and mystery and terror that I had received.

— ARTHUR MACHEN: *Far Off Things.*

I. Ratmiroff gazed gloomily after his wife — even then he could not fail to observe the enchanting grace of her figure, or her movements — and crushing his cigarette with a heavy blow against the marble slab of the chimney-piece, he flung it far from him. His cheeks suddenly paled, a convulsive quiver flitted across his chin, and his eyes wandered dully and fiercely over the floor, as though in search of something. . . . Every trace of elegance had vanished from his face. That must have been the sort of expression it had assumed when he flogged the White Russian peasants.

— IVAN TURGENEV: *Smoke.*

J. He was a Mr. Cornelius Vanslyperken, a tall, meagre-looking person-age, with very narrow shoulders and very small head. Perfectly straight up and down, protruding in no part, he reminded you of some tall parish pump, with a great knob at its top. His face was gaunt, cheeks hollow, nose and chin showing an affection for each other, and evidently lamenting the gulf between them which prevented their meeting. Both appear to have fretted themselves to the utmost degree of tenuity from disappointment in love; as for the nose, it had a pearly round tear hanging at its tip, as if it wept. — FREDERICK MARRYAT: *The Dog Fiend.*

K. Her heart seemed so full, that it spilt its new gush of happiness, as it were, like rich and sunny wine out of an overbrimming goblet.
— NATHANIEL HAWTHORNE: *The Marble Faun.*

L. But I eat. I gradually lose all knowledge of particulars as I eat. I am becoming weighed down with food. These delicious mouthfuls of roast duck, fitly piled with vegetables, following each other in exquisite rotation of warmth, weight, sweet and bitter, past my palate, down my gullet, into my stomach, have established my body. I feel quiet, gravity, control. All is solid now. Instinctively my palate now requires and anticipates sweetness and lightness, something sugared and evanescent; and cool wine, fitting glove-like over those finer nerves that seem to tremble from the roof of my mouth and make it spread (as I drink) into a domed cavern, green with vine leaves, musk-scented, purple with grapes. Now I can look steadily into the mill-race that foams beneath. By what particular name are we to call it? Let Rhoda speak, whose face I see reflected mistily in the looking-glass opposite; Rhoda whom I interrupted when she rocked her petals in a brown basin, asking for the pocket-knife that Bernard had stolen. Love is not a whirl-pool to her. She is not giddy when she looks down. She looks far away over our heads, beyond India. — VIRGINIA WOOLF: *The Waves.*

M. The nether sky opens and Europe is disclosed as a prone and ema-ciated figure, the Alps shaping like a backbone, and the branching moun-tain-chains like ribs, the peninsular plateau of Spain forming a head. Broad and lengthy lowlands stretch from the north of France across Russia like a grey-green garment hemmed by the Ural mountains and the glistening Arctic Ocean. — THOMAS HARDY: *The Dynasts.*[6]

N. I studied M. de Charlus. The tuft of his grey hair, the eye, the brow of which was raised by his monocle to emit a smile, the red flowers in his buttonhole formed, so to speak, the three mobile apices of a convulsive and striking triangle. — MARCEL PROUST: *The Guermantes Way.*

O. In search of a place proper for this, I found a little plain on the side of a rising hill, whose front towards this little plain was steep as a house-side, so that nothing could come down upon me from the top; on the side of this rock there was a hollow place, worn a little way in, like the entrance

---

6 From Thomas Hardy: *The Dynasts.* Copyright, 1904, by The Macmillan Company and used with their permission.

or door of a cave; but there was not really any cave, or way into the rock at all.

On the flat of the green, just before this hollow place, I resolved to pitch my tent. This plain was not above an hundred yards broad, and about twice as long, and lay like a green before my door, and at the end of it descended irregularly every way down into the low grounds by the seaside. It was on the NNW. side of the hill, so that I was sheltered from the heat every day, till it came to a W. and by S. sun, or thereabouts, which in those countries is near the setting. — DANIEL DEFOE: *Robinson Crusoe*.

P. We live on a large farm in southern Tuscany — twelve miles from the station and five from the nearest village. The country is wild and lonely; the climate harsh. Our house stands on a hillside, looking down over a wide and beautiful valley, beyond which rises Monte Amieta, wooded with chestnuts and beeches. Nearer by, on this side of the valley, lie slopes of cultivated land — wheat, olives, and vines. Among them still stand some ridges of dust-colored clay hillocks, the *crete senesi*, as bare and colorless as elephants' backs, as mountains of the moon. The wide riverbed in the valley holds a rushing stream in the rainy season, but during the summer a mere trickle, in a wide desert of stones. Then, when the wheat ripens and the alfalfa has been cut, the last patches of green disappear from the landscape. The whole valley becomes dust-colored — a land without mercy, without shade. If you sit under an olive tree you are not shaded; the leaves are like little flickering tongues of fire. At evening and morning the distant hills are misty and blue, but under one's feet the dry earth is hard. The cry of the cicadas shrills in the noonday. — IRIS ORIGO: *War in Val d'Orcia*.

CHAPTER EIGHT

Narration

Narration is the kind of discourse concerned with action, with events in time, with life in motion. It answers the question, " What happened? " It tells a story.[1] In our sense of the word here, a story is a sequence of events — historically true or false — so presented that the imagination is appealed to. This is not a full definition of narration, but we can take it as a first step.

The kind of narration we are here talking about is to be distinguished from expository narration (page 110), which appeals to the understanding. Expository narration, as we have seen, is the kind found in, say, the account of a laboratory experiment or in the directions for making or doing something. In these things the method of narration is, in fact, used — a process is outlined stage by stage, event by event, in time sequence — but the intention is not that of narration as a type of discourse. Expository narration aims to give information, to explain something. It does not appeal to the imagination. It does not aim to give us a sense of things actually happening, concretely, before us.

The distinction between narration and expository narration may involve differences between the kinds of material being treated, but fundamentally it involves a difference in intention in the treatment and, therefore, a difference in method. Sometimes, as a matter of fact, the same material may be treated either way. Let us make up an example:

George Barton, a poor boy about twelve years old, was forced to sell the mastiff, which he had reared from a puppy and was much attached to, for

---

[1] We ordinarily think of storytelling as the special province of the writer of fiction, but fiction is only one type of narration, and here we shall be concerned with narration in general — narration as a kind of discourse. Fiction involves many special considerations which will not be touched on in this book, but there is some discussion of them in Appendix Six (page 839).

two reasons. First, having lost his job, he could no longer buy proper food for a dog of such size. Second, after it had frightened a child in the neighborhood, he was afraid that someone would poison it.

This paragraph involves an action, the fact that the boy sells the dog, but its primary concern is with the causes of the action and with what the action illustrates rather than with the immediate presentation of the action in time. Let us rewrite the passage:

George Barton owned a mastiff which he had reared from a puppy. He loved it very much. But he lost his job and could no longer buy proper food for it. Then the dog frightened a little child of the neighborhood, who was eating a piece of bread. George was afraid that someone would poison the dog. So he sold it.

Here, as before, the causes of the action are given, but now they are absorbed into the movement of the action itself. When we wrote in the first version that George sold the dog for two reasons, we violated the whole nature of narrative — the movement in time — because we made the causes of the action, not the action itself, the primary interest. The first piece of writing is primarily expository; it explains why the boy sold the dog. The second is primarily narrative; it tells us what happened.

Narration gives us a moving picture, objects in operation, life in motion, the transformation of life from one moment to the next. It does not tell *about* a story. It *tells* a story. It aims to give immediacy, a sense of the event before our eyes, involving us, our interest, and perhaps our sympathy. Description, too, aims to give immediacy, but its purpose is to give the quality of an action, not the movement of the action itself. Action is what narration presents.

We shall talk about action under the heads of *time* and *meaning*.

Time

An action takes place in time. The movement of an event is from one point in time to another. But narration gives us a *unit* of time, not a mere fragment of time. A unit is a thing which is complete in itself. It may be part of a larger thing, and it may contain smaller parts, which themselves are units, but in itself it can be thought of as complete. A unit of time is that length of time in which a process fulfills itself.

We must now emphasize, not the mere fact of movement in time, but the movement from a beginning to an end. We begin a story at the moment when something is ripe to happen, when one condition prevails but is unstable, and end it when something has finished happening, when a new condition prevails and is, for the moment at least, stable. In between the beginning and the end are all the moments which mark the stages of change, that is to say, the process of the event.

We move, as it were, from A to Z, A the beginning, Z the end; and every item in between has a necessary order in time. We can make a little chart to indicate this natural sequence in time:

Natural
order   A B C D E F G H I – etc. – U V W X Y Z
in time

But we recall narratives which do not begin with the first moment when something was ripe to happen, that is, with our A. For instance, a narrative may begin with a man in the very midst of his difficulties and problems, say on the battlefield, in a moment of marital crisis, or at a time when he hears that he has lost his fortune, and then it may cut back to his previous history and experience to explain how he came to be in such a situation. Such a narrative does not move in an orderly fashion from A to Z. It begins, instead, with G, H, and I and then cuts back to A, B, and C. But we must distinguish here between two things: how the narrator treated the sequence in time and how the sequence existed in time. The narrator may have given us G, H, and I first in order to catch our interest. He may have thought that A, B, and C would not be interesting to us until we knew what they were to lead to. But when he does finally cut back to A, B, and C, we become aware of the full sequence in time and set it up in our imaginations A, B, C, . . . G, H, I, ... In other words, we must distinguish between the *way* (G, H, I – A, B, C, . . .) in which the narrator presents an action to us and the *action* (A, B, C, D, E, F, G, . . .) which he presents.

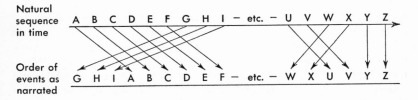

Natural
sequence   A B C D E F G H I – etc. – U V W X Y Z
in time

Order of
events as   G H I A B C D E F – etc. – W X U V Y Z
narrated

This is a distinction that we easily grasp, for we have long been acquainted with it in all sorts of narration, from conversation, newspaper stories, novels, and so on. But it is an important distinction, because when we talk about action as we shall use the word here, we are talking about action as referring to events in the *natural order* in time and not in the *narrative order,* unless the two orders happen to coincide.

Meaning

An action, as we are using the word, is not merely a series of events; it is a *meaningful* series. We have already implied this in saying that narration gives us a unit of time, with a beginning and an end. In other words, the events must be stages in a process and not merely a random collection held together in time. They must have a unity of meaning. Suppose that we should read:

President Wilson presented his war message to Congress on April 6, 1917. War was declared. Thus the United States embarked on its first great adventure in world affairs. On April 8, 1917, just two days later, Albert Mayfield was born in Marysville, Illinois. He was a healthy baby and grew rapidly. By the time of the Armistice he weighed 22 pounds. On December 12, 1918, the troopship *Mason,* returning to New York from Cherbourg, struck a floating mine off Ireland and sank. Two hundred and sixteen men were lost.

Several events are chronologically recounted in this passage, but as they are presented to us, nothing holds those events together. They have no significant relation to one another. Merely a sequence in time, they do not constitute an action. But suppose we rewrite the passage:

President Wilson presented his war message to Congress on April 6, 1917. War was declared. Thus the United States embarked on its first great adventure in world affairs. On April 8, 1917, just two days later, Albert Mayfield was born in Marysville, Illinois. Scarcely before the ink had dried on the headlines of the extra of the Marysville *Courier* announcing the declaration of war, Albert embarked on his own great adventure in world affairs. He was a healthy baby and grew rapidly. By the time of the Armistice he weighed 22 pounds. On December 12, 1918, the troopship *Mason,* returning to New York from Cherbourg, struck a floating mine off Ireland and sank. Two hundred and sixteen men were lost. Among those men was Sidney Mayfield, a captain of artillery, a quiet, unobtrusive, middle-aged insurance salesman, who left a widow and an infant son. That son was Albert Mayfield. So Albert grew up into a world which the war — a war he could not remember — had defined. It had defined the little world of his home, the silent, bitter woman who was his mother, the poverty and the cheerless discipline, and it had defined the big world outside.

Now we are moving toward an action. The random events are given some relationship to one another. We have unity and meaning. We may want to go on and find out more about Albert and about the long-range effects of the war on his life, but what we have is, as far as it goes, an action in itself as well as part of a bigger action, the story of Albert's life.

We have said that an action must have unity of meaning. This implies that one thing leads to another or that both things belong to a body of related events, all bearing on the point of the action. For instance, in the paragraph about Albert Mayfield, the declaration of war by the United States did not directly cause the floating mine to be in a particular spot off Ireland, but both events belong in the body of events contributing to the formation of Albert's character.

In seeking the unity of an action, we must often think of the persons involved. Events do not merely happen to people; people also cause events to happen. People have desires and impulses, and these desires and impulses are translated into deeds. Therefore, human motives may contribute to the unity of an action. This human element, **motivation,** may provide the line which runs through the individual events and holds them together. When motivation does not provide us with the line, we must think of the events as leading to some human response. For example, no motivation in the sense just used binds the little story of Albert Mayfield together, but the effect of the events on Albert Mayfield, his response to them, provides the unity and the meaning.

If we summarize what we mean by an action, we arrive at something like this. It is a connected sequence of events. It involves a change from one condition to another. It must have unity and meaning.

For illustration, let us look back at our paragraph about George Barton and his dog:

George Barton owned a mastiff which he had reared from a puppy. He loved it very much. But he lost his job and could no longer buy proper food for it. Then the dog frightened a little child of the neighborhood, who was eating a piece of bread. George was now afraid that someone would poison it. So he sold it.

This is a very poor, dull, and incomplete piece of narration. For one thing, it can scarcely be said to *present* an event at all. It gives us little sense of the immediacy of the event. It is so bare of detail that the imagination of the reader finds little to work on. For another thing, we do not know what it means. It has no point.

Let us rewrite a bit to try to answer the first objection:

George Barton was a nondescript little boy, scarcely to be distinguished from the other boys living in Duck Alley. He had a pasty face, not remarkable in any way, eyes not blue and not brown but some vague hazel color, and a tangle of neutral-colored hair. His clothes were the drab, cast-off things worn by all the children of Duck Alley, that grimy street, scarcely a street at all but a dirt track, which ran between the bayou and a scattering of shanties. His life there was cheerless enough, with a feeble, querulous father, a mother who had long since resigned herself to her misery, and a sullen older brother, with a mean laugh and a hard set of knuckles, who tormented George for amusement when he was not off prowling with his cronies. But this home did not distinguish George from the other children of Duck Alley. It was like many of the others. What distinguished George was his dog.

One day two years back — it was the summer when he was ten — George had found the dog. It was a puppy then, a scrawny, starving creature with absurd big paws, sniffing feebly in the garbage dump at the end of Duck Alley. No one could have guessed then that it would grow into a sleek, powerful animal, as big as a pony.

George brought it home and defended it against the protests and jeers and random kicks of the family. " I'll feed him," he asserted. " He won't never eat a bite I don't make the money to pay for." And he was as good as his word. There was no job too hard for him, for he could look forward to evening when he would squat by the old goods box which served as a kennel and watch Jibby gnaw at the hunk of meat he had bought.

Suppose we begin the narrative in that way. We have added several elements to the bare synopsis given before. We know now why the dog is so important to the boy. There is no direct statement on this point, but we see that he lives an isolated and loveless life and that the dog satisfies a craving of his nature for companionship and affection. We also see that now George has a reason for his efforts, a center for his life. In other words, we can imaginatively grasp his state of mind. The reason for George's attachment to the dog, as we have just stated, is given as explanation, as exposition, but in the narrative itself this expository element is absorbed into situation and action. Similarly, the little bits of description are woven into the narrative to help us visualize the scene and George himself.

What should be emphasized here is that the narrative is concerned to make us sense the fullness of the process, to make us see, hear, feel, and understand the event as a unit. Description alone might make us see or hear some aspect of the event. Exposition might make us understand its meaning, its causes, or results. But narrative, when it is fully effective, makes us aware directly of the event as happening.

To return to our little narrative: Suppose we should carry on our suggested revision to the moment when George sells his dog. Would there be anything still lacking to make the narrative fully satisfactory? Perhaps there would be. Perhaps the meaning of the action would not be very clear. Let us pick it up at a point after George has lost his job and the dog has frightened the child.

George sold the dog to John Simpson, a boy who lived in one of the big brick houses on the hill back of town. John Simpson's father was rich. John could feed Jibby. John could take care of him. No one would poison Jibby up at John Simpson's house, behind the high iron fence. George comforted himself with these thoughts.

Sometimes, however, they did not comfort him enough, and he felt the old loneliness and emptiness which he had felt before Jibby came. But he was getting to be a big boy now, big and tough, and he put those feelings out of his mind as well as he could. He did not work regularly now, but hung around with the Duck Alley gang in the railroad yards. He almost forgot Jibby.

One day on the main street of town he met John Simpson and the dog, such a big, powerful, sleek dog now that he scarcely recognized him. He went up to the dog. " Hi, Jibby! Hi, boy! " he said and began to pull the dog's ears and scratch his head as he had done three years before, in the evenings, back by the goods box, after Jibby had bolted his supper. The dog nuzzled him and licked his hands. George looked up at the other boy and exclaimed, " Jeez, look at him. Look at him, will ya. Ain't he smart? He remembers me! "

John Simpson stood there for a moment and did not utter a word. Then he said, " Take your hands off that dog. He belongs to me."

George stepped back.

" Come here, Blaze," John Simpson ordered, and the dog went to him. He fondled the dog's head, and the dog licked his hands.

George turned around and walked off.

This is somewhat more extended than the previous version. If we stop with the sale of the dog, we have an example of narration, but the reader no doubt is somewhat confused about the exact meaning of the event presented. Perhaps the reader feels sorry for the boy. Perhaps he is aware that poverty is the cause of the boy's loss of the dog. Those reactions may be taken as meanings of the piece of narration given. But they are not brought to focus. The reader may not be sure exactly what is intended. He is certain to feel that the narrative is rather fragmentary.

With the addition of the section dealing with the meeting of

George and John Simpson, however, the reader is more certain of the direction of the narrative, of the significance. The contrast between John Simpson, who owns the dog, and George, who merely loves it, gives us a point which is clear even without any comment.

We may observe, however, that more is involved than the mere contrast between the two boys. The dog licks John Simpson's hands, too. How does this fact tie in with what we have just said? This act is, as it were, a kind of betrayal of George's affection for the dog. Another question: What is George's attitude as he turns and walks off? Perhaps the reader senses the boy's resentment at the betrayal. But the writer might want more. He might want a more positive conclusion. For example, he might want to make this event a kind of turning point in George's growing up, a seemingly trivial event which had a far-reaching effect on his life. He might continue:

> The next day George hunted for a job. He found one at the lumberyard where he had worked before, when Jibby was a puppy. He worked as steadily now as he had worked in the old days when he looked forward to getting home to feed the dog and squat by him in the dusk, or, if it were winter, in the dark. But he did not love the dog now. He was through with that.
>
> But he worked because he had learned one thing. It was a thing which he was never to forget. He had learned that even love was one of the things you cannot get unless you have the money to pay for it.

These paragraphs give us a positive conclusion. They give the effect of the event on George, not merely the first reaction of resentment or hurt feelings, but the effect which prevails over a long period of time. Neither the reader nor the writer may agree that what George learns is the truth — that money is the basis of everything, even of such things as love and loyalty and kindness — but what George learns is the " truth " for him, the rule by which he will conduct his life for a time to come.

The important thing to understand here is that a point is made, whether or not the reader accepts the point as true. The narrative is complete. It is not complete merely because a summarizing statement has been made by the writer. Certainly, the summarizing statement would not make the narrative complete if what it says were not something which could grow reasonably out of the event for a person in George's situation. Many narratives imply rather than state their meaning. But a full narrative does involve significance, a meaning, a point, which grows out of the sequence of events.

We have just said that the narrative is complete. This does not necessarily mean that George will never change his mind about the meaning of the experience he has had. The narrative might well be part of a long story or novel which showed how for thirty years George conducted his life by the hard, materialistic " truth " he had learned and then found, even in the moment of his practical success, when he had grown rich and powerful, that his " truth " was really a profound mistake and that he had to learn a new truth.

To summarize, we may say that the idea of completeness as applied to narrative always involves the idea of an interpretation, stated or implied, of the events narrated. The interpretation may be made by a character in the narrative, as by George in this case, or it may be made by the reader on the basis of the presentation of the material, or it may be stated by the writer. But in all cases of fully developed narrative, an interpretation is involved. This means that our understanding, as well as our imagination, is appealed to, but appealed to through the presentation of an action. It is appealed to because the action has a point.

There are many kinds of point an action may have. We have seen that the narrative about George and the dog gives the point of what George has learned — or thinks he has learned — about life. Let us look at a little narrative from a sports magazine, a report of a wrestling match:

WRESTLING: THE NEW MAN

The new man wore a plain white towel over his shoulders in lieu of a robe. His weight was announced at 240 pounds, his opponent's at 323. The referee, Joe Walcott, a former heavyweight boxing champion, called both men to the center of the ring, and, after a moment's talk, the bell rang and the action started.

The 323-pounder, billed as Cowboy Rocky Lee, reached for the new man's shoulders. The new man fell back, held up his fists like a boxer and the fat cowboy stopped dead in his tracks in apparent terror. The crowd of 4,200 in the Washington, D.C., arena laughed and cheered.

The new man was awkward. When he went down, he fell heavily as though he were not used to falling.

The cowboy pounced on the new man, grabbed his leg and twisted it. Ringsiders heard the cowboy whispering in the new man's ear. It sounded like " Hold on, hold on now! " The new man looked like he wanted to yawn.

It went on that way. The cowboy persisted in mean tricks, villainous ways, but always retreated in terror when the new man held up his fists like a boxer. And always the crowd cheered and laughed at the fat cowboy's terror.

Then the cowboy went too far. While Referee Walcott's back was turned, he rubbed his bandaged hand across the new man's eyes. Then he dropped the new man with an arm-twist and punched him in the stomach while he was down. Walcott tried to intervene and the cowboy gave him a hard shove. Again the new man put up his fists like a boxer. He hit the cowboy full in the midsection. Not hard, but hard enough to put the cowboy down for the count of 10. It was all over. Time: 11 minutes. The crowd cheered and laughed.

Later, the new man talked to reporters in his dressing room. They asked him what he thought of wrestling after his first match.

" It's an honest living," said Joe Louis, boxing's greatest champion since Dempsey. " It's not stealing."

The promoter said he could make Joe $100,000 a year if he would agree to wrestle three times a week. Joe couldn't promise. He would have to think it over, he said, and talk it all over with his wife.

— From *Sports Illustrated,* March 26, 1956.[2]

In this account of the come-down of a great figure, the point is to make us feel the pathos of the situation, to give us some sense of the courage of the aging Louis, not as a fighter but as a human being making the best of his bad circumstances, descending from his glory to get along in the rather shabby world of wrestling. " It's not stealing," he says, and the irony of that remark sums up the meaning of the narrative.

And here is a student theme. What is the point here?

A TRUE EPISODE

I live in New Orleans, which is getting to be a big industrial town, but which is still a good-time place and center for tourists. The biggest attraction for tourists is, of course, the old part, called French Town. It is full of bars and night clubs and antique shops and restaurants, with the bars well out ahead, about one per capita for the regular population of the city. Something strange happened to me there this last Christmas when I went home for the holidays.

I have two good friends I went to school with in New Orleans. Both of them now go East to school, one of them to Amherst and the other to Princeton. We had been having a big reunion that first afternoon home, just wandering around, going to a movie, taking on a little beer, but mostly just talking about what had been happening all fall and planning our vacation now. Along about six-thirty we were on our way home, passing down Royal Street toward Canal Street. Outside a bar I saw a man on crutches leaning against a lamp post. He was not a man who just happened to be recovering from an injury. You could tell that he was a real cripple, a victim of polio or something like that. He was a well-dressed man, about thirty-five.

Just as we passed him, his crutches slipped, or something, and down he came, every which way. We did what anybody expects to do in a case like

<hr>

[2] From *Sports Illustrated,* © 1957. Time Inc.

that. We found he wasn't hurt, just shaken a little. He sort of grinned, and said, " No bones broken, boys." We assembled his things and got him back on his crutches and propped against the lamp post. He thanked us very politely and wished us a Merry Christmas.

We had not gone more than six feet away, when we heard it again. He had slipped down again. Naturally we did a repeat performance on our good Samaritan act. He made some kind of joke about how the city ought to provide foam-rubber curbstones for the tourist trade. I don't want to imply that he was drunk. He had had something to drink, of course, but if it hadn't been for the falling down, you would never have known it. We put him back together, and he again wished us Merry Christmas.

This time we got all of ten feet away. We ran back to him. He wasn't hurt, but he was worse shaken than before. He waited a little longer before he made his new joke. We were about to lift him up to his feet and prop him against the lamp post when he said, " Boys, maybe that will be above my standard of living. Just let me stay down here. Put me against the post where it's nice and comfortable."

We tried everything. We wanted to get a cab for him. We wanted to call somebody. But he would not let us. He was as bright and casual about it all as could be. " Boys," he said, " it's just three days till Christmas. You don't want to be so worn out by then that you'll oversleep Christmas morning."

So we finally left him. He was whistling " Jeannie with the Light Brown Hair " as we went on away. We felt bad about leaving him, but there didn't seem to be anything we could do by then.

• **Applications** •

I. In the Readings, study " Three Views of Mary Todd Lincoln " (pages 680–700). What are the differences of interpretation among these three accounts of the same character? What details can you find in each to support its special interpretation?

II. Write a short narrative, about 300 words, about some experience which taught you something. Here are some topics which may suggest an experience:

> You Can't Tell by Appearances
> I Thought I Was a Big Shot
> Bark and Bite
> Why I Kept the Summer Job
> True Friendship
> Brave — If You Can't Help It
> Hot Rod
> Success That Counts
> What My Father Did That Makes Me Admire Him

Pattern

In the course of time we hear and read many different kinds of narratives — jokes, novels, short stories, anecdotes, newspaper reports — and they seem to have many different kinds of organization. Is there some fundamental pattern which underlies all the various kinds of narrative? If we can find such a pattern, then we have taken an important step toward being able to write good narrative.

At this point let us remind ourselves of a distinction that we have already made — the distinction between the natural order of events in time and the order of narration (page 233) — and remind ourselves that this distinction applies as well to imaginary events as to events which have actually occurred. We must remind ourselves of this distinction because in discussing patterns of action here we shall be referring to the natural order in time, that is, to the order of the material from which narrative is to be made, and not to any artificial order employed as a device by a narrator.

We have defined an action as a meaningful sequence of events in time. Such a sequence may be real or imaginary, but in either case the events must embody a meaning if they are to be taken as constituting an action. The principle of pattern applies equally well to either real or imaginary action, and in seeking illustrations we shall sometimes draw from factual material and sometimes from imaginary. In both kinds of examples, we shall be asking, " What is the shape events take in order to constitute an action?"

We can answer our question by saying that an action has a beginning, a middle, and an end. Let us try to analyze what is really meant by this answer.

Beginning

An action does not spring from nothing. It arises from a situation. The situation, however, must be an unstable one, ready to lead to change and containing in it the seeds of future developments.

A situation may be very simple or very complicated. In the joke we begin, " Two Irishmen met on a bridge at midnight in a strange city. The first Irishman said. . . ." We have a minimum of information here, but all we may need for the joke. The situation could not be simpler. But the principle is the same as that in an enormously complicated situation; for instance, the situation from which German Nazism developed, a situation that contained more elements than we can hope to enumerate. There was the conflict between capital and labor, the insecurity of the lower middle class, the fear of Bolshevism, the economic collapse and the inflation of currency, the tradition of German militarism, the demand for revenge after the defeat in World War I, the example of Italian Fascism, the personality of Hitler, his bitterness and frustration. An interaction of all these factors and many more led to the unstable situation which worked itself out in Nazism.

Given this material, the writer of an account of Nazism must first present the situation clearly enough for the reader to see how the rest will follow. In dealing with matters of fact, as such a writer of history would be doing, his first task would be to analyze the body of material to be sure he knew what was really significant for future developments, and his second task would be to present the material so that the reader would see the relation among the various elements. It is true that the reader may not understand the significance of the situation when it is first presented to him, but he must be given enough to go on, to rouse and sustain his interest, to show that there is a line of possible development. And he must be given enough for him to feel, when he looks back over the whole narrative, that the action is really a logical development from the situation.

The problem is essentially the same for a writer who is dealing with imaginary events. The only difference is that he does not have to analyze factual materials already given him but has to create or adapt his materials. If we glance at Act I of Shakespeare's *Romeo and Juliet,* we find a good example of a beginning. We learn that there is a feud between the houses of Capulet and Montague, that bloodshed and violence are imminent, that Romeo is an idealistic young man eager to fall in love. Very early we have enough information to account for the future events. Or, to go back to our own improvised narrative of George and the dog, the situation presenting the misery and lovelessness of the boy's life gives us enough to account for the later importance of the dog to the boy.

The beginning, the presentation of the situation, enables us to understand the narrative. Therefore, that part of the narrative is often given the name of **exposition.** But we must keep the word in this special sense distinct from the more general sense in which it signifies one of the kinds of discourse.

It is not to be understood, however, that the exposition of a narrative is merely a kind of necessary evil, a body of dull information which the reader must absorb before he can settle down to the real story. It need not be explanatory or descriptive material in isolation or a colorless summary of the situation from which the action stems. Instead, the exposition may appear as an episode, a fragment of action, interesting in itself. If we think back on the opening scene of *Romeo and Juliet,* we remember that in it we see a street fight. We are not *told about* the feud between the rival houses of Capulet and Montague, but actually see it in operation. Not all kinds of exposition can take a direct form, but in general it can be said that whenever possible exposition should be dramatically presented, that is, directly presented.

Middle

The middle is the main body of the action. It is a series of stages in the process. It involves the points of mounting tension, or increasing complication, developing from the original situation. *Romeo and Juliet* will illustrate. In spite of the hostility of their two families, Romeo and Juliet meet, pledge their love to each other, and are secretly married by Friar Laurence. But the action receives a most important complication when Romeo kills Juliet's kinsman and is banished from the city; and further complication still when Juliet's father decides to force her into marriage with the young nobleman, Paris. In this crisis of tension, Friar Laurence sees only one way out: Juliet must risk death by taking a potion which will put her into a deathlike sleep. She will then be placed in the tomb — from which Romeo will rescue her. Juliet's resolution to take the risk might be regarded by many readers as the climax of the play; that is, the point of greatest intensity or greatest suspense. The climax is the focal point, the turning point of the narrative.

History as well as fiction may be used to illustrate the nature of the " middle " of an action. To return to our example of the rise of Nazism, we would find such points of mounting tension as the beer hall *Putsch* in Munich, Hitler's imprisonment and the writing of *Mein Kampf,* the street fights against the German Communists, the election of Hitler as Chancellor, the Reichstag fire, the purge of the party, the claims on Sudetenland. Looking back on the events of the past thirty or forty years, we can see the points of crisis, the stages at which new tensions emerged. If a historian were writing an account of those years, he might center his attention on those stages. They might provide him with natural chapter divisions.

The same principle applies in any narrative, the simple joke or the elaborate novel. If one is telling or writing about real events, one tries to focus attention on those which mark real stages of development. And if one is making up a narrative, he arranges his imaginary material in the same way. He wants to create suspense, to hold the interest of his audience. If his narrative seems to be a mere drift of events, he cannot hold his readers' interest. He can do so only in so far as the narrative emerges in well-defined stages of increasing complication.

We have seen this very clearly in the main body of *Romeo and Juliet:* Romeo meets Juliet; the marriage takes place; Romeo kills Juliet's kinsman Tybalt while trying to stop a duel; Romeo is banished; and so on. And we can see it in the little account of the boy and the dog: George gets a job to feed the dog; the dog becomes the center of his life; he loses the job; the dog frightens the child; George sells the dog; and so on.

Just as we have a technical name for the beginning of a narrative (exposition) , so we have one for the middle: **complication.**

End

As for the end of an action, it is not simply the point at which the action stops. It is, rather, the point at which the forces implicit in the situation have worked themselves out. Whether it is the gag line of the joke or Berlin shattered under British and American bombs and Russian shells, the principle is the same. The end of an action, however, is not necessarily the physical victory of one set of forces over another. It may be the reconciliation of forces, or it may be in the fusion of previously opposing forces to create a new force. As a matter of fact, the end of an action may simply be a new awareness on the part of a person involved, directly or indirectly, in the action. We know how we can look back on an experience and recognize the point at which an attitude we held was changed by it.

When we come to writing a narrative, we regard the end as the point where the action achieves its full meaning. It is the point at which the reader is willing to say, " Oh, yes, I see what it is all about." If we look back on our narrative of the boy and the dog we see that if we had stopped with the sale of the dog, the meaning would have been blurred. The reader would not have been quite sure what was at stake. He might have felt sorry for the boy in a vague sort of way. But the meeting with John Simpson and the dog gives us in direct terms, as a contrast, a much more sharply defined meaning. This episode could be an end. We, as readers, see that there is an issue, a question, raised by the narrative — the question of legal ownership of the dog opposed to the demands of affection.

The narrative now has a point. If we go on to write the last paragraph, we simply indicate the fact of George's awareness and the effect on him. By means of George's awareness we have made the point more explicit, but it *was* implicit at the moment when the two boys had their little encounter. The technical term for the end of a narrative is **denouement.** The word means an "untying." With the denouement, the complications are finally untangled and resolved. In *Romeo and Juliet,* for example, the lovers consummate in death their ill-starred love, and their families remorsefully give up the enmity that has destroyed their children.

Examples of Narrative Pattern

Let us look at a few examples of narrative with the idea of indicating the structure, or pattern, of each. The first is the account of how Robinson Crusoe, who fancied himself absolutely alone on his desert island, found a footprint:

> It happened one day about noon, going towards my boat, I was exceedingly surprised with the print of a man's naked foot on the shore, which was very plain to be seen in the sand. I stood like one thunderstruck, or as if I had seen an apparition: I listened, I looked around me, but I could hear nothing, nor see anything. I went up to a rising ground, to look farther; I went up the shore and down the shore, but it was all one; I could see no other impression but that one. I went to it again to see if there were any more, and to observe if it might not be my fancy; but there was no room for that, for there was exactly the print of a foot, toes, heel, and every part of a foot; how it came thither I knew not, nor could I in the least imagine; but, after innumerable fluttering thoughts, like a man perfectly confused and out of myself, I came home to my fortification, not feeling, as we say, the ground I went on, but terrified to the last degree; looking behind me at every two or three steps, mistaking every bush and tree, and fancying every stump at a distance to be a man. Nor is it possible to describe how many various shapes my affrighted imagination represented things to me in, how many wild ideas were found every moment in my fancy, and what strange unaccountable whimsies came into my thoughts by the way. — DANIEL DEFOE: *Robinson Crusoe.*

A piece of narrative could scarcely be simpler than this, but we see that it follows the basic pattern. The situation is given, as are the time and place. The complication follows on the discovery of the print — the first reaction, the looking about and listening, the going to higher ground for a wider view, the returning to verify the existence of the print. Then follow the flight and the terror consequent upon the discovery. And it is this terror, changing the whole aspect of the familiar landscape, which constitutes the denouement. Crusoe's life cannot be the same again. This fact is not specified, but it is strongly implied.

Our next example makes its point more explicitly:

> And also Mohammet loved well a good Hermit that dwelled in the Deserts a Mile from Mount Sinai, in the Way that Men go from Arabia toward Chaldea and toward Ind, one Day's journey from the Sea, where the Merchants of Venice come often for Merchandise. And so often went Mohammet to this Hermit, that all his Men were wroth; for he would gladly hear this Hermit preach and make his Men wake all Night. And therefore his Men thought to put the Hermit to Death. And so it befell upon a Night, that Mohammet was drunken of good Wine, and he fell asleep. And his Men took Mohammet's Sword out of his Sheath, whiles he slept, and therewith they slew this Hermit, and put his Sword all bloody in his Sheath again. And at the Morrow, when he found the Hermit dead, he was fully sorry and wroth, and would have done his Men to Death. But they all, with one accord, said that he himself had slain him, when he was drunk, and showed him his Sword all bloody. And he trowed that they had said Truth. And then he cursed the Wine and them that drink it. And therefore Saracens that be devout drink never any Wine.
>
> — SIR JOHN MANDEVILLE: *Travels.*

This, too, falls into the pattern. The exposition is a little less simple here than in our earlier example, for now we are concerned not only with the physical facts but with human motives leading up to the action — Mohammet's love of the hermit, his custom of listening to the sermons, the irritation of the men. The complication falls into three divisions — the killing of the hermit, the discovery of the deed and Mohammet's anger, the lie and the bloody sword in his own scabbard. The denouement has two divisions — Mohammet's curse on wine and, as the main point, the result among devout followers in later times.

Our next example is an anecdote told about an argument between the Duke of Windsor and Winston Churchill before World War II. We have here merely a clash of opinion:

> The Windsors' dinner was very grand, and the guests consisted of assorted notables from up and down the coast, mostly English people of high rank who were holidaying in the South. My Lords Rothermere and Beaverbrook had been prevented from attending by colds. (Lord Beaverbrook's cold did not prevent his attendance at the Casino, where we saw him afterward.) When some of the more overpowering guests had departed, after the long and stately meal in the white-and-gold dining room, the Duke of Windsor and Mr. Churchill settled down to a prolonged argument with the rest of the party listening in silence. The Duke had read with amaze-

ment Mr. Churchill's recent articles on Spain and his newest one (out that day, I believe) in which he appealed for an alliance with Soviet Russia. "You of all people, Winston," was the gist of his argument, "you cannot wish to make friends of these murderers and thieves." At one point Mr. Churchill, who was defending his point of view stubbornly and with undiplomatic vigor, said: "Sir, I would make a friend of the devil himself, if it would save England." It resulted plainly from the statements on the two sides that the self-willed, pleasure-loving little Prince, filled to the fingertips with royal prejudice, had no conception of the deadly danger to England involved in his dalliance with Hitler, while Mr. Churchill, disliking the Bolshevik theory and practice as much as ever, was so thoroughly aware of England's peril that he would seek the alliance of Stalin at once. We sat by the fireplace, Mr. Churchill frowning with intentness at the floor in front of him, mincing no words, reminding H.R.H. of the British constitution, on occasion — "when our kings are in conflict with our constitution we change our kings," he said — and declaring flatly that the nation stood in the gravest danger of its long history. The kilted Duke in his Stuart tartan sat on the edge of the sofa, eagerly interrupting whenever he could, contesting every point, but receiving — in terms of the utmost politeness so far as the words went — an object lesson in political wisdom and public spirit. The rest of us sat fixed in silence; there was something dramatically final, irrevocable about this dispute.

— VINCENT SHEEAN: *Between the Thunder and the Sun.*[3]

This is scarcely a narrative at all, simply a little incident almost buried in the comment with which the author has surrounded the event. But the author has hinted at the action and has given enough for us to grasp its natural structure and order (as contrasted with the way the author has told it, for the author has not stuck to the chronological order of events).

SITUATION:

Dinner with Windsors. Nature of gathering. World of pleasure and privilege. Churchill and his articles on Spain.

COMPLICATION:

Prolonged argument. The Duke's amazement at Churchill's articles, especially his demand for an alliance with Russia. The Duke's stubbornness. He eagerly leans forward from sofa, contesting every point. Churchill's remarks on relation of kingship to English constitution, the danger to England, and so forth. The Duke's statement: "You of all people, Winston, cannot wish to make friends of these murderers and thieves."

DENOUEMENT:

Churchill's reply: "Sir, I would make a friend of the devil himself, if it would save England."

---

[3] From *Between the Thunder and the Sun* by Vincent Sheean. Reprinted by permission of Random House, Inc.

We do not know all that occurred at that conversation. We do not need to know it to have a notion of the action, in our sense of the word. For, in this connection, action is the word we apply to a meaningful event, and the things which merely happened and have no bearing on the meaning of the event are not, properly speaking, a part of the action. The writer has omitted them from his account.

Here is a more fully developed narrative, the story of Andrew Jackson's most famous duel, the duel with Charles Dickinson, who had made some remarks reflecting on the character of Rachel Jackson, Andrew Jackson's wife.

EXPOSITION:

On Thursday, May 29, 1806, Andrew Jackson rose at five o'clock, and after breakfast told Rachel that he would be gone for a couple of days and meanwhile he might have some trouble with Mr. Dickinson. Rachel probably knew what the trouble would be and she did not ask. Rachel had had her private channels of information concerning the Sevier affray. At six-thirty Jackson joined Overton at Nashville. Overton had the pistols. With three others they departed for the Kentucky line.

Mr. Dickinson and eight companions were already on the road. " Goodby, darling," he told his young wife. " I shall be sure to be home tomorrow evening." This confidence was not altogether assumed. He was a snap shot. At the word of command and firing apparently without aim, he could put four balls in a mark twenty-four feet away, each ball touching another. The persistent tradition in the countryside, that to worry Jackson he left several such examples of his marksmanship along the road, is unconfirmed by any member of the Dickinson or Jackson parties. But the story that he had offered on the streets of Nashville to wager he could kill Jackson at the first fire was vouchsafed by John Overton, the brother of Jackson's second, a few days after the duel.

Jackson said he was glad that " the other side " had started so early. It was a guarantee against further delay. Jackson had chafed over the seven days that had elapsed since the acceptance of the challenge. At their first interview, Overton and Dr. Hanson Catlett, Mr. Dickinson's second, had agreed that the meeting should be on Friday, May thirtieth, near Harrison's Mills on Red River, just beyond the Kentucky boundary. Jackson protested at once. He did not wish to ride forty miles to preserve the fiction of a delicate regard for Tennessee's unenforceable statute against dueling. He did not wish to wait a week for something that could be done in a few hours. Dickinson's excuse was that he desired to borrow a pair of pistols. Overton offered the choice of Jackson's pistols, pledging Jackson to the use of the other. These were the weapons that had been employed by Coffee and McNairy.

As they rode Jackson talked a great deal, scrupulously avoiding the subject that burdened every mind. Really, however, there was nothing more to be profitably said on that head. General Overton was a Revolutionary soldier of long acquaintance with the Code. With his principal he had canvassed every possible aspect of the issue forthcoming. "Distance . . . twenty-four feet; the parties to stand facing each other, with their pistols down perpendicularly. When they are READY, the single word FIRE! to be given; at which they are to fire as soon as they please. Should either fire before the word is given we [the seconds] pledge ourselves to shoot him down instantly." Jackson was neither a quick shot, nor an especially good one for the western country. He had decided not to compete with Dickinson for the first fire. He expected to be hit, perhaps badly. But he counted on the resources of his will to sustain him until he could aim deliberately and shoot to kill, if it were the last act of his life.

COMPLICATION:

On the first leg of the ride they traversed the old Kentucky road, the route by which, fifteen years before, Andrew Jackson had carried Rachel Robards from her husband's home, the present journey being a part of the long sequel to the other. Jackson rambled on in a shrill voice. Thomas Jefferson was "the best Republican in theory and the worst in practice" he had ever seen. And he lacked courage. How long were we to support the affronts of England — impressment of seamen, cuffing about of our ocean commerce? Perhaps as long as Mr. Jefferson stayed in office. Well, that would be two years, and certainly his successor should be a stouter man. "We must fight England again. In the last war I was not old enough to be any account." He prayed that the next might come "before I get too old to fight."

General Overton asked how old Jackson reckoned he would have to be for that. In England's case about a hundred, Jackson said.

He spoke of Burr. A year ago, this day, Jackson had borne him from the banquet at Nashville to the Hermitage. He recalled their first meeting in 1797 when both were in Congress. Jackson also met General Hamilton that winter. "Personally, no gentleman could help liking Hamilton. But his political views were all English." At heart a monarchist. "Why, did he not urge Washington to take a crown! "

Burr also had his failings. He had made a mistake, observed Jackson, with admirable detachment, a political mistake, when he fought Hamilton. And about his Western projects the General was none too sanguine. Burr relied overmuch on what others told him. Besides, there was Jefferson to be reckoned with. "Burr is as far from a fool as I ever saw, and yet he is as easily fooled as any man I ever knew."

The day was warm, and a little after ten o'clock the party stopped for refreshment. Jackson took a mint julep, ate lightly and rested until mid-afternoon. The party reached Miller's Tavern in Kentucky about eight o'clock. After a supper of fried chicken, waffles, sweet potatoes and coffee, Jackson repaired to the porch to chat with the inn's company. No one guessed his errand. At ten o'clock he knocked the ashes from his pipe and went to bed. Asleep in ten minutes, he had to be roused at five in the morning.

The parties met on the bank of the Red River at a break in a poplar woods. Doctor Catlett won the toss for choice of position, but as the sun had not come through the trees this signified nothing. The giving of the word fell to Overton. Jackson's pistols were to be used after all, Dickinson taking his pick. The nine-inch barrels were charged with ounce balls of seventy caliber. The ground was paced off, the principals took their places. Jackson wore a dark-blue frock coat and trousers of the same material; Mr. Dickinson a shorter coat of blue, and gray trousers.

" Gentlemen, are you ready? " called General Overton.

" Ready," said Dickinson quickly.

" Yes, sir," said Jackson.

" *Fere!* " cried Overton in the Old-Country accent.

DENOUEMENT:

Dickinson fired almost instantly. A fleck of dust rose from Jackson's coat and his left hand clutched his chest. For an instant he thought himself dying, but fighting for self-command, slowly he raised his pistol.

Dickinson recoiled a step horror-stricken. " My God! Have I missed him? "

Overton presented his pistol. " Back to the mark, sir! "

Dickinson folded his arms. Jackson's spare form straightened. He aimed. There was a hollow " clock " as the hammer stopped at half-cock. He drew it back, sighted again and fired. Dickinson swayed to the ground.

As they reached the horses Overton noticed that his friend's left boot was filled with blood. " Oh, I believe that he pinked me," said Jackson quickly, " but I don't want those people to know," indicating the group that bent over Dickinson. Jackson's surgeon found that Dickinson's aim had been perfectly true, but he had judged the position of Jackson's heart by the set of his coat, and Jackson wore his coats loosely on account of the excessive slenderness of his figure. " But I should have hit him," he exclaimed, " if he had shot me through the brain."

-— MARQUIS JAMES: *The Life of Andrew Jackson.*[4]

The event narrated above is historically true. It had causes running back before the episode of the duel (Dickinson had insulted Jackson's wife) and was to have consequences long after the duel. But the writer is not immediately concerned with causes or effects. He is concerned with rendering the episode itself, the duel, and through the duel, something of the character of Jackson himself. We can see that in doing so he naturally gives his account in three sections — the exposition, the complication, and the denouement.

The exposition describes the attitudes of the two duelists as they make ready and gives the terms of the duel. The complication seems

---

[4] From *The Life of Andrew Jackson* by Marquis James. Copyright 1938. Used by special permission of the publishers, the Bobbs-Merrill Company, Inc.

to have a good deal of material off the point — Jackson's long conversation about politics — but we shall see that even this apparent digression is related to the point the author wishes to make in his narrative: Jackson's cool certainty and confidence. Then the complication gives the details as the opponents face each other and Dickinson fires. The denouement falls into two related parts, Jackson's self-command when hit and his shooting of Dickinson, and his remark after the event.

Both Vincent Sheean and Marquis James are using narrative to make a point, a point more important than the event narrated. Sheean is interested in illustrating one aspect of the political background of World War II; and James, in exhibiting an aspect of Jackson's character, his iron will. But the essential narrative structure underlies both accounts. It underlies them because the action to be narrated had that natural structure, and not because the writer imposed it. The thing to remember is that events, real or imaginary, in so far as they constitute an action in our sense of the word, fall into that pattern. The writer may make shifts of order in his presentation, may add digressions, and may make his own comments, but the essential structure of the action remains.

In the Applications on page 241 you were asked to write a short theme about some experience which has taught you something. Here is a theme written for that assignment.

SOMETHING I LEARNED

What I am going to tell about happened last summer at camp in Vermont, the Bateway Camp for boys, where I had gone for three years. I suppose I learned as much from this event as from anything that ever happened to me. At least, it makes me think twice now before I do a certain kind of thing, which I hope I will never do again.

There was a boy at camp named Alex Flinders. He wasn't exactly a beauty, because he was sort of pale and scrawny. He might have been getting a good build if he could fill out, but he sure didn't have it yet. We got to calling him Spindly, the way kids will call each other names. I am no beauty either, and I know it, not with my nose. If I happened to try to forget I am no beauty, some guy calling me Nosey would remind me quick enough. There's not much harm in such name-calling, if you don't rub it in, and maybe Spindly would have been all right if something else hadn't happened.

Spindly was not much good at any sport, just sort of slow and not well coordinated. But he did have a knack for swimming. He had the makings of a nice crawl, once he developed some power. One day we were all diving in the lake, from the next to lowest board. You could see that Spindly was sort of afraid to go up, but couldn't keep from hanging around. So the fellows sort of gave it to him, daring him and all. I confess I took the lead, for diving is the one thing I do pretty well. Enough I mean to get noticed a little, and it sort of goes to my head. That is the way I figure it now.

Spindly finally went up and took a dive. It might have been all right if he hadn't got panicked just as he was leaving the board; so he took a flop. The fellows all laughed, but it might have been forgotten if I hadn't gone right up to the next highest board and done a comic take-off on Spindly, yelling in a highpitched voice, " Oh, Mommy, save your Flopsy." So the boys kept calling him Flopsy and daring him every day to try again. He wouldn't do it. He just clammed up and didn't say a word.

About a week later, Sam Burrus told me a secret. He had waked up and gone out in the middle of the night and there was Flopsy practicing diving on the sly. He was diving pretty good, Sam said, for a surprise. We cooked up something to fix him, because we were sore, or pretended to be sore, that he was doing it on the sly. It seemed to make everything all right, if we said we were teaching him a lesson.

The next night we had tipped off the boys to come out to the lake around the other side where the brush is, so Flopsy wouldn't see us until too late. We sneaked up behind the brush and saw him take a pretty good dive from the second board from the bottom. It was not wonderful, but it was all right. Then just as he got out the next time on that board, we all broke out of the brush and started yelling falsetto at him, " Oh, Mommy, save your Flopsy! "

He stood there like he was a gatepost or something. Then he started back off the board. The fellows then, me included, started yelling " Chicken! " I don't know what he had intended to do. He may have intended to do what he did. Anyway, he went back off the board but he didn't go down. He went up. He went up to the next board, but he didn't stop there. He went on. The fellows had stopped yelling " Chicken " by then. Nobody made a sound.

I got the impulse to run out there and stop him. I did start out, but I heard somebody titter behind me expecting I was up to some kind of joke. So I turned it into a joke. I saw that Flopsy had hesitated, looking down. So I yelled some foolishness and climbed up to the board just below him and ran out and jumped off as awkward as I could, yelling " Flopsy, save me! " and then knifed out into as pretty a dive as I ever made. I felt mighty good about that one. I wished the coach for the Olympics could have seen that one.

When I came up, I saw Flopsy on the top board, just standing there. Then he backed out of my sight, and I figured he was going to go chicken. But he was just getting back to run off, the exact way I had, starting all tangled up and awkward like me. He tried to knife out. But what chance would a kid like that have? Well, he got it.

I don't mean he killed himself or anything. But it turned out that he had had a back operation not too long before and wasn't supposed to exert himself too much. He had been ashamed to tell anybody. Well, he has had another one now. They say it will be all right, but it taught me a lesson. It taught me not to think I was God's gift to the entertainment world, even if I could dive some. And it taught me to try to figure out why somebody else does something before you start criticizing and making jokes.

• Application •

Study the student theme above. Has the writer learned the principle of narrative organization? To prove your answer, break down the theme into exposition, complication, and denouement. How many stages in the complication are there?

 # Proportion

The relation of the parts of a narrative to one another raises the question of **proportion**. In one way this term is misleading, for it implies a mere mechanical ratio in the size of the parts. Actually, we cannot look at the question in that way. We cannot say, for instance, that the complication should be three times longer than the exposition or five times longer than the denouement.

We need to ask, rather, whether the parts are adequate to the needs of the special narrative we are dealing with. What would be a satisfactory proportion for one narrative might be quite unsatisfactory for another. In any given instance, does the exposition give all the information necessary to establish the situation for the reader? Is it burdened with information which is really unnecessary and distracting? Does the complication give the reader the essential stages of the development of the action? Does it confuse the reader by presenting material which does not bear on the development of the action? Does the denouement give the reader enough information to make the point of the narrative clear? Does it blur the point by putting in irrelevant material or by so extending relevant material that a clear focus is lost? But these questions cannot be answered unless we are sure of the intention of the particular narrative.

Let us, with these questions in mind, look back at the story of Jackson's duel. To answer these questions we must remember the author's basic intention. He is not writing a tract against dueling. He is not concerned with the sad death of a promising young man. He is not trying to evoke our sympathy for the young Mrs. Dickinson. All of these considerations may be present in his mind (and a little after the point at which our excerpt concludes he goes on to tell how Mrs. Jackson exclaimed, " Oh, God have pity on the poor wife — pity on the babe in her womb! "), but the main intention of the narrative is to show an aspect of Jackson's character — his iron will.

The exposition, therefore, tells merely what we need to know to establish this point: how Jackson took a natural, casual farewell from his wife; how Dickinson was confident in his mere skill, in contrast to Jackson's deadly inner certainty. The exposition also tells us, of course, something about the procedure agreed on for the duel, but this is primarily a mechanical matter. The complication builds the suspense by details of Jackson's journey to the Kentucky line, of how he discussed political questions, enjoyed his meals and his julep, talked with the guests at the inn, and slept well. These things do not bear directly on the business of the duel, and might be considered by some critics not properly part of the complication but an aside, a digression from the main line of action. But they do help to build the suspense and do indicate the qualities of self-control and certainty in Jackson.

Then the details of the actual duel lead us to the climax, the moment when Dickinson's bullet strikes and Jackson reels but recovers and, with deadly deliberation, lifts his weapon.

The denouement falls into two parts, the first presenting the actual shooting of Dickinson, the second presenting Jackson's behavior after the act, his indifference to his own wound, and his final remark when it is discovered why Dickinson had missed the heart. All the way through, of course, we notice that there is a building up of suspense about the outcome of the physical event, but along with this goes the unfolding of Jackson's character, which is summarized by the grim, last remark.

The narrative of Jackson's duel is part of a full-length biography, and it might be said that we have arbitrarily chosen to limit the exposition, for instance, to the part quoted here. It is true, of course, that in the full biography there is a great deal of explanation of the quarrel leading up to the duel. But is that really a part of the exposition of the narrative when the episode is considered solely as an episode? No; for what we are concerned with here is not the cause of the duel, the character of Rachel Jackson, or her husband's attitude toward her. In the episode itself we are concerned with the single, significant flash which exhibits Jackson's will. What preceded or followed the duel is not relevant to that consideration, taken in itself. Even though this little narrative is part of a much larger narrative, the account of Jackson's entire life, we are justified in interpreting it as a unit in so far as it is dominated by one basic intention.

A word of caution should be given before we leave the topic of proportion. In many narratives, one cannot draw a single hard and fast line between, say, the exposition and complication. Instead, there may be some overlapping or an intermingling of the two elements. A certain amount of exposition is always necessary early in a narrative, but we can recall instances, especially of extended narratives, in which the complication is interrupted by the insertion of bits of exposition. A biographer, for instance, may interrupt his narrative to explain a political situation, or a novelist may give what is called a **cutback** to an earlier scene or situation needed to explain a present action (page 233).

· **Applications** ·

I. In the Readings, study "The Hickman Story" (page 496) and "Il Plœːr dã mõ Kœːr" (page 719). Indicate the general divisions of the action. In the middle, the complication, how many stages do you distinguish? Does the denouement have more than one element?

II. Select some subject, real or imaginary, which you think would make an interesting narrative. Make a set of informal notes dividing up the material and indicating the basic pattern which a narrative would take. What would be necessary in the exposition? In the complication? In the denouement? You might set these details and topics down under the proper heads in the order you feel they should appear in a finished narrative. When you have finished the notes, write a statement in a sentence or two giving what you consider to be the idea or point of the narrative to be written. Looking back over your notes, ask yourself if the material indicated would really make that point.

Selection

Selection is as important for narration as it is for description. Skillful selection permits a large action to be presented in relatively brief space. But selection is not merely a matter of saving space; it is a matter of vividness. If a narrative is cluttered, the over-all shape will be lost. A writer wants to present only those details that will clarify the line of action and contribute to his point. No stage of the action should be omitted, and yet no details should be included which distract from the real concern of the narrative. There is no arbitrary rule in such a matter. A writer must keep firmly in mind what his real concern is and judge for himself. For example, in the episode of Jackson's duel, it might seem at first glance that the section about Jackson's conversation on the road is unnecessary and distracts from the real concern of the narrative. But this would be so only if the duel itself were taken to be the real concern. Actually, since the real intent of the author is the revelation of Jackson's character, the conversation on the way, illustrating his calmness and confidence, is relevant to the effect intended.

Even in a narrative dealing with fact the author may heighten the interest by leaving out merely casual material. In treating the episode of Jackson's duel, Marquis James may know that after his opponent was hit Jackson actually said more than is given here. The author, however, presents just those remarks which contribute to our awareness of Jackson's character. In dealing with matters of fact, a writer does not want to distort the truth by omissions, but neither does he want to lose the significance of the action by obscuring it behind a screen of mere facts. Certainly, the narrator is concerned with facts, but primarily with significant facts. When he is dealing with imaginary events, the writer has a freer hand and a greater responsibility; for now he cannot rely on the interest which mere fact as fact can sometimes evoke in the reader. With the imaginary narrative a detail can never pay its way simply because it is interesting in itself. It must contribute to the main business or to the vividness of the impression.

A narrative is a more or less immediate presentation of events. Therefore, vividness is important — the detail, the small gesture, the trivial word which can stir the imagination. And the details which, strictly speaking, are descriptive may be absorbed into the narrative effect. For instance, the cut and color of Jackson's and Dickinson's clothes, the kind of woods by which the meeting took place, and the Irish accent of General Overton when he gave the command to fire contribute to the impression of reality. Marquis James is much concerned to give an immediate presentation. But if we turn back to Vincent Sheean's anecdote of the Duke of Windsor and Churchill, we find that immediacy is not very important to the author. He is chiefly concerned to present a clash of opinions. Even here, however, we do get the details of the Stuart tartan which the kilted Duke wears, his posture on the sofa, and Churchill's position staring at the floor.

We have said that a narrative is a more or less immediate presentation of events and that therefore vividness is important. In order to support this effect of immediate presentation, writers sometimes substitute the present tense, the so-called "historical present," for the past tense. For example, this is the way in which a Confederate soldier described Pickett's charge at Gettysburg:

Over the plain we marched. Surely the hill has fallen. No, look! They are bringing artillery to bear upon us. Again the shrieking shot and bursting shell, and now the blazing musketry. Forward, still forward. How thin the ranks are getting. Down the gradual descent we hurry. Over the fence we scramble. We bound diagonally across the Emmetsburg Pike and feel that the hill has fallen.   — WILLIAM NATHANIEL WOOD: *Reminiscences of Big I.*

Sometimes, as in the passage just quoted, the use of the historical present seems natural, and in that case it may be rhetorically effective. But the use must not be forced. The student will probably find that normally he will want to use the past tense for narration.

• Applications •

I. In the Readings, study "Reveries over Childhood" (page 714) to locate details which are especially vivid or contribute to the main concern of the narrative chosen.

II. Take the outline of a narrative which you have prepared in the last exercise and from it write a narrative of some 500 or 600 words. Then criticize your selection of details on the basis of significance and vividness. If you are not satisfied, revise your composition.

Point of View

The term **point of view** implies some of the most important considerations of narration. In ordinary speech this phrase has a meaning different from the meaning of the technical term to be discussed here. In ordinary speech we say: " From my point of view, I think James was perfectly right." Or: " I understand Sarah's point of view, but I don't agree with it." What we understand by point of view in these two statements is an attitude, a set of values, or a body of ideas. We could rewrite the sentences above in these terms and not change the meaning: " According to my set of values (or my ideas, or my attitude), I think James was perfectly right." Or: " I understand Sarah's ideas (or set of values, or attitude), but I don't agree with them." But in discussing narration we shall use the term to mean the point from which the action of a narrative is viewed.

When we use the term point of view in description (see above, pages 217–20), we mean a physical point from which the specified or implied observer looks at the thing described. In discussing it in narration we do not mean a physical point; we mean, rather, a person who bears some relation to the action, either as observer or participant, and whose intelligence serves the reader as a kind of guide to the action. Point of view, then, involves two questions: " Who tells the story? What is his relation to the action? "

In broad terms, there are two possible points of view, the first person and the third person. When we read, " That summer when we were staying at Bayport, I had the most astonishing experience of my life," we know that we are dealing with the first-person point of view. When we read, " When Jake Millen, at the age of sixty, surveyed the wreck of his career, he knew that only one course was left open to him," we know that we are dealing with a third-person point of view. That is, in the first example, an " I," real or fictitious, is telling us about an experience in which he himself was involved; in the second example, an author, writing impersonally, is telling us about an experience in which another person was involved.

There are, however, certain shadings and variations possible within these two broad general divisions of point of view.

What are the variations possible within the first person? The distinctions here are to be made on the basis of the relation of the first-person narrator to the action which he narrates. Two extreme positions are possible. First, the narrator may tell of an action in which he is the main, or at least an important, participant. That is, he tells his " own story." We are all familiar with this type of treatment. Most autobiographies are of this kind; for example, " Il Plœ:r dã mõ Kœ:r " by Hortense Calisher (see Readings, page 719) . Occasionally we encounter a piece of informal history using this method; for example, T. E. Lawrence's *Seven Pillars of Wisdom*. Many short stories and novels create an imaginary " I " who is the main character of the story and who tells the story; for example, Defoe's *Robinson Crusoe* and Hemingway's *A Farewell to Arms*.

At the other extreme, the narrator, either real or imaginary, recounts an action of which he is merely an observer. This, also, is a familiar type of treatment. Memoirs tend to take this form, for frequently the writer of memoirs has not himself played a conspicuous role in affairs but has been in a position to observe important events. The account of General Eisenhower by his aide, Captain Butcher, is a good example of this type. The same type of treatment appears of course, in fiction. Poe's " The Fall of the House of Usher " is a notable instance, and Ring Lardner's story " Haircut " is another.

Thus we may have the two types of the first-person point of view: *narrator — main character* and *narrator — mere observer*. But in between these two extremes many variations are possible, cases in which the narrator participates directly in the action and has something at stake in its outcome but is not the main character.

But what of the variations possible within the third-person point of view?

In this point of view the narrative is given by an author writing impersonally, that is, as a kind of disembodied intelligence before whom the events are played out. What is the relation of this impersonal author, this disembodied intelligence, to the action? In the first place, he does not participate in the action; he is merely an observer. The question then becomes this: " How much of the action does the author observe? " And here, as in dealing with the first-person point of view, we can define the two extreme positions.

One extreme we may call the **panoramic** point of view. In this method the author may report any aspect or all aspects of an action and may go into the head of any or all of the characters involved in the action. His eye, as it were, sweeps the entire field and he reports whatever is interesting or relevant. In an imaginary narrative there is no limit to what may be seen or reported according to this method; the most private acts and the most secret thoughts or sensations of any or all of the characters may be reported, for the author is the creator of the whole. But when a writer is using this method in presenting a nonimaginative narrative, say a piece of history, he is, of course, limited by what facts or plausible deductions are available to him. He cannot be as thoroughgoing in applying the method as the writer of an imaginary narrative, though within the limits of the facts available to him he may do so. Many pieces of historical and biographical writing use this method, and, of course, it is not uncommon in fiction. For instance, it appears in the following scene from Thackeray's novel *Vanity Fair,* presenting the city of Brussels when the false news comes that Napoleon has won the Battle of Quatre Bras, an engagement just before Waterloo:

We of peaceful London city have never beheld — and please God shall never witness — such a scene of hurry and alarm as that which Brussels presented. Crowds rushed to the Namur gate, from which direction the noise proceeded, and many rode along the level *chaussée,* to be in advance of any intelligence from the army. Each man asked his neighbor for news; and even great English lords and ladies condescended to speak to persons whom they did not know. The friends of the French went abroad, wild with excitement, and prophesying the triumph of their Emperor. The merchants closed their shops, and came out to swell the general chorus of alarm and clamor. Women rushed to the churches, and crowded the chapels, and knelt and prayed on the flags and steps. The dull sound of cannon went on rolling, rolling. Presently carriages with travellers began to leave the town, galloping away by the Ghent barrier. The prophecies of the French partisans began to pass for facts. " He has cut the army in two," it was said. " He is marching straight on Brussels. He will overpower the English, and be here tonight." " He will overpower the English," shrieked Isidor to his master, " and will be here tonight." The man bounded in and out from the lodgings to the street, always returning with some fresh particulars of disaster. Jos's face grew paler and paler. Alarm began to take entire possession of the stout civilian. All the champagne he drank brought no courage to him. Before sunset he was worked up to such a pitch of nervousness as gratified his friend Isidor to behold, who now counted upon the spoils of the owner of the laced coat.

The women were away all this time. After hearing the firing for a moment, the stout Major's wife bethought her of her friend in the next chamber, and ran in to watch, and if possible to console, Amelia. The idea that she had that helpless and gentle creature to protect, gave additional strength to the natural courage of the honest Irishwoman. She passed five hours by her friend's side, sometimes in remonstrance, sometimes talking cheerfully, oftener in silence, and terrified mental supplication.

— WILLIAM MAKEPEACE THACKERAY: *Vanity Fair.*

At the other extreme from the panoramic point of view we find what we may call the point of view of **sharp focus.** The author does not sweep the entire field of the action, but keeps his, and his reader's, attention focused on one character and on that character's relation to the action. Accordingly, the parts of the action not directly participated in by the selected character are not reported by the author. To use a figure of speech, the character may be regarded as a kind of prism through which the action is refracted. Here is an example of the method:

He was hungry, for, except for some biscuits which he had asked two grudging curates to bring him, he had eaten nothing since breakfast-time. He sat down at an uncovered wooden table opposite two work-girls and a mechanic. A slatternly girl waited on him.

" How much is a plate of peas? " he asked.

" Three halfpence, sir," said the girl.

" Bring me a plate of peas," he said, " and a bottle of ginger beer."

He spoke roughly in order to belie his air of gentility, for his entry had been followed by a pause of talk. His face was heated. To appear natural he pushed his cap back on his head and planted his elbows on the table. The mechanic and the two work-girls examined him point by point before resuming their conversation in a subdued voice. The girl brought him a plate of grocer's hot peas, seasoned with pepper and vinegar, a fork and his ginger beer. He ate his food greedily and found it so good that he made a note of the shop mentally. When he had eaten all the peas he sipped his ginger beer and sat for some time thinking of Corley's adventure.

In his imagination he beheld the pair of lovers walking along some dark road; he heard Corley's voice in deep energetic gallantries, and saw again the leer of the young woman's mouth. This vision made him feel keenly his own poverty of purse and spirit. He was tired of knocking about, of pulling the devil by the tail, of shifts and intrigues. He would be thirty-one in November. Would he never get a good job? Would he never have a home of his own? He thought how pleasant it would be to have a warm fire to sit by and a good dinner to sit down to. He had walked the streets long enough with friends and with girls. He knew what those friends were worth: he knew the girls too. Experience had embittered his heart against the world. But all hope had not left him. He felt better after having eaten than he had felt before, less weary of his life, less vanquished in spirit. He might yet be able to settle down in some snug corner and live happily if he could only come across some good simple-minded girl with a little of the ready.   — JAMES JOYCE: " Two Gallants," *Dubliners*.[5]

In between the extremes of the panoramic point of view and the point of view of sharp focus there are, of course, all sorts of grada-tions and mixtures of the two methods. The choice of one of the methods or the mixing of the two is not a matter to be settled arbi-trarily, for the method should reflect a special interest involved in the narrative. For instance, the panoramic point of view is well suited to the rendering of some large and complicated action — a battle, a mob scene, the burning of a city — in which the interest lies in the sweep of events. The point of view of sharp focus is suited to a narrative in which the interest is primarily in the psychology of a single character. A narrative may well involve both such inter-ests, and then the writer may mix his methods according to the needs of the moment.

But the use of the panoramic point of view is not restricted to action which covers a physically broad field, such as a battle. Take, for example, this section from a student theme:

It isn't hard for me to imagine how the family was sitting around waiting for my brother to come home. My brother was the youngest of us children, and in a way they were all partial to him. And now he was the first of us ever to get picked up by the police, and the family didn't even know what it was about. They had to sit there and wait for the news.

Waiting wasn't ever very easy for my father, to begin with. I bet he was pacing around, picking up a newspaper, glancing at it as though nothing was on his mind, then throwing it down. He was probably chewing his under lip the way he does when something is building up inside him. He

---

5 From *Dubliners* by James Joyce, copyright, 1925, by The Viking Press, Inc., and now included in *The Portable James Joyce,* published by The Viking Press, Inc., New York.

is a man who is built for action, and waiting is not his dish. He was probably about to lose his temper, too, at some little trifle.

My mother was sure to be in the rocking chair. She would pretend to be sewing, but all the time her mind would be on Jack. She is a religious woman, but not in any sickening way, and, if her lips were moving, she was praying. Then she would finally say to my father, " John, why don't you sit down; you're wearing out the carpet," which is an old joke between them.

Susie, my sister, came in about nine. She is a goodie-good if there ever was one. When they told her, she cried, and said, " Poor Jackie, poor Jackie, I've always cautioned him about that car." Then she began to rearrange flowers, and Bill says she was humming the gayest little tune to herself under her breath. She came too close and he heard her.

" You're damned pleased about it all, aren't you? " he said, and she flounced out of the room. But she came back in a minute and wanted to know if she couldn't get a glass of milk and some cake for my father. That is always a bad sign, a sign she is cooking up one of her fast ones. She was sure getting ready to pull a fast one that night.

Here we find the event rendered as it would appear to the mere observer, in its externals only. The scene is restricted, but the use of the panoramic method gives a sense of distance and impersonality, which corresponds to the sense of physical distance and impersonality we find in the panoramic rendering of a scene that is physically large. That is, here we seem to stand back from the scene while the family is waiting, seeing them all, one after another, as if a movie camera slowly swept the room, catching each person in some significant gesture or word.

• Applications •

I. In the Readings, what point of view is used in " The Dog That Bit People " (page 595)? In " A Stillness at Appomattox " (page 661)? In " Reveries over Childhood " (page 714)?

II. Write a brief narrative of about 250 words, in the third person, with a sharp focus, presenting a character's feelings and thoughts as well as his actions.

Narration and the Other Kinds of Discourse

We have been discussing narration (and narrative) as a thing in itself. But it bears certain relations to the other kinds of discourse — description, exposition, and argument. What are these relations?

We can break this general question down into two other questions:

1. How does narration use other kinds of discourse?
2. How do other kinds of discourse use narration?

Let us take up the first question. A narrative may have within it descriptive, argumentative, or expository elements. In fact, any rather full narrative will almost certainly have them, but if the prevailing motive of the piece of writing is narrative, they will be absorbed into the narrative intention.

A narrative presents us with an action. But an action implies things or persons that act and are acted upon. And the word *presents* implies that we are not told about those things or persons but are given some sense of their actual presence, their appearance, their nature. This means that, in a greater or lesser degree, they are described. So description comes in to give us that impression of immediacy which is important for all narrative except the most bare and synoptic kind.

The same line of reasoning leads us to an awareness of the importance of exposition in narrative. A narrative involves an action, and we have defined an action as a sequence of events related to create a meaning. One thing leads to another. There is a connection of cause and effect, or at least the events are connected with each other by means of some idea.

Exposition is the kind of discourse concerned with explanation, with making us understand something, and in so far as a narrative employs explanation to bring us to an understanding of its point, it involves exposition. Some narratives, it is true, may simply arrange their materials so that the reader is aware of the point without having to depend on any explanation, but in any fully developed narrative some element of exposition, even though a very slight one, is apt to appear.

As for our second question, " How do other forms of discourse use narration? " common sense and a little observation give us the answer very readily.

Strictly speaking, description can scarcely be said to use narration as an aid. It is, of course, possible to find cases in which description involves movement — a man's habitual acts, for instance, in a description of a character. But we must keep in mind the distinction between an act and an action in the sense in which we have been using the word *action*. A character description might even involve an action, but our interest in action is so much more vital than our interest in mere appearance that we should probably feel that the description was incidental to the narration rather than that the narration was incidental to the description. An object in motion catches the eye.

The situation, however, is different in regard to exposition and argument. Frequently in extended discourses which are primarily intended to explain something to us or convince us of something, we find bits of narrative used to dramatize an attitude, to illustrate a point, to bring an idea home to us. Sermons and speeches are often full of anecdotes. The preacher tells his congregation the story of a deathbed confession. The politician tells his audience how such and such a law, which he is pledged to help repeal if elected, has ruined the life of John Doe over in Murray County. The after-dinner speaker tells the club members a joke. But the story of the deathbed confession or of the ruin of John Doe over in Murray County or of the two Irishmen must have a point related to the main business in hand. If it does not have such a relation, the listeners feel that the speaker has dragged it in by the tail, merely to catch their attention — that somehow he has not played fair.

What is true of the sermon or political address or after-dinner speech is true of informal essays, informational articles, character sketches, travel books, philosophical essays, essays of opinion, memoirs, historical studies, and many other types of writing. And here, too, the narrative may be used to bring directly home to the reader what argument or exposition can give only in general terms. For instance, observe how the general statement with which the following paragraph begins takes on significance in narrative:

Undergraduate life at Cambridge [Massachusetts] has not lacked for bitter passages, which compel notice from any anatomist of society. On the one hand there has long been a snobbery moulded of New England pride and juvenile cruelty which is probably more savage than any known to Fifth Avenue and Newport. Its favorite illustration is the time-worn tale of the lonely lad who to feign that he had *one* friend used to go out as dusk fell over the yard and call beneath his own windows, " Oh, Reinhardt! " And on the other it has moments of mad, terrible loyalty — exampled by the episode which is still recalled, awesomely without names, over the coffee and liqueurs when Harvard men meet in Beacon Street or in the South Seas. It is the true story of a Harvard senior at a party in Brookline, who suddenly enraged by a jocular remark made concerning the girl whom he later married, publicly slapped the face of his best friend — and then in an access of remorse walked to an open fire and held his offending hand in the flame until it shrivelled away to the wrist.

— DIXON WECTER: *The Saga of American Society.*

Or let us take the following passage, which has the same basic pattern, the movement from a general proposition to an illustration in narrative:

There are men of all nations who feel the fascination of a life unequally divided between months of hardship and short days of riot and spending; but in the end it is the hardship that holds them. The Chinese, taking them as they come, are not like this. They frankly detest hard work. A large belly among them is an honorable thing, because it means that the owner of it does not swink for his living. I never met a Chinese outside of the caravans who was what we should call sentimental about his work. Camel pullers alone have a different spirit, a queer spirit. Time and again when the men were talking around the fire and cursing the weather, the bad taste of the water, or the dust blown into their food, I have heard one ask, rhetorically, "What is a camel puller?" . . .

Then another would say, "Yes, but this is the good life — do we not all come back to it?" and be approved in a chorus of grunts and oaths. Once a veteran said the last word: "I put all my money into land in the newly opened country Behind the Hills, and my nephew farms it for me. My old woman is there, so two years ago when they had the troubles on the Great Road and my legs hurt I thought I would finish with it all — defile its mother! I thought I would sleep on a warm *k'ang* and gossip with the neighbors and maybe smoke a little opium, and not work hard any more. But I am not far from the road, in my place, and after a while in the day and the night when I hear the bells of the *lien-tze* go by, *ting-lang, ting-lang*, there was a pain in my heart — *hsin-li nan-kuo*. So I said, "Dogs defile it! I will go back on the Gobi one more time and pull camels."

— OWEN LATTIMORE: *The Desert Road to Turkestan.*

• Applications •

I. Study the following selections in the Readings. To what different uses is narrative put in "The Hickman Story" (page 496), "The Story of an Eye-Witness" (page 512), "A Lark's Flight" (page 570), and "Saturday's Smells" (page 611)? Is narrative used merely to give information? To amuse? To bring about a reform? To express an attitude toward life?

II. Keeping in mind the various models under Reportage in the Readings, write a narrative of some event which you have witnessed.

CHAPTER NINE

The Paragraph and the Sentence

So far in discussing the problems of writing we have talked about whole themes. We have focused upon such problems as how to describe the process of training a dog or of how to direct another person through the steps of gluing felt to wood; that is, the problems have been of the sort that require several hundred words for the working out; we have not been concerned with the smaller units of composition — paragraphs and sentences — as such.

There is something to be said for postponing the discussion of the smaller elements. Most of us do not write by painfully building up sentences into paragraphs and the paragraphs in turn into larger wholes. Few of us think our compositions out in that fashion. We write in large units of thought and *revise* by paragraph and sentence. It is easier to deal with the shaping principles of composition when one keeps the larger architecture in view. Nevertheless, the smaller elements should be studied apart from the whole composition. As a unit of thought, for example, a paragraph has a certain structure, achieved through unity, coherence, and emphasis. As a part of the larger structure that is the total composition, the paragraph contributes to the unity, coherence, and emphasis of the whole.

The Paragraph as a Convenience to the Reader

A paragraph, mechanically considered, is a division of the composition, set off by an indentation of its first sentence or by some other conventional device, such as extra space between paragraphs. In manuscript it may be marked by the sign ¶. Paragraph divisions signal to the reader that the material so set off constitutes a unit of thought.

For the reader this marking off of the whole composition into segments is a convenience, though not a strict necessity. A truly well-organized, well-written piece of prose would presumably be no worse as a piece of prose if it were printed with no paragraph divisions whatsoever. Printed thus, it would say precisely what it said before. But the reader would certainly be irritated, and rightly so, because the writer had failed to provide these pointers to the organization of his thought. Since communication of one's thought is at best a difficult business, it is the part of common sense (not to mention good manners) to mark for the reader the divisions of one's thought and thus make the thought structure visible upon the page.

Where should these divisions occur? How long should a paragraph be? In answering these questions, let us again begin by adopting the position of the reader. For him, a composition consisting of one- or two-sentence paragraphs might as well be printed without paragraph divisions at all. Segmentation on this scale would tell the reader little more about organization than the segmentation already given by the division into sentences.

Common sense dictates that the length of the normal paragraph will lie between the extremes of very short paragraphs and no paragraphs at all. But this is not to say that an *occasional* very short paragraph — even a paragraph of only one sentence — may not tell the reader a great deal. The shortness of the paragraph emphasizes its importance. Similarly, an occasional long paragraph does no damage and may serve to emphasize the unity of a long passage, always provided, of course, that the long passage actually constitutes a unit. We may sum up, then, by saying that there is no formula for ascertaining the length of paragraphs. Only common sense and the requirements of the occasion can determine how long any paragraph ought to be.

The Paragraph as a Unit of Thought

Paragraphing, obviously, can be of help to the reader only if the indicated paragraphs are genuine units of thought — not faked units nor mere random bits of writing arbitrarily marked off as units. *For a paragraph undertakes to discuss one topic or one aspect of a topic.* Nevertheless, any realistic definition must be rather loose and gen-

eral. Fortunately, we do not construct paragraphs by applying defini
tions. In his actual writing, the student will find his best approach
is to remind himself that the paragraph is a *part* of the composition.
A paragraph thus has its " part " to play, its own particular job to
do, in the larger structure of meaning.

The Structure of the Paragraph

The paragraph, however, has its own structure, and there are
various ways of indicating that structure. One of these ways is to
build the paragraph around one sentence, the **topic sentence**, which
states the central thought of the whole paragraph. We may think of
the topic sentence as a kind of backbone, or spine, which supports
the body of the paragraph and around which the rest of the structure is formed. Here is an example:

> *The reader of a novel — by which I mean the critical reader — is himself*
> *a novelist; he is the maker of a book which may or may not please his*
> *taste when it is finished, but of a book for which he must take his own*
> *share of the responsibility.* The author does his part, but he cannot transfer
> his book like a bubble into the brain of the critic; he cannot make sure
> that the critic will possess his work. The reader must therefore become,
> for his part, a novelist, never permitting himself to suppose that the crea-
> tion of the book is solely the affair of the author. The difference between
> them is immense, of course, and so much so that a critic is always inclined
> to extend and intensify it. The opposition that he conceives between the
> creative and the critical task is a very real one; but in modestly belittling
> his own side of the business he is apt to forget an essential portion of it.
> The writer of the novel works in a manner that would be utterly impossi-
> ble to the critic, no doubt, and with a liberty and with a range that would
> disconcert him entirely. But in one quarter their work coincides; both
> of them make the novel.   — PERCY LUBBOCK: *The Craft of Fiction.*

In this paragraph the first sentence is the topic sentence. It states
the thesis which the paragraph as a whole develops. It is frequently
said that every paragraph contains a topic sentence, stated or *implied.* A more accurate statement, however, is that some paragraphs
have topic sentences and that others do not; for an " implied " topic
sentence is one which the reader is able to construct for himself as
a way of summarizing the paragraph in question. Obviously any
piece of composition possessing even a minimum of unity may be
summed up in some kind of sentence. The " implied " topic sen-

tence, therefore, is an abstraction — a not very useful kind of ghost sentence. In the pages that follow we shall mean by *topic sentence* only an actual sentence; and though insisting that every paragraph have unity, we shall admit the existence of paragraphs that do not embody a topic sentence.

We have just looked at a paragraph that begins with a topic sentence. Here follows a paragraph in which the topic sentence concludes the paragraph:

The artistic temperament is a disease that afflicts amateurs. It is a disease which arises from men not having sufficient power of expression to utter and get rid of the element of art in their being. It is healthful to every sane man to utter the art within him; it is essential to every sane man to get rid of the art within him at all costs. Artists of a large and wholesome vitality get rid of their art easily, as they breathe easily, or perspire easily. But in artists of less force, the thing becomes a pressure, and produces a definite pain, which is called the artistic temperament. Thus, very great artists are able to be ordinary men — men like Shakespeare or Browning. There are many real tragedies of the artistic temperament, tragedies of vanity or violence or fear. *But the great tragedy of the artistic temperament is that it cannot produce any art.*

— G. K. CHESTERTON: " On the Wit of Whistler," *Heretics.*

The last sentence of this paragraph makes a generalized statement of the point developed in the preceding sentences. The topic sentence serves, in this instance, as a kind of summary. Although the beginning and the end of a paragraph constitute emphatic positions for the topic sentence, it may, in fact, occur at any place in the paragraph.

• Applications •

I. Do the following paragraphs contain topic sentences? If so, what are they?

A. Popular amusements had more generally evolved from diversions that were originally available only to the wealthy. The theatre in America had at first been primarily class entertainment, the democratic audiences in the large playhouses of the mid-nineteenth century, as we have seen, offering a marked contrast to the more exclusive theatre patronage of the colonial period. And from this gradually democratized theatre had developed the even more popular minstrel shows, burlesques, and vaudeville. But the first appeal of moving pictures was to the masses rather than the classes. They were cheap and popular from the very beginning. The support which in time enabled them to raise their standard of entertainment came entirely from their nickel-paying customers.

— Foster R. Dulles: *America Learns to Play.*

B. Such was the man who, at the age of thirty-three, became headmaster of Rugby. His outward appearance was the index of his inward character: everything about him denoted energy, earnestness, and the best intentions. His legs, perhaps, were shorter than they should have been; but the sturdy athletic frame, especially when it was swathed (as it usually was) in the flowing robes of a Doctor of Divinity, was full of an imposing vigour; and his head, set decisively upon the collar, stock and bands of ecclesiastical tradition, clearly belonged to a person of eminence. The thick, dark clusters of his hair, his bushy eyebrows and curling whiskers, his straight nose and bulky chin, his firm and upward-curving lower lip — all these revealed a temperament of ardor and determination. His eyes were bright and large; they were also obviously honest. And yet — why was it? — was it the lines of the mouth or the frown on the forehead? — it was hard to say, but it was unmistakable — there was a slightly puzzled look upon the face of Dr. Arnold.

— Lytton Strachey: " Dr. Arnold," *Eminent Victorians.*

C. It is odd that American men are so frequently presented in European caricatures of the type, in fiction, plays, and films, as being extremely ill-mannered, loud, rough customers. Such Americans exist, of course, just as sneering Englishmen, bullying Teutons, insolent Latins also exist. But it has always seemed to me that American manners in general tend to err on the side of formality and solemnity. They are rather like those of elderly English dons and clergymen. The ordinary English are much more casual. We do not take enough trouble, for example, with our introductions. Terrified of appearing pompous, we hastily mumble names or hastily accept a mumble of names, so that our introductions do not serve their purpose, and often, not knowing to whom we are talking, we saunter into the most dreadful traps. The deliberate ceremony that most Americans make of introductions protects them from these dangers and errors. — J. B. Priestley: *Midnight on the Desert.*

Look back at the student theme " Training a Dog " (page 42). How many of its eight paragraphs may be said to contain topic sentences?

II. Construct paragraphs which will incorporate several of the following as topic sentences:

1. A person can become accustomed to almost anything.
2. Baseball still remains our national sport.
3. The enormous prestige of the entertainer in our day is evidence of a decline in taste.
4. Television is the death of the imagination.
5. Television is the hope of the arts.
6. Modern man grows increasingly dependent upon his machines.
7. Familiarity breeds contempt.

Methods of Paragraph Organization

With or without a topic sentence, there is always the problem of arranging the material of a paragraph. What are the typical organizational principles? We can answer by saying that they are, by and large, the same as those that govern the composition as a whole. In the chapter on Exposition, for example, we noticed such methods of organization as classification and division, comparison and contrast, illustration, and definition. These methods can determine the make-up of the smaller as well as the larger units of composition. For example, we have already used Thomas Henry Huxley's " The Herring " (page 78) as an instance of illustration, and this instance constitutes, as it happens, a single paragraph. We have offered Della Lutes's essay, " Are Neighbors Necessary? " (page 85) as another instance of illustration used as an organizing principle. In this essay individual paragraphs, notably the first, second, and sixth, are specifically organized to be illustrations.

In the same way, organization by means of comparison and contrast can be applied to the paragraph as well as to longer units of composition. The excerpt from *An American at Oxford* (quoted on page 92) happens to be just one paragraph long and thus provides a specific instance of comparison and contrast as a method of paragraph construction.

Further instances are provided by some of the paragraphs in G. Lowes Dickinson's " Red-bloods and Mollycoddles " (page 94). Considered as a whole, Dickinson's essay may be said also to make a classification, but the basic development of the essay is through comparison and contrast. The first paragraph begins with a suggested definition and proceeds to elaborate and particularize that definition by comparison and contrast. The next paragraph emphasizes the traits of the Mollycoddle (as opposed to the Red-blood), but in illustrating the nature of the Mollycoddle it uses a series of contrasts with the Red-blood. The third paragraph extends the classification from individuals to nations. Its first sentence, which we may take as the topic sentence, reads: " Nations, like men, may be classified roughly as Red-blood and Mollycoddle." The rest of the paragraph illustrates this generalization through a series of contrasts of national characteristics.

We can say that in general the more complex methods of exposition and argument, such as functional analysis, chronological analysis, causal analysis, and deductive reasoning, rarely determine the structure of a single paragraph. Their very complexity prevents their doing so, for the structure of the paragraph is usually simple. It consists of the statement and elaboration of a point, or of a contrast made between two points, or of the illustration of an argument, or of the application of some principle.

Some paragraphs, however, do have a rather explicit logical structure in which the topic sentence states a conclusion which follows from premises stated in the body of the paragraph. Here is a paragraph so constructed:

A really great pitcher must have control. Charles Ramsey had wonderful speed and a curve that broke as sharply as any that I have ever seen. He dazzled opposing batters with his fireball or made them break their backs reaching for pitches that broke sharply away from the plate. Charles had nearly everything — he even fielded his position brilliantly — but he lacked control. Even on his best days his control was less than certain. Shrewd batters learned this, and waited him out, frequently successfully, for a base on balls. On his worst days he simply couldn't find the plate. A pitcher without control cannot win close games. For this reason I do not consider Ramsey a great pitcher.

This is a rather simple paragraph on a simple subject; yet it is characterized by a logical structure. We can see this plainly by stating its argument in the form of a conclusion deduced from premises (see pages 167–76) :

A great pitcher must have control. (major premise)
Charles Ramsey lacks control. (minor premise)
Therefore Charles Ramsey is not a great pitcher. (conclusion)

Thus far we have examined paragraph structure primarily in the light of the methods of organization discussed in the chapters on Exposition and Argument. But the chapters on Description and Narration suggest other ways in which paragraphs may be organized; indeed, some of the simpler kinds of organizations, such as time sequence or the sequence of objects arranged in space.

Consider first a paragraph from Joseph Conrad's story, "The Secret Sharer":

On my right hand there were lines of fishing-stakes resembling a mysterious system of half-submerged bamboo fences, incomprehensible in its division of the domain of tropical fishes, and crazy of aspect as if abandoned for ever by some nomad tribe of fishermen now gone to the other end of the ocean; for there was no sign of human habitation as far as the eye could reach. To the left a group of barren islets, suggesting ruins of stone walls, towers, and blockhouses, had its foundations set in a blue sea that itself looked solid, so still and stable did it lie below my feet; even the track of light from the westering sun shone smoothly, without that animated glitter which tells of an imperceptible ripple. And when I turned my head to take a parting glance at the tug which had just left us anchored outside the bar, I saw the straight line of the flat shore joined to the stable sea, edge to edge, with a perfect and unusual closeness, in one levelled floor half brown, half blue under the enormous dome of the sky.

Here we have a fixed observer. He tells us what he sees on his right hand, then on his left, and finally, turning his head, what he sees behind him. (There is even an implied look upward: "the . . . dome of the sky.") The order of composition is simple and even mechanical, though the writing itself is not mechanical. Note, for example, the sense of finality and completeness given by the last sentence. The observer's survey comes to rest in "the straight line" of shore and sea "under the enormous dome of the sky." The paragraph thus rounds out and completes its chosen topic. It is thoroughly unified, though it does *not* contain a topic sentence.

We may also have a paragraph describing a scene through the eyes of an observer who is shifting his position. The paragraph from Lawrence's *Seven Pillars of Wisdom* (page 219) furnishes an illustration of this. Or a scene may be described in terms of an image which provides a frame of reference. Thomas Hardy, for example, describes the continent of Europe through the figure of a human being (see page 229).

Various other ways in which descriptions of a scene may be organized have been discussed in Chapter 7. They may be keyed to some sense, hearing or touch or sight; dominated by a special mood; focused upon a particular detail; and so on. All these methods of describing a scene apply to descriptive paragraphs as well as to the larger units of description. In fact, the examples that we used in Chapter 7 to illustrate methods of presenting description turn out to be, almost without exception, distinct paragraphs. The student can learn from them, therefore, a great deal about paragraph development (see especially pages 226–30).

By the very fact of discussing the typical ways in which paragraphs may be organized, we have assumed that a paragraph has unity, for a formless blob of writing would require no organization at all. Organization implies a unifying purpose; and unity implies coherence. (See the discussion of the relation of unity and coherence on page 26.) Note too that coherence imposes its own problems upon the inexperienced writer, for even when he has carved out a paragraph that relates to *one* idea and does *one* job within the composition, the parts of it may not actually hang together. It is possible for a paragraph to have an ascertainable unity and yet lack coherence. The following paragraph has unity of a sort — it is all about one thing, the herring — but it is scarcely coherent:

The body, tapering to each end, is covered with thin, flexible scales, which are very easily rubbed off. The taper head, with its underhung jaw, is smooth and scaleless on the top; the large eye is partly covered by two folds of transparent skin, like eyelids — only immovable and with the slit between them vertical instead of horizontal; the cleft behind the gill-cover is very wide, and, when the cover is raised, the large red gills which lie underneath it are freely exposed. If anyone wants to exemplify the meaning of the word "fish," he cannot choose a better animal than a herring. The rounded back bears the single moderately long dorsal fin about its middle.

The student might try to see what rearrangement of the sentences will improve the coherence of the paragraph. Then he should turn back to page 78 to compare this version and his improvement on it with the original.

Or consider what happens to the coherence of the paragraph quoted from Chesterton on page 270 when we rearrange it to read as follows:

Artists of a large and wholesome vitality get rid of their art easily, as they breathe easily, or perspire easily. It is healthful to every sane man to utter the art within him; it is essential to every sane man to get rid of the art within him at all costs. The artistic temperament is a disease that afflicts amateurs. It is a disease which arises from men not having sufficient power of expression to utter and get rid of the element of art in their being. Thus, very great artists are able to be ordinary men — men like Shakespeare or Browning. But in artists of less force, the thing becomes a pressure, and produces a definite pain, which is called the artistic temperament. There are many real tragedies of the artistic temperament, tragedies of vanity or violence or fear. But the great tragedy of the artistic temperament is that it cannot produce any art.

The paragraph as rearranged makes a kind of sense. It is "about" one general topic, the nature of the artistic temperament. But a careful comparison of the rearranged paragraph with the original will illustrate how much blurring of thought occurs when we do not think out the relation of sentence to sentence within the paragraph. (But it is only fair to observe that much of the finer articulation of part with part can come only with revision — when we reread our first draft and then subject it to a careful rewriting. See Chapter 14.)

We have briefly discussed unity and coherence within the paragraph, but even a brief discussion should not omit all mention of the third member of the triad — emphasis. In general, emphasis is a function of coherence; that is, only when we have made our thought truly coherent can we expect that it will express a proper scale of emphasis. (The rewriting of Chesterton's paragraph, for example, destroys the emphasis as well as the coherence of his thought.) We can further observe that two places in a paragraph, the beginning and the end, tend to be those of greatest emphasis. It is no accident that topic sentences — obvious devices for emphasis within the paragraph — tend to occur at the beginning or the end of the paragraph.

A review of these schemes for paragraph development serves to reinforce a point made earlier: There is no formula by which the length or structure of a paragraph may be determined. The student must use his best judgment, his common sense, and his taste. Unless he is very sure of his ground, he will tend to employ paragraphs of medium length and to use the more conventional paragraph structures. But in following these common-sense rules he must not conceive of paragraphs as mechanical units of even length and of homogeneous make-up. He should feel free, on occasion, to formulate paragraphs of " felt unity," relying upon his own impression of the " rightness " of the structure. For the student must never forget that the paragraph is a part — a meaningful part — of a larger structure and therefore cannot be formulated mechanically any more than can the larger structure of which it is a part.

• Applications •

I. Reread the essay " The Seven Deadly Fallacies " (Readings, page 551), which is organized as a classification. How are the paragraphs related to this general function? Are any of them constructed as classifications? Do any provide illustrations? Attempt to state the structural principles to be found in the first ten paragraphs of this selection.

II. What structural principles are to be found in each of the following paragraphs? If you judge that the paragraph has no real structure, say so and indicate why.

1. The second of the two paragraphs from Leo Tolstoy's *War and Peace* quoted on page 117
2. The first paragraph from Melville's " The Encantadas " quoted on page 197
3. The paragraph from John Burroughs' *Leaf and Tendril* quoted on page 209
4. The paragraph from Millikan's " Science, Freedom, and the World of Tomorrow " quoted on page 121
5. The second paragraph from Melville's *Moby-Dick* quoted on page 102
6. The paragraph from Vincent Sheean's *Between the Thunder and the Sun* quoted on page 247

III. Reread the student theme " Training a Dog " (page 42) or " Careers for Girls " (page 185). Attempt to state the structural principle of each of the paragraphs in these themes.

Linking Paragraph with Paragraph

Since paragraphs are parts of a whole work, elements in an ordered sequence, it is important that they be properly linked together. Even when the chain of development embodied in the series of paragraphs has been thought out carefully, the reader will still be grateful for signposts to direct him. The judicious use of transitional words and phrases, such as *therefore, consequently, hence, thus, accordingly, on the contrary, however, nevertheless, furthermore, finally, in the same way,* and *moreover,* constitutes one way of helping the reader. (In this connection the student might reread pages 30–31.) The writer may also make use of the coordinate conjunctions *for, and, but, or,* and *nor* as signs of the connection between paragraphs. Since, however, we ordinarily use these conjunctions to join the parts of a sentence, or to join sentence with sentence, we employ them less frequently to tie a paragraph to a preceding paragraph.

If we do provide the reader with transitional words as signposts, obviously we must use them accurately. We must not begin a paragraph by writing " In the same way " unless what follows *is* " in the same way "; we must not write " Consequently " unless what follows is a consequence of the preceding paragraph.

An obvious device for linking paragraphs is the repetition of a key word or phrase. It is a useful device, especially if we wish to avoid the formality of style suggested by the employment of transitional words and the abruptness occasioned by the use of *and, but,* or *or.* To illustrate: T. H. Huxley in his " The Method of Scientific Investigation " (see page 466) effects the transition between his eighth and ninth paragraphs in the following manner (we have italicized the key words here and in the examples that follow) :

You mean to say exactly what you know; but in reality you are giving expression to what is, in all essential particulars, an hypothesis. You do not know it at all; it is nothing but an hypothesis rapidly framed in your own mind. And it is an *hypothesis* founded on a long train of *inductions* and *deductions.*

What are those *inductions* and *deductions,* and how have you got at this *hypothesis?* You have observed in the first place. . . .

The exact word or phrase, of course, need not be repeated if the idea is carried over. Here is Huxley's transition from paragraph five to six:

He sees that the experiment has been tried under all sorts of conditions, as to time, place, and people, with the same result; and he says with you, therefore, that the law you have laid down must be a good one, and he must believe it.

In science we *do the same thing.* . . .

Here is a series of three paragraphs from a story in *Time* magazine:

A buzzard coasting high in the air over Central America last week would have seen nothing unusual. The mountainous, forest-matted isthmus lay quietly in the greasy November sun. Among the many human realities invisible to the buzzard were the boundary lines — the imaginary but very actual barriers that said: "This is Costa Rica; this is Guatemala; this is Nicaragua."

Far below the *coasting buzzard,* in the gray-green jungles of northern Nicaragua, more was stirring than his great bird's-eye view could catch. Snaking through the scrub, *guerilla riflemen made short, sharp little raids* against government outposts. In and out of the piny mountain country on Nicaragua's northern flank, armed, machete-toting *men filtered mysteriously.* In Guatemala and Costa Rica dusty little *companies,* in faded denim and khaki, *marked time in the tropic heat.*

All this scattered activity added up to one gathering purpose. That purpose called itself the Caribbean Legion.

Here is a series of three paragraphs from Dorothy Sayers' *The Mind of the Maker:*

It is for this reason that I have prefixed to this brief study of the creative mind an introductory chapter in which I have tried to make clear the difference between *fact* and *opinion,* and between the so-called "laws" based on *fact* and *opinion* respectively.

In the creeds of Christendom, we are confronted with a set of documents which purport to be, not expressions of *opinion* but statements of *fact.* Some of these *statements* are historical, and with these the present book is not concerned. Others are theological — which means that they claim to be statements of fact about the nature of God and the universe; and with a *limited number of these I propose to deal.*

The selected statements are those which aim at defining the nature of God, conceived in His capacity as Creator. They were originally. . . .

Another obvious device for linking paragraphs is the use of the demonstrative pronouns *this* (*these*) and *that* (*those*); but these words must be used with care. We are frequently tempted to employ them vaguely, hoping that the idea or object to which they refer will be clear from the context. Frequently it is not clear, and, instead of a tight and neat coupling of the two paragraphs, we have only the vague and clumsy suggestion of a tie. For example, consider the problem of making a transition between the second and third paragraphs of "The Colors That Animals Can See" (page 478). The second paragraph ends thus:

After we have arranged these new cards, we have not long to wait. Very soon bees arrive again, and it can be seen that they fly straight on to the blue card; none go to the red card.

Now we might be tempted to begin the next paragraph with: "This seems to indicate two things. The first is. . . ." But what the author wrote was: "This behavior of the bees seems to indicate two things. . . ." A little reflection will indicate that his judgment was sound. The author intends to state clearly a process of proof. He has been wise therefore to state very precisely what "this" refers to. The mistake of vague and indefinite reference is so common in student themes that the student should check each composition he writes to make certain that "this" or "that" standing at the beginning of a paragraph or at the beginning of a sentence refers unmistakably to some specific noun.

About the part-to-whole relationship (the paragraph as related to the whole composition), a further word may be said. As parts of a larger structure, paragraphs often have specialized functions. The opening paragraph (or paragraphs), for example, must introduce the whole essay;[1] the final paragraph (or paragraphs) must bring it to a suitable conclusion. Within the essay itself, there may be many paragraphs of specialized function: one paragraph states a particular argument; another provides an illustration; still another effects a transition between two sections of the essay.

These part-to-whole relationships cannot be studied by considering the paragraph in isolation. Here, too, the student will learn most by studying whole essays. Study of the paragraph, therefore, always leads us back to the general problems of composition.

• Applications •

I. In the following paragraphs from the selections in the Readings, indicate the topic sentences (if any) and the devices for connecting one paragraph with another.

1. The first ten paragraphs of "It Was a Stable World" (pages 653–57)
2. The first eight paragraphs of "The Thinking of Men and Machines" (pages 482–83)

---

[1] On pages 15–20 we discussed a series of typical introductory paragraphs.

3. The first ten paragraphs of " How To Write Like a Social Scientist "
(pages 623–25)

II. The paragraphs referred to below exemplify some of the following
structures: (a) identification and illustration, (b) comparison and contrast,
(c) causal analysis, (d) frame image, and (e) disposition of details from
a fixed point of view. Which method of organization is exemplified in each
paragraph?

1. Paragraph five in " The Marxian Philosophy of History " (page 524)
2. Paragraph six in " Dickens " (page 631)
3. Paragraph two in " It Was a Stable World " (page 654)
4. Paragraph five in " It Was a Stable World " (page 655)

Rhetoric and Grammar of the Sentence

Having applied the principles of rhetorical organization to the
composition as a whole and to its parts (the paragraphs), we next
apply them to the smallest rhetorical unit, the **sentence.**

With this smallest rhetorical unit, however, we encounter another
problem — the problem of grammar. In earlier chapters we could
take the problem of grammar for granted; for, since the larger units
of a composition are made up of sentences, we could assume that the
demands of grammar had been met.[2] But in this section, although we
shall still be primarily concerned with how to make our sentences
effective (the rhetorical problem), we shall have to touch upon specifically grammatical problems, which concern the rules and conventions that govern English sentence structure.

The basic distinction between grammar and rhetoric might be illustrated from the game of football. The " grammar " of the game
would be the rules and conventions that determine the conduct of
the game, including the system of scoring. The " rhetoric " of the
game would be the knowledge of strategy and maneuver that leads
to effective play and a winning game. To play the game correctly
would not *necessarily* be to play it effectively, though effective play
would certainly have to conform to the rules of the game. Let us consider the sentence, then, in both its rhetorical and grammatical
aspects.

---

[2] By this time the student will have discovered whether his knowledge of
grammar can safely be taken for granted. In any case, the brief Handbook of
Grammar on pages 727–811 is there to be consulted when needed.

The sentence is usually defined as a complete thought, expressed through a subject and a predicate; that is, a sentence "says something"—makes a predication—about another "thing," the subject. The foregoing is a grammatical definition, but it will not be too difficult to relate it to the three basic principles of rhetorical structure — unity, coherence, and emphasis. A sentence obviously has *unity* (is a complete thought), and its parts *cohere* (that is, are related to one another in special ways so as to produce that unity). The relationship of *emphasis* to the pattern of sentence structure may not be so obvious. But the term *emphasis* is applicable, for every complete sentence must have a special focus, a specific center of emphasis, around which the parts cohere.

This center of emphasis is the finite verb. Verbals, that is, nouns and adjectives derived from the verb, will not serve, even though, as derivatives of the verb, they express an action, condition, or state of being and even though they retain enough of the power of the verb to take a direct object. (See the Handbook, page 767.) It is not enough that we connect the thing about which we are talking (the subject) with some action. The following phrases make such connections: "the volcano belching clouds of sulphurous smoke"; "lastly to stop their ears against the heart-moving pleas of their suffering fellows"; "by crossing the border that separates manly pride from mean vanity." But none of these strings of words is a sentence; the action is not pinned down to a specific subject, singular or plural, first, second, or third person, acting at a given time. "The volcano belched smoke." "Stop!" "He crossed the border." These are sentences, for each of the three contains a finite verb.[3] In English, as well as in most other languages, the finite verb is the signal of predication. A phrase like "the volcano belching clouds of sulphurous smoke" remains unfocused. It lacks a point of emphasis around which the other parts of the sentence may be made to cohere so as to give us that special kind of unity which characterizes the kind of complete thought that is a sentence.

---

[3] The student is to be reminded that a finite verb literally means a *limited* verb, that is, limited with reference to person, number, tense, and so on. Thus *goes* may be used only with a singular noun in the third person and with reference to present or future time; whereas the "infinite" forms, such as the participle *going* and the infinitive *to go,* refer to the general idea of going. Two things tend to obscure this distinction: (1) the fact that forms such as the participle and the infinitive do have some limitations, such as tense distinctions; and (2) the fact that in modern English so many of the inflections of the verb — inflections that show tense, number, and so on — have been lost, so that most of the finite forms are exactly alike. But the general distinction holds, nevertheless. As contrasted with the infinite forms of the verb, the finite forms are limited and specific and, because specific, can be used to provide a focus for the sentence.

The Fixed Word Order of the Normal Sentence

In discarding many of the inflections that characterized the language at an earlier period, English has come to depend very heavily for expressing its meaning upon the position that words occupy in the sentence pattern. In some instances, change of position means a radical change in meaning. Thus, " The boy hit the ball " means something very different from " The ball hit the boy." Most of the shifts of meaning accomplished by rearrangement of words and word groups within a sentence are far less drastic than that in the example just cited. Yet, even the slight alterations and shadings to be gained by manipulations of word order are important if we value the clarity and force of our writing.

At this point the student should turn to the Handbook and read the section having to do with order (page 772). There he will find the statement that the normal order of the English sentence consists of:

Subject + verb + inner complement + outer complement
                        (if any)   (if any)

He will find also that the shifts from this order are treated as means for securing emphasis (since they are variations from *normal* order), justified when a particular emphasis is wanted and worse than useless when it is not. The student will also find the passive voice described as essentially a way of emphasizing the complement of the verb, and the expletives *It is* and *There is* described as a way of throwing emphasis upon the subject.

In addition to this discussion of the normal order of the main elements of the sentence, the Handbook contains a discussion of the normal positions occupied by adjectival modifiers and adverbial modifiers (see pages 775–79). The gist of this discussion may be summed up in this fashion:

1. Adjectival modifiers are relatively fixed: variation from the normal position constitutes a means of emphasizing the modifier.

2. Adverbial modifiers are rather freely movable: careful placing of these modifiers constitutes a means for controlling fine shadings of expression.

When the student has looked through the Handbook section on word order, he should try the following exercises.

• Applications •

I. Convert the following sentences to normal word order; that is, re-establish the pattern of *subject, verb, inner and outer complements,* and, where necessary, eliminate *expletive* and *passive* constructions.

1. Icebergs, he could see wherever he looked.
2. There was a man once that was bored with his life.
3. The arrival of five cruisers and twenty destroyers was reported.
4. The great bear was surrounded by a horde of yapping, excited dogs.
5. It was a great bear that was surrounded by the horde of yapping, excited dogs.
6. When I was five year old, I was given my first book by my grandmother.
7. My first book was given to me by my grandmother when I was five years old.
8. It was a book that was my first present.
9. Books, he had treasured from the earliest period of his life.
10. Ways and means for handling the peak late-afternoon traffic through Westville and Lakeville were discussed.

II. In the following sentences, some of the adjectival modifiers are improperly placed. Rearrange the modifiers, and, where necessary, rewrite the sentences to improve clarity and effectiveness.

1. Bird cage and parrot offered by refined young lady, having green feathers and yellow beak for what have you? — The Salt Lake *Tribune.*
2. A two-story house was for sale with green shutters.
3. A man in the army that I served with gave me this book.
4. It was the man I knew whom I now saw.
5. The lady whom I knew from Boston has not returned.
6. Boy is missing in first pair of long pants. — The Detroit *Free Press.*
7. Rex Parsons laid an egg on our table that had been previously laid on the nest by a little white Leghorn hen that was three inches in length and 6½ inches in circumference the smallest way. — The Farmington *Franklin Journal.*
8. Slowly filling with water, we saw the ship go down.
9. The ducks on the pond with ringed necks swam in lazy circles.
10. The ducks were still undisturbed on the pond; those in the nearby meadow quacked noisily.
11. Walking sedately before the bride, came her small nephew George Slaughter 3rd, carrying the ring and two little nieces of the groom. — The Roswell *Dispatch.*
12. The man in the automobile that I recognized was Jim.
13. Laughing through tears, we heard the hysterical girl try to tell her story.

14. The jumbled-up awards system has caused bitter criticism in the past, and taking on the job of revising it doesn't require a bit more courage than tackling a hungry tiger armed with a dull toothpick. — Los Angeles *Examiner*.

III. The following sentences contain dangling participles. Remove them (a) by rewriting the sentence so that the participle is given some word to modify and (b) by rewriting the dangling participle into a subordinate clause. For example:

" Ringing the doorbell, the house answered us with silence." Correct to (a) " Ringing the doorbell, we could hear from the house only the answer of silence." Or (b) " Although we rang the doorbell, the house answered us with silence."

1. Hurrying and out of breath, scurrying up the depot stairs, the 9:01 for Grand Central swept past us.
2. The afternoon drowsed on to an end, sipping lemonade and listening to records.
3. Reading the thrilling ghost story, the grandfather clock ticked insistently in our ears.
4. Hanging on for dear life, the car careened to the edge of the road.
5. Walking up the last steps of the drive, the first mutterings of thunder were heard.

IV. Some of the following sentences include dangling modifiers. In others, the modifiers have been shifted out of the order in which they were originally written. Remove dangling modifiers, and rearrange the italicized modifiers so as to improve the clarity and effectiveness of each sentence.

1. Though the Greek scientist Eratosthenes had, *with only a small error,* calculated the distance of the sun from the earth and the earth's circumference at the equator, his theory of a global world was received by men of common sense *with polite scorn*.
2. Singing merrily and happily, our music put the whole company into a jolly mood.
3. In myriad private hotel rooms of myriad hotels the Alumni Weekly Lunch is, *today,* being celebrated, *as every day*.
4. *Because their maxims would not have expressed their hearts,* they would not have been perfect moralists *then, even if their theory had been correct* (which, I think it was, *though not in statement,* in intention).
5. Thinking as hard as we could, the answer still could not be found.
6. Eight men were drowned, *however,* and *from that memory* my grandfather *at intervals all his life* suffered and never read anything but the shipwreck of St. Paul *if asked to read the family prayers*.
7. There can be no miracles *unless there exists something else which we may call the supernatural, in addition to Nature*.

8. Calling and calling again as we wandered over the fields, not a sound was heard from the lost child.
9. Turning the corner, the gigantic skeleton of New York's newest and the world's highest building comes into view. — The New York Herald Tribune.
10. There are wild woods and mountains, marshes and heaths, even in England. But *only on sufferance* are they there, *because we have chosen to leave them their freedom, out of our good pleasure.*
11. For Nature is always alien and inhuman, *even in the temperate zone*, and diabolic *occasionally*.
12. Joan Fontaine plays a European countess who returns to her home town in Ohio and charms a young married man *tonight at 9 on GE Theater.*

General Principles of Sentence Structure

PARALLELISM

Thus far we have considered the structure of the sentence from one point of view: that of the arrangement of its basic constituents and of the various kinds of modifiers. But other principles may determine the structure of a sentence. One of these is **parallelism**, a method of adjusting grammatical pattern to rhetorical pattern. In its simplest terms, parallelism means no more than that elements of like meaning should be put in like constructions.

The very richness of English tempts us to violate parallelism. For example, we have two noun forms of the verb. We can use the infinitive *to swim* or the gerund *swimming*. Consequently, the careless writer may blunder into a sentence like this: " *To swim* and *hunting* are my favorite sports." But the distinction between infinitive and gerund awkwardly distracts the reader from what is a coordinate relation. We ought to write: " *Swimming* and *hunting* are my favorite sports." Or: " *To swim* and *to hunt* are my favorite sports."

It is our great variety of movable modifiers, however, that most tempts us into violations of parallelism. We may write, for example: " *Being lazy by nature* and *because I am clumsy,* I have never liked tennis." Such violations of parallelism easily creep into first drafts — even into the first drafts of a good writer. Careful rewriting is the remedy.

In learning to avoid these blunders, we must not forget, however, that the principle of parallelism is a positive one. It is, in fact, a powerful rhetorical device. By using parallel constructions, we emphasize parallel ideas, and we can thus play off one sort of meaning against the other. Sentences constructed on this principle are some-times called " balanced sentences." Here are some examples:

1. As the hart panteth after the water brooks, so panteth my soul after Thee, O God.

2. He was sick of life, but he was afraid of death; and he shud-dered at every sight or sound which reminded him of the inevitable hour.

3. To examine such compositions singly cannot be required; they have doubtless brighter and darker parts; but when they are once found to be generally dull, all further labor may be spared; for to what use can the work be criticized that will not be read?

The parallel elements may be represented in the following scheme:

1. as	so
hart	soul
panteth	panteth (repetition)
water brooks	Thee

2. sick	afraid
life	death

3. singly	generally
required	spared
once found	all further
be criticized	be read

COORDINATION AND SUBORDINATION[4]

Coordination may be regarded as an aspect of parallelism. We have seen that elements of like meaning should be put in like con-structions. Conversely, *only* elements of like importance should be linked together as equals. A less-important element must be made subordinate to a more important one. Consider the following sen-tence: " I stayed at home; I was ill." What is the relation between the two statements? The writer has merely associated them. He has not defined the relation of one to the other. He might define the relationship in various ways:

Because I was ill, I stayed at home.
While I was staying at home, I was ill.
Although I stayed at home, I was ill.
Feeling ill, I stayed at home.
I stayed at home, quite ill.

Simple, uncritical writing, such as that of a child, tends to pre-sent a succession of coordinate units: " Then the bear got hungry.

---

4 See Handbook, page 770.

He came out of his den. He remembered the honey tree. And he started walking toward the honey tree." The mature and discriminating writer indicates the relation of his statements, one to another, by subordinating, thus:

Having done this, she thought it prudent to drop a few words before the bishop, letting him know that she had acquainted the Puddingdale family with their good fortune so that he might perceive that he stood committed to the appointment.

The writer who points up relationships, instead of leaving them to be inferred by the reader, obviously makes the reader's task easier. He gives not only facts but an interpretation of facts: the very pattern of subordination is an interpretation. When, however, the writer, by using subordination, assumes this burden of interpretation, he must not falsify his interpretation by careless and thoughtless subordination. He must think through the relation of part to part. Unless he does so, he may write sentences like this: " My head was feeling heavy when I took an aspirin." In this sentence the motive for the act is treated as though it were the matter of importance; the act itself has been relegated to the subordinate position. Rather than confuse the reader with a subordination which inverts the real relationship, the writer would have done better simply to have written: " My head was feeling heavy; I took an aspirin." But it is obvious, of course, that the proper subordination would be: " Because my head was feeling heavy, I took an aspirin." Or: " When my head began to feel heavy, I took an aspirin."

Here are two further examples of improper subordination:

The workman snored loudly and he had a red face.

Alter to:
The workman, who had a red face, snored loudly.

Or to:
The red-faced workman snored loudly.

Mr. Jones is our neighbor and he drove by in a large automobile.

Alter to:
Mr. Jones, who is our neighbor, drove by in a large automobile.

Or to:
Mr. Jones, our neighbor, drove by in a large automobile.

Though subordination is important as a means for tightening up a naïve and oversimple style, the student ought not to be browbeaten into constant subordination. In certain contexts a good writer might prefer:

The workman snored loudly. He had a red face.

This form of the statement does bring into sharp focus the detail of the red face. It might even suggest a leisurely observer, looking on with some amusement. For instances of some other effects secured by a simple and uncomplicated style, the student might look at pages 221 and 222.

We may sum up this topic as follows: Grammatical subordination must conform to the rhetorical sense; it must not mislead by inverting it. Positively, it is an important means for securing economy. Careful subordination tends to give the sense of a thoughtful observer who has sifted his ideas and arranged them with precision.

WORD ECHO AND JINGLING REPETITION

Before leaving the related topics of parallelism and coordination, we must mention the problems of word echo, repetition, and rhyme. Perhaps these problems seem out of place here and would be more appropriately treated under some such heading as euphony or vowel harmony. That they do bear upon the problem of parallelism, however, can speedily be made evident.

A recent newspaper story on the golden retriever breed of dogs has the following passage:

The golden retriever made his first American appearance before the first World War. Interest flagged for quite a *spell;* then several American sportsmen fell under their *spell* and brought in top stock for breeding." [*Italics ours.*]

Two paragraphs further on we find:

. . . it is relatively easy for them to pick up honors in *field* and obedience, *field* and *show,* and some have *shone* in all three." [*Italics ours.*]

The echo of *spell* is somewhat disconcerting and gives a mild shock when the reader realizes that the echo is pointless and meaningless. The partial echo of *show — shone* is just as pointless, and the defect is much more noticeable by being associated with a repetition (*field — field*) that *is* meaningful.

Though we may be tempted to dismiss these blemishes as merely a matter of sounds, they actually irritate us by promising a parallelism of meaning which they later deny. Mr. W. K. Wimsatt [5] is helpful on this point. He quotes the sentence " To read his tales is a

---

' *The Prose Style of Samuel Johnson,* Yale University Press, 1941, p. 13.

baptism of optimism . . ." and goes on to comment upon the nasty jingle of " -ptism " and " -ptimism." The jingling effect is, as he says, nasty " just because the two combinations so nearly strive to make these words parallel, whereas they are not; one qualifies the other." That is, the style is bad because the diction (baptism . . . optimism) suggests a parallelism between terms that are not parallel, just as *spell* and *spell* are not, and the reader feels that what pretended to be an expressive element — the *-ism* link between the terms — has proved to be meaningless, even misleading. (The reader will not necessarily make this analysis, of course; he will probably merely *feel* it, hearing the *-ism* repetition as an irritating jingle.)

The student writer should be chary of verbal ornament. He will do well to avoid " fine writing " and highfalutin tricks. But he must do more. The man writing about the golden retriever was probably not trying to work out melodic patterns; he was simply careless and did not revise his copy with sufficient care. The student must depend largely upon revision to rid his style of such blunders. The best way to avoid them is to read the manuscript aloud. Silly verbal echoes then make themselves apparent, and awkwardly misplaced modifiers betray their presence by the very awkwardness that they impose on the reading.

LOOSE SENTENCES AND PERIODIC SENTENCES

We can view sentence structure in still another way. We can distinguish between those sentences in which the sense of the sentence is held up until almost the end **(periodic sentences)** and those in which it is not held up **(loose sentences).** Holding up the sense creates suspense: we do not know how the sentence is " coming out " until we have reached, or nearly reached, the end of it. Here are some examples:

It was partly at such junctures as these and partly at quite different ones that with the turn my matters had now taken, my predicament, as I have called it, grew most sensible. — HENRY JAMES.

If we convert the sentence to loose structure, we get something like this:

With the turn my matters had now taken, my predicament, as I have called it, grew most sensible, partly at such junctures as these and partly at quite different ones.

But of all those Highlanders who looked on the recent turn of fortune with painful apprehension the fiercest and the most powerful were the Macdonalds. — LORD MACAULAY.

Converted to loose structure, the sentence reads:

But the Macdonalds were the fiercest and the most powerful of all those Highlanders who looked on the recent turn of fortune with painful apprehension.

The loose sentence is the " normal " sentence in English; the structure of the periodic sentence is " abnormal." As we noted above, deviation from the norm always tends to be emphatic. The periodic sentence, in skillful hands, is powerfully emphatic. By inversion, by use of the " It was " construction, or by interposition of movable modifiers between subject and predicate, the sentence and its primary statement are made to end together. But like all deviations from the norm, the periodic sentence — and the balanced sentence — are somewhat artificial. Overused, such sentences soon weary the reader.

SENTENCE LENGTH AND SENTENCE VARIATION

How long should a sentence be? It may be as short as one word. " Go! " is a perfectly good sentence; it has a predicate with subject implied. On the other hand, a sentence may be forty or fifty words long. In fact, by tacking together elements with *and*'s and *but*'s, we can construct sentences of indefinite length. These are the possible extremes. But with the sentence, as with the paragraph, common sense and taste set reasonable limits. A succession of very short sentences tends to be monotonous. Extremely long sentences tend to bog down the reader in a quagmire of words.

This is not, of course, to say that the writer should not feel free to use a one-word sentence whenever he needs it or even a succession of short sentences to gain special effects (see the latter part of page 601 for an example) . By the same token, he ought to feel free to use very long sentences to gain special effects. The following sentence from Lytton Strachey's *Queen Victoria* will illustrate:

Perhaps her fading mind called up once more the shadows of the past to float before it, and retraced, for the last time, the vanished visions of that long history — passing back and back, through the cloud of years, to older and ever older memories — to the spring woods at Osborne, so full of primroses for Lord Beaconsfield — to Lord Palmerston's queer clothes and high demeanour, and Albert's face under the green lamp, and Albert's first stag at Balmoral, and Albert in his blue and silver uniform, and the Baron coming in through a doorway, and Lord M. dreaming at Windsor with the rooks cawing in the elm-trees, and the Archbishop of Canterbury on his knees in the dawn, and the old King's turkey-cock ejaculations, and Uncle Leopold's soft voice at Claremont, and Lehzen with the globes, and her mother's feathers sweeping down towards her, and a great old repeater-watch of her father's in its tortoise-shell case, and a yellow rug, and some friendly flounces of sprigged muslin, and the trees and the grass at Kensington.   — LYTTON STRACHEY: *Queen Victoria.*

Strachey is imagining what may have passed through the old Queen's dying mind as she slipped from consciousness. He imagines the succession of memories as going backward in time, from those of adult life to those of youth, and on back to the memories of childhood. The loosely linked series of clauses which constitute the sentence can be justified on two counts: the memories are presented as those of a dying mind, and, as the memories go backward in time, they become those of a child. Thus dramatically considered, the jumping from scene to scene (as suggested by the dashes) and the loose tacking on of additional scenes (by *and*'s) are justified. This sentence, which closes Strachey's book with what amounts to a recapitulation of Victoria's life, is thus used to gain a special effect.

The normal limitations and requirements of the human mind dictate how much can be taken in satisfactorily " at one bite." Unless the writer is striving for some special effect, he ought to regard with suspicion very short and, especially, very long sentences. The human mind also requires variety: the sentences should not all be monotonously of the same length.

Let us consider a particular case. Look back at the paragraph from Virginia Woolf quoted on page 229. These thirteen sentences range in length from three words to fifty-two. The fourth sentence is quite long; the seventh sentence, very long. But three short sentences lead up to the fourth sentence, and two short sentences separate the fourth and seventh sentences.

Santayana's " Dickens " (page 663) will repay close study for the skill in which sentence variety is maintained. Santayana's sentences tend to be long. They are carefully constructed and are frequently quite complex. But he is careful not to tire the reader. The following passage will illustrate: " Having humility, that most liberating of sentiments, having true vision of human existence and joy in that vision, Dickens had in a superlative degree the gift of humour, of mimicry, of unrestrained farce." But after this sentence, we are given the simple statement: " He was the perfect comedian." And having thus had time to catch our breaths, we are ready to go on with " When people say Dickens. . . ."

Alternation of long and short sentences is but one means, however, by which to secure variety. Another, and a most important, means consists in varying the structure of the sentence. The examples from Santayana will illustrate: The sentence " He was the perfect comedian " is not only shorter than the sentence that precedes it; it represents, after the quite complex structure of the preceding sentence, a return to the simplest type of structure (subject + predicate + predicate complement).

Sentences that repeat a pattern become monotonous. Here is an example:

I was twenty that April and I made the glen my book. I idled over it. I watched the rhododendron snow its petals on the dark pools that spun them round in a swirl of brown foam and beached them on a tiny coast glittering with mica and fool's gold. I got it by heart, however, the dripping rocks, the ferny grottos, the eternal freshness, the sense of loam, of deep sweet decay, of a chain of life continuous and rich with the ages. I gathered there the walking fern that walks across its little forest world by striking root with its long tips, tip to root and root to tip walking away from the localities that knew it once. I was aware that the walking fern has its oriental counterpart. I knew also that Shortia, the flower that was lost for a century after Michaux found it " *dans les hautes montagnes de Carolinie*," has its next of kin upon the mountains of Japan. I sometimes met mountain people hunting for ginseng for the Chinese market; long ago the Chinese all but exterminated that herbalistic panacea of theirs, and now they turn for it to the only other source, the Appalachians.

The " I was — I idled — I gathered " formula is relieved somewhat by the long descriptive phrases and relative clauses. Even so, it is irritatingly monotonous. Here is the way in which Donald Culross Peattie actually wrote the passage:

The glen was my book, that April I was twenty. I idled over it, watching the rhododendron snow its petals on the dark pools that spun them round in a swirl of brown foam and beached them on a tiny coast glittering with mica and fool's gold. But I got it by heart, the dripping rocks, the ferny grottos, the eternal freshness, the sense of loam, of deep sweet decay, of a chain of life continuous and rich with the ages. The walking fern I gathered there, that walks across its little forest world by striking root with its long tips, tip to root and root to tip walking away from the localities that knew it once, has its oriental counterpart; of that I was aware. And I knew that Shortia, the flower that was lost for a century after Michaux found it, " *dans les hautes montagnes de Carolinie*," has its next of kin upon the mountains of Japan. Sometimes I met mountain people hunting for ginseng for the Chinese market; long ago the Chinese all but exterminated that herbalistic panacea of theirs, and now they turn for it to the only other source, the Appalachians.

             — DONALD CULROSS PEATTIE: *Flowering Earth.*

There are many ways in which to vary sentence structure. Nearly everything said earlier in this chapter can be brought to bear on this problem. We can invert the normal pattern, or rearrange the pattern to throw emphasis on what is normally the subject or complement; we can subordinate severely or rather lightly. Most of all, we can dispose the modifiers, particularly the movable modifiers, so as to vary the pattern almost indefinitely. The effort to secure variety should never be an overriding consideration. A sentence should take the structure best adapted to its special job. The writer will usually find that he is thoroughly occupied in discharging this obligation. Yet it is well to remind ourselves here again of the claims of the whole composition. We never write a "collection of sentences"; we write an essay, a theme, a total composition. The good sentence honors the claims exerted upon it by the total composition. And in our writing, and especially in our *rewriting,* we need to see that we have avoided monotony of sentence length or of sentence structure.

• Applications •

I. Try to determine which of the following sentences are periodic in structure and which are loose. Rewrite the periodic sentences into loose sentences, and the loose into periodic. Pick out the balanced sentences, if any.

1. The power, and the restriction on it, though quite distinguishable when they do not approach each other, may yet, like the intervening colors between white and black, approach so nearly as to perplex the understanding, as colors perplex the vision in marking the distinction between them. — John Marshall

2. Peace cannot be secured without armies; and armies must be supported at the expense of the people. It is for your sake, not for our own, that we guard the barrier of the Rhine against the ferocious Germans, who have so often attempted, and who will always desire, to exchange the solitude of their woods and morasses for the wealth and fertility of Gaul. — Edward Gibbon.

3. The night, the earth under her, seemed to swell and recede together with a limitless, unhurried, benign breathing. — Katherine Anne Porter.

4. And it is precisely because of this utterly unsettled and uncertain condition of philosophy at present that I regard any practical application of it to religion and conduct as exceedingly dangerous. — Charles S. Peirce.

5. If we begin with certainties, we shall end in doubts; but if we begin with doubts, and are patient in them, we shall end in certainties. — Francis Bacon.

6. The mania for handling all the sides of every question, looking into every window, and opening every door, was, as Bluebeard judiciously pointed out to his wives, fatal to their practical usefulness in society. — Henry Adams.

7. Bubbling spontaneously from the artless heart of a child or man, without egoism and full of feeling, laughter is the music of life. — William Osler.

8. Every night I pulled my flag down and folded it up and laid it on a shelf in my bedroom, and one morning before breakfast I found it, though I had folded

it up the night before, knotted around the bottom of the flagstaff so that it was touching the grass. — W. B. Yeats.

9. The hunger and thirst for knowledge, the keen delight in the chase, the good-humored willingness to admit that the scent was false, the eager desire to get on with the work, the cheerful resolution to go back and begin again, the broad good sense, the unaffected modesty, the imperturbable temper, the gratitude for any little help that was given — all these will remain in my memory, though I cannot paint them for others. — F. W. Maitland.

10. If he be my enemy, let him triumph; if he be my friend, as I have given him no personal occasion to be otherwise, he will be glad of my repentance. It becomes me not to draw my pen in the defense of a bad cause, when I have so often drawn it for a good one. — John Dryden.

II. The following paragraphs are taken from *Time*. *Time* style is celebrated for its inversions of, and its drastic departures from, normal sentence order. The motive, presumably, is a desire for condensation and emphasis. Rewrite these paragraphs so as to restore normal sentence order. Can you justify the departures from normal order? Is emphasis intelligently used? Or does too much emphasis result in no emphasis?

An abandoned lime quarry at Makapangsgat, Transvaal, yielded two bones last year to Dart's diggers: part of an occiput (the back part of the skull) and a lower jaw, from a pygmy moppet who had died while still getting his second teeth. Near by were many baboon skulls, bashed in from above or behind with a club which had a ridged head (the distal end of the humerus).

Most startling was Dart's evidence, from a number of charred bones, that the little man had learned to use fire. He lived in the early Ice Age, from 300,000 to 500,000 years before Peking Man, hitherto the earliest known user of fire. In honor of both his fire-bringing record and his prophetic skills, the new little man was named *Australopithecus prometheus*.

III. The following paragraph is from Ring Lardner's *You Know Me, Al,* which purports to be a series of letters from Jack, the rookie pitcher, to his friend. As a revelation of character and of speech " in character," it is quite perfect. But rewriting it may provide us with a useful exercise in sentence structure and proper subordination. Put it into formal English.

We was to play 2 games here and was to play 1 of them in Tacoma and the other here but it rained and so we did not play neither 1 and the people was pretty mad a bout it because I was announced to pitch and they figured probily this would be there only chance to see me in axion and they made a awful holler but Comiskey says No they would not be no game because the field neither here or in Tacoma was in no shape for a game and he would not take no chance of me pitching and may be slipping in the mud and straneing myself and then where would the White Sox be at next season. So we been laying a round all the p.m. and I and Dutch Schaefer had a long talk to gether while some of the rest of the boys was out buying some cloths to take on the trip and Al I bought a full dress suit of evening cloths at Portland yesterday and now I owe Callahan the money for them and am not going on no trip so probily I wont never get to ware them and it is just $45.00 throwed a way but I would rather throw $45.00 a way then go on a trip a round the world and leave my family all winter.

CHAPTER TEN

Diction

Good diction is the choice of the right words. Accurate, effective expression obviously requires the right words, the words which will represent — not nearly, not approximately, but exactly — what we want to say. This is a simple rule; but to apply it is far from simple. The good writer must choose the right words, yes; but how does he know which are the right words?

Diction would be no problem if there existed for each object and each idea just one word which denoted specifically that object or idea — if there were one name and one name only for each separate thing. But language is not like that. Most words are not strictly denotative, that is, they do not merely point to a specific object. Some words in English, it is true, particularly scientific words, do represent the only name we have for a specific object or substance. *Lemming,* for example, is the only name we have for a certain mouse-like rodent; *purine* is the only name of a compound the chemical formula of which is $C_5H_4N_4$. The language of science ideally is a language of pure denotation. But this constitutes a special case, and its problems are different from those of more ordinary language.

Primary Meaning and Implied Meaning

Actually, instead of one word and only one word for each thing, the writer finds competing for his attention a number of words, all of which denote exactly or approximately the same thing. Moreover, even those words which have exactly the same denotation, that is, those which explicitly refer to the same thing, may have different connotations — different shades of meaning.

For example, *brightness, radiance, effulgence,* and *brilliance* may be said to have the same general denotation, but there is a considerable difference in what they connote. *Radiance* implies beams radiating from a source, as the words *brilliance* or *brightness* do not. *Brilliance,* on the other hand, suggests an intensity of light which *effulgence* and *brightness* do not. Again, *brightness* is a more homely, everyday word than are *radiance, brilliance,* and *effulgence.* These are only a few suggested contrasts among the connotations of these words, all of which describe a quality of light.

Varying connotations in words with the same denotation may also be illustrated from words which refer to concrete objects. Compare the simple words *bucket* and *pail.* The primary meanings are much the same. We might apply either word to naming the same vessel. But in most of present-day America *bucket* is more likely to be the ordinary word, with associations of everyday activity; whereas *pail* will seem a little more old-fashioned and endowed with more " poetic " suggestions. It connotes for some readers a bygone era of pretty milkmaids in an idyllic setting. But *bucket,* too, may have sentimental associations, someone will exclaim, remembering the song entitled, " The Old Oaken Bucket." For words change in meaning from period to period, and their associated meanings change, as a rule, much more rapidly than do their primary meanings.

Words, then, are not static, changeless counters but are affected intimately, especially on the level of connotation, by the changing, developing, restless life of the men who use them. Some words wear out and lose their force. Some words go downhill and lose respectability. Other words rise in the scale and acquire respectability.

In 1710, Jonathan Swift, the author of *Gulliver's Travels,* poked fun at some of the clipped and slang forms of English which were coming into vogue in his day. Some of these words — for example, *mob* (a clipped form of *mobile*) and *banter* (origin unknown) — have since acquired respectability and now perform useful functions in our language. But other words upon which Swift cast scorn, such as *pozz* (for *possible*), *plenipo* (from *plenipotentiary,* " big shot " in modern slang), and *phiz* (from *physiognomy,* that is, *face*), have disappeared, as Swift hoped they would. One can observe a similar process at work in our own day. Some of the slang of fifty years ago — indeed, in some circles that of ten years ago — may now seem oddly quaint.

The process of growth and decay in language is so strong that many words in the course of generations have shifted not only their associations but their primary meanings as well; some have even reversed their original meanings.[1]

---

[1] Later in this chapter we shall have occasion to return to the history of words when we discuss the use of the dictionary. (See also pages 304–08.)

The history of word change is interesting in itself, but we are concerned here with the light that it throws upon the nature of words. Words shift meaning because they are not static but are dynamic. The secondary and associated meanings of a word are powerful, and it is not surprising that sometimes one of them becomes the new primary meaning. It behooves the writer to take into account these important associated meanings of a word as well as its precise denotation. Indeed, the writer has the task of controlling both dimensions of his language. Thus in a romantic tale one might appropriately use the word *steed* rather than *horse*. But in ordinary contexts one certainly would not say or write, " Saddle my steed," unless he were being deliberately playful or ironic. On the other hand, there are still other contexts in which, instead of the rather neutral word *horse*, it might be appropriate to use words like *plug* or *nag*, terms which are as derisive or humorous in tone as *steed* is poetic and " literary."

Two Distinctions: General and Specific; Abstract and Concrete

A general word refers to a group, a class, and a specific word refers to a member of that class. *Tree* is a general word, but *oak, elm, poplar* are specific. We must remember, however, that the terms **general** and **specific** are relative, not absolute. *Coat,* for example, is more specific than *garment,* for a coat is a kind of garment. But *coat,* on the other hand, is more general than *hunting jacket,* for a hunting jacket is a kind of coat. So with our trees above. *Oak* is more specific than *tree* but more general than *black oak* or *water oak* or *post oak.*

The specific word tends to give color and tang, tends to appeal to the imagination. Suppose we write: " He saw a ship on the horizon." What can our reader's imagination do with that? It can put some sort of floating object, large, man-made, and designed for transportation, on the imagined horizon. But what is the shape of the object? Will there be a smudge of smoke or the glint of white sail? The word *ship* is a general word and, therefore, cannot give a vivid image in that split second in which the reader's eye rests upon the sentence. Suppose we substitute *liner, schooner, brig, tanker, brig-schooner, junk,* or some other specific word. Then there is something for the imagination to seize on. There is no blur on the horizon; there is a shape.

But suppose, one may object, that we write *brig* and that the reader does not know what rig such a craft carries. Does he then have a shape on the horizon? Most readers would get the glint of sail and not the smudge of smoke, for their information might go that far. The specific word, however, does more than give, or appeal to, information. The mere fact of the use of the specific word gives some sort of nudge to the imagination, gives some sense of knowingness, makes the reader kid himself a bit. If we use the word *brig,* even the reader totally ignorant of nautical matters, as most of us are, feels, just for the moment, a little like an old salt.

There is another distinction which is important in our choice of words. It has to do with concreteness and abstraction. *Peach, pear, quince, apple,* and *apricot* are **concrete** words. The word *peach* implies certain qualities: a certain shape, a certain color, a certain kind of sweetness. But *peach* implies these qualities as " grown together," as we should actually find them embodied in a peach. (The Latin word from which *concrete* derives means literally " grown together.") We can, of course, *abstract* (this word literally means " take away ") these qualities from the actual peach and refer to them in isolation: *sweetness, fuzziness, softness.* Isolating these qualities in such fashion, we get a set of **abstract** words. *Sweetness* isolates a quality common to peaches, of course, and to many other things; the quality is thought of as an idea in its own right.

Words that refer to ideas, qualities, and characteristics *as such* are usually abstract. Words that name classes of objects and classes of actions are usually general. Words that refer to particular objects and particular actions are usually both concrete and specific. These are, on the whole, our most vivid words; they reflect immediately the world of things known to our senses. This comment is not meant to imply that concrete and specific words are somehow " better " than abstract and general words. For some purposes they are indeed better, but for others, not. The world of ideas and concepts requires its terms just as urgently as does the world of particular things.

• Applications •

I. Make a list of the concrete words in the passages of description quoted on pages 218, 219, and 221. Make another list of the concrete words in the passages quoted on pages 94, 106, and 121. Which tend to use the greater proportion of concrete words? Why?

II. Compare, in the matter of abstract-general and concrete-specific diction, the passage quoted from *Far Off Things* (page 228) with that quoted from *Robinson Crusoe* (page 229). Can you account for the choice of diction in terms of what each author is trying to do? About which of the two scenes described do you have more facts? Which do you visualize more vividly?

III. Let us assume that, in a theme describing incidents upon a motor trip, you have written the following paragraphs:

Although there is a bridge across the Mississippi River at Baton Rouge, we decided to cross the river by ferryboat, simply to say that we had been on a river ferry. My head was full of what I had read from Mark Twain about life on the Mississippi when he was a pilot on the great river. So naturally I wanted to see what a Mississippi steamboat was like. I wondered how much conditions had changed in a hundred years.

The river was big and brown-colored. I could see a few things drifting in the water. There did not seem to be much current, though the companion ferry coming from the other side to meet us was obviously steering to counteract drift. The western bank of the river was low-lying and covered with trees of some sort. As I watched the river, I heard the noise of the chain barrier going into place and I knew that we were about ready to start. The whistle blew, and I heard the engines begin to make their characteristic noise. As I looked toward the sound, I saw the fireman throw up the door of the furnace and begin to shovel in coal. The fire under the boiler was visible.

Even if you have never seen the Mississippi or have never been on a river packet, you should be able to improve the sample paragraphs. You are acquainted with other rivers; you have been to the movies; you may even have read Mark Twain.

Rewrite these paragraphs to make them more vivid, substituting concrete and specific words. (You need not, of course, restrict your revision to diction; make whatever other changes seem called for.)

IV. Assume that, in an account of a motor trip through one of the New England states, you have written the following paragraphs:

We stopped the car beside the stone wall near the gate that had led to the farmhouse door. The house was gray and unpainted. It must have been unlived in for years. Some of the windows were broken. The roof was in disrepair.

The house was set in what had been a thriving apple orchard, and now on this October day, the old trees were worth looking at. A majority of them were filled with fruit. The sun was shining, and the sight was very pretty, even though some of the trees were rotted. A lot of them had vines growing up their trunks, and Jim said it was poison ivy.

Rewrite this passage so as to make the reader see the scene. Your revision will certainly call for changes in diction, but do not hesitate to make more extensive changes.

The Misuse of Abstract and General Words

Much writing that is woolly and clouded, difficult to read, clogged and ineffective, is writing that is filled with general and abstract words. For example:

Quite significantly, the emphasis is being placed upon vocational intelligence, which is based upon adequate occupational information for all pupils in secondary schools. . . . This emphasis upon vocational guidance for the purpose of making young people intelligent concerning the world of occupations and the requirements for entering occupations need not conflict seriously with other views of guidance that take into account everything pertaining to the education of the pupil.

There are a number of things wrong with this flabby statement, among them, the large number of abstract words. The author might have written:

High schools today insist that the student learn enough about jobs to choose his own job wisely. The student needs to learn what various jobs pay, what training they require, and what kinds of people find them interesting. He can learn these things while he is learning the other things that schools are supposed to teach. Both kinds of learning are preparations for life, and one need not interfere with the other.

The rewritten version still makes use of general and abstract words (*training, preparation,* and so on); but some of the cloudiest of the abstractions (*vocational intelligence, occupational information*) have been removed, and the rewritten version is not only simpler but has more force.

Many subjects, however, require general and abstract words. For example, compare these two ways of saying the same thing: (1) " A child needs sympathy." (2) " A child does not like frowns. Cold looks cow him. He is fearful when he hears harsh words." The second account is long-winded; even so, the concrete words do not manage to give fully the meaning of the one abstract word *sympathy.*

Or, compare (1) " He lived in a house of medium size " with (2) " His home did not have the suburban air of a bungalow, and it certainly had nothing of the rustic style of a lodge. It was much smaller than a mansion, but somewhat larger than a cottage." *Mansion, cottage, bungalow,* and *lodge* (not to mention *cabin, hut, villa,* and *château*) are overspecific for the writer's purpose here; he needs the simple, general term *house.* Our pronouns provide another illustration. The English personal pronouns sometimes prove to be overspecific. In some contexts, it would be most convenient if we had a pronoun which could mean either " he " or " she " (" his " or " her," " him " or " her ") , without forcing us either to specify, or to use the masculine form with the understanding that it applies to either sex: " Someone has left his (or her) pen " (or " his pen ") .

The writer cannot, and need not try to, avoid abstract and general words. But he ought not to fall into the slovenly habit of using them without thought. In any case, he should remember that a sprinkling of concrete and specific words can be used to lighten the numbing weight of piled-up abstractions. To illustrate, compare:

(1) A child needs sympathy. Tolerance of his mistakes and the sense of understanding and comradeship provide the proper stimulus for his developing personality. Conversely, an environment defective in sympathy and understanding can be positively thwarting; it can lead to repressions and thus lay the foundation for ruinous personality problems.

(2) A child needs sympathy. He didn't intend to smash the vase or to hurt the cat when he pulled its tail. Tolerance of mistakes and some understanding is necessary if he is to feel that he is a comrade. Acceptance as a comrade stimulates him to become a better comrade. He grows and develops toward responsibility. But he finds it hard to grow normally in a cold and repressive atmosphere. The meaningless spanking — meaningless to him, since he had no intention of breaking the vase — drives him in on himself. He becomes confused and repressed. Some of these confusions and repressions may linger into adult life.

In choosing our words, the overriding consideration, of course, will always be the particular effect that the writer wishes to obtain. Description and narration, for example, thrive on the concrete and the specific. Note the number of concrete and specific terms in the following passage:

He knew the inchoate sharp excitement of hot dandelions in young Spring grass at noon; the smell of cellars, cobwebs, and built-on secret earth; in July, of watermelons bedded in sweet hay, inside a farmer's covered wagon; of cantaloupe and crated peaches; and the scent of orange rind, bitter-sweet, before a fire of coals.
— THOMAS WOLFE: *Look Homeward, Angel.*

Exposition and argument, on the other hand, by their very nature, call for a diction in which general and abstract words are important.

Marx's interpretation of the past is explicit and realistic; his forecast of the future seems to me vague and idealistic. I have called it utopian, but you object to that word. I do not insist on it. I will even surrender the word " idealistic." But the point is this. Marx finds that in the past the effective force that has determined social change is the economic class conflict. He points out that this economic class conflict is working to undermine our capitalistic society. Very well. If then I project this explanation of social changes into the future, what does it tell me? It seems to tell me that there will be in the future what there has been in the past — an endless economic class conflict, and endless replacement of one dominant class by another, an endless transformation of institutions and ideas in accordance with the changes effected by the class conflict.

— CARL BECKER: 'The Marxian Philosophy of History,"
Everyman His Own Historian: Essays on History and Politics.

Language Growth by Extension of Meaning

We have said that a word has not only a specific meaning but also implied meanings. The implied meanings are obviously less definite than the specific meaning, and therefore less stable and more amenable to change. In scientific language the specific meanings are rigidly stabilized, and the hazy and shifting implied meanings are, in so far as possible, eliminated. In a colorful and racy use of everyday language, just the reverse is the case. The implied meanings are rich and important. We are often tempted to use a word, not **literally** (that is, adhering strictly to the specific meaning), but **figuratively,** stressing the associations of the word. It is through such a process that words have shifted their meanings in the past; but this process of extension of meaning is constantly at work even in our own time. Let us consider an illustration of the process.

The casual and unthinking view of language sees each word as fastened neatly and tightly to a certain specific object: *weasel* means a certain kind of small, furry mammal of slender body, that moves furtively, preys on birds, rats, and rabbits, sucking their blood, and occasionally also sucking eggs; *cooking* means the preparation of food by exposing it to heat; *spade* means an instrument for digging in the earth. But words are not actually so neatly fastened to the objects for which they stand. Even when we are determined to speak forthrightly and " call a spade a spade," we rarely do so. It is against the nature of language that we should be able to do so.

For example, Bob, who is determined to call a spade a spade, says: " Well, Joe has weaseled out on us again. Yesterday when I told him the Collins deal was finally cooking, he pretended he had never heard of it and said he wouldn't buy a pig in a poke." But obviously one is not calling a spade a *spade* when he attributes to

another human being the actions of a weasel, describes the preparation of a business deal as a piece of cookery, and makes the agreement to be signed the purchase of a pig enclosed in a bag.

Weasel and *cooking* — not to mention the pig — are not being
used literally here; their meanings have been extended through analogy. In the case of *cooking* the extension of meaning is very easy
to grasp: one sort of preparation — cooking — is extended to mean
another and more general sort of preparation. *Weaseling* is more
difficult. There may be some implication of "weasel words," that is,
words that have had the substance sucked out of them, like eggs
sucked by a weasel; but the more probable analogy here is that between Joe's wriggling out of his promise and the weasel's bodily
movements as it glides through apparently impossibly small aper-
tures.

The situation we have just considered is thoroughly typical. Many
common words have been extended from their original meanings in
just this fashion. We speak of the "eye" of a needle, the "mouth"
of a river, the "legs" of a chair, the "foot" of a bed. The hole in
the end of a needle might have been given a special name; instead,
men called it an "eye" because of its fancied likeness to the human
eye. So, too, with examples such as these: a *keen* mind, a *bright* disposition, a *sunny* smile, a *black* look. Someone saw an analogy between the way in which a keen blade cut through wood and the
way in which a good mind cut into the problem with which it was
concerned. The smile obviously does not really shed sunlight, but
it may seem to affect one as sunlight does, and in a way quite the
opposite of the black look.

But the point to be made here does not concern the basis for the
analogy, whether of physical resemblance (the *jaws* of a vise), similarity of function (the *key* to a puzzle), similarity of effect (a *shining* example), or anything else. The point to be made is, rather,
that people normally use words in this way, extending, stretching,
twisting their meanings, so that they apply to other objects or actions or situations than those to which they originally applied. This
is the **metaphorical** process, about which we shall have more to say
in the next chapter. The essence of metaphor inheres in this transfer of meaning, in the application of a word that literally means one
thing to something else.

Thus far we have taken our illustrations from common words. But
less common words and learned words will illustrate the same process of extension of meaning. Indeed, most of our words that express
complex ideas and relationships have been built up out of simpler
words. For example, we say, "His generosity caused him to over-

look my fault." *Overlook* here means to " disregard or ignore in-
dulgently." But *overlook* is obviously made up of the simple words
look and *over*. To look over an object may imply that one does not
let his gaze rest upon that object: his eyes pass over it without no-
ticing it. *Overlook,* then, in the sense of " disregard " is an extension
and specialization of one of the implied meanings of *look over*. We
have said " one of the meanings," for *look over* obviously implies
other possible meanings. Consider the nearly parallel expression " to
see over." From it we get the word *oversee*. This word normally
means today *to direct, to supervise* — something quite different from
" overlook." *Supervise* is built out of the same concepts as *oversee,*
for *super* in Latin means " over," and *-vise* comes from the Latin
verb *videre* (past participle *visus*) which means " to see." A bishop,
by the way, is literally an *overseer*. For *bishop* comes originally from
two Greek words: *epi,* which means " over," and *skopein,* which
means " to look." Thus, such diverse words as *overlook, oversee,
overseer, supervise,* and *bishop* represent particular extensions of
much the same primitive literal meaning.

The Dictionary: A Record of Meanings

The etymology (that is, the derivation and history) of a word is
often highly interesting in itself, but knowledge of word origins is
also of great practical usefulness. The full mastery of a particular
word frequently entails knowing its root meaning. Possessing that
meaning, we acquire a firm grasp on its various later meanings, for
we can see them as extended and specialized meanings that have
grown out of the original meaning.

Here, for example, is the entry in *The American College Dictionary* for the word *litter:* [2]

> **lit·ter** (lĭt′ər), *n.* **1.** things scattered about; scattered
> rubbish. **2.** a condition of disorder or untidiness. **3.** a
> number of young brought forth at one birth. **4.** a
> framework of canvas stretched between two parallel
> bars, for the transportation of the sick and the wounded.
> **5.** a vehicle carried by men or animals, consisting of a
> bed or couch, often covered and curtained, suspended
> between shafts. **6.** straw, hay, etc., used as bedding for
> animals, or as a protection for plants. **7.** the rubbish of
> dead leaves and twigs scattered upon the floor of the
> forest. —*v.t.* **8.** to strew (a place) with scattered ob-
> jects. **9.** to scatter (objects) in disorder. **10.** to be
> strewed about (a place) in disorder (fol. by *up*). **11.** to
> give birth to (young): said chiefly of animals. **12.** to
> supply (an animal) with litter for a bed. **13.** to use
> (straw, hay, etc.) for litter. **14.** to cover (a floor, etc.)
> with litter, or straw, hay, etc. —*v.i.* **15.** to give birth to
> a litter. [ME *litere,* t. AF, der. *lit* bed, g. L *lectus*] —**Syn.**
> **3.** See **brood.**

[2] From *The American College Dictionary,* ed. by Clarence L. Barnhart, copyright, 1956, by Random House, Inc.

The word is first listed as a noun (*n.*). Seven meanings of the noun are given. But the word is also a transitive verb (*v.t.*), for which seven meanings are given. For *litter* as an intransitive verb (*v.i.*), only one meaning is given. The word first occurs in Middle English (ME *litere*), was taken from Anglo-French (t. AF), derived from a word meaning bed (der. *lit* bed), and goes back finally to the Latin word for bed, *lectus* (g. L *lectus*). Synonyms (words of nearly the same meaning) for the third meaning of *litter* will be found under *brood* (Syn. 3. See brood).

Let us consider the various meanings given for *litter*. At first glance there seems little to connect meaning 2, " a condition of disorder or untidiness," with meaning 3, " a number of young brought forth at a birth," and even less with meaning 4, " a framework of canvas . . . for the transportation of the sick and the wounded." But once we grasp the fact that *litter* comes originally from a Latin word meaning " bed," it is fairly easy to see how the various apparently unconnected meanings of *litter* developed. Meanings 4 and 5 obviously refer to special sorts of portable beds; and the term *bedding* in definition 6 provides a link to meanings 12, 13, and 14. For if beds originally consisted of straw or rushes heaped together, it is easy to see how any scattering of straw or hay might come to be called a *litter,* and the process of strewing it a process of *littering.* Meanings 1, 2, 8, and 9 are obvious further extensions, for in these meanings the emphasis has been shifted from the purpose of making a kind of bed to an aimless and untidy strewing about.

Meanings 3, 11, and 15 derive from the original meaning " bed " by another chain of development. The mother animal frequently makes a sort of rude bed in which she lies to give birth, and by association the rude bed (*litter*) comes to be used for what is found in the bed, the young animals themselves.

Let us consider another example, this time from *Webster's Collegiate Dictionary.* Here is the dictionary entry for the common word *sad:*

> **sad** (săd), *adj.;* SAD′DER (-ẽr); SAD′DEST. [AS. *sæd* satisfied, sated.]
> **1.** *Archaic.* Firmly established. **2.** Affected with or expressive of grief; downcast; gloomy. **3.** Characterized by or associated with sorrow; melancholy. **4.** Afflictive; grievous. **5.** Dull; somber; — of colors. **6. a** Shocking; wicked; — often playfully. **b** *Slang.* Inferior.

By permission. From Webster's New Collegiate Dictionary
Copyright, 1949, 1951, 1953, 1956
by G. & C. Merriam Co.

The word is an adjective (*adj.*). The forms of the comparative and superlative degrees are given; then its derivation (from Anglo-Saxon *saed*). Next, the dictionary lists six meanings of this word, one of which it designates as archaic (1) and another as slang (6*b*).

Even so brief an account as this suggests a history of shifting meanings. Inspection of a larger dictionary, such as *Webster's New International Dictionary* or the *Oxford English Dictionary* (also known as *A New English Dictionary*), with its fuller information as to the derivation of the word and its finer discrimination of meanings (including the various earlier meanings), enables us to make out a detailed history of the meanings of the word.

Sad is closely related to the German word *satt* ("full to repletion") and to the Latin word *satis* ("enough"), from which we get such modern English words as *satiate* and *satisfied*. But a man who has had a big dinner is torpid and heavy, not lively or restless, and so *sad* came to carry the suggestion of *calm, stable, earnest*. Shakespeare frequently uses it to mean the opposite of "trifling" or "frivolous." But a person who seems thus sober and serious *may* be so because he is grieved or melancholy, and the word thereby gradually took on its modern meaning of "mournful" or "grieved." But we must not end this account without mentioning other lines of development. The sense of *torpid* or *heavy* was extended from animate beings, which can eat to repletion, to inanimate things which cannot — to bread, for example, that fails to rise, or to a heavy laundry iron. In this connection the student should look up the word *sadiron*. (*Webster's Collegiate Dictionary* indicates that the element *sad* has an obsolete sense of *heavy*.)

Meaning 5 (dull; somber; — of colors) represents still another such extension. It means the kind of color which a sobersides (as opposed to a gay and sprightly person) would wear, that is, dull, sober colors.

Has the process of extension now ceased? Hardly. Meaning 6*a* represents a fairly late instance of it. In mock deprecation, a young fellow might be called "a sad young dog," as though his conduct caused horror and grief. Meaning 6*b* is a later extension still, one that has not yet been approved by careful speakers as "good English." In such a phrase as "sad sack" this meaning of *sad* has temporarily gained wide currency (though in formal American English we tend to prefer the word *sorry:* a sorry team, a sorry outfit, a sorry job). If meaning 6*b* ever establishes itself in standard English, the dictionary will remove the characterization "slang." (Some terms which began as slang have found their way into the language and into good usage; but a vastly greater number have enjoyed a brief popularity, have been discarded, and are now forgotten. See page 296.)

Here is a third example of a dictionary listing, this time from *Webster's New World Dictionary:* [3]

de·grade (di-grād'), *v.t.* [DEGRADED (-id), DEGRADING], [ME. *degraden;* OFr. *degrader;* LL. *degradare,* to reduce in rank < L. *de-,* down + *gradus;* see GRADE], **1.** to lower in rank or status; take a position of honor from: as, the sergeant was *degraded* to the rank of private. **2.** to lower or corrupt in quality, moral character, etc. **3.** to bring into dishonor or contempt. **4.** to lower in value, price, quality, etc. **5.** in *biology,* to place in a lower classification. **6.** in *geology,* to lower (a surface) by erosion. *v.i.* to sink to a lower position or type; degenerate.
SYN.—**degrade** literally means to lower in grade or rank, but it commonly implies a lowering or corrupting of moral character, self-respect, etc.; **abase** suggests a loss, often merely temporary and self-imposed, of dignity, respect, etc. (he *abased* himself before his employer); **debase** implies a decline in value, quality, character, etc. (a *debased* mind); to **humble** is to lower the pride or increase the humility, especially of another, and, unqualified, suggests that such lowering is deserved (*humbled* by the frightening experience); to **humiliate** is to humble or shame (another) painfully and in public (*humiliated* by their laughter).—*ANT.* exalt, dignify.

The word is a transitive verb (*v.t.*). Its derivation is traced through Middle English (ME. *degraden*), Old French (OFr. *degrader*), Late Latin (LL. *degradare*), back to Latin (*de + gradus*). Five meanings are distinguished; and since *degrade* may also appear as an intransitive verb (*v.i.*), one further intransitive meaning. There is a discussion of the differences in meaning between *degrade* and four of its synonyms. Two antonyms (words of opposed meaning) are listed.

The definition of a word is, then, a somewhat more complex business than one might suppose. It consists frequently not just of *the* meaning, but of interrelated sets of meanings, some of which are current and some of which are not, and some of which have been accepted into good society and some of which are merely clinging to the fringes of society. A word which is appropriate in one context obviously might be grossly out of place in another.

• **Applications** •

I. Look up the origin of the following words:

nostril	enthusiasm	fast (adj.)
aristocracy	urbane	egregious
plutocracy	Bible	sympathetic
complicate	fine (adj.)	malaria
thrilling	infant	starboard
vivid	silly	melancholy
gerrymander	laconic	bourgeois

---

[3] From *Webster's New World Dictionary of the American Language,* College Edition, copyright, 1957, by The World Publishing Company.

Does knowledge of its origin clarify the meaning of any word? Does it enable you to understand the relationship between current discrepant meanings (that is, " He made a *fast* trip," and " The boat was made *fast* to the pier "; or " This *fine* print hurts my eyes " and " He was a big, *fine,* upstanding man ")? Does knowledge of the origin of the word help account for such uses as " legal *infant* " and " the *Book* " (as applied to the Bible)?

II. With the help of the dictionary discriminate as carefully as you can among the words in the following groups:

1. sulky, petulant, peevish, sullen, morose, crabbed, surly
2. skeptic, infidel, atheist, freethinker, agnostic
3. reasonable, just, moderate, equitable, fair-minded, judicial
4. rebellion, revolt, insurrection, revolution
5. belief, faith, persuasion, conviction, assurance, reliance
6. sneak, skulk, slink
7. trick, fool, hoodwink, bamboozle, deceive, beguile, delude, cheat, mislead
8. brave, daring, courageous, fearless, valiant, dauntless
9. dawdle, idle, loiter, linger, lag
10. solemn, sober, serious, grave, reverential, earnest

Does a knowledge of the origin of the word throw light upon the special connotations of any of these words?

The Company a Word Keeps: Colloquial, Informal, and Formal

Earlier, in discussing the implied meanings of words, we touched briefly upon the way in which these meanings may determine the appropriateness of a word for a particular context (page 297). The word *steed,* we saw, would be proper for some contexts, *nag* for others, and *horse* for still others. But the problem of appropriateness is important and deserves fuller treatment.

In the first place, there is what may be called the dignity and social standing of the word. Like human beings, a word tends to be known by the company it keeps. Words like *caboodle* and *gumption* are good colloquial words and perfectly appropriate to the informal give-and-take of conversation. But they would be out of place in a dignified and formal utterance. For example, a speech welcoming a great public figure in which he was complimented on his " statesman-like gumption " would be absurd. To take another example, many of us use the slang term *guy,* and though, like much slang, it has lost what pungency it may once have had, its rather flippant breeziness is not inappropriate in some contexts. But it would be foolish to welcome our elder statesman by complimenting him on being a " wise and venerable guy." The shoe, it is only fair to say, can pinch the other foot. Certain literary and rather highfalutin terms, in a *colloquial* context, sound just as absurd. We do not praise a friend for his " dexterity " or for his " erudition," not, at least, when we meet him on the street or chat with him across the table.

The fact that words are known by the company they keep does not, however, justify snobbishness in diction. Pomposity is, in the end, probably in even worse taste than blurting out a slang term on a formal occasion. Words must be used with tact and common sense. But the comments made above do point to certain areas of usage of which most of us are already more or less aware. The various kinds of diction (and their necessary overlappings) are conveniently represented in the following diagram: [4]

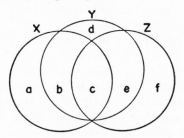

The three circles X, Y, Z, represent the three sets of language habits indicated above.
  X—formal literary English, the words, the expressions, and the structures one finds in serious books.
  Y—colloquial English, the words, expressions, and the structures of the informal but polite conversation of cultivated people.
  Z—illiterate English, the words, the expressions, and the structures of the language of the uneducated.
  b, c, and e represent the overlappings of the three types of English.
  c—that which is common to all three: formal literary English, colloquial English, and illiterate English.
  b—that which is common to both formal literary English and colloquial English.
  e—that which is common to both colloquial English and illiterate English.
  a, d, and f represent those portions of each type of English that are peculiar to that particular set of language habits.

Modern slang, for example, falls into segment *e* — and possibly *d.* It would be properly available for colloquial and informal writing.

[4] From *The American College Dictionary,* ed. by Clarence L. Barnhart, copyright, 1956, by Random House, Inc.

(But segments *d* and *e,* of course, include more than slang: they include colloquial terms of all kinds that do not occur in formal literary English.) Segment *a* includes the terms that occur only in formal literary English, but the overlap of formal literary English with colloquial and illiterate English is large — so large that most of the words used in writing of the most formal style are to be found in writings at the other extreme of style.

It would be misleading, therefore, to suggest that there is a mechanical rule for selecting the diction that one uses in an informal essay, or in a formal treatise, or to express the dialogue of "low characters" in a novel. The degrees of height and lowness of style and shadings of formality and informality are so many — and vary so much even within one work — that we cannot hope to find our appropriate diction segregated for us in one compartment. But our chart should make plain that in this matter of levels of diction, the dictionary can be of real help. It marks, as such, colloquial words, slang, technical words, and so on. Yet recourse to the dictionary is not a substitute for the student's developing a feeling for language. The dictionary can help, but wide reading and practice in writing can help even more.

The student already has a more sensitive feeling for language than he realizes. It would not occur to the student — except as a joke — to say to a friend: "I am trying to ascertain the assignment for next week in English. The amiable pedagogue who directs our labors was inaudible to me, though I think he must have mumbled something. Can you advise me?" Even though the student is not likely to err in the direction of the pompous and the highfalutin, he may very well be tempted into a colloquial and slangy style. He *might* write for his history instructor: "I think that Andrew Johnson got a raw deal from Congress. He was a pretty cantankerous customer, I have to admit, and mighty stubborn. Lots of people just didn't like the cut of his jib. But I think he was honest as the devil."

• Applications •

I. Rewrite the short passage about Andrew Johnson above to make it more formal.

II. Rewrite the following sentences, removing (a) any stilted diction and (b) any slang or illiterate diction. In general try to make the diction fit an informal standard.

1. We approached Emporium City from Route 60, driving like a bat out of hell.

2. Miss Warner was a young creature of patrician elegance and of disdainful hauteur but really pretty dumb.
3. It sure was picturesque! Titanic vistas solicited our view. It was all mighty grand.

III. The following passage is quite informal — even colloquial — in diction and expression. Rewrite the passage so as to make it as formal as possible.

I could recognize big changes from Commerce down. Beaver Dam Rock was out in the middle of the river now, and throwing a prodigious " break "; it used to be close to the shore, and boats went down outside of it. A big island that used to be away out in mid-river has retired to the Missouri shore, and boats do not go near it any more. The island called Jacket Pattern is whittled down to a wedge now, and is booked for early destruction. Goose Island is all gone but a little dab, the size of a steamboat. The perilous " Graveyard," along whose numberless wrecks we used to pick our way so slowly and gingerly, is far away from the channel now, and a terror to nobody. One of the islands formerly called the Two Sisters is gone entirely; the other, which used to lie close to the Illinois shore, is now on the Missouri side, a mile away; it is joined solidly to the shore, and it takes a sharp eye to see where the seam is — but it is Illinois ground yet, and the people who live on it have to ferry themselves over and work the Illinois roads and pay Illinois taxes: singular state of things!
— Samuel L. Clemens: *Life on the Mississippi.*

IV. This passage is much more formal than that by Clemens. Attempt to rewrite the passage so as to make it less formal.

The reader has been informed, that we were running along the coast, within a mile of it, to enable us to keep sight of the land. The object of this was to make the proper landfall for running into the Gulf of Paria, on which is situated the Port of Spain, in the island of Trinidad, to which we were bound. We opened the gulf as early as nine A.M., and soon afterward identified the three islands that form the *Bocas del Drago*, dragon's mouth. The scenery is remarkably bold and striking at the entrance of this gulf or bay. The islands rise to the height of mountains, in abrupt and sheer precipices, out of the now muddy waters — for the great Orinoco, traversing its thousands of miles of alluvial soil, disembogues near by. Indeed, we may be said to have been already within the delta of that great stream.

Memory was busy with me, as the *Sumter* passed through the Dragon's Mouth. I had made my first cruise to this identical island of Trinidad, when a green midshipman in the Federal Navy. A few years before, the elder Commodore Perry — he of Lake Erie memory — had died of yellow fever when on a visit in one of the small schooners of his squadron up the Orinoco. The old sloop-of-war *Lexington,* under the command of Commander, now Rear-Admiral Shubrick, was sent to the Port of Spain to bring home his remains. I was one of the midshipmen of that ship. A generation had since elapsed. An infant people had, in that short space of time, grown old and decrepit, and its government had broken in twain. But there stood the everlasting mountains, as I remembered them, unchanged!
— Admiral Raphael Semmes: *Service Afloat.*

How Associations Control Meanings

Thus far we have seen how associated meanings determine what may be called the social tone of a word. But we must go on to consider the very important way in which these meanings actually determine, though sometimes subtly, the effect of the word, that is, the way in which they actually determine meaning. In our time especially, propaganda and advertising have made this whole matter very important.

A group of words that point to more or less the same thing may range in their associations from highly favorable to highly unfavorable. For example, we may call an agriculturist a "farmer," a "planter," a "tiller of the soil," or, in more exalted fashion, "the partner of Mother Nature"; but we can also refer to him as a "rube," a "hayseed," or a "hick." Few of our words merely *name* something. They imply a judgment about its value as well. They make a favorable or an unfavorable evaluation. Consider, for example, the following table of rough synonyms:

FAVORABLE	NEUTRAL	UNFAVORABLE
highest military leadership	general staff	army brass
motor sedan, cabriolet, convertible	automobile	jalopy
secret agent	informant	stool pigeon
cherub	child	brat
Democratic (or Republican) statesman	party leader	political boss
self-control	discipline	regimentation

By choosing terms with the right associations, we can easily color our whole account of a man or a happening or an idea. Much of the effectiveness of this method depends upon the fact that the writer ostensibly is only pointing to certain things, only naming them: the damaging (or ennobling) implications are, as it were, smuggled in surreptitiously. This was the method frequently used by such writers as Westbrook Pegler and H. L. Mencken. Notice how heavily the following passage from one of Mencken's essays leans upon this device. (The italics are supplied by the present authors.)

"The Ride of the Valkyrie" has a certain intrinsic value as pure music; played by a competent orchestra it may give civilized pleasure. But as it is commonly performed in an opera house, with a *posse* of fat *beldames* throwing themselves about the stage, it can produce the effect of a dose of ipecacuanha. The sort of person who actually delights in such spectacles is the sort of person who delights in plush furniture. Such half-wits are in a majority in every opera house west of the Rhine. They go to the opera, not to hear music, not even to hear bad music, but merely to see a more or less obscene *circus*.   — H. L. MENCKEN: " Opera," *Prejudices: Second Series.*

As a matter of fact, Mencken has here so clearly expressed his attitudes that the use of damaging implications may be obscured. With such a trumpeting of his prejudices, the phrase " smuggled in surreptitiously " may seem a misnomer, even though the effect depends upon implications as well as upon denunciation. In the following passage the attitude is also clearly marked, but note the effect of the italicized terms in strengthening and filling out the expression of the attitude:

Rome was now a great *jackdaw's* nest, with temples and mansions newly built in solid, vulgar, imitation-Greek architectural style — much of it concrete with a thin marble facing — *stuffed* with *loot* from more ancient and beautiful cities. Typical scenes of " the grandeur that was Rome " at the sack of Corinth. A group of smoke-blackened Roman infantrymen *squatting* on a priceless old master — Aristides's " The God Dionysus " — and *shooting craps* for possession of sacred chalices looted from Dionysus's temple. Others *hacking* souvenirs from the most famous relic of antiquity, the stern of the ship " Argo " which had brought back the Golden Fleece from the Caucasus more than a thousand years before. The Army commander impressing on the transport captains detailed to convey unique works of art back to Rome — " Mind you, my men, anything you lose you'll have to replace."   — ROBERT GRAVES: " It Was a Stable World."

The power of association is also illustrated by our recourse to **euphemisms.** Certain words, even necessary words, which refer to unpleasant things, are avoided in favor of softening expressions or indirect references. In many contexts " bastard " is felt to be too brutal; so " illegitimate " is substituted for it. Even a word like " died " may be shunned in favor of " deceased," or " passed away," or " went to his reward." Undertakers have taken to calling themselves " morticians," and butchers in some parts of the country prefer to be known as " meat-cutters." Whatever one may think of the substitutions, they at least testify to the power of past associations and the desire of men to avoid words with unpleasant or disparaging associations.

The power of association is illustrated positively in our tendency to disparage human beings by associating them with unpleasant animals or insects. Thus, we express contempt by calling a man a " rat," a " louse," or a " worm "; a certain admiration for his cleverness, by calling him a " fox "; hatred (and perhaps fear), by calling him a

" snake." In general, the animal creation is a rich source of expressions of attitude toward other human beings, particularly of hostile or contemptuous attitudes. But we may use associations drawn from all sorts of areas: " He is a tower of strength "; " He is as hard as flint "; " She is as neat as a pin." (In the next chapter, we shall discuss in detail the uses of figurative language of this sort.)

Here follows the account of an incident as it might be reported by a relatively impartial writer:

> Democratic (or Republican) Senator Briggs expressed surprise at being met by reporters. He told them that he had no comment to make on the " Whitlow deal." He said that he had not known that Whitlow was in the employ of General Aircraft and observed that the suggestion that he had received favors from Whitlow was an attempt to discredit him.

How might a hostile reporter describe the incident? He would perhaps give an account something like this:

> Senator Briggs, Democratic (or Republican) wheelhorse, was obviously startled to find himself confronted by newspapermen. He stubbornly refused to comment on what he called the " Whitlow deal " and professed not to have known that Whitlow was a lobbyist. The Senator complained that he was being smeared.

The second account seems to be substantially the same as the first. The " facts " are not appreciably altered. But the emotional coloring, and, with it, the intended effect on the reader, have been sharply altered. The senator is now a " wheelhorse," with its suggestions of a hardened and (probably) calloused political conscience. Whitlow is a " lobbyist," and again suggestions of political corruption are insinuated. Moreover, the senator's actions and speech (" obviously startled," " stubbornly refused," " professed not to have known," and " complained ") are made to suggest guilt.

Now the point in this comparison of the two accounts is not to indicate that the drier, more objective account is necessarily " truer " and therefore to be preferred. Our estimable fictitious senator may, in fact, be quite guilty, and the writer of the second account may have given us the more accurate account of what actually happened in the interview. (It is even conceivable that the first account was written by a reporter who was pretty certain of the senator's guilty conduct but whose editor had ordered him to play down any suggestion of guilt. In that event, the first account would have to be regarded as biased.) The point to be made is this: The coloring of attitudes in a piece of writing is extremely important and is, indeed, an integral part of its "meaning." (In this general connection, the student should read "How To Detect Propaganda," page 518.)

ⁱons •

ʋing words, try to find synonyms (or generally synony-
ɪrases) of opposite associations:

n	harsh	dictator
	reformer	liberal
nt	conventional	ward leader
mination	diplomacy	theoretical
dom	practical	aroma
ice officer	vacillating	radical
soteric	strait-laced	canard

II. Alter the diction of the following passages in order to gain (a) a more favorable tone; (b) a less favorable tone. (The sample sentence, with its optional terms, will illustrate the kind of alteration which the student is to make.)

The veteran (*still-youthful, aging*) movie star walked (*swept, minced*) into the strong (*brilliant, harsh*) light and paused for a moment to look at (*glance at, ogle*) the crowd.

1. The old woman walked up to the counter and priced the scarf. She hesitated, seemed to think for a moment, and then opened her black purse, and extracted a five-dollar bill. She laid it on the counter and began to finger the bright piece of cloth.
2. The mayor, a stocky man of middle age, stepped forward to the microphone with a sheaf of papers in his hand. He placed these on the lectern and cleared his throat. His face was serious as he began his speech.
3. The two boys, fifteen and seventeen, were ill at ease when they appeared before Judge Baker, who regarded them impersonally from the bench. An atmosphere of tension prevailed in the courtroom as lawyers began shuffling their papers.

Worn-out Words and Clichés

We began this chapter by saying that the problem of diction is that of finding the right words, the words which will say exactly what the writer wants to say. But we have seen that exactness in language cannot be attained simply and mechanically, that the exactness works on a number of levels and in a number of different ways. Words are not static. They have a history; they have biographies; and even have, one is tempted to say, personalities. Most of all, since they are not changeless and inflexible, but to some extent plastic, changing their shape a little under the pressure of the context in which they occur, they offer a continual stimulus and challenge to the imagination of the writer.

Language, as we have seen, changes, develops, grows, and, by the same token, language wears out. We are not thinking, however, of the normal sloughing off of words that have died natural deaths and now either do not occur in a modern dictionary at all or, if they do occur, are marked *obsolete* (*shoon* for *shoes*) or *archaic* (*e'en* for *even*) . We are thinking rather of words that have been thoughtlessly used in certain contexts so often that they have lost nearly all their force. Whether we call these threadbare expressions " trite " or " hackneyed " or term them " stereotypes " and " clichés " is of little importance.

Common Stereotypes, Including Slang

Jargon is produced by writers who do not think out what they want to say but find a worn groove in the language down which they let their thoughts slide. Books on rhetoric sometimes supply lists of threadbare expressions against which the student is warned: " the more the merrier," " last but not least," " to trip the light fantastic toe." Hackneyed phrases of this sort have probably by now become too literary, too old-fashioned, to offer much temptation to a modern student — even to a lazy one. But stereotyping continues, and much of the writing and conversation to which we are constantly exposed is a tissue of trite expressions. The sports page, for example, will yield stereotypes in abundance. Mr. Frank Sullivan amusingly exhibits some of these in question-and-answer form:

Q. If [the teams] don't roll up a score what do they do?
A. They battle to a scoreless tie.
Q. What do they hang up?
A. A victory. Or, they pull down a victory.
Q. Which means that they do what to the opposing team?
A. They take the measure of the opposing, or take it into camp.
Q. And the opposing team?
A. Drops a game, or bows in defeat.
Q. This dropping, or bowing, constitutes what kind of blow for the losing team?
A. It is a crushing blow to its hopes of annexing the Eastern championship. Visions of the Rose Bowl fade.

Q. So what follows as a result of the defeat?

A. A drastic shakeup follows as a result of the shellacking at the hands of Cornell last Saturday.

Q. And what is developed?

A. A new line of attack.

Q. Mr. Smith, how is the first quarter of a football game commonly referred to?

A. As the initial period.　　　— FRANK SULLIVAN: "Football Is King."

Society-page editors have their own brand of stereotypes: "social function," "society bud," "gala affair." To come still closer home, there is slang. Some slang expressions may once have been pungent and colorful. The sportswriter who first described the strike-out of a slugging batter by saying "he made three dents in the atmosphere" conveyed the scene sharply and humorously. When slang is thus "tailor-made" for the occasion, it may be bright and perceptive, though, if it is still fresh and vivid, it is a question whether it ought to be viewed as "slang" at all. But, as most of us use it, slang is a worn and impoverished language, not bright and irreverent and lively, but stale and dead: "the party was a washout"; "I'm fed up"; "he crabbed a lot"; "he blew his top." The real sin committed here is not so much that of bringing slang's flippant associations into a serious context. We do not often commit this fault. The real sin in using slang consists in using a thin and inexpressive language — slang that has lost the edge of slang.

Jargon: *The Degenerative Disease of Prose*

We have to step up, however, to a somewhat more exalted plane to find the stereotypes which most damage modern prose and which are likely to do the student most harm. These stereotypes are such expressions as "along the lines of," "in the last analysis," "socioeconomic considerations," "the world of business affairs," "according to a usually reliable source." Such locutions puff out many an official document, many a political speech, and it must be admitted, many a professor's lecture or article.

This wordy, woolly style is sometimes called "officialese." Former Congressman Maury Maverick, a few years ago, called it "gobbledygook," submitting as a horrible sample the following extract:

Whereas, national defense requirements have created a shortage of corundum (as hereafter defined) for the combined needs of defense and private account, and the supply of corundum now is and will be insufficient for defense and essential civilian requirements, unless the supply of corundum is conserved and its use in certain products manufactured for civilian use is curtailed; and it is necessary in the public interest and to promote the defense of the United States, to conserve the supply and direct the distribution and use thereof. Now, therefore, it is hereby ordered that. . . .

Here follows a paragraph of jargon with a more academic smack:

This relationship would define certain linkages between the social and physical structure of the city. It would also provide a precise definition of the commonalities among several spatial distributions. By the same token, the correlation between the residential desirability scale and the continuum of socio-economic status would provide an estimate of the predictive value of aerial photographic data relative to the social ecology of the city.

Mr. Malcolm Cowley, who garnered the specimen of jargon just quoted, comments as follows:

Mr. Green has used 160 words — counting "socio-economic" as only one — to express an idea that a layman would have stated in thirty-three. As a matter of fact, he has used many more than 160 words, since the whole article is an elaboration of this one thesis. Whatever may be the virtues of the sociological style, or Socspeak, as George Orwell might have called it — it is not specifically designed to save ink and paper.

— "Sociological Habit Patterns in Linguistic Transmogrification," *The Reporter*, Sept. 20, 1956.

But whether we call it officialese when it emanates from some government bureau, or gobbledygook, or simply jargon, its empty wordiness is characteristic. Here are two somewhat more respectable samples culled from *College English* — a fact which should warn us that anyone can fall prey to jargon, even those who undertake to teach others how to write effective English.

(1) If we start at one of the extremes of the continuum, we shall find a grouping around a point of great vitality and wide appeal. Keenly aware of the painstaking scholarship and of the high creative effort that over the centuries has accumulated the body of subject matter we call "English," a group of our ablest teachers conceive their role to be to transmit this product of human endeavor, this hard-won store of learning and of art, this rich portion of man's heritage of culture, to the oncoming generations, and to imbue them with some perception of its worth.

(2) But whether we are trained statisticians or not, we can improve the results of our examination speeches and themes. First of all, we can, without great difficulty, develop better controlled problems. There are various degrees of control possible in examination speeches and themes, and, within reasonable limits, it would seem as though the greater the control the more meaningful the test results. Complete freedom of choice of topic

and material puts a premium upon accidental inspiration and upon glib-ness rather than thoughtfulness. A single assigned topic is palpably unfair since it may strike the interest and experience of some and yet leave others untouched.

These two passages have been somewhat unfairly taken out of context. Moreover, the topics discussed are not precisely colorful and exciting. Is it fair, then, to condemn their authors for having written jargon? How else could either writer have said what he had to say?

It is true that we have torn the passages out of context and that the subject matter is difficult. Yet, even so, the symptoms of jargon are present. Consider the second excerpt: Both " puts a premium upon " and " palpably unfair " are clearly stereotypes. Moreover, what does the author gain by specifying " without great difficulty " and " within reasonable limits "? Are these specifications necessary? Could they not be assumed? Has not the writer put them in for rhetorical purposes, that is, to " dress up " his statement rather than to make necessary qualifications?

The persistence of jargon and the way in which it obscures thought are powerfully demonstrated in Joseph Warren Beach's rewriting of a paragraph by the philosopher John Dewey. Mr. Beach records his sympathy with many of Dewey's opinions and recognizes his very great reputation as a philosopher, but finds him a careless writer. He cites the following paragraph from *Human Nature and Conduct* as an instance of Dewey's muddy and confused style. Here is Dewey's paragraph:

But no matter how much men in authority have turned moral rules into an agency of class supremacy, any theory which attributes the origin of rule to deliberate design is false. To take advantage of conditions after they have come into existence is one thing; to create them for the sake of an advantage to accrue is quite another thing. We must go back to the bare fact of social division into superior and inferior. To say that accident produced social conditions is to perceive that they were not produced by intelligence. Lack of understanding of human nature is the primary cause of disregard of it. Lack of insight always ends in despising or else unreasoned admiration. When men had no scientific knowledge of physical nature they either passively submitted to it or sought to control it magically. What cannot be understood cannot be managed intelligently. It has to be forced into subjection from without. The opaqueness of human nature to reason is equivalent to a belief in its intrinsic irregularity. Hence a decline in the authority of social oligarchy was accompanied by a rise of scientific interest in human nature. This means that the make-up and working of human forces affords a basis for moral ideas and ideals. Our science of human nature in comparison with physical sciences is rudimentary, and morals which are concerned with the health, efficiency and happiness of a development of human nature are correspondingly elementary. These pages are a discussion of some phases of the ethical change involved in positive respect for human nature when the latter is associated with scientific knowledge.

Here follows Beach's rewriting of the paragraph, with his changes indicated in italics:

But no matter how much men in authority have turned moral rules into an agency of class supremacy, *it would be a mistake to suppose that these rules were created originally with the* deliberate design *of using them for this purpose.* It is one thing to take advantage of conditions after they have come into existence; it is quite another thing to create them for the sake of an advantage to accrue. *To understand a system of morals,* we must go back to the division into classes — into superior and inferior. *We shall find that social conditions grew up spontaneously, and that is as much as to say that they were not the product of deliberate thought. Just the contrary, they were the product of a want of intelligence in interpreting human nature. Human nature was disregarded in framing moral rules because it was not understood.* Lack of insight *into anything* leads to its being despised or else admired unreasonably. *It is so with* physical nature; when men had no knowledge of it, they either passively submitted to it or sought to control it magically. What cannot be understood cannot be understood intelligently. It has to be forced into subjection from without. *In the case of* human nature, *the difficulty of understanding it leads to the assumption that it is essentially arbitrary in its action, only to be controlled from without. This is the assumption of all social oligarchy, and it is an assumption which social oligarchy finds it to its advantage to maintain. And this in turn prevents the growth of any scientific study of human nature. But* a decline in the authority of social oligarchy is *naturally* accompanied by the rise of *that* scientific interest in human nature *to which social oligarchy has been opposed. The scientific assumption is that the principles of morality should be sought in the very constitution of human nature, and based on a study of* the make-up and *actual* working of human forces. *It must be acknowledged that,* in comparison with the physical sciences, our science of human nature is rudimentary, and morals — *which are concerned with the development of human nature into something* healthful, efficient and happy — are correspondingly elementary. These pages *will be taken up with* a discussion of some phases of the ethical change involved in *that* respect for human nature *which results from its being studied in connection* with scientific knowledge *in general.*

Here are Beach's comments on the revision:

It would be too long an undertaking to explain the necessity of the several dozen changes made in order that the course of this thought may be clear to the reader, if indeed I have succeeded in making it clear. But it would be worth our while to analyze, through several sentences, the process of trial and error, of guess and reconstruction, in which the reader must at every point engage in order to make any connected sense. Let us begin with the sentence a little below the middle of the passage, "The opaqueness of human nature to reason is equivalent to a belief in its intrinsic irregularity." The first thing the reader does instinctively is to get rid of the words "equivalent to." No fact about human nature is equivalent to any belief about it. Facts are one thing, beliefs another. The general connection makes the reader understand that the author means to say, "The opaqueness of human nature to reason leads to a belief in its intrinsic irregularity." The reader then approaches the phrase, "the opaqueness of human nature to reason." He first translates the figurative phrase into one more consistent with English idiom, and has, "the imperviousness of human nature to reason." He supposes it to mean the fact that human nature is dense and irrational, that reason cannot penetrate into it. And so he reads, for simplification, "The irrationality of human nature leads to a belief in its intrinsic irregularity." But that, in the particular connection, makes no sense, and the reader tries again. He takes his cue from the statement two sentences back that what cannot be understood cannot be managed intelligently. Perhaps the author means, not the imperviousness of human nature to reason in the abstract, the irrationality of human nature, but its imperviousness to the understanding of the observer — the difficulty of understanding it. So he tries that. "The difficulty of understanding human nature leads to a belief in its intrinsic irregularity." That does make sense in the connection, providing one develops a little the connotations of the word "irregularity." A thing that is irregular is arbitrary in its action, not to be controlled by reference to its own laws, but only to be forced into subjection from without. So the reader puts the sentence into a form that will suggest that connection, and he proceeds to the following sentence: "The difficulty of understanding human nature leads to an assumption that it is essentially irregular, or arbitrary, in its action. Hence a decline in the authority of social oligarchy was accompanied by a rise of scientific interest in human nature."

— JOSEPH WARREN BEACH: "Unripe Fruits,"
The Outlook for American Prose.[5]

Jargon: Some Antidotes

Jargon, of course, involves more than stereotypes. Jargon is nearly always compounded of clusters of general and abstract words. Though there is no certain prescription against jargon, it is easy to state one or two practical antidotes.

[5] From *The Outlook for American Prose* by Joseph Warren Beach, published 1926 by the University of Chicago Press. Reprinted by permission of the author.

1. The student should try to use words that are as specific and concrete as possible; that is, he should never use a word more general and indefinite than he has to. Hazy and indefinite expressions represent the easy way out for a writer who is too timid to commit himself or too lazy to think through what he wants to say.

2. The student should avoid stereotypes of all kinds — prefabricated phrasings which come easily to mind but which may not represent precisely his own ideas and emotions. But note this carefully: He should never avoid an *individual* word because it seems simple and common. If the sense calls for a simple, common word, it is generally best to repeat the word, if necessary, again and again. There is little to be said in favor of what is sometimes called **elegant variation,** that is, the substitution of some synonym in order to avoid repetition. Here is an example: " Mr. Jones was a powerful *financier.* As a *tycoon* he had a deep suspicion of socialism. He shared the feelings of his associates who were also *bankers.*" The variations are irritating and can be confusing. Either recast the sentence or repeat *financier.*

On the other hand, the student should try to avoid *words strung together* — that is, phrasings — which are common and, for that very reason, probably stereotyped. He cannot avoid all common expressions, nor should he try to avoid them, but he should learn to inspect them carefully before he decides to use them. If he really needs to say " along the lines of," or if something is really " in consideration of " something else and an emphasis on *consideration* is relevant, then let him use the expression by all means. But it is a good rule to remember that though he need never shy away from an individual *word* because it is common, he ought to be very shy of *phrases* that are common.

3. The student should try to use live words, remembering that finite verbs are the most powerful words that we have. We can find an instance of the failure to do so in the second sentence of the first excerpt quoted on page 318:

Keenly aware of the painstaking scholarship and of the high creative effort that over the centuries has accumulated the body of subject matter we call " English," a group of our ablest teachers conceive their role to be to transmit this product of human endeavor, this hard-won store of learning and of art, this rich portion of man's heritage of culture, to the oncoming generations. . . .

This sentence is packed with ideas, but the only finite verb in it (aside from *has accumulated* and *call,* in the two relative clauses) is the verb *conceive.* A participle, *aware,* is made to carry the weight of the first twenty-six words; and the whole latter part of the sentence hangs from two successive infinitives, " to be " and " to transmit." The sentence has so little stamina that it sprawls. It sprawls because the writer has starved it of finite verbs. The author might better have written:

> Our ablest teachers realize what effort has gone into the making of that body of subject matter we call " English." They know it is a precious thing, for it embodies the effort of painstaking scholars and of great poets and novelists. They want to transmit this heritage of culture to the oncoming generations.

Finite verbs are more powerful than strings of participles, gerunds, or infinitives. Moreover, a specific verb is usually stronger than a more general verb qualified by modifiers. Compare " He walked along slowly " with " He strolled," " He sauntered," " He dawdled," " He lagged." Frequently, it is true, we need the qualifiers. But we ought not to forget the wealth of concreteness which the English language possesses in its great number of verbs which name specifically, and therefore powerfully, certain modes of action.

4. Finally, the student ought to remember that simple sentences in normal sentence order (see page 282) rarely degenerate into jargon. An essay so written may be childishly simple, and it can become monotonous; but it will seldom collapse into the spineless flabbiness of jargon.

Jargon, however, is not to be dealt with summarily. It is our most pervasive kind of " bad " style, and, like style in general, it is the product of the interplay of many elements. We shall have to recur to this topic in some of the chapters that follow, especially in the discussion of metaphor.

• Applications •

I. The following passages are badly infected with jargon. Try to determine what the author in each case means to say, and then put it into English for him. (You might apply the four antidotes to jargon described on pages 321–23.)

A. The chemical age gives every highly technical nation a choice between self-sufficiency and trade on whatever barter or bargaining basis it desires, thus upsetting time-honored geographical alignments of monopolies of certain natural products and altering the whole concept of imperialism. This is an entirely new situation for agriculture. For centuries the threat of eventual scarcity of food and land hung over the world. Within a few decades the march of science has brought about a complete reversal. On the one hand the chemist and the technologist have made possible the production of greater and greater quantities of products on less and less land, resulting in enormous surpluses of acreage, crops, and labor. At the same time, ironically enough, the chemist is removing one product after another from the soil into the laboratory, throwing still more land out of cultivation and further reducing the amount of labor needed.

B. The maintenance of democracy will, I believe, require not only a deflation of executive power and its restoration to popular control but a public vigilance greater than that heretofore manifest. Whether it is possible to expect private citizens to make the necessary sacrifices of time and effort to see to it that representative government is not frustrated, only time can tell. But if the electorate will not insist upon congressional control of public policy, executive government will come by default and the historical cycle through which other countries have passed may well be reflected here.

As a way of life our people have heretofore valued the freedom and respect for the human personality which the Constitution was designed to insure. Even that has suffered inroads, necessarily because of legitimate legislative restraints but unnecessarily also because the protection of civil liberties lies for the most part with the local communities, and many elements of our population are becoming indifferent to the fundamental importance of civil liberties. Some people insist that economic well-being explains the luxury of democracy, and that hard times and insecurity promote the surrender of freedom. This only means that the effort to maintain democracy is now more difficult. It should not be allowed to go by default.

II. List the clichés and stereotyped phrasings in the following letters. Attempt to rewrite Dorothy Dix's answer in simple, clear English, free of slang and hackneyed expressions.

Dear Miss Dix:
The time has come when I feel that I need some personal advice. I am a woman 32 years old. A little more than a year ago I met a man 45 years old and fell madly in love with him. I gave him his meals and was thrilled to do it. But now I wonder if I have just had a case of infatuation, for this man never pays any of the bills, or takes me to any place of amusement, or does anything to make me happy.

He says he loves me and wants to marry me some time, but when I suggest that we settle on a date, he always postpones it. Will a man who does nothing for me before marriage support me after marriage?

Perplexed

Answer:

Of course, he won't. The dumbest woman in the world would know that a man who grafted his living off a woman before marriage would continue his deadbeat tactics after marriage, if she only would give her brains a chance to function now and then.

Strange and unaccountable are the ways a woman's mind works its wonders to perform. Of all loathsome human beings, the worst is the male parasite who lives on women, instead of working and supporting himself, and how any woman can find anything to love in such a creature, passes all comprehension.

Don't deceive yourself into thinking that this man will ever marry you. He hasn't the slightest intention of doing so. He will leave you as soon as some woman who works a little harder and makes a little more money and is a little better graft comes along. Yet there are thousands of women who fall for this racket.

You ask if I think what you feel for this man is " infatuation "? I'd say that what ails you is just lack of plain, ordinary common sense.

III. The author of the following passage is attempting to treat with some sprightliness a subject which for most people is abstruse and painfully dry. Is he successful? If so, how does his choice of diction contribute to his success? How many concrete words does Hogben use? How many abstract words? How does Hogben avoid the sense of formality? Illustrate from his choice of diction. What are the connotations of *bowling, petrol, car, tank,* and *motorcycle*? What are the connotations of *Greeks, abacus,* and *counting frame*? Does Hogben actually want the contrast between the associations of the two groups of words? What purpose does it serve? Do the associations of *Good Friday* and *All Fools' Day* clash? What purpose is served by this clash?

[Euclid] was limited by the social culture in which he lived. The Greeks did not live in a world of interest and petrol consumption and bowling analysis. Ratios were not familiar quantities. They represented a process of division which was carried out with a very stiff instrument, the abacus. Proportion did not sit lightly on Euclid's pupils. You can easily see the difficulty of Euclid's pupils. Suppose I know that the petrol consumption of a car is 35 miles to the gallon. I can get the number of miles I can run before filling up by multiplying the number of gallons in the tank by 35. I can get the number of gallons I require by dividing the number of miles I intended to run by 35. The two processes are equally easy in our arithmetic. The arithmetic of the counting frame is different. Multiplying one proper number by another always gives you an exact result which you get by repeated addition. Dividing one proper number by another means finding how many times you can take one away from the other. Usually you have some beads left over on the counting frame. You rarely get an exact answer. So division was a much more difficult process to grasp when people thought that all real numbers were proper numbers. Euclid had to devote a whole book (Book V) to illustrate the simple rules of proportion which are all summed up in the diagonal rule given in the last chapter. Draw two right-angled triangles, one with the two shorter sides 3 and 4 centimetres long, the other with the two shorter sides of 1½ and 2 inches; compare them, and you will see without difficulty that two triangles having corresponding sides whose lengths are in the same ratio is a situation no more difficult to grasp than the fact that a motorcycle has the same petrol consumption on Good Friday and All Fools' Day.

— Lancelot Hogben, *Mathematics for the Million.*[6]

IV. The student will probably conclude that the writing in the following passage is quite effective. It is, on the whole, rather straightforward prose. The sentences are simple in structure. How much of the effectiveness of the passage depends upon the choice of diction? How many hackneyed expressions does it contain, if any? Does the writer make use of slang? If so, is it justified? Why?

[6] Reprinted from *Mathematics for the Million* by Lancelot Hogben, by permission of W. W. Norton & Company, Inc. Copyright 1937, 1940 by the publishers.

Dutchmen don't get excited over nothing. I was in an airliner over Holland, when the Dutch aboard started crowding each other at the windows: below us, green and shining, was a farm landscape that has only just recently come out of the sea. It is the first piece of a whole new province (a new state, we would say) that Holland is adding to itself: " Flevoland."

I went back later, by car, by boat, by Piper Cub, and looked into this land-making operation. It's the pride of the Dutch. It's what makes their eyes shine.

The main method is this: you build an earthen dam from shore out into the shallow sea and back to shore, so as to fence in part of the sea. Then you pump the water out. You wait a few years for the rains to wash the salt out of the soil. Then you start farming! Such a piece of land — saucer-shaped, lying below sea level, is called a " polder." It's a necessary word, and not translatable. Nobody has polders but the Dutch. They have been making them for five hundred years — small ones — and now, with big money and big machines, they make them big.

I drove out on a dyke that is fencing off one future piece of Flevoland. You drive on the top of the dyke, and you do sixty. We went out of sight of land, and still the road kept going. I thought: " This is big." You hold it against the American scale of things — Hoover Dam, TVA, Empire State Building — and it still is big. You hold it against the size of Holland — six Hollands wouldn't fill the State of Kansas — and it becomes colossal. It's as if we wanted to push the Gulf of Mexico back and build a second Texas. . . .

And this is what makes Holland Holland. Windmills, for instance: land below sea level doesn't drain. You have to keep pumping the rain out. The windmills do that — still do it, though most of the pumping now is electric, or diesel. And those wooden shoes? (You still see them quite a bit.) Why? Much of the soil is always wet, and wooden shoes are watertight and warm. You can't run in them — but then, a Dutchman is well organized; he starts early and has no need to run. Little boys who feel like running have a special Dutch boys' gesture: you take your shoes off and carry them both in your left hand, and run. ·

— J. Wolfgang Langewiesche: " The Dutch Hustle,"
Harper's Magazine, April, 1956.

V. In the passage quoted from *Service Afloat* (page 311), Semmes uses the term *disembogues*. Consult the dictionary for the etymology of this word. Does the root meaning of the word indicate why Semmes chose it rather than some other for the particular passage in which it occurs?

VI. In the passage quoted from *Life on the Mississippi* (page 311), an island " has retired," another island is " booked for early destruction," the division between still another island and the mainland is a " seam." What are the literal or normal meanings of " retire to," " book for," and " seam "? Are the metaphorical extensions involved here justified? Attack or defend them.

CHAPTER ELEVEN

Metaphor

In metaphor there is a transfer of meaning — the Greek word from which metaphor is derived means " to transfer." A word that applies literally to one kind of object or idea is applied by analogy to another. Thus a ray of sunshine *cuts* the gloom (as if it were a knife) ; a ship *courses* the seas (its motion likened to that of a grey-hound) ; a man *weasels* out of his promise (as a ferret-like animal wriggles through a small hole) .[1]

In the preceding chapter we considered some of the simpler kinds of metaphor. Thus on page 303 we spoke of the *eye* of a needle, the *legs* of a chair, the *bed* of a river. As we saw, language normally grows by a process of metaphorical extension; we extend old names to new objects. But when, in this process of extension, a metaphor is really absorbed into common language, like the *bed* of a river, it loses its metaphorical force; it becomes a dead metaphor. Compare, for example, " the bed of a river " with " the dance of life." The first phrase carries no suggestion that the bed is a place of repose or that the river is sleepy! We use " the bed of a river " as a pure denotation from which the associated meanings that apply to *bed* in its usual senses are quite absent. But it is very different with the phrase " the dance of life." This metaphor is still alive. (At least, when a certain writer, Havelock Ellis, used it as the title of one of his books, he must have hoped that it would seem alive.) Here the suggestions, the associations, are thoroughly relevant to Ellis's purpose. The suggestions (of something rhythmic, of patterned move-

---

[1] In this chapter we have used *metaphor* in the largest and most inclusive sense. We have not distinguished metaphor proper from *simile* (an *explicit* comparison, usually introduced by *like* or *as:* " she glided into the room *like a swan,*" " he was as bald *as an egg* ") , or *metonymy* (the use of a part to designate the whole: " he employed twenty *hands* on his farm ") , or other such specializations of the metaphoric principle. Such classifications are, in our considered opinion, of little practical importance to the writer.

ment, even, perhaps, of gaiety and happiness) are meant to be associated with life.

The term "dead metaphor" can itself illuminate the problem now being considered. With "dead" metaphors, we can say, *rigor mortis* has set in: they have no flexibility, no force; they have stiffened into one meaning. Metaphors that are still alive prove that they are alive by their flexibility; and because they are still alive, they can be used to give color and life to a piece of writing. They are concrete and particular; they reflect the world of the senses. They can still excite the imagination.

In metaphors that are still recognizably metaphoric, there are, of course, varying degrees of life. The following examples are not very lively, but they do show that metaphor is a perfectly normal and important part of our normal speech: we say, for example, "John is a good egg"; "Jane is a peach"; "He ran out on the deal"; "That remark threw him for a loss." Such expressions are rather worn and faded. But their original metaphorical character is plain enough, and we still think of them, and use them, as metaphors. The list of expressions that are badly shopworn but are still recognizably metaphors could be extended almost indefinitely: "hot as the devil," "independent as a hog on ice," "lazy as a dog," "crazy as a bat," and so on.

Importance of Metaphor in Everyday Language

Our preference for the concrete and the particular, as these examples show, is not only normal; it is deeply and stubbornly rooted in the human mind. Consider the following situation: It is a hot day. We can say, "It is hot" or "It is very hot," or, piling on the intensives, we can say, "It is abominably and excruciatingly hot." But most of us, afflicted with the heat, will resort to metaphor of some kind: "It's hot as hell," or more elaborately, "It's hot as the hinges of hell." Evidently metaphor is felt to add forcefulness, and evidently the forcefulness has some relation to sharpness of detail and concreteness of expression.

That is one point, then: In metaphor, force and sharpness of detail, especially of sensory detail, tend to go together. Indeed, we are usually attracted to metaphor in the first place because ordinary language seems worn and abstract. A second point to be made is this: Metaphor tends to accompany the expression of emotions and attitudes. A strictly scientific purpose would find entirely adequate expression in the statement that it is now 97.6 degrees Fahrenheit and that the humidity is 88.

Let us consider another simple case. Suppose we feel an especial kind of happiness and try to express our feelings. We can say, " I feel happy." Or we can try to find a word which more accurately hits off this special feeling: *merry, gay, ecstatic, cheerful, glad, jolly,* or *joyous*. There are many synonyms for *happy*, as the dictionary will quickly reveal, and they differ in their shades of meaning. For example, *jolly* suggests heartiness and the good humor that go with comfortable living; *ecstatic* suggests an elevating rapture; *gay* suggests sprightliness, a nimble lightheartedness. We shall do well to consult the dictionary to learn (or remind ourselves of) the wealth of resources at our disposal. Even so, we rarely find an adjective which exactly expresses our feelings. We tend to resort to metaphor. We say " I'm happy as a June bug," or " I feel like a million dollars," or " I'm walking on air this morning," or " I feel like a colt in springtime."

If the feeling is very special or complex, we are usually *forced* to resort to metaphor. Here are the ways in which two writers of fiction express the special kind of happiness which each of their characters experiences.

The first is the happiness of a young soldier when the brilliant woman who has dazzled him shows him a small attention:

She regarded him with her kindly glances, which made something glow and expand within his chest. It was a delicious feeling, even though it did cut one's breath short now and then. Ecstatically he drank in the sound of her tranquil, seductive talk full of innocent gaiety and of spiritual quietude. His passion appeared to him to flame up and envelop her in blue fiery tongues from head to foot and over her head, while her soul appeared in the center like a big white rose. . . .

— JOSEPH CONRAD: " The Warrior's Soul," *Tales of Hearsay*.

The author tries to do justice to the emotion of almost physical intensity that the young soldier feels, and in doing so, he twice resorts to metaphor. The first is a rather simple and even conventional metaphor of a feeling of warmth within his chest — something that seems to " glow " and to " expand." The second attempts to interpret as well as present the quality of the emotion — the lady is encircled in flame, but the flames, though fierce ("blue fiery tongues "), do not injure her and may even be said to protect her. The white rose, which in his ecstatic vision stands for her soul, is not scorched or shriveled.

The second example has to do with the experience of a little girl in a Maine village sixty years ago:

It was a day in spring, and it must have been in early spring, for we had not as yet been allowed to cast off our winter underwear, and as the warmth of the morning increased, it felt cumbrous and uncomfortable. I have no remembrance of where I had been when the peculiar and essential meaning of the day stole over me, but probably on some errand to the village. I know that I was coming up the board sidewalk which led past the picket fence surrounding our orchard when all at once I felt an odd quickening within me.

There had been a white mist in the early morning from a heavy rainfall during the night, and the sun was just then breaking through it in long rays of light. I felt suddenly surrounded by light and half frightened by the equally sudden perception of it. I walked slowly up the sidewalk until I reached the white gate, where I stopped, for I was puzzled and bewildered.

Light to me before this had been the absence of darkness, the assurance of safety, of the ordinary and the familiar; and I could not understand why these rays of light dispelling the mist, this unexpected, sudden effulgence, seemed so different from daylight in its usual sense. I felt as though something were happening inside me, for I seemed all at once incomprehensibly alive and new, even as if I had just been born.

— MARY ELLEN CHASE: *The White Gate.*

Again, this passage is made effective by the re-creation of the scene in our imagination. The writer is careful to have us visualize the scene in all its detail. If the reader can be made to see what the little girl saw, he is on the way to understanding the experience. But ultimately the writer has to resort to metaphor in order to tell us what the experience was. It was like a transfiguration — it was like a rebirth.

• Application •

Choose metaphors which will describe *how you feel* in the following situations. Do not necessarily take the first metaphor which comes to mind; try to avoid worn-out metaphor; try to find a metaphor which describes as accurately as possible your own feelings.

1. On getting an A when you would have been happy to settle for the grade of C.
2. On getting well splashed by a passing car when on your way to an appointment.
3. On your first experience of stage fright.
4. On seeing a serious accident.

5. On first discovering that a close friend has betrayed your friendship.

6. On coming to realize that you have been guilty of a serious fault.

Slang as Metaphor

In connection with metaphor it may be profitable to consider again two abuses of language, slang and jargon, which have already been touched upon in the preceding chapter (pages 316–23). The impulse to use slang springs from our preference for the concrete and the particular. Slang expressions are originally metaphoric, and the problem of the misuse of slang cannot properly be solved apart from the more general problem of the use and abuse of figurative language. That is why it does very little good for the instructor to tell the student — or for the student to tell himself — not to use slang, for this advice is essentially negative. The student is right in wanting to make his writing warm, colorful, and lively. What he needs to do, therefore, is not to discard figurative language in favor of abstract expressions; but rather to inspect all his figurative language, *including slang,* in order to improve it as metaphor. He will try to eliminate all metaphors that are worn and trite, or that seem pretentious, or that are discordant with the rest of the composition. The practical result, of course, will be that in this process most of the slang will be sloughed off, but sloughed off *because it proves to be poor and ineffective metaphor,* not because it is figurative. The writer will scarcely be able to avoid the use of metaphor even if he tries. But he wants it to be alive rather than dead, responsible and controlled rather than irresponsible and wild.

Jargon and Worn-out Metaphor

But why recur to the second general abuse of language, jargon, in this chapter on metaphor? What possible connection can jargon have with metaphor? The first answer to this question can be put simply: There is an important negative relation. It is the very lack of concrete words and of metaphorical vividness and particularity that makes jargon cloudy and ineffective. A primary way to avoid jargon, then, is to use concrete language, including its extension into metaphor. The spinelessness of jargon is in part the result of the writer's timid avoidance of vigorous metaphor. Even the most timid writer, however, is not actually able to avoid all metaphor; and with this observation we can give a second answer to the question. Jargon characteristically involves stereotypes of all kinds, including stereotyped, and therefore lifeless, metaphor. This connection of jargon with secondhand metaphor is forcefully put by the British writer, George Orwell:

Prose (nowadays) consists less and less of *words* chosen for the sake of their meaning, and more and more of *phrases* tacked together like the sections of a prefabricated henhouse. . . . There is a huge dump of worn-out metaphors which have lost all evocative power and are merely used because they save people the trouble of inventing phrases for themselves. . . . Modern writing at its worst . . . consists in gumming together long strips of words which have already been set in order by someone else.

The student will observe that Orwell himself uses metaphor very effectively: "sections of a prefabricated henhouse," "dump of worn-out metaphors," "gumming together long strips of words." Orwell thus vividly suggests his two points of indictment: the lazy and careless craftsmanship of the writer of jargon and the second-hand quality of the materials he uses.

Orwell goes on to illustrate his point by suggesting how a modern writer of hand-me-down phrases would express the following passage from Ecclesiastes: "I returned, and saw under the sun, that the race is not to the swift, nor the battle to the strong, neither yet bread to the wise, nor yet riches to men of understanding, nor yet favor to men of skill; but time and chance happeneth to them all."

Such a writer, says Orwell, would probably turn it out like this: "Objective consideration of contemporary phenomena compels the conclusion that success or failure in competitive activities exhibits no tendency to be commensurate with innate capacity, but that a considerable element of the unpredictable must invariably be taken into account."

Confused Metaphor and Half-dead Metaphor

Orwell has hardly exaggerated, and the faults which he points out are found just as frequently in America as in Great Britain. The following passage is an excerpt from a newspaper advertisement for a savings and loan association:

The little squirrel, with a God-given instinct to prepare for tomorrow, stores away nuts and has plenty to eat . . . when winter comes.

Is he smarter than *you* are? Think about this.

Now, today, is the time to start "salting away" that nest egg you'll need sure as fate.

In this advertisement three metaphors for the savings that we are urged to make jostle oddly with one another — the nut, the salted meat, and the nest egg. In the days before modern refrigerating methods, meat was laid down in salt to preserve it for the winter and times of scarcity generally. Men came to extend the phrase " to salt away " to all sorts of things that were to be reserved and preserved for future use.

A " nest egg " was the egg that one left in the nest so that the hen would continue to lay in that nest and not desert it for another. Again an analogical extension has been made to anything that, in the interests of good husbandry, one refuses to gather or harvest for immediate use. But the metaphors, already trite, are woefully mixed: You can't *salt away a nest egg* — the nut-burying squirrel is not doing that and one ought not to ask a human being to try.

Of course we know what the ad writer *means* to say. But that is not the point. The point is the ineffectiveness of his way of saying it. He evidently wanted to use concrete expressions in the interest of vividness and therefore wrote three successive metaphors for " save " and " savings."

The writer of the passage that follows is attempting to describe the effect of " comic books ' :

They defy the limits of accepted fact and convention, thus amortizing to apoplexy the ossified arteries of routine thought. But by these very tokens the picture-book fantasy cuts loose the hampering debris of art and artifice and touches the tender spots of universal human desires and aspirations, hidden customarily beneath long accumulated protective coverings of indirection and disguise.

But can one defy a limit? One can, of course, defy another person to set a limit. The comic books may break across boundaries, may exceed limits, and their authors may defy authorities to set any limits that they will respect. But here it is the comic books that are made to " defy limits," probably because the author was looking for a strong metaphor, and was willing to accept, without asking too many questions of it, the first strong metaphor that he found. The defiance hinted by the comic books has violent results. The comic books amortize the " ossified arteries of routine thought." To " amortize " is to cancel a mortgage. And " amortize," like " mortgage," is related etymologically to Latin *mors,* death. Even so, how can a defiance extinguish a mortgage on the arteries of thought — to the point of apoplexy? People who suffer from hardening of the arteries are subject to strokes of apoplexy. Perhaps the writer is trying to say that the outrageous breaking of the conventions drives certain readers to apoplexy. But he has his apoplectic stroke affect the creaky and antiquated thoughts themselves. The result is a rather amazing mix-up.

In the next sentence, the comic books, having by their defiance ruptured the arteries of conventional thought, proceed to cut loose the " debris of art and artifice." Or rather, it is the fantasy which cuts this debris loose. But " debris " means a scattered mass of materials. Can one cut a person loose from debris? Does one not rather dig a victim *out of* the debris which has fallen upon him? And how can such debris be *worn,* as is evidently the case here, as a " protective covering "? The cutting loose of wreckage, the pulling off of a disguise, and the removal of a protective shell are thoroughly scrambled. And the confusion is not helped when we remember that the debris in question is composed of " art and artifice " and that the agent which cuts it loose is fantasy — something which one usually regards as associated with both art and artifice.

There is much to be said for a rich and concrete idiom. In return for it, we might be willing to disregard a few metaphorical loose ends. But there are limits, even though the comic books are said to defy limits. The writer here is evidently buried up to his ears in a debris which may be artifice but certainly is not art.

The instance of mixed metaphor that we have just examined was published in a " quality " magazine, and that fact should constitute a warning to the student writer. Try to think out what you want to say. Then be sure that your metaphors are consistent with it, and when they are closely connected, are consistent with one another.

• Application •

The following passages are taken from articles in reputable magazines. Make a criticism of the use of metaphor in these passages. Where the metaphors seem garbled or inappropriate, rewrite the passage, substituting consistent or appropriate metaphors.

1. As his fame was slowly ascending, partly because of this social skill of his, into more illustrious circles, so was it trickling down among the more numerous obscure.
2. Today Hitler has rolled time back to the grim days of pillage and purge, building, not a " greater Germany that will last a thousand years," but the greatest hate ever brewed in the hearts of men.
3. It's not the hurt the other fellow does you that keeps on rankling; it's the hurt you do yourself by your own remembering. That sticks in your skin and infects your mind.
   I guess that's the secret of all successful forgetting. Don't let it break

through your insulation at the start. Don't let it make a deep and lasting brand on the sensitive recording plate of your consciousness.

4. The emancipation of the slaves withdrew the Negroes from the maternal wing of the plantation system and threw them into the labor market.

5. Therefore, when he championed his middle class, he instinctively set his face against everything that threatened to substitute quantity for quality — against the encroachments of commerce and the new imperialism which the progressively minded among both Whigs and Tories were imbibing from Chatham. And the caveat against the dangers lurking in materialistic panaceas is not without implications that carry beyond the time and the place.

The Function of Metaphor

Thus far we have given our attention to some of the abuses of figurative language. It is high time to give a more positive account of metaphor and to show some of the uses of figurative language. After all, why do we use metaphor? What purpose does it serve? We have already assumed in earlier pages that it has its value in contributing color and liveliness, but if we are to understand why it is one of the great resources of the writer, we shall need to define more clearly what its function is. This is all the more necessary since the conventional account of the uses of metaphor is calculated to mislead. For example, we are in the habit of saying that the purpose of metaphor is to illustrate or to embellish; but these terms can easily suggest that figurative language is a kind of " extra " which may be usefully or gracefully " added on " to a statement, but which is never essential to the statement, never a direct part of what is being said. In accordance with this conventional view, the practical function of metaphor is to give a concrete illustration of some point which has been put more abstractly. Metaphor provides a pleasing decoration, like an attractive wallpaper pasted onto the wall or like a silk ribbon tied around a box of candy. But the trouble is that, in either case, the figure of speech seems to be something which can be left off; and if we misconceive the purposes of metaphor by thinking of it as something external and additional, we shall never come to understand why an understanding of metaphor is absolutely essential to good writing — and to good reading, too.

Why Scientific Statement Does Not Require Metaphor

Let us begin by disposing of a special kind of writing in which metaphor is indeed unnecessary and is merely an addition. If we wish to say " $2 + 2 = 4$ " or that " the square of the hypotenuse of a right triangle is equal to the sum of the squares of the other two sides," we shall not require metaphor. Metaphor would be in the way. Such statements as these, however, are very special; the terms used in them are (or aspire to be) pure denotations. As we pointed out in the preceding chapter, if such terms have associations at all, the associations are surely irrelevant. Thus the " words " employed are not being used as words in the usual sense; for most words are capable of metaphorical extension. These scientific terms are, by contrast, rather special symbols, and the purest scientific statements are able to dispense with words altogether: thus $2 + 2 = 4$, or $H_2SO_4 + Fe \rightarrow FeSO_4 + H_2 \uparrow$.

But important as such statements are, they represent a stringently specialized discourse. Most of the discourse which interests us as human beings and which we must use as writers goes far beyond abstract relationships of this kind. Most of our discourse has to do with the " full " world of our human experience, not with the colorless, soundless, abstract world of modern physics, say, or of mathematics.[2]

Metaphor as Illustration

It ought to be noted, however, that even the scientific writer very often needs to go beyond this stringently limited abstract discourse, and for him too, metaphor, though frankly employed as illustration, may be highly necessary and useful. The following passage from Bertrand Russell's *The Scientific Outlook* will illustrate this point. The book is addressed to a general audience, and Russell is attempting to convince his reader that " what is actually experienced is much less than one would naturally suppose." He proceeds to analyze a typical experience for us — what happens scientifically when we " see " someone:

You may say, for example, that you see your friend, Mr. Jones, walking along the street: but this is to go far beyond what you have any right to say.

---

[2] This is not, of course, to question the importance or the reality of such worlds. The scientist can deal with his material only in this abstract way. His language is neither more nor less real than the language of the poet or the novelist. It is merely different. In this connection, the student might reread the discussion of abstract and concrete words (pages 297–302).

You see a succession of coloured patches, traversing a stationary background. These patches, by means of a Pavlov conditioned reflex, bring into your mind the word " Jones," and so you say you see Jones; but other people, looking out of their windows from different angles, will see something different, owing to the laws of perspective: therefore, if they are all seeing Jones, there must be as many different Joneses as there are spectators, and if there is only one true Jones, the sight of him is not vouchsafed to anybody. If we assume for a moment the truth of the account which physics gives, we shall explain what you call " seeing Jones " in some such terms as the following. Little packets of light, called " light quanta," shoot out from the sun, and some of these reach a region where there are atoms of a certain kind, composing Jones's face, and hands, and clothes. These atoms do not themselves exist, but are merely a compendious way of alluding to possible occurrences. Some of the light quanta, when they reach Jones's atoms, upset their internal economy. This causes him to become sunburnt, and to manufacture vitamin D. Others are reflected, and of those that are reflected some enter your eye. They there cause a complicated disturbance of the rods and cones, which, in turn, send a current along the optic nerve. When this current reaches the brain, it produces an event. The event which it produces is that which you call " seeing Jones." As is evident from this account, the connection of " seeing Jones " with Jones is a remote, roundabout causal connection. Jones himself, meanwhile, remains wrapped in mystery. He may be thinking about his dinner, or about how his investments have gone to pieces, or about that umbrella he lost; these thoughts are Jones, but these are not what you see.

— BERTRAND RUSSELL: *The Scientific Outlook.*[3]

The passage may be regarded as an instance of the expository method of illustration. (See pages 78–86.) Notice that Russell has completed his analysis with the last statement of the passage; yet apparently he felt that the account might prove too technical and that his reader might fail to understand. Therefore he adds the following statement: " To say that you see Jones is no more correct than it would be, if a ball bounced off a wall in your garden and hit you, to say that the wall had hit you. Indeed, the two cases are closely analogous." Most readers will be grateful for this illustration. Most minds find abstractions so alien to them that they need a concrete statement such as the analogy provides. This is a truth which the writers of all books of scientific popularization know. Even if the writer is able, as Bertrand Russell is able here, to state his analysis directly, the extra illustration — the concrete analogy drawn from daily experience — is helpful.

---

[3] From *The Scientific Outlook* by Bertrand Russell, by permission of George Allen and Unwin, Ltd.

• Applications •

I. The authors of the following passages originally supplied illustrative or summarizing comparisons to make clearer or more emphatic what they had to say. Here, however, these summarizing comparisons have been omitted. Try to supply an appropriate comparison.

A. These molecules move with very high speeds; in the ordinary air of an ordinary room, the average molecular speed is about 500 yards a second. This is roughly the speed of a rifle-bullet, and is rather more than the ordinary speed of sound. As we are familiar with this latter speed from everyday experience, it is easy to form some conception of molecular speeds in a gas. It is not a mere accident that molecular speeds are comparable with the speed of sound. Sound is a disturbance which one molecule passes on to another when it collides with it, rather like. . . .   — Sir James Jeans: *The Universe Around Us.*[4]

B. An insect, therefore, is not afraid of gravity; it can fall without danger, and can cling to the ceiling with remarkably little trouble. It can go in for elegant fantastic forms of support like that of the daddy-long-legs. But there is a force which is as formidable to an insect as gravitation to a mammal. This is surface tension. A man coming out of a bath carries with him a film of water of about one-fiftieth of an inch in thickness. This weighs about a pound. A wet mouse has to carry about its own weight of water. A wet fly has to lift many times its own weight and, as everyone knows, a fly once wetted by water or any other liquid is in a very serious position indeed. An insect going for a drink is in as great danger as. . . .   — J. B. S. Haldane: " On Being the Right Size," *Possible Worlds.*

II. In the following passages the authors have made much use of illustrative metaphor. Try to restate what is said in language as unmetaphorical as you can devise. Do not be surprised if you find that the rewritten version requires a good many more words than the original passage.

A. We, then, the animals, consume those stores in our restless living. Serenely the plants amass them. They turn light's active energy to food, which is potential energy stored for their own benefit. . . .

Animal life lives always in the red; the favorable balance is written on the other side of life's page, and it is written in chlorophyll. All else obeys the thermodynamic law that energy forever runs down hill, is lost and degraded. In economic language, this is the law of diminishing returns, and it is obeyed by the cooling stars as by man and all the animals. They float down its Lethe stream. Only chlorophyll fights up against the current. It is the stuff in life that rebels at death, that has never surrendered to entropy, final icy stagnation. It is the mere cobweb on which we are all suspended over the abyss.

      — Donald Culross Peattie: *Flowering Earth.*[5]

B. The passage beginning " And just at that instant " and ending " Let there be light," in " Dawn over Zero " (Readings, page 490).

---

[4] From *The Universe Around Us*, 4th ed., by Sir James Jeans. Copyright, 1944 by The Macmillan Company and used with their permission.

[5] From *Flowering Earth* by Donald Culross Peattie. Copyright 1939, by Donald Culross Peattie. Courtesy of G. P. Putnam's Sons.

Metaphor as Essential Statement

In strict scientific statement, then, metaphor would seem to have no place, and in less strict scientific discussion it would seem to be auxiliary and optional. But we shall make a serious mistake if we conclude that in other kinds of writing metaphor is a device of as little fundamental importance. The truth is quite to the contrary! In most of the writing with which we are concerned — political speeches, articles on international affairs, letters to friends, expressions of opinion, attempts to persuade and convince, essays in which we invite other people to share our experiences and evaluations of life — in these and in nearly all the writing that we shall do, metaphor is a primary device of expression.

The common misconception of metaphor makes it, as we have seen, a mere ornament, and therefore an inessential part of expression. But metaphor is not a mere decoration, an " extra." It often represents not only the most compact and vigorous way of saying a thing -- it represents sometimes the only way in which the particular thing can be said at all. This last remark holds especially true when " the thing to be said " involves an interpretation or evaluation. Metaphor is indeed an indispensable instrument for interpreting experience.

Let us illustrate. In the sentence that follows, Helen Keller describes what tactile sensation means to a person who has always been blind and deaf: " The immovable rock, with its juts and warped surface, bends beneath my fingers into all manner of grooves and hollows." The rock, of course, does not literally bend; it is " immovable." But under her sensitive fingers, which do duty for eyes, the rock itself seems to respond dynamically to her touch. For what is being described is not the fumbling of an ordinary person who is blindfolded. We are, rather, being let into Helen Keller's " world," a world of exciting qualities which most of us do not know at all. Metaphor here is the only means by which it may be made known to us, since this world does not exist in our experience and cannot be pointed to; it can only be created for us. (The student should compare Helen Keller's account of touch, as given in fuller detail on page 200, with Bertrand Russell's account of sight, page 336. They are radically different in purpose, and therefore in method.)

Consider what metaphor does in the following two verses from Ecclesiastes. " It is better to bear the rebuke of the wise, than for a man to hear the song of fools. For as the crackling of thorns under a pot, so is the laughter of the fool; this also is vanity."

This comparison, as we see, uses the dry, crackling sound of burning thorn branches to describe the laughter of a fool. Now, there is a certain realistic basis for the comparison, but the metaphor is far more than a phonetic description. It makes a value judgment, too· The fool's laughter, it implies, is brittle, hollow, meaningless; it is the noise that attends the going up in smoke of something quite worthless, the rubbish of dried thorn branches. This implication is the justification for the last clause, " this (the fool's laughter) also is vanity." But the metaphor does much more than " illustrate " the vanity. It is the metaphor itself that defines vanity and realizes it for us — its specious brightness, its explosive chatter, its essential emptiness.

Consider what metaphor does in the following passages. In the first passage Arthur Koestler is describing Western Europe. But he is doing more than that — he is interpreting its state of mind:

Western Europe is a patient in an iron lung. American economic and military aid provide it with oxygen, but it cannot live and breathe by itself. The sickness which paralyses it is not of an economic nature. Nor is it social strife; nor the Communist phantom creed. These are symptoms of the disease, but not its cause. The cause is both deeper and simpler: Europe has lost faith in itself.   — ARTHUR KOESTLER: *The Trail of the Dinosaur*.[6]

Note how much work the iron-lung comparison does. The social and economic structure of Western Europe is able to function mechanically just as the polio victim's body is able to do, but the impulses have to come from without — the process is not self-sustaining. There is a paralysis of the will, so Koestler argues, that parallels the paralysis of the chest muscles of the iron-lung patient. Try to say all that this paragraph says without using Koestler's comparison, and you will begin to see how much the comparison accomplishes.

In the following passage E. B. White comments upon the way in which the true Christmas has all but disappeared beneath the commercialized Christmas. Note the extended comparison through which he makes his point:

To perceive Christmas through its wrapping becomes more difficult with every year. There was a little device we noticed in one of the sporting-goods stores — a trumpet that hunters hold to their ears so that they can hear the distant music of the hounds. Something of this sort is needed now to hear the incredibly distant sound of Christmas in these times, through the dark, material woods that surround it. " Silent Night," canned and dis-

⁶ From *The Trail of the Dinosaur* by Arthur Koestler. Copyright 1947, 1948, 1951, 1953, 1955 by Arthur Koestler. Reprinted by permission of The Macmillan Company.

tributed in thundering repetition in the department stores, has become one of the greatest of all noise-makers, almost like the rattles and whistles of Election Night.　　　　　　— E. B. WHITE: *The Second Tree from the Corner.*

One of the most effective things about this passage is that White's main metaphor and the subsidiary metaphors that flank it are taken from the literal details of the commercialized Christmas — the shops, the gift wrappings, the blare of Christmas hymns and carols from advertising loudspeakers. There is a visual image: We have concealed Christmas almost too well beneath its gaudy wrappings — we see the colored paper and not the true gift. Then White shifts to what will be his main image, the hunter's hearing trumpet, which might itself be on display in some exclusive shop as a Christmas present for a sportsman. An analogous device is required to hear the spiritual music of Christmas because we have got so far away from it ("distant sound . . . in these times") and because its sound is blocked off by "dark, material woods." And, finally, another detail from Christmas shopping is used to give a further twist to this last figure: what might be thought to be the very music of Christmas ("Silent Night") has become one of the noises (the hymn "canned and distributed in thundering repetition") that makes it impossible to hear Christmas's true music.

This sequence of related images seems to mirror the very scene which it judges; a faithful description of the commercialized Christmas is made to contribute to a searching criticism of it. This economy of means has its counterpart in forcefulness of effect. Again, the student might try to say all that White is saying *without* benefit of such comparisons. The attempt will show how much this chain of metaphors accomplishes.

We must not, however, allow our choice of examples to make the process of using metaphor seem too complicated and "literary." Consider a passage from a student theme, which was quoted in full on page 215:

Off yonder, beyond the glitter of the water where the sun still struck, you could see the clouds piling up like a cliff, black and slate-colored, streaked with purple. I said like a cliff, but it was like a cliff that somehow, momentarily, grew taller while you looked at it, looking awfully solid but somehow swelling and coiling upward at the same time.

The comparison to a swelling and coiling cliff enables the reader to visualize what the storm cloud looked like as it boiled up. But it does more; it goes far to suggest the awe and fright that the storm cloud excited in the mind of the girl who describes it.

One more example, this one again selected to combat the conventional notion that metaphor is somehow "literary." Here is the way in which "Bugs" Baer describes the collapse of a prize fighter: "Zale folded as gracefully as the Queen's fan and fell on his battered face alongside the ropes. His seconds carried him to his corner like three window-dressers packing a melted dummy off during a heat wave on the sunny side of Broadway." This description may be judged to be good writing or bad, but it is easy to see why Baer used figurative language. He was not trying to "tell" us about the scene; he was trying to make us *see* the scene, vividly, freshly, fully, as a somewhat cynical but highly interested observer might have seen it.

The nature and function of metaphor can be further illustrated from passages quoted in the earlier chapter on Description. It might be useful for the student to go back and review some of the descriptive passages there. He may well be struck with the amount of metaphor in these passages and also with the *amount of work* that the metaphors actually do. For a starter, the student might reread the description of the Arabian town on page 208, where the heat is "like a drawn sword," or the account of Mr. Chadband on page 209, a man who "moves softly and cumbrously, not unlike a bear who has been taught to walk upright," or, on page 211, Faulkner's picture of Miss Emily, whose eyes are like "two small pieces of coal pressed into a lump of dough."

A few paragraphs above we cited a passage written by Helen Keller in which she gives an account of her sense of touch. We must admit that the world of Helen Keller's experience is a special world which can be conveyed to us only through suggestion and analogy. Yet, a little reflection will show us that the world of experience belonging to each of us is far more special than we may think, for our world is to a great extent determined by our values, moods, and emotional biases. The world as seen by the girl watching the storm cloud is special in this sense, and so too is that of the Hebrew preacher who speaks in Ecclesiastes. If we are to communicate our experience with any accuracy, figurative language is frequently the only way by which it can be conveyed. By means of metaphor we grasp not only the experience as an entity but its "meaning," its value to us as well.

What Makes a "Good" Metaphor?

In judging the value of a metaphor, the physical similarity of the items compared is easily overestimated. In many finely effective comparisons the degree of physical similarity is not very great. Some element of resemblance there must be, of course. But a good comparison is not necessarily one in which there is close resemblance, since "illustration," as we have seen, is not the primary purpose of metaphor. Moreover, even a great deal of dissimilarity does not necessarily render the comparison strained or forced.

The Element of Similarity in Metaphor

To realize this last point, let us consider one of the tritest comparisons of all: " Her eyes were like stars." Far from seeming strained or overingenious, the comparison will seem to most of us entirely too simple and easy. Yet even in this well-worn analogy the objects compared are really very dissimilar. Certainly the human eyeball and the flaming mass of elements that make up the stars have very little in common. If this examination, which compares the two objects as scientifically considered, seems somewhat unfair, we can go on to point out that the eyes, even those of a lovely woman, do not much resemble the glinting points of light which are the stars as we see them. The truth of the matter is that what supports this oldest and most hackneyed of comparisons is not the physical resemblances so much as the associations: the associations of stars with brilliance, with the high and celestial. It is these associations which make the stars seem " like " the glances of the eyes of someone loved.

Thus, every comparison has a very important subjective element in it; its proper task is to interpret, to evaluate — not to point to physical analogies. Its proper function is, as we have said, to define attitude.

Let us consider one of the celebrated comic comparisons in English literature. In his satire " Hudibras," Samuel Butler describes the rosy sky of dawn:

> And like a lobster, boyl'd, the morn
> From black to red began to turn.

We think of this as an absurd comparison, and so it is — appropriately so — for " Hudibras " is a humorous poem, and Butler is casting good-humored scorn upon his hero. Yet it is worth asking why the comparison strikes us as absurd. We are likely to say that it is absurd because the dawn does not in the least resemble a boiled lobster. But the colors to be seen in the shell of a boiled lobster may very closely resemble the exact shade of red to be seen on some mornings. The absurdity does not come from the lack of physical resemblance; it comes from the absurd contrast of the small with the large, the commonplace and homely with the beautiful and grand, the grotesque creature in the steaming pot with the wide, fresh expanse of the dawn sky. Butler has, for humorous effect, deliberately played them against each other.

Here is an extended comparison which goes far toward making a certain judgment and setting up a certain attitude, but the *physical* resemblance between the things compared is (one hopes) very slight indeed.

> The teachers of Benton were like sheep, where money was concerned, and the President was their shepherd: he had to scramble around looking, and worrying, and leading them to greener pastures if he could see any, while they walked on munching their scanty feed and baaing — piteously, but contentedly and accustomedly, too. Sometimes the President seemed to me not a shepherd but a scapegoat, and a willing one: the sheep had all the inconveniences and vexations of doing without money, but all the guilt of getting it had been put on his own . . . shoulders.
>   — RANDALL JARRELL: *Pictures from an Institution.*

The Element of Contrast in Metaphor

We think of metaphors (and related figurative expressions) as "comparisons," and yet it is plain that we might as accurately refer to them as "contrasts." For the elements of dissimilarity between the terms of a metaphor may be of just as much importance as the elements of likeness. One can go further still: In an effective metaphor there must be a *considerable degree of contrast*. If we say "the river roared like a flood" or "the dog raged like a wild beast," we feel that the metaphor in each case is weak or nonexistent. A river is too much like a flood, and a dog, though a tame beast, too much resembles a wild beast. If, on the other hand, we say, "the fire roared like a flood" or "the fire raged like a wild beast," we feel that these are metaphors, even though actually rather poor metaphors. Fire and flood or fire and beast are sufficiently dissimilar for us to feel that some metaphorical transfer occurs; in these cases there are the "new namings" which constitute metaphor.

We are inclined to reject what we rather awkwardly call "farfetched " comparisons. (The term is awkward because it suggests that the terms of a good comparison are close together, though we have seen that even " eyes " and " stars " are not really very close.) But if comparisons must not be too " farfetched," neither must they be too " nearly fetched." They have to be fetched some distance if we are to have a recognizable metaphor at all.

• Applications •

I. Consider carefully the metaphors in " A Lark's Flight " (Readings, page 570). What is the justification of the author's using so much figurative language? (In this connection one might observe that B. F. Skinner in " Freedom and the Control of Men," page 536, uses comparatively little metaphor. Do you see why the one writer should use so much, the other so little?)

II. On page 655 Graves compares Rome to a " great jackdaw's nest." What is the justification of this comparison? In its associations the comparison certainly clashes with the scope and grandeur of the Roman world as described in the earlier paragraphs. Is the clash an intentional one? What purpose, if any, is served by it? Attempt to rewrite the paragraph in which the jackdaw's-nest metaphor occurs, making use of some other metaphor of your own choosing in order to give another effect.

III. Notice that although Yeats is a poet, his "Reveries" do not contain any large amount of metaphor (page 714). Can you account for this fact? Do the metaphors that occur in the selection throw any light on this problem?

IV. Santayana's prose will repay careful reading for its treatment of metaphor. The student might look carefully for three things in particular: (1) the occasional extended metaphor, which may dominate a whole section of the essay; (2) the revivification of what would ordinarily be dead metaphor; and (3) the constant pointing up of abstractions by some concrete detail. For example, the passage beginning " In his love of roads " (page 631) and ending " love and laughter " (page 633), is rather abstract in its ideas. Moreover, Santayana has risked using such apparent clichés as " never see the wood for the trees," " pendulum soon swings back," and the " vain tides " of things. Mark the metaphors in this passage, and attempt to state how the metaphors are related to one another. Are there any actual clichés? If there are not, what prevents some of the expressions from affecting us as clichés do? What is the relation to the whole pattern of the two or three extended metaphors that occur?

V. The following metaphors are primarily *illustrative*, that is, the metaphor makes something plain by comparing it with a simpler or more familiar thing. But are they *merely* illustrative? Are any of the metaphors used to *state* a meaning as well as to *illustrate* a meaning? Test them on this point by trying to restate precisely " the thing said " in nonmetaphorical language.

A. On each side of the [bee's] abdomen are four little wax-pockets situated in the joints of the hard-surfaced body; and here the supply of wax may be seen issuing, the flat, light-colored wax appearing somewhat like a letter which a man has tucked up under his waistcoat.　— Charles D. Stewart: " The Bee's Knees."

B. Intellectual assimilation takes time. The mind is not to be enriched as a coal barge is loaded. Whatever is precious in a cargo is taken carefully on board and carefully placed. Whatever is delicate and fine must be received delicately, and its place in the mind thoughtfully assigned.
　　— Arlo Bates: " Reading on the Run," *Talks on the Study of Literature.*

C. Bed is the perfect laboratory — just the right degree of withdrawal from the world, yet with the comforts at hand, and errands delegated to someone else. The toast crumbs, accumulating among the sheets, set up the irritation inside the shell and start the pearl growing.　　— E. B. White: " Peavy, Book and Guitar."

D. When I am dead, the chance that my bones will become fossilized is very remote. Bones decay away like the rest of our bodies unless a lot of very unlikely things happen. First of all, a dead body will not leave any permanent remains in the form of a fossil unless it happens to be covered up and thus protected from decay. That is fairly easy in the case of animals in the sea. Rivers are always carrying sediment out and depositing it, and tides and currents shift the sediment and cover up the bodies of dead animals. But even in this case it is by no means likely that the bones will be fossilized. Much more probably they will gradually dissolve away and leave no trace of themselves. Fossilization is rather a complicated process. It involves the replacement of each particle of bone, as it dissolves away, by a less soluble and therefore more permanent substance. When that has happened, the chances are still very remote that anyone will find the fossil thousands or millions of years later. Our quarries and mines and cuttings are mere scratches on the surface of the earth. With terrestrial animals the chances of fossilization are still less than with marine ones. They are likely to die and decay without being covered up. It would be quite absurd to look with any great hopefulness for the fossil remains of the ancestors of any given animal. It would not simply be like looking for the proverbial pin in a haystack, for then you are supposed to have the advantage of knowing that the pin is there. But in this case you are looking for a soluble pin in a haystack in a thunderstorm, and you always have at the back of your mind the disconcerting thought that perhaps it is no longer there. — John R. Baker: " Missing Links," *Science in a Changing World.*[7]

E. This man was hunting about the hotel lobby like a starved dog that has forgotten where he had buried a bone.
　　— O. Henry: " A Municipal Report," *Strictly Business.*

F. . . . [the ship's] middle structure was like a half-tide rock awash upon a coast. It was like an outlying rock with the water boiling up, streaming over, pouring off, beating round — like a rock in the surf to which shipwrecked people cling

---

[7] From " Missing Links " by John R. Baker, in *Science in a Changing World,* ed. by Mary Adams. Used by permission of Appleton-Century-Crofts, Inc.

before they let go — only it rose, it sank, it rolled continuously, without respite and rest, like a rock that should have miraculously struck adrift from a coast and gone wallowing upon the sea. — Joseph Conrad: *Typhoon*.

VI. Do any of the following metaphors seem farfetched and extravagant? Do any seem tame and flat? What principle, if any, seems to determine the matter of acceptability?

Are any of the passages ineffective because the metaphors are " mixed "? Is it possible to shift rapidly from one metaphor to another without producing confusion? Are we never to mix metaphor? What principle, if any, seems to determine this matter?

A. The chickens he raised were all white meat down through the drumsticks, the cows were tended like children, and the big ram he called Goliath had horns with a curl like a morning-glory vine and could butt through an iron door. But Dan'l wasn't one of your gentleman farmers; he knew all the ways of the land, and he'd be up by candlelight to see that the chores got done. A man with the mouth of a mastiff, a brow like a mountain and eyes like burning anthracite — that was Dan'l Webster in his prime.
— Stephen Vincent Benét: *The Devil and Daniel Webster*.

B. A smile lit the eyes of the expiring Kentuck. " Dying! " he repeated; " he's a-taking me with him. Tell the boys I've got the Luck with me now "; and the strong man, clinging to the frail babe as a drowning man is said to cling to a straw, drifted away into the shadowy river that flows forever to the unknown sea. — Bret Harte: " The Luck of Roaring Camp."

C. Due to the great increase in the importance of social and economic problems during the past generation, philosophy is giving more attention than heretofore to the social and economic aspects of life. Also, esthetics is receiving greater consideration as the problem of civilization's goal becomes more pressing.
— John Geise: *Man and the Western World*.

D. Over in the corner Zale was rounding as slowly as the Queen Mary docking in the Hudson. He had taken a beating that would have busted the light in a night club bass drum. . . . In the sixth both sluggers were plugging away like a thirty-six cylinder car at a gasoline pump with the motor running. Neither the car nor the pump had gained an inch . . . The seventh was as tough as a spelling bee as ever missed out on cat. They were moving around like a Fiji fire dancer wearing celluloid sox. And banging both hands to the equator. — " ' Bugs ' Baer Says."

E.   Take the instant way;
          For honor travels in a strait so narrow,
          Where one but goes abreast: keep then the path;
          For emulation hath a thousand sons,
          That one by one pursue: if you give way,
          Or hedge aside from the direct forthright,
          Like to an enter'd tide they all rush by,
          And leave you hindmost: —
          Or like a gallant horse fallen in first rank,
          Lie there for pavement to the abject rear,
          O'er-run and trampled on: Then what they do in present,

Though less than yours in past, must o'ertop yours:
For time is like a fashionable host,
That slightly shakes his parting guest by the hand;
And with his arms out-stretch'd, as he would fly,
Grasps in the comer: Welcome ever smiles,
And farewell goes out sighing.

— Shakespeare: *Troilus and Cressida.*

F. . . . Even with the most virtuous at the levers, how can control be exercised for the good of all when there are so many voices emerging from different conditions, inheriting different traditions, committed to different ideals, and demanding different solutions. Every man wants to realize the opportunities of human knowledge, but each is inclined to believe that all will benefit if knowledge is mobilized in the service of his ideals and his traditions. Though their own powers are universal, men's values are local and mired in the mud of history. Power is too often untamed by responsibility to the world.

Few want to turn back the clock of science and technology. Most approve the trend toward an integration of the world so that its resources, its experience, its knowledge will be available to everyone, but they do not want to turn their backs entirely on the customs, the morals, the language, the institutions which they have inherited from their ancestors. . . .

— Quincy Wright: " The Universities and the World Order," *A.A.U.P. Bulletin.*

G. But perfection has one grave defect: it is apt to be dull. Swift's prose is like a French canal, bordered with poplars, that runs through a gracious and undulating country. Its tranquil charm fills you with satisfaction. . . . Dryden flourished at a happy moment. He had in his bones the sonorous periods and the baroque massiveness of Jacobean language and under the influence of the nimble and well-bred felicity that he learnt from the French he turned it into an instrument that was fit not only for solemn themes but also to express the light thought of the passing moment. He was the first of the rococo artists. If Swift reminds you of a French canal, Dryden recalls an English river winding its cheerful way round hills, through quietly busy towns and nestling villages, pausing now in a noble reach and then running powerfully through a woodland country. It is alive, varied, windswept; and it has the pleasant open-air smell of England.

— Somerset Maugham: *The Summing Up.*

H.   And he shall be like a tree planted by the streams of water,
That bringeth forth its fruit in its season,
Whose leaf also doth not wither;
And whatsoever he doeth shall prosper.
The wicked are not so,
But are like the chaff which the wind driveth away.

— Psalms, 1:3–4.

I. We must be vigilantly on our guard to protect our sacred institutions against the boring from within of subversive elements, those blood-thirsty termites who like to fish in troubled waters.   — From a commencement address.

VII. George F. Carter, in " The American Civilization Puzzle " (Readings, pages 666–79), writes the following passages:

A. " Pandora's box was open. The moat was crossed. The Independent Interventionists' vessel had sprung a leak."

B. " But this was an uneasy peace. For facts are a bit like the fires of a volcano. They may lie dormant, but actually they are smoldering away, awaiting only the touch of an investigator's hand to spring into life, capable of destroying the most elaborate of philosophical structures."

Are these mixtures of metaphors justifiable? Has the author made any preparation for them?

VIII. What is the function of each of the following metaphors? Are any of them merely decorative? What does each metaphor " say "? Try to restate in nonmetaphorical language the exact shade of meaning that each conveys.

A. The furnished room received its latest guest with a first glow of pseudo-hospitality, a hectic, haggard, perfunctory welcome like the specious smile of a demirep.   — O. Henry: " The Furnished Room," *Strictly Business.*

B. A late moon had cut a round, white hole in the sky off to the east, shedding enough light so that down below I could see the thin smoke-like scattered clouds floating halfway between me and the chromium-plated highway of the Potomac.   — Beirne Lay, Jr.: *I Wanted Wings.*

C. Her bones felt loose, and floated around in her skin, and Doctor Harry floated like a balloon around the foot of the bed. He floated and pulled down his waistcoat and swung his glasses on a cord.
     — Katherine Anne Porter: " The Jilting of Granny Weatherall."

D. Thus we see what a tree really is. It is a sheath of life spread over the dead trees of other years. Generation stands within generation, successively wrapped about. The outer life of cambium and leaf and bud uses this as a trellis to go up and reach out sunward and skyward.
     — Charles D. Stewart: " The Tree as an Invention."

E. And so the dance whizzed on with cumulative fury, the performers moving in their planet-like courses, direct and retrograde, from apogee to perigee, till the hands of the well-kicked clock at the bottom of the room had travelled over the circumference of an hour.   — Thomas Hardy: " The Three Strangers."

Material for further exercises on metaphor may be found in Applications at the end of Chapter 7, pages 226–30.

CHAPTER TWELVE

Tone and Other Aspects of Style

▶ ## Tone as the Expression of Attitude

Every piece of discourse implies a particular situation. A politician is attempting to convince a hostile audience; or a mother is attempting to coax a child into doing something which the child dislikes; or a legislator who can assume agreement on ends is trying to persuade his colleagues that certain procedures constitute the best means by which to secure these ends. Even technical treatises, which attempt no persuasion, imply a special situation; the writer assumes that he is writing for people whose interest in the truth is so absorbing that rhetorical persuasions would be unnecessary and even positively irritating.

Just as every discourse implies a situation in which the writer is related to his audience, so every discourse also implies a certain **tone**. This term " tone " is based frankly on a metaphor. We all know how important in speech the tone of voice may be in indicating the precise meaning of the words. For instance, the words " very well," uttered in a certain tone of voice, may imply enthusiastic agreement, but spoken in another tone of voice they may indicate nothing more than surly compliance. The " tone " of a piece of writing, in the same way, may show the writer's attitude, and in so doing may heavily qualify the literal meaning of the words.

The importance of tone is easily illustrated by the misunderstandings which personal letters so often provoke. In conversation, even a rather clumsy and inadequate knowledge of language can be so supplemented by the actual tone of the voice that little serious misunderstanding will occur. But when such a speaker writes a letter — where, of course, the " tone of voice " has to be implied by the words themselves — all sorts of misunderstandings can, and frequently do, occur. The practiced writer, on the other hand, is able even in this medium to control what we have called the " tone."

All through this book we have been dealing with the problem of tone, although we have rarely used the word. For example, when, in the chapter on Argument (page 193), we talked about the occasion of an argument and the right way to present it, we were concerned with the problem of tone. In the chapter on Diction (page 312), we touched upon the problem of tone when we discussed the associations of words and the way in which certain words are colored by our attitude — the word *cop* used to refer to a police officer, or *rube* used to refer to a farmer. Again, we saw in the chapter on Metaphor (page 328) the ways in which comparisons — " He's a good egg," " She's a peach " — express our attitudes. All such devices represent means for controlling tone. But tone is more than these devices; it is a pervasive thing which characterizes the whole composition, and it is a matter so important in its own right that it deserves special discussion.

The Importance of Tone

In most of our writing an important part of what we are trying to " communicate " is our attitude itself. This is certainly true of poetry and fiction, but it is also true of most essays, sermons, orations, and letters. It is even true of much of what we are inclined to regard as pure exposition. For even in expository writing the author is rarely content to give us mere facts, or mere propositions. He feels that to do this is to be painfully and technically " dry."

A glance at the so-called articles of information in magazines like the *Atlantic* and *Harper's* will indicate that even when the stress is on information, the establishing of the appropriate tone is of the highest importance. For example, Wolfgang Langewiesche's " Making the Airplane Behave," a typical expository article in *Harper's,* makes very special use of tone, and is thus anything but a mechanically " dry " piece of exposition. The author assumes that the reader is a reasonably intelligent person who has a fairly wide acquaintance with the modern world; specifically, that he knows how to drive an automobile, that he does not have a technical knowledge of physics, but that he does have enough common sense to follow a clear illustration. The exposition does not insist on technicalities any more than the writer stands on his dignity. His attitude toward his reader is definitely informal. The tone of his article suggests that flying is interesting and important, but that his attitude toward it is lively. How do we know all this? Well, consider the following paragraph:

You try, for instance, steep turns in a strong wind. The ship will go in some crazy, wrong-looking attitude; but when you check your instruments you find that it is doing a correct job of flying and that the seat of your pants and your eyes would have tricked you had you been allowed to do the " co-ordinating."

The informal " you try " rather than the more formal " one tries "; the phrase " the seat of your pants " rather than the more formal " tactile pressure of the plane "; the informal " tricked " rather than the more formal " deceived " — all of these point to the tone; that is, they indicate the author's attitude.

What Determines Tone?

If, however, we are to define tone as the reflection of the author's attitude, it is necessary to make a simple distinction. Of what attitude is it the reflection? His attitude toward the material? Or his attitude toward the reader?

We have already indicated that both considerations are important. In the paragraph from the article " Making the Airplane Behave," we have said that the writer's attitude is informal toward both his material and his reader. The writer knows his subject to be important, but he can take it and his own superior information about it with some lightness, and he writes as though he were in casual conversation with a good friend. Here we have the informality of tone reflecting an easy attitude toward the subject and toward the reader.

Attitude Toward Subject

We are well acquainted, however, with subjects which scarcely permit informality of tone, even when being presented to intimates. To take an extreme case, here is a quotation from a sermon by the great seventeenth-century preacher John Donne:

Make haste to have these spiritual graces; to desire them is to begin to have them: But make not too much haste in the way. Do not think thy self purer than thou art because thou seest another do some such sins as thou hast forborne.

Beloved, at last, when Christ Jesus comes with his scales, thou shalt not be weighed with that man, but every man shall be weighed with God: *Be pure as your Father in heaven is pure,* is the weight that must try us all; and then, the purest of us all that trusts to his own purity must hear that fearful *Mene Tekel Upharsin,* Thou art weighed, thou art found too light. . . .

Donne addresses his congregation intimately and directly. He even calls them " beloved," but no matter how close a relation the preacher assumes to exist, the urgency of the subject forbids informality. He may use simple and realistic language, that is true, but the seriousness of the subject pervades his language.

If, again, we take the essay " A Lark's Flight " (Readings, page 570) we immediately feel that the gravity and painfulness of the situation, the execution of the ignorant Irish workmen, demand a certain seriousness of tone. Banter and jesting at their expense would offend us; and it would certainly indicate that the writer was silly or callous. This is not to say, however, that humor or wit is not possible about serious subjects, even about death itself. When, in an old anecdote, the condemned man is being led out to the gallows in the cold dawn and asks for a handkerchief to put around his neck to keep from catching cold, we are not offended by the levity — we laugh. When Mercutio, in Shakespeare's *Romeo and Juliet,* makes a joke about his death wound and says that it is " not so deep as a well nor so wide as a church door: but 'tis enough, 'twill serve," we aren't offended. For one thing, both the condemned man and Mercutio are making light of their own distress, and we too feel a sense of release with them. Humor can work, and often does work, in both literature and life as a way of rising above distress, an antidote for self-pity. Humor thus employed works as a kind of understatement, undercutting the expected note of seriousness.

But suppose that the author of " A Lark's Flight " had written in the tone of the joke about the man condemned to be hanged, or even in the tone of Mercutio. What would be the difference? For one thing, just as a suggestion, a starting point, we may say that he would be making light, not of his own distress, but of the distress of somebody else, and that is never a very attractive thing. Levity about serious subjects is acceptable when somehow the writer recognizes his own share, directly or merely by sympathy, in some human situation and by humor rises above it. For example, jokes, and humor in general, about sex and death are universal; they can be universal subjects for humor only because they are of universal importance and involve us all. We have enormously complicated attitudes toward those subjects, and humor, for the moment, strikes through to something simple, the flash of release from complication. We must remember that humor about a serious subject always requires tact and discrimination. The writer may understand this need for tact and discrimination if he thinks of the occasion of his writing as analogous to a social situation. What kind of reader can he assume? One who can respond to the humor or one who will be shocked by it? But perhaps the writer wants to shock. Then he should ask himself whether he wants to shock just to show off, or whether the shock is to make a point, to bring some new awareness. And always we can recognize that there are certain situations where levity can only be offensive and, worse, silly. To take a most extreme instance, it is hard to imagine a person who would show levity in discussing the Passion of Christ. Blasphemy would be, in a sense, comprehensible, for, in a backhand way, blasphemy always recognizes the seriousness of the thing blasphemed. It is like an inverted prayer, we might say. But levity here would be comprehensible only as an indication of a vain, silly, and unimaginative person.

We have been dealing with extreme instances simply because the extreme cases make the principles involved come readily clear. When we come, however, to ordinary subjects we can still see how tone may be related to subject. The material dealt with in the excerpt from C. S. Lewis's " The Abolition of Man " (Readings, page 545) cannot be treated breezily if one believes, as Lewis does, that the threat to man is a serious one. Or if the writer should treat it breezily, he would have to set the lightness, the humor, against the basic seriousness of his intention. " The Hickman Story " (Readings, page 496), to take another example, raises similar considerations. Here the writer treats a situation of human misery and injustice, a situation in which even the immediate villain of the piece is, in a way, a victim too. The writer is aware of the human distress involved, the distress of defenseless people, and of the urgency of the social dangers. His response to the subject permits no trifling. If he did permit himself humor, it would have to be a way of highlighting the basic seriousness, perhaps a sarcastic, biting humor. He might, of course, exhibit the humor of the people whom he writes about, which is a sort of escape from their misery. But that would be another kind of highlighting.

If we turn from serious to light subjects, the same general principles apply. The light subject requires light treatment, not deadpan solemnity — unless, of course, that solemnity is indeed part of the joke. Thurber's " The Dog That Bit People " (page 595) is a semifabulous creature whose story has to be told with a certain lightness of touch if it is to be told at all. The beauty of the story is a combination of the preposterousness of the subject and the calm precision of the way of telling, a combination, too, of the humor and the sympathy. Or to look ahead (page 359), observe the serious, almost mock-heroic elements in the passage from "Farewell, My Lovely," Lee Strout White's essay on the Model T Ford. Thus far we have concerned ourselves with two extremes: seriousness and levity. Needless to say, there are hundreds of shadings between these extremes. The possible variations of tone are almost infinite.

Attitude Toward the Audience

Until now we have, for the most part, emphasized tone as indicating the writer's attitude toward his subject, or the attitude which the subject might dictate from the writer. But the writer's attitude toward the audience is equally important. It is so important that, as we can see by the previous section, one can scarcely talk about the attitude toward the subject without drifting over into a discussion of the audience.

Let us suppose that we are writing in support of the American policy toward Red China. The subject itself would, of course, allow certain different kinds of tone. We know that there is no merely mechanical equation between subject and tone. But the subject is a serious one, and though humor and satire might enter, flippancy could not. The demands of the subject would, however, be only the beginning of the study of tone. The treatment for a friendly audience, one that assumed the basic policy to be correct and that merely wanted further clarification, would scarcely be adequate for a hostile audience. We might want to persuade the hostile audience and lead them bit by bit to agreement. We might want to find the common ground (page 126) and try to show that once they recognize it they will have to follow, step by logical step, to the present policy. We might want to shock them into an awareness of the necessity of the present policy. We might, in fact, try any number of approaches, and each approach, or combination of approaches, would imply a different tone. And each possible tone would, of course, be different from the merely explanatory tone taken toward the friendly audience.

Furthermore, considerations of friendliness and hostility are not the only ones that determine the writer's attitude toward his audience. The knowledge which a special audience possesses and its interests and concerns are also determining factors. Suppose that we are writing about China. It will make a difference if our essay is to appear in a technical journal edited for specialists in political science; or in *Fortune* Magazine edited for prosperous businessmen; or on a newspaper editorial page; or in *Harper's* Magazine. It will make a difference if we read our paper before a college forum, or a California audience with its keen awareness of the Orient, or a Midwestern Chamber of Commerce dinner. The same tone would not serve for all. What is good for everything is not very good for anything.

The advertising page will furnish another kind of example of the way in which a writer's attitude toward his audience determines tone. Advertising puts a special premium upon catching and holding the interest of the reader. The advertising copy writer who did not understand some of the elementary principles of the control of tone would soon be on his way to the nearest government unemployment relief office.

Here is an advertisement for a dandruff remover. Above a picture of two young women talking there is the caption: " It's Listerine, for you chum . . . but *quick!* Those innocent-looking flakes and scales you see on scalp, hair or dress-shoulders, are a warning. . . . This is no time to fool around with smelly lotions or sticky salves that can't kill germs. You need antiseptic action . . . and you need it quick."

The young women in the picture are clearly friends, and the opening caption is represented as the comment of one to the other. But the advice as given to a chum is meant to carry over to the reader. As the advertisement frankly goes on to address the reader, " This is no time to fool around with smelly lotions. . . . You need antiseptic action. . . ."

What is the attitude toward the reader, then? The attitude is that of a sprightly, intimate friend whose advice can be frank and straight from the shoulder.

Let us look at another advertisement. This one, printed in color, depicts a young woman on a luxurious bed looking dreamily at a handsome blanket. The caption begins: " For you to whom beauty is a necessity. . . . Yours is a nature that thrives on beauty. . . . Seize it as a vital factor in your daily living. To you a blanket should be more than a source of warmth. Exquisite colors, luxuriously deep nap, rich, virgin-wool loveliness — these awaken in you an emotional response far beyond the material."

These statements, of course, are not addressed merely to the young woman pictured in the advertisement. They are addressed to the reader as well, and they make certain flattering assumptions about the reader: that she is a young woman of means who is at home with the luxurious and who has a soul which deserves and requires beauty as a necessity. Coarser natures may buy blankets simply for warmth, but you, dear and lovely reader, ought to have something more — even in a blanket.

The attitude toward the reader, of course, need not be flattering. Here follows an example of a very different tone, though like the advertisements just discussed, the tone here also is primarily conditioned by the writer's attitude toward his reader. The example is a letter written by Dr. Samuel Johnson to James Macpherson. In the 1760's Macpherson had published several volumes of poetry which he claimed to have translated from Gaelic [1] originals. Dr. Samuel Johnson refused to believe in the existence of any Gaelic originals. He openly pronounced his opinion that they were Macpherson's own composition. In reply to Macpherson's demands that he retract this charge Johnson wrote the following letter:

Mr. James Macpherson:
I received your foolish and impudent letter. Any violence offered me I shall do my best to repel; and what I cannot do for myself, the law shall do for me. I hope I shall never be deterred from detecting what I think to be a cheat, by the menaces of a ruffian.

What would you have me retract? I thought your book an imposture; I think it an imposture still. For this opinion I have given my reasons to the publick, which I here dare you to refute. Your rage I defy. Your abilities, since your *Homer*,[2] are not so formidable; and what I hear of your morals, inclines me to pay regard not to what you shall say, but to what you shall prove. You may print this if you will.   — SAM. JOHNSON.

A most important part of this letter is the attitude taken toward Macpherson. For Johnson might have stated the " facts " in a form as simple as this: " I continue to hold the view that the Macpherson translations are fraudulent " or " I repeat that I shall not believe in any Gaelic originals until they are produced." And if we argue that Johnson's expression of fearlessness is a " fact " with which the letter concerns itself, even this fact might have been expressed very differently; thus, " I have no intention of expressing a retraction " or " I mean to stand my ground on this matter " or " I am sorry that I can make no retraction since I feel that there is nothing to retract."

The tone of the letter is of the utmost importance, then. How shall we characterize it? No paraphrase of the letter will do justice to it; for the full realization we shall have to return to the letter itself. But one can point to some of its important elements: a manly contempt of threats, a confidence in truth and in his own integrity, perhaps even a trace of sardonic amusement at baffled and petty rage.

---

[1] The original Celtic language of the Scottish Highlands.
[2] Macpherson had published a translation of Homer.

I. Select five advertisements from current magazines and state what is the primary basis of the appeal made to the reader. What attitude is taken toward the reader? What statements or devices in the advertisement suggest this attitude?

II. What kind of audience does Thomas Huxley address in "The Method of Scientific Investigation" (Readings, page 463)? How do you infer this from the tone of the essay? What adjustments to a particular audience are indicated by the style of his essay?

III. In "The Decline of the Graces" (Readings, page 605), Max Beerbohm makes a special allusion to a possible reader: "I except from my indictment any young lady who may read these words." But is not the essay addressed primarily to such a young lady? To what audience is the essay addressed? What is the tone of the essay?

IV. Reread the student theme "Teachers I Have Known" (page 75) and imagine that you are writing it for a teacher who you think probably knows something about his subject but who is quite dull in the classroom. Perhaps you might turn in this draft to him as it stands. Perhaps it will not hurt his feelings, or the hurt may actually be good for him. But with him in mind, could you render this theme more persuasive? Try rewriting some sections of it, particularly paragraphs 3 and 4, to see whether you can improve the tone as directed toward the special reader we have described.

Tone as a Qualification of Meaning

We began our discussion of tone with special emphasis upon tone as a reflection of the author's attitude -- his specification as to how we are to " take " what he is saying. But it should be apparent by now that tone also represents a qualification of meaning -- a shaping of what is to be said. Indeed, a little reflection will show that full meaning is rarely conveyed by merely literal statement. We constantly find that we must " read between the lines " in order to understand a letter; or that we must take into account the tone of voice and the facial expression if we are to understand fully a conversation with a friend. The importance of tone as a guide to meaning comes out particularly in essays that deal with our valuations and judgments.

For example, consider how important is the tone in the following passage describing the old Model T Ford:

I see by the new Sears Roebuck catalogue that it is still possible to buy an axle for a 1909 Model T Ford, but I am not deceived. The great days have faded, the end is in sight. Only one page in the current catalogue is devoted to parts and accessories for the Model T; yet everyone remembers springtimes when the Ford gadget section was larger than men's clothing, almost as large as household furnishings. The last Model T was built in 1927, and the car is fading from what scholars call the American scene — which is an understatement, because to a few million people who grew up with it, the old Ford practically *was* the American scene.

It was the miracle God had wrought. And it was patently the sort of thing that could only happen once. Mechanically uncanny, it was like nothing that had ever come to the world before. Flourishing industries rose and fell with it. As a vehicle, it was hard-working, commonplace, heroic; and it often seemed to transmit those qualities to the persons who rode in it. My own generation identifies it with Youth, with its gaudy, irretrievable excitements; before it fades into the mist, I would like to pay it the tribute of the sigh that is not a sob, and set down random entries in a shape somewhat less cumbersome than a Sears Roebuck catalogue.

The Model T was distinguished from all other makes of cars by the fact that its transmission was of a type known as planetary — which was half metaphysics, half sheer friction. Engineers accepted the word " planetary " in its epicyclic sense, but I was always conscious that it also means " wandering," " erratic." Because of the peculiar nature of this planetary element, there was always, in Model T, a certain dull rapport between engine and wheels, and, even when the car was in a state known as neutral, it trembled with a deep imperative and tended to inch forward. There was never a moment when the bands were not faintly egging the machine on. In this respect it was like a horse, rolling the bit on its tongue, and country people brought to it the same technique they used with draft animals.

— LEE STROUT WHITE: " Farewell, My Lovely." [3]

To enjoy the passage just quoted one must be aware that the author laments the passing of the Model T with mock seriousness. The game that the author plays is to invest with literary allusions and sentimental clichés a piece of machinery which seems to belong to a nonliterary and nonsentimental world. Suppose we remove the tone of mock lament and simply state the facts literally and directly. Here is what we might have if we treated the first paragraph in this fashion.

The new Sears Roebuck catalogue indicates that one may still purchase an axle for a 1909 Model T Ford. But this possibility, though interesting, does not mean that the Model T Ford is any longer an important factor in American transportation. The section of the catalogue devoted to Ford

[3] From " Farewell, My Lovely " by Lee Strout White. Copyright 1936 The New Yorker Magazine, Inc. (formerly The F-R Publishing Corporation).

parts, once larger than that devoted to men's clothing, has now shrunk to a single page. No Model T's have been built since 1927, and this model is rapidly disappearing from the American highway.

The rewriting, by altering the tone, destroys the humor. It does even more. It destroys a good deal of what the passage says. For the real content of the passage is the presentation of a certain complex attitude toward some aspects of American life. The author's real concern is with American social history, but he presents that history, not clinically and "sociologically," but affectionately and a little whimsically. The tone, then, is a most important element in "what" the author is saying. Lest the last example be thought a rather special case, consider the importance of tone in the following definition of a weed:

What is a weed? I have heard it said that there are sixty definitions. For me, a weed is a plant out of place. Or, less tolerantly, call it a foreign aggressor, which is a thing not so mild as a mere escape from cultivation, a visitor that sows itself innocently in a garden bed where you would not choose to plant it. Most weeds have natal countries, whence they have sortied. So Japanese honeysuckle, English plantain, Russian thistle came from lands we recognize, but others, like gypsies, have lost all record of their geographic origin. Some of them turn up in all countries, and are listed in no flora as natives. Some knock about the seaports of the world, springing up wherever ballast used to be dumped from the old sailing ships. Others prefer cities; they have lost contact with sweet soil, and lead a guttersnipe existence. A little group occurs only where wool waste is dumped, others are dooryard and pavement weeds, seeming to thrive the more as they are trod by the feet of man's generations. Some prized in an age of simpler tastes have become garden *déclassés* and street urchins; thus it comes about that the pleasant but plebeian scent of Bouncing Bet, that somewhat blowsy pink of old English gardens, is now one of the characteristic odors of American sidewalk ends, where the pavement peters out and shacks and junked cars begin.

— DONALD CULROSS PEATTIE: *Flowering Earth.*[4]

We could describe a weed as follows:

A weed may be defined as a plant that, though growing in cultivated ground, is economically useless and is a detriment to the crop being cultivated. Yet, it must be conceded that this definition is somewhat subjective, for a plant considered useless by one person might be counted useful by another, and a plant ordinarily cultivated for its own sake might be regarded as a nuisance when found in a field planted to some other crop.

[4] From *Flowering Earth* by Donald Culross Peattie. Copyright 1939, by Donald Culross Peattie. Courtesy of G. P. Putnam's Sons.

But there is general agreement on most of the plants that we call weeds. Some examples would be dog fennel, dock, mullein, and ragweed.

This paragraph gives substantially the same definition as that given in the paragraph by Peattie. But it is relatively toneless. The author is not visualizing any particular person for whom he is writing, and he does not seem to have a particular attitude toward his subject. As a consequence, this paragraph is quite without personality.

Notice how much of the writer's personality comes through in the original passage. Peattie evidently possesses a great deal of botanical information. He is undoubtedly familiar with the various " flora " and knows which plants are listed in them and which are not. But this passage is not intended to be a technical description; rather it is a more desultory and amiable account of weeds. Peattie is a man of perception, with keen senses (" the pleasant but plebeian scent of Bouncing Bet," " the characteristic odors of American sidewalk ends "). He evidently has a sense of humor. He is aware of current politics (" foreign aggressor "). He has a sense of history.

In short, in this passage we get the play of an informed and sensitive mind — a mind which special knowledge has not made stuffy — and of a personality which savors, with evident enjoyment, the varied and amusing world. In this connection notice how a central metaphor which treats the weed as a human being who has broken bounds runs through the whole passage, and how this metaphor is varied through the passage to express the varying aspects of weeds in general and of certain weeds in particular. One weed may be like a " foreign aggressor " to be resisted; another, like an immigrant or colonist from another land; still another, like a gypsy whose original homeland is lost in obscurity. Some weeds, like groups of immigrants, remain near the seaports where they made their first entry. The migration of other weeds has been from country to city. They have moved in from the provinces and have become citified and now lead a " guttersnipe " existence. Still other weeds are like human beings who have come down in the world and, having lost pride of class and dignity, are now happily and frowsily plebeian. The general comparison of the weed to the human migrant is flexible enough to provide quite specific illustrations of the various kinds of weeds. The metaphor not only renders the abstract definition concrete, but it suggests Peattie's own attitude toward weeds and, in fact, the world in general — an attitude of genial and good-humored amusement.

Notice, too, how the diction unobtrusively but powerfully supports the variations of the basic metaphor. " Foreign aggressor " is pointed up by the use of the word "sortied." (A "sortie" suggests a military raid.) "Guttersnipe existence" sharpens the hint given by "others prefer cities." "Plebeian" and "somewhat blowsy" support and extend the suggestions made by "déclassé."

The diction, of course, does something more. Though Peattie is willing to use a technical term like *flora,* most of his words are specific and concrete. Moreover, he does not hesitate to use colloquial expressions like "knock about" and "peters out." Peattie is not at all like the fabled scholar who knew all the pedantic terms but could not address a dog in his own dialect. His diction is accommodated to the wholesome vulgarity of his subject.

The preceding account of Peattie's paragraph on the weed may seem to be overelaborate, but it is usually difficult to define a particular tone without using many more words than the author himself used to achieve it. There is, moreover, a justification for the attention which we have given to this one paragraph. We have wanted to illustrate the fact that a particular tone depends upon various factors — diction, metaphor, as well as the larger principles of composition. Tone, indeed, represents a kind of final integration of all the elements that go into a piece of writing. Writing that is toneless or confused in tone is usually bad writing.

• Applications •

I. In the following description we get an impression of Jidda. It possesses a definite quality, a special atmosphere. What is the author's attitude toward this city? Does he loathe it? Admire it? Feel affection for it? Is his writing florid? Studiedly dry? What is the tone?

The style of architecture was like crazy Elizabethan half-timber work, in the elaborate Cheshire fashion, but gone gimcrack to an incredible degree. Housefronts were fretted, pierced and pargetted till they looked as though cut out of cardboard for a romantic stage-setting. Every story jutted, every window leaned one way or other; often the very walls sloped. It was like a dead city, so clean underfoot, and so quiet. Its winding, even streets were floored with damp sand solidified by time and as silent to the tread as any carpet. The lattices and wall-returns deadened all reverberation of voice. There were no carts, nor any streets wide enough for carts, no shod animals, no bustle anywhere. Everything was hushed, strained, even furtive. The doors of houses shut softly as we passed. There were no loud dogs, no crying children: indeed, except in the bazaar, still half asleep, there were few wayfarers of any kind; and the rare people we did meet, all thin, and as it were wasted by disease, with scarred, hairless faces and screwed-up eyes, slipped past us quickly and cautiously, not looking at us. Their skimp, white robes, shaven polls with little skull-caps, red cotton shoulder-shawls, and bare feet were so same as to be almost a uniform.

The atmosphere was oppressive, deadly. There seemed no life in it. It was not burning hot, but held a moisture and sense of great age and exhaustion such as seemed to belong to no other place: not a passion of smells like Smyrna, Naples or Marseilles, but a feeling of long use, of the exhalations of many people, of continued bath-heat and sweat. One would say that for years Jidda had not been swept through by a firm breeze: that its streets kept their air from year's end to year's end, from the day they were built for so long as the houses should endure.

— T. E. Lawrence: *Seven Pillars of Wisdom.*[5]

II. For what audience is the following paragraph written? Has the audience been visualized by the writer? Could it be said that the writing is relatively " toneless "? If so, is its tonelessness a defect or a virtue?

Before intelligent criteria can be developed for the selection of superimposed leaders, the organization, through its professional staff, must first clearly define the objectives of its group program and establish qualifications for group leadership. Second, these objectives must be made clear to the leaders. In group work terminology the concept *socialization* appears as the central objective, but in the experience of the writer little effort has been made to define this concept so as to be understandable to the leader.   — From a magazine of social research.

III. What kind of audience is the author addressing in the passage below? How do you know? Compare the tone of this paragraph with the tone of the fifth and sixth paragraphs of " Method of Scientific Investigation " (Readings, pages 464–65).

When the quest is for a material of inexplicable behavior, of unique and spectacular qualities, water has all other chemicals licked for first place. True, it is the most abundant material on the Earth's surface. If suddenly all the water on the Earth could be broken into its constituent gases and released into the air, the atmospheric pressure (now 15 pounds) would become 6,000 pounds to the square-inch. That's how much water there is. And its quality is increasing continually. Every fire we light, every explosion we set off, every puff of a cigarette, combines some particles of oxygen to build new water and release it to the air. Yes, water is common, and continually becoming more so.

— George W. Gray: " Little Drops of Water." [6]

Literal Statement and Ironical Statement

Irony always involves a discrepancy between the literal meaning of a statement and its actual meaning. On the surface, the ironical statement says one thing; in actuality it says something rather different. In the lighthearted, laughingly ironical statement, the literal meaning may be only partially qualified; in a bitter and obvious irony (such as that which we call sarcasm) the literal meaning may

---

[5] From *Seven Pillars of Wisdom* by T. E. Lawrence. Copyright 1925, 1935 by Doubleday & Company, Inc.

[6] From " Little Drops of Water " by George W. Gray. Copyright, 1938, by Esquire, Inc.

be entirely reversed. An example of rather lighthearted and affectionate irony occurs in the discussion of the Model T Ford by Lee Strout White (see page 359). The little car is treated in almost mock heroic style ("It was the miracle God had wrought. . . . it was patently the sort of thing that could only happen once. . . . before it fades into the mist, I would like to pay it the tribute of the sigh that is not a sob. . . ."). The informal essay frequently makes use of some form of gentle irony such as this.

A sample of ordinary sarcasm might be represented by a student's outburst at his roommate: "A fine friend you turn out to be, borrowing my car and taking my girl on a date." The literal meaning which proclaims the roommate to be a fine young man is just the opposite of what his now irate friend means to say about him.

Between the more delicate ironical qualifications and the sarcastic reversal there are a thousand shadings possible, and it is a pity that we do not have specific terms by which to describe them. Yet, on second thought, our lack of such terms may be no real handicap. We can develop these qualifications of meaning without in the least needing to give them a label. What is important is not that we have a glossary of terms, but that we be aware of the fact of ironical qualification. Here are a few samples of ironical statement. The first is from a novel, Thackeray's *Vanity Fair:*

Being an invalid, Joseph Sedley contented himself with a bottle of claret, besides his Madeira at dinner, and he managed a couple of plates full of strawberries and cream, and twenty-four little rout cakes, that were lying neglected in a plate near him, and certainly (for novelists have the privilege of knowing everything), he thought a great deal about the girl upstairs. "A nice, gay, merry young creature," thought he to himself. "How she looked at me when I picked up her handkerchief at dinner! She dropped it twice. Who's that singing in the drawing-room? Gad! shall I go up and see?"

This is rather obvious irony, but certainly not severely sarcastic. Thackeray tells us a good deal about Joseph Sedley's state of invalidism by describing his diet. But the joke is not so simple as this: Thackeray suggests something of Sedley's general character, and more economically than he might have done by giving a fully explicit description.

The next example is from *The Exurbanites.* Exurbia (from Latin *ex urbe,* meaning outside the city) is the name that the author assigns to those districts beyond the suburbs of New York City in which many people connected with the communications and entertainment industries live.

How do they spend their money?

Well, variously. In some cases, even as you and I. Being exurbanites, they hustle in to town, to see the latest play, or to hear the latest concert. They deal heavily in the metropolitan specialty shops and department stores: they average better than six charge accounts per family. There are book-stores, in this exurb, and these folk are highly literate: they buy books, some of which they may place in prominent positions on their coffee tables. They buy paintings, sometimes as investments; if they conceive it to be im-portant to achieve status as hi-fi buffs, they buy expensive and intricate equipment, and subsequently records. (Standard classics, yes; plus some modern and off-beat classical types like Poulenc; Friml, no. Show tunes by Porter, Coward, etc., yes; Victor Herbert, no. Jazz, yes — if it's authentic; Liberace, no. And, importantly, a heavy play to off-color records, those for example, dubbed off the master on which the recording artist fluffed and in consequence, exchanged blue epithets with the boys in the band.)

— A. C. SPECTORSKY: *The Exurbanites.*

The irony expressed in this passage is primarily an *irony of situa-tion;* that is, the people described pretend to be interested in litera-ture and music but are really concerned only with giving the im-pression of being high-brow. But this irony of situation is at least partially converted into an *irony of statement* by the way in which the writer describes the situation. It is as though he did not himself see the implications of such phrases as " sometimes as investments," " if they conceive it to be important to achieve status," and so on. The writer's refusal to make comments upon what he is depicting — his affecting not to see the implications of what he is describing — in itself constitutes irony.

The third example is from Katherine Anne Porter's essay on Ger-trude Stein's account of her life in *Everybody's Autobiography:*

Still earlier she was a plump solemn little girl abundantly upholstered in good clothes, who spent her allowance on the works of Shelley, Thackeray, and George Eliot in fancy bindings, for she loved reading and *Clarissa Harlowe* was once her favorite novel. These early passions ex-hausted her; in later life she swam in the relaxing bath of detective and murder mysteries, because she liked somebody being dead in a story, and of them all Dashiell Hammett killed them off most to her taste. Her first experience of the real death of somebody had taught her that it could be pleasant for her, too. " One morning we could not wake our father." This was in East Oakland, California. " Leo climbed in by the window and called out that he was dead in his bed and he was." It seems to have been the first thing he ever did of which his children, all five of them, approved. Miss Stein declared plainly they none of them liked him at all: " As I say, fathers are depressing but our family had one," she confessed, and conveys the notion that he was a bore of the nagging, petty sort, the kind that worries himself and others into the grave.

Considering her tepid, sluggish nature, really sluggish like something eating its way through a leaf, Miss Stein could grow quite animated on the subject of her early family life, and some of her stories are as pretty and innocent as lizards running over tombstones on a hot day in Maryland.

— KATHERINE ANNE PORTER: *The Days Before.*

In this passage, to be sure, there is a certain amount of perfectly direct commentary. But what gives the passage its biting power is the calm assumption of the author that what she is describing in Miss Stein's conduct is somehow proper and normal for her. The tone of almost clinical commentary sets up an ironic contrast with the material she is discussing, and so becomes powerfully expressive.

• Applications •

I. Robert Graves' " It Was a Stable World " (Readings, page 653) may be said to be characterized by irony. What is the tone of Edward Gibbon's account of Rome (Readings, page 646)? In comparison with Gibbon's formality and solemnity, Graves may seem somewhat flippant. Is there any hint of irony in Gibbon's account of Rome? Compare and contrast the tone of these two selections as carefully as you can. Be specific. Give concrete illustrations.

II. The scene described below is a British club in India, some decades ago. The orchestra has just played " God Save the King." What is the author's attitude toward his fellow countrymen? The passage is obviously ironic, but what is the precise shading of irony? Is the author indignant? Mocking? Bitter? Or what?

Meanwhile the performance ended, and the amateur orchestra played the National Anthem. Conversation and billiards stopped, faces stiffened. It was the Anthem of the Army of Occupation. It reminded every member of the club that he or she was British and in exile. It produced a little sentiment and a useful accession of will-power. The meager tune, the curt series of demands on Jehovah, fused into a prayer unknown in England, and though they perceived neither Royalty nor Deity they did perceive something, they were strengthened to resist another day. They poured out, offering one another drinks.

— E. M. Forster: *A Passage to India.*

III. Here is a piece of advice on how to go about social climbing:

Even Emily Post offers a few demure suggestions to the " outsider ": " The better, and the only way if she [a woman with social ambition] has not the key of birth, is through study to make herself eligible. Meanwhile, charitable or civic work will give her interest and occupation as well as throw her with ladies of good breeding, by association with whom she cannot fail to acquire some of those qualities before which the gates of society always open." The patronage of charity, church settlement work (Episcopalian), the financial support of hospitals, clinics, and opera are probably the safest route which the newcomer can travel. After she has given her cheque for a substantial sum and shown her eagerness to work for the cause, she will be asked to become a sustaining member and sit on the board with women she has wanted to know. Probably they will begin to ask her to tea, then to large parties and luncheons, and finally to dinner. If fortune has blessed her with a small daughter, let her be sent to a fashionable day school, where she will have classmates to be invited to a birthday party, and given expensive souvenirs; in this way a little child may lead them. No climber should overlook the broadening influences of travel; in crossing the Atlantic, cruising the Mediterranean, or circumnavigating the globe, one may get a good table by generous tipping and promptness, and then maneuver eligible acquaintances and celebrities into sitting there. Deck stewards also can do much for one, since during the course of a long voyage propinquity is almost irresistible.

— Dixon Wecter: *The Saga of American Society.*[7]

What is the quality of the irony employed in this passage? Define it as precisely as you can. What are some of the ironical devices employed?

IV. The student theme " Teachers I Have Known " (page 75) has some traces of irony in it. For example, the student asks: " Did they become teachers because they were really interested in their subject and in young people, or did they just drift into the profession through indifference or necessity? " But in general, the judgments are given directly and explicitly. Would there be any advantages in presenting the judgment against such teachers indirectly and ironically? Try rewriting this theme, making use of an ironical approach. Pretend, for example, that you are praising all teachers; or try to give a deadpan account of the teachers' faults as if you did not realize that they were faults.

Overstatement and Understatement

We have been occupied with a distinction between a literal and nonliteral (including the ironic) use of words. It is useful to consider the problem of tone in the light of another distinction, that between **overstatement** and **understatement**. Overstatement, as the term implies, is redundancy; but it is much more than mere repetition. The term connotes gushiness and floweriness — a straining after effects. The following passage consists of the last two paragraphs of Bret Harte's story, " The Outcasts of Poker Flat." In the story a gambler and a prostitute rise to heroism as they try to shelter and protect an innocent girl who has fallen into their company when

[7] From *The Saga of American Society* by Dixon Wecter. Copyright 1937, by Charles Scribner's Sons.

the whole party is overtaken by a severe snowstorm in the mountains. The paragraphs that follow describe the last days of the two women, the innocent girl and the prostitute.

The wind lulled as if it feared to waken them. Feathery drifts of snow, shaken from the long pine boughs, flew like white-winged birds, and settled about them as they slept. The moon through the rifted clouds looked down upon what had been the camp. But all human stain, all trace of earthly travail, was hidden beneath the spotless mantle mercifully flung from above.

They slept all day that day and the next, nor did they waken when voices and footsteps broke the silence of the camp. And when pitying fingers brushed the snow from their wan faces, you could scarcely have told from the equal peace that dwelt upon them which was she that had sinned.

Here the author, in his anxiety to stress the pathos of the scene and the redemption of the fallen woman, is not content to let the scene speak for itself. The wind lulls the two women; the moon looks down upon them; a " spotless mantle " is " mercifully flung from above." The pseudopoetic language, the suggestion that nature mercifully hides " all human stain," the general absence of restraint and reserve — all indicate that the tone here is one of **sentimentality**; that is, emotion in excess of the occasion.

What was Bret Harte's own attitude? One has to conclude that either he himself was " soft " (that is, that he was taken in by his own attempt to " work up " an effect), or else he was cynically trying to seduce his reader into an emotional response which is not itself justified by the dramatic occasion that he provided. Whatever Harte's attitude, most sensitive readers will feel that the tone is sentimental. Sentimentality usually betrays itself by a straining to work up the reader's feelings. Of course, in a sense, any appeal to our emotions represents an attempt " to work up " an effect. But it is one thing to do this legitimately by presenting a scene with imaginative power, and it is quite a different thing to try to bully the reader into the desired emotional response. Readers may disagree on whether the response has been evoked legitimately or illegitimately (that is, sentimentally), but the principle involved is crucial. Otherwise any writer, however tawdry or mawkish, could demand our response simply by making a direct assault on our feelings.

The student may feel that in the kind of writing that he does there is little danger of his " gushing "; and it is quite true that the particular temptations to which Bret Harte yielded are not likely to tempt him. But student themes present their own opportunities for overwriting. The theme in which a student tries to describe his grandfather and his mother (page 91) will illustrate. A few phrases like " the dearest Mom in all the world " would alter the effect much for the worse. The student's affection for his mother comes out quite clearly, but he lets us infer it from the way in which he writes about her. (The student themes quoted earlier in this text are in general admirably free from gush.)

We must not, however, associate overwriting merely with the softer emotions of love and pity. It can show itself in a strained attempt at humor or a hectic gaiety or a pretentious heartiness. Advertising copy will provide obvious instances (see page 356).

Understatement does not constitute a true antithesis to overstatement. Though overstatement, as it is commonly used, is a term of adverse criticism, understatement is not. It does not necessarily mean statement that is starved and deficient, poor because of its meagerness. Instead it tends to mean statement of a calculated bareness or a studied dryness. Indeed, understatement is often a powerful device for obtaining certain effects. One may illustrate by a passage from *Seven Pillars of Wisdom* in which T. E. Lawrence describes an incident that occurred in Arabia during World War I while he was serving with the Arabs in their revolt against Turkey. The incident took place while Lawrence was leading a raiding party of Arab tribesmen.

My followers had been quarrelling all day, and while I was lying near the rocks a shot was fired. I paid no attention; for there were hares and birds in the valley; but a little while later Suleiman roused me and made me follow him across the valley to an opposite bay in the rocks, where one of the Ageyl, a Boreida man, was lying stone dead with a bullet through his temples. The shot must have been fired from close by; because the skin was burnt about one wound. The remaining Ageyl were running frantically about; and when I asked what it was, Ali, their head man, said that Hamed the Moor had done the murder. I suspected Suleiman, because of the feud between the Atban and Ageyl . . . but Ali assured me that Suleiman had been with him three hundred yards further up the valley gathering sticks when the shot was fired. I sent all out to search for Hamed, and crawled back to the baggage, feeling that it need not have happened this day of all days when I was in pain.

As I lay there I heard a rustle, and opened my eyes slowly upon Hamed's back as he stooped over his saddle-bags, which lay just beyond my rock. I covered him with a pistol and then spoke. He had put down his rifle to lift the gear; and was at my mercy till the others came. We held a court at once; and after a while Hamed confessed that, he and Salem having had words, he had seen red and shot him suddenly. Our inquiry ended. The Ageyl, as relatives of the dead man, demanded blood for blood. The others supported them; and I tried vainly to talk the gentle Ali round. My head was aching with fever and I could not think; but hardly even in health, with all eloquence, could I have begged Hamed off; for Salem had been a friendly fellow and his sudden murder a wanton crime.

Then rose up the horror which would make civilized man shun justice like a plague if he had not the needy to serve him as hangmen for wages. There were other Moroccans in our army; [Hamed the Moor was a Moroccan] and to let the Ageyl kill one in feud meant reprisals by which our unity would have been endangered. It must be a formal execution, and at last, desperately, I told Hamed that he must die for punishment, and laid the burden of his killing on myself. Perhaps they would count me not qualified for feud. At least no revenge could lie against my followers; for I was a stranger and kinless.

I made him enter a narrow gully of the spur, a dank twilight place overgrown with weeds. Its sandy bed had been pitted by trickles of water down the cliffs in the late rain. At the end it shrank to a crack a few inches wide. The walls were vertical. I stood in the entrance and gave him a few moments' delay which he spent crying on the ground. Then I made him rise and shot him through the chest. He fell down on the weeds shrieking, with the blood coming out in spurts over his clothes, and jerked about till he rolled nearly to where I was. I fired again, but was shaking so that I only broke his wrist. He went on calling out, less loudly, now lying on his back with his feet towards me, and I leant forward and shot him for the last time in the thick of his neck under the jaw. His body shivered a little, and I called the Ageyl; who buried him in the gully where he was. Afterwards the wakeful night dragged over me, till, hours before dawn, I had the men up and made them load, in my longing to be set free of Wadi Kitan. They had to lift me into the saddle. — T. E. LAWRENCE: *Seven Pillars of Wisdom*.[8]

What is Lawrence's attitude toward Hamed? Toward the Arabs and their blood feuds? Most of all, toward himself? Is he ashamed of himself? Proud of himself? Complacent and untroubled about himself?

The incident is told with detachment and an almost studied dryness. But it is evident that Lawrence is not glossing over the incident casually and briefly. He develops it fully, giving us even minute details: e.g., "bullet through his temples," "as he stooped over his saddle-bags," "shot him for the last time in the thick of his neck under the jaw." Even the scene of the execution, the gully, is described carefully and precisely: "Its sandy bed had been pitted by trickles of water down the cliffs in the late rain."

The narrator evidently remembers the whole incident vividly, and knows how to make the incident vivid to his reader. Why, then, is he not more explicit about his own feelings and attitudes? Would anything have been gained if Lawrence had added a long paragraph describing the feelings that passed through his mind as he decided

8 From *Seven Pillars of Wisdom* by T. E. Lawrence. Copyright 1925, 1935 by Doubleday & Company, Inc.

that he must act as executioner? Would anything have been lost? Notice that Lawrence is willing to use the word "horror," but he does not write, "As a civilized man I was overwhelmed with horror," but rather, "Then rose up the horror which would make civilized man shun justice like a plague if he had not the needy to serve him as hangmen for wages." Why does Lawrence, in this most explicit account of his own feelings, prefer the generalized statement?

A little meditation on these questions is likely to result in some such conclusion as this: that Lawrence, far from remaining cool and detached, was indeed terribly shaken by the experience, but that, nevertheless, he preferred to make his *account* of the experience as detached and objective as was possible. He chose to give a restrained description of his actions, leaving his reader to infer from the actions themselves what his feelings must have been.

This restraint itself has an important effect on the tone: it implies a certain modesty (his own mental anguish is not allowed to dominate the story as if he thought his anguish the important thing in the episode) and it implies a certain confidence in the reader's maturity and sensitiveness — the reader need not be "told" what Lawrence was feeling. But the restraint here is of still further importance; the restraint manifested in Lawrence's *account* of his action is a reflection of, and a type of, the disciplined control which he imposed on his followers and on himself in the desert. The man who relates the action is the man who acted, and his manner of writing about the event suggests his attitude toward the event itself.

The foregoing incident may seem a little too exalted to be of much service to the student writer. But it puts for us only more fully and more dramatically a device that the student will constantly be using in his own work. It has already appeared in some of the student themes that we have read in earlier sections of this book. The last paragraphs of "Something I Learned" (page 253) use understatement to present the writer's sense of horror at Alex Flinders' accident and his sense of guilt in being partially responsible for it:

. . . But what chance would a kid like that have? Well, he got it.

I don't mean that he killed himself or anything. But it turned out that he had had a back operation not too long before and wasn't supposed to exert himself too much. He had been ashamed to tell anybody. Well, he has had another one now.

The writing is a little clumsy, but clearly the method aimed at is that of understatement. The writer consciously says *less* than he might have been expected to say — not because he feels no guilt, but because he feels more than he dares to try to express directly.

In the student theme "Getting Engaged" (page 215), the basic technique is again that of understatement. The writer's fear at the coming of the storm and her excitement at the dangerous trip from the island to the mainland are not developed. They are implied, certainly, but the writer has preferred to "understate" both of them. She has chosen to convey her own emotions about the former by giving us a detailed description of the storm cloud and then a detailed description of Joseph's face as he watches. About her excitement at the perils of the trip home, she writes merely this:

To make a long story short, we did manage to get in, but it was a tough trip. That evening we got engaged.

The engagement is the climax of the events of the day. Therefore, the writer has quite properly insisted upon putting it into sharp focus. But the announcement of the fact of the engagement also tells us all that we need to know about it, for obviously it was the experience of real danger shared that brought about the engagement. The foregoing should not leave the student with the feeling that he should not on occasion write as vividly as he can about exciting experiences. But first things should come first, and underplaying certain aspects of a composition may be a necessary way of putting certain other aspects into proper focus. Understatement is, among other things, a means of bringing about a proper proportioning of the various elements of the composition.

SOME PRACTICAL DONT'S

The problem of tone, then, is most important. There are obviously too many shadings of tone for us to be able to set down elaborate rules for achieving the proper tone. But it is possible to set down a few "don'ts" which have a very general application.

1. Writing down. One must not "write down" to his audience. The sense of oversimple statement and painfully careful explanation can disgust the reader as quickly as any offense of which the writer is capable. Prose which is properly suited to an audience of eight-year-olds would prove completely tiresome or, on the other hand, unintentionally funny, to a mature audience. Take into account your reader's lack of special knowledge of your subject, but never underestimate your reader's intelligence.

2. False enthusiasm. The reader is also likely to resent any hint of synthetic breeziness and false camaraderie. It is a fault into which modern advertising is tending to press the whole civilization. Bug-eyed young matrons oo-la-la-ing over the purchase of sheets or tooth-

brushes, and the all-too-infectious joviality of supersalesmen more and more fill the advertisements. The student obviously wishes to gain a kind of liveliness and warmth in his style, but an artificial concoction of informality and sprightliness can be more depressing than a rather painful dryness.

3. Sentimentality. This third fault is hardly likely to appear in most simple expository writing, but as we have seen in earlier chapters, there is very little writing which is " simply expository." Sentimentality may show itself as pure gushiness or as a kind of hair-trigger emotional sensitiveness. But whatever form it takes, sentimentality always involves an implied demand on the part of the writer for more emotional response than the situation warrants; and it implies, on the part of the sentimental reader, a willingness to respond emotionally when the response is not actually justified.

The Special Audience and the Ideal Audience

Earlier in this chapter we spoke of tone as reflecting the author's attitude toward his audience *and* toward his material, but the student may well ask: " When should attitude toward the audience dominate, and when attitude toward the material? "

Writing which demands that the author take into account his particular audience is, as we have seen, always " practical " writing — writing designed to effect some definite purpose. The advertiser is trying to persuade the housewife to buy something. The politician hopes that his speech will induce citizens to vote for him. Or, to take a more exalted case (for there need be no self-interest) , a statesman urges a nation (through his writing and his speeches) to adopt a certain course of action. Yet these cases all have one thing in common: they are designed to secure a practical end. An audience is to be won to agreement or urged to action.

If such writing is to be effective, the author must, of course, keep his specific audience constantly in mind. An approach calculated to win the suffrage of one audience may very well repel another. The age, the intelligence, the amount of education, the interest, the habits and prejudices of the audience, must all be taken into account. The skillful management of such problems is an aspect of rhetoric, and for many people rhetoric has come to mean largely the art of persuasion. The pure scientist may be thought to escape the need for using rhetoric. The scientist writing strictly as a scientist does not persuade his reader, he "just tells him." The facts speak for themselves, and in purely technical writing they are allowed to speak for themselves. But they speak fully only to a specially trained audience. In a work like "The Method of Scientific Investigation" (page 463), Thomas Huxley is writing for an audience that is not so trained, and the tone which he adopts toward his readers quite properly takes that fact into account.

But what about the student who has no special audience in view? Addressing himself to a general rather than a specific reader, he may find that the problem of tone becomes difficult simply because he lacks a definite target at which to aim. Yet all good writing is addressed to a reader, even though that reader is an ideal reader, not a limited and special one. One could argue, in fact, that because the ideal reader is ideal, his intelligence, his sensitivity, his general discrimination, are to be honored and respected all the more. This is to say what has been said earlier — that we do not evade the problem of tone by addressing ourselves to the reader-in-general rather than to Tom, Dick, or Harry. Actually, the problem of tone here becomes more important, not less important.

Yet the student, even though he agrees with what has just been argued, may find that the ideal reader remains too shadowy to furnish him something definite at which to aim. In that case it may be useful for him to imagine himself writing for some particular person — the most intelligent and discriminating person that he knows. If he can please that person and be convincing to that person, the problem of tone will probably have been taken care of quite adequately.

There is another practical way of considering the problem: The author writes for a particular audience, but he also writes for himself. There is his own sense of fitness that must be satisfied. The writer himself becomes the audience at which he aims. The question which he asks himself is not, "Have I made this convincing to Tom, or to Dick, or to Harry?" but rather, "Have I made this convincing to myself?"; or, to put the matter more succinctly still, "Have I made this convincing?"

In writing for this "ideal" reader, then, the author can transpose all problems of tone into the problem of handling the material itself. The problem of tone alters only when the writing is addressed specifically to Tom or to Dick — not to just any reader — and in proportion as Tom or Dick differs from the ideal reader.

Let us look at the passage quoted from *Seven Pillars of Wisdom* (page 369). The passage, as we saw, tells us a good deal about Lawrence's character, and it makes a commentary on a number of things:

on the Arabs, on justice, and on capital punishment. But as we have already observed, such writing makes its points by implication, and it assumes that the reader is mature. For the *ideal* reader, no alteration of tone is required, and Lawrence has managed his problem of tone in probably the most satisfactory way possible.

But let us suppose that Lawrence were relating the episode to an audience which was complacent in its contempt for the "barbarian" Arabs. Unless his attitude toward the Arabs were to be completely distorted, Lawrence would have to alter the tone to take the prejudices of his audience into account. In particular, he would have to make much more explicit the fact that the Arabs honestly faced up to their imposition of the death penalty as the more sentimental, but ultimately more callous, citizen of England or America refuses to face it.

Or suppose that Lawrence were standing for a seat in Parliament, and a garbled account of the incident were being used against him. He might be content to rely upon the relation which he has given in *Seven Pillars*. Properly read, it shows him to be anything but callous and insensitive. But the politician cannot afford to risk what the artist can. The objectivity of his account might have to be qualified. What his feelings and attitudes were could not safely be left to inference. Lawrence would have to state them explicitly. In general, the rewritten account would be focused not on the drama of the scene itself, but on Lawrence's personal feelings and his struggle with duty.

Tone and Other Components of Style

It should be apparent that a particular tone is achieved by the interplay of various elements. Sentence structure, diction, and metaphor are only a few of those involved. Indeed, in discussing tone we have dealt in one way or another with nearly all the components of literary style. The only notable exception is that of rhythm. Since the tone of a work, taken in the deepest sense, most nearly embodies the organizing intelligence of a work — the "spirit" of a work — a brief discussion of rhythm would go far toward rounding out a simple account of the whole notion of literary style. (We shall mean by *style* the organization of meaning through form. Style represents "how" a thing is said, and how it is said goes far to determine what is said.)

Rhythm

In discussing tone we pointed out that in actual conversation the tone of voice, gesture, and facial expression supplement the words and do much to set the particular tone which the speaker intends — playfulness, seriousness, irritability, and so on. If we use the written word, however, the " tone " has to be established by the choice of words and the patterning of those words. But it will have occurred to the student that in moving from actual conversation to the written word the speaker relinquishes still another very important element — the matter of emphasis. Consider the following simple sentence: " Are you going to town? " If we stress the word *are,* the sentence becomes an emphatic question; and if we stress it heavily, it may even suggest surprise. But if we stress *you,* the question becomes centered upon whether it is *you* who are going rather than someone else. If we stress *town,* we get a third variation; the question then emphasizes the destination.

Thus the rhythmic inflection of a sentence, with its various stresses on particular words, is a very important way in which we express our meanings. When we put the sentence on paper, we can, of course, indicate some of this stress by underlining the words to be emphasized. But mere underlining is a relatively crude substitute for the living voice, and it is the mark of a clumsy writer to have to rely upon constant underlining. The skilled writer, by his control of the rhythm of his sentences, suggests where the proper emphases are to fall; for emphasis is an element of rhythm.

Rhythm and Clarity of Meaning

Control of rhythm, then, is important for clarity of meaning. This fact is illustrated by the muddled and monotonous rhythms of technological jargon. Look back at Maury Maverick's example of gobbledygook (page 317). Jargon of this sort is difficult to read for a variety of reasons. It is fuzzy, abstract, and dull. It lacks flavor. But it lacks clarity as well; for there are no natural emphases, no obvious points of primary stress.

Compare with the passage quoted by Maverick, the following:

Nor had Dickens any lively sense for fine art, classical tradition, science, or even the manners or feelings of the upper classes in his own time and country: in his novels we may almost say there is no army, no navy, no church, no sport, no distant travel, no daring adventure, no feeling for the watery wastes and the motley nations of the planet, and — luckily, with his notion of them — no lords and ladies.

— GEORGE SANTAYANA: *Soliloquies in England.*[9]

Santayana's sentence is long and relatively complex, but it is rhythmical. The heavy stresses come where they should, on words like " Dickens," " lively," " fine," " classical," " even." Moreover, phrase balances phrase: " no distant travel " balances " no daring adventure "; " watery wastes " sets off " motley nations." Even the parenthetical phrase, " with his notion of them," is prepared for. (Notice that the rhythm is destroyed if we alter the ending to read " and — with his notion of them — luckily no lords and ladies.")

We have observed that lack of rhythm is frequently a symptom of disordered discourse; an easily grasped rhythm, on the other hand, is often the sign of good order and proper disposition of words and phrases. But rhythmic quality is much more, of course, than a mere index of clarity.

Emphatic rhythms tend to accompany emotional heightening. It is no accident that eloquent prose — prose that makes a strong appeal to the feelings — tends to use clearly patterned rhythms, or that poetry is commonly written in the systematized rhythm which we call " verse." The association of formal rhythm with emotional power is based on a perfectly sound psychological fact. Fervent expression of grief, rage, or joy tends to fall into rhythmic patterns — whether it be the sobbings of a grief-stricken woman or the cursing of an irate cab driver.

The student may feel, however, that rhythm is much too intricate an instrument for him to try to use *consciously*. It almost certainly is. We do not suggest that the student consciously try for rhythmic effects. Yet a very practical use of rhythm can be made; the student may learn to use rhythm in order to test his composition. As he rereads it aloud, he should learn to listen for the break in the rhythm, the jangling discord, the lack of smoothness that signals to him that something in the sentence is awry. This comment applies particularly to the disposition of modifiers, prepositional phrases, and the like. The student may find that reading his composition aloud and listening to its rhythms proves to be one of the best practical means for spotting sentence elements that are not in the best order.

Consider the following sentence:

Oriental luxury goods — jade, silk, gold, spices, vermilion, jewels — formerly had come by way of the Caspian Sea overland; and a few daring

9 From *Soliloquies in England and Later Soliloquies* by George Santayana. Copyright 1922, by Charles Scribner's Sons.

Greek sea captains, now that this route had been cut by the Huns, catching the trade winds, were sailing from Red Sea ports and loading up at Ceylon.

The sentence is passable, and is not perhaps noticeably unrhythmical. But if we read this sentence in the form in which Robert Graves actually wrote it, we shall find that it is not only clearer, it is much more rhythmical and much easier to read:

Oriental luxury goods — jade, silk, gold, spices, vermilion, jewels — had formerly come overland by way of the Caspian Sea and now that this route had been cut by the Huns, a few daring Greek sea captains were sailing from Red Sea ports, catching the trade winds and loading up at Ceylon.

Style

The real difficulty in discussing style comes at this point. Style, as we have already had occasion to point out, is an over-all effect. It is an effect determined by the working together of sentence structure, vocabulary, figures of speech, rhythm, and many other elements. It is not always easy for a reader to pick out the element which is most important, or even largely important, in giving the style of the writer its special quality. It is quite impossible for a writer to produce a given quality of style by mechanically measuring out so much of this element and so much of that. A modern author has put the matter in this way: " Style is not an isolable quality of writing; it is writing itself."

Like tone, rhythm represents the harmonious interplay of many diverse elements. Style itself, of which tone and rhythm are aspects, represents such an interplay. That is why it is difficult to discuss a style *as such*. Yet there are a few general considerations with regard to style that are worth saying to the student. In the first place, style is never to be thought of as a mere veneer, a decorated surface laid over the content. In the second place, a writer's real difficulty in composition is to know what he really wants to say — not, as we are often tempted to think, merely how to say it. For in a good composition, form and content interpenetrate each other and are inseparable. In the third place, a bad style always reveals itself in some disharmony or cleavage between what is said and what we guess the author actually meant to say.[10] The discordant elements " stick out " — they call attention to themselves.

---

[10] Ironic effects may seem to invite confusion with bad style since, as we have observed earlier (page 363) , irony always involves a discrepancy, a " disharmony," between what is apparently said and what is actually meant. But the confusion, if it occurs, is usually only momentary. The ironic discrepancy proves to be a device under the writer's control — not an ineptitude.

These last considerations bear upon another aspect of style: the originality of the writer. We properly take originality to be a symptom of a good style. If we see that the style is not a veneer, but rather the informing principle of content, we can understand why good style is always indelibly impressed with the personality of the writer. But the student needs to be warned against any excessive striving for originality as such. It is not enough to urge him to be his unique self, for frequently he finds that true self only through a process of exploration. Originality, the impress of personality, fortunately can be left to take care of itself if the writer manages to take care of what he can consciously control in his composition.

• Applications •

I. The following are general questions which the student should ask himself as he considers the passages quoted below.

1. What is the author's attitude toward the reader? In what way is this shown?
2. What is the author's attitude toward his material?
3. Are there any instances of sentimentality? In what way is it revealed? Are there any instances of other kinds of overstatement? Is the overstatement justified or unjustified?
4. Which of the passages, if any, makes use of understatement?
5. Do any of the passages make use of irony? Try to characterize the kind of irony in each case — sarcasm, light mocking irony, bitter irony, gay irony, and so on.
6. Are there any passages which are relatively toneless? Are there any which are confused in tone?

A. [The mate] felt all the majesty of his great position, and made the world feel it, too. When he gave even the simplest order, he discharged it like a blast of lightning, and sent a long reverberating peal of profanity thundering after it. I could not help contrasting the way in which the average landsman would give an order with the mate's way of doing it. If the landsman should wish the gangplank moved a foot farther forward, he would probably say: " James, or William, one of you push that plank forward, please "; but put the mate in his place, and he would roar out: " Here, now, start that gang-plank for'ard! Lively, now! What're you about! Snatch it! There! There! Aft again! aft again! Don't you hear me? Dash it to dash! are you going to sleep over it! 'Vast heaving. 'Vast heaving, I tell you! Going to heave it clear astern? Where're you going with that barrel! for'ard with it 'fore I make you swallow it, you dash-dash-dash-dashed split between a tired mud-turtle and a crippled hearse-horse! " I wished I could talk like that.
— Samuel L. Clemens: *Life on the Mississippi.*

Characterize the tone of the mate's speech. Characterize the author's attitude toward the mate. Be as specific as you can.

B. It wasn't the bully amateur's world any more. Nobody knew that on armistice day, Theodore Roosevelt, happy amateur warrior with the grinning teeth, the shaking forefinger, naturalist, explorer, magazine writer, Sundayschool teacher, cowpuncher, moralist, politician, righteous orator with a short memory, fond of denouncing liars (the Ananias Club) and having pillowfights with his children, was taken to the Roosevelt hospital gravely ill with inflammatory rheumatism.

Things weren't bully any more;

T.R. had grit;

he bore the pain, the obscurity, the sense of being forgotten as he had borne the grilling portages when he was exploring the River of Doubt, the heat, the fetid jungle mud, the infected abscess in his leg.

and died quietly in his sleep
at Sagamore Hill,
on January 6, 1919
and left on the shoulders of his sons
the white man's burden.   — John Dos Passos: " The Happy Warrior," *1919.*[11]

C. No man could have been more bitter against opponents, or more unfair to them or more ungenerous. In this department, indeed, even so gifted a specialist in dishonorable controversy as Dr. (Woodrow) Wilson has seldom surpassed him. He never stood up to a frank and chivalrous debate. He dragged herrings across the trail. He made seductive faces to the gallery. He capitalized his enormous talents as an entertainer, his rank as a national hero, his public influence and consequence. The two great law-suits in which he was engaged were screaming burlesques upon justice. He tried them in the newspapers before ever they were called; he befogged them with irrelevant issues; his appearances in court were not the appearances of a witness standing on a level with other witnesses, but those of a comedian sure of his crowd. He was, in his dealings with concrete men as in his dealings with men in the mass, a charlatan of the very highest skill — and there was in him, it goes without saying, the persuasive charm of the charlatan as well as the daring deviousness, the humanness of naivete as well as the humanness of chicane. He knew how to woo — and not only boobs. He was, for all his ruses and ambuscades, a jolly fellow.

— H. L. Mencken: " Roosevelt: An Autopsy," *Prejudices: Second Series.*[12]

Both Dos Passos and Mencken exhibit definite attitudes toward Theodore Roosevelt; compare and contrast them. How does the attitude in each case color the writer's account? Cite specific instances.

II. A. The worst experience I ever had was being trapped in a cave. The idea of being all alone and in the dark and unable to move is enough to make most grown men afraid, and I was only fourteen. Even though the chances were I'd be found soon, I couldn't be dead sure. But I kept my head and this probably saved me from serious injury. The doctor said later that if I had tried to pull my foot loose I probably would have injured it severely. It was bad enough as it was, and the sprained ankle kept me on crutches for several weeks. My friends

---

11 From *1919,* second volume of *U.S.A.* by John Dos Passos. Published by Houghton Mifflin Company.

12 From " Roosevelt: An Autopsy " by H. L. Mencken. Reprinted from *Prejudices: Second Series* by H. L. Mencken, by permission of Alfred A. Knopf, Inc. Copyright 1920 by Alfred A. Knopf, Inc. Copyright 1948 by H. L. Mencken.

began kidding me about them after a while, but I think it's better to be safe than sorry. The doctor had told me to use the crutches as long as I wanted to.

B. Getting trapped in a cave is no fun, but it's not the worst thing that can happen to you if you keep your head. After telling myself over and over " Keep your head, now," it struck me that it wasn't my head I was in danger of losing, it was my foot. I had to laugh, even in the fix I was in, and started telling myself, " Keep your foot, now." It sort of cheered me up and kept me from doing anything stupid.

When it was all over, people kept saying, " I'll bet you were scared to death." And my mother, after she got over her crying spell, would say, " Jimmie's not scared of anything." They were both wrong. I was scared, all right, but I kept seeing the funny side of it.

How would you characterize the tone of the first version? Of the second? Finish the account of the experience, continuing the tone of the first or the second version. Attempt to rewrite this account, giving it still another tone — say one that might be used by a much younger child, or by a philosophical old man.

III. A.
Dear Phyllis,

Laura tells me that you are thinking of joining us on our trip through the South. I hope you can, though I wish you could have decided earlier. I will write Aunt Agnes and Mrs. Stillwell and ask them if they can find a bed for you, too. But I hope you're not expecting a deluxe suite!

I can't imagine why your mother and father should have any objections. After all, we're old enough to take care of ourselves, though our parents are a little stuffy about admitting it. I'm really looking forward to being off on our own for once.

If you do decide to come, please try to be polite to Doris. I know she gets in your hair, but after all, she's my cousin and there's no use starting trouble for me.

Love,

Evelyn

How would you characterize the writer of this letter, judging from the tone? Would the letter persuade Phyllis to go on the trip? Would it persuade her parents? Can you rewrite the letter, using a more persuasive tone?

B.
Dear Phyllis,

Laura tells me that you are thinking about joining us for our trip through the South. I gather that you are all for it and it's just a question of whether your parents approve. Knowing them as I do, I'm sure they will not decide this arbitrarily. My mother, too, was a little leery at first, but after I had gone over all our plans with her, she agreed that they were perfectly sound.

The fact that we have a new car, which should eliminate any road trouble, and the fact that we'll be staying with relatives or friends every night convinced her that we'll be perfectly safe.

I remember so well the trip I made with you and your family when we were children. The old Packard may have had its weak moments, but your father's ingenuity and good spirits kept us all going merrily along — to say nothing of your mother's unerring ability to spot the perfect place for stopping each night. I hope our trip turns out to be half as much fun as that one. Please give my love to everyone.

Evelyn

Compare the tone of this letter with that given above. How would you characterize its tone. What objections is it designed to overcome? Is it designed to be shown to Phyllis's parents? If there were no parental objection to be overcome, how differently could the ideas of the letter be expressed? Try to rewrite it.

IV. Select one of the following three subjects and write a theme of 500 to 700 words, imitating the style of the selection listed. The imitation should not be slavish, but the student should attempt to apply to his own writing all that he can learn from his model.

1. The present state of the United States (depicted as one of stability or instability) on the model of " It Was a Stable World " (Readings, page 653).
2. An essay on a favorite pet on the model of " The Dog That Bit People " (Readings, page 595).
3. A description of some simple process on the model of " The Colors That Animals Can See " (Readings, page 478).

V. Making use of Williamson's rules (" How To Write Like a Social Scientist," page 623), rewrite the first three paragraphs of " The Colors That Animals Can See " (page 478). Here, for a start, is the first paragraph rewritten:

I propose in the following study to examine the question of what hues are visually significant to animals. As compared with human beings, do other mammals, and, for that matter, other creatures with visual sense organs, make fine or less fine color discriminations? In order to produce valid findings with reference to this question, scientists have performed a number of experiments. The essence of all these experiments consists in training the animals to respond to different hues, usually by associating a particular hue with some food lure to which the animal normally responds. There is a high ratio of similarity between this method of testing color discrimination and experiments used in the past to test responsiveness to sound.

PART 4 THE RESEARCH PAPER

CHAPTER THIRTEEN

Preparation and Note-taking

Most of the longer papers that the student will be asked to write in his college courses will be research papers. That is, the student will be asked to make a study of some particular subject, to assemble materials, organize them, and incorporate them into a unified composition, with footnotes to indicate his authority for the various statements that he makes.

The research paper is a form, and a most important form, of expository discourse. We may want to investigate hydroponics or the architecture of Crusader castles or the nineteenth-century whaling industry or the Battle of Hastings or the present-day do-it-yourself vogue or a thousand and one other things. But at the end of our research, after we have read our books and magazines or have gone on our field trip or carried out our experiments in the laboratory, there remains the problem of organizing the results. Our facts and opinions need to be organized so as to present their meaning as lucidly and as tellingly as possible. Even if our investigation has been extensive and thorough, it may be wasted if we present its fruits in a muddled and confusing form.

Such a muddled presentation may indeed mean that we ourselves do not know what to make of the facts we have discovered. For facts do not automatically crystallize about a meaning. We have to find what the facts mean, and this involves thinking about them, analyzing them, and working out their implications. The problems to be faced then are those that we have already studied in earlier chapters, and particularly in such chapters as those on Exposition and Argument with their topics on classification, definition, comparison and contrast, the various kinds of analysis, the nature of evidence, and the principles of induction and deduction. We should, therefore, by this time already know a great deal about the processes involved in working out a research paper; and by the same token, the research paper should provide us at this point with a fine opportunity to review what we have learned in studying exposition.

We need not, however, confine our review to those chapters. As we have had occasion to remark many times in this book, the four modes of discourse are rarely met with in a pure form. In even predominantly expository writing, there are elements of the other modes: we have occasion to argue a point; a piece of description is called for; or we need to tell the story of a man or a process or a development. The research paper should give us an opportunity to review many of the important methods of organization on which we have been at work throughout the course.

In this chapter and the following chapter we shall take up the problems of gathering material and writing a research paper. Here we shall be particularly concerned with the mechanics of research; in Chapter 14 we shall actually write and revise the paper.

▶ ## Sources

The aim of the research paper is to assemble facts and ideas from various sources, and by studying them, to draw new conclusions or to present the material in the light of a new interest. For instance, a military historian who wanted to understand why General Lee lost the Battle of Gettysburg would study the written records of orders and events, the correspondence and memoirs of witnesses, the actual terrain, and the interpretations of other historians. In the light of that evidence, he would try to frame an explanation. Or a literary critic who wanted to understand why a certain novelist often used certain themes would study the facts of the novelist's life as found in whatever sources were available (letters, memoirs, public records, biographies), the kind of education he received, the kind of ideas current in his particular place and time, and so forth. Such material would be his evidence. The researcher might discover new facts, and new facts can easily upset old theories. But he might have to depend on facts which were already available but were available only in scattered sources. Then his task would be to collect these facts and shape them into a new pattern of interpretation.

The book written by the professional historian or literary critic and the term paper written by a student use the same basic method: they collect the facts and interpret them. The term paper can be intelligent, well informed, interesting, and original. To make it so, the student must be systematic.

The first step toward making his paper systematic is to learn how to investigate his subject. There are two kinds of sources which he can use: primary and secondary. The historian going to the order book of a general or the terrain of a battlefield, the anthropologist observing the Indian tribe, or the literary scholar studying the manuscripts or letters of an author are using what are called primary sources; that is, firsthand information, the original documents. The college student must usually use secondary sources; that is, secondhand information, a report on, or analysis of, the original documents. He reads the report of the anthropologist or he studies an edition of a poet prepared by a scholar. There are also tertiary sources — the digest of, or commentary on, the anthropologist's report (e.g., *The Reader's Digest* and *The Book Review Digest*). These the student should not use unless he cannot get access to the secondary or primary sources. Even when he has no choice but to cite a tertiary source, he should do so with great caution. Get as close to the facts as possible. No matter how good your reasoning is, it is useless if the facts on which it works are not dependable.

Bibliography

The research paper, we have said, draws its material from many sources. It is not a digest of one book or article. But how do you get at the useful sources?

Reference books give a good starting point — standard encyclopedias and dictionaries, and such compilations as the *American Yearbook*, the *Statesman's Yearbook,* and the *World Almanac*. In addition to such general reference works, there are those devoted to special fields; for example, the *Dictionary of National Biography* (limited to the British), the *Dictionary of American Biography, Living Authors, Who's Who* (British), *Who's Who in America,* the *Encyclopedia of the Social Sciences,* the *Catholic Encyclopedia,* the *Oxford Companion to English Literature,* the *Oxford Companion to American Literature,* the *Cambridge History of English Literature,* the *Cambridge History of American Literature,* Bartlett's *Familiar*

Quotations, and the *Readers' Guide to Periodical Literature.* Reference books are so numerous and sometimes so specialized that it is often helpful to consult the *Guide to Reference Books,* by Constance M. Winchell, to know where to go in the first place.

The reference book will give an introduction to a subject and certain basic facts. Best of all for the student, it will usually offer a list of other works — books or articles less limited in scope than the treatment in the reference book itself. With this as a starting point the student can make up his own *working bibliography* for his subject. As he reads into his subject he will encounter references to other works, and can gradually extend the range of his working bibliography. The subject catalogue of the library will also provide new items.

The working bibliography should be kept on convenient cards of uniform size, with only one entry to a card. This allows the student to arrange them in alphabetical or other order (by topics, for example), according to his need. The entry on the card should contain all the basic information about a book or article: the author's name with the last name first, the title of the work, the volume number, if any, the place of publication, the publisher, the date of publication. If the work appears in a periodical or collection, that fact should be indicated with volume number, the date, and the pages occupied by the work.

This form of card entry is to be retained in making up the final bibliography to be attached to your finished paper. There the order will be alphabetical by authors. Your final bibliography may be shorter than your working bibliography, for the final bibliography should contain no entry from which you have not taken material for the actual paper, whereas certain items in your working bibliography may have been dropped as more valuable items came to light.

Entry for a book

> Strachey, Lytton, <u>Elizabeth</u> <u>and</u> <u>Essex</u>, London, Chatto and Windus, 1928.

Entry for an article

> Barrington, Margaret, "The Censorship in Eire," <u>Commonweal</u>, XLVI, August 15, 1947, 429–32.

What items should be included in the student's working bibliography? The professional scholar may want to work through all the material on his subject, but the student preparing a term paper scarcely has the time for such a program. Many items in the bibliographies he encounters are antiquated or trivial. So to save his time and energy, he should try to select the items which will best repay his attention. There is no rule for selecting a bibliography. The student, however, can sometimes get ideas from a similarly selected bibliography in a textbook or other book on his subject. Sometimes an author will refer with special respect to certain other works on his subject. The student can also take his working bibliography to his instructor and ask for comment.

• **Applications** •

I. Perhaps the instructor in one of your courses has already assigned a general topic for a research paper. If not, choose a general topic. The following list may give you some ideas:

Paul Revere's Ride
The Evacuation of Dunkirk
The Sinking of the *Andrea Doria*
How a Dude Ranch Is Run
Hybrid Corns and Their Effect on American Agriculture
Turbojet Engines
Running a Mink Farm
John Keats in Italy
History of the Bowie Knife
The Plymouth Settlement
Custer's Last Stand
Running an Antique Shop
Sports Cars
Organizing a Club

See also the list of topics printed on page 46.

II. Having chosen your topic, make a preliminary bibliography for it.

Notes

Unless you take notes on your reading you will probably not be able to remember much of the relevant material and will certainly not be able to organize it well when you write your paper. If you have taken your notes carefully, you will be able to lay out before you the whole subject and put it in order. Then the paper will almost write itself. If the notes are to give you the most help, they must have a convenient mechanical form. Notes can be put on note cards (usually 4″ x 6″ or 5″ x 7″). As already mentioned, not more than one note, however brief, should be on a card. This rule should be strictly adhered to, even when the notes are on the same topic; for when you take the notes, you cannot be sure in what order you will eventually use them. Only if each note is independent can you arrange them in the order desired when you write your paper. Each note should carry at the top, at the left or toward the center, some indication of the precise content — not the general subject of your investigation, but some subtopic. And at the top right or at the bottom, the note should carry an adequate reference to the source from which it is drawn. Presumably the full bibliographical information about that source is already in your working bibliography, and so some skeleton notation will be adequate here. (When you are taking notes not related to a working bibliography — when, for example, you are doing general reading — you should record full bibliographical information with the note.) Below is a specimen card:

```
American success worship    Chesterton, What I Saw
                            in America, pp. 107-10

American worship of success not materialistic.  Fact
of worship means a mystic rather than a materialist.
Frenchman who saves money to retire and enjoy his
omelet more of a materialist.  American does not work
for the enjoyment of things, but for some ideal vision
of success.  He does not want the dollar for what it
will buy but as a symbol.  Phrase "making good" il-
lustrates the fact;   carries a moral connotation by
a "sort of ethical echo in the word" good (p. 108).
Not necessarily an admirable morality, but a morality
implied, and idealism of a kind.
```

When we look at the actual note on the card we see that several other phrases might have been used to indicate the topic discussed; for instance, "American business mysticism," or "American materialism." All that is needed is a word or phrase which will remind the note-taker of the content. We notice, too, that after the direct quotation there is a parenthesis with the page number. The note-taker apparently feels that this is a telling phrase worth remembering and perhaps using. If he quotes it, he will want the exact page reference.

As for the bibliographical indication at the upper right, he might have reduced it simply to "Chesterton" if there was no Chesterton other than G. K. Chesterton on his bibliography and no other book by that author. This, like the topic indication, is for his own convenience and need tell no more than he himself has to know to identify the source.

So much for the mechanics of note-taking. As for the process, you should make your notes relevant, accurate, and clear. To make them relevant you must keep constantly in mind the main purpose of your investigation. You are studying a particular subject with particular limits. (Remember in this connection what was said on page 14 with regard to a "true subject.") You are not concerned with anything only casually associated with the subject. If, for instance, when your subject is the economic background of the American Revolution, you are reading a general history of the period, you should not be distracted by military strategy of the French and Indian Wars or an analysis of Puritan theology. Your job is to follow your main purpose through a body of various materials, and often what is major for you will be minor in the work you are investigating.

It is possible to take notes prematurely. Therefore, it is always best to become acquainted with a work before you take notes from it. In your first reading you may indicate material for possible notes and pass on. When you have finished the work, or those parts relevant to your interest, you can then better assess the material for possible notes. In this way you will get from any particular work only the most pertinent notes, and you will avoid duplication.

The note itself may be direct quotation or summary. If direct quotation is used, it is sometimes valuable to record the context of the quotation. What leads the author to make his statement? What point does he try to establish by it? You do not want to misinterpret your author by implication. For instance, suppose a critic should write:

Although Herman Melville has created in Captain Ahab of *Moby-Dick* a character of intense interest and monumental proportions, he has in general little sense of the shadings of personality and motive. Most of his creations are schematic, mere outlines without flesh. He lacks that basic gift of the novelist, a sense of character.

If you, assembling material for a paper on Melville as a novelist, should merely quote, "Herman Melville has created in Captain Ahab of *Moby-Dick* a character of intense interest and monumental proportions," you would have a misleading note. An accurate note would run something like this:

> Even though this critic believes that Melville in general lacks a sense of character, he admits that Captain Ahab is a " character of intense interest and monumental proportions."

This principle of context holds good for both the note by summary and the note by quotation.

When you are taking notes by summary, the kind of summary to be used depends on the special case. In one case, the author's method of reasoning may be very important, and then the summary should be of a form to indicate the logical structure of the original text. In another case, where mere facts or scattered opinions are involved, the summary need record merely these facts and opinions. As for the scale of the summary, there is no guiding principle except the note-taker's need. Try to forecast what you will need when you actually come to write your paper; not merely what you will want to incorporate in the paper, but what you will need in order to understand your subject fully.

Once your notes are taken, how do you use them? This again depends on the kind of subject with which you are dealing. Some subjects suggest a chronological order, others a logical order. For instance, if you are doing a paper on Keats's development as a poet you might first arrange your notes chronologically — notes on early poems, notes on middle poems, notes on late poems. But if your subject is an analysis of the themes of Keats's poems, you might try to arrange your notes by themes, running various classifications until you have one that seems to make sense. Or you might find, sometimes, that two levels of organization are necessary. For instance, certain themes of Keats's poems might be characteristic of certain periods. Then having established one type of classification (by theme), you might run another type (by chronology). Notes are flexible. You can use them as a device to help your thinking, or to help you organize your material.

Notes record questions and issues. The different authors you have consulted have had individual approaches to the general subject, different interests, different conclusions. As you work over your cards you can locate these differences and try to see what they mean to you in your special project. Ask yourself if there is any pattern of disagreement among the authors you have consulted. List the disagreements. Are they disagreements of fact or of interpretation? Compare the evidence and reasoning offered by the authors who are in disagreement. Can you think of any new evidence or new line of reasoning on disputed points? Can you think of any significant points not discussed by your authors? What bearing would such points have on their conclusions? Again, use your notes as a device to help your thinking.

• Application •

Study " The American Civilization Puzzle " (Readings, page 666). Though this is not in any formal sense a research essay, it embodies and summarizes a great deal of research in various fields brought to bear on a single historical question. Observe carefully how the author has analyzed disagreements and assessed evidence.

Outline

By working over your notes and thinking about ideas suggested in them you will probably strike on some vague general plan for your paper. But do not commit yourself to the first plan that comes into your head. Consider various possibilities. Then when you have struck on the most promising, try to work up an outline on that basis. You will undoubtedly start with a sort of rough suggestive outline, the barest shadow of the paper you want to write. By checking back on your material you can begin to fill in the outline and determine the relation among the facts and ideas you wish to present. So you will arrive at a more fully organized outline. Perhaps a topic outline will serve your purpose, but at some stage a sentence outline will probably be helpful, for to make it you will have to state clearly and exactly what you mean.

Once you have an outline prepared you can begin the actual composition. Use your outline as a guide, but do not consider yourself bound by it. As you write, new ideas will probably come to you, and if they are good ideas you should revise your outline to accommodate them. The outline is not sacred. Like your notes, it is simply a device to help you think. And remember that your paper should be a fully rounded composition, unified and coherent, emphasizing matters according to the scale of their importance. The outline is only a start toward creating a fluent, well-proportioned discussion.

Your paper should be more than a tissue of facts and quotations from your notes. It should represent your handling of a subject and not a mere report on what other writers have said. Naturally, a large part of your material will be derived from other writers, but you should always ask yourself just what a fact or idea means in relation to your own purpose. If there is no proper place for it in your pattern, it should be excluded. A writer who has studied his subject always has more material than he can well use.

Footnotes

Full credit should be given for the source of every fact or idea derived from another writer. In your own text you will want to acknowledge any important item as a matter of help to your reader. It is easy to introduce a statement or a quotation by a clear explanatory phrase or sentence. We are all accustomed to such introductory remarks as these:

Charles A. Beard has proved that . . .
James Truslow Adams maintains that . . .
An excellent statement of this view is given by James Truslow Adams in his *Epic of America:* . . .
As Sinclair Lewis shows in *Main Street,* the culture of the American town is . . .
On the other hand, a liberal economist such as Paul Douglas holds that . . .
As Thomas Wolfe observed . . .

Some facts or ideas can simply be stated in your text if the fact or idea is not especially to be associated with the particular writer from whom you derived it. But in all cases, authority should be given in a footnote.[1]

Exactly what must be footnoted? First, every direct quotation is identified in a footnote. Second, every statement of fact is referred to its source in a footnote. The student must use his discretion about documenting commonly known facts that are available in many sources. It is not necessary, for example, to cite an authority for the fact that the world is round. But it is probably necessary to document an assertion that the world is actually the shape of a grape-

---

[1] Detailed instructions for writing footnotes will be found in the Appendix on footnoting, pages 825–29.

fruit or a slightly squishy cantaloupe, the theory of present-day scientists. Third, every opinion or interpretation drawn from another writer should be referred to its source in a footnote, *even if the opinion or interpretation is one which you have independently come upon in your own thinking.* In cases where a group of facts or opinions treated together in one paragraph is drawn from the same source, one note at the end of the paragraph will serve for all the material. In cases where more than one source is involved for a single item in the text, one note will serve to acknowledge the several sources.

Sample Research Paper

A good research paper is certainly not merely an affair of organized quotations and footnotes. It is not necessarily dull and dry. It can be, and it ought to be, well written. Consider the example of a research paper that follows. As a concrete example it may tell us more about the make-up of a good research paper than the abstract discussion that has preceded.

THE YANKEE SCHOOL

By

George Lyman Kittredge

You should add ▶
course and section,
date, and other in-
formation your
instructor requests.

OUTLINE

THE YANKEE SCHOOL

THESIS: The popular <u>Farmer's Almanack</u>
          offers a key to the under-
          standing of the Yankee school
          and its masters in the period
          just after the Revolution, the
          time when the universal,free
          school system was recognized
          by many observers as the chief
          institution in forming Amer-
          ican virtues and talents.

◄ The central idea or
thesis is stated in
one sentence.

I.   Good schooling was equated by the
     early Yankees with necessities of
     life.

     A.   A foreign observer, Harriet
          Martineau, was struck by this
          emphasis on popular educa-
          tion.

     B.   The common concern with
          schooling is signally re-
          flected in the pages of the
          <u>Farmer's Almanack</u>.

          1.   The Old Farmer advises
               his readers to include
               the hiring of a good
               schoolmaster with the
               other tasks of getting
               ready for winter.

          2.   He could speak with the
               authority of one who had
               been a successful
               teacher.

          3.   His advice to parents —
               to keep their children in
               school and to leave au-
               thority to the teachers
               — is still apposite.

               [i]

Small Roman
numeral in brackets
for first page pre-
◄ ceding the text.

II. "The chief glory of New England is in her schools," recited pupils of the last century.

    A. Laws regarding compulsory free education were passed early in colonial times.

        1. Although the laws were sometimes flouted, their observance was a matter of concern to the clergy, revealing the importance attached to them.

        2. There is evidence that the laws were generally kept and were a matter of pride to such figures as John Adams.

            a. Adams attributed the virtues of American character to the meeting—house, the school—house, and the militia training field.

            b. The true New England drive towards education is revealed in Rufus Putnam's struggle to acquire learning.

    B. The Massachusetts law of 1789, which remained unchanged until 1824, provided for both elementary and grammar schools.

        1. The three R's plus "decent behaviour" composed the elementary curriculum.

        2. These were expanded to a study of Latin and Greek as well as English in grammar school.

C. Foreign observers were favorably impressed by the Yankee schools.

D. The Academies were founded to fill the gap in the educational system created by smaller towns that could not afford schools of their own.

III. Education for girls at first lagged behind that for boys, but after 1789 advances were made.

A. Caleb Bingham is commonly credited with opening the first private school for girls in Boston.

1. His success led to town support of a girls' school in 1789 with Bingham as master.

2. He also wrote best-selling texts.

B. Schools for girls soon opened elsewhere.

1. Jedediah Morse, writer of a popular geography text, opened such a school in New Haven.

2. Others followed in Pennsylvania, New York, and Massachusetts with "female academies."

IV. But it is the grammar school with its master that best represents the Yankee school.

A. Ezekiel Cheever of the Boston Latin School is typical.

1. Discipline and student rivalry as illustrated by two anecdotes could be

iv

> > > problems that sometimes
> > > drove a student away.
> >
> > 2. The good master could,
> >   however, bow magnani-
> >   mously to youthful learn-
> >   ing.
>
> B. After nearly forty years as
> master, Cheever died in 1708,
> eliciting in tribute a broad-
> side ballad — "The Gram-
> marian's Funeral."

V. A final quotation from the _Farm-
er's Almanack_ ends on the wry
note of the uneducable quality of
a non-typical Yankee, neighbor
Braggadocia.

THE YANKEE SCHOOL*

◀ Title in caps
repeated on page 1

In 1834 Miss Harriet Martineau
came to America in search of mental
refreshment and change of scene. She
spent a couple of years in this country
and has left a record of her experiences and impressions in two books
which have won a respectable place in
the great class of miscellaneous literature — Society in America, and Retrospect of Western Travel — besides the
minute account of her connection with
the anti-slavery movement which she
gives in her Autobiography. With the
mass of these writings we have at this
moment no particular concern, but one
incident must not pass without notice.
In an idle hour — or let us say rather
in a moment of peculiar inspiration —
Miss Martineau had recourse to a certain "old almanack," where she discovered something to point an excellent
moral. Here is her account of the discovery:

◀ Formal introduc-
tion to a long
quotation.

> All young people in
> these [New England] villages
> are more or less instructed.
> Schooling is considered a
> necessary of life. I hap-
> pened to be looking over an
> old almanack one day, when I

---

* From G. L. Kittredge, The Old
Farmer and His Almanack (1904, 1920).
By permission of the Harvard University
Press.

[1]

2.

found, among the directions   F
relating to the preparations
for a winter on a farm, the
following: "Secure your
cellars from frost. Fasten
loose clap—boards and shingles. Secure a good schoolmaster." It seemed doubtful, at the first glance,
whether some new farming
utensil had not been thus
whimsically named; as the
brass plate which hooks upon
the fender, or upper bar of
the grate, is called "the
footman"; but the context
clearly showed that a man
with learning in his head was
the article required to be [1]
provided before the winter.

Reference number, ▶
above the line, is
placed at end of
quotation.

It must be admitted, even by Miss
Martineau's warmest admirers, that she
did not always comprehend the American
character. Indeed, she had the good
sense not to suppose that she could
comprehend it. Just before she sailed
for the United States, James Mill asked
her, quizzically, whether she "expected to understand the Americans" in
two years. "He was glad to find,"
writes Miss Martineau, "that I had no
such idea, and told me that five—and-
twenty years before, he had believed
that he understood the Scotch: and that
in another five—and—twenty, he should
no doubt understand the English; but
that now he was quite certain that he
understood neither the one nor the

Informal quota- ▶
tion woven into
text.

———————
[1] Society in America (London,
1837), I, 264.

other."[2] It was hardly this warning
that sent Miss Martineau to the old
almanac, but rather her own sagacity,
or perhaps a happy accident. At all
events, she lighted upon a highly characteristic passage, and it is to her
credit that she did not fail to perceive what it signifies — that to procure a schoolmaster is as much a matter
of course to a Yankee farmer as any
other provision for the winter season.
To his mind there is nothing incon-
gruous between attention to loose
shingles and solicitude for primary
education.

◄ Significance of previous quotation is discussed.

It does not appear what almanac
Miss Martineau consulted. Very possibly it was that of Mr. R. B. Thomas.
The precise passage, to be sure, has
not been discovered in the sayings of
the Old Farmer; but she may have been
quoting from memory, and the form and
the sentiment both suggest the admonitions of the Farmer's Calendar. That
column contains, along with its pre-
cepts of practical agriculture, much
exhortation on the subject of schools
and schoolmasters. Some of the entries
are characteristic enough to deserve
reproduction. Besides, they are not
without value as bits of country life
at the end of the eighteenth and the
beginning of the nineteenth century.

◄ Smooth transition to *Farmer's Almanack.*

◄ Reference to work in more than one volume.

[2] Autobiography (Boston, 1877), I,
329.

4.

A passage which comes very near to Miss Martineau's quotation occurs in the Farmer's Calendar for November, 1804:

No footnote ▶ needed since documentation is given in text.

> Now let the noise of
> your flail awake your drowsy
> neighbours.
> Bank up your cellars.
> Now hire a good school-
> master, and send your chil-
> dren to school as much as
> possible.

Series of ▶ pertinent quo- tations, each introduced and identified.

In November, 1810, there is also a near approach to what Miss Martineau read:

> Bank your cellars unless
> your underpinning is such as
> renders it unneedful. Drive
> all your loose nails; and if
> the boys have broken any
> glass during the summer in
> the windows, you find it more
> comfortable to have the hole
> stopped up, than to let it go
> over winter. Send your chil-
> dren to school. Every boy
> should have a chance to pre-
> pare himself to do common
> town business.

In December, 1801, we have a good piece of proverbial philosophy:

> "A cheap school—master
> makes a dear school," says
> Common Sense. As this is the
> season for opening schools in
> the country, the above adage
> may be worthy of attention.
> Experience teaches, that the
> master, who will keep for 8
> dollars per month, is not
> worth keeping: yet some

towns, to save 2 dollars,
give away 10.

Again, in December, 1803 and 1805:

     It is hoped that every
town and village is now supplied with a wise and virtuous
school-master; not ten dollar
men — such pitiful pedants
are too plenty. (1803.)
     Attend to your schools.
Hire not what neighbor Simp-
kins calls a <u>four dollar
master</u> to instruct your children; it will be throwing away
money. He who deprives his
children of education, at once
robs himself and society.
(1805.)

◀ Long quotations
single spaced
and indented,
no quotation
marks.

But the liveliest passage of the
kind is in the Calendar for November,
1820, where we have not only a full
account of the acquirements of a five-
dollar master, but also an eloquent
speech from one of the advocates of
ill-judged economy:

     This is the last month
of Autumn, and it is now the
business of the prudent man
to be making his calculations
about winter matters. I have
often mentioned the importance of schooling to the
rising generation. Few, if
any countries, are blest like
New-England, with public
school establishments. No
stinginess about the business. See that you have an
able master, and pay him
well. Here my neighbour
Hugpurse and I can never
agree; for he says,"So much
of this here larnin is alto-

◀ Punctuation of
source followed
exactly (New-
England).

6.

gether useless and expensive.
There is Joe Simple is good
enough for our school. He
has cyphered through com-
pound interest, and that's
fur enough for any man. He
knows nothing about Jogrify
and Grammar and such stuff;
but he can write as good a
hand as I can; and as for
reading, he is far better
than Squire Puff. In spelling they say he is curious.
I have often heard that when
a boy he could spell <u>Nebu-
chadnezzar</u> quicker than any
one in school. I move,
Mr. cheersman, that we hire
Joe Simple to keep our school
this winter. Give him five
dollars a month and board
himself, which is all he
axes."

Authority of source ▶
is established.

  Mr. Thomas knew what he was talking about. He had been a country
pedagogue himself; and, though he did
not fall in love with the profession —
in fact, he tells that he grew heartily
tired of it — he had always been successful in his schoolmastering. He
felt a proper contempt for the shortsighted stinginess of ignorant com-
mitteemen, and cherished no illusions
as to the quality of the cheap pretenders to learning whose services they
secured for little or nothing. He must
Literary allusion ▶
to Irving's Ichabod
Crane used
effectively.
have known many Ichabod Cranes and
Joe Simples in his day. But schoolmasters like Joe Simple were not the
only pretenders whom Mr. Thomas sati-
rized. He was equally severe on those

who aped the follies of fine gentlemen.
Thus in December, 1815, we read:

> It is all important now
> that you send your children
> to school; but take care that
> you have a good instructor
> for them. It is not every-
> one who apes the gentleman
> that is fit for this under-
> taking. To strut in white
> top boots, brandish a cane,
> drink brandy, and smoke se-
> gars, are not the most essen-
> tial qualifications for a
> school-master. It is a seri-
> ous misfortune that in many
> parts our country schools are
> exceedingly neglected; and it
> would seem that were it not
> for the law's obliging them
> to have at least the appear-
> ance of schools, there would
> be no provision at all for
> this purpose made for years!
> What better estate can you
> give your off-spring than a
> good education? I would not
> urge you to send them to
> college — neither to an
> academy; but see that you
> have the best of teachers in
> your town schools; be not
> stingy about the price — let
> not your children suffer for
> shoes and other clothing to
> make them comfortable and
> decent — Town schools are of
> the first importance, for
> here and in the family at
> home is laid the foundation
> of the future man, whether
> he be great, or mean, an
> honest man, or a scoundrel.

Top boots and cigar-smoking seem
to have gone together. Robert Sut-
cliff, the English Quaker, who travelled in America from 1804 to 1806,

8.

shared Mr. Thomas's suspicion of both articles. "I have remarked," he writes, "that some people in America have a great predilection for wearing boots, and for smoking segars. Even children of five or six years of age, are sometimes seen, in their boots smoking segars."[3] Most of Mr. Thomas's early readers, if they smoked at all, doubtless smoked pipes, for the cigar (or segar, as there was a tendency to spell the word about this time) was not only citified, but was regarded as indicative of riotous living. Perhaps, therefore, the following entry, honestly meant as it certainly was, suggested no roguish thoughts to the contemporary agriculturist. To the modern smoker it has a sinister sound. It occurs in the Farmer's Calendar for June 12, 1796:

    Set cabbages and tobacco.

And, as if a word to the wise were not always sufficient in tricks of the trade, we have, a year later, in June, 1797, an additional injunction:

    Set more cabbages and tobacco.

---

[3] *Travels in some Parts of North America, in the years 1804, 1805, and 1806*, 2d ed., York, 1815, p. 103.

The word <u>more</u> has some significance.
It involves a pleasant suggestion of
the "constant reader," the "old sub-
scriber." In consulting the Calendar
for June of one year, the farmer who is
faithful to the admonitions of the
<u>Almanac</u> will surely remember what he
did, or shunned, the year before.
"<u>More</u> cabbages and tobacco," then, must
not be taken as the helpless reitera-
tion of an almanac—writer at his wit's
end. It implies, rather, that the
author believes in himself and has
reason to think that his public has
confidence in him. "You planted cabbages and tobacco last year, no doubt,
as I advised. Very well! Plant some
more now. You see my counsel was
good."

A lesson for parents, as apposite
now as it ever was, may be found in the
December Calendar for 1807. Here also
Mr. Thomas was speaking from experience:

> Let your children go to
> school as much as possible;
> and do not interfere with the
> orders and regulations of the
> master. When your little
> darling Jemmy is whipt at
> school it is a miserable way
> to give him gingerbread, and
> call the master puppy, ras-
> cal, &c. &c.

And again, in February, 1809:

> Keep the boys at school
> as much as possible, and take

◄ Separate quotations
on same topic
arranged together.

10.

care not to rail against the
master in their presence.
Some people are eternally
complaining about the schoolmaster or mistress. Let the
school be never so well kept,
they will be dissatisfied.

Another kind of admonition, in the
Calendar for December, 1812, sounds
strange to modern ears:

Now you have an oppor-
tunity for schooling your
children; and what can you
give them to more profit?
Riches and honors will fly
away, but a good education,
with habitual improvement,
will abide by them, and be
a source of pleasure and
profit, when business and
money, and friends fail them.
But do not let them be prevented from going to school
for want of shoes, &c. They
should have been well shod
before this time.

This observation about staying at
home for lack of shoes recalls the fact
that going barefoot was far commoner a
hundred (or even thirty) years ago than
it is to—day. "Old enough to go to
meeting barefooted" is a Yankee proverb
not yet forgotten, though not, of
course, to be taken seriously. An old
New Englander who, in 1837, wrote
reminiscences of his youth for the Old
Colony Memorial, is very clear on this
matter. He is speaking of ordinary
attire in the country districts. "Old
men," he says, "had a great coat and a

pair of boots. The boots generally
lasted for life . . . Shoes and stockings were not worn by the young men,
and by but few men in farming business." As for the young women, he
informs us that in the summer, when
engaged in their ordinary work, they
"did not wear stockings and shoes."[4]
  We may close our series of ex-
tracts with two eloquent utterances of
a generally admonitory character:

> Let your children go to
> school. No country in the
> world is so blest with
> schooling as New—England;
> then neglect not to improve
> this excellent advantage.
> (December, 1806.)

> It is a duty to educate
> our children in the ways of
> frugality and economy, as
> well as industry. In some it
> is owing to inattention, in
> others to parsimony that
> their children are kept from
> school. The heedless man
> who can just write his name
> and pick out a chapter or
> two in his bible [sic] and
> perhaps find the changes of
> the moon in his almanack,
> thinks that his children and
> his children's children are
> to go on the same way with
> himself, and so is regardless
> of their education; but the
> penurious man, if it cost a
> cent, will see them hanged
> before they shall be taught
> to spell Caleb. (March, 1813.)

◀ Editorial word
sic indicates
faithful following
of capitalization
practice of
source.

[4] Collections of the New—Hampshire
Historical Society, 1837, V, 226-7.

12.

A generation ago there was a stock question which used to be asked of school children: "What is the chief glory of New England?" And the reply was a matter of clockwork: "The chief glory of New England is in her public schools." The children had their doubts, but they answered dutifully. This kind of catechising is out of fashion now, and the mere thought of it provokes a smile among educational theorists; but it had its uses. In the case in hand, it called attention to the fact that schools do not spring up of themselves; and it may now and then have reminded the rising generation of certain items of indebtedness to the Puritan past. This whole subject of New England schooling is not easy to discuss without losing one's equilibrium. On the one hand, we are habituated to a good deal of undiscriminating eulogy of our ancestors, as if they never faltered in their zeal for education. On the other, there are the iconoclasts, who make much of the difficulty there was in enforcing the school laws.[5] There is evidence of such difficulty. A Massachusetts Act of 1701 declares that the previous

> [5] The Massachusetts laws which particularly concern us are those of 1647 (Mass. Colony Records, II, 203), 1692 (4 Wm. and Mary, ch. xi), 1701 (13 Wm. III, ch. xx), 1789 (Acts, ch. xix), and 1824 (Acts, ch. cxi, amending the Act of 1789).

Conflicting views of authorities indicated.

statute "is shamefully neglected by
divers Towns." In an Election Sermon
for 1709 the Rev. Grindal Rawson, of
Mendon, exclaims: "How little care is
there generally taken, especially in
Country Towns, to promote the Liberal
Education of Children? How much is it
become the Practice of many Towns, to
Study Tricks and Shifts whereby the
Law of the Land obliging to the uphold-
ing and maintaining of Schools, may be
wholly evaded and lose its Efficacy?
And is not this Provoking to God, and
disserviceable to the interest of
Posterity?"[6] In 1713 Cotton Mather, in
one of his innumerable jeremiads —
called Advice from the Watch Tower, in
a Testimony against Evil Customs —
censures the evasion of this law:
"To Elude the Law about Schools, is too
Customary. It argues, that a due sense
of that Grand Concern, the Education of
Children, is too much laid aside among
us. — Tis Wonderful! Tis Wonderful!
That a People of our Profession would
seem so unconcerned, Lest the next
Generation be miserably Uncultivated,
and have hideous Barbarity grow upon
it!"

All this, however, should not mislead us. The facts are clear enough
and the anxiety of the preachers is
really a favorable symptom. The sig-

◀ Notice preserva-
tion of original
form of quota-
tion, even to
italicized
words.

◀ Author's inter-
pretation of
sources above.

---

[6] The Necessity of a Speedy and
Thorough Reformation (Boston, 1709),
p. 36.

14.

nificant thing is not that the laws
were not always obeyed, but that the
colonial and provincial authorities
made an honest attempt to enforce them,
and that the outcome of their efforts
was, when time was ripe, a public
school system which, though not perfect, is at all events a remarkable
achievement. We should regard the
general tendency and the final results.
We have a good many diaries kept by
soldiers in the Revolutionary War.
Most of these are rudely spelled and
not very exact in point of grammar.
They show that the rank and file were
not highly educated, and they have
often been cited as proof that the
schools and schoolmasters of the eighteenth century were poor things. What
they really prove, however, is that
almost every New Englander could read
and write, and this, after all, is a
pretty creditable showing. When John
Adams was in England in 1786, he fell
in with a Virginian, Major Langbourne,
who had "taken the whim of walking all
over Europe, after having walked over
most of America." The Major lamented
"the difference of character between
Virginia and New England." "I offered," writes Adams, "to give him a
receipt for making a New England in
Virginia. He desired it; and I recommended to him town meetings, training
days, town schools, and ministers,

Long anecdote ▶
is introduced
to support
opinion.

giving him a short explanation of each
article. The meeting-house and the
school-house and training field are the
scenes where New England men were
formed. Colonel Trumbull, who was
present, agreed that these are the
ingredients. In all countries and in
all companies, for several years, I
have, in conversation and in writing,
enumerated the towns, militia, schools,
and churches, as the four causes of the
growth and defence of New England. The
virtues and talents of the people are
there formed; their temperance, patience, fortitude, prudence, and justice, as well as their sagacity,
knowledge, judgment, taste, skill,
ingenuity, dexterity and industry."[7]

Here is an uncommonly interesting
bit of autobiography from the middle of
the eighteenth century. The writer,
Rufus Putnam, was an officer of distinction, whom Washington pronounced
the best engineer on the American side
in the Revolution. No one can doubt
that the New England spirit finds a
truer expression in the boy's struggles
to learn something than in the non-
chalance of his guardians.

◀ Quotation
introduced, its
author identified,
and inferences
drawn.

> In Sept 1747, I went to
> live with my Step Father,
> Capt John Sadler (at Upton)

---

[7] "Diary," July 21, 1786, in
Works, ed. C. F. Adams (Boston, 1850-
56), III, 400.

◀ Reference to a
section of a
larger work.

16.

Author wisely ▶
omits *sic* in passage
revealing unique
grammar and
spelling.

and continued with him untill
his death (in September or
october 1753)
      during the six year I
lived with Capt Sadler, I
never Saw the inside of a
School house, except about
three weeks. he was very illiterate himself, and took no
care for the education of his
family; but this was not all
I was made a ridecule of,
and otherwise abused for my
attention to books, and attempting to write, and learn
Arethmatic, however, amidst
all those discouragements I
made Some advances in writing and Arethmatic, that is I
could make Letters that could
be under stood, and had gon
as far in Arethmatic as to
work the rule of three (without any teacher but the
book) ── Oh! my Children be-
ware you neglect not the
education of any under your
care as I was neglected. ──
      In March 1754 I was
bound apprentice to Daniel
Matthews of Brokfield, to the
Millw[r]ights trade; by him
my education was as much neglected, as by Capt Sadler,
except that he did not deny
me the use of a Light for
Study in the winter eve-
nings ──
      I turned my attention
chiefly to Arethmatic, Geography, and history; had I ben
as much engaged in Learning
to write well, with Spelling, and Gramer, I might
have ben much better qualified to fulfill the duties
of the Succeeding Scenes of
Life, which In providence I
have ben called to pass
through. I was zealous to
obtain knowledge, but having
no guide I knew not where to

Editorial letter ▶
added between
brackets to make
sense of the
word.

> begin nor what course to pur-
> sue, — hence neglecting Spell-
> ing and gramer when young I
> have Suffered much through
> life on that account.[8]

◀ Quotation given
in full to
illustrate by its
spelling and gram-
mar the author's
point about need
of education.

The Constitution of Massachusetts, adopted in 1781, laid
special emphasis on the duty of
the Commonwealth with regard to
education. In the same year the
legislature passed an elaborate
law providing for both elementary and
grammar schools.[9] By grammar schools,
we should remember, was always meant
what we now call Latin or High Schools.
If we compare this act of 1789 with the
original law of 1647, we shall find
that it is less exacting. Instead of
requiring a grammar school in every
town of one hundred families, it raises
the limit to two hundred. This change
is estimated to have released one
hundred and twenty towns from an obligation under which they had lain for
many years.[10] Doubtless, however, it
was as rigorous a rule as the country
could bear. What had seemed possible
in the compact and homogeneous Colony
was no longer practicable in the growing State.

◀ Footnote used
to document
fact.

---

[8] _Memoirs_, ed. Rowena Buell
(Boston, 1903), pp. 9–11.
[9] Acts of 1789, ch. xix.
[10] George H. Martin, _The Evolution
of the Massachusetts Public School
System_ (New York, 1894), lecture iii.

18.

This act of 1789 brings us down to the time of the _Farmer's_ _Almanack_. It defines the conditions which Mr. Thomas had in mind in his constant exhortations.[11] In the lower schools the master was "to teach children to read and write, and to instruct them in the English language, as well as in arithmetic, orthography, and decent behaviour." The higher schools were to be provided with "a grammar schoolmaster of good morals, well instructed in the Latin, Greek and English languages."

An idea of the impression which the schools of New England made upon a highly cultivated and philosophical foreigner may be got from a passage in Rochefoucauld's _Travels_ _in_ _North_ _America_. The distinguished Frenchman, who belonged to the school of Arthur Young, is speaking of Connecticut in 1795:

Ellipsis mark to ▶ indicate words omitted from source.

> There is . . . no instance of a town or parish, remaining, negligently, without a school. Many communities maintain their schools for a greater part of the year, than they are, by law, obliged to do. The selectmen and the deputations from the communities manage the farms and other revenues of the schools.
> The teachers are commonly young men from the col-

Footnote used to ▶ explain and support statement in text.

---

[11] There was no further law until 1824: Acts of 1824, ch. cxi (amending the act of 1789).

leges, students of law or
theology. Their salaries are
at the pleasure of the different parishes, from two to
three hundred dollars. Almost all those who now act a
distinguished part in the
political business of New
England, began their careers
as teachers in these schools;
a situation that is accounted
exceedingly honourable.
Sometimes, where the salary
is small, women are chosen to
be the teachers. Even these
must, in this case, be well
qualified to teach reading,
writing, and arithmetic.
        Every county must have
a school for Greek and Latin.
A fine of three dollars is
exacted from parents neglect-
ing to send their children to
school. The select-men have
authority to levy it.[12]

No account of our schools, however
brief and incidental, can ignore the
Academy — that peculiarly New England
institution which has played so important a part in the social and educational life of America. The smaller
towns had found it impossible to support classical schools; but there was
no actual falling-off in the zeal for
education. Academies were founded,
partly by bequests from public-
spirited citizens, partly by voluntary contributions from subscribers.
These multiplied exceedingly in the

---

[12] *Travels through the United
States of North America*, trans.
H. Neuman (London, 1799), I, 530.

◀ Author's name, given in text, not repeated in note.

20.

late eighteenth and the early nineteenth century, and many of them were
subsidized by the States. Most of them
have gone out of existence, becoming
unnecessary as wealth increased and the
towns were able once more to assume
the duty of maintaining high schools.
But the stronger institutions of the
kind, which are also among the oldest,
have survived and flourished. They are
a distinctive feature of the educational system of the whole United
States. Their importance is no longer
merely local; it is national.

Mr. Thomas makes an amusing remark
about academies in the Farmer's Calendar for December, 1808:

> Now let your boys and
> girls attend school. Send
> them to the common town
> school, rather than to an
> academy. Fun, frolick' and
> filigree are too much prac-
> tised at the academies for
> the benefit of a farmer's
> boy. Let them have a solid
> and useful education.

This should not be misunderstood.
It is not an assault on the academy as
an institution. It is merely a caution
against sending a boy to an inappropriate school. Academies, in Mr. Thomas's
opinion, were not meant for those who
were to spend their lives on the farm.
He was no enemy to ambition, but he
wished to see it intelligently guided.

It will be noticed that Mr. Thomas mentions girls as well as boys in this last exhortation. The education of girls was neglected in the early days. In 1782 the Rev. John Eliot wrote from Boston to Jeremy Belknap, then minister at Dover, New Hampshire:

> We don't pretend to teach ye female part of ye town anything more than dancing, or a little music perhaps, (and these accomplishmt. must necessarily be confined to a very few,) except ye private schools for writing, which enables them to write a copy, sign their name, &c., which they might not be able to do without such a priviledge & with it I will venture to say that a lady is a rarity among us who can write a page of commonplace sentiment, the words being well spelt, & ye style & language kept up with purity & elegance.[13]

Two years later Caleb Bingham opened a private school for girls, commonly said to have been the first girls' school ever known in Boston. The letter just quoted shows that this idea is not strictly correct. Yet Bingham's establishment was so far in advance of the mere writing classes which Mr. Eliot mentions that it de-

---

[13] Feb. 1, 1782. Collections of the Massachusetts Historical Society, 6th Series, IV, 223.

◄ Notice the smooth transition from academies to education of girls.

◄ Date and printed source of the letter are given.

22.

serves its reputation. "He taught not
only writing and arithmetic, but reading, spelling, and English grammar,"
thus meeting precisely the needs which
Mr. Eliot refers to. Bingham's successful experiment soon led the town
to make some provision for the education of girls. This was in 1789, and
Bingham was employed in one of these
new public schools. He was the author
of several text-books which rivalled
those of Noah Webster in popularity.
His American Preceptor, published in
1794, had by 1832 sold to the number of
nearly six hundred and fifty thousand
copies, and his Columbian Orator, published in 1797, to the number of more
than two hundred thousand. He also
prepared, for his private school, a
little English grammar, The Young
Lady's Accidence, of which a hundred
thousand copies were sold by 1832. It
was the first English grammar used in
the schools of Boston.[14] Several other
private schools for girls were established toward the end of the eighteenth
century. In 1784 Dr. Jedediah Morse,
the well-known geographer, opened such
a school at New Haven, and in 1790 a
Mr. Woodbridge, who gave himself the
grandiloquent title of "the Columbus

One reference ▶
suffices to cover
the various facts
given in the
paragraph up to
this point.

___

[14] See George E. Littlefield,
Early Schools and School-Books of New
England (Boston, 1904), pp. 156, 158,
229-30.

of female education," followed his example. Three years before, the Moravian brethren had founded a "female seminary" at Bethlehem, Pennsylvania. The opposition to any kind of higher education for women is amusingly illustrated by the experience of Miss Emma Willard, who opened a seminary for girls at Troy, New York, in 1821. She had previously conducted what she called a "female academy" at Waterford, in the same state. A friendly minister, who felt it his duty to mention this institution in his public prayers, styled it a "seminary," not wishing to offend his hearers by speaking of it as an "academy" or a "college." Bradford Academy, in Massachusetts, which still flourishes, was founded in 1803.[15]

But chronology is dull work. Let us revert to anecdote, and, in so doing, to the old-fashioned grammar school. The Rev. John Barnard of Marblehead (who was born at Boston in 1681), after attending the instruction of a school mistress in the town and another in the country, was sent to the Latin School in his eighth year, where he was under the tuition of "the aged, venerable, and justly famous

----

[15] See a paper on "The Early History of Schools and School-Books," by R. N. Meriam, Collections of the Worcester Society of Antiquity, IX, no. 27, pp. 93f.

24.

Mr. Ezekiel Cheever," one of the most noted of New England preceptors. In his autobiography, written when he was eighty-five years old, Mr. Barnard tells a pretty little story of "an odd accident" which "drove him from the school after a few weeks": "There was," he says, "an older lad entered the school the same week with me; we strove who should outdo; and he beat me by the help of a brother in the upper class, who stood behind master with the accidence open for him to read out off; by which means he could recite his [MS. illegible] three and four times in a forenoon, and the same in the afternoon; but I who had no such help, and was obliged to commit all to memory, could not keep pace with him; so that he would be always one lesson before me. My ambition could not bear to be outdone, and in such a fraudulent manner, and therefore I left the school."[16]

But he soon returned and got on very well in his studies, not withstanding he was, as he confesses, "a very naughty boy, much given to play." At length Mr. Cheever resorted to an ingenious device. "You, Barnard," said he, "I know you can do well enough if you will; but you are so full of play

Subsequent reference ▶ uses abbreviated form of title.

[16] Coll. Mass. Hist. Soc., 3d Series, V, 178.

that you hinder your classmates from
getting their lessons; and therefore,
if any of them cannot perform their
duty, I shall correct you for it."
"One unlucky day, one of my classmates
did not look into his book, and therefore could not say his lesson, though
I called upon him once and again to
mind his book; upon which our master
beat me. I told master the reason why
he could not say his lesson was, his
declaring he would beat me if any of
the class were wanting in their duty;
since which this boy would not look
into his book, though I called upon him
to mind his book, as the class could
witness. The boy was pleased with my
being corrected, and persisted in his
neglect, for which I was still corrected, and that for several days. I
thought, in justice, I ought to correct
the boy, and compel him to a better
temper; and therefore, after school was
done, I went up to him, and told him I
had been beaten several times for his
neglect; and since master would not
correct him I would, and I should do so
as often as I was corrected for him;
and then drubbed him heartily. The boy
never came to school any more, and so
that unhappy affair ended."[17]

The temptation to go on with

---

[17] Coll. Mass. Hist. Soc., 3d
Series, V, 178.

◄ Anecdote compiled
from sporadic
parts of the
source is docu-
mented at end.

26.

Mr. Barnard's delightful anecdotes of
his boyhood is great, but must be resisted. Still, we may indulge ourselves in one more extract, which is
very brief, and gives a charming picture of the little boy and the veteran
schoolmaster:

> I remember once, in mak-
> ing a piece of Latin, my
> master found fault with the
> syntax of one word, which was
> not so used by me heedlessly,
> but designedly, and therefore
> I told him there was a plain
> grammar rule for it. He
> angrily replied, there was no
> such rule. I took the gram-
> mar and showed the rule to
> him. Then he smilingly said,
> "Thou art a brave boy; I had
> forgot it." And no wonder;
> for he was then above eighty
> years old.[18]

Mr. Cheever was master of the
Boston Latin School for nearly forty
years. He died in 1708, at the age of
ninety-three, and was honored with a
singular poetical tribute from the
pen of Benjamin Thompson, "the re-
nowned poet of New England." It bore
a title prophetic of Browning, "The
Grammarian's Funeral," and was printed
as a broadside.[19] It begins:

---

[18] Coll. Mass. Hist. Soc., 3d
Series, V, 180.
[19] Reproduced by Samuel A. Green
in his Ten Facsimile Reproductions
(Boston, 1902), No. III.

> Eight Parts of <u>Speech</u> this Day
>   wear <u>Mourning Gowns</u>
> Declin'd <u>Verbs</u>, <u>Pronouns</u>, <u>Parti-</u>
>   <u>ciples</u>, <u>Nouns</u>.
> And not declined, <u>Adverbs</u> and
>   <u>Conjunctions</u>,
> In <u>Lillies</u> Porch they stand to do
>   their functions.
> With <u>Preposition</u>; but the most
>   affection
> Was still observed in the <u>Inter-</u>
>   <u>jection</u>.

This is quaint enough, but the oddest thing about the verses is that they are announced in the broadside as having been originally "composed upon the Death of Mr. <u>John</u> <u>Woodmancy</u>, formerly a School—Master in <u>Boston</u>: But now Published upon the Death of the Venerable Mr. Ezekiel Chevers." In other words, a second—hand elegy!

The chapter may close with a bit from the <u>Almanack</u> for 1807 (July), which will serve as a fitting epilogue to our pedagogical miscellany:

> <u>I have more pork in my</u>
> <u>cellar</u>, said neighbor Brag-
> gadocia, <u>than all the Al-</u>
> <u>manack makers in christendom</u>.
> <u>Fie on your larnin, and all</u>
> <u>that stuff</u>; <u>I wants none of</u>
> <u>your nonsense. No man shall</u>
> <u>teach me, faith</u>. Now I for-
> bore to dispute with this
> great man; for the proverb
> says, <u>you cannot make a</u>
> <u>silken purse of a sow's ear</u>.

28.

SELECTED BIBLIOGRAPHY

Since the list is not ▶
exhaustive,
"Selected" qualifies
"Bibliography."

Adams, John. Works, ed. Charles
   Francis Adams. 10 vols. Boston:
   Little, Brown and Company, 1850–56.

Work issued in ▶
volumes over
several years.

Green, Samuel A. Ten Facsimile Reproductions Relating to New England.
   Boston: n.p., 1902.

No publisher ▶
given.

La Rochefoucauld Liancourt, Francois
   Alexandre Frederic, Duc de. Travels
   through the United States of North
   America, trans. H. Neuman. 2 vols.
   London: R. Phillips, 1799.

Translator of ▶
foreign work
included.

Littlefield, George E. Early Schools
   and School-Books of New England.
   Boston: The Club of Odd Volumes,
   1904.

Martin, George H. The Evolution of the
   Massachusetts Public School System.
   New York: D. Appleton and Company,
   1894.

Martineau, Harriet. Autobiography, ed.
   Maria Weston Chapman. 2 vols.
   Boston: J. R. Osgood and Company,
   1877.

Edited work in more ▶
than one volume.

——————————————. Society in America. London: Saunders and Otley,
   1937.

Long dash used ▶
instead of name
in second reference.

Massachusetts Historical Society, Collections of. Boston, 1792––.

Dash after date ▶
indicates series is
still being published.

Putnam, Rufus. Memoirs, ed. Rowena
   Buell. Boston and New York: Houghton
   Mifflin and Company, 1903.

Work published ▶
in two places.

Rawson, Grindal. The Necessity of a
   Speedy and Thorough Reformation.
   Boston: B. Green, 1709.

Worcester Society of Antiquity, Collections of. Worcester, Mass., 1881–
   99.

Serial publication ▶
of a Society, listed
alphabetically.

Though the marginal notes that we have made on " The Yankee School " stress problems of mechanics, particularly problems concerning quotations and footnotes, they also call attention to certain features of the organization of this paper: they point out such things as the happy use of a literary allusion (page 404) or a smooth transition from one idea to another (page 401). Yet a good deal more about the rhetorical organization of this paper remains to be said.

" The Yankee School " presents a rather systematic account of the character and importance of the early New England school. As we can see from the sentence outline that precedes this paper (see page 395), the author has founded his paper upon five main headings arranged in a coherent pattern, and these main headings, where necessary, are logically divided and subdivided. But though this paper is logically organized, it does not seem pedestrian or mechanical. The writing has color and personality. The author gives the impression of moving easily from one anecdote or concrete illustration to another. Indeed, though the logical skeleton of the paper firmly articulates part with part, the writer has found the means — the student may be tempted to say " gimmick " — to give another and additional sort of unity, a unity of feeling and tone. The principal device for achieving this unity is the *Farmer's Almanack*.

The *Almanack* is quoted in the very first paragraph of the paper and again in the last, supplying, as the author himself puts it, " a fitting epilogue " to the essay. Generous quotations from the *Almanack* occur throughout the body of the paper. The *Almanack* serves, in short, as a powerful unifying device, though of a special sort. It is typical of the kind of testimony to the character of the Yankee school that the paper sets out to assemble from the letters, diaries, and reminiscences of the eighteenth and early nineteenth centuries. The *Almanack* can properly keynote these, for it is typical of the character and opinion of New England throughout this period.

Professor Kittredge, of course, does not bind himself slavishly to the *Farmer's Almanack*. He goes farther afield to garner evidence for the regard in which early New England held her schools. This is natural and proper since his paper is, after all, not on the *Almanack* as such but on the Yankee school. The *Almanack* quotations are skillfully related to the other evidence. For example, a foreign observer, Miss Martineau, gives her testimony, but in so doing she quotes " an old almanack " and thus introduces the first of the quotations by the Old Farmer. It is quite likely that Professor Kittredge planned his paper around quotations from the *Farmer's Almanack,* and then later discovered that Miss Martineau had quoted it, at that point deciding to use the Martineau quotation to introduce the paper. But whether the result of original planning or of revision, the introductory paragraph is very skillfully handled.

In general, the paper is admirable for the way in which the various passages that are quoted are introduced and knit together. The introductory comments do a good deal to point the significance of the particular quoted passages. The skill with which they effect this, because it is self-effacing, may easily escape our attention. But the problem of how to introduce quotations will appear in nearly every research paper (see page 392), and the student can learn a great deal from considering very carefully the way in which Professor Kittredge introduces the various passages that he quotes.

One further comment on " The Yankee School " seems worth making. The logical structure of this paper is well set forth in the outline. The system of subdivisions in particular shows the way in which the material is logically organized. But an outline cannot so graphically indicate how the *main* headings are related to each other, and this matter deserves a further word. The materials subsumed under headings II and III represent what are essentially developments of the assertion made in heading I. The material under heading II deals with such matters as the laws governing public education and the academies, which were private, not public, schools. Section III takes up the matter of education for girls. These are normal and proper developments, but the author is rightly concerned to bring his paper back firmly to the central idea and so headings IV and V return us to the original thesis. There is a practical lesson here for the student. Research papers easily fray out into subsidiary points and " ramble " away from the main point. It will be well worth studying how Professor Kittredge keeps his paper properly focused.

• **Applications** •

I. Describe some of the methods Kittredge uses to introduce quotations.

II. What is the chief form of discourse used here? Are any other forms used?

III. Comment on the diction and tone of the paper.

CHAPTER FOURTEEN

The Final Version: Writing and Rewriting

Throughout this book we have been insisting that in good writing all the elements are interrelated. There is no such thing as " good " diction apart from the context in which it occurs, or " correct " tone abstracted from a specific occasion. In good writing the principles of unity, coherence, and emphasis apply at all levels — not only to the larger blocks of the composition, but to the individual phrases and even the individual words.

Though this principle of interrelation, if clearly understood by the student, can illuminate the problems of writing, it can also be inhibiting. Confronted with the demand that every item in his composition be ultimately related to everything else, the student writer may not know where to start. He may feel that in a fabric so intricately interwoven, there are no seams — no natural divisions with which to begin. It may be well, therefore, in this last chapter to do two things. The first will be to review the typical methods by which one builds up a composition. The second thing will be to point out the importance of *rewriting*. Even professional writers rarely achieve an adequate unification of elements with the first draft. In this chapter we shall want to examine very carefully — and with concrete examples — what is involved in the process of rewriting.

Writing the Paper

Let us assume that the student has been assigned a term paper that is to deal with some aspect of contemporary American culture. He can write about the movies, if he likes, or football, or the World

Series, or the New York stage, or any other such topic that may engage his interest. Let us assume that he decides to write about jazz. Though he is not a talented musician, he is interested in music, and he thinks that jazz represents a characteristic aspect of American popular music and popular culture.

Jazz, however, as he begins to think about it, is a large subject which could be treated in very many different ways. He is up against the problem which we dealt with earlier in this book (page 14), the problem of finding the " true subject." Is he to write about the origins of jazz, or the geographical variations in the development of jazz — " the Chicago period," for example? The student does not, however, try immediately to make a final limitation of his subject. He decides that a further exploration of the subject in the library will help him decide just what he wants to write about and which aspects of the subject he has sufficient material to write about.

Bibliography

By using the card catalogue in his library and some of the general aids referred to on page 385, plus some help from the reference librarian, and by having the good fortune to find a special bibliography entitled *Books and Periodicals on Jazz from 1928 to 1932* (issued by the School of Library Service, Columbia University, June 6, 1933), he comes up with the following list of books and articles:

BOOKS:

Armstrong, Louis. *Satchmo: My Life in New Orleans*. New York: Prentice-Hall, Inc., 1954.

Grossman, W. L., and Farrell, J. W. *The Heart of Jazz*. New York: New York University Press, 1956.

Hobson, Wilder. *American Jazz Music*. New York: W. W. Norton & Co., 1939.

Sargeant, Winthrop. *Jazz, Hot and Hybrid*. New York: E. P. Dutton & Co., 1946.

Ulanov, Barry. *A History of Jazz in America*. New York: Viking Press, 1952.

ARTICLES:

Copland, Aaron. " Jazz Structure and Influence." *Modern Music,* IV, No. 2 (January—February, 1927), 9–14.

Engel, Carl. " Jazz: A Musical Discussion." *Atlantic Monthly,* CXXX (August, 1922), 183–189.

Knowlton, Don. " The Anatomy of Jazz." *Harper's,* CLII (April, 1926), 578–585.

Thomson, Virgil. " Jazz." *American Mercury,* II (August, 1924) , 465–467.

Turner, W. J. " Waltz Kings and Jazz Kings." *New Statesman,* XXVII (April 17, 1926) , 13–14.

(The student actually found many more books and articles, but these were the ones he actually got out and sampled or read through carefully. Note that he did not use all these sources in his final draft.)

Note-taking

Here are some sample notes taken by our student:

```
Amount of improvisation in jazz  Grossman and Farrell,
                                 The Heart of Jazz,
                                 p. 42

". . . compositions as performed in traditional Jazz
are, as a rule, neither wholly worked out in advance
nor wholly created in the course of performance.  The
importance of prearrangement, habitual residue,
specific traditional material, and extemporization,
respectively, varies from band to band."
```

```
Improvisation fundamental to music  Sargeant, Jazz,
                                    Hot and Hybrid,
                                    p. 15

"Actually, improvisation — the art of creating music
directly with vocal or instrumental means — is far
more fundamental to music than is the complex, diffi-
cult, and specialized art of planning compositions on
paper."
```

```
Individualism of some recent jazz    Gerry Mulligan,
                                     "The Importance of
                                     Jazz Tradition,"
                                     Down Beat (Sept.
                                     21, 1955), p. 14

Gerry Mulligan, a leading modern jazz artist, cites
Ellington, Lester Young, Dizzy Gillespie, Charlie
Parker and Woody Herman as the "tradition" in which he
works.
```

(Note that in this third card there is full bibliographical information. The first two cards could omit it, for they refer to works already mentioned in the bibliography, where full information is given.)

• **Applications** •

If you have already done the exercise on page 387, Chapter 13, you are ready to reduce your topic to a true subject. If you have not done this exercise, turn back to it now; select a topic, and make a preliminary bibliography.

I. Take notes on your subject, following the suggestion outlined in Chapter 13, pages 387–91.

II. With the help of the notes you have assembled, fix upon the limited subject on which you will write.

Outline

When our student had finished his research in books and magazines he jotted down the following scratch outline:

1. Origins of jazz obscure but three sources fairly certain: spirituals, brass-band music, and ragtime piano.
2. Too much attention given to primitive African sources of jazz.
3. Basic structure of the blues.
4. Band music important in New Orleans life — even in religion.

5. Every piece of music has subject matter and content.
6. The first jazz band formed by Buddy Bolden about 1885–1900. Other early jazzmen.
7. True jazz overwhelmed by pseudo-jazz — the big bands of Whiteman, Dorsey, and others.
8. Jazz in New York in the 1940's and bop.
9. What is essential in jazz, and the rebirth of true jazz.

First Draft

Our student was aware that his scratch outline did not give him as clear an idea of the organization of the paper as might be desired. Still the scratch outline got down on paper many of the ideas that he wanted to deal with and he hoped that in the actual process of writing, his ideas would become adequately clarified. At any rate, he decided to begin writing without going farther with his outline. The following paragraphs represent the first twelve paragraphs of his paper.

JAZZ

Much has been written concerning the origins of jazz. As with any folk art, perhaps, its origins must of necessity remain obscure. One cannot expect documentation where there was practically no knowledge of musical notation among the earliest performers. Three main sources for the beginnings of jazz may be suggested with some precision, however: spirituals, brass-band music, and ragtime piano.

It should be noted at this point that no mention has been made of African rhythms, particularly drum-beat rhythms, which are supposed to be the source of the inherent rhythmic sense which the Negro brought with him to America. The theory is an attractive one, but unfortunately it is difficult, if not impossible, to demonstrate any real parallels between the African milieu and the rhythms in jazz.

In fact it should be emphasized that jazz is a peculiarly American art form. Thus it is only natural to search for its origins in the American music prevalent around the end of the Civil War. To search farther seems to me a mistake, even though a theory which champions the " noble savage " as the real secret behind jazz expression seems to have much appeal. Even if it were not factually wrong, nevertheless this theory denies to jazz much of its order and discipline. The fact is that jazz is by no means simply a spontaneous, unrehearsed emotional outlet. It has a definite discipline, elements of which will be dealt with below, but of which for the moment, let it suffice to say that it exists.

One of the strongest arguments, in fact, against the African theory of jazz origin may be derived from a study of the actual sources of jazz. Mentioned above in this connection were spirituals, brass-band music, and ragtime piano. To these must be added the tradition of blues, as this latter is perhaps most important of all, not only harmonically, but also from the point of view of feeling.

The basic structure of blues is a simple one, musically speaking. Blues consist, historically, of a twelve-bar chorus. The first four bars state the theme, the second four contain slight variations on that theme, and the third set of four bars contain significant variations of the theme. One observer, Richard Wright, has likened the blues structure " to a man walking around a chair clockwise (the first four bars), then walking around it again counterclockwise (the next four), and then standing aside and pronouncing final judgment upon it." [1] The harmonics of the blues are simple, and are based on the usual chord arrangement of the folk song; i.e., the first four bars are usually based upon the chord of the tonic, the second four bars are usually based upon the chord of the subdominant, and the last four on the chord of the dominant. The melody, of course, derives from the blues chords, but its tonal concept is unique: the blues scale is the usual one, plus the addition of a flatted third and seventh; these are known as " blue notes." Thus the scale looks like this (for C major):

$$C - D - E\flat - E - F - G - A - B\flat - B - C$$

This structure is exceptionally important in the structure of jazz.

This is because there are many recognized pitch variations in the playing of jazz, and there can be no question but that the idea for most of them came from the blues. This is not capricious, either emotionally or musically, and occurs with regularity in jazz. It is of course very marked in much " modern " jazz, but here there is also a concomitant self-consciousness which tends to make what should be a natural effect become one which is instead merely a kind of trick. This will be dealt with at greater length further on. Perhaps the best source for study of the blues' assault on pitch would be the old Bessie Smith recordings, many of the best of which have been re-released on LP's. Attention to the flatted notes will reveal the blues scale (usually five notes of it) very nearly as depicted above. So much for blues and their effect on jazz.

We must remember too that the early New Orleans bands played more religious and church music than we would think. In New Orleans, as well as elsewhere, the band was a necessary adjunct of church services, funerals, weddings, as well as lodge outings, bawdy-house parlors, and just parades. An anecdote related by Louis Armstrong will illustrate. He wrote as follows about Joe (King) Oliver's original band as it played at a funeral:

> It was a real sad moment when the Onward Brass Band struck up the funeral march as Arthur Brown's body was being brought from the church to the graveyard. Everybody cried, including me. Black Benny beat the bass drum with a soft touch, and Babe Mathews put a handkerchief under his snare to deaden the tone. *Nearer My God to Thee* was played as the coffin was lowered into the grave. . . .

---

[1] Barry Ulanov, *A History of Jazz in America* (New York, 1952), p. 27.

The funerals in New Orleans are sad until the body is finally lowered into the grave and the Reverend says, "ashes to ashes and dust to dust." After the brother was six feet under ground the band would strike up one of those good old tunes like *Didn't He Ramble,* and all the people would leave their worries behind. Particularly when King Oliver blew that last chorus in high register.[2]

The main point I wish to make here is that, even at this primitive state in jazz history, the music which is later to become a definite form already is associated with a strong emotional state, a fact which is of crucial importance for the later development of jazz into a full expression.

Closely associated with such an emotional situation is religious music of all kinds, particularly spirituals and church music. It must be remembered that almost all of the musicians who were later to become jazzmen were brought up on this sort of music. W. C. Handy, for instance, was brought up learning to play the organ, in fact his father financed lessons on this instrument, but was forbidden to play the guitar because it was "one of the devil's playthings."[3] (Handy composed the first published blues, "Memphis Blues," in 1909.[4] It was the first of many compositions of his which have become jazz stand-bys.)

There is not much of a problem in linking religion, at least on this level, with an emotional state. The specific relationship between music in general and religion poses a more subtle question.

The general problem of the religious content of music is beyond the scope of this paper. It will have to suffice merely to suggest the nature of the problem by making the point that, for instance, the music of Handel's Hallelujah Chorus from the *Messiah* would serve fittingly indeed for, say, the celebration of a great victory, or any other sort of triumph. Here it might be added that the words, not the music, lend the religious content. As has been pointed out by Grossman and Farrell,[5] there are many examples of secular music having been taken over and used for religious purposes. The point that has to be made in this connection is that one may expect differences in the method of playing the music, differences which will depend on the feeling which the musicians find they are to be responsible for at the moment. "The Battle Hymn of the Republic" might sound

---

[2] Louis Armstrong, *Satchmo: My Life in New Orleans* (New York, 1954), pp. 90–91.

[3] W. L. Grossman and J. W. Farrell, *The Heart of Jazz* (New York, 1956), p. 62.

[4] This was published by Handy as a campaign song for E. H. Crump, a reform candidate for mayor of Memphis. Handy's words:

> Mr. Crump won't 'low no easy riders here:
> Mr. Crump won't 'low no easy riders here:
> I don't care what Mr. Crump won't 'low,
> I'm gonna bar'l-house anyhow,
> Mr. Crump can go and catch himself some air.*

* Quoted by permission of W. C. Handy. Copyright 1912 by W. C. Handy. Copyright renewed, 1940.

[5] Grossman and Farrell, p. 47.

one way if it were played at one of those New Orleans funerals, and quite another way if played later in the day by the same band in a honky-tonk. It is this which leads one to the conclusion that jazz, while not obviously primarily religious, nevertheless has a Christian content. This is a fact which the very origins of the music make unavoidable.

It may be said of any piece of music that it has both subject matter and content, the first being specific, the second including all the emotional aura which will come to surround it. In general it is in this latter area where one will have to search for the Christian elements in jazz. To be sure, there are many overtly Christian elements: the most famous, if over-rated, piece of the jazz repertoire is undoubtedly " When the Saints Go Marching In." But less obvious than this is the preoccupation, in many blues numbers, with death and redemption, a tradition which of course comes from the spirituals. " St. James' Infirmary," particularly its last verse, is a good example of this. And in this connection it is well to remember another overworked but perhaps useful convention about jazz, which is that the instruments " talk " as they play, particularly the cornet and the clarinet. This may serve to bring the musicians closer to the words of a piece of music than they may even be conscious of, and thus the emotion involved is modified by the feelings of the performer.

This brings us to a crucial point in the study of jazz, where one must consider the nature of the music involved. At this point, however, I should like to introduce some more of the early history of the music itself, in order to perhaps arrive at some idea of what jazz is and where its responsibilities to its tradition lie today.

Rewriting

At this point, however, our student stopped, for it had become plain that his plan was muddled, and that the paper was going in no particular direction. He had made the mistake of not settling on his true subject before he began to write. This failure had got him into difficulties. As he looked back over the paragraphs that he had written, he tried to analyze the points that he had made or had tried to make. As he now saw them, they turned out to be these. (1) Though the origins of jazz are obscure, at least three sources of jazz can be identified: spirituals, band music (as played in New Orleans), and ragtime piano. (2) The frequently alleged African origins of jazz have been overstressed. (3) The theory of African origins is part of a theory that conceives of jazz as a spontaneous emotional outpouring and fails to take into account its discipline. (4) " Blues " music has a certain harmonic and melodic structure. (5) This structure is important in the structure of jazz, for (6) the pitch variations in the playing of jazz come from the blues. (7) It is difficult to determine precisely the religious content of any piece of music, and (8) this difficulty applies fully to jazz even though (9) jazz clearly has some religious elements in it.

These nine statements do not represent all that is said in the twelve paragraphs, but they are the most important statements made; and to list them is to make quite plain the poor organization of the opening section of the research paper, for the relation of the nine numbered items is far from clear. Is the writer trying to characterize jazz, attacking one definition and offering another? Or does he simply mean to give us a short history of jazz? Both purposes are represented in his paper. Moreover, some kind of relation obviously exists between the material on sources and origins and the argument that jazz is not merely primitive and an emotional outpouring. Indeed, in the first sentence of the fourth paragraph, he writes: " One of the strongest arguments, in fact, against the African theory of jazz origin may be derived from a study of the actual sources of jazz."

But the argument is not clearly made. The relation between the sources of jazz and the essential character of jazz remains confused, and the confusion is reflected in the organization of the paper. This general defect in the paper ultimately springs from the fact that the writer has not yet really decided what he wants to write about. The defect shows in the title. " Jazz " is too vague to be a true subject. Once the student has really decided what he wants to say about jazz — once he has found his true subject — he will be able to shape the outlines of his paper. Notice that the issue here is not that the paper shall deal *merely* with a definition of jazz or *merely* with its history. We cannot properly give its history unless we are able to say what it is and, on the other hand, it is plain that its history may indeed throw much light upon the definition. The problem is not that of removing one or the other of these considerations from the paper; it is rather one of proper subordination and proper emphasis.

After going over his notes and his scratch outline again, the student decided that his true subject could be described under the title " The Development of Jazz." (He was tempted to add a subtitle, writing " The Development of Jazz: an American Phenomenon." " An American Phenomenon " would suggest that he was going to argue against the importance of the alleged primitive African origins in favor of formative influences to be found on this continent. But he felt that for a short paper, the subtitle might seem pretentious. He decided, however, to try to state the general point that he hoped to make, his " thesis," and to include it in his outline. (Note that Professor Kittredge includes a thesis in the outline of his paper. See page 395.)

Having chosen a new and more restricted title, our student decided to revise his first outline, and in the process of revision, turn it into a sentence outline. (Note that some of the headings in his original scratch outline disappear from the new outline, discarded in view of the change of plan.)

Before working on his new outline, our student turned back to the chapter on Exposition and reread the various sections including that on **expository narration,** page 110, for it was apparent that a discussion of the development of jazz would need to make use of expository methods. But he was well aware that in most actual writing there is a mixture of modes. His own paper would have elements of argument — see above: " he was going to argue against the importance of the alleged primitive African origins " — and it would include at least one fairly developed piece of description. Expository narration — assuming that it appeared to be a method likely to be of most use in writing this paper — is itself a kind of blending of two of the primary forms of discourse. (It will be interesting to note, as you read this research paper on jazz, just what expository methods — and others — our student actually did use.)

THE DEVELOPMENT OF JAZZ

Thesis: If one reviews the history of jazz, it becomes plain that jazz is a novel development of American cultural forces, that it had defined itself before the so-called jazz age began, and that genuine jazz will survive the dilutions and commercializations that it has suffered.

I. The sources of jazz are to be found in American culture at the end of the Civil War.
   A. Three main sources of jazz are to be found in the blues, in the spirituals, and in the small New Orleans brass bands.
   B. The theory of African origins is difficult to substantiate.
      1. There is little real evidence to connect African drum-beat rhythms with American jazz.
      2. The emphasis on African origins often comes from misconceiving of jazz as a " primitive " and undisciplined loosing of emotion.
II. Jazz took from the blues the twelve-bar chorus, a certain harmonic pattern, and a certain melodic pattern.
   A. The chorus represents three variations on a four-bar theme.
   B. The melody is based on the blues scale, which has two accidentals plus the seven-note scale.

C. The three variations employ tonic, subdominant, and dominant chords.

III. Jazz was influenced in its content by spirituals and other religious music.
   A. This influence is vague and difficult to pinpoint, as it must be when we consider any music apart from its accompanying words.
   B. The influence does show itself powerfully, however, in terms of
      1. The preoccupation with such themes as death and redemption, and
      2. The strong emotional quality of the music.
   C. The influence of religion and religious music is to be expected if one knows the cultural situation in New Orleans, where jazz originated.

IV. The history of the early brass bands furnishes one of the best means for following the development of jazz, for
   A. The band was a necessary adjunct of church services, funerals, weddings, lodge outings, and bawdy-house parlors, and
   B. From the earliest beginnings down to the lavish " big " bands of a later period, jazz music was " band " music.

V. The first jazz band, formed by Buddy Bolden, dates from 1895–1900.
   A. Bolden's band included cornet, clarinet, trombone, bass, guitar, and drums.
   B. The early jazzmen frequently played in one another's bands.
   C. There was from the beginning a real continuity of methods and techniques — a point to be remembered by those who regard jazz as mere capricious improvisation.
   D. The career of Louis Armstrong constitutes a link between the early New Orleans style of jazz and the Chicago and other later styles.

VI. In the so-called jazz age true jazz was overwhelmed by pseudo-jazz.
   A. Big bands like Whiteman's and the Dorseys' turned out a commercial product, " sweetened," made easier and more facile.
   B. Benny Goodman represents another instance of great technical ability and versatility too often employed to " smooth " over the authentic patterns of jazz.

VII. In New York in the 1940's there were further distortions of the original jazz.
   A. Bop was the beginning of so-called " cool jazz."
   B. The faults of this new jazz may be described as
      1. Self-conscious individual daydreaming, and
      2. Empty formalism.

VIII. In retrospect it is easier to see some of the important features of jazz:
   A. Jazz is not mere brilliant improvisation by the musician.
   B. Jazz is not merely rebellion against the patterns and rules of more conventional music.
   C. There is evidently a body of traditions that represents the core of jazz form.

IX. In view of some of the meaningless developments, not to say distortions of later so-called "jazz," it is easy to see why there has been of late a return to the style of "New Orleans" jazz.

• Application •

Write a sentence outline of the paper for which you have taken notes. (See pages 429–32.)

THE DEVELOPMENT OF JAZZ

1. As with any folk art, the origins of jazz must of necessity remain obscure. One cannot expect documentation when there was practically no knowledge of musical notation among the earliest performers. But we can be reasonably sure of three main sources for the beginnings of jazz: the spirituals, the blues, and the brass-band music of the turn of the century. I have not included one frequently cited source, ragtime, because I see it as a cousin of jazz, not an ancestor. As Wilder Hobson puts it, " Jazz is often referred to as if it were a development of ragtime. This is incorrect, although, as we shall see, these kinds of music had common ancestry." [6] Jazz is a peculiarly American art form.

2. The last sentence may seem strange in view of the fact that so much has been said in the past about African rhythms, particularly drum-beat rhythms, which are supposed to be the source of the inherent rhythmic sense that the Negro is alleged to have brought with him to America. But though the theory is attractive and has consequently been popular, it is unfortunately difficult, if not impossible, to demonstrate any real parallels between native African rhythms and the characteristic rhythms of jazz.[7]

3. Part of the attraction of the African theory is that it seems to support the popular conception of jazz as a primitive emotional expression, an undisciplined release of emotion, uninhibited and untrammeled with the fusty trappings of civilization. Jazz is thought of as going back to the experience of the " noble savage," a being who has somehow remained uncorrupted by civilization and close to the rhythms of nature. The anthropologists, of course, have never discovered the noble savage of the romantic dream, but the notion dies hard. The real harm done by this theory is the misconception that it fosters with reference to jazz itself. For it strengthens the prejudices of those who would deny that jazz is a disciplined art.

4. When we turn from the romantically mistaken notion of where jazz comes from to its actual sources in nineteenth-century American culture, we come up against formal patterns and traditional moods and attitudes. Indeed, the best refutation of the alleged African origin of jazz is supplied

---

[6] Wilder Hobson, *American Jazz Music* (New York, 1939) , p. 21.

[7] Winthrop Sargeant, *Jazz, Hot and Hybrid* (New York, 1946), pp. 182–91. See especially the chapter entitled " Influences from the Dark Continent."

by an examination of the actual sources. One of the most important of these is that complex of forms and structural patterns that goes by the name of " the blues."

5. Musically speaking, the basic structure of the blues is a simple one. Blues consist, historically, of a twelve-bar chorus. The first four bars state the theme, the second four contain slight variations on the theme, and the third set of four bars contains significant variations on the theme. The harmonics of the blues are simple, and are based on the usual chord arrangement of the folk song; i.e., the first four bars are based upon the chord of the tonic, the second four on the chord of the subdominant, and the last four on the chord of the dominant. The melody, of course, derives from the blues chords, but its tonal concept is unique: the blues scale is the usual one, plus the addition of a flatted third and seventh; these are known as " blue notes." Thus the scale looks like this (for C major) :

$$C - D - E\flat - E - F - G - A - B\flat - B - C$$

This scale is exceptionally important in the structure of jazz.

6. This is because there are many recognized pitch variations in the playing of jazz, and there can be no question but that the idea for most of them came from the blues. This is not capricious, either emotionally or musically, and occurs with regularity in jazz. It is of course very marked in much " modern " jazz, but here there is also an accompanying self-consciousness which tends to make what should be a natural effect become one which is instead merely a kind of trick.

7. The general problem of the religious content of music is beyond the scope of this paper. It will have to do to suggest the nature of the problem by making the point that, for instance, the music of Handel's Hallelujah Chorus from the *Messiah* would serve fittingly indeed for, say, the celebration of a great victory, or any other sort of triumph. For it is the words, not the music, that lend the specific religious content. Moreover, the occasion and the circumstances of a rendition of a piece of music make a great deal of difference. " The Battle Hymn of the Republic " might sound one way if it were played at one of those New Orleans funerals, and quite another way if played later in the day by the same band in a honky-tonk. It is this which leads one to the conclusion that jazz, while not obviously primarily religious, nevertheless derives heavily from religious music. This is a fact which the very origins of the music make unavoidable.

8. So much for the difficulty of pointing out specifically religious elements in jazz, but they are there nonetheless, some of them even overtly religious. The most famous, if overrated, of them is undoubtedly " When the Saints Go Marching In." But less obvious than this is the preoccupation, in many blues numbers, with death and redemption, a tradition which of course comes from the spirituals. " St. James' Infirmary," particularly its last verse, is a good example of this.

9. In this general connection, it must be remembered that almost all of the musicians who were later to become jazzmen were brought up on religious music. W. C. Handy, for instance, was brought up learning to play

the organ, in fact his father financed lessons on this instrument, but was forbidden to play the guitar because it was " one of the devil's playthings." [8] (Handy composed the first published blues, "Memphis Blues," in 1909.[9] It was the first of many compositions of his which have become jazz stand-bys.)

10. We must remember too that the early New Orleans bands played more religious and church music than we would think. In New Orleans as well as elsewhere, the band was a necessary adjunct of church services, funerals, weddings, as well as lodge outings, bawdy-house parlors, and just parades. An anecdote related by Louis Armstrong will illustrate. He wrote as follows about Joe (King) Oliver's band as it played at a funeral:

> It was a real sad moment when the Onward Brass Band struck up the funeral march as Arthur Brown's body was being brought from the church to the graveyard. Everybody cried, including me. Black Benny beat the bass drum with a soft touch, and Babe Mathews put a handker-chief under his snare to deaden the tone. *Nearer My God to Thee* was played as the coffin was lowered into the grave. . . .
>
> The funerals in New Orleans are sad until the body is finally lowered into the grave and the Reverend says, "ashes to ashes and dust to dust." After the brother was six feet under ground the band would strike up one of those good old tunes like *Didn't He Ramble,* and all the people would leave their worries behind. Particularly when King Oliver blew that last chorus in high register.[10]

11. The ubiquitous nature of the early brass bands in New Orleans and their involvement in the full range of the various forms and traditions that were to go to make up jazz suggests that we trace the history of the development of jazz through its bands. There is general agreement that the jazz band as we know it today was first formed between 1895 and 1900 by Buddy Bolden. His group included the cornet, the clarinet, trombone, bass, guitar, and drums. Not only this, but Bolden himself being a cornet player (as well as a barber, which may indicate that band employment had not yet become very steady), originated the tradition of the cornet lead, to which the rest of the band (particularly, as later, the clarinet) provides a counterpoint structure. But of course there are no recordings of this band,

---

[8] W. L. Grossman and J. W. Farrell, *The Heart of Jazz* (New York, 1956), p. 62.

[9] This was published by Handy as a campaign song for E. H. Crump, a re-form candidate for mayor of Memphis. Handy's words:

> Mr. Crump won't 'low no easy riders here;
> Mr. Crump won't 'low no easy riders here;
> I don't care what Mr. Crump won't 'low,
> I'm gonna bar'l-house anyhow,
> Mr. Crump can go and catch himself some air.*

* Quoted by permission of W. C. Handy. Copyright 1912 by W. C. Handy. Copyright renewed, 1940.

[10] Louis Armstrong, *Satchmo: My Life in New Orleans* (New York, 1954), pp. 90–91.

a fact which may in fact account for the fact that Bolden has become sort of a myth in jazz circles, a man who could, and did, do everything which has been thought of since. After Bolden came the famous Olympia Band, including, at the beginning, Keppard, Alphonse Picou (who invented the traditional clarinet break in *High Society*), and John Vean, who invented the first four-beat drum part. Later, the famous clarinetist Jimmy Noone and the cornet player Bunk Johnson came to this band.

12. By 1918, Oliver's Creole Jazz Band became famous in New Orleans, and it was this group which was responsible for bringing jazz to Chicago to stay. Other musicians had tried it and come back broke. It is interesting, in this general connection, to look at the progression of musicians at Pete Lala's café, starting around 1915: Kid Ory's band begins there, followed by King Oliver, and Bechet. When Oliver goes to Chicago, he is replaced in his band by the young and presumably awed Louis Armstrong.[11] When Bechet went on tour, his place was taken by Johnny Dodds. The point I am trying to make here is that it is pretty true that all the great early New Orleans jazzmen played with one another's groups at one time or another.

13. This circulation of the influential early jazzmen through the various bands had important consequences. As one would expect, there developed a real unanimity of feeling and technique that is characteristic of early jazz. This fact constitutes an important argument against the person who insists that jazz is nothing more than a capricious improvisation resulting in loud noise and frantic rhythms. The fact is quite the contrary: there is a strong agreement about methods, brought about by this unanimity at the beginnings of jazz.

14. A kind of focal point in the history of jazz is represented by the famous Louis Armstrong. Although the latter-day image of this man has perhaps been somewhat compromised by his fabulous success and his willingness to sacrifice some of his musicianship to the popular notion of what is expected of him, nevertheless it is true that he is in a sense at the crossroads of the history of jazz, a figure which strides the gap, if there really is one, between New Orleans and Chicago jazz, and who, in doing so, merges in his own technique the elements of both traditions. Armstrong's mentor in New Orleans was, of course, King (then Joe) Oliver, whose place he took over, as has been pointed out already. Oliver requested him to come to Chicago in 1922 to play second cornet to Oliver's first. This he did, but it was not in Louis's nature to play second cornet to anybody, not even to the great Oliver, for very long. It is this need for solo expression, a need which was only sporadically met in the New Orleans style, that led Louis to try to find an individual outlet.

15. This he did in 1924, where he was first cornet for Fletcher Henderson's band. With this he had a great recording success (a new factor in jazz, it should be pointed out) and he went on his own, making the famous "Hot Five" and "Hot Seven" recordings in 1925 and 1927 for Okeh records. Even in these early recordings it is possible to note some modifica-

---

[11] *Ibid.*, p. 103.

tions of the New Orleans style, but it was not until the addition of Earl Hines on piano that the solo style of Armstrong really came into its own. This was because of the technique of Hines, which itself was extremely individual, for Hines refused to treat the piano purely as a rhythmic adjunct, as Lillian Hardin had on the Hot Five records.

16. Beginning at this time is the so-called " jazz age," a misnomer if there ever was one, because the true jazz got buried under a welter of pseudo-jazz, created to arrangement by big bands, such as Paul Whiteman's, the Dorseys', and others. It was the music of Gershwin in combination with these bands that made for a loss of the essential emotional and spiritual values that characterized the early jazz. This music was a commercial product, trading on a kind of cheap romanticism. And, as if to make matters even worse, there was swing, and Benny Goodman. Now no one would deny to Goodman a tremendous technical versatility, and no one would deny to his kind of music a compelling emotion and sound. But these things are not jazz, and his music is the more dangerous because it sometimes sounds, to the uninitiated, like traditional jazz. In fact it is a popular, cleaned-up sound designed to sound sort of like jazz but without the "rough edges" which seemed to the Goodman arrangers, and perhaps to Benny himself, characteristic of jazz. A point might be made in Goodman's defense, however: he had to eat. But it is too bad that there should be this large body of music set up as a deception on the road to traditional jazz — a body of music which a lot of people accept in its place.

17. In the 1940's, New York, long a financial foster home for Chicago and New Orleans jazzmen, produced, for better or worse, an idiom which it could call its own. This was bop. Now bop, as handled by Ellington, Hodges, et al., was the beginning of so-called " cool " jazz, and it is the direct forerunner of modern jazz, also called " progressive." Bunk Johnson has probably summed up the resultant problem, when he asked, " What is this music for? " It is significant to note that among the exponents of this music there is no awareness of the tradition outlined above. Many of the men are music-school trained, and the architectonics of music seem more fascinating than any emotional possibilities. Thus, instead, the music contains, very often, little more than a kind of self-conscious, *individual* reverie, a kind of random personal eclecticism; this cannot lead to anything positive.

18. It can be seen that the lack of a tradition of unity is of importance. It is interesting to note that one of the leading modern jazz artists, Gerry Mulligan, cited Ellington, Lester Young, Dizzy Gillespie, Charlie Parker, and Woody Herman as the " tradition " in which he works.[12] The music he makes can only turn to itself, and toward nothing positive. It is interesting to watch this music being played. I remember a session with Chico Hamilton in Boston, where the people sat like statues and Mr. Hamilton announced new composition after new composition, by his drummer, his

---

[12] Gerry Mulligan, " The Importance of Jazz Tradition," *Down Beat* (Sept. 21, 1955) , p. 14.

guitarist, and so on. Nobody reacted. Nobody did anything. The music clearly fulfilled no need. As Winthrop Sargeant has pointed out,[13] " Actually, improvisation — the art of creating music directly with vocal or instrumental means — is far more fundamental to music than is the complex, difficult, and specialized art of planning compositions on paper." At this point it may be well to return from what *The New Yorker* has called " Pixieland " jazz, and repeat some of the principles that underlie traditional jazz, as well as to try to suggest something in the way of a definition, however impossible the latter chore may indeed prove to be.

19. There are, obviously, various unique elements in the performance of jazz. The layman would say that the basic element is improvisation, but as we have earlier pointed out, this is by no means the whole story. Some of the psychology involved in this insistence is outlined by Grossman and Farrell: [14]

> . . . compositions as performed in traditional jazz are, as a rule, neither wholly worked out in advance nor wholly created in the course of the performance. The importance of prearrangement, habitual residue, specific traditional material, and extemporization, respectively, varies from band to band. . . . One wonders why writers on jazz who have access to the facts nevertheless promulgate the proposition which the facts controvert. In at least some cases the reason for this curious inconsistency appears to be the desire to buttress another proposition, which is less than a half-truth, viz., that jazz is a sort of rebellion against old ideas and impediments to freedom, both aesthetic and social or political. In other cases the reason may well be in the desperate need of some jazz lovers to participate vividly in an act of creation.

It is most important to note the effect of tradition and habit, two elements not susceptible to arrangement. It is from these two elements that the content of traditional jazz derives its greatest amount of meaning.

20. The elements of tradition and habit are lacking in the modern idiom. And more than anything else, perhaps, it is the fact that we find these two elements in New Orleans jazz that accounts for its present-day revival. Novelty is of little value if it is not based on something real, and instinctively, it seems, the listeners of a generation which could not have heard the beginnings of the jazz movement are demanding that there be a rebirth. Enjoyment is not, in the end, a question of novelty but a question of inherent value. ". . . the old profundities remain. Music that effectively conveys them will survive generation after generation of the latest thing." [15]

---

[13] Sargeant, p. 15.
[14] Grossman and Farrell, p. 163.
[15] *Ibid.*, p. 87.

• Application •

Write the first draft of the paper for which you have made an outline. (See page 440.)

At this point the student had before him a completed draft of his paper. (The first section of it actually represented a rewriting – a second draft.) But the paper was far from finished, and as the student went over it, he found many paragraphs that called for revision and even drastic rewriting. Consider paragraph 6, for example. Though the student thought that he knew what he wanted to say, he had to admit to himself when he read over paragraph 6 that he had not really said it. The obscurity and confusion shows itself quite clearly in the fact that each sentence in the paragraph begins with a word which has no clear reference. To what do the first two " This's " refer? What is it that " is because " and what is it that " is not capricious "? The antecedent of " it " is also quite vague. (See page 441.)

In order to revise the paragraph the student had to make the antecedents clear, and this meant thinking out much more precisely what it was that he meant to say. He began his revised paragraph as follows:

That the occurrence of the blues scale in jazz is not an accident is proved by other similarities. There are, for example, many recognized pitch variations in playing jazz, the originating idea for most of which seems unquestionably to have come from the blues.

These sentences, once he had put them down, seemed rather strained and awkward. So he decided to try again and this is the paragraph that he managed to write:

That the typical blues scale should be found also in so much jazz is not an accident. The proof would lie in the fact that there are so many other technical similarities. There are, for example, many recognized pitch variations in the playing of jazz, and the idea for most of these variations unquestionably came from the blues. The choice of certain pitch variations is not capricious; those pitch variations occur in jazz with a good deal of regularity. In much " modern " jazz this regularity is very marked, though it must be admitted that citations from the most recent jazz do not necessarily prove much about the essential characteristics of jazz. (Much " modern " jazz has become so self-conscious that it has turned what ought to be natural effects into special tricks.)

The revised paragraph is not altogether satisfactory. It begins by commenting on further relationships between the blues and jazz, but then goes on to anticipate some of the criticisms of recent jazz that the student plans to make in the latter part of his paper. Our student thought first of dropping the last two sentences but finally decided that if he made it plain that these sentences consisted of a kind of anticipatory remark they might be retained. (In order to stress the anticipatory nature of these remarks, he had inserted the parenthetical statement " it must be admitted " and had enclosed the last sentence in parentheses.)

Paragraph 7 seemed sound structurally but the second sentence was obviously too wordy. Instead of " It will have to do to suggest the nature of the problem by making the point that, for instance, the music," etc., he wrote, " One example must suffice: the music," etc. In the fifth sentence there is a reference to " one of those New Orleans funerals." The kind of funeral referred to is that described quite vividly in paragraph 10, but this description, of course, occurs further on in the paper. So the student decided to make the phrase read " one of those New Orleans burial-society funerals." In the last sentence of the paragraph there is an instance of careless diction. It is not a " fact " but a " conclusion " which the " very origins of the music make unavoidable."

In paragraph 9 the second sentence needs attention on several counts. " Brought up learning " is distinctly awkward, and besides the words " brought up " are repeated from the preceding sentence. Moreover, the sentence is badly punctuated. (See pages 786–87 in the Handbook.) Our student corrected it to read, " W. C. Handy, for instance, grew up learning to play the organ; in fact, his father had him take organ lessons, but the little boy was forbidden to play the guitar because it was ' one of the devil's playthings.' "

In paragraph 14 the long second sentence caught our student's attention as he reread the paper. Not only is it questionably long, but it involves some very trite and possibly quite inappropriate metaphors. Louis Armstrong is said to be " at the crossroads of the history of jazz " and he is described also as " a figure which strides the gap . . . between New Orleans and Chicago jazz." The general idea would seem to be that Louis Armstrong is a link between two jazz traditions. But the awkward expression " figure which strides the gap " says this clumsily – and the clumsiness becomes the more evident when our writer indicates that he is not sure that there really is a gap between New Orleans and Chicago jazz. In any case the metaphor involving " the crossroads of the history " seems to be out of place. A person standing where the roads cross has to decide which of the roads to take, and his decision may be momentous for his future career. There is no intimation that Armstrong made any conscious choice, or even that his going to Chicago was momentous for jazz. The writer simply wishes to emphasize Armstrong's centrality in the jazz tradition. It would be well if the student could find a forceful figure of speech which described succinctly and vividly Armstrong's role in the development of jazz. (Perhaps some such figure will suggest itself to you, the reader.) But as we have seen in the chapter on Metaphor (pages 327–45), there is no way to contrive a metaphor by formula or rule. As Aristotle said, the true poet shows his genius most characteristically in his ability to find metaphors; and most of us do not have this kind of genius. But all of us can at least be expected to clear out the jargon that is created by dead metaphors. Our student decided to rewrite the second sentence as follows: "Although we may feel that the present-day image of this man has been somewhat tarnished by his fabulous success and by his willingness to sacrifice some of his musicianship to the popular notion of what is expected of him, nevertheless, he remains one of the central figures in the history of jazz. Louis Armstrong constitutes a link between New Orleans and Chicago jazz and he was a great enough artist to merge in his own technique elements of both styles."

Paragraph 16 caused our student a certain amount of trouble, particularly in getting the diction right, and in clearing away some of the disturbing echoes of the same sound. Because this paragraph was important in making clear his case against the distortions of jazz, our student decided to make a careful rewriting of the whole paragraph. This is the way in which he rewrote it:

At this time commences the so-called "jazz age," a misnomer if ever there was one. For the true jazz was smothered under a welter of pseudo-jazz, a synthetic product created through elaborate arrangements by big bands such as those of Paul Whiteman, the Dorseys, and others. The music of Gershwin also made for a loss of the essential emotional and spiritual values that had characterized the early jazz. Music of this sort was distinctly a commercial product; it traded upon a kind of cheap romanticism. And then, as if to make matters still worse, swing appeared, and with it, Benny Goodman. Let us be just. No one would deny to Goodman tremendous technical versatility nor would one deny to his kind of music a compelling emotion and sound. But these things are not jazz, and Gershwin's music is the more dangerous because it sometimes sounds to the uninitiated like traditional jazz.

If you look back at the first draft you will find that the next sentence echoes the word "sound" twice — "cleaned-up sound" and "to sound sort of like jazz." (See page 444.) These disturbing and meaningless echoes obviously must be removed. So our student continued the paragraph with these revisions:

In fact it is a popular, cleaned-up music designed to resemble jazz but with a smoothing-off of the "rough edges" which seemed to the Goodman arrangers, and perhaps to Benny himself, characteristic of jazz. A point must be made in Goodman's defense: he had to eat. But it is unfortunate that this large body of music has been set up as a deceptive attraction — a glittering but false semblance of traditional jazz calculated to mislead the unwary.

Notice that the student has decided to remove a rather confused metaphorical expression: "a deception *on the road* to traditional jazz." Either the idea of a road with people on it seeking true jazz must be meaningfully developed or it had better be dropped altogether.

• Applications •

I. The various revisions of the first draft of " The Development of Jazz " have had to do with such matters as diction, metaphor, and paragraph and sentence structure. Having cursorily referred to Chapters 9, 10, and 11, see what revisions, if any, you feel need to be made in paragraphs 3, 4, 10, 11, 13, 15, 17, 18, and 19. (You may very well have further changes to suggest for paragraphs 7, 9, 14, and 16.)

II. Go over your own research paper with a view to making the kind of revision that has been demonstrated. In this connection you may find it useful to review the topic headings for the chapters on The Paragraph and the Sentence, Diction, and Metaphor. These headings may suggest the errors for which you are to be on the alert.

Thus far we have said little about the problem of tone, and perhaps at this stage of the paper it is rather late to begin revisions undertaken primarily in the interest of tone. For as we have seen earlier (pages 352–58), tone is a reflection of the author's whole attitude toward his material and toward his audience.

In the research paper that we have been revising, the writer has assumed that his reader knows something about jazz and that he will recognize at least the more celebrated names connected with jazz. He assumes too that his typical reader will know a little about music, though the writer has been rather careful not to presume upon this knowledge. He does not ask the reader to deal with many technicalities of musical structure.

On the other hand, the writer evidently does count upon his reader's having a general background in cultural history. For example, he refers to the " noble savage " and to the concept of primitivism, and he seems to expect that his reader can be counted upon to understand certain basic elements to be found in any genuine art.

In making this last assumption, perhaps the writer goes too far, and in paragraph 17 he may be asking his reader to translate out of his special knowledge what comes close to being arty jargon. See, for example, the following passage: ". . . the music contains, very often, little more than a kind of self-conscious, *individual* reverie, a kind of random personal eclecticism." Unless he can assume a reader possessed of a good general knowledge of the arts, some of these statements may need to be translated into simpler terms.

The relative tonelessness of this paper probably springs from the fact that it *is* a research paper — that is, a paper to be written merely for the instructor or for some faceless and anonymous ideal reader. A personal essay or an informal essay allows for a more intimate and warmly personal relation between the author and reader. Yet we must not manufacture needless difficulties here. This paper is by no means completely toneless and some of its blurrings and confusion of tone can can be remedied by the writer's sharpening and clarifying for himself the nature of his reader.

Let us try once more to visualize that reader as he is implied by the paper. He is probably a college student with some interest in literature and the arts, though he is not necessarily trained in music. He knows something about the history of ideas and of culture, and has presumably some notion about what distinguishes genuine art from spurious art. One guesses that he has heard a good deal of jazz at one time or another, but he is not necessarily a jazz enthusiast and has not thought deeply about the nature of jazz or its development as an art. He is likely to have been taken in by some of the misconceptions that surround the subject.

If this is the reader that our writer has principally in mind, are there any further adjustments of tone likely to make this paper more effective and attractive to him? Perhaps not a great deal can be done at this point without extensive detailed revision; but there are two things that can clearly be improved. The concluding paragraph can be reshaped with this reader in mind and the beginning of the essay can be revised to catch this particular reader's attention.

I discovered jazz a few months ago. Like most people of my generation, I have been listening to jazz all my life, or so I thought. I have danced to it, heard it on the record player and the radio, at parties and on dates, and have even gone to hear a few of the name bands of our day. But I hadn't discovered jazz. That discovery occurred one afternoon last spring when a friend had me in to listen to his collection of early jazz records — things like "Dippermouth Blues" by King Oliver's band, and "West End

Blues " by Louis Armstrong. Perhaps I was ready for the experience; perhaps my friend was skillful in what he chose to play and in his suggestions about what to listen for. At any rate, then and there I made my discovery of the genuine idiom as distinguished from the sweetened dilutions and the smoothed-out commercializations and the other kinds of pseudo-jazz. From that time on I have been interested in helping others to make that discovery — or at least to dispel some of the misconceptions of what jazz is.

This new introductory paragraph has the merit of suggesting the writer's own interest in the subject and of making some claim upon the reader's interest in it. It sets a certain tone for the discussion. But there are other merits. The paragraph suggests, if it does not actually state, the line of argument which the writer is going to take in this essay: that is, that he regards the early jazz as the genuine thing, to be distinguished from later sophistications of it.

That this new introductory paragraph fits the paper well enough and that the paragraphs above numbered 1 and 2 follow on from it can be ascertained by turning back and rereading them. There is the temptation, however, in the light of our new introductory paragraph, to alter their tone to something a bit more informal. For example, they might be made to read as follows:

The origins of jazz, like those of any other folk art, are bound to be obscure. In view of the fact that most of the earliest jazzmen didn't know how to read music, it would be folly to expect much documentation. Yet we can be pretty sure of three main sources for the beginnings of jazz: the spirituals, the blues, and the New Orleans brass-band music of the turn of the century. Jazz is as American as apple pie and corn on the cob.

This assertion that jazz is essentially American may seem odd in view of all that we have heard about African rhythms and the throbbing of the talking drums. The Negro, we have been told over and over again, brought these special rhythms with him to America. The theory is certainly attractive and it is intriguingly romantic. The only trouble is that it has been impossible to show any real parallels between native African rhythms and the rhythms of jazz.

It may be interesting for the student who is reading these passages to try his own hand at rewriting several of the paragraphs that follow so as to sustain the tone of the paragraphs we have just rewritten. To do so would be to carry out an exercise in the manipulation of tone. But it ought to be made perfectly clear that there is no virtue as such in the more informal and colloquial tone. Indeed, the reader may very well feel that the tone of the original paragraphs 1 and 2 accords better with the general purposes of this research paper. For research papers tend on the whole to make use of a somewhat more formal tone. In any case, as we have already pointed out, our new introductory paragraph will fit well enough with the original paragraphs 1 and 2.

Whether or not we decide to rewrite the whole paper for the sake of developing a somewhat more informal tone, paragraph 17, for reasons suggested a little earlier, still stands in need of revision. The revision that we contemplate may seem to be more appropriately called a simplification of style than a revision of tone. Yet the simplification of style has been called for by our more clearly focused notion of the character of the reader to whom this paper is addressed. And with that reader clearly in mind — we have tried to characterize him on page 450 — we can the more successfully make the revision. Paragraph 17 rewritten might sound like this:

> In the 1940's, New York, for years the financial foster home for Chicago and New Orleans jazzmen, at long last produced an idiom which it could call its own. This was bop. As handled by Ellington, Hodge, et al., bop was the beginning of " cool " jazz; it was furthermore the direct forerunner of modern, also called " progressive," jazz. But progressive jazz sets a problem, one that Bunk Johnson put very pointedly when he asked, " What is this music for? " One might have trouble in saying just *what* the earlier jazz was for, but there was no doubt that it was for something, and that its hearers participated in it with a full emotional commitment. But progressive jazz seems to be characterized by a certain formal emptiness. It provides a means for its exponents, often music-school trained, to dally with the architectonics of music. Indeed, progressive jazz often seems to be nothing more than the reflection of the performer's highly self-conscious, quite private daydreaming. The performer does not seem to be working in a tradition; instead, he assembles musical ornaments and arabesques in random fashion at the promptings of a quite personal taste.

There are other paragraphs of the research paper which perhaps require simplification of style. The student should attempt such simplifications. In doing so, he will find it helps to keep clearly in mind the kind of reader for whom he is writing. In view of our clearer focus upon that reader, the concluding paragraph certainly needs some revision. The reader that we have visualized probably does not know enough about music to follow what is said in paragraphs 19 and 20. We need to simplify and clarify these statements. We need in addition to make the concluding paragraph fulfill a little more emphatically what was promised by implication in our new introductory paragraph. In particular, our student author of this paper decided to try to work in an explanation for the fact that he had not been able to give the reader a perfectly clear definition of jazz. With all this in mind, he produced the following paragraph as a substitute for paragraph 20:

The term "traditional jazz" may seem rather lame, coming as it does at the end of this paper. Has it not been possible, after all, in the course of this paper to arrive at a clear definition of jazz? Frankly, it has not been possible to do so, for, as Hobson puts it, jazz is a language and "a language of course cannot be defined." [16] But it is just because jazz is a language itself that mere personal idiom, mere novelty, are of little importance. Instinctively the listeners of a generation that could not have heard the beginnings of the jazz movement are now reacting against the private talk and empty formalism of modern jazz and are demanding the full language and what can be said in it. They are, in brief, demanding the revival of genuine jazz. Enjoyment is much more than the surprise at novelty. ". . . the old profundities remain. Music that effectively conveys them will survive generation after generation of the latest thing." [17]

As a last Application, the student should set himself the task of reworking his own research paper with special regard to improving and making consistent the tone, though he should certainly not, in making his final touches, *restrict* his revisions to problems of tone. This is the time also to make a careful proofreading of the manuscript, with special attention to sentence structure, agreement of subjects and verbs, sequence of tenses, the position of modifiers, and, not least, spelling and mechanics! Any clarification of style, smoothing of transitions, perfecting of rhythms that he can effect will probably be worth the trouble. The writer, whether novice or veteran, must not become weary in well doing. Good writing is mostly rewriting. The sweat is worth as much as the inspiration.

---

[16] Hobson, p. 16.
[17] Grossman and Farrell, p. 87.

A
BOOK
OF
READINGS

CONTENTS

INTRODUCTION

What can reading do for us? It can do many things for us, but for immediate purposes, we may list three. It can help us think. It can give us things to think about. And it can help us to express our thoughts.

Is there some sort of a system for reading which will help the student? There is no foolproof system. For one thing, different kinds of writing may call for different systems of reading. What may work for fiction may not, and probably will not, work for writing that is primarily expository. Moreover, a system which works for one person may not work for another. In the end the student may have to develop his own system. But any system must take into account such questions as these:

1. What is the material?

2. What understanding do I already have of such material? That is, do I have any basis for comparison and criticism?

3. What is the author's motive? Is he trying to inform me, convince me, persuade me, or make me participate in an imaginative experience — the experience of a novel, say, or of a poem or play?

4. What is the author's basic idea or theme?

5. How is this idea developed in the organization of the work? In other words, what is the author's method of thinking?

6. What are the tone and style of the work? Do I understand the intention and the effect of the language as used in the work?

7. What enlightenment does the work give me? New facts? New ideas? New methods of thought? New sense of character? Deeper awareness of human experience?

Number 1 is the easiest question. The book, or whatever it is, is about something. The material (as opposed to the author's interpretation of that material — the idea or theme) may be tribal life in Polynesia, co-operative marketing, the theory of relativity, the program of the Republican Party, socialism, the nature of the good. It is fairly easy to identify the material — the "raw material" — the author worked with.

Number 2 also seems easy, but it is sometimes harder than it looks.

To answer these questions, the reader must look honestly into his own knowledge. It is easy to delude oneself. A person hears about something and in the end assumes that he knows something about it. But he merely has the words, and perhaps has one accidental or arbitrary interpretation. He must ask: What do I know about Polynesia? What do I know about the ways in which the good has been conceived? What are some of the problems involved in defining it? Certainly, we want to read about subjects we do not know about, and for any subject there must always be the first acquaintance. We have to start somewhere. The point is simply this: The reader must try to know where he stands, what background and equipment he possesses for dealing with a subject.

Number 3 seems relatively easy, and usually is. Often an author will state quite flatly what he intends to do — to inform the reader about tribal life in Polynesia, to persuade the reader to vote the Republican ticket. But all cases are not so simple. Sometimes there are concealed motives. For instance, what seems to be a piece of history may actually be written from a point of view that would imply your adopting some attitude or line of action, here and now. The life of Abraham Lincoln might work as an appeal to support the Republican Party in the next election, or the life of George Washington might work as an argument against political co-operation with Great Britain. In both of these examples, the apparent motive would be to inform but the real motive would be to convince or persuade. Try to see whether the author has something up his sleeve.

In regard to question 4, sometimes an author will state very explicitly his main idea, or theme. This idea is to be distinguished sharply from the mere material. It is what the author *thinks about* the material, his interpretation of it, the line of action that he proposes be taken in regard to it. But sometimes he is not explicit. The reader must arrive at it by the course of the discussion. Furthermore, even if an author does state the idea, it is sometimes a good thing for the reader to put it into his own words, to state it as it would appear to him, and to try to see how it might apply to other instances and situations than those used by the author.

When we think we have some grasp of the theme of the work in hand, we should try to answer question 5, to see in some detail how the theme is developed in the structure of that work. How does one idea lead to another, what is the handling of explanation or argument? Why are things put in this particular order? Do illustrations really illustrate the point intended by the author? Is the work consistent, or does it contain self-contradictions? Are the author's conclusions the only conclusions which could be derived from the evidence he presents? Questions such as these — and the student can frame others of the same sort — will give some notion of the structure of the whole.

As for question 6, we seem to come to this late in the day. How do we get anything from a piece of writing if we do not really understand the language? But there are degrees of understanding. After we think we have understood well enough to get the main drift — to state, for instance, the theme and to work out something of the structure of the whole composition — we can return to a closer inspection of the language itself. Upon this inspection we may find that we had not really understood many things. We may have even missed the basic notion of the whole work. So we may have to revise our answers to earlier questions.

When we read we are constantly being affected, whether we know it or not, by the slight qualifications of meaning in the language, and these slight shadings are in the end of enormous importance. Attention to such matters in our reading leads us to a skill in our own use of language.

The answer to the last question, number 7, really summarizes all the other answers. But it does more. It puts what the student has gained from the present work into the context of what he has gained from all his past reading and experience. It may be that he has gained nothing — for several possible reasons. The work may be bad or trivial in itself. Or the work may be good in itself, but be a thing which is too elementary for the student's present development. Or the student may simply not be prepared to profit from the work; his background may not qualify him to grasp it. Or it may be that the student simply hasn't given enough time and effort to it. But if you discover that you have failed to gain anything from something you have read, try honestly to understand why.

The questions have been numbered, one to seven, but this does not mean that there is any order of importance here. All are important, and if you as reader cannot answer one, you probably cannot answer others. They are all interrelated, and in the end have to do with the unit which is the work. As there is no order of importance here, so there is no necessary order in which the questions should be considered. With one reservation: perhaps numbers 1 and 2 should always be first and second, and number 7 last. But the others may have to be considered in different orders at different times. Occasionally, for instance, the reader might have to work hard at the language before he could get at the theme and organization. Or he might find the reverse true. Fumble with the thing until you find a key. If one approach fails, try another. The random touch may spring the secret latch.

The Method of Scientific Investigation

T. H. Huxley

The method of scientific investigation is nothing but the expression of the necessary mode of working of the human mind. It is simply the mode at which all phenomena are reasoned about, rendered precise and exact. There is no more difference, but there is just the same kind of difference, between the mental operations of a man of science and those of an ordinary person, as there is between the operations and methods of a baker or of a butcher weighing out his goods in common scales, and the operations of a chemist in performing a difficult and complex analysis by means of his balance and finely graduated weights. It is not that the action of the scales in the one case, and the balance in the other, differ in the principles of their construction or manner of working; but the beam of one is set on an infinitely finer axis than the other, and of course turns by the addition of a much smaller weight.

You will understand this better, perhaps, if I give you some familiar example. You have all heard it repeated, I dare say, that men of science work by means of induction and deduction, and that by the help of these operations, they, in a sort of sense, wring from Nature certain other things, which are called natural laws, and causes, and that out of these, by some cunning skill of their own, they build up hypotheses and theories. And it is imagined by many, that the operations of the common mind can be by no means compared with these processes, and that they have to be acquired by a sort of special apprenticeship to the craft. To hear all these large words, you would think that the mind

THE METHOD OF SCIENTIFIC INVESTIGATION: From *Collected Essays,* " Darwiniana," by T. H. Huxley.

of a man of science must be constituted differently from that of his fellow men; but if you will not be frightened by terms, you will discover that you are quite wrong, and that all these terrible apparatus are being used by yourselves every day and every hour of your lives.

There is a well-known incident in one of Molière's plays, where the author makes the hero express unbounded delight on being told that he had been talking prose during the whole of his life. In the same way, I trust that you will take comfort, and be delighted with yourselves, on the discovery that you have been acting on the principles of inductive and deductive philosophy during the same period. Probably there is not one here who has not in the course of the day had occasion to set in motion a complex train of reasoning, of the very same kind, though differing of course in degree, as that which a scientific man goes through in tracing the causes of natural phenomena.

A very trivial circumstance will serve to exemplify this. Suppose you go into a fruiterer's shop, wanting an apple — you take up one, and on biting it, you find it is sour; you look at it, and see that it is hard and green. You take up another one and that too is hard, green, and sour. The shopman offers you a third; but, before biting it, you examine it, and find that it is hard and green, and you immediately say that you will not have it, as it must be sour, like those that you have already tried.

Nothing can be more simple that that, you think; but if you will take the trouble to analyse and trace out into its logical elements what has been done by the mind, you will be greatly surprised. In the first place you have performed the operation of induction. You found that, in two experiences, hardness and greenness in apples went together with sourness. It was so in the first case, and it was confirmed by the second. True, it is a very small basis, but still it is enough to make an induction from; you generalise the facts, and you expect to find sourness in apples where you get hardness and greenness. You found upon that a general law that all hard and green apples are sour; and that, so far as it goes, is a perfect induction. Well, having got your natural law in this way, when you are offered another apple which you find is hard and green, you say, " All hard and green apples are sour; this apple is hard and green, therefore this apple is sour." That train of reasoning is what logicians call a syllogism, and has all its various parts and terms — its major premiss, its minor premiss, and its conclusion. And, by the help of further reasoning, which, if drawn out, would have to be exhibited in two or three other syllogisms, you arrive at your final determination, " I will not have that apple." So that, you see, you have, in the first place, established a law by induction, and upon that you have founded a deduction, and reasoned out the special particular case. Well now, suppose, having got your conclusion of the law, that at some time afterwards, you are discussing the qualities of apples with a friend: you will say to him, " It is a very curious thing, but I find that all hard and green apples are sour! " Your friend says to you, " But how do you know that? " You at once reply, " Oh, because I have tried them over and over again, and have always found them to be so." Well, if we were talking science instead of common sense, we should call that an experimental verification. And, if still opposed, you go further, and say, " I have heard from the people in Somersetshire and Devonshire, where a large number of apples are grown, that they have observed the same thing. It is also found to be the case in Normandy, and in North America. In short, I find it to be the universal experience of mankind wherever attention has been directed to the subject." Whereupon, your friend, unless he is a very unreasonable man, agrees with you, and is convinced that you are quite right in the conclusion you have drawn. He believes, although perhaps he does not know he believes it, that the more extensive verifications are — that the more frequently experiments have been made, and results of the same kind arrived at — that the more varied the conditions under which the same results are attained, the more certain is the ultimate conclusion, and he disputes the question no further. He sees that the experiment has been tried under all sorts of conditions, as to time, place, and people, with the same result; and he says with you, therefore, that the law you have laid down must be a good one, and he must believe it.

In science we do the same thing — the philosopher exercises precisely the same faculties, though in a much more delicate manner. In scientific inquiry it becomes a matter of duty to expose a supposed law to every possible kind of verification, and to take care, moreover, that this is done intentionally, and not left to a mere accident, as in the case of the apples. And in science, as in common life, our confidence in a law is in exact proportion to the absence of variation in the result of our experimental verifications. For instance, if you let go your grasp of an article you may have in your hand, it will immediately fall to the ground. That is a very common verification of one of the best established laws of nature — that of gravitation. The method by which men of science establish the existence of that law is exactly the same as that by which we have established the trivial proposition about the sourness of hard and green apples. But we believe it in such an extensive, thorough, and unhesitating manner because the universal experience of mankind verifies it, and we can verify it ourselves at any time; and that is the strongest possible foundation on which any natural law can rest.

So much, then, by way of proof that the method of establishing laws in science is exactly the same as that pursued in common life. Let us now turn to another matter (though really it is but another phase of the same question), and that is, the method by which, from the relations of certain phenomena, we prove that some stand in the position of causes towards the others.

I want to put the case clearly before you, and I will therefore show you what I mean by another familiar example. I will suppose that one of you, on coming down in the morning to the parlour of your house, finds that a tea-pot and some spoons which had been left in the room on the previous evening are gone — the window is open, and you observe the mark of a dirty hand on the window-frame, and perhaps, in addition to that, you notice the impress of a hob-nailed shoe on the gravel outside. All these phenomena have struck your attention instantly, and before two seconds have passed you say, " Oh, somebody has broken open the window, entered the room, and run off with the spoons and the tea-pot! " That speech is out of your mouth in a moment. And you will probably add, " I know there has; I am quite sure of it! " You mean to say exactly what you know; but in reality you are giving expression to what is, in all essential particulars, an hypothesis. You do not *know* it at all; it is nothing but an hypothesis rapidly framed in your own mind. And it is an hypothesis founded on a long train of inductions and deductions.

What are those inductions and deductions, and how have you got at this hypothesis? You have observed in the first place, that the window is open; but by a train of reasoning involving many inductions and deductions, you have probably arrived long before at the general law — and a very good one it is — that windows do not open of themselves; and you therefore conclude that something has opened the window. A second general law that you have arrived at in the same way is, that tea-pots and spoons do not go out of a window spontaneously, and you are satisfied that, as they are not now where you left them, they have been removed. In the third place, you look at the marks on the window-sill, and the shoe-marks outside, and you say that in all previous experience the former kind of mark has never been produced by anything else but the hand of a human being; and the same experience shows that no other animal but man at present wears shoes with hob-nails in them such as would produce the marks in the gravel. I do not know, even if we could discover any of those " missing links " that are talked about, that they would help us to any other conclusion! At any rate the law which states our present experience is strong enough for my present purpose. You next reach the conclusion that, as these kinds of marks have not been left by any other animal than man, or are liable to be formed in any other way than by a man's hand and shoe, the marks in question have been formed by a man in that way. You have, further, a general law, founded on observation and experience, and that, too, is I am sorry to say, a very universal and unimpeachable one — that some men are thieves; and you assume at once from all these premises — and that is what constitutes your hypothesis — that the man who made the marks outside and on the windowsill, opened the window, got into the room, and stole your tea-pot and spoons. You have now arrived at a *vera causa* — you have assumed a cause which, it is plain, is competent to produce all the phenomena you have observed. You can explain all these phenomena only by the hypothesis of a thief. But that is a hypothetical conclusion, of the justice of which you have no absolute proof at all; it is only rendered highly probable by a series of inductive and deductive reasonings.

I suppose your first action, assuming that you are a man of ordinary common sense, and that you have established this hypothesis to your own satisfaction, will very likely be to go off for the police, and set them on the track of the burglar, with the view to the recovery of your property. But just as you are starting with this object, some person comes in, and on learning what you are about, says, " My good friend, you are going on a great deal too fast. How do you know that the man who really made the marks took the spoons? It might have been a monkey that took them, and the man may have merely looked in afterwards." You would probably reply, " Well, that is all very well, but you see it is contrary to all experience of the way tea-pots and spoons are abstracted; so that, at any rate, your hypothesis is less probable than mine." While you are talking the thing over in this way, another friend arrives, one of the good kind of people that I was talking of a little while ago. And he might say, " Oh, my dear sir, you are certainly going on a great deal too fast. You are most presumptuous. You admit that all these occurrences took place when you were fast asleep, at a time when you could not possibly have known anything about what was taking place. How do you know that the laws of Nature are not suspended during the night? It may be that there has been some kind of supernatural interference in this case." In point of fact, he declares that your hypothesis is one of which you cannot at all demonstrate the truth, and that you are by no means sure that the laws of Nature are the same when you are asleep as when you are awake.

Well, now, you cannot at the moment answer that kind of reasoning. You feel that your worthy friend has you somewhat at a disadvantage. You will feel perfectly convinced in your own mind, however, that you are quite right, and you say to him, " My good friend, I can only be guided by the natural probabilities of the case, and if you will be kind enough to stand aside and permit me to pass, I will go and fetch the police." Well, we will suppose that your journey is successful, and that by good luck you meet with a policeman; that eventually the burglar is found with your property on his person, and the marks correspond to his hand and to his boots. Probably any jury would consider those facts a very good experimental verification of your hypothesis, touching the cause of the abnormal phenomena observed in your parlour, and would act accordingly.

Now, in this supposititious case, I have taken phenomena of a very common kind, in order that you might see what are the different steps in an ordinary process of reasoning, if you will only take the trouble to analyse it carefully. All the operations I have described, you will see, are involved in the mind of any man of sense in leading him to a conclusion as to the course he should take in order to make good a robbery and punish the offender. I say that you are led, in that case, to your conclusion by exactly the same train of reasoning as that which a man of science pursues when he is endeavouring to discover the origin and laws of the most occult phenomena. The process is, and always must be, the same; and precisely the same mode of reasoning was employed by Newton and Laplace in their endeavours to discover and define the causes of the movements of the heavenly bodies, as you, with your own common sense, would employ to detect a burglar. The only difference is, that the nature of the inquiry being more abstruse, every step has to be most carefully watched, so that there may not be a single crack or flaw in your hypothesis. A flaw or crack in many of the hypotheses of daily life may be of little or no moment as affecting the general correctness of the conclusions at which we may arrive; but, in a scientific inquiry, a fallacy, great or small, is always of importance, and is sure to be in the long run constantly productive of mischievous if not fatal results.

Do not allow yourselves to be misled by the common notion that an hypothesis is untrustworthy simply because it is an hypothesis. It is often urged, in respect to some scientific conclusion, that, after all, it is only an hypothesis. But what more have we to guide us in nine-tenths of the most important affairs of daily life than hypotheses, and often very ill-based ones? So that in science, where the evidence of an hypothesis is subjected to the most rigid examination, we may rightly pursue the same course. You may have hypotheses, and hypotheses. A man may say, if he likes, that the moon is made of green cheese: that is an hypothesis. But another man, who has devoted a great deal of time and attention to the subject, and availed himself of the most powerful telescopes and the results of the observations of others, declares that in his opinion it is probably composed of materials very similar to those of which our own earth is made up: and that is also only an hypothesis. But I need not tell you that there is an enormous difference in the value of the two hypotheses. That one which is based on sound scientific knowledge is sure to have a corresponding value; and that which is a mere hasty random guess is likely to have but little value. Every great step in our progress in discovering causes has been made in exactly the same way as that which I have detailed to you. A person observing the occurrence of certain facts and phenomena asks, natually enough, what process, what kind of operation known to occur in Nature, applied to the particular case, will unravel and explain the mystery? Hence you have the scientific hypothesis; and its value will be proportionate to the care and completeness with which its basis had been tested and verified. It is in these matters as in the commonest affairs of practical life; the guess of the fool will be folly, while the guess of the wise man will contain wisdom. In all cases, you see that the value of the result depends on the patience and faithfulness with which the investigator applies to his hypothesis every possible kind of verification.

Mother Sea: The Gray Beginnings

Rachel L. Carson

> *And the earth was without form, and void; and darkness was upon the face of the deep.*
> — GENESIS

Beginnings are apt to be shadowy, and so it is with the beginnings of that great mother of life, the sea. Many people have debated how and when the earth got its ocean, and it is not surprising that their explanations do not always agree. For the plain and inescapable truth is that no one was there to see, and in the absence of eyewitness accounts there is bound to be a certain amount of disagreement. So if I tell here the story of how the young planet Earth acquired an ocean, it must be a story pieced together from many sources and containing many whole chapters the details of which we can only imagine. The story is founded on the testimony of the earth's most ancient rocks, which

MOTHER SEA: THE GRAY BEGINNINGS: From *The Sea Around Us* by Rachel L. Carson. Copyright 1951 by Rachel L. Carson. Reprinted by permission of Oxford University Press, Inc.

were young when the earth was young; on other evidence written on the face of the earth's satellite, the moon; and on hints contained in the history of the sun and the whole universe of star-filled space. For although no man was there to witness this cosmic birth, the stars and the moon and the rocks were there, and, indeed, had much to do with the fact that there is an ocean.

The events of which I write must have occurred somewhat more than 2 billion years ago. As nearly as science can tell that is the approximate age of the earth, and the ocean must be very nearly as old. It is possible now to discover the age of the rocks that compose the crust of the earth by measuring the rate of decay of the radioactive materials they contain. The oldest rocks found anywhere on earth — in Manitoba — are about 2.3 billion years old. Allowing 100 million years or so for the cooling of the earth's materials to form a rocky crust, we arrive at the supposition that the tempestuous and violent events connected with our planet's birth occurred nearly 2½ billion years ago. But this is only a minimum estimate, for rocks indicating an even greater age may be found at any time.

The new earth, freshly torn from its parent sun, was a ball of whirling gases, intensely hot, rushing through the black spaces of the universe on a path and at a speed controlled by immense forces. Gradually the ball of flaming gases cooled. The gases began to liquefy, and Earth became a molten mass. The materials of this mass eventually became sorted out in a definite pattern: the heaviest in the center, the less heavy surrounding them, and the least heavy forming the outer rim. This is the pattern which persists today — a central sphere of molten iron, very nearly as hot as it was 2 billion years ago, an intermediate sphere of semi-plastic basalt, and a hard outer shell, relatively quite thin and composed of solid basalt and granite.

The outer shell of the young earth must have been a good many millions of years changing from the liquid to the solid state, and it is believed that, before this change was completed, an event of the greatest importance took place — the formation of the moon. The next time you stand on a beach at night, watching the moon's bright path across the water, and conscious of the moon-drawn tides, remember that the moon itself may have been born of a great tidal wave of earthly substance, torn off into space. And remember that if the moon was formed in this fashion, the event may have had much to do with shaping the ocean basins and the continents as we know them.

There were tides in the new earth, long before there was an ocean. In response to the pull of the sun the molten liquids of the earth's whole surface rose in tides that rolled unhindered around the globe and only gradually slackened and diminished as the earthly shell cooled, congealed and hardened. Those who believe that the moon is a child of earth say that during an early stage of the earth's development something happened that caused this rolling, viscid tide to gather speed and momentum and to rise to unimaginable heights. Apparently the force that created these greatest tides the earth has ever known was the force of resonance, for at this time the period of the solar tides had come to approach, then equal, the period of the free oscillation of the liquid earth. And so every sun tide was given increased momentum by the push of the earth's oscillation, and each of the twice-daily tides was larger than the one before it. Physicists have calculated that, after 500 years of such monstrous, steadily increasing tides, those on the side toward the sun became too high for stability, and a great wave was torn away and hurled into space. But immediately, of course, the newly created satellite became subject to physical laws that sent it spinning in an orbit of its own about the earth. This is what we call the moon.

There are reasons for believing that this event took place after the earth's crust had become slightly hardened, instead of during its partly liquid state. There is to this day a great scar on the surface of the globe. This scar or depression holds the Pacific Ocean. According to some geophysicists, the floor of the Pacific is composed of basalt, the substance of the earth's middle layer, while all other oceans are floored with a thin layer of granite, which makes up most of the earth's outer layer. We immediately wonder what became of the Pacific's granite covering and the most convenient assumption is that it was torn away when the moon was formed. There is supporting evidence. The mean density of the moon is much less than that of the earth (3.3 compared with 5.5), suggesting that the moon took away none of the earth's heavy core, but that it is composed only of the granite and some of the basalt of the outer layers.

The birth of the moon probably helped shape other regions of the world's ocean besides the Pacific. When part of the crust was torn away, strains must have been set up in the remaining granite envelope. Perhaps the granite mass cracked open on the side opposite the moon scar. Perhaps, as the earth spun on its axis and rushed on its orbit through space, the cracks widened and the masses of granite began to drift apart, moving over a tarry, slowly hardening layer of basalt. Gradually the outer portions of the basalt layer became solid and the wandering continents came to rest, frozen into place with oceans between them. In spite of theories to the contrary, the weight of geologic evidence seems to be that the locations of the major ocean basins and the major continental land masses are today much the same as they have been since a very early period of the earth's history.

But this is to anticipate the story, for when the moon was born there was no ocean. The gradually cooling earth was enveloped in heavy layers of cloud, which contained much of the water of the new planet. For a long time its surface was so hot that no moisture could fall without immediately being reconverted to steam. This dense, perpetually renewed cloud covering must have been thick enough that no rays of sunlight could penetrate it. And so the rough outlines of the continents and the empty ocean basins were sculptured out of the surface of the earth in darkness, in a Stygian world of heated rock and swirling clouds and gloom.

As soon as the earth's crust cooled enough, the rains began to fall. Never have there been such rains since that time. They fell continuously, day and night, days passing into months, into years, into centuries. They poured into the waiting ocean basins, or, falling upon the continental masses, drained away to become sea.

That primeval ocean, growing in bulk as the rains slowly filled its basins, must have been only faintly salt. But the falling rains were the symbol of the dissolution of the continents. From the moment the rains began to fall, the lands began to be worn away and carried to the sea. It is an endless, inexorable process that has never stopped — the dissolving of the rocks, the leaching out of their contained minerals, the carrying of the rock fragments and dissolved minerals to the ocean. And over the eons of time, the sea has grown ever more bitter with the salt of the continents.

In what manner the sea produced the mysterious and wonderful stuff called protoplasm we cannot say. In its warm, dimly lit waters the unknown conditions of temperature and pressure and saltiness must have been the critical ones for the creation of life from non-life. At any rate they produced the result that neither the alchemists with their crucibles nor modern scientists in their laboratories have been able to achieve.

Before the first living cell was created, there may have been many trials and failures. It seems probable that, within the warm saltiness of the primeval sea, certain organic substances were fashioned from carbon dioxide, sulphur, nitrogen, phosphorus, potassium, and calcium. Perhaps these were transition steps from which the complex molecules of protoplasm arose — molecules that somehow acquired the ability to reproduce themselves and begin the endless stream of life. But at present no one is wise enough to be sure.

Those first living things may have been simple microorganisms rather like some of the bacteria we know today — mysterious borderline forms that were not quite plants, not quite animals, barely over the intangible line that separates the non-living from the living. It is doubtful that this first life possessed the substance chlorophyll, with which plants in sunlight transform lifeless chemicals into the living stuff of their tissues. Little sunshine could enter their dim world, penetrating the cloud banks from which fell the endless rains. Probably the sea's first children lived on the organic substances then present in the ocean waters, or, like the iron and sulphur bacteria that exist today, lived directly on inorganic food.

All the while the cloud cover was thinning, the darkness of the nights alternated with palely illumined days, and finally the sun for the first time shone through upon the sea. By this time some of the living things that floated in the sea must have developed the magic of chlorophyll. Now they were able to take the carbon dioxide of the air and the water of the sea and of these elements, in sunlight, build the organic substances they needed. So the first true plants came into being.

Another group of organisms, lacking the chlorophyll but needing organic food, found they could make a way of life for themselves by devouring the plants. So the first animals arose, and from that day to this, every animal in the world has followed the habit it learned in the ancient seas and depends, directly or through complex food chains, on the plants for food and life.

As the years passed, and the centuries, and the millions of years, the stream of life grew more and more complex. From simple, one-celled creatures, others that were aggregations of specialized cells arose, and then creatures with organs for feeding, digesting, breathing, reproducing. Sponges grew on the rocky bottom of the sea's edge and coral animals built their habitations in warm, clear waters. Jellyfish swam and drifted in the sea. Worms evolved, and starfish, and hard-shelled creatures with many-jointed legs, the arthropods. The plants, too, progressed, from the microscopic algae to branched and curiously fruiting seaweeds that swayed with the tides and were plucked from the coastal rocks by the surf and cast adrift.

During all this time the continents had no life. There was little to induce living things to come ashore, forsaking their all-providing, all-embracing mother sea. The lands must have been bleak and hostile beyond the power of words to describe. Imagine a whole continent of naked rock, across which no covering mantle of green had been drawn — a continent without soil, for there were no plants to aid in its formation and bind it to the rocks with their roots. Imagine a land of stone, a silent land, except for the sound of the rains and winds that swept across it. For there was no living voice, and no living thing moved over the surface of the rocks.

Meanwhile, the gradual cooling of the planet, which had first given the earth its hard granite crust, was progressing into its deeper layers; and as the interior slowly cooled and contracted, it drew away from the outer shell. This shell, accommodating itself to the shrinking sphere within it, fell into folds and wrinkles — the earth's first mountain ranges.

Geologists tell us that there must have been at least two periods of mountain building (often called " revolutions ") in that dim period, so long ago that the rocks have no record of it, so long ago that the mountains themselves have long since been worn away. Then there came a third great period of upheaval and readjustment of the earth's crust, about a billion years ago, but of all its majestic mountains the only reminders today are the Laurentian hills of eastern Canada, and a great shield of granite over the flat country around Hudson Bay.

The epochs of mountain building only served to speed up the processes of erosion by which continents were worn down and their crumbling rock and contained minerals returned to the sea. The uplifted masses of the mountains were prey to the bitter cold of the upper atmosphere and under the attacks of frost and snow and ice the rocks cracked and crumbled away. The rains beat with greater violence upon the slopes of the hills and carried away the substance of the mountains in torrential streams. There was still no plant covering to modify and resist the power of the rains.

And in the sea, life continued to evolve. The earliest forms have left no fossils by which we can identify them. Probably they were soft-bodied, with no hard parts that could be preserved. Then, too, the rock layers formed in those early days have since been so altered by enormous heat and pressure, under the foldings of the earth's crust, that any fossils they might have contained would have been destroyed.

For the past 500 million years, however, the rocks have preserved the fossil record. By the dawn of the Cambrian period, when the history of living things was first inscribed on rock pages, life in the sea had progressed so far that all the main groups of backboneless or invertebrate animals had been developed. But there were no animals with backbones, no insects or spiders, and still no plant or animal had been evolved that was capable of venturing onto the forbidding land. So for more than three-fourths of geologic time the continents were desolate and uninhabited, while the sea prepared the life that was later to invade them and make them habitable. Meanwhile, with violent tremblings of the earth and with the fire and smoke of roaring volcanoes, mountains rose and wore away, glaciers moved to and fro over the earth, and the sea crept over the continents and again receded.

It was not until Silurian time, some 350 million years ago, that the first pioneer of land life crept out on the shore. It was an arthropod, one of the great tribe that later produced crabs and lobsters and insects. It must have been something like a modern scorpion, but, unlike some of its descendants, it never wholly severed the ties that united it to the sea. It lived a strange life, half-terrestrial, half-aquatic, something like that of the ghost crabs that speed along the beaches today, now and then dashing into the surf to moisten their gills.

Fish, tapered of body and stream-molded by the press of running waters, were evolving in Silurian rivers. In times of drought, in the drying pools and lagoons, the shortage of oxygen forced them to develop swim bladders for the storage of air. One form that possessed an air-breathing lung was able to survive the dry periods by burying itself in mud, leaving a passage to the surface through which it breathed.

It is very doubtful that the animals alone would have succeeded in colonizing the land, for only the plants had the power to bring about the first amelioration of its harsh conditions. They helped make soil of the crumbling rocks, they held back the soil from the rains that would have swept it away, and little by little they softened and subdued the bare rock, the lifeless desert. We know very little about the first land plants, but they must have been closely related to some of the larger seaweeds that had learned to live in the coastal shallows, developing strengthened stems and grasping, rootlike holdfasts to resist the drag and pull of the waves. Perhaps it was in some coastal lowlands, periodically drained and flooded, that some such plants found it possible to survive, though separated from the sea. This also seems to have taken place in the Silurian period.

The mountains that had been thrown up by the Laurentian revolution gradually wore away, and as the sediments were washed from their summits and deposited on the lowlands, great areas of the continents sank under the load. The seas crept out of their basins and spread over the lands. Life fared well and was exceedingly abundant in those shallow, sunlit seas. But with the later retreat of the ocean water into the deeper basins, many creatures must have been left stranded in shallow, landlocked bays. Some of these animals found means to survive on land. The lakes, the shores of the rivers, and the coastal swamps of those days were the testing grounds in which plants and animals either became adapted to the new conditions or perished.

As the lands rose and the seas receded, a strange fishlike creature emerged on the land, and over the thousands of years its fins became legs, and instead of gills it developed lungs. In the Devonian sandstone this first amphibian left its footprint.

On land and sea the stream of life poured on. New forms evolved; some old ones declined and disappeared. On land the mosses and the ferns and the seed plants developed. The reptiles for a time dominated the earth, gigantic, grotesque, and terrifying. Birds learned to live and move in the ocean of air. The first small mammals lurked inconspicuously in hidden crannies of the earth as though in fear of the reptiles.

When they went ashore the animals that took up a land life carried with them a part of the sea in their bodies, a heritage which they passed on to their children and which even today links each land animal with its origin in the ancient sea. Fish, amphibian, and reptile, warm-blooded bird and mammal — each of us carries in our veins a salty stream in which the elements sodium, potassium, and calcium are combined in almost the same proportions as in sea water. This is our inheritance from the day, untold millions of years ago, when a remote ancestor, having progressed from the one-celled to the many-celled stage, first developed a circulatory system in which the fluid was merely the water of the sea. In the same way, our lime-hardened skeletons are a heritage from the calcium-rich ocean of Cambrian time. Even the protoplasm that streams within each cell of our bodies has the chemical structure impressed upon all living matter when the first simple creatures were brought forth in the ancient sea. And as life itself began in the sea, so each of us begins his individual life in a miniature ocean within his mother's womb, and in the stages of his embryonic development repeats the steps by which his race evolved, from gill-breathing inhabitants of a water world to creatures able to live on land.

Some of the land animals later returned to the ocean. After perhaps 50 million years of land life, a number of reptiles entered the sea about 170 million years ago, in the Triassic period. They were huge and formidable creatures. Some had oarlike limbs by which they rowed through the water; some were web-footed, with long, serpentine necks. These grotesque monsters disappeared millions of years ago, but we remember them when we come upon a large sea turtle swimming many miles at sea, its barnacle-encrusted shell eloquent of its marine life. Much later, perhaps no more than 50 million years ago, some of the mammals, too, abandoned a land life for the ocean. Their descendants are the sea lions, seals, sea elephants, and whales of today.

Among the land mammals there was a race of creatures that took to an arboreal existence. Their hands underwent remarkable development, becoming skilled in manipulating and examining objects, and along with this skill came a superior brain power that compensated for what these comparatively small mammals lacked in strength. At last, perhaps somewhere in the vast interior of Asia, they descended from the trees and became again terrestrial. The past million years have seen their transformation into beings with the body and brain and spirit of man.

Eventually man, too, found his way back to the sea. Standing on its shores, he must have looked out upon it with wonder and curiosity, compounded with an unconscious recognition of his lineage. He could not physically re-enter the ocean as the seals and whales had done. But over the centuries, with all the skill and ingenuity and reasoning powers of his mind, he has sought to explore and investigate even its most remote parts, so that he might re-enter it mentally and imaginatively.

He built boats to venture out on its surface. Later he found ways to descend to the shallow parts of its floor, carrying with him the air that, as a land mammal long unaccustomed to aquatic life, he needed to breathe. Moving in fascination over the deep sea he could not enter, he found ways to probe its depths, he let down nets to capture its life, he invented mechanical eyes and ears that could re-create for his senses a world long lost, but a world that, in the deepest part of his subconscious mind, he had never wholly forgotten.

And yet he has returned to his mother sea only on her own terms. He cannot control or change the ocean as, in his brief tenancy of earth, he has subdued and plundered the continents. In the artificial world of his cities and towns, he often forgets the true nature of his planet and the long vistas of its history, in which the existence of the race of men has occupied a mere moment of time. The sense of all these things comes to him most clearly in the course of a long ocean voyage, when he watches day after day the receding rim of the horizon, ridged and furrowed by waves; when at night he becomes aware of the earth's rotation as the stars pass overhead; or when, alone in this world of water and sky, he feels the loneliness of his earth in space. And then, as never on land, he knows the truth that his world is a water world, a planet dominated by its covering mantle of ocean, in which the continents are but transient intrusions of land above the surface of the all-encircling sea.

The Colors That Animals Can See

H. Munro Fox

What colors can animals see? Is the world more brightly colored or duller to animals than it is to us? To find out the answers to these questions scientists have used a method of training the animals to come to different colors, which is similar in principle to the method used in studying the sense of hearing in animals.

Let us take bees first of all, partly because more exact scientific research has been done on the color-sense of bees than of almost any other animal. It is especially interesting to know what colors bees can see because these insects visit flowers to get sweet nectar from them to make honey, and in so doing the bees incidentally carry pollen from flower to flower. On the face of it, it would seem very likely that bees are attracted to flowers by their bright colors. But possibly it is the scents that attract the bees, or perhaps it is both color and scent. So, among other things, we want to know whether bees can really see the colors of flowers, and if so, what colors they can see. Exactly how is this found out?

A table is put in a garden, and on the table a piece of blue cardboard is placed, on which there is a watch-glass containing a drop of syrup. After a short while bees come to the syrup and suck up some of it. The bees then fly to their hive and give the syrup to other bees in the hive to make honey. Then they return to the feeding-place which they have discovered. We let the bees go on doing this for a while, after which we take away the blue cardboard with the syrup on it. Instead of this card we now put on the table a blue card on the left side of the first feeding-place, and a red card to the right of the first feeding-place. These new cards have no syrup on them but only an empty watch-glass lying on each. Thus, the blue card is on the left, the red card on the right, and there is nothing where the first blue feeding-card used to be. After we have arranged these new cards, we have not long to wait. Very soon bees arrive again, and it can be seen that they fly straight on to the blue card; none go to the red card.

This behavior of the bees seems to indicate two things. The first is that the bees remember that blue means syrup and so they fly to the blue. Since they did not go to the place on the table where the syrup used to be, but flew to the blue card which had been placed on the left, it really was the blue card that attracted them, not the place where the syrup had previously been. We have trained the bees to come to

THE COLORS THAT ANIMALS CAN SEE: From *The Personality of Animals* by H. Munro Fox. Copyright 1940. Reprinted by permission of the author and Penguin Books, Ltd.

the blue card. And the second thing our experiment seems to mean is that bees can tell blue from red.

But can they? This is not yet quite certain. The reason for our doubt is as follows. It is well known that there are a few people in the world, very few, who cannot see colors at all. These people are totally color-blind. To them all colors look like different shades of grey. They may be able to tell red from blue, because red will perhaps look darker and blue lighter in shade, but the colors are not red or blue. It might be, then, that bees are really color-blind, and that in the experiment they came to the blue card not because they saw it as blue but just because it appeared lighter in shade than the red card. Perhaps they had really been trained to come not to blue, but to the lighter of two shades. We can find out quite simply if this is so by another training experiment.

On our table in the garden we put a blue card, and all around this blue card we put a number of different grey cards. These grey cards are of all possible shades of grey, from the extremes of white to black. On each card a watch-glass is placed. The watch-glass on the blue card has some syrup in it; all the others are empty. After a short time bees find the syrup as before, and they come for it again and again. Then, after some hours, we take away the watch-glass of syrup which was on the blue card and put an empty one in its place. Now what do the bees do? They still go straight to the blue card, although there is no syrup there. They do not go to any of the grey cards, in spite of the fact that one of the grey cards is of exactly the same brightness as the blue card. Thus the bees do not mistake any shade of grey for blue. In this way we have proved that they really do see blue as a color.

We can find out in just the same way what other colors bees can see. It turns out that bees see various colors, but these insects differ from us as regards their color-sense in two very interesting ways. Suppose we train bees to come to a red card, and having done so we put the red card on the table in the garden among the set of different grey cards. This time we find that the bees mistake red for dark grey or black. They cannot distinguish between them. Thus it appears that red is not a color at all for bees; for them it is just dark grey or black. In reality further experiments have shown that bees can see red as a color but only when it is very brilliantly illuminated: They are relatively insensitive to red.

That is one strange fact: here is the other. A rainbow is red on one edge, violet on the other. Outside the violet of the rainbow there is another color which we cannot see at all. The color beyond the violet, invisible to us, is called the ultra-violet. Although invisible, we know that the ultra-violet is there because it affects a photographic plate. Now, although we are unable to see ultra-violet light, bees can do so; for them ultra-violet is a color. Thus bees see a color which we cannot even imagine. This has been found out by training bees to come for syrup to various different parts of a spectrum, or artificial rainbow, thrown by a quartz prism on a table in a dark room. In such an experiment the insects can be taught to fly to the ultra-violet, which for us is just darkness.

We will leave the bees now and turn to birds. Cocks have striking colors in their plumage — striking to us, at any rate — while hens only possess dull tints. But can hens see the colors of the cock as we can see them? Can the peahen, for instance, see the wonderful colors of the peacock? To answer this question we must know what colors a bird can actually see. This has been studied in the following manner. A lamp and prism are set up to throw a spectrum of rainbow colors on the floor of a dark room. On the different colors of the spectrum grains of corn are sprinkled, and then a hen is brought in. She pecks at the grains of corn and gobbles up all she can see. After a time we remove the hen and take note of what grains are left untouched by her. We find that the hen has eaten nearly all the grains which were in the red, in the yellow, and in the green regions of the spectrum. We find that she has taken a few of the grains in the blue light, but the hen leaves the grains in the violet untouched. This means that she cannot see the grains which are in the violet light, and she is not able to see those in the blue very well either, for she did not pick up many of them. So violet is just like black to the hen, and blue is not a very bright color.

This has been confirmed with homing pigeons on which colored spectacles were fitted; with red and yellow specs the birds flew home normally, but with green, and especially blue, they were unable to do so. A human being could see clearly through the blue celluloid of which the spectacles were made, but evidently blue is like a black-out to the bird, and it is well known that homing pigeons cannot find their way in dim light or darkness.

Other birds are like this, too, which seems strange at first, because some birds are themselves blue. The kingfisher, for instance, is blue. Are we to conclude that the kingfisher is unable to see the beautiful color of its mate? This does not follow; the kingfisher can probably see his mate's blue plumage, for our experiments do not show that birds are unable to see blue at all. Birds just do not see this color very well; for them to see blue, the blue must be intense. And indeed the color of the kingfisher is very bright. Yet it is not all birds that have such difficulty in seeing blue; owls, on the contrary, are more sensitive than we ourselves to the blue end of the spectrum.

And what can dogs see? The answer to this question is disappointing: dogs apparently see no colors. The answer is disappointing because many owners of dogs will naturally be sorry that their dogs cannot see colors which to them are beautiful. But then, they may reflect that dogs have an extraordinarily keen sense of smell. The dogs' world is rich in enjoyable smells, even if it may be colorless.

How do we know if dogs are color-blind? This has been tested in the same way that it has been discovered what dogs can hear. The attempt has been made to train dogs to salivate when they are shown certain different colors, just as they were trained so that their mouths watered when definite musical notes were sounded. Such experiments have turned out failures; it has been found impossible to make dogs distinguish colors from one another as signals for their dinner. This question requires further testing with other techniques, but so far as the available scientific evidence goes, dogs seem to be color-blind. Many dog-owners will disagree with this, being convinced that their dogs know, for instance, the color of a dress. But the evidence given for this has never been sufficiently rigid for a scientist, who is not certain that the dog did not really respond to some other clue or sign than the color — to a smell, for instance, or to the particular behavior of the wearer of the dress.

Experiments have been made, too, to test the color-sense of cats; although these experiments may not yet be conclusive, they have indicated, so far, that cats are color-blind. Different cats were trained to come for their food in response to signals of each of six different colors. But the cats always confused their particular color with one of a number of shades of grey, when these were offered at the same time as the color.

Monkeys, on the other hand, are able to distinguish colors. They have been trained successfully to go for their meal to a cupboard, the door of which was painted in a certain color, and to ignore other available cupboards with differently colored doors, in which there was no food. Apart from monkeys and apes, however, most mammals seem to be color-blind, at any rate those which have been scientifically tested. Even bulls have been shown not to see red as a color. In spite of popular belief they are not excited by red, and they cannot distinguish red from dark grey. No doubt any bright waving cloth excites a high-spirited bull.

Color-blindness in mammals, other than monkeys, is comprehensible when one considers the lives of the animals in a wild state. For nearly all wild mammals are nocturnal or crepuscular. Wolves and lions hunt mostly at night, while antelopes and wild cattle graze at night, or in the evening when colors are dim. But monkeys, in the forests where they live, are awake and about in the daytime, and there are abundant colors for them to see in the bright tropical light.

Moreover, the color-blindness of mammals other than monkeys accords with the fact that the animals themselves are more or less dull colored; their coats are brown or yellow, black or white. Only in monkeys are greens, bright reds, and blues found. These are colors which recall the brilliant tints of birds and of fish, animals which also possess color-vision.

The Thinking of Men and Machines

John H. Troll

1

The uneasy, half-embarrassed rivalry between man and machine has reached a peak with the thinking machine. We have become used to machines that are more powerful, more durable, more accurate, and faster than we are, but machines that challenge our intelligence are hard to take. At this point the competition becomes uncomfortable.

Machines and tools have always been created in the image of man. The hammer grew from the balled fist, the rake from the hand with fingers outstretched for scratching, the shovel from the hand hollowed to scoop. As machines became more than simple tools, outstripping their creators in performance, demanding and obtaining increasing amounts of power, and acquiring superhuman speeds and accuracies, their outward resemblance to the natural model disappeared; only the names of the machine's parts show vestiges of their human origin. The highly complex machinery of the modern industrial age has arms that swing, fingers that fold, legs that support, teeth that grind, and male and female parts that mate. Machines feed on material, run when things go well, and spit and cough when they don't.

But the newest machines possess human traits that had always been considered far beyond mechanization. Here we find not only electric eyes that see and sensing devices that feel, but also memories that recall and logic sections that classify, arrange, and select. These machines can make choices, comparisons, and decisions, learn from past ex-

THE THINKING OF MEN AND MACHINES: From *The Atlantic Monthly*, July 1954. Reprinted by permission of the author.

perience, and reach logical conclusions on the basis of premises. It may no longer be denied: these machines can really think.

This realization has renewed the furtive rivalry between man and machine. The battle is being fought underground because even to conceed the existence of such a contest would be undignified. Like a small child jealous of the attention paid a puppy, men do not often admit openly that this inhuman contrivance of nuts and bolts and evilly gleaming electron tubes is a threat. But as the child will get even with the puppy by tweaking its tail when no one is looking, so man, consciously or unconsciously, likes to throw monkey wrenches into machines and see them get their comeuppance.

Newspaper editors a few years back felt that there would be interest in a story about a Japanese arithmetician who, with an abacus — a simple device made of a few counting beads — won a race against a mechanical calculating machine. The story was prominently featured in the world press. If the mechanical calculator had won, there would have been no story.

No one likes to depend on a rival. Consequently there is a general desire to distrust and by-pass machines. Pilots during the Second World War preferred to fly by the seat of their pants — a device so notoriously insensitive that it won't tell the pilot when he flies upside down — rather than by their highly precise and reliable instruments. Many posters and disciplinary actions were necessary to make pilots use their instruments.

When Univac, one of the computers used on election night, made an amazingly accurate prediction of the outcome on the basis of very early returns, it was disbelieved by the experts who designed and constructed it. Even when by all rational standards it becomes evident that the machine knows better, man is reluctant to let it have the last word.

An even more telling sign of this half-secret battle of man and the technical monster of his creation is the character of the Utopias of our time. Where Thomas More of the sixteenth century and Edward Bellamy of the nineteenth found ideal, beautifully harmonious societies in their imaginary travels, with satisfactory solutions to the pressing problems of their days, George Orwell and Aldous Huxley in our age see only a nightmarishly heightened outgrowth of the modern world. In their Utopias, standardization, an integral part of the machine culture, extends to the hygienically controlled production of humans; machines take all the major roles in human enjoyment, dominating even sex and simple sports; machines write all novels and plays and newspapers and create all art and entertainment; machines watch and spy day and night, destroying all vestiges of human individuality. Is the arrival of the thinking machine the first sign that these nightmares are about to become a reality? Is man hopelessly outmatched in this bout with the machine?

Take for instance the calculation involved in the design of photographic lenses. Before the arrival of computers, one could design lenses by painstaking pencil and paper work. By this method an experienced lens designer took about six years to design one of the complicated lenses. The desk calculator cut this time to about fifteen weeks, and now a giant computer like the Bureau of Standards SEEAC does the job in a single hour.

2

Let us look at this lens design problem a little closer to learn something about the way such a machine operates. A good optical lens like those used in the best cameras differs from simple lenses or from eyeglasses mainly in that it consists of many glasses of various shapes all cemented together. The designers must prescribe the exact shape of each of these glasses making up a lens so that all rays originating from a point, say from a star we want to photograph, will meet in another point behind the lens, forming an image of the star. Actually, these rays cannot be made to meet in a point, which would be ideal, but will all fall within a circle. The smaller the circle, the better defined the image and the better the lens.

The design procedure is part calculation, part trial and error. There are, of course, an infinite number of angles at which the rays may enter the lens. A good many of these must be traced through the lens. That is, we must find the change in angle for each ray as it enters and leaves each glass. As a result, we know the angle of the ray when it leaves the last glass surface and therefore where it will meet the other rays. Though the arithmetical procedure to find these changes of angles for each ray is not complicated, it requires accuracies to about seven decimals, and many rays have to be considered. After all the required rays are traced we find the diameter of the circle within which they meet. If we find it small enough to suit our requirements, the job is done. But if it appears too large, we must change by a slight amount one of the shapes of the glass surfaces. Now we trace all the rays for the new condition and see whether we have improved the design or made it worse. It used to take a man six years to complete such a job.

How much of this work can the computer take over for us? Almost all of it. It requires only an adequate set of instructions. These must contain a formula which shows what the angle of a ray is when leaving a surface if we know the angle of entrance, some properties of the glass, the shape of the surface, and the color of the ray. In addition, the instructions tell the computer how good a lens it must design and what initial shapes to start with.

Next, we tell the machine how to proceed. Our program may read: " Start with a ray 45° off to the center axis. Figure its entrance and exit angles through each of the eleven surfaces. Note the angle of exit from the last surface; do the same with the ray at 44°, then 43°, and so forth, in intervals of one degree until the ray at 0° has been traced. Compare the resulting circle where the rays meet with the desired one; if it is the same size or smaller, print out the answer; if it is larger, change the shape of the first surface and repeat the ray tracing. If the new answer is better than the old one but still not right, change the surface again in the same direction. If the new answer is worse, change in the opposite direction. When the best answer is still not right, change the second surface the same way, and so through all other surfaces until the answer is right."

The actual instructions to the computer appear not in words but in a mathematical shorthand written on magnetic tape or in the form of punched holes in a paper tape very much like the good old player piano roll — quite a remarkable device in days when no one thought of computers. It could memorize long piano pieces, know which notes to play, when and how loud, and yet no one worried about its being a thinking machine.

Now that the machine has received its instructions, it can go to work. Strangely enough, it performs in an eerie silence. There are no motors whirring, no bells clanging, not even a hum as it races through millions of trial-and-error calculations with a speed that is literally close to that of lightning. Only the even red glow of the tubes shows that anything is going on. When the computer is finished, there is the clacking of an electric typewriter printing out the solution.

If anything goes wrong, the machine stops and types out what is the matter. Often it can tell which of its many tubes has failed or what additional information it requires to complete the problem. Most computers are designed so that they never give wrong answers; if something fails, the machine gives no answer. Once an answer is printed, you can depend upon it. Moreover, computers constantly check their work and will repeat any calculation that appears incorrect.

Can we call such a process thinking? We have seen that it involves remembering, sorting, classifying, and choosing alternatives on the basis of logic. When men do this sort of work, it has always been considered thinking. And so in fairness to the machine we must concede that within the usual meaning of the word it can and does think. And since in the course of its work the machine discards solutions in favor of better ones, acting on past experience, it cannot be denied that it also learns. Since it thinks fast, it learns fast — much faster than man. Moreover, it makes no mistakes and while working on a problem never forgets. Does this mean that the machine is more intelligent than man?

To state it generally, today's thinking machines are in their element and truly superior to men when they draw conclusions about particular cases to which a general rule applies. There are computers in development that can make quick and accurate strategic decisions in air battles, taking into consideration the positions of the friendly and enemy aircraft — provided they are given a basic tactical rule they can follow. And by the same token, there is no reason why tomorrow's computer could not predict the sales volume for an article corrected for season, weather, the general state of prosperity, Mr. Dior's dictates, and the prevailing feminine mood, as long as it has past sales trends that it can use as a rule.

But the unquestioned obedience to the initial rules which makes for the machine's superhuman precision also sets a limit to its general intelligence. For the results of its thinking can only be as good as the rules that it has been taught to follow. If the rules showed themselves to be totally wrong for the situation, the machine would cling to them stubbornly, threatening, like the broom of the sorcerer's apprentice, destruction for its master and itself.

3

There is another kind of thinking — the thinking that sees relations between individual events and forms rules on this basis, and, having formed them, discards or modifies what no longer fits. Men do this kind of thinking so effortlessly that we often do not even consider it thought. If we see a circle, for instance, we immediately recognize it as such regardless of its material or its size. We need not examine each point on the circle separately and compare it with a formula. Moreover, we can tell things that are approximately circular without much strain. Machines cannot sense shapes that are not given point by point or as a mathematical formula.

It is this form of thinking that we use when we recognize someone on the street. We do not, computer fashion, check a lot of details: " 5 feet 7 inches tall, size 32 blouse, brown eyes, blond hair, arm length 33 inches, finger lengths 3 inches, 4 inches," and so forth; we can say immediately, " Hello, Mary." It matters little whether Mary has lost or gained weight, has grown taller or dyed her hair. In fact, we need no precise quantitative information about her at all. On a purely statistical basis, the amount of information required to distinguish her definitely among the 75 million females living in this country would be formidable. Yet we need to know astonishingly little to be quite certain that this is Mary. We may recognize her on a cold winter day though she is covered with bulky clothes from head to foot and nothing shows but the tip of a red nose — or we might recognize her from the rear without even this meager clue. People can recognize one another at unexpected meetings after twenty years, when they have last seen one another in grammar school and when they have grown, acquired beards or figures, changed their voices and their clothing — when, in fact, not a particle of their bodies is the same.

Despite the nearly miraculous feat involved in recognition, it requires no outstanding mental ability. Children and even pets are quite good at it. Yet such an activity exceeds the capabilities of the most complex thinking machines. It depends entirely on forming a general picture, an idea — something more than a simple checking off, or adding, or averaging of all the individual parts.

How we form such ideas or generalizations has always been considered one of the most puzzling aspects of the human mind. The ancient Greeks and particularly Plato saw it closely related to the recognition process. He believed that true reality in the form of ideas was stored in a place visited by man's soul before birth, and that the earthly realization of particular objects was a recall of memories acquired during this prenatal experience. Ideas can not only serve in helping us to recognize what we have seen but can be applied to predict the unknown on the basis of similarity. A cab driver in New York told me that he was able to cut his working day to a respectable eight hours while most of his colleagues had to work ten or twelve. Yet he made just as much money and had as many fares as they did. His secret: he learned to recognize the peculiar characteristics of people making up their minds to take a cab. He could spot such people in a crowd or walking out of a building. Before he let me off, he pointed to a man who was just walking along and said, " He wants a cab." He pulled up next to him and the man got in as I got out.

Most good salesmen know who can be called by his first name and slapped on the back after a few minutes' acquaintance and who must always be addressed as " Mr." and treated with formality. Confidence men are very adept at determining what kind of man makes a good " mark," and they don't have at their disposal a set of standardized psychological tests. Their occupation is safe from the intrusion of the thinking machine.

All of us form definite first impressions and adjust our behavior accordingly. We feel whether the new acquaintance is friendly, whether he is a threat or harmless, whether he is bright or dull, and how we may best be able to get along with him. We recognize and adjust to behavior just as we recognize a person, not by the busy examination of many detailed facts but by organizing these facts into a new entity.

A similar process is involved when a doctor makes a diagnosis. There are really an infinite number of possible diseases that a doctor may be faced with, and if he had to proceed entirely on serial examination of all the symptoms, most of his patients would die — most likely of old age — before he was able to make a single diagnosis; yet the good diagnostician often identifies a disease immediately, and at other times requires only relatively few specific tests to come to a conclusion. His mental picture of the disease is a whole, not a collection of many details, and he can therefore recognize it when he sees something that matches this mental picture.

A singular human attribute is not only the formation of ideas but the ability to connect such ideas in a useful fashion. The human memory is a filing system that has a far greater capacity than that of the largest thinking machine built. A mechanical brain that had as many tubes or relays as the human brain has nerve cells (some ten billion) would not fit into the Empire State Building, and would require the entire output of Niagara Falls to supply the power and the Niagara River to cool it. Moreover, such a computer could operate but a fraction of a second at a time before several thousand of its tubes would fail and have to be replaced.

One of the largest of today's computers, the Eniac, has about 10,000 tubes and has therefore about as many brain cells as a flatworm.

The human brain, with one million times as many cells, is unique not only for its ability to store vast amounts of information in a small storage space and for requiring vanishing amounts of operating power, but also for the speed and ease with which any remembered item can be produced. The human filing system is so flexible that it can be reshuffled instantly from an infinity of new viewpoints. The most elaborate filing systems or library catalogues are arranged by author, subject, and sometimes date of publication, with cross references between these files. The human file of ideas, however, classifies each idea in an infinite variety of ways; the word " red " can be connected with " green " or " hot " or " blush " or " Skelton" or " Communist " or " blood " or " herring," to mention only a few. Computers can refer to their memories only in a systematic fashion well planned and explained beforehand but cannot create new cross indexing for themselves.

Yet connection of ideas forms an important aspect of thinking. Without it, Newton could not have associated the apocryphal apple with the motion of the planets because the cross index, " apple falling

— *see* rate — *see* square law — *see* planets' motion," had not existed. Nor could Norbert Wiener and Shannon have seen that there is a similarity between the way a message loses intelligibility in transmission and an object loses heat to the surrounding area. Nor could physicists have seen that there are similarities in the ways sound, light, and heat behave, so that picturing them as waves would work for all. Nor could Freud have recognized a connection between accidental slips of the tongue and jokes, dreams, and neuroses.

The sort of thinking that can be called truly creative is such forming and organizing of ideas and the connecting of these ideas into new larger entities. And this is precisely what falls beyond the computer's scope. With its electronics, memories, logic systems, lightning speeds, accuracy, and infaliibility, a computer cannot create an idea or ask a question that could form a basis for a new outlook.

Nor does it seem likely that tomorrow's computers will do this. The machines of the future may overcome some of the other handicaps, such as their enormous size and power requirements. There are signs that they may even beget their own kind — but never ideas.

True, a computer could be designed which would randomly and madly connect all sorts of facts and then test them for internal consistencies. It would certainly come up with a million theories. But it would have no criterion for selecting the ones that are meaningful.

For what is meaningful is a function of man's need to survive and to create a world for himself that he can manage physically and mentally.

Thinking machines, more than any other invention in the history of mankind, can aid this creation of a workable and understandable environment by checking man's ideas for validity and internal consistency, by saving him millions of trials and errors, and by speeding up immeasurably the acquisition of new facts and knowledge. But it always takes a human to come up with the approach, the generalization, the idea which furnishes the basis for the machine's lightning checking, applying, and finding of new facts. How such basic ideas are conceived we do not know. Yet only they can be called truly creative thought — a process which must forever remain in the province of the human spirit. The bad dreams of our Utopians will not come true; even the most complex, advanced thinking machines will not replace or dominate this spirit.

Dawn over Zero

William L. Laurence

The Atomic Age began at exactly 5.30 mountain war time on the morning of July 16, 1945, on a stretch of semi-desert land about fifty air-line miles from Alamogordo, New Mexico, just a few minutes before the dawn of a new day on that part of the earth. At that great moment in history, ranking with the moment when man first put fire to work for him, the vast energy locked within the heart of the atoms of matter was released for the first time in a burst of flame such as had never before been seen on this planet, illuminating earth and sky, for a brief span that seemed eternal, with the light of many super-suns.

The elemental flame, first fire ever made on earth that did not have its origin in the sun, came from the explosion of the first atomic bomb. It was a full-dress rehearsal preparatory to dropping the bomb over Hiroshima and Nagasaki — and other Japanese military targets, had Japan refused to accept the Potsdam Declaration for her surrender.

The rehearsal marked the climax in the penultimate act of one of the greatest dramas in our history and the history of civilized man — a drama in which our scientists, under the direction of the Army Corps of Engineers, were working against time to create an atomic bomb ahead of our German enemy. The collapse of Germany marked the end of the first act of this drama. The successful completion of our task, in the greatest challenge by man to nature so far, brought down the curtain on the second act. The grand finale came three weeks after-

DAWN OVER ZERO: Reprinted from the book *Dawn over Zero* by William L. Laurence, by permission of Alfred A. Knopf, Inc. Copyright 1946 by William L. Laurence.

ward in the skies over Japan, with a swift descent of the curtain on the greatest war in history.

The atomic flash in New Mexico came as a great affirmation to the prodigious labors of our scientists during the past four years. It came as the affirmative answer to the until then unanswered question: " Will it work? "

With the flash came a delayed roll of mighty thunder, heard, just as the flash was seen, for hundreds of miles. The roar echoed and reverberated from the distant hills and the Sierra Oscuro range near by, sounding as though it came from some supramundane source as well as from the bowels of the earth. The hills said yes and the mountains chimed in yes. It was as if the earth had spoken and the suddenly iridescent clouds and sky had joined in one affirmative answer. Atomic energy — yes. It was like the grand finale of a mighty symphony of the elements, fascinating and terrifying, uplifting and crushing, ominous, devastating, full of great promise and great forebodings.

I watched the birth of the era of atomic power from the slope of a hill in the desert land of New Mexico, on the northwestern corner of Alamogordo Air Base, about 125 miles southeast of Albuquerque. The hill, named Compania Hill for the occasion, was twenty miles to the northwest of Zero, the code name given to the spot chosen for the atomic bomb test. The area embracing Zero and Compania Hill, twenty-four miles long and eighteen miles wide, had the code name Trinity.

I joined a caravan of three busses, three automobiles, and a truck carrying radio equipment at 11 P.M. on Sunday, July 15, at Albuquerque. There were about ninety of us in that strange caravan, traveling silently and in the utmost secrecy through the night on probably as unusual an adventure as any in our day. With the exception of myself the caravan consisted of scientists from the highly secret atomic bomb research and development center in the mesas and canyons of New Mexico, twenty-five miles northwest of Santa Fe, where we solved the secret of translating the fabulous energy of the atom into the mightiest weapon ever made by man. It was from there that the caravan set out at 5.30 that Sunday afternoon for its destination, 212 miles to the south.

The caravan wound its way slowly over the tortuous roads overlooking the precipitous canyons of northern New Mexico, passing through Espagnola, Santa Fe, and Bernalillo, arriving at Albuquerque at about 10 P.M. Here it was joined by Sir James Chadwick, who won the Nobel Prize and knighthood for his discovery of the neutron, the key that unlocks the atom; Professor Ernest O. Lawrence of the University of California, master atom-smasher, who won the Nobel Prize for his discovery of the cyclotron; Professor Edwin M. McMillan, also of the University of California, one of the discoverers of plutonium, the new atomic energy element; and several others from the atomic bomb center, who, like me, had arrived during the afternoon.

The night was dark with black clouds, and not a star could be seen. Occasionally a bolt of lightning would rend the sky and reveal for an instant the flat semi-desert landscape, rich with historic lore of past adventure. We rolled along on U. S. Highway 85, running between Albuquerque and El Paso, through sleeping ancient Spanish-American towns, their windows dark, their streets deserted — towns with music in their names, Los Lunas, Belen, Bernardo, Alamillo, Socorro, San Antonio. At San Antonio we turned east and crossed " the bridge on the Rio Grande with the detour in the middle of it." From there we traveled ten and one half miles eastward on U. S. Highway 380, and then turned south on a specially built dirt road, running for twenty-five miles to the base camp at Trinity.

The end of our trail was reached after we had covered about five and one fifth miles on the dirt road. Here we saw the first signs of life since leaving Albuquerque about three hours earlier, a line of silent men dressed in helmets. A little farther on, a detachment of military police examined our special credentials. We got out of the busses and looked around us. The night was still pitch-black save for an occasional flash of lightning in the eastern sky, outlining for a brief instant the Sierra Oscuro Range directly ahead of us. We were in the middle of the New Mexico desert, miles away from nowhere, with hardly a sign of life, not even a blinking light on the distant horizon. This was to be our caravansary until the zero hour.

From a distance to the southeast the beam of a searchlight probed the clouds. This gave us our first sense of orientation. The bomb-test site, Zero, was a little to the left of the searchlight beam, twenty miles away. With the darkness and the waiting in the chill of the desert the tension became almost unendurable.

We gathered in a circle to listen to directions on what we were to do at the time of the test, directions read aloud by the light of a flashlight:

At a short signal of the siren at minus five minutes to zero, " all personnel whose duties did not specifically require otherwise " were to prepare " a suitable place to lie down on." At a long signal of the sirens at minus two minutes to zero, " all personnel whose duties did not specifically require otherwise " were to " lie prone on the ground immediately, the face and eyes directed toward the ground and with the head away from Zero. Do not watch for the flash directly," the directions read, " but turn over after it has occurred and watch the cloud. Stay on the ground until the blast wave has passed (two minutes). At two short blasts of the siren, indicating the passing of all hazard from light and blast, all personnel will prepare to leave as soon as possible.

" The hazard from blast is reduced by lying down on the ground in such a manner that flying rocks, glass and other objects do not intervene between the source of blast and the individual. Open all car windows.

" The hazard from light injury to eyes is reduced by shielding the closed eyes with the bended arms and lying face down on the ground. If the first flash is viewed a ' blind spot ' may prevent your seeing the rest of the show.

" The hazard from ultraviolet light injuries to the skin is best overcome by wearing long trousers and shirts with long sleeves."

David Dow, assistant to the scientific director of the Atomic Bomb Development Center, handed each of us a flat piece of colored glass such as is used by arc welders to shield their eyes. Dr. Edward Teller of George Washington University cautioned us against sunburn. Someone produced sunburn lotion and passed it around. It was an eerie sight to see a number of our highest-ranking scientists seriously rubbing sunburn lotion on their faces and hands in the pitch-blackness of the night, twenty miles away from the expected flash. These were the men who, more than anybody else, knew the potentialities of atomic energy on the loose. It gave one an inkling of their confidence in their handiwork.

The bomb was set on a structural steel tower one hundred feet high. Ten miles away to the southwest was the base camp. This was G.H.Q. for the scientific high command, of which Professor Kenneth T. Bainbridge of Harvard University was field commander. Here were erected barracks to serve as living-quarters for the scientists, a mess hall, a commissary, a post exchange, and other buildings. Here the vanguard of the atomists, headed by Professor J. R. Oppenheimer of the University of California, scientific director of the Atomic Bomb Project, lived like soldiers at the front, supervising the enormously complicated details involved in the epoch-making tests.

Here early that Sunday afternoon gathered Major General Leslie R. Groves, commander in chief of the Atomic Bomb Project; Brigadier General T. F. Farrell, hero of World War I, General Groves's deputy; Professor Enrico Fermi, Nobel Prize winner and one of the leaders in the project; President James Bryant Conant of Harvard; Dr. Vannevar Bush, director of the Office of Scientific Research and Development; Dean Richard C. Tolman of the California Institute of Technology; Professor R. F. Bacher of Cornell; Colonel Stafford L. Warren, University of Rochester radiologist; and about a hundred and fifty other leaders in the atomic bomb program.

At the Base Camp was a dry, abandoned reservoir, about five hundred feet square, surrounded by a mound of earth about eight feet high. Within this mound bulldozers dug a series of slit trenches, each about three feet deep, seven feet wide, and twenty-five feet long. At a command over the radio at zero minus one minute all observers at Base Camp, lay down in their assigned trenches, " face and eyes directed toward the ground and with the head away from Zero." But most of us on Compania Hill remained on our feet.

Three other posts had been established, south, north, and west of Zero, each at a distance of 10,000 yards (5.7 miles). These were known, respectively, as South-10,000, North-10,000, and West-10,000, or S-10, N-10, and W-10. Here the shelters were much more elaborate — wooden structures, their walls reinforced by cement, buried under a massive layer of earth.

S-10 was the control center. Here Professor Oppenheimer, as scientific commander in chief, and his field commander, Professor Bainbridge, issued orders and synchronized the activities of the other sites. Here the signal was given and a complex of mechanisms was set in motion that resulted in the greatest burst of energy ever released by man on earth up to that time. No switch was pulled, no button pressed, to light this first cosmic fire on this planet.

At forty-five seconds to zero, set for 5.30 o'clock, young Dr. Joseph L. McKibben of the University of California, at a signal from Professor Bainbridge, activated a master robot that set off a series of other robots, until, at last, strategically spaced electrons moved to the proper place at the proper split second.

Forty-five seconds passed and the moment was zero.

Meanwhile at our observation post on Compania Hill the atmosphere had grown tenser as the zero hour approached. We had spent the first part of our stay eating an early morning picnic breakfast that we had taken along with us. It had grown cold in the desert, and many of us, lightly clad, shivered. Occasionally a drizzle came down, and the intermittent flashes of lightning made us turn apprehensive glances toward Zero. We had had some disturbing reports that the test might be called off because of the weather. The radio we had brought with us for communication with Base Camp kept going out of order, and when we had finally repaired it some blatant band would drown out the news we wanted to hear. We knew there were two specially equipped B-29 Superfortresses high overhead to make observations and recordings in the upper atmosphere, but we could neither see nor hear them. We kept gazing through the blackness.

Suddenly, at 5.29.50, as we stood huddled around our radio, we heard a voice ringing through the darkness, sounding as though it had come from above the clouds: " Zero minus ten seconds! " A green flare flashed out through the clouds, descended slowly, opened, grew dim, and vanished into the darkness.

The voice from the clouds boomed out again: " Zero minus three seconds! " Another green flare came down. Silence reigned over the desert. We kept moving in small groups in the direction of Zero. From the east came the first faint signs of dawn.

And just at that instant there rose from the bowels of the earth a light not of this world, the light of many suns in one. It was a sunrise such as the world had never seen, a great green super-sun climbing in a fraction of a second to a height of more than eight thousand feet, rising ever higher until it touched the clouds, lighting up earth and sky all around with a dazzling luminosity.

Up it went, a great ball of fire about a mile in diameter, changing colors as it kept shooting upward, from deep purple to orange, expanding, growing bigger, rising as it expanded, an elemental force freed from its bonds after being chained for billions of years. For a fleeting instant the color was unearthly green, such as one sees only in the corona of the sun during a total eclipse. It was as though the earth had opened and the skies had split. One felt as though one were present at the moment of creation when God said: " Let there be light."

To another observer, Professor George B. Kistiakowsky of Harvard, the spectacle was " the nearest thing to doomsday that one could possibly imagine. I am sure," he said, " that at the end of the world — in the last millisecond of the earth's existence — the last man will see what we have just seen! "

A great cloud rose from the ground and followed the trail of the great sun. At first it was a giant column, which soon took the shape of a supramundane mushroom. For a fleeting instant it took the form of the Statue of Liberty magnified many times. Up it went, higher, higher, a giant mountain born in a few seconds instead of millions of years, quivering convulsively. It touched the multicolored clouds, pushed its summit through them, kept rising until it reached a height of 41,000 feet, 12,000 feet higher than the earth's highest mountain.

All through this very short but extremely long time-interval not a sound was heard. I could see the silhouettes of human forms motionless in little groups, like desert plants in the dark. The newborn mountain in the distance, a giant among the pygmies of the Sierra Oscuro Range, stood leaning at an angle against the clouds, a vibrant volcano spouting fire to the sky.

WILLIAM L. LAURENCE / 495

Then out of the great silence came a mighty thunder. For a brief interval the phenomena we had seen as light repeated themselves in terms of sound. It was the blast from thousands of blockbusters going off simultaneously at one spot. The thunder reverberated all through the desert, bounced back and forth from the Sierra Oscuro, echo upon echo. The ground trembled under our feet as in an earthquake. A wave of hot wind was felt by many of us just before the blast and warned us of its coming.

The big boom came about one hundred seconds after the great flash — the first cry of a newborn world. It brought the silent, motionless silhouettes to life, gave them a voice. A loud cry filled the air. The little groups that had hitherto stood rooted to the earth like desert plants broke into a dance — the rhythm of primitive man dancing at one of his fire festivals at the coming of spring. They clapped their hands as they leaped from the ground — earthbound man symbolizing the birth of a new force that for the first time gives man means to free himself from the gravitational pull of the earth that holds him down.

The dance of the primitive man lasted but a few seconds, during which an evolutionary period of about 10,000 years had been telescoped. Primitive man was metamorphosed into modern man — shaking hands, slapping his fellow on the back, all laughing like happy children.

The sun was just rising above the horizon as our caravan started on its way back to Albuquerque and Los Alamos. We looked at it through our dark lenses to compare it with what we had seen.

" The sun can't hold a candle to it! " one of us remarked.

The Hickman Story

John Bartlow Martin

1

The oldest son of the Hickman family, Willis, twenty years old, went to the barber shop after work and got home about 8:15, and then they all were home who were coming home that night, the seven children and the parents. Another son was working. The father, James Hickman, a cleancut Negro of thirty-nine, serious of mien and small

THE HICKMAN STORY: Copyright 1948 by John Bartlow Martin. Reprinted by permission of Harold Ober Associates.

but tightly-knit of body, was getting ready to go to his night job. He " had bad feet " and he sent Willis to the floor below to get a bucket of water to bathe them. (The Hickmans had no running water in their attic room atop the tenement.) About nine o'clock Hickman left for the steelmill. He was the head of this family.

Willis, and Charles, who was nineteen, and their mother helped the younger children with their lessons. The three in school — Leslie, fourteen, Elzena, nine, and Sylvester, seven — were really studying and Velvena was playing at studying, though she was only four. After half an hour Mrs. Hickman, a thin quiet woman, went to bed. Soon the four younger children crawled in with her. Willis and Charles got into the other bed, first turning off the kerosene heater, cookstove, and lamp. They all fell asleep. It was then about 10:00 P.M. on January 16, 1947.

An hour and a half later Mrs. Hickman was wakened by fire. " I heard the paper popping " in the ceiling. She ran to the door to the only stairway and " the fire and the smoke hit me, fire came right to me, in the face," and she slammed the door and went to get the children up. Charles leaped through the fiery doorway naked and escaped down the stairs. Mrs. Hickman was about to collapse. Willis wakened, " fire was over my head, in the door, I threw the cover back, and burned my hand." He rolled out of bed, crawled beneath the smoke to the front window, kicked it out, started out, hesitated, looked back.

Dimly through the smoke and flame he saw his mother huddled in the corner near her four smallest children. The flames were upon them. He pulled her to the window. It was three floors straight down the bare face of the old brick tenement to the street. He straddled the sill and hung her outside and told her to kick out the glass on the third floor below. She was too short, so Willis climbed out and, hanging by one hand, lowered her down. She scrambled to the second-floor window. He grabbed the third-floor window frame, but it gave way and he fell to the ground, breaking his collar bone and leaving her dangling. A man below yelled to her to let go, and she did, and he caught her. Later a fire chief said, " I cannot understand how she escaped . . . it was a miracle," and the coroner said, " The Lord was with her." But her four children were dead.

The night was cold, snow lay on the ground, but a great crowd gathered, this was a slum fire. Other tenants of the building streamed out, maybe forty of them. Neighbors took Mrs. Hickman and Willis to the hospital. The fire chief recalled, " It was a holocaust, it was one mass of fire rolling across that roof." But the firemen put it out in five minutes. Soon the street in the slum was deserted again.

Hours later, about 7:30 in the morning, gray daylight, a man alone came walking up the street, James Hickman the father. He had been told at work that he " had trouble in my home." Out in front of the tenement a man was tinkering with an automobile, he had the hood up, and another man was pouring water over the steps of the building. Hickman started upstairs, ". . . a policeman hailed me and asked where I was going. I said I was going upstairs where I live. ' You can't go up there,' he said. ' Man, you tell me I can't go up there, what's the trouble? I am James Hickman, I live there.' " The policeman asked cautiously what floor he lived on. " I said the fourth and he said, ' Ah, you can't go up there, we had a big fire.' I asked him where were my children, he said he didn't know." Another tenant had appeared. " He said, ' Mr. Hickman, I hate to tell you this, four of your children is burnt to death.' And I weakened down to the ground." They carried him into the basement. Presently, Hickman recalls, " My mind referred back." He remembered that his landlord David Coleman, had threatened to burn down the building if the tenants didn't clear out. A neighbor recalls, " Mr. Hickman was walking back and forth. He said nothing. There were tears in his eyes. Mr. Hickman looked pretty bad, like he was losing his mind. After about one half-hour, some officers helped Mr. Hickman away."

Our story is about James Hickman, a Negro. It is about his landlord, David Coleman, likewise a Negro, and their combat. It is also about slums and housing and race discrimination, the plight of the Negroes in the northern ghettos, the segregation that keeps them there and generates explosions, explosions like this fire and what came after it.

James Hickman, a man of rich brown color, was born February 19, 1907, " in the country " near Louisville, Mississippi. His mother and father were sharecroppers raising cotton and corn. They lived in a four-room shack. He was the youngest of four children; one was killed, the others left. At ten he went to work in the fields. At twelve he experienced a religious conversion. Forever after he was deeply religious. His mother and father separated when he was fourteen and he quit school. At sixteen he married a neighbor girl, Annie Davis. They lived with his mother and took care of her; she had tuberculosis. (She died in 1926 and for half a year Hickman grieved.) Their first child was born on August 2, 1924. They named her Arlene and Hickman made a vow to God: " I was the head of this family and had to make a support for them, I was a guardian to see for them as long as the days I should live on the land." He was then seventeen.

They moved to Fern Spring, " sharecropping cotton and corn, and vegetables for ourselves," his wife remembers. " We started farming at sun-up and stopped at sun-down. We were in the hilly part of Mississippi. I chopped cotton myself. . . ." They moved often, making a crop and giving birth to a child, then moving on, trying to better their lot. Some owners were fair, some were not. " We never could own the land." They moved to the Delta, land of milk and honey. They farmed the Delta seventeen years. One year, 1942, they made $935, their greatest earnings in the South. Before the war they often made only $100, one year $28, some years nothing at all. When they had a bad year "the bossmen . . . claimed that the cotton prices had failed." " When we got paid, Smith and Wiggins took their money first for food, clothes, fertilizer." Hickman says, " The landlord furnished everything. But you pays for it. And he don't work."

After the children were eight or nine, they rarely attended school more than four or five months a year, sometimes only one; for if the parents didn't send them to the fields, Hickman recalls, " the landlord'd be a-grumblin'. He'd say, get 'em busy, your grass is growin', this, that, or else he'd put a bunch in the fields, and it'd come out of your pay in the fall. Work is all they look for you to do. They don't look for no school. The plow and hoe and such'll keep knowledge out of a person's head." Mrs. Hickman says, " We was very anxious to get up North where they had the opportunity to go to school and all these privileges," meaning by " privileges " freedom for a black person.

Nine children were born and the Hickmans reared them all, an achievement for Negroes in the South. One, Corene, was born blind and never talked, the only one afflicted. Hickman said, " We couldn't help her but I loved her just like I loved the rest of them." Hickman was stern with his children but he loved them with a surpassing love. Upon the birth of each he repeated his vow to God to protect them and set them free. He wanted to take them North. He felt they were destined for great things. The ones born first disappointed him. " The oldest was taken in the Army. The next one was kicked out of school. The daughter married. I said all right. These youngest children — I had told them all one night — ' It seems like I can see a future for you.' I see in those four children that they possibly would be great men and great women some day. . . . I had a vision and the spirit said they would be great."

The Navy ordered Hickman to report for induction April 12, 1944, but the day before, men of his age were exempted " until further notice." He didn't know what to do, but the North had been tugging at him for a long time, so he went up there, worked ten months in a shipyard, went back South, then in the spring of 1945 went alone to Chicago, intending to find a job and a home and to bring his family North to stay.

How did Chicago look to this countryman? He'd visited Southern cities, but Chicago was different. Bigger, of course, but more than that. "Here, it was quite different when I'd see peoples riding in the cars together, buses — in the banks and post office colored would be working," he said recently in his slow, deep, deliberate voice. His oldest daughter, who had married, was living in Chicago, and Hickman stayed with her. "A gentleman picking up labor carried us over to a place to work"; Hickman thought it was the factory where his son-in-law worked but it was the stockyards, and he left. He got a job at Wisconsin Steel, far out at the Indiana line. He worked "on the crib," guiding the hot steel as it came off the hotbed. He was paid about $1.25 an hour, an awful lot to him. Better still, "I could see what I was gittin'. On the farm I'd be charged for a lot of things, I couldn't see what it was for. In the factory work it comes to my hand."

But soon the pleasures of earning good money and riding white men's buses palled. "I would see so many old raggedy buildings I'd say my goodness, I see so many nice buildings and then others just propped, folks livin' in just to have some place to live." He was hunting a place for his family. Finding one proved difficult. Hickman was bucking what may be the nation's worst housing problem.

Chicago's Black Belt is a narrow strip of land seven miles long and a mile and a half wide on the South Side, in spots almost — but not quite — touching the gilded lakefront. This is America's second biggest Negro city. Here, and in several scattered communities, dwell 400,000 Negroes, a tenth of Chicago's population. When a housing project of 1,658 units was opened in 1941, more than 19,000 people applied to live in it. Since then about 100,000 more Negroes, drawn by the war boom and Northern freedom, have come to live in Chicago. Why do they all crowd into this one area? Poverty? Yes, to a certain extent; but well-to-do Negroes live here too. The law? No, our laws imply the opposite, freedom. Ethnological attraction, then, which draws any immigrant group together? Again, yes, to a certain extent. Ah, but here we can see the truth: the European immigrants, as their earnings and adaptation increased, scattered throughout the city, disappearing into the general population. "Disappearing" — how can a black man disappear? He is not wanted. He is condemned to inhabit the areas that nobody else wants. Around the Negroes we have welded an iron ring of restrictive covenants and less formalized segregation enforced by violence. Thus trapped they turn upon one another. In this artificially restricted market, people of means bid high for hovels; rentals skyrocket; landlords gouge. Some of the landlords are white, some are black, all profit by the race-hate that makes their hovels desired. The Black Belt landlords squeeze tighter, and sometimes an eruption occurs, as in the Hickman case.

James Hickman got off the night shift at 7:00 A.M. " I would leave the job and just ride, hunting for a place for my folks," till dark, rest a few hours, then go back to work. " Ride and ride, walk and walk. I'd knock on a door and ask. Workin' and lookin'." Ignorant of Chicago, he often got into strange neighborhoods. " Sometimes I'd get to where they wasn't nothin' but white folks, I'd be the only colored man walkin' down the street. I'd see houses and I didn't know who was living there till I'd knock on the door and they'd say white folks only. They'd tell me which hundred block was for the colored. I'd catch the car and go back and get off there." Did he experience any unpleasantness? " My race talked more rougher than the other race. I was born in a country where there's nothin' but white folks and I knowed how to talk and carry myself and they treated me mighty fine."

He found plenty of empty flats. " But they didn't want nobody with children." Even a public housing project refused him because he had so many children. Real estate offices took his money and produced nothing. Their usual fee was between $1 and $5 " to enlist," plus a month's rent if they found you a place. One landlord wanted to rent a four-room flat for $45 a month and sell the furniture for $1,200. Another asked " a thousand dollars down and $55 for twenty-five years, I didn't have that kind of money." But he had saved $260 since coming to Chicago and he was willing to pay up to $100 a month rent.

After six months, a barber offered to rent him a room in his own house. Hickman paid him a month's rent, $30, and sent train fare to his wife. She arrived with all the children on January 10, 1946, and Hickman met them at the station and took them out to their daughter's flat. Next day their furniture arrived from Mississippi, all their belongings, " meat and lard and everything but bread."

But the barber said the room wasn't ready yet. They put their furniture in their daughter's basement. Time passed. The Hickmans began looking for another place. A " real estate " lady found them one and they gave her $25 and paid the landlady $25 but the landlady returned their money; they couldn't have the apartment. They resumed their search, streetcars, pavements, want ads, realtors, all spring long. In June the barber called: they could have the room. They hired a truck for $18 and took their belongings to the barber's home. The barber's wife met them. She said they couldn't move in; " she was the boss." They went away. They put their furniture in a warehouse. And started all over again, looking.

Hickman's daughter's landlord said there were too many of them, they'd have to get out. " We scattered," he recalls. On August 19, their daughter heard about a five-room basement flat where children were acceptable. Immediately Mr. and Mrs. Hickman caught a streetcar to the real estate office, paid $5 a room " for listing " — $23 cash and $2 owed — received the landlord's address, 2720 Prairie and hurried there by taxi. It proved to be a stone relic of the Gold Coast's splendor, drawing rooms and even butler's pantries now rented out as " apartments." Far at the back, in a recess dark even at noonday, lived the man the Hickmans had come to see, David Coleman. He only rented a room here, this was not his building. He took them outdoors to talk things over. They sat down in his half-brother's two-tone Buick taxicab parked in the glass-strewn street in front of the mansion's iron gates.

Coleman was a very black man, twenty-five years old, about five-feet-ten, solidly built. He asked $200 rent in advance. Hickman said he couldn't pay so much. Coleman asked if he could pay $150. " Then he stopped, he looked at me, he said you look like I see you somewhere Hickman." They had lived only about three miles apart in the Delta. Coleman said. " Well now. Maybe we can get together. You can give me $100, can't you? " Hickman said he could but he wanted to see the apartment first. The three of them caught a streetcar.

2

Now David Coleman had been born January 12, 1922, at a flag-stop on the railroad in the Mississippi Delta. He was the last of eleven children; all but three of them died in infancy. " They just died," his mother says. " I don't know what of." He went to the fields full-time at twelve; later got a job driving a truck; married and had a child; and in 1943, lured by tales of freedom and high wartime wages, drove with his family to Chicago. They got along fine. The mother says, " We had a good job and a place to live. Nobody can do better." They came earlier than the Hickmans, before the housing screws were tightened quite so much, and they had fewer children. Coleman's wife died in bearing his second child. He married again; learned arc welding and once earned $2.10 an hour; liked to think of himself as a business man and tried to dress like one.

In July 1946, he met a woman with a building to sell. He borrowed money and leased the building and later he bought it " on contract " for $8,000, paying $300 down, the rest monthly. He had a lot of trouble over this deal, as we shall see; indeed it led to his death.

The building is on the West Side in an area once called Little Italy but now almost solidly Negro except for a few Mexicans. The best buildings are the churches and the factories. The buildings where people live are high brick tenements, patched-up wooden tenements, sheds. In between are vast wastelands, desolate open areas where buildings have collapsed or been torn down, the excavations partly filled with rubble. Broad Roosevelt Road, busy with traffic, cuts the section cleanly. A half block south is Washburne Street, our scene. It is a quiet street. A man is sitting idly on the iron railing in front of a house, tossing a pair of dice in the air and catching them, and a woman is sweeping the sidewalk with a broom, and now and then a child skates past, and that is all. The doorways of many houses are open, open onto a black void, the doors may be open or they may have vanished, and the houses look abandoned; but a woman is leaning on the railing, a hint of humanity packed inside. At the streetcorners are a Jewish delicatessen, a drugstore selling " Dream Books," the Temptation Cleaners, the iron structure of the El. In midblock, one of many in a row, is No. 1733, David Coleman's building. It is old, perhaps forty or fifty years old. It is huge and narrow — it stands three stories high above an English basement but, built on a twenty-five-foot lot, it is only thirty-one brick lengths wide. Two perpendicular rows of windows run up its face; in each is a panel of stained glass. To reach the upstairs flats you have to walk down a narrow gangway and enter a doorway halfway back along the side.

It was to this building on August 20, 1946, that David Coleman, as landlord, took Mr. and Mrs. Hickman. He showed them the basement apartment, offered at $50 a month. Hickman recalls, ". . . the water was half a leg deep in the basement . . . no windows, no lights, no nothing in there." A man who has since visited it says, " It was a woodshed really. The only impression it made on me was, this is how rats live." Hickman said it wouldn't do. Coleman said that in nine days a flat on the second floor would be available at $50 a month, and in the meantime they could have a room in the attic for $6 a week. Hickman testified later: " We walked up the stairs, it was so dark . . . we almost had to feel our way. . . . I am walking around looking at it, I don't like this. She said, I don't neither but surely we can stay here because we ain't got no place." They went outdoors and Hickman paid Coleman $30 " to hold us." He went to the South side, withdrew $70 from his postal savings, and took it to Coleman. He got his furniture out of storage and that night he and his wife hired a taxi and took their six youngest children there — the two older boys moved in later — and they all slept there that night.

And so now, after more than a year, they had a home. It was an attic room about fourteen by twenty-one feet but the roof sloped so that you could stand up only in a fourteen-foot-square space. The three smallest children slept with Mr. and Mrs. Hickman and the rest slept in the other bed. There was no electricity; they used a kerosene lamp. There was no gas; they used a stove and heater burning kerosene. There was one window. There was no water; they had to go down to the third floor to use the toilet or to get water for washing or cooking. But it was shelter, and a place they could all be together with their things. And it was, they thought, only temporary.

The nine days passed, however, and ten more, and Hickman asked Coleman about the second-floor flat. " He said, Hickman wait until the 18th and if those folks don't move out, I'll give you back your $100." Hickman agreed. But " on September 18th, he dodged me." Hickman began to suspect a runaround. Other tenants told him they'd had trouble with Coleman. On September 22 Hickman caught up with Coleman. He asked for his $100 so he could use it to find another place to live. Coleman replied, " I won't pay you until I get ready." Hickman recalls, " I said I'd go to the law and make him give it back. He said he had a man on the East Side ready to burn the place up if . . . I had him arrested. . . . He said go ahead and have me arrested, I would be sorry. And," Hickman now says, " I really was sorry." But that day he said nothing, he went back upstairs. " I looked at my family, looked at my small children. . . . I . . . told my wife what David Coleman told me downstairs, I said I wanted peace, I have lived in peace forty years, I asked her if there was laws in Chicago to take care of men like that, she said yes." On September 24 they got a warrant for Coleman's arrest. But the police never served it.

Coleman had leased the building July 27 from the owner, Mrs. Mary Porter Adams, a county social worker. About October 7 he took possession under his purchase contract. He had paid a rather high price and to meet the monthly payments he decided to cut the building up into more lucrative " kitchenette " apartments. He sent a contractor to the building, but the tenants obstructed him. Coleman arrived. An argument ensued. If he wanted to cut up the flats, they said, he would have to have the court evict them first. One recalled later, " He said: ' I am the owner, I don't have to go to court to do that, I will get everybody out of here when I want to if it takes fire.' "

Another family man, Albert Jones, had rented the dismal basement for $300, six months at $50 a month. Coleman had promised to repair it but he didn't. The main water line into the building was broken and so the water ran onto the floor of Jones's " apartment "; to alleviate this condition the other tenants turned off the main valve outside the building, and by prearrangement one of them would go outdoors and turn on the valve for a few minutes each day while the others flushed all the toilets and drew water into slop jars and buckets.

The Hickmans took their blind backward child, Corene, to a State hospital at Lincoln, Illinois. That left nine Hickmans in the room. " I worried about it night and day. I didn't want to bring them up in such living conditions." Hickman later testified that he never had lived so poorly in Mississippi as he had to live in Chicago.

Coleman refused to make repairs. Perhaps he hoped that hardship would drive the tenants out. Many bitter wrangles ensued. The tenants appealed to the OPA, the police, the fire department, the board of health, the water inspector. The only results: a policeman " come and looked and said it was awful," and the waterman shut off the water (probably because the bill wasn't paid). Nor was all this anything new; one tenant said, " We had been calling [the authorities] for the last few years," and violation of fire or building regulations — including insufficient fire exits — had been charged to various owners of this building but only one fine — of $25 — had been levied. In December 1946, after a routine department inspection, Mrs. Adams was ordered to make certain repairs and to remove papers, lumber, rags, and combustible rubbish, and a little later the city building department ordered her and Coleman to exterminate rats, reduce illegal overcrowding, repair the plumbing, and place " premises in habitable condition or vacate same." But nothing was done and there was no evidence that the building department took any steps toward enforcement — until after the fire.

As we have seen, Coleman bought the building on a shoestring. In November he leased it to Anthony Lee Barnett, Jr., who paid him $425. But then Barnett discovered that Jones already had a lease on the basement and Hickman had a $100 claim, so Barnett went to the State's Attorney and was advised to get a warrant for Coleman's arrest. Coleman fell behind in his monthly payments to Mrs. Adams. She visited the building about January 1, 1947, and was surprised to learn of Barnett's lease. The thing was a terrible muddle. That Sunday there was a fire in the flue. It did little damage but it aroused the tenants. They telephoned Mrs. Adams. She too wanted to get them out. One of them testified that she said, " Well, you are not paying enough rent there. . . . I am not going to fix anything. . . . It is not my fault because you got children. . . . Just find yourself another place." Another tenant told Mrs. Adams he was going to have the plumbing fixed " and pay it out of the rents." She sent him an eviction notice. She told the Hickmans there were too many of them in one room. Hickman said he didn't know what to do; and she suggested he find another home.

The same week the fire chief, on a routine inspection, found nineteen people living in the attic: another family had moved into the rear room. The chief ordered this other family out, and they went.

On three nights that week the Hickmans heard "somebody tipping up the stairs to the door and tipping down." Hickman asked his wife, "I wonder what they are up to. Do you reckon that somebody would burn us up here?" Coleman had lived for a time in a small room at the head of the stairs and had left an old bed frame and mattress and a trunk; now he came up and moved his trunk away. But he left the old bed frame and the mattress, the mattress rolled up in the corner. A week later the fire started where the mattress was.

3

Hickman was at work when the fire occurred. The police telephoned the steelmill and the foreman called for Hickman and a white man named Hicks went home by mistake. Not till almost 4:00 A.M. did they reach the right person. They told him he was wanted at the DesPlaines Street police station. The streetcar motorman told him where to get off but it was the wrong place and he walked around, lost. A man told him to go back to State Street and take a car up to Roosevelt Road and transfer. He still couldn't find the station so he went home.

The police investigation was lackadaisical (a deputy coroner remarked: "If this fire happened over on Sheridan Road some place, we would have half the police force in here"). Coleman denied having threatened to burn the building. There was no direct evidence that he had set it afire. But nobody could figure out an innocent origin and evidence indicated a strong possibility of arson. In the little room at the head of the stairs, investigators found a five-gallon can that nobody in the building recognized and it was half full of kerosene; one witness had seen a strange man running down the stairs the night of the fire; Coleman had removed his trunk a week earlier; firemen thought the fire moved suspiciously fast. But the coroner's jury, while "vigorously" condemning the condition of the building, confessed itself unable to determine whether the fire was accident or arson and recommended that the State's Attorney investigate further. The State's Attorney's investigation was feeble. The Coroner dropped the case. Nothing at all resulted. In April Coleman was fined $350 and costs and Mrs. Adams was fined $250 and costs for violations of the city building code — charges that could have been instituted months earlier, before the fire, but were not.

Hickman was convinced that Coleman had fired the building. And he felt justice had not been done. He was bitter. "Paper was made to burn, coal and rags. Not people. People wasn't made to burn." His son Willis remembers, "Before the fire he was out-going. Not after the fire. He wouldn't eat. He had nothing to say. He would sit with his eyes closed, but was not asleep." One night in April, Willis heard him in the bedroom, " talkin' to Elzena," the child of nine who had burned to death, and to Velvena, the dead child of four. He talked " at first faintly and then excitely." Then he jumped out of bed and cried, " The Lord have mercy," and ran from the room.

People of sympathy had got the Hickmans into a housing project, and Hickman had gone back to work, but his wife remembers, " He used to carry on practically every day. He would come home from work, sit down, and start talking about the children. ' My children got no cause to be dead. Other children are playing. My children have a right to play too. They didn't do any harm.' The more we talked about it, the more I would get worried. He would say: ' I know what Coleman told me. After he said it would happen, it did happen.' " Coleman's threat " went through my mind like a clock, over and over again." He bought a thirty-two caliber automatic pistol, telling his wife it was " for home use "; he always had kept a gun around the house. A strike at the steelmill July 10 made him idle. He brooded more. " When I looked around, the oldest ones was gone and the youngest ones were too. It used to be if we wanted a drink of water the baby would get it. Now there was no one there. No one to say: ' Daddy have you any candy? ' There would be no happiness again until I would get in camp with God." He and his wife were officers of the Liberty Baptist Church. On July 15, Hickman said, " I got no mind to go to church," but they went. His wife recalls, " We had a Morning Star Club meeting." They got home about midnight. Hickman went to bed, got up, went into the boys' room, looked at them sleeping, looked at the pictures of the dead children. He got out his gun and polished it. He " turned the radio on — it didn't play so good. I started a verse to a hymn. I walked back and sat down on the studio couch. When I got to summing up my life, I saw my life was unhappy. I was in grief and sorrow." Next morning, his wife recalls, " he got up quiet."

Hickman remembers that day: " I drunk a half a cup of tea and part of a sandwich, I was filled up. I wasn't mad, I wasn't glad, I walked in the . . . living room, I reached under the bed in the cash box, I took the key off my side and unlocked it, reached in for this automatic, picked it up and laid it down. You just got to go through with it. I laid it down again. I walked back and sat down beside my wife, I ain't spoke nothing to her. I walked back to the cash box, I picked up this gun, I knocked the safety off of it and wanted to see if it would hang. I put it back down, I can't go through with this. The voice kept speaking, you know your promise." The " promise " was the vow he had made to God to protect his children. " The third time I picked up this gun, I put eight in the magazine, knocked the safety off and threw one in the barrel." Still he paced the house and yard in torment; once he got a block away. But he came back: " The word was so sharp it was cutting like a two edge sword. . . . The third time I didn't return no more."

He caught a bus, transferred to a streetcar, and got off at 26th and Indiana. Coleman lived a few blocks away. " I stood there on the street. I didn't want to go through with what it was telling me. . . . [But] this was a vow that I made to this family in 1923 . . . and the answer is I wouldn't back up. So I walked on down to Prairie." It was a little before 1:00 P.M. Out in front of the big dilapidated mansion at 2720 Prairie, David Coleman was sitting behind the wheel of his half-brother's big Buick taxicab, reading a newspaper, reading aloud an account of a raid to Percy Brown, who was leaning through the window.

Hickman came up the sidewalk. " He had some rent tickets in his lap . . . I walked up to him and spoke to him and friendly talked. I wanted peace with all mankind. ' How do you do, how are you feeling this morning, Coleman? ' ' What do you want with me? ' ' I come to ask you something about this arrest warrant, of the $100 and causing this disturbance,' " that is, the fire. Coleman replied, " Yes, but I ain't going to pay you." Hickman recalls, " My mind got scattered. I took out my automatic and blazed him twice. He said: ' I'll pay you.' I said: ' It's too late now. God is my secret judge.' I said: ' You started that fire.' He said: ' Yes, I did.' I shot him twice more. . . . I thought he was dead." He wasn't but he died three days later.

Hickman walked down the street and away, the automatic still in his hand. He missed a streetcar, walked on, farther than he needed. " I had put a heavy load down and a big weight fell off of me and I felt light." He took a streetcar home and asked his son Charles, " Where is your mother? " " He said, ' down to Arlene's.' I said, ' Tell her to come here, I got something to tell her,' so she came. . . . She said . . . ' They will find you.' ' I know.' " He waited till 4:15 P.M. before the Homicide Squad arrived. They arrested him and took his gun. He confessed immediately. A coroner's jury bound him to the Grand Jury, which indicted him for first degree murder. He was jailed without bond. He had no money for a lawyer. It looked like at least fourteen years in the penitentiary and he could have been electrocuted.

4

But suddenly to his rescue came some citizens — an organizer for the Socialist Workers party, Mike Bartell, and two labor union men, Willoughby Abner, a Negro and first vice president of the central CIO

Council in Chicago, and Charles Chiakulas, president of the United Auto Workers (CIO) local. (Hickman was not then a CIO member.) Bartell had visited Hickman the day after the fire and at his behest a civil-rights lawyer, M. J. Myer, had represented Hickman at the inquest (subsequently, when Mrs. Adams had filed suits to evict the other tenants who kept on living in the burned building without paying rent, Myer and Leon M. Despres represented them, presenting the interesting defense that the building was unfit for human habitation and therefore no rent was due). Now Abner, Chiakulas, and Bartell formed a Hickman Defense Committee.

Myer, Despres, and William H. Temple agreed to defend Hickman. Abner recalls " We had two objectives — to raise money for the defense and to educate the public to the horrible conditions these people lived in and the tragedies that can result." Others active were the Reverend James Luther Adams, a Unitarian minister and a board member of the Independent Voters of Illinois; Gerald Bullock, chairman of the Committee on Racial Equality; Franklin Field, a unionist active in the AVC; and Sidney Lens, head of an AF of L local. Many such groups degenerate into luncheons and resolutions. Hickman's defenders worked hard, effectively, fast, and according to plan. One traveled all over the East on $100, setting up local committees. They held rallies (Tallulah Bankhead, the actress, appeared) and put donation jars in Black Belt stores. Each member obtained mailing lists, publicity, and money from organizations he had access to.

Hickman's trial began on November 10, 1947, before a white judge and a white jury, with four white lawyers out of five on both sides. The prosecution proved that Hickman killed Coleman, the defense claimed he did so while temporarily insane. Hickman himself occupied the witness chair for a day and a half, a small black man behind an oak panel, speaking freely in flowing narrative, sometimes in language almost biblical.

He said: " My feelings was that I was mistreated without a cause. I felt that my children was without a guardian, that they suffered death, that they ought to be free on land and living."

He said: " This was God fixed this. I had raised these children up and God knowed that vow I made to him . . . that these children was a generation to be raised up. God wasn't pleased what happened to them."

His lawyer asked him about blind Corene who had been taken to an institution: " Mr. Hickman, while you were up in the attic before the fire, did one of the children leave the family and go live elsewhere? " and he said, " Leave the family? Yes, sir," and the lawyer said, " Will you describe her — when was she born, what happened to her? " and Hickman began, " She was born in June and she was beautiful."

His lawyer asked him to describe " your feelings " between the fire and the shooting, and he replied: " I had two sons and two daughters who would some day be great men and women, some day they would have married, some day they would have been fathers or mothers of children; these children would have children and then these children would have children and another generation of Hickmans could raise up and enjoy peace."

The jury was out for nineteen hours and then reported hopeless disagreement. All six men and one woman reportedly voted for acquittal, the other five women were for conviction. The jury was discharged. Hickman was sent back to jail to await a new trial.

But by this time the Hickman Defense Committee's work had taken hold. Letters were rolling in on the State's Attorney from all over the United States. The Defense Committee finally reached an agreement with Assistant State's Attorney Samuel L. Freedman, and on December 16 Judge Rudolph F. Desort dismissed the murder charge, found Hickman guilty of manslaughter and placed him on probation for two years. A few hours later Hickman went home to his family for Christmas.

Before disbanding, the Defense Committee held its only luncheon meeting. Abner, a quiet softspoken man, recalls, " Mr. and Mrs. Hickman thanked us from the the bottom of their hearts, said they were very grateful." Abner said recently, " I don't know — at the start, you knew the thing was there, you couldn't just sit back and do nothing about it, it got inside you. We really felt good when it was over. It shows everything isn't in vain, it isn't all injustice, people will rally, it shows what can be done."

Not quite everybody had rallied. Some organizations declined to do so. The Communists and the organizations they control or influence would not participate. The American Civil Liberties Union felt that no civil-rights issue was involved and the National Association for the Advancement of Colored People that no race issue was involved. Attorney Myer said recently, " Sure Hickman and Coleman were both Negroes — but there wouldn't have been any fire or shooting either if it hadn't been for restrictive covenants and the Negro slums."

And in truth Coleman as well as Hickman seems the victim of a system. The system of segregation that creates such tremendous housing pressures also creates opportunity for men weak by nature to exploit their fellows. Coleman happened to be black but it was white man's race prejudice that enabled him to exploit Hickman. And he was only the last of many men who had oppressed Hickman because of Hickman's color. The white planters of Mississippi had driven him to Chicago. Here Coleman took over. And he was able to take over because of the prejudice of Northern whites. The North had failed the Negro no less than the South, there is no place in this country for a black man to go. In Chicago after the 1917–18 war the tremendous population pressure burst the bounds of the Black Belt despite bombings, arsons, and a major race riot. The same thing is happening today. And the greater the pressure of the blacks, the greater white resistance — more hurried meetings of " improvement " associations to draw new restrictive covenants, more rocks and bombs and " Molotov cocktails " thrown at newly-purchased Negro homes, more suspect fires that already within the past three years have killed a score of Negroes, more " streetcar incidents " and " bathing beach incidents," more political speeches promising " racial purity." Even the government's efforts in the Negroes' behalf, public housing, have been resisted stoutly. It is profitable to rent firetraps. The vested — and highly respectable — real estate interests of this city draw the iron ring ever tighter. (Who cares if they are corroding away the heart of the city? They also are pandering to our own prejudices.) Chicago's postwar housing record is one of complete failure; indeed, despite innumerable editorials and civic luncheons, bond issues, and tub-thumping, in 1946 the city actually lost more dwelling units through fire and simple decay than it erected. The housing problem is bad everywhere in America; in no major city is it worse than in Chicago, and Negroes are at the bottom of the heap because we put them there and we keep them there. Now after a " people's war " Negroes are becoming restive; and on at least one occasion since V–J Day only Negro restraint has prevented a major race riot; and the Mayor's Commission on Human Relations, which has done much to ease the dangerous tensions, has warned: " Unless more homes are provided, no one, regardless of good will or police power, can check the social conflicts which are inherent in this situation . . . we have all of the ingredients for social destruction."

The Defense Committee helped to get Hickman a new job. He and his wife and the remaining children, the three boys, eighteen, twenty, and twenty-two, are living in a housing project near the airport, close to another project where in 1946 one of Chicago's most dangerous race flare-ups occurred. They intend to stay in Chicago. Mrs. Hickman says, " I like Chicago. I used to like it very much when I had my children."

A year after the fire the old building at 1733 Washburne was deserted. After the shooting the tenants had quit resisting eviction and moved away, and almost at once another fire gutted the building. The windows have been boarded up, the attic is open to the weather, charred black timbers and jagged bricks and boards askew against the sky. In the alley dirty newspapers blow gently by a wrecked car, a woman is burning trash in a salamander, and in the center lies a dead rat. On a little mound of rubble behind 1733, an old Negro squats amid piles of junk, hat brim up, shoes broken, denim jacket patched; he is tending a little fire to burn the wood from barrel hoops, burning tin cans and buckets clean with fire. He moved here in 1919 from the South Side, the only Negro in his block, and for a time white kids broke his windows, " though I guess their folks put them up to it." It isn't as nice here as on the South Side. Why do people move over here? " Looking for some place to go." There's talk that the owner of 1733 is going to fix the building up and sell it. Will people live in it? " Sure," and he laughs. " If they fix it up, they'll soon be lined up here, putting in their application. People got no place to go."

The Story of an Eye-Witness

Jack London

Upon receipt of the first news of the earthquake, Collier's telegraphed to Mr. Jack London — who lives only forty miles from San Francisco — requesting him to go to the scene of disaster and write the story of what he saw. Mr. London started at once, and has sent the following dramatic description of the tragic events he witnessed in the burning city.

The earthquake shook down in San Francisco hundreds of thousands of dollars' worth of walls and chimneys. But the conflagration that followed burned up hundreds of millions of dollars' worth of property. There is no estimating within hundreds of millions the actual damage wrought. Not in history has a modern imperial city been so completely destroyed. San Francisco is gone. Nothing remains of it but memories and a fringe of dwelling-houses on its outskirts. Its industrial section is wiped out. Its business section is wiped out. The factories and warehouses, the great stores and newspaper buildings, the hotels and the palaces of the nabobs, are all gone. Remains only the fringe of dwelling-houses on the outskirts of what was once San Francisco.

Within an hour after the earthquake shock the smoke of San Fran-

THE STORY OF AN EYE-WITNESS: Reprinted by permission. Originally published in *Collier's* Magazine, May 5, 1906.

cisco's burning was a lurid tower visible a hundred miles away. And for three days and nights this lurid tower swayed in the sky, reddening the sun, darkening the day, and filling the land with smoke.

On Wednesday morning at a quarter past five came the earthquake. A minute later the flames were leaping upward. In a dozen different quarters south of Market Street, in the working-class ghetto, and in the factories, fires started. There was no opposing the flames. There was no organization, no communication. All the cunning adjustments of a twentieth century city had been smashed by the earthquake. The streets were humped into ridges and depressions, and piled with the debris of fallen walls. The steel rails were twisted into perpendicular and horizontal angles. The telephone and telegraph systems were disrupted. And the great water-mains had burst. All the shrewd contrivances and safe-guards of man had been thrown out of gear by thirty seconds' twitching of the earth-crust.

The Fire Made Its Own Draft

By Wednesday afternoon, inside of twelve hours, half the heart of the city was gone. At that time I watched the vast conflagration from out on the bay. It was dead calm. Not a flicker of wind stirred. Yet from every side wind was pouring in upon the city. East, west, north, and south, strong winds were blowing upon the doomed city. The heated air rising made an enormous suck. Thus did the fire of itself build its own colossal chimney through the atmosphere. Day and night this dead calm continued, and yet, near to the flames, the wind was often half a gale, so mighty was the suck.

Wednesday night saw the destruction of the very heart of the city. Dynamite was lavishly used, and many of San Francisco's proudest structures were crumbled by man himself into ruins, but there was no withstanding the onrush of the flames. Time and again successful stands were made by the fire-fighters, and every time the flames flanked around on either side, or came up from the rear, and turned to defeat the hard-won victory.

An enumeration of the buildings destroyed would be a directory of San Francisco. An enumeration of the buildings undestroyed would be a line and several addresses. An enumeration of the deeds of heroism would stock a library and bankrupt the Carnegie medal fund. An enumeration of the dead — will never be made. All vestiges of them were destroyed by the flames. The number of the victims of the earthquake will never be known. South of Market Street, where the loss of life was particularly heavy, was the first to catch fire.

Remarkable as it may seem, Wednesday night, while the whole city crashed and roared into ruin, was a quiet night. There were no crowds.

There was no shouting and yelling. There was no hysteria, no disorder. I passed Wednesday night in the path of the advancing flames, and in all those terrible hours I saw not one woman who wept, not one man who was excited, not one person who was in the slightest degree panic-stricken.

Before the flames, throughout the night, fled tens of thousands of homeless ones. Some were wrapped in blankets. Others carried bundles of bedding and dear household treasures. Sometimes a whole family was harnessed to a carriage or delivery wagon that was weighted down with their possessions. Baby buggies, toy wagons, and go-carts were used as trucks, while every other person was dragging a trunk. Yet everybody was gracious. The most perfect courtesy obtained. Never, in all San Francisco's history, were her people so kind and courteous as on this night of terror.

A Caravan of Trunks

All night these tens of thousands fled before the flames. Many of them, the poor people from the labor ghetto, had fled all day as well. They had left their homes burdened with possessions. Now and again they lightened up, flinging out upon the street clothing and treasures they had dragged for miles.

They held on longest to their trunks, and over these trunks many a strong man broke his heart that night. The hills of San Francisco are steep, and up these hills, mile after mile, were the trunks dragged. Everywhere were trunks, with across them lying their exhausted owners, men and women. Before the march of the flames were flung picket lines of soldiers. And a block at a time, as the flames advanced, these pickets retreated. One of their tasks was to keep the trunk-pullers moving. The exhausted creatures, stirred on by the menace of bayonets, would arise and struggle up the steep pavements, pausing from weakness every five or ten feet.

Often, after surmounting a heart-breaking hill, they would find another wall of flame advancing upon them at right angles and be compelled to change anew the line of their retreat. In the end, completely played out, after toiling for a dozen hours like giants, thousands of them were compelled to abandon their trunks. Here the shopkeepers and soft members of the middle class were at a disadvantage. But the working-men dug holes in vacant lots and backyards and buried their trunks.

The Doomed City

At nine o'clock Wednesday evening I walked down through the very heart of the city. I walked through miles and miles of magnificent buildings and towering skyscrapers. Here was no fire. All was in perfect order. The police patrolled the streets. Every building had its watchman at the door. And yet it was doomed, all of it. There was no water. The dynamite was giving out. And at right angles two different conflagrations were sweeping down upon it.

At one o'clock in the morning I walked down through the same section. Everything still stood intact. There was no fire. And yet there was a change. A rain of ashes was falling. The watchmen at the doors were gone. The police had been withdrawn. There were no firemen, no fire-engines, no men fighting with dynamite. The district had been absolutely abandoned. I stood at the corner of Kearney and Market, in the very innermost heart of San Francisco. Kearney Street was deserted. Half a dozen blocks away it was burning on both sides. The street was a wall of flame, and against this wall of flame, silhouetted sharply, were two United States cavalrymen sitting their horses, calmly watching. That was all. Not another person was in sight. In the intact heart of the city two troopers sat their horses and watched.

Spread of the Conflagration

Surrender was complete. There was no water. The sewers had long since been pumped dry. There was no dynamite. Another fire had broken out further uptown, and now from three sides conflagrations were sweeping down. The fourth side had been burned earlier in the day. In that direction stood the tottering walls of the Examiner building, the burned-out Call building, the smoldering ruins of the Grand Hotel, and the gutted, devastated, dynamited Palace Hotel.

The following will illustrate the sweep of the flames and the inability of men to calculate their spread. At eight o'clock Wednesday evening I passed through Union Square. It was packed with refugees. Thousands of them had gone to bed on the grass. Government tents had been set up, supper was being cooked, and the refugees were lining up for free meals.

At half-past one in the morning three sides of Union Square were in flames. The fourth side, where stood the great St. Francis Hotel, was still holding out. An hour later, ignited from top and sides, the St. Francis was flaming heavenward. Union Square, heaped high with mountains of trunks, was deserted. Troops, refugees, and all had retreated.

A Fortune for a Horse!

It was at Union Square that I saw a man offering a thousand dollars for a team of horses. He was in charge of a truck piled high with trunks from some hotel. It had been hauled here into what was considered safety, and the horses had been taken out. The flames were on three sides of the Square, and there were no horses.

Also, at this time, standing beside the truck, I urged a man to seek safety in flight. He was all but hemmed in by several conflagrations. He was an old man and he was on crutches. Said he, " Today is my birthday Last night I was worth thirty thousand dollars. I bought five bottles of wine, some delicate fish, and other things for my birthday dinner. I have had no dinner, and all I own are these crutches."

I convinced him of his danger and started him limping on his way. An hour later, from a distance, I saw the truck-load of trunks burning merrily in the middle of the street.

On Thursday morning, at a quarter past five, just twenty-four hours after the earthquake, I sat on the steps of a small residence on Nob Hill. With me sat Japanese, Italians, Chinese, and Negroes — a bit of the cosmopolitan flotsam of the wreck of the city. All about were the palaces of the nabob pioneers of Forty-nine. To the east and south, at right angles, were advancing two mighty walls of flame.

I went inside with the owner of the house on the steps of which I sat. He was cool and cheerful and hospitable. " Yesterday morning," he said, " I was worth six hundred thousand dollars. This morning this house is all I have left. It will go in fifteen minutes." He pointed to a large cabinet. " That is my wife's collection of china. This rug upon which we stand is a present. It cost fifteen hundred dollars. Try that piano. Listen to its tone. There are few like it. There are no horses. The flames will be here in fifteen minutes."

Outside, the old Mark Hopkins residence, a palace, was just catching fire. The troops were falling back and driving the refugees before them. From every side came the roaring of flames, the crashing of walls, and the detonations of dynamite.

The Dawn of the Second Day

I passed out of the house. Day was trying to dawn through the smoke-pall. A sickly light was creeping over the face of things. Once only the sun broke through the smoke-pall, blood-red, and showing quarter its usual size. The smoke-pall itself, viewed from beneath, was a rose color that pulsed and fluttered with lavender shades. Then it turned to mauve and yellow and dun. There was no sun. And so dawned the second day on stricken San Francisco.

An hour later I was creeping past the shattered dome of the City Hall. Than it there was no better exhibit of the destructive forces of the earthquake. Most of the stone had been shaken from the great dome, leaving standing the naked framework of steel. Market Street was piled high with the wreckage, and across the wreckage lay the overthrown pillars of the City Hall shattered into short crosswise sections.

This section of the city, with the exception of the Mint and the Post-Office, was already a waste of smoking ruins. Here and there through the smoke, creeping warily under the shadows of tottering walls, emerged occasional men and women. It was like the meeting of the handful of survivors after the day of the end of the world.

Beeves Slaughtered and Roasted

On Mission Street lay a dozen steers, in a neat row stretching across the street, just as they had been struck down by the flying ruins of the earthquake. The fire had passed through afterward and roasted them. The human dead had been carried away before the fire came. At another place on Mission Street I saw a milk wagon. A steel telegraph pole had smashed down sheer through the driver's seat and crushed the front wheels. The milkcans lay scattered around.

All day Thursday and all Thursday night, all day Friday and Friday night, the flames still raged.

Friday night saw the flames finally conquered, though not until Russian Hill and Telegraph Hill had been swept and three-quarters of a mile of wharves and docks had been licked up.

The Last Stand

The great stand of the fire-fighters was made Thursday night on Van Ness Avenue. Had they failed here, the comparatively few remaining houses of the city would have been swept. Here were the magnificent residences of the second generation of San Francisco nabobs, and these, in a solid zone, were dynamited down across the path of the fire. Here and there the flames leaped the zone, but these fires were beaten out, principally by the use of wet blankets and rugs.

San Francisco, at the present time, is like the crater of a volcano, around which are camped tens of thousands of refugees. At the Presidio alone are at least twenty thousand. All the surrounding cities and towns are jammed with the homeless ones, where they are being cared for by the relief committees. The refugees were carried free by the railroads to any point they wished to go, and it is estimated that over one hundred thousand people have left the peninsula on which San Francisco stood. The Government has the situation in hand, and, thanks to the immediate relief given by the whole United States, there is not the slightest possibility of a famine. The bankers and business men have already set about making preparations to rebuild San Francisco.

How To Detect Propaganda

Institute for Propaganda Analysis

If American citizens are to have clear understanding of present-day conditions and what to do about them, they must be able to recognize propaganda, to analyze it, and to appraise it.

But what is propaganda?

As generally understood, *propaganda is expression of opinion or action by individuals or groups deliberately designed to influence opinions or actions of other individuals or groups with reference to predetermined ends*. Thus propaganda differs from scientific analysis. The propagandist is trying to " put something across," good or bad, whereas the scientist is trying to discover truth and fact. Often the propagandist does not want careful scrutiny and criticism; he wants to bring about a specific action. Because the action may be socially beneficial or socially harmful to millions of people, it is necessary to focus upon the propagandist and his activities the searchlight of scientific scrutiny. Socially desirable propaganda will not suffer from such examination, but the opposite type will be detected and revealed for what it is.

We are fooled by propaganda chiefly because we don't recognize it when we see it. It may be fun to be fooled but, as the cigarette ads used to say, it is more fun to know. We can more easily recognize propaganda when we see it if we are familiar with the seven common propaganda devices. These are:

HOW TO DETECT PROPAGANDA: From *Propaganda Analysis,* November 1937. Copyright 1937 by The Institute for Propaganda Analysis, Inc.

1. The Name Calling Device
2. The Glittering Generalities Device
3. The Transfer Device
4. The Testimonial Device
5. The Plain Folks Device
6. The Card Stacking Device
7. The Band Wagon Device

Why are we fooled by these devices? Because they appeal to our emotions rather than to our reason. They make us believe and do something we would not believe or do if we thought about it calmly, dispassionately. In examining these devices, note that they work most effectively at those times when we are too lazy to think for ourselves; also, they tie into emotions which sway us to be " for " or " against " nations, races, religions, ideals, economic and political policies and practices, and so on through automobiles, cigarettes, radios, toothpastes, presidents, and wars. With our emotions stirred, it may be fun to be fooled by these propaganda devices, but it is more fun and infinitely more to our own interests to know how they work.

Lincoln must have had in mind citizens who could balance their emotions with intelligence when he made his remark: ". . . but you can't fool all of the people all of the time."

Name Calling

" Name Calling " is a device to make us form a judgment without examining the evidence on which it should be based. Here the propagandist appeals to our hate and fear. He does this by giving " bad names " to those individuals, groups, nations, races, policies, practices, beliefs, and ideals which he would have us condemn and reject. For centuries the name " heretic " was bad. Thousands were oppressed, tortured, or put to death as heretics. Anybody who dissented from popular or group belief or practice was in danger of being called a heretic. In the light of today's knowledge, some heresies were bad and some were good. Many of the pioneers of modern science were called heretics; witness the cases of Copernicus, Galileo, Bruno. Today's bad names include: Fascist, demagogue, dictator, Red, financial oligarchy, Communist, muckraker, alien, outside agitator, economic royalist, Utopian, rabble-rouser, troublemaker, Tory, Constitution wrecker.

" Al " Smith called Roosevelt a Communist by implication when he said in his Liberty League speech, " There can be only one capital, Washington or Moscow." When " Al " Smith was running for the presidency many called him a tool of the Pope, saying in effect, " We must choose between Washington and Rome." That implied that Mr. Smith, if elected President, would take his orders from the Pope. Likewise Mr. Justice Hugo Black has been associated with a bad name, Ku Klux Klan. In these cases some propagandists have tried to make us form judgments without examining essential evidence and implications. " Al Smith is a Catholic. He must never be President." " Roosevelt is a Red. Defeat his program." " Hugo Black is or was a Klansman. Take him out of the Supreme Court."

Use of " bad names " without presentation of their essential meaning, without all their pertinent implications, comprises perhaps the most common of all propaganda devices. Those who want to *maintain* the status quo apply bad names to those who would change it. . . . Those who want to *change* the status quo apply bad names to those who would maintain it. For example, the *Daily Worker* and the *American Guardian* apply bad names to conservative Republicans and Democrats.

Glittering Generalities

" Glittering Generalities " is a device by which the propagandist identifies his program with virtue by use of " virtue words." Here he appeals to our emotions of love, generosity, and brotherhood. He uses words like truth, freedom, honor, liberty, social justice, public service, the right to work, loyalty, progress, democracy, the American way, Constitution defender. These words suggest shining ideals. All persons of good will believe in these ideals. Hence the propagandist, by identifying his individual group, nation, race, policy, practice, or belief with such ideals, seeks to win us to his cause. As Name Calling is a device to make us form a judgment to *reject and condemn,* without examining the evidence, Glittering Generalities is a device to make us *accept and approve,* without examining the evidence.

For example, use of the phrases, " the right to work " and " social justice," may be a device to make us accept programs for meeting labor-capital problems, which, if we examined them critically, we would not accept at all.

In the Name Calling and Glittering Generalities devices, words are used to stir up our emotions and to befog our thinking. In one device " bad words " are used to make us mad; in the other " good words " are used to make us glad.

The propagandist is most effective in the use of these devices when his words make us create devils to fight or gods to adore. By his use of the " bad words," we personify as a " devil " some nation, race, group, individual, policy, practice, or ideal; we are made fighting mad to destroy it. By use of " good words," we personify as a godlike idol some nation, race, group, etc. Words which are " bad " to some are " good " to others, or may be made so. Thus, to some the New Deal is " a prophecy of social salvation " while to others it is " an omen of social disaster."

From consideration of names, " bad " and " good," we pass to institutions and symbols, also " bad " and " good." We see these in the next device.

Transfer

" Transfer " is a device by which the propagandist carries over the authority, sanction, and prestige of something we respect and revere to something he would have us accept. For example, most of us respect and revere our church and our nation. If the propagandist succeeds in getting church or nation to approve a campaign in behalf of some program, he thereby transfers its authority, sanction, and prestige to that program. Thus we may accept something which otherwise we might reject.

In the Transfer device, symbols are constantly used. The cross represents the Christian Church. The flag represents the nation. Cartoons like Uncle Sam represent a consensus of public opinion. Those symbols stir emotions. At their very sight, with the speed of light, is aroused the whole complex of feelings we have with respect to church or nation. A cartoonist by having Uncle Sam disapprove a budget for unemployment relief would have us feel that the whole United States disapproves relief costs. By drawing an Uncle Sam who approves the same budget, the cartoonist would have us feel that the American people approve it. Thus the Transfer device is used both for and against causes and ideas.

Testimonial

The " Testimonial " is a device to make us accept anything from a patent medicine or a cigarette to a program of national policy. In this device the propagandist makes use of testimonials. " When I feel tired, I smoke a Camel and get the grandest ' lift.' " " We believe the John L. Lewis plan of labor organization is splendid; C.I.O. should be supported." This device works in reverse also; counter-testimonials may be employed. Seldom are these used against commercial products like patent medicines and cigarettes, but they are constantly employed in social, economic, and political issues. " We believe that the John L. Lewis plan of labor organization is bad; C.I.O. should not be supported."

Plain Folks

" Plain Folks " is a device used by politicians, labor leaders, business men, and even by ministers and educators to win our confidence by appearing to be people like ourselves — " just plain folks among the neighbors." In election years especially do candidates show their devotion to little children and the common, homey things of life. They have front porch campaigns. For the newspaper men they raid the kitchen cupboard, finding there some of the good wife's apple pie. They go to country picnics; they attend service at the old frame church; they pitch hay and go fishing; they show their belief in home and mother. In short, they would win our votes by showing that they're just as common as the rest of us — " just plain folks " — and, therefore, wise and good. Business men often are " plain folks " with the factory hands. Even distillers use the device. " It's our family's whiskey, neighbor; and neighbor, it's your price."

Card Stacking

" Card Stacking " is a device in which the propagandist employs all the arts of deception to win our support for himself, his group, nation, race, policy, practice, belief, or ideal. He stacks the cards against the truth. He uses under-emphasis and over-emphasis to dodge issues and evade facts. He resorts to lies, censorship, and distortion. He omits facts. He offers false testimony. He creates a smoke screen of clamor by raising a new issue when he wants an embarrassing matter forgotten. He draws a red herring across the trail to confuse and divert those in quest of facts he does not want revealed. He makes the unreal appear real and the real appear unreal. He lets half-truth masquerade as truth. By the Card Stacking device, a mediocre candidate, through the " build-up," is made to appear an intellectual titan; an ordinary prize fighter, a probable world champion; a worthless patent medicine, a beneficent cure. By means of this device propagandists would convince us that a ruthless war of aggression is a crusade for righteousness. Some member nations of the Non-Intervention Committee send their troops to intervene in Spain. Card Stacking employs sham, hypocrisy, effrontery.

The Band Wagon

The " Band Wagon " is a device to make us follow the crowd, to accept the propagandist's program en masse. Here his theme is: " Everybody's doing it." His techniques range from those of medicine show to dramatic spectacle. He hires a hall, fills a great stadium, marches a million men in parade. He employs symbols, colors, music, movement, all the dramatic arts. He appeals to the desire, common to most of us, to " follow the crowd." Because he wants us to " follow the crowd " in masses, he directs his appeal to groups held together by common ties of nationality, religion, race, environment, sex, vocation. Thus propagandists campaigning for or against a program will appeal to us as Catholics, Protestants, or Jews; as members of the Nordic race or as Negroes; as farmers or as school teachers; as housewives or as miners. All the artifices of flattery are used to harness the fears and hatreds, prejudices, and biases, convictions and ideals common to the group; thus emotion is made to push and pull the group on to the Band Wagon. In newspaper article and in the spoken word this device is also found. " Don't throw your vote away. Vote for our candidate. He's sure to win." Nearly every candidate wins in every election — before the votes are in.

Propaganda and Emotion

Observe that in all these devices our emotion is the stuff with which propagandists work. Without it they are helpless; with it, harnessing it to their purposes, they can make us glow with pride or burn with hatred, they can make us zealots in behalf of the program they espouse. As we said at the beginning, propaganda as generally understood is expression of opinion or action by individuals or groups with reference to predetermined ends. Without the appeal to our emotion — to our fears and to our courage, to our selfishness and unselfishness, to our loves and to our hates — propagandists would influence few opinions and few actions.

To say this is not to condemn emotion, an essential part of life, or to assert that all predetermined ends of propagandists are " bad." What we mean is that the intelligent citizen does not want propagandists to utilize his emotions, even to the attainment of " good " ends, without knowing what is going on. He does not want to be " used " in the attainment of ends he may later consider " bad." He does not want to be gullible. He does not want to be fooled. He does not want to be duped, even in a " good " cause. He wants to know the facts and among these is included the fact of the utilization of his emotions.[1]

Keeping in mind the seven common propaganda devices, turn to today's newspapers and almost immediately you can spot examples of them all. At election time or during any campaign, Plain Folks and Band Wagon are common. Card Stacking is hardest to detect because

---

[1] For better understanding of the relationship between propaganda and emotion see Chapter One of *Folkways* by William Graham Sumner. This shows why most of us tend to feel, believe, and act in traditional patterns. See also *The Mind in the Making* by James Harvey Robinson. This reveals the nature of the mind and suggests how to analyze propaganda appealing to traditional thought patterns.

it is adroitly executed or because we lack the information necessary to nail the lie. A little practice with the daily newspapers in detecting these propaganda devices soon enables us to detect them elsewhere — in radio, news-reel, books, magazines, and in expression of labor unions, business groups, churches, schools, political parties.

The Marxian Philosophy of History

Carl L. Becker

I sometimes find myself discussing communism with those who profess that faith; and not infrequently I note an implicit assumption on their part that I, as an intelligent person with some knowledge of history, ought either, (1) to refute the Marxian philosophy of history, or (2) in all honesty to support the communist cause. In such discussions I have maintained, (1) that an intelligent person may regard the Marxian philosophy of history as an illuminating interpretation of the past without subscribing to it as a law of history, and (2) that even if convinced that the Marxian doctrine is a valid law of history, one might still with excellent reasons refuse to support the communist cause. Such discussions, developed more fully and presented more formally, may for convenience be put in the form of a discussion between a communist and a liberal.

COMMUNIST: Don't you think, Professor, that history proves that social progress, or change if you prefer, is the result of an inevitable class conflict?

LIBERAL: Put in that precise way, no. I can't see that history proves anything except that what happened did happen, or that anything is inevitable except what happened; but what happened is precisely the question at issue. In using the words " prove " and " inevitable " you are, as the logicians say, begging the question.

COMMUNIST: I don't insist on those precise words.

LIBERAL: Very well. I agree then that history does support, or can easily be made to support, the Marxian doctrine in a general way. For

THE MARXIAN PHILOSOPHY OF HISTORY: From *Everyman His Own Historian: Essays on History and Politics* by Carl L. Becker. Copyright 1935 by F. S. Crofts & Company, Inc. Reprinted by permission of Appleton-Century-Crofts, Inc.

example, in the middle ages the chief source of wealth was certainly land; and it is obvious that at that time the land-owning aristocracy was the ruling class. No great ingenuity is required to show that political, social, and religious customs and ideas at that time were suited to maintaining the political and economic ascendancy of the aristocracy. Likewise, it is obvious that during the last three centuries land has gradually been replaced by capital as the chief source of wealth; and the history of this time may easily be regarded as a conflict between the middle-class capitalist and the land-owning aristocracy, as a result of which the former have replaced the latter as the ruling class and have substituted, in their interest, a new set of institutions and ideas (representative government, individual liberty, popular sovereignty, free competition) for the old. Yes, as an interpretation of the last thousand years of European history, the Marxian theory is most illuminating.

COMMUNIST: Isn't it a bit more than merely illuminating? Can you deny that it is a more convincing and realistic interpretation than any other?

LIBERAL: I could very easily deny it, but I have no wish to do so. Let us admit that it is the most convincing interpretation. I will go farther. For purposes of argument I will admit that it is the only valid interpretation.

COMMUNIST: Very well then. If you admit that Marx has correctly interpreted the past, why not admit that he has correctly interpreted the future? Why not admit that just as the bourgeois-capitalist class displaced the land-owning aristocracy as the ruling class, so the proletariat will in its turn replace the bourgeois-capitalist class? And if they do so, isn't it reasonable to suppose that the characteristic ideas of the present society (representative government, freedom of speech, *laissez-faire*) will in turn give way to others suited to the interests of the proletariat?

LIBERAL: If I accept Marx's interpretation of the past it is because I know what it is, and can test it. If I hesitate to accept his interpretation of the future it is partly because I do not know precisely what it is, and partly because, even if I know what it is, I cannot test it. I willingly admit that the future will, in some way that can after the event be rationalized, resemble the past. Certainly change is the law of life, and it is obvious that the institutions and the ideas of the nineteenth century, which were so well suited to the interests of the capitalist class, will not suffice without modification for the needs of the complex mechanized society of the twentieth. I willingly admit also that the ideas and institutions of today will be changed in such a way as to conform more closely with the economic interests of the workers, the mass of the people, the proletariat. But that is not to say that the change will come about in the way predicted by Marx, or that the result will be the sort of utopia predicted by him.

COMMUNIST: Utopia! I am not aware that Marx predicted any utopia.

LIBERAL: Well, let us say that he didn't. What then did he predict?

COMMUNIST: He predicted that the capitalist régime would by its own nature destroy itself. Its nature is to be ruthlessly competitive, so that in any industrial society the tendency is for wealth to be more highly concentrated in the hands of the few, while the mass of the people tend to fall to the condition of wage slaves. When this process reaches a certain point, the system breaks down, as it is now breaking down because it has deprived the people of the means of buying the commodities which it is the sole aim of the capitalistic class to make and sell for a profit. When the system ceases to work the people will necessarily take control, and, since it is their interest to do so, they will establish a classless society based upon the common ownership of instruments of production, and a more equitable distribution of the product. This is the social revolution that Marx predicted, and it has already begun — in Russia.

LIBERAL: In Russia, yes. In Russia, that is to say, not the most highly industrialized society but the least highly industrialized society. That is surely not according to Marx.

COMMUNIST: No, it is not. But you cannot maintain that because Marx's prediction is not verified in every detail it is not therefore valid in its general outline. The Great War created a special set of circumstances which were peculiarly favorable to the social revolution in Russia.

LIBERAL: Very true. The social revolution clearly occurred before its time in Russia. Providence, or Dialectic Materialism, or whatever it is that regulates social changes, certainly did a very curious thing in bringing the social revolution to Russia before it brought it to more highly industrialized countries, such as England. For my part, I don't think the Russian revolution does anything to verify the predictions of Marx; to me it indicates only that in a country in which the people were accustomed to being ruled by a dictatorship, a country moreover in which the prevailing form of dictatorship was especially corrupt and incompetent, it was very easy to establish a dictatorship of a different sort. But let that pass. My reluctance to accept the Marxian doctrine arises from something far more fundamental than the Russian accident. There are two difficulties which have always troubled me. Perhaps you can solve them. One is that it is extremely difficult to predict the future on the basis of past experience; or rather it is extremely easy to find in the past support for diverse predictions of the future. The other difficulty is to understand why a persistent economic class conflict in the past justifies us in predicting a classless society in the future.

As to the first difficulty. What little I know of history makes me chary of any prediction as to the form which social institutions will take in the future. Especially so when such predictions, based upon a realistic view of the past, take an idealistic view of the future. During the last two thousand years all the saints and sages of the world, deploring greed and strife, poverty and injustice, have looked forward to the time when a more just society would be established. They have many times predicted the coming of a classless society in which everyone would have enough; but the course of events has never yet verified their hopes. This generalization is as solidly based on historical fact as any that Marx has made, and it is more widely based; and if I am to judge the future by the past, I see no reason for discarding this generalization for that which Marx offers me. The less so, since Marx's interpretation of the past, if projected into the future, seems to refute his own prediction.

COMMUNIST: I don't understand that.

LIBERAL: Perhaps it will become clear if I elaborate the second difficulty I just mentioned. Marx's interpretation of the past is explicit and realistic; his forecast of the future seems to me vague and idealistic. I have called it utopian, but you object to that word. I do not insist on it. I will even surrender the word " idealistic." But the point is this. Marx finds that in the past the effective force that has determined social change is the economic class conflict. He points out that this economic class conflict explains the rise of the present capitalistic society. He shows, or at least his disciples show, how this economic class conflict is working to undermine our capitalistic society. Very well. If then I project this explanation of social changes into the future, what does it tell me? It seems to tell me that there will be in the future what there has been in the past — an endless economic class conflict, an endless replacement of one dominant class by another, an endless transformation of institutions and ideas in accordance with the changes effected by the class conflict. But this is not what Marx predicts. What he predicts is the end of the economic class conflict, the establishment of a classless society. What you and he are asking me to accept is an explanation of history that will explain it only up to a certain point. Marx criticised Hegel for that very weakness. Hegel explained past history as a transformation effected by the Transcendent Idea realizing itself in the actual events of history; according to him the great objective of history was the complete realization of the Idea in the form of Freedom, and this great objective had already been in some sense attained in the Prussian state. Marx wanted to know what the Transcendent Idea would find to do in the future, now that it was entirely realized. That is a sound criticism. Now, my difficulty is to know how Marx has improved on Hegel. To be sure Marx does not say that the great objective of history has already been attained. He says the economic class conflict will bring about another social revolution. But after the social revolution, what then? What becomes of the economic class conflict after the revolution has established a classless society? I can't find that it will have anything more to do than Hegel's Transcendent Idea. A law of history which, at some determinate moment, ceases to explain history, a law of history which is required, at the appropriate moment, to commit hari-kari on the doorstop of the ideal, surely leaves something to be desired.

COMMUNIST: Well, that's a point. But really, Professor, you know very well that this objection has been noted before, and that there is a good answer to it. Marx was not so blind as to overlook it. How could he have done so, since he pointed out that very weakness in Hegel's philosophy of history?

LIBERAL: I should be glad to learn how Marx avoids that difficulty.

COMMUNIST: I am not sure that Marx does altogether avoid it. But you must allow Marxian philosophy to be elaborated and interpreted by his followers in the light of later experience. You have no objection to that?

LIBERAL: None at all. We must by all means discuss Marxianism at its best, as it is now interpreted by the most expert exegesis available.

COMMUNIST: Very well. According to a recent interpreter of Marxianism, history is explainable in terms of a dialectic of transformation, in which conflicts appear only to be resolved in a higher synthesis. This conflict is not necessarily always an economic class conflict. After the classless society is established the conflict will continue, but on a different level. According to Professor Sidney Hook, a recent interpreter of Marx, the dialectic in a communistic, classless society, will not be " historically conditioned in the same sense " as in earlier times. " It finds expression . . . on a more elevated plane. Although in advance no one can describe the detailed forms it will take, it is clear that its general locus is individual and personal." In other words, having solved the economic problem by establishing a classless society, men will be occupied with the higher, spiritual problems of human development.

LIBERAL: Well, I must confess that this greatly surprises me. A while back you would not allow me to apply the term " utopian " to the future society predicted by Marx, and yet this sounds to me very similar to all the utopian societies I ever heard of. Throughout the past men have been engaged in brutal conflict for material gain; but this brutal conflict is somehow to bring about a classless society in which men will suddenly change their natures and devote themselves to the nobler things of life. A dialectic materialism will be replaced by what we may call a dialectic spiritualism; or to put it in simple English, conflict will cease on the economic plane, and continue only on the moral plane.

Well, it may be so; and if it should turn out so, it would be grand. I point out merely that this is what all the idealistic prophets of the world have always hoped would happen. It is what the early prophets of democracy predicted. It is what all humane liberals may hope for. But what I don't understand is how the Marxian philosophy permits us to hope for it. I suppose it to be a fundamental tenet of Marxian philosophy that the conduct of men is strictly conditioned; and if their conduct in the past has been strictly conditioned by the economic class conflict, how can it cease to be so conditioned in the future?

COMMUNIST: Your difficulty arises from a false assumption — an assumption that is made by many of the hostile critics of Marx. The assumption is that Marx accepted the nineteenth-century doctrine of mechanistic determinism. That is not so. Marx always insisted that " man makes his own history." He contributes something novel to the conditions that determine his own conduct. Marx says explicitly: " By acting on the external world man changes his own nature." This means that man can, by acquiring knowledge, modify his environment, and so modify also his own ways of submitting to the environment. Therefore it is quite possible that men might for a very long time submit blindly to the influence of the economic class conflict; for a long time, but not necessarily forever; since, having become aware that they had been in the past submitting to the economic class conflict, they would, in the future, even if they submitted to it, not be submitting to it blindly. This awareness that their conduct has been determined by the economic class conflict becomes a new element in the conditions, and so changes the conditions that will determine men's conduct in the future. One might say that the great object of Marx was just this: to make men aware of the conditions that made social revolutions in the past, so that in the coming social revolution, being aware of what was happening, they could consciously direct it. To quote once more from Professor Sidney Hook: " Once man acquires control of the conditions of social life, he can consciously make over his own nature in accordance with a morally free will, in contradistinction to men in the past, whose nature has been unconsciously made over by the economically determined will of the economic class."

LIBERAL: I see; at least I think so, in spite of Professor Hook's somewhat obscure academic phraseology. But what it comes to, I suppose, is this. In the physical world a law operates forever in the same way because the physical object is not aware of, and is indifferent to, what happens. A billiard ball (to use the classic example) has no desire to make over its nature. But man is aware of, and is not indifferent to, what happens. His acts are indeed strictly conditioned, but as soon as he becomes aware of what it is that conditions them, his awareness enables him to react differently; his acts are then not less strictly conditioned than formerly, but his own awareness becomes a new element that changes and complicates the conditions. For a long time men may worship the sun; when they become aware of the influences that make them worship the sun, this awareness may become an influence that will make them cease to worship the sun. Freedom of the will, as Engels said, is no more than man's knowledge that his acts are conditioned.

Very well, Marx then (or perhaps his disciples) applies this principle of freedom to the social changes or revolutions that occur in history. In the past, social revolutions have been conditioned by the economic class conflict. As long as men are not aware of this fact, social revolutions will continue to be conditioned by the economic class conflict. But when men become fully aware, through the great discovery of Marx, that social revolutions in the past have been conditioned by the class conflict, this knowledge will enable them to react differently — to react in such a way as to abolish the class conflict. This, I take it, is how you interpret Marx.

COMMUNIST: Yes, that is right.

LIBERAL: Well, I agree with this idea of free will. It seems to me obvious that as men acquire knowledge of the influences that determine their acts, this knowledge becomes a new influence that enables them to act differently. But if we accept this principle it seems odd to me that men shouldn't have acquired, before the time of Marx, some knowledge of the fact that their conduct was determined by the economic class conflict. I should have supposed that this element of awareness would have been steadily modifying the conditions that determine social change from the time of the Neanderthal man down to the present. How does it happen that this element has had no appreciable influence up to the time of Marx? Marx must have been a much greater man than I have always thought — a veritable Messiah, who at a single stroke has given mankind this epoch-making revelation that is to transform so radically the conditions that determine human history. I find it difficult to believe that. It seems more reasonable to believe that knowledge has been steadily modifying the economic influences that have determined social changes in the past, and that in the future further knowledge, knowledge unknown to Marx, will continue to modify those influences in ways not dreamed of by Marx.

But that is a minor point. Let us assume that up to the time of Marx men have been submitting blindly to the economic class conflict, and that now, thanks to Marx, they are in the way of becoming aware of that fact, and that being aware of it they are in a position to modify profoundly the conditions that will determine social changes. What then? Well, it seems to me that this great revolution made by Marx is precisely what makes it impossible for him to predict the character of the coming social revolution. If we did not know that social changes had been conditioned by the economic class conflict, the coming social revolution would presumably follow the course of previous ones, in which case no classless society would emerge from it. But since we do know that social revolutions in the past were conditioned by the class conflict, this very knowledge, according to Marx, will make the coming social revolution follow some different course, in which case we may hope, but cannot be sure, that a classless society will emerge from it. In short, in so far as Marx has made men aware of the influence of the economic class conflict in the past, he has destroyed the very conditions that would have enabled him to predict the nature of the social revolution in the future. If Marx wished to predict correctly the nature of the coming social revolution, he should not have told us what it is that makes social revolutions: since he has told us, the secret is out, and hence no one can predict it. The great secret is out, thanks to Marx, and this knowledge will enable us to make of the coming social revolution something different than it otherwise would have been. Marxian philosophy presents his disciples with a dilemma which they either do not see or refuse to meet. It is this. Either social changes are always determined by the same conditions, in which case we may be sure that the coming social revolution will be similar to those in the past — it will transform the present class conflict only to create the conditions that will issue in a new one. Or else knowledge of the conditions that have determined social revolutions in the past introduces a novel influence in the conditions that will determine social revolutions in the future, in which case we cannot predict with any certainty the nature of those revolutions. The profound conviction of Communists that the proletariat is destined to establish a classless society on the ruins of the present capitalistic régime is not justified by Marxian philosophy: if you interpret Marx in terms of mechanistic determinism, this profound communist conviction is a pure delusion; on the other hand, if you interpret Marx in terms of free will, this conviction is no more than splendid hope. That is why I cannot accept the Marxian philosophy as a law of history.

COMMUNIST: Very well. Suppose, for purposes of argument, that the communist conviction is only a splendid hope. You yourself have said that the present capitalist régime must be changed in such a way as to harmonize better with the interests of the mass of the people, the proletariat. That is just what the Communists want. Since you sympathize with their object and believe that it will in some measure be realized, why not join the Communists and help to realize this splendid hope?

LIBERAL: I refuse to join the Communists because, while I sympathize with their desire to make a better world for the mass of the people, I have no faith in the methods which they propose for obtaining this object. If I understand them, they claim that nothing really worth while can be done until conditions are ripe for the application of the revolutionary technique. When that time comes, they propose, following the example of the Bolshevists in Russia, to seize control of the government, forcibly expropriate the bourgeois class, and ruthlessly suppress the expression of all opinion that a dictatorial government judges to be hostile to the welfare of the community of workers.

Now I have no faith in force and repression as the *primary* means of achieving the good life. I am not as yet a non-resistant pacifist. Any government is probably better than none, and all governments rest at last on force. But I believe that the essential test of civilized society is the extent to which law and public authority rest on free discussion and voluntary consent. A resort to force as a means of obtaining consent may be sometimes necessary to prevent a society from falling into virtual anarchy, but the resort to force in place of persuasion is so far a confession of failure. I have no faith in the possibility of abolishing oppression by oppressing oppressors. I have no faith in the infallibility of any man, or of any group of men, or of the doctrines or dogmas of any man or group of men, except in so far as they can stand the test of free criticism and analysis. I agree with Pascal that " thought makes the dignity of man "; and I believe therefore that all the great and permanently valuable achievements of civilization have been won by the free play of intelligence in opposition to, or in spite of, the pressure of mass emotion and the effort of organized authority to enforce conformity in conduct and opinion. I do not believe that there has been, or that there will be, a high civilization in any country in which the mind of man is limited to the expression of ideas authorized by public authority. Dictatorship is as old as European society; and whether it be the dictatorship of a Stalin, a

Mussolini, or a Hitler, it does not become something new and admirable by being dressed up in a new and mystical ideology. I recognize it as a possibility that our modern, complex, machine civilization may so far fall into confusion that a dictatorship will in fact replace the present régime; but I refuse to recognize this outcome as inherently desirable, and I refuse to join in any effort to make it inevitable.

This is why I do not join the Communists. I believe that profound changes in our economic and industrial system are necessary; but I believe that they can and I hope that they will be made, in this country, without resorting to violent revolution, without resorting to dictatorship, without abandoning our traditional reliance on free discussion and criticism of public authority and of the measures it proposes for the solution of social ills. And there is nothing in the Marxian philosophy, as you expound it, that makes it illogical for me to take this position. According to you, now that Marx has made us aware of the influence of the economic class conflict in the past, this very awareness will enable us to master and modify the class conflict in the future. I agree. But why is it necessary to assume that this knowledge which Marx has revealed to us is the exclusive possession of the proletariat? After all, the bourgeoisie have a certain amount of intelligence. They can read Marx, or at least Sidney Hook. They can observe what has occurred in Russia, in Italy, in Germany. It is possible for them, too, to understand that the capitalist competitive system is in a fair way of destroying itself. Marxian doctrine tells me that capitalists, like proletarians, are motivated by their economic class interest; it does not tell me that they, any more than the proletarians, must forever be motivated by a blind illusion as to what that interest is. At the present moment it obviously is not to the interest of the capitalist class that the mass of the people should be without the means of buying the goods which the capitalist class produces in order to sell. It is still possible that the capitalist system in this country, subjected to the pressure of economic necessity and the force of public discontent, may by reasonably peaceful procedure be sufficiently transformed into a coordinated and planned economic system to make it, not a utopia indeed, but at least a decently workable system. And a decently workable system which preserves our traditional liberty of discussion and criticism will, in my opinion, be superior in the long run to any system that can be established by the repressive measures now employed by the Communists of Russia, the Fascists of Italy, or the Nazis of Germany.

COMMUNIST: A decently workable system. That's certainly vague enough — as vague as Marx's idealistic society of the future which you derided. No doubt a decently workable system is one which you would prefer to something which you don't like, such as the Russian communist state.

LIBERAL: It is. But you must permit me to prefer a decently workable system which I like to a decently workable system which I don't like. You can hardly expect me to become a Communist until I am convinced that communism would be preferable to the system under which I live.

COMMUNIST: No. But you have already admitted that the " decently workable system " which you hope will be established may fail to be established — that the present system may end in a dictatorship. That I think is the more probable outcome. It is likely that in the long run the capitalist class, confronted by the rising power of the proletariat, will resort to force, as it has done in Italy and Germany. If then you are faced with the alternative of supporting a dictatorship of the proletariat or a dictatorship of the bourgeoisie what will you do? What then will become of freedom of speech and the appeal to persuasion? Since you sympathize with the objectives of the Communists, will you not then be forced to join them? Why wait till then? Why not join now the side which is bound to win in the long run because it is in harmony with the dominant trend of social forces?

LIBERAL: I do not admit that communism is necessarily in harmony with the dominant trend of social forces. I see that when it suits your argument you, like most Communists, fall back on the doctrine of a fatalistic determinism which makes the communist revolution inevitable whatever men do about it; but when your argument requires another doctrine you admit that the social revolution may be mastered and directed by the conscious purposes of men. You ought really to accept one doctrine or the other, and stick to it. But no matter. Accept one docrine or both, as you like. In either case I see no good reason for joining the Communists. If the communist revolution is inevitable, whatever men do about it, why do anything? Why join either side, if you know beforehand that one side is bound to win anyway? But if the communist revolution is not inevitable, then the proletariat can indeed do something to hasten it, and by the same token the bourgeoisie can do something to retard it. And in that case why should I join the Communists? I am a professor; and the Communists are never weary of telling me that professors as a class support the capitalistic régime because it is their economic interest to do so. Very well, I will be a sufficiently good Marxian to accept the doctrine that men's actions are motivated by their economic class interest. If then my economic interests are bound up with the capitalist régime, and I can do something to retard the communist revolution, I should be, according to Marx himself, a poor humanitarian fool to desert my class and work for a revolution which, if successful, would ruthlessly suppress me. As a liberal humanitarian, or a Christian mystic, I might logically sacrifice myself and my class for the welfare of the masses; but as a Marxian that would be to adopt the very " utopian " attitude which Marx never ceased to ridicule. You really ask too much. The Marxian philosophy teaches me either that the communist revolution is inevitable, in which case I merely resign myself to it: or else it teaches me that the communist revolution can be hastened or retarted by the conscious efforts of men, in which case I stick to my class and do what I can to retard it. In either case I have the profound consolation of knowing that my conduct is based on the solid foundation of the Marxian philosophy of history.

These, you are to understand, are choices logically open to me on the assumption that I accept the Marxian philosophy of history. But life is less simple than logic. In logic you can present me with clear-cut alternatives. You can ask me whether I will " choose " to support the dictatorship of the proletariat or the dictatorship of the bourgeoisie, quite as if some day, the two contending parties being lined up in battle array on a *champs de mars,* I should be asked to step out and join one side or the other. In actual life it does not seem to me that I am ever confronted with choices as simple or as dramatically staged as that. When I voted for Mr. Roosevelt (if I *did* vote for him — I can't be sure now) I made a choice, without being certain (any more than Mr. Roosevelt himself was) what would come of it. I am now " supporting " (so far as I am supporting anything) the Roosevelt administration, and it is possible that in 1936 I shall vote for the reelection of Mr. Roosevelt. Does this mean that I am " choosing " to support a fascist rather than a communistic regime? Thoroughgoing Communists appear to know that I am: the New Deal, they say, is obviously an American species of fascist technique. But I am sufficiently naive not to be aware of having made any choice between communism and fascism. And very glad I am that it is so. I should dislike very much to be confronted with a clear-cut choice between a dictatorship of the proletariat and a dictatorship of the bourgeoisie. I should be inclined to say, " A plague on both your houses! " I find Mussolini as offensive as Stalin, and Hitler more offensive than either.

COMMUNIST: That is all very well, but a real revolution is not impossible. There are plenty of Russians who could assure you that the alternative you so much dislike has been presented to them in a quite sufficiently clear-cut and dramatic manner. If it should be similarly presented in this country, it seems to me that you would, however much you might dislike it, have to choose one side or the other.

LIBERAL: Not necessarily. There would still be another possibility.

COMMUNIST: What would that be?

LIBERAL: I might still refuse to join either side. I might persist in the futility of expressing my faith in the superior virtues of persuasion.

COMMUNIST: That would have serious consequences for you. You would be suppressed.

LIBERAL: True enough. But I might accept the consequences. I might choose to be suppressed rather than to support what I object to. In short, I might, as a last refuge from imbecility, become a Christian and practise the precept that it is better to suffer evil than to do it.

COMMUNIST: That would be to fall back upon a far more mystical type of idealism than Marx ever contemplated, and I fail to see that it would get you anywhere.

LIBERAL: I dare say it wouldn't. But as I said before, I am a professor, and a professor, as the German proverb has it, is " a man who thinks otherwise ": if he is not permitted to talk freely he cannot get anywhere anyway.

from Freedom and the Control of Men

A PSYCHOLOGIST PRESENTS THE CASE FOR THE BEHAVIORAL SCIENCES

B. F. Skinner

The second half of the twentieth century may be remembered for its solution of a curious problem. Although Western democracy created the conditions responsible for the rise of modern science, it is now evident that it may never fully profit from that achievement. The so-called " democratic philosophy " of human behavior to which it also gave rise is increasingly in conflict with the application of the methods of science to human affairs. Unless this conflict is somehow resolved, the ultimate goals of democracy may be long deferred.

1

Just as biographers and critics look for external influences to account for the traits and achievements of the men they study, so science ultimately explains behavior in terms of " causes " or conditions which lie beyond the individual himself. As more and more causal relations are demonstrated, a practical corollary becomes difficult to resist: it

From FREEDOM AND THE CONTROL OF MEN: Reprinted by permission of author and publisher, from *The American Scholar,* Winter 1955–56.

should be possible to *produce* behavior according to plan simply by arranging the proper conditions. Now, among the specifications which might reasonably be submitted to a behavioral technology are these: Let men be happy, informed, skillful, well behaved, and productive.

This immediate practical implication of a science of behavior has a familiar ring, for it recalls the doctrine of human perfectibility of eighteenth- and nineteenth-century humanism. A science of man shares the optimism of that philosophy and supplies striking support for the working faith that men can build a better world and, through it, better men. The support comes just in time, for there has been little optimism of late among those who speak from the traditional point of view. Democracy has become " realistic," and it is only with some embarrassment that one admits today to perfectionistic or utopian thinking.

The earlier temper is worth considering, however. History records many foolish and unworkable schemes for human betterment, but almost all the great changes in our culture which we now regard as worthwhile can be traced to perfectionistic philosophies. Governmental, religious, educational, economic, and social reforms follow a common pattern. Someone believes that a change in a cultural practice — for example, in the rules of evidence in a court of law, in the characterization of man's relation to God, in the way children are taught to read and write, in permitted rates of interest, or in minimal housing standards — will improve the condition of men: by promoting justice, permitting men to seek salvation more effectively, increasing the literacy of a people, checking an inflationary trend, or improving public health and family relations, respectively. The underlying hypothesis is always the same: that a different physical or cultural environment will make a different and better man.

The scientific study of behavior not only justifies the general pattern of such proposals; it promises new and better hypotheses. The earliest cultural practices must have originated in sheer accidents. Those which strengthened the group survived with the group in a sort of natural selection. As soon as men began to propose and carry out changes in practice for the sake of possible consequences, the evolutionary process must have accelerated. The simple practice of making changes must have had survival value. A further acceleration is now to be expected. As laws of behavior are more precisely stated, the changes in the environment required to bring about a given effect may be more clearly specified. Conditions which have been neglected because their effects were slight or unlooked for may be shown to be relevant. New conditions may actually be created, as in the discovery and synthesis of drugs which affect behavior.

This is no time, then, to abandon notions of progress, improvement, or, indeed, human perfectibility. The simple fact is that man is able, and now as never before, to lift himself by his own bootstraps. In achieving control of the world of which he is a part, he may learn at last to control himself.

2

Timeworn objections to the planned improvement of cultural practices are already losing much of their force. Marcus Aurelius was probably right in advising his readers to be content with a haphazard amelioration of mankind. " Never hope to realize Plato's republic," he sighed, ". . . for who can change the opinions of men? And without a change of sentiments what can you make but reluctant slaves and hypocrites? " He was thinking, no doubt, of contemporary patterns of control based upon punishment or the threat of punishment which, as he correctly observed, breed only reluctant slaves of those who submit and hypocrites of those who discover modes of evasion. But we need not share his pessimism, for the opinions of men can be changed. The techniques of indoctrination which were being devised by the early Christian Church at the very time Marcus Aurelius was writing are relevant, as are some of the techniques of psychotherapy and of advertising and public relations. Other methods suggested by recent scientific analyses leave little doubt of the matter.

The study of human behavior also answers the cynical complaint that there is a plain " cussedness " in man which will always thwart efforts to improve him. We are often told that men do not want to be changed, even for the better. Try to help them, and they will outwit you and remain happily wretched. Dostoievsky claimed to see some plan in it. " Out of sheer ingratitude," he complained, or possibly boasted, " man will play you a dirty trick, just to prove that men are still men and not the keys of a piano. . . . And even if you could prove that a man is only a piano key, he would still do something out of sheer perversity — he would create destruction and chaos — just to gain his point. . . . And if all this could in turn be analyzed and prevented by predicting that it would occur, then man would deliberately go mad to prove his point." This is a conceivable neurotic reaction to inept control. A few men may have shown it, and many have enjoyed Dostoievsky's statement because they tend to show it. But that such perversity is a fundamental reaction of the human organism to controlling conditions is sheer nonsense.

So is the objection that we have no way of knowing what changes to make even though we have the necessary techniques. That is one of the great hoaxes of the century — a sort of booby trap left behind in the retreat before the advancing front of science. Scientists themselves have unsuspectingly agreed that there are two kinds of useful propositions about nature — facts and value judgments — and that science must confine itself to " what is," leaving " what ought to be " to others. But with what special sort of wisdom is the nonscientist endowed? Science is only effective knowing, no matter who engages in it. Verbal behavior proves upon analysis to be composed of many different types of utterances, from poetry and exhortation to logic and factual description, but these are not all equally useful in talking about cultural practices. We may classify useful propositions according to the degrees of confidence with which they may be asserted. Sentences about nature range from highly probable " facts " to sheer guesses. In general, future events are less likely to be correctly described than past. When a scientist talks about a projected experiment, for example, he must often resort to statements having only a moderate likelihood of being correct; he calls them hypotheses.

Designing a new cultural pattern is in many ways like designing an experiment. In drawing up a new constitution, outlining a new educational program, modifying a religious doctrine, or setting up a new fiscal policy, many statements must be quite tentative. We cannot be sure that the practices we specify will have the consequences we predict, or that the consequences will reward our efforts. This is in the nature of such proposals. They are not value judgments — they are guesses. To confuse and delay the improvement of cultural practices by quibbling about the word *improve* is itself not a useful practice. Let us agree, to start with, that health is better than illness, wisdom better than ignorance, love better than hate, and productive energy better than neurotic sloth.

Another familiar objection is the " political problem." Though we know what changes to make and how to make them, we still need to control certain relevant conditions, but these have long since fallen into the hands of selfish men who are not going to relinquish them for such purposes. Possibly we shall be permitted to develop areas which at the moment seem unimportant, but at the first signs of success the strong men will move in. This, it is said, has happened to Christianity, democracy, and communism. There will always be men who are fundamentally selfish and evil, and in the long run innocent goodness cannot have its way. The only evidence here is historical, and it may be misleading. Because of the way in which physical science developed, history could until very recently have " proved " that the unleashing of the energy of the atom was quite unlikely, if not impossible. Similarly, because of the order in which processes in human behavior have become available for purposes of control, history may seem to prove that power will probably be appropriated for selfish purposes. The first techniques to be discovered fell almost always to strong, selfish men. History led Lord Acton to believe that power corrupts, but he had probably never encountered absolute power, certainly not in all its forms, and had no way of predicting its effect.

An optimistic historian could defend a different conclusion. The principle that if there are not enough men of good will in the world the first step is to create more seems to be gaining recognition. The Marshall Plan (as originally conceived), Point Four, the offer of atomic materials to power-starved countries — these may or may not be wholly new in the history of international relations, but they suggest an increasing awareness of the power of governmental good will. They are proposals to make certain changes in the environments of men for the sake of consequences which should be rewarding for all concerned. They do not exemplify a disinterested generosity, but an interest which is the interest of everyone. We have not yet seen Plato's philosopher-king, and may not want to, but the gap between real and utopian government is closing.

3

But we are not yet in the clear, for a new and unexpected obstacle has arisen. With a world of their own making almost within reach, men of good will have been seized with distaste for their achievement. They have uneasily rejected opportunities to apply the techniques and findings of science in the service of men, and as the import of effective cultural design has come to be understood, many of them have voiced an outright refusal to have any part in it. Science has been challenged before when it has encroached upon institutions already engaged in the control of human behavior; but what are we to make of benevolent men, with no special interests of their own to defend, who nevertheless turn against the very means of reaching long-dreamed-of goals?

What is being rejected, of course, is the scientific conception of man and his place in nature. So long as the findings and methods of science are applied to human affairs only in a sort of remedial patch-work, we may continue to hold any view of human nature we like. But as the use of science increases, we are forced to accept the theoretical structure with which science represents its facts. The difficulty is that this structure is clearly at odds with the traditional democratic conception of man. Every discovery of an event which has a part in shaping a man's behavior seems to leave so much the less to be credited to the man himself; and as such explanations become more and more comprehensive, the contribution which may be claimed by the individual himself appears to approach zero. Man's vaunted creative powers, his original accomplishments in art, science, and morals, his capacity to choose and our right to hold him responsible for the consequences of his choice — none of these is conspicuous in this new self-portrait. Man, we once believed, was free to express himself in art, music, and literature, to inquire into nature, to seek salvation in his own way. He could initiate action and make spontaneous and capricious changes of course. Under the most extreme duress some sort of choice remained to him. He could resist any effort to control him, though it might cost him his life. But science insists that action is initiated by forces impinging upon the individual, and that caprice is only another name for behavior for which we have not yet found a cause.

In attempting to reconcile these views it is important to note that the traditional democratic conception was not designed as a description in the scientific sense but as a philosophy to be used in setting up and maintaining a governmental process. It arose under historical circumstances and served political purposes apart from which it cannot be properly understood. In rallying men against tyranny it was necessary that the individual be strengthened, that he be taught that he had rights and could govern himself. To give the common man a new conception of his worth, his dignity, and his power to save himself, both here and hereafter, was often the only resource of the revolutionist. When democratic principles were put into practice, the same doctrines were used as a working formula. This is exemplified by the notion of personal responsibility in Anglo-American law. All governments make certain forms of punishment contingent upon certain kinds of acts. In democratic countries these contingencies are expressed by the notion of responsible choice. But the notion may have no meaning under governmental practices formulated in other ways and would certainly have no place in systems which did not use punishment.

The democratic philosophy of human nature is determined by certain political exigencies and techniques, not by the goals of democracy. But exigencies and techniques change; and a conception which is not supported for its accuracy as a likeness — is not, indeed, rooted in fact at all — may be expected to change too. No matter how effective we judge current democratic practices to be, how highly we value them, or how long we expect them to survive, they are almost certainly not the *final* form of government. The philosophy of human nature which has been useful in implementing them is also almost certainly not the last word. The ultimate achievement of democracy may be long deferred unless we emphasize the real aims rather than the verbal devices of democratic thinking. A philosophy which has been appropriate to one set of political exigencies will defeat its purpose if, under other circumstances, it prevents us from applying to human affairs the science of man which probably nothing but democracy itself could have produced.

4

Perhaps the most crucial part of our democratic philosophy to be reconsidered is our attitude toward freedom — or its reciprocal, the control of human behavior. We do not oppose all forms of control because it is " human nature " to do so. The reaction is not characteristic of all men under all conditions of life. It is an attitude which has been carefully engineered, in large part by what we call the " literature " of democracy. With respect to some methods of control (for example, the threat of force), very little engineering is needed, for the techniques or their immediate consequences are objectionable. Society has suppressed these methods by branding them " wrong," " illegal," or " sinful." But to encourage these attitudes toward objectionable forms of control, it has been necessary to disguise the real nature of certain indispensable techniques, the commonest examples of which are education, moral discourse, and persuasion. The actual procedures appear harmless enough. They consist of supplying information, presenting opportunities for action, pointing out logical relationships, appealing to reason or " enlightened understanding," and so on. Through a masterful piece of misrepresentation, the illusion is fostered that these procedures do not involve the control of behavior; at most, they are simply ways of " getting someone to change his mind." But analysis not only reveals the presence of well-defined behavioral processes, it demonstrates a kind of control no less inexorable, though in some ways more acceptable, than the bully's threat of force.

Let us suppose that someone in whom we are interested is acting unwisely — he is careless in the way he deals with his friends, he drives too fast, or he holds his golf club the wrong way. We could probably help him by issuing a series of commands: don't nag, don't drive over sixty, don't hold your club that way. Much less objectionable would be " an appeal to reason." We could show him how people are affected by his treatment of them, how accident rates rise sharply at higher speeds, how a particular grip on the club alters the way the ball is struck and corrects a slice. In doing so we resort to verbal mediating devices which emphasize and support certain " contingencies of reinforcement " — that is, certain relations between behavior and its consequences — which strengthen the behavior we wish to set up. The same consequences would possibly set up the behavior without our help, and they eventually take control no matter which form of help we give. The appeal to reason has certain advantages over the authoritative command. A threat of punishment, no matter how subtle, generates emotional reactions and tendencies to escape or revolt. Perhaps the controllee merely " feels resentment " at being made to act in a given way, but even that is to be avoided. When we " appeal to reason," he " feels freer to do as he pleases." The fact is that we have exerted *less* control than in using a threat; since other conditions may contribute to the result, the effect may be delayed or, possibly in a given instance, lacking. But if we have worked a change in his behavior at all, it is because we have altered relevant environmental conditions, and the processes we have set in motion are just as real and just as inexorable, if not as comprehensive, as in the most authoritative coercion.

" Arranging an opportunity for action " is another example of disguised control. The power of the negative form has already been exposed in the analysis of censorship. Restriction of opportunity is recognized as far from harmless. As Ralph Barton Perry said in an article which appeared in the Spring, 1953, *Pacific Spectator,* " Whoever determines what alternatives shall be made known to man controls what that man shall choose *from*. He is deprived of freedom in proportion as he is denied access to *any* ideas, or is confined to any range of ideas short of the totality of relevant possibilities." But there is a positive side as well. When we present a relevant state of affairs, we increase the likelihood that a given form of behavior will be emitted. To the extent that the probability of action has changed, we have made a definite contribution. The teacher of history controls a student's behavior (or, if the reader prefers, " deprives him of freedom ") just as much in *presenting* historical facts as in suppressing them. Other conditions will no doubt affect the student, but the contribution made to his behavior by the presentation of material is fixed and, within its range, irresistible.

The methods of education, moral discourse, and persuasion are acceptable not because they recognize the freedom of the individual or his right to dissent, but because they make only *partial* contributions to the control of his behavior. The freedom they recognize is freedom from a more coercive form of control. The dissent which they tolerate is the possible effect of other determiners of action. Since these sanctioned methods are frequently ineffective, we have been able to convince ourselves that they do not represent control at all. When they show too much strength to permit disguise, we give them other names and suppress them as energetically as we suppress the use of force. Education grown too powerful is rejected as propaganda or " brainwashing," while really effective persuasion is decried as " undue influence," " demagoguery," " seduction," and so on.

If we are not to rely solely upon accident for the innovations which give rise to cultural evolution, we must accept the fact that some kind of control of human behavior is inevitable. We cannot use good sense in human affairs unless someone engages in the design and construction of environmental conditions which affect the behavior of men. Environmental changes have always been the condition for the improvement of cultural patterns, and we can hardly use the more effective methods of science without making changes on a grander scale. We are all controlled by the world in which we live, and part of that world has been and will be constructed by men. The question is this: Are we to be controlled by accident, by tyrants, or by ourselves in effective cultural design?

The danger of the misuse of power is possibly greater than ever. It is not allayed by disguising the facts. We cannot make wise decisions if we continue to pretend that human behavior is not controlled, or if we refuse to engage in control when valuable results might be forthcoming. Such measures weaken only ourselves, leaving the strength of science to others. The first step in a defense against tyranny is the fullest possible exposure of controlling techniques. A second step has already been taken successfully in restricting the use of physical force. Slowly, and as yet imperfectly, we have worked out an ethical and governmental design in which the strong man is not allowed to use the power deriving from his strength to control his fellow men. He is restrained by a superior force created for that purpose — the ethical pressure of the group, or more explicit religious and governmental measures. We tend to distrust superior forces, as we currently hesitate to relinquish sovereignty in order to set up an international police force. But it is only through such countercontrol that we have achieved what we call peace — a condition in which men are not permitted to control each other through force. In other words, control itself must be controlled.

Science has turned up dangerous processes and materials before. To use the facts and techniques of a science of man to the fullest extent without making some monstrous mistake will be difficult and obviously perilous. It is no time for self-deception, emotional indulgence, or the assumption of attitudes which are no longer useful. Man is facing a difficult test. He must keep his head now, or he must start again — a long way back.

from The Abolition of Man

C. S. Lewis

Human nature will be the last part of Nature to surrender to Man. The battle will then be won. We shall have " taken the thread of life out of the hand of Clotho " and be henceforth free to make our species whatever we wish it to be. The battle will indeed be won. But who, precisely, will have won it?

For the power of Man to make himself what he pleases means, as we have seen, the power of some men to make other men what *they* please. In all ages, no doubt, nurture and instruction have, in some sense, attempted to exercise this power. But the situation to which we must look forward will be novel in two respects. In the first place, the power will be enormously increased. Hitherto the plans of educationalists have achieved very little of what they attempted and indeed, when we read them — how Plato would have every infant " a bastard nursed in a bureau," and Elyot would have the boy see no men before the age of seven and, after that, no women,[1] and how Locke wants children to have leaky shoes and no turn for poetry [2] — we may well thank the beneficent obstinacy of real mothers, real nurses, and (above all) real children for preserving the human race in such sanity as it still possesses. But the man-moulders of the new age will be armed with the powers of an omnicompetent state and an irresistible scientific technique: we shall get at last a race of conditioners who really can cut out all posterity in what shape they please. The second difference is even more important. In the older systems both the kind of man the teachers wished to produce and their motives for producing him were prescribed by the *Tao* [3] — a norm to

From THE ABOLITION OF MAN: From the book *The Abolition of Man*, by C. S. Lewis, Copyright 1947 by The Macmillan Company. Reprinted by permission of The Macmillan Company and Geoffrey Bles Ltd.

[1] *The Boke Named the Governour*, I. iv: " Al men except physitions only shulde be excluded and kepte out of the norisery." I. vi: " After that a childe is come to seuen yeres of age . . . the most sure counsaile is to withdrawe him from all company of women."

[2] *Some Thoughts concerning Education*, 7: " I will also advise his *Feet to be wash'd* every Day in cold Water, and to have his Shoes so thin that they might leak and *let in Water*, whenever he comes near it." 174: " If he have a poetick vein, 'tis to me the strangest thing in the World that the Father should desire or suffer it to be cherished or improved. Methinks the Parents should labour to have it stifled and suppressed as much as may be." Yet Locke is one of our most sensible writers on education.

[3] [The Chinese term *Tao* means Reality. Nature, the Road, the Way — the way in which the universe goes on and things emerge into space and time. It is also the way which men should tread in imitation of this progression. It is a harmony of Man with the Universe. Ed.'s note.]

which the teachers themselves were subject and from which they claimed no liberty to depart. They did not cut men to some pattern they had chosen. They handed on what they had received: they initiated the young neophyte into the mystery of humanity which overarched him and them alike. It was but old birds teaching young birds to fly. This will be changed. Values are now mere natural phenomena. Judgments of value are to be produced in the pupil as part of the conditioning. Whatever *Tao* there is will be the product, not the motive, of education. The conditioners have been emancipated from all that. It is one more part of Nature which they have conquered. The ultimate springs of human action are no longer, for them, something given. They have surrendered — like electricity: it is the function of the Conditioners to control, not to obey them. They know how to *produce* conscience and decide what kind of conscience they will produce. They themselves are outside, above. For we are assuming the last stage of Man's struggle with Nature. The final victory has been won. Human nature has been conquered — and, of course, has conquered, in whatever sense those words may now bear.

The Conditioners, then, are to choose what kind of artificial *Tao* they will, for their own good reasons, produce in the Human race. They are the motivators, the creators of motives. But how are they going to be motivated themselves? For a time, perhaps, by survivals, within their own minds, of the old " natural " *Tao*. Thus at first they may look upon themselves as servants and guardians of humanity and conceive that they have a " duty " to do it " good." But it is only by confusion that they can remain in this state. They recognize the concept of duty as the result of certain processes which they can now control. Their victory has consisted precisely in emerging from the state in which they were acted upon by those processes to the state in which they use them as tools. One of the things they now have to decide is whether they will, or will not, so condition the rest of us that we can go on having the old idea of duty and the old reactions to it. How can duty help them to decide that? Duty itself is up for trial: it cannot also be the judge. And " good " fares no better. They know quite well how to produce a dozen different conceptions of good in us. The question is which, if any, they should produce. No conception of good can help them to decide. It is absurd to fix on one of the things they are comparing and make it the standard of comparison.

To some it will appear that I am inventing a factitious difficulty for my Conditioners. Other, more simple-minded, critics may ask " Why should you suppose they will be such bad men? " But I am not supposing them to be bad men. They are, rather, not men (in the old sense) at all. They are, if you like, men who have sacrificed their own share in traditional humanity in order to devote themselves to the task of deciding what " Humanity " shall henceforth mean. " Good " and " bad," applied to them, are words without content; for it is from them that the content of these words is henceforward to be derived. Nor is their difficulty factitious. We might suppose that it was possible to say, " After all, most of us want more or less the same things — food and drink and sexual intercourse, amusement, art, science, and the longest possible life for individuals and for the species. Let them simply say, ' This is what we happen to like,' and go on to condition men in the way most likely to produce it. Where's the trouble? " But this will not answer. In the first place, it is false that we all really like the same things. But even if we did, what motive is to impel the Conditioners to scorn delights and live laborious days in order that we, and posterity, may have what we like? Their duty? But that is only the *Tao,* which they may decide to impose on us, but which cannot be valid for them. If they accept it, then they are no longer the makers of conscience but still its subjects, and their final conquest over Nature has not really happened. The preservation of the species? But why should the species be preserved? One of the questions before them is whether this feeling for posterity (they know well how it is produced) shall be continued or not. However far they go back, or down, they can find no ground to stand on. Every motive they try to act on becomes at once a *petitio.* It is not that they are bad men. They are not men at all. Stepping outside the *Tao,* they have stepped into the void. Nor are their subjects necessarily unhappy men. They are not men at all: they are artefacts. Man's final conquest has proved to be the abolition of Man.

Yet the Conditioners will act. When I said just now that all motives fail them, I should have said all motives except one. All motives that claim any validity other than that of their felt emotional weight at a given moment have failed them. Everything except the *sic volo, sic jubeo* has been explained away. But what never claimed objectivity cannot be destroyed by subjectivism. The impulse to scratch when I itch or to pull to pieces when I am inquisitive is immune from the solvent which is fatal to my justice, or honour, or care for posterity. When all that says " it is good " has been debunked, what says " I want " remains. It cannot be exploded or " seen through " because it never had any pretensions. The Conditioners, therefore, must come to be motivated simply by their own pleasure. I am not here speaking of the corrupting influence of power nor expressing the fear that under it our Conditioners will degenerate. The very words *corrupt* and *degenerate* imply a doctrine of value and are therefore meaningless in this context. My point is that those who stand outside all judgments of value cannot have any ground for preferring one of their own impulses to another except the emotional strength of that impulse. We may legitimately hope that among the impulses which arise in minds thus emptied of all " rational " or " spiritual " motives, some will be benevolent. I am very doubtful myself whether the benevolent impulses, stripped of that preference and encouragement which the *Tao* teaches us to give them and left to their merely natural strength and frequency as psychological events, will have much influence. I am very doubtful whether history shows us one example of a man who, having stepped outside traditional morality and attained power, has used that power benevolently. I am inclined to think that the Conditioners will hate the conditioned. Though regarding as an illusion the artificial conscience which they produce in us their subjects, they will yet perceive that it creates in us an illusion of meaning for our lives which compares favourably with the futility of their own: and they will envy us as eunuchs envy men. But I do not insist on this, for it is mere conjecture. What is not conjecture is that our hope even of a " conditioned " happiness rests on what is ordinarily called " chance " — the chance that benevolent impulses may on the whole predominate in our Conditioners. For without the judgement " Benevolence is good " — that is, without re-entering the *Tao* — they can have no ground for promoting or stabilizing their benevolent impulses rather than any others. By the logic of their position they must just take their impulses as they come, from chance. And Chance here means Nature. It is from heredity, digestion, the weather, and the association of ideas, that the motives of the Conditioners will spring. Their extreme rationalism, by " seeing through " all " rational " motives, leaves them creatures of wholly irrational behaviour. If you will not obey the *Tao,* or else commit suicide, obedience to impulse (and therefore, in the long run, to mere " nature ") is the only course left open.

At the moment, then, of Man's victory over Nature, we find the whole human race subjected to some individual men, and those individuals subjected to that in themselves which is purely " natural " — to their irrational impulses. Nature, untrammelled by values, rules the Conditioners and, through them, all humanity. Man's conquest of Nature turns out, in the moment of its consummation, to be Nature's conquest of Man. Every victory we seemed to win has led us, step by step, to this conclusion. All Nature's apparent reverses have been but tactical withdrawals. We thought we were beating her back when she was luring us on. What looked to us like hands held up in surrender was really the opening of arms to enfold us for ever. If the fully planned and conditioned world (with its *Tao* a mere product of the planning) comes into existence, Nature will be troubled no more by the restive species that rose in revolt against her so many millions of years ago, will be vexed no longer by its chatter of truth and mercy and beauty and happiness. *Ferum victorem cepit:* and if the eugenics are efficient enough there will be no second revolt, but all snug beneath the Conditioners, and the Conditioners beneath her, till the moon falls or the sun grows cold.

My point may be clearer to some if it is put in a different form. Nature is a word of varying meanings, which can best be understood if we consider its various opposites. The Natural is the opposite of the Artificial, the Civil, the Human, the Spiritual, and the Supernatural. The Artificial does not now concern us. If we take the rest of the list of opposites, however, I think we can get a rough idea of what men have meant by Nature and what it is they oppose to her. Nature seems to be the spatial and temporal, as distinct from what is less fully so or not so at all. She seems to be the world of quantity, as against the world of quality: of objects as against consciousness: of the bound, as against the wholly or partially autonomous: of that which knows no values as against that which both has and perceives value: of efficient causes (or, in some modern systems, of no causality at all) as against final causes. Now I take it that when we understand a thing analytically and then dominate and use it for our own convenience we reduce it to the level of " Nature " in the sense that we suspend our judgements of value about it, ignore its final cause (if any), and treat it in terms of quantity. This repression of elements in what would otherwise be our total reaction to it is sometimes very noticeable and even painful: something has to be overcome before we can cut up a dead man or a live animal in a dissecting room. These objects *resist* the movement of the mind whereby we thrust them into the world of mere Nature. But in other instances too, a similar price is exacted for our analytical knowledge and manipulative power, even if we have ceased to count it. We do not look at trees either as Dryads or as beautiful objects while we cut them into beams: the first man who did so may have felt the price keenly, and the bleeding trees in Virgil and Spenser may be far-off echoes of that primeval sense of impiety. The stars lost their divinity as astronomy developed, and the Dying God has no place in chemical agriculture. To many, no doubt, this process is simply the gradual discovery that the real world is different from what we expected, and the old opposition to Galileo or to " body-snatchers " is simply obscurantism. But that is not the whole story. It is not the greatest of modern scientists who feel most sure that the object, stripped of its qualitative properties and reduced to mere quantity, is wholly real. Little scientists, and little unscientific followers of science, may think so. The great minds know very well that the object, so treated, is an artificial abstraction, that something of its reality has been lost.

From this point of view the conquest of Nature appears in a new light. We reduce things to mere Nature *in order that* we may " conquer " them. We are always conquering Nature, because " Nature " is the name for what we have, to some extent, conquered. The price of conquest is to treat a thing as mere Nature. Every conquest over Nature increases her domain. The stars do not become Nature till we can weigh and measure them: the soul does not become Nature till we can psycho-analyse her. The wresting of powers *from* Nature is also the surrendering of things *to* Nature. As long as this process stops short of the final stage we may well hold that the gain outweighs the loss. But as soon as we take the final step of reducing our own species to the level of mere Nature, the whole process is stultified, for this time the being who stood to gain and the being who has been sacrificed are one and the same. This is one of the many instances where to carry a principle to what seems its logical conclusion produces absurdity. It is like the famous Irishman who found that a certain kind of stove reduced his fuel bill by half and thence concluded that two stoves of the same kind would enable him to warm his house with no fuel at all. It is the magician's bargain: give up our soul, get power in return. But once our souls, that is, our selves, have been given up, the power thus conferred will not belong to us. We shall in fact be the slaves and puppets of that to which we have given our souls. It is in Man's power to treat himself as a mere " natural object " and his own judgements of value as raw material for scientific manipulation to alter at will. The objection to his doing so does not lie in the fact that this point of view (like one's first day in a dissecting room) is painful and shocking till we grow used to it. The pain and the shock are at most a warning and a symptom. The real objection is that if man chooses to treat himself as raw material, raw material he will be: not raw material to be manipulated, as he fondly imagined, by himself, but by mere appetite, that is, mere Nature, in the person of his dehumanized Conditioners.

The Seven Deadly Fallacies

Arthur Koestler

The war hysteria from which a considerable number of people seem to suffer here in the United States is not a sign of mature awareness. Nor is the mentality of appeasement. Appeasement of an expanding power creates a fog in which neither of the opponents knows where he is; the aggressor, having grabbed positions A, B and C, hopes to get away with grabbing D — and why should he not hope so with all the encouragement that he receives from the opponent's camp? But position D — Poland in 1939, and maybe Italy to-day — has meanwhile come to be regarded by the other side as a *casus belli,* and so the world slides into war — without either of the opponents wanting it. Appeasement means playing poker; a firm, clearly outlined, principled policy means playing chess.

These are platitudes, the type of platitude which every reader of the *New Republic* or *The New Statesman and Nation* knew by heart in the 1930's. To-day they have forgotten it, and arguing against them means regressing to the kindergarten level. I hope that in this meeting we shall remain at least on the level of the primary school. So I shall take it for granted henceforth that war hysteria and appeasement are our Scylla and Charybdis, and that the liberal's precarious task is to navigate like Ulysses between the two.

Allow me, as an aid to navigation, to point out some of the logical fallacies and emotional eddies in which young idealists frequently get shipwrecked. I have listed for myself seven of them — the seven deadly fallacies of what you may allow me to call Left Babbittism. Here they are:

First is *the confusion of Left and East.* Some sections of the reactionary Press are unable or unwilling to distinguish between liberals, New Dealers, Social Democrats and Communists; they are all damned Reds. Naturally we are indignant at such poisonous imbecility. But the Left itself is partly responsible for this confusion. The Left Babbitt assumes that there is a continuous spectrum stretching from pale pink liberals to deeper red socialists and so on to purple Communists. It is time that he got it into his head that Moscow is not to his left but to his east. The Soviet Union is not a socialist country, and Com-

THE SEVEN DEADLY FALLACIES: From *The Trail of the Dinosaur* by Arthur Koestler; published 1955 by The Macmillan Company. Copyright 1947 by Arthur Koestler and reprinted with his permission. Compressed version of a lecture in Carnegie Hall, New York, March, 1948.

inform policy is not socialist policy. So let us bear in mind that " East is east and Left is left " and if the twain sometimes still meet, the meeting is purely coincidental.

The second fallacy is *the soul-searching fallacy.* The other day there was a press conference at which I mentioned that the frightened people in Italy and France look upon you Americans as their only hope of salvation, both from the economic point of view through E. R. P., and from the military point of view against open or disguised Russian aggression. Thereupon one of the reporters present said, " Do you really believe that we can help Europe with our dirty hands? " I asked: " What do you mean by ' dirty hands '? " He said: " Well, I mean our policy in Greece, and in Palestine, and backing up Franco, and the way we treat Negroes and Jews. We are dirty all over, and when we pose as defenders of democracy it is sheer hypocrisy."

The answer to this fallacy is to project the argument back to 1938. Then it would have run as follows: " We have no right to fight Hitler's plan of sending the Jews to the gas chambers so long as there are ' restricted ' hotels in America and so long as Negroes do not have absolute equality here. Once American democracy has become a perfect democracy, then and then only shall we have a right to defend what remains of Europe. And if Europe goes to the dogs before we have finished, that's just too bad and cannot be helped."

Third, and closely related to the soul-searching fallacy, is *the fallacy of the false equation.* Its European version runs: " Soviet totalitarianism is bad. American imperialism is equally bad. There is nothing to choose between them, so let us stay in No Man's land until fate catches up with us." To prove that the American system is " just as bad " as the Russian system, to make the two sides of the equation balance, your purist has recourse to half-conscious little subterfuges. He equates the Hollywood purges with the Moscow purges. He has never lived under a totalitarian régime, so when he draws comparisons he does not know what he is talking about. His conscience is in revolt against the appalling slums of Chicago, in which the Negro workers of the slaughter-house industry live like rats. I have spent a few days in Chicago, and I was appalled by what I saw and heard and smelled. Do not think I am a naïve tourist, a romantic admirer of your system. But now compare your treatment of racial minorities at its worst, with the Soviet treatment of the minorities of the Crimean Republic, the Chechen Republic, the Volga-German Republic, whose total populations were deported because they had, as the official Soviet communiqué said, " proved themselves unreliable during the war." Even the babes in their cradles were unreliable and had to go to Siberia. In Chicago I saw men on strike, and sympathised with them. In Russia strikes, or incitement to strike, are qualified as high treason and punished by the maximum penalty. In American elections political machines corrupt and distort the People's will. In Russian elections 99½ per cent. vote for the one official list — the remaining ½ per cent. presumably being in bed with influenza. Your enlightened Babbitt equates an imperfect democracy with a perfect totalitarian régime; his philosophy boils down to the maxim that there is nothing to choose between measles and leprosy.

Fallacy number four is *the anti-anti attitude*. It runs: " I am not a Communist. In fact, I dislike Communist politics, but I don't want to be identified with anti-Communist witch-hunting. Hence I am neither a Communist nor an anti-Communist, but an anti-anti-Communist. If W. R. Hearst says that twice two is four, I shall automatically hold that twice two is five, or at least 4½." The $2 \times 2 = 4½$ mathematicians are usually Henry Wallace voters.

Don't laugh, for the roots of this fallacy are very deep in all of us, myself included. I remember how painful it was when a doddering elder in a London club walked up to me and said with a tap on my shoulder: " Well, young man, I am glad that at last you have come round to see reason. I myself knew twenty-five years ago what Bolshevism means, and it's never too late to repent."

You can't help this sort of thing; you can't help people being right for the wrong reasons. In the last war we fought in the name of democracy in an alliance with Dictator Metaxas of Greece, Dictator Chiang Kai-shek and Dictator Stalin. At that time Nazism was the main menace to the world, and politics is based on forming alliances. But there is a fundamental difference between a war-time alliance, and political identification with one's allies. Being allied to Chiang did not mean that we wished to imitate the Chinese régime. Being against our will in one camp with the Hearst press or Senator McCarthy does not mean that we identify ourselves with their ideas and methods. This fear of finding oneself in bad company is not an expression of political purity; it is an expression of a lack of self-confidence. If you are sure of yourself — politically and ideologically — you will no longer be frightened to say that twice two makes four, even if Colonel McCormick says the same.

Fallacy number five is *the sentimental fallacy*. For years we were allied to Communists in the struggle against Nazism, and now when we have to part company, the roots of past loyalty are difficult to tear out. Our bedfellows of yesterday do not share this sentimental squeamishness. Over the slightest disagreement they will denounce us as Fascists, traitors and cannibals. These emotional ties are one-way ties, and it is essential to bear in mind that they are entirely irrational and conservative in nature.

Fallacy number six is *the fallacy of the perfect cause*. It is related to number two, the soul-searching fallacy. Only absolutely clean hands have a right to reach out to protect and save what remains of Europe. Only an absolutely perfect cause is worth fighting for. And the search for the perfect cause becomes an excuse for quietism.

History knows no perfect causes, no situation of white against black. Eastern totalitarianism is black; its victory would mean the end of our civilisation. Western democracy is not white but grey. To live, even to die for a perfect cause is a luxury permitted to few. In 1942 or '43 I published an article which began with the words: "In this war we are fighting a total lie in the name of a half-truth." The total lie was Hitler's New Order. The half-truth was our democracy. To-day we face a similar emergency and a similar predicament. Once more the choice before us is merely that between a grey twilight and total darkness. But ask the refugees who manage to escape, at the risk of their lives, from behind the iron curtain into our grey twilight world whether this choice is worth fighting for. They know. You don't.

The last fallacy, number seven, is the *confusion between short-term and long-term aims*. It is the most dangerous of all. By long-term aims I mean the age-old struggle for reform, for social justice, for a more equitable system of government. By short-term aims I mean the necessity of fighting an immediate emergency.

The danger of confusion is twofold. Your leftist Babbitt may refuse to fight against the short-term emergency until he has finished the job of creating a perfect government in his country, in a century or two. The opposite danger is to become so obsessed with the immediate emergency, that all principles of the long-term struggle are thrown overboard. Ex-Communists and disappointed radicals are in particular danger of toppling over to the other extreme. It is essential that we should keep in mind that there are two distinct levels involved in our struggle; that to defend our system against a deadly threat does not imply acceptance of everything in this system, does not imply giving up the long-term fight to improve it; and *vice versa,* that our criticism of the shortcomings of this system does not free us from the duty to defend it, despite its ambiguous greyness, against the total corruption of the human ideal.

This talk was mainly addressed to the progressive Left. I may have been harsh to the Left Babbitt; it was a brotherly harshness. To the Babbitt of the Right I have nothing to say; we have no language in common.

The power-vacuum which two world wars have created in Central and Western Europe, has inescapably linked your fate with that of the European continent. I feel the enormous burden which is falling on your shoulders. For there will either be a *Pax Americana* in the world, or there will be no pax. Never has such a burden and such a responsibility been borne by any single nation in history. It is the more unfair to you as yours is an adolescent civilisation, with adolescent enthusiasms and adolescent pimples. The task of the progressive intelligentsia of your country is to help the rest of the nation to face its enormous responsibilities. It is time for the American liberal to grow up.

Motes, Beams, and Foreigners

Dorothy Canfield

1

Breathes there a man — breathes there a woman — with soul so dead as never to have thrown a plate across the table at the graciously condescending person who has just remarked, " Why, nobody would ever think *you* were an American! "

When I was younger that well-meant phrase roused me to throw metaphorical plates, to boil inwardly, to stamp away, to slam doors behind me. " How would *he* like it," I used to mutter under my breath, " how would he like it if I told *him* with a congratulatory grin, ' why nobody in the world would ever dream you were English (or German, or French, or what not)! ' "

I used to flatter myself on my superior international broad-mindedness, until one day not long ago it occurred to me that, though I didn't say them aloud, I was constantly thinking those very words myself.

If I met an Englishman (one does occasionally) who was sensitive to nuances of all kinds, with quick, kind intuitions about other people's feelings, who did not lose all human decency if he couldn't get his afternoon tea, who did not assume that God must be English or he wouldn't be God, who did not take it for granted that English homes

MOTES, BEAMS, AND FOREIGNERS: From *Harper's Magazine,* March, 1931. Permission to reprint granted by Paul R. Reynolds & Son, 599 Fifth Avenue, New York, N.Y.

are the only real homes, into whose voice there did not creep when he spoke of or to a person with a title that peculiar quality we have all heard in English voices when a title is in the offing, and who did not think that the adjective " un-English " was a synonym for degradation — whenever I happened to meet such a prodigy, what did I say to myself about him? You know what I said, " Well, who'd ever think that man was English! "

And the Frenchman or French woman who could pass a door marked *" entrée interdite "* without pushing it open, who refrained from using personal influence to get some special privilege unshared by others, who did not glare murderous hate at a traveler entering his railway compartment, who did not fly off the handle to one or the other acrimonious extreme on the Clerical question, who did not lose all human decency if he hadn't hot soup in the evening, who did not consider French mothers the only preservers of sacred home life, who did not conceive of all civilization, past, present and future, as centering exclusively in Paris — had I not a thousand times murmured to myself my conviction, " There simply must be some Alsatian, or Flemish, or Swiss, or Jewish blood in that family! "

I ran rapidly through all my personal experiences of other nationalities. Every instance convicted me of being just as provincial and complacent as the people I had laughed at and hated. And you who read this article are just as bad as I, no matter who you may be! Consider the quiet, slim, reserved, gentlemanly person across the table from us on the steamer coming home. He had no roll of fat at the back of his neck; his manner to his wife was courteous and gentle; he did not lean over his plate and breathe hard when he ate; even when home-life was mentioned he did not show that he considered German homes the only ones left alive in the twentieth century — if you had been there, you as well as I would repeatedly have suppressed the exclamation, " To think of that man's hailing from Prussia! " Don't tell me you wouldn't! I know better.

Conscience-struck, I realized that my urbanity had been only surface-deep. What others blurted out, I hotly thought and felt. Who was I to resent the phrase, " Nobody would ever think you were an American," with its clearly understood implication: " Unlike your fellow-countrymen, you respect grammar, never say, ' Whoopee ' or ' O. K.,' seem to conceive of other bases for civilization than a bathtub for every bedroom, ignore toothpicks, do not attend revival meetings, retain some semblance of humanity even if you do not have cereal for breakfast, do not proclaim that American homes are the only ones where ' true home life ' is to be found."

" Well, well, what is the matter with us all? " I wondered, laying down my plate and closing the door gently. " Are we so one-sided that we all — not only ordinary folk but enlightened people like myself — consider other nations' objectionable qualities (mostly universal to humanity) as the characteristic traits which make them what they are and different from us? And when a foreigner tries his hand at the same game about *our* nation, have we the face to cry out at his obvious shocking injustice? "

At first sight it looked very familiar — and hopeless. Just another manifestation of plain human cussedness about which there is no arguing. But the change away from the " God-I-thank-thee " attitude to the honest humility of " Lord be merciful " carries one a long way towards a little fairness and understanding of human nature. The more I thought about the problem the less certain I was that contempt for people in all nations except our own is solidly based on the bedrock of inevitable hatefulness. We do not, for example — no, not even the least civilized of us — feel this same complacent contempt for all other humans except ourselves, or take unquestioningly this outrageous attitude towards individual human beings. When people of our own circle act disagreeably we do not assume that it is only their real nature coming out. Nor when they meet with our approval do we instinctively register the odious surprise which we find so natural when we occasionally approve of other nations. Mr. Emmet, your neighbor, stops his car and calls out, " I'm going down to the station to meet the six-ten, and I'll bring Ned home for you. Might as well, since I'm going anyhow. It'll save you the trip." You do not as a natural way of praising his thoughtful friendliness shout heartily back, " Well, well, who'd ever dream you were Roland Emmet! " Except in rare exceptional cases, and in rare, exceptionally cantankerous moods, such a formula does not even cross your thoughts, hapless member of the human race though you are.

If then we have — most of us most of the time — got beyond the baseness of thinking and expecting the worst of individual humans close to us, why are the octopus suckers of international prejudice still so firmly fastened in the depths of our hearts? We can think of Roland Emmet as a fellow human; why do we lump together millions of other fellow humans, as comic or objectionable Frenchmen, Germans, Englishmen? If we could find out the bad mental habits back of that injustice perhaps we could find out a way to pry those hateful tentacles loose — at least from our own hearts. And that would be worth doing. For as long as they are fixed there they suck away every faint beginning of international understanding and friendliness. Our unconscious hostility to a foreigner merely because he is a foreigner wedges the nations apart. It is as real an obstacle to decent feeling between nations as tariff walls, immigration problems, hostile armaments — as real, and perhaps more dangerous because it is so intimately a part of everybody's personal life.

You think I'm overstating the case, don't you? You've said to yourself, "Oh, there are lots of people who react just the other way. How about the Anglomaniacs, the Francophiles, the German-Americans one meets on the Rhine boats who proclaim themselves about one hundred and fifty per cent American; the Londoner or Chicagoan who goes Oriental and becomes more Chinese or Indian than any real Chinaman or Hindu?" They certainly show, don't they, that cosmopolitan good feeling is common enough? I thought of that apparent contradiction, too, and explored it for a moment. But it turned out, of course, to be only a by-pass of the main road leading to the same horrid goal of offensive complacency and unfairness. Such people, the fanatic converts to one or another civilization not their own by birth, do not judge any nation more fairly than the rest of us. They have merely changed the point of view from which they judge unfairly. A Francophile is only an American (or an Irishman, a German or whatever) who takes over the egregious cocksureness of a Frenchman; an Anglomaniac is only a foreigner who transfers his unreason to the English base; the blatant German-American merely says to his German kin (instead of to an American) "Well, nobody would ever think *you* were . . . etc."

2

I could spare no more time to these perverse transplanted jingoes, for through the fog of my discouraged bewilderment I thought I saw looming vaguely ahead a "principle." I don't know what your definition of a principle is; I define it as a tool which helps me make sense out of a mass of facts till then chaotic. When I finally caught up to this principle it turned out not such a very big one, nothing grand or epic about it; it never would have dug the Panama Canal. But it was big enough for my purpose. The moment I took it into my hand dirt began to fly and order began to come into the facts piled up in my mind, higgledy-piggledy, still lying in illogical confusion just where many years of transatlantic comings and goings had tumbled them in.

There are in your mind, too, I am sure, just such uncatalogued heaps of inexplicable facts. Haven't you wondered, sometimes with laughter at his absurdity, sometimes with profanity at the bad blood he stirs up, how the American traveler, after an expensive round of Paris-pleasures-for-sale, can have the nerve to report (as he often does) that "French women" are heartless gold-diggers? Haven't you turned the same wonder, laughter, and profanity on the French lecturer, who after a flight across country, or a month or two in New York, writes a book to show that " American women " are heartless gold-diggers? Haven't you asked yourself, not rhetorically but in honest amazement, how people can be so outrageous as to apply to other nations a method of judging which, when applied to their own, they recognize as downright unfair? Take the " American business man " (that pet scarecrow of European journalists), the dollar-making-machine with no personality outside his office, knowing nothing but how to run his factory, touching in no way the lives of his wife and children except to furnish money for them to spend. You are annoyed perhaps by this aged, fly-specked caricature but you do not take it seriously. Because the moment it is brought out in your presence your mind flies to the flesh-and-blood American business men you really know, all of them something more than successful industrialists; one is a collector of first editions, another a Gibraltar of helpfulness to local social service, an expert on the wild-life of his region, an explorer of some phase of American history, or a pretty good second violin in a string quartette. But wait a moment before you congratulate yourself on your wisdom. If you hear somebody remark carelessly that Frenchmen, of course, have no moral standards, does your experience with the falsity of sweeping generalization prompt you to protest? Aren't you apt to wag your head with the air of a man who knows life for what it is, and say in unison with the French voice from across the sea, " No indeed, I shouldn't want my daughter to marry a Frenchman (an American) "?

Why, only this last summer when I was visiting a Danish friend near Copenhagen, didn't she ask me challengingly, " You're always standing up for the French. I want to ask you straight — could you have brought yourself ever to *marry* a Frenchman? " I could see that she felt for a decent woman there could be but one answer, " No, heavens, no! Of course not." Through my mind ran the thought of one after another of the serious, exemplary Frenchmen of my acquaintance, devoted, magnanimous husbands, delightful companions, impassioned fathers. But I did not try to convert her, for even as I recoiled from the injustice of her prejudice, I thought, " If she had asked me if I could ever have married a Bulgarian, wouldn't my instant impulse have been to answer, " No, no, of course not! " Now that Danish friend is one of the wisest, most deep-hearted women I know. And I don't consider myself altogether provincial, either. How had we two, on most subjects open-minded, strayed so far from fairness?

We have plenty of company, and of the best. In the last book of Georges Duhamel — one eloquent wail of sorrow over Christopher Columbus' betrayal of humanity — he recounts the following incident as part of the evidence he collected here of the loathsome, hypocritical, Puritanical spirit of America. The fine, distinguished woman who was secretary of the Maison Française of Columbia received for him some mail from France. Knowing that he was anxious about the health of a member of his family, she went with it herself down to the Pennsylvania Hotel, where he was staying, and — presumably to spare him the shock of receiving bad news in the midst of strangers — took it up to his room. One of the letters did announce the death he feared. While he was still holding it in his hand, too stricken to speak, the central office of the hotel called his room by telephone, told him that men guests are not allowed to take women to their rooms, and would the strange lady seen entering his bedroom please go away.

The little episode is recounted with the dramatic skill of the wonderfully gifted writer that Duhamel is, charged to the last word with his power for making his readers share the suffering of his heroes. You, the reader, stand there, too, staring at the tragic words, your heart wrung with grief, your thoughts far on the other side of the Atlantic, with the stricken family there. Your nerves as well as his are shattered by the hateful, intrusive American jangle of the telephone. Only half-conscious of what you are doing, you take down the receiver and, with him, you shudder at the brutality of the insulting suspicion that lies back of the brusque summons in the harsh foreign language. You are swept along over the edge to the conclusion where Duhamel wants to land you, that a country where a sensitive, self-respecting man can be subjected to such a humiliation is indeed a crass, coarse, materialistic, hypocritical place which it was a great mistake ever to have discovered. What is wrong with this picture?

Well, one thing that is wrong with it is that good European hotels aren't any too enthusiastic about having men guests receive women in their bedrooms. Even the Grand Hotel of Vicki Baum, which certainly did not err on the side of Puritanism, drew the line at women secretaries in business men's bedrooms. Still more to the point, in M. Duhamel's home country the better class of café will not allow a woman alone, or with another woman, to sit down to a table and order a glass of lemonade (or anything else) no matter how thirsty she is. Many and many an American school-teacher, in France to absorb some of that fine civilization she has heard so much about, stopping at a café to get a drink of something cool on a hot day, has shuddered as much (though not as eloquently) as M. Duhamel, on being told plainly by the *garçon* that they do not serve women unaccompanied by men; the presumption of the country being that women who go alone to cafés are prostitutes, likely to annoy men patrons with solicitations. I have heard women recounting the humiliation to which they have been subjected, claim passionately that a country where such a thing could happen to a sensitive, self-respecting woman can be nothing but a putrid mass of moral corruption, just as they always heard before going there. Strange, isn't it, that Duhamel in holding up the Pennsylvania Hotel rule as proof of depraved Anglo-Saxon hypocrisy, should ignore the strikingly similar rule in Parisian cafés; strange that the school-teachers crying out upon French foul-mindedness should forget that in parallel circumstances their own country is as suspicious as any other!

3

It is more than strange, it is illuminating. Just set those two oddly assorted shudderers side by side before you and look at them with an analytical eye. Look at them fairly, even if you think them a little over-squeamish. To be sure, a hard-boiled commercial traveler in M. Duhamel's place would not have registered indignation and a lasting hatred of the United States. Instead he would have laughed the matter off with some such words as, " Trot along, Cutie. Anthony Comstock down in the office has got us wrong, but just the same, beat it." And at the café any of the youngish American women who try to keep in water hot enough to boil them might have taken the hint that she was no better than she should be as a welcome tribute to the chicness of her costume and make-up. Still the fact remains that our sensitive, not-at-all-hard-boiled M. Duhamel and the school-teacher did suffer and were perfectly right in feeling wounded and resentful. But they were hardly right in jumping to the conclusion that their suffering was caused by a beastliness *peculiar to the country each was visiting*. Why did they jump to that conclusion? Well, the first reason that leaps to visibility, of course, is that each found in the visited country just what he had been taught to expect. We all know that the American school-teacher's mind, before ever she saved up her passage money, was loaded to the gunwales and awash with the tradition of French immorality. And with all due respect to M. Duhamel's very superior mind, we may be equally sure that any Frenchman brings with him to the U. S. A. an attitude very receptive to any evidence of Puritan nasty-niceness. After all what happened to them? It was about the same thing, wasn't it? Each was humiliated by being told by a foreigner that he (or she), a decent, self-respecting person, had by a harmless, unconsidered action quite natural under the circumstances, put himself in a position which by the dirty-minded custom of the country laid him open to the suspicion of sexual irregularity. Their very reactions are similar. Each hates and despises the country where the humiliation happened. Each refuses to believe that anything similar could happen in the homeland. Why, oh why, that last assumption?

Yes, yes, patience! I am approaching that " principle." According to the best pedagogic practice I am taking you through the steps which led me to it. We have seen that on arriving in the country each held a prepared label in his hand, ready-licked so to speak, to paste on whatever happened. But much more than this, it is quite possible, it is probable, it is almost certain that they did not consciously and unfairly turn their eyes away from the custom in their own country corresponding to the one they encountered abroad, because they honestly had never heard of it — or so vaguely that it made no personal impression on their minds. How would the American school-teacher ever have run into that rule in American hotels? It is the rarest thing in the world for her, I am sure, to go to a hotel in the States at all, and it certainly never would occur to her to invite a strange gentleman to come up to her bedroom. In fact, though I am past fifty and have been around to American hotels myself a good deal, and have repeatedly patronized the Pennsylvania Hotel, I never heard of that rule till I read it in the book of the French traveler. I ask you, how should I? On the other side, M. Duhamel has certainly sat down a great many times at a café table to order a cool drink on a hot day. But he probably would have heard vaguely if at all of the reception given self-respecting American school-teachers who try to do the same thing. How would he? No French school-teacher or any other well-bred French woman of any class would get into such a situation. If she wanted a cool drink, she'd step into a *pâtisserie,* where she would be welcome.

Everybody knows his way around his own country and does not step through those invisible high-tension wires which fence off what " is done " from what " isn't done." But when he is in a foreign country he doesn't see them till he has blundered through and is writhing in misery from the consequent electric shock. All travelers in the nature of things constantly find themselves in foreign countries in positions which do not correspond with anything that ever happens to them in their own. But humans — you know their habits — cannot encounter a thing, not the smallest thing, without passing judgment on it. We are made that way. For good and for bad, that is one of our most marked qualities. And you can't judge anything unless you have something to compare it with. So our wounded or indignant or contemptuous travelers usually — *faute de mieux* — compare what happens to them in a foreign country with *something entirely different from it in their own.*

And there's my principle. I'll put it like a mathematical formula.

" Much, perhaps most, international misunderstanding and dislike is not inherent and inevitable, but comes from the comparison of customs and people in our country not with corresponding customs and people in another, but with others totally different." I'll make it clearer. Since everything is put down in graphs nowadays, I'll make a graph of it. It's so simple even I can draw it.

What the enlightened, perfectly just (and almost nonexistent) tourist should do, in judging the customs of the country where he is visiting, is expressed in the following graph, in which A represents the foreign custom he is trying to evaluate, and A' the corresponding custom in his own country, and the other letters, B', C', D', other customs, that have no relation to the one he is encountering.

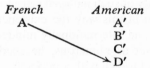

> French   American
> A————————→A'
>   B'
>   C'
>   D'

The straight line drawn from a foreign custom to the one corresponding to it in America expresses, of course, the route that should be traveled by the fair-minded traveler. The graph below expresses the route his mind usually does follow.

> French   American
> A   A'
>   B'
>   C'
>   →D'

Perhaps you can follow me better if I diagram a concrete case already familiar to you, the American visitor to Montmartre night life. He feels the impulse, universal, human, inevitable, to make some estimate of the life he is encountering. Now you can estimate or measure a thing only by setting it up against something the dimensions or value of which you already know. As a standard of comparison for the night-life women in Paris, the visiting American knows, say, the night-life women of New York, the women who taught school when he went to school, the women employees in his office, his own mother, wife, and daughter, etc., etc.

Here is the graph:

French	American
French night-life women	American night-life women
	School-teachers
	Employees
	Mothers, wives, etc.

With no more explanation of my principle, I can trust you to draw his line anywhere but straight across to where it should go. Just draw it anywhere you think he's likely to have drawn it and see graphically what is wrong with that man's report on what " French women " are like.

Here's another concrete case, in which I applied the principle and the graph to my own enlightenment, this very day. I was reading a witty, Heinelike article by a German about France, about the fact that whoever fights France must be prepared to find God on the other side, about the complacent French assumption that whoever fights for France fights for humanity, etc., etc. I couldn't help laughing at the picture he drew of embattled French self-righteousness, the likeness was so deftly caught. But after a time, I stopped reading to exclaim, " But see here! How ever has he the nerve to consider that characteristic of the French alone! Didn't he ever hear about *Gott mit uns,* and *unser alte Deutsche Gott?* Not to speak of English cathedrals ringing sonorously with the certainty that God is in danger when England is. How *can* a man have . . ." But, of course, I saw at once how he could. He had drawn his line crookedly, namely from the large number of self-centered, savagely nationalistic people in France, not to the similar large group in his own country with exactly similar views, but to the small number of broad-minded, fair people capable of seeing the murderous absurdity of such national self-glorification. And having hidden from his vision in this way the existence of a small group in France, just as broad and internationally minded as the similar circle in Germany, and about as numerous, he sped on his way making clear and open the road to hell with a perfectly good conscience.

Our unfortunate American school-teacher got herself misunderstood and insulted by assuming in her mental graph that a smart French café is equivalent to an American soda water fountain, which is about as sensible as to assume that a leopard, because it has four legs like a lap dog, can be treated in the same manner.

4

I said that the fair-minded traveler is almost nonexistent, almost but not quite. M. Dubreuil represents the intelligent minority. A French skilled mechanic, he came to this country and worked in various factories (Ford's among others) to see for himself the life the American workingman really leads. His graphs are not crazy quilts. He draws them with the skill and intelligence of a craftsman. On one page he describes the Sunday of an American working family. They spend their morning like dumb driven cattle, reading the comic strips in the newspapers and listening to the radio. After dinner they sit for a while, listening to the phonograph playing jazz, and then, utterly barren of any inner resources, incapable of any conversation except trivial personalities, leave the house and climb into yet another machine in which they spend the rest of the day, racing through scenery at which they do not look. So far his account sounds exactly like the usual European recipe for pictures of American life — the main ingredients of the dish being plenty of stupefying mechanism well stirred together with ignorance, seasoned by the European cook with contempt and a dash of fear, and served piping hot. But M. Dubrueil gives an O. Henry twist at the end simply by drawing his line with accuracy straight across the Atlantic. He does not compare this family with a group of intellectuals in Paris (as subconsciously most French writers do because that is the group they personally know) but with a similar workingman's family such as he alone among French writers on America has lived with. In France he tells us such a family would not have any radio, phonograph, or Ford car. But it wouldn't have had any conversation either. Sitting out on the porch with the wife and children of a summer evening and calling across to your next-door neighbor once in a while is flat and banal and American, but the talk is about on a level with that of a French family *of the same class* sitting around that much admired center of civilization, a table in a café. Civilized, cultivated conversation is everywhere, alas! restricted to very small groups, and most of the time even they don't bring it off.

But my Danish friend, my wise, fine Danish woman, who has as a matter of fact scarcely traveled at all in France and has never personally had a French friend, how can my formula and my graph apply to her? Ah, so easily, so completely, even more perfectly than in any other case. She, like hundreds and thousands of well-read people, was making the fatal, the abysmal mistake of comparing people she met in foreign books with the real people in her own country. Ah, what a fault was that, my countrymen — everybody's countrymen! The greatest. And we all do it. Even those who have written books themselves commit that fault, although they, if anybody, ought to know how little the people in books represent the general run of humanity as it is found. We are never sufficiently on our guard against the danger of judging foreign countries from their fiction because we are never seriously misled by the people in the books of our own native tongue. As we read, we mentally set back of them and around them the millions of real people who, if they existed in real life, would surround, modify, and dilute them to a recognizable humanity. But when we see them in a foreign book we take them for all there is. A Frenchman turns from Flaubert's white-hot indictment of small-town narrowness, meanness, stupidity, cruelty, and aridity of soul, as shown in

Madame Bovary, saying to himself, " What a strong, true picture of *one* aspect of human nature." The same man lays down *Main Street,* remarking, " So this is American nature! "

Do you read Scandinavian fiction? If you do, you must have noticed what violent, dark, morbid goings-on fill the days in the old Nordic part of Europe. Infanticide, melancholia, brooding, murderous moods, religious mania, all-pervading despair is the chief of their diet, isn't it? My Danish friend, of course, also reads and admires those books. But she knows perfectly well what relation they bear to the reliable, pleasant-mannered good citizens in real life all around her, devoted to their healthy, fun-loving children, fond of their wives, good bridge players, with tennis courts on their lawns, wet bathing suits hanging on the line, civilized books on their shelves, and radio loud-speakers in their living rooms. Yet she goes right on comparing the Frenchmen she meets in books, subtle, devilish, sex-tormented fellows, not with the Scandinavians she meets in books, but with her own agreeable circle of Nordic friends, relatives, and neighbors. Her graph line being all wrong, it's no wonder she comes to the oddest conclusions about the French — as odd as those we have about Scandinavians or those held by the French about America.

Do I mean that people are just alike everywhere, with no national traits at all? That's a rhetorical not a real question on your part. You know I can't mean that. Even if, as the Watsonites would have it, a Chinese baby and a Norwegian baby are made of the very same protoplasm (or whatever it is Watson thinks babies are made of), Norway and China soon arrange that protoplasm into different patterns. I mean that we can't make the faintest beginning at accuracy in knowing anything about national traits, customs, habits, or individuals as long as we keep trying to measure the flavor of string beans by comparing it to the rain-resisting qualities of roofing paper, so to speak. I mean considerably more than that, too, as I hope you'll see in a moment.

We cannot have the most approximate idea of what another nation is if we do not realize, and with all our fibers, that it is made up of all kinds of folks; that, for instance, France is not inhabited solely by French people but mostly by human beings. We shall always harbor absurd and unfair ideas of other peoples and other races so long as we think we know something about any given individual human being when we have been told what his race or nationality is, instead of comprehending that we still know nothing, nothing, nothing! One authentic fact about him himself, the smallest, the most baroque — such as that he is apt to be late at appointments, or that he likes green neckties — gives you just one hundred per cent more reliable information about the flesh-and-blood individual he is than to know that he is Swedish, or Swiss, or Jewish. Because, doggedly as our minds set themselves against the idea, there are all kinds of Swedes and Swiss and Jews.

Perhaps one reason why we so mulishly balk at this idea is that we do not really admit it in the case of our own country. We know, of course, there are in our own nation a great many people who are " not our kind." Pennsylvania believers in witchcraft and hex-masters, Southern lynch-mobs, New England back-road degenerates, California religious maniacs, to mention a few. But when we speak of " Americans " we don't include them. We mean by Americans those we know, and we naturally gather around us those who are our kind, because we don't like to have anything to do with the others if we can help it. It does not occur to us, for instance, to look about us in the day-coach of a railway train, or in the subway, or on the station-platform of a country junction, to " see what Americans look like." We already know what Americans look like — our kind; and we keep our eyes glued to our magazine. Going abroad to a new country we leave behind " our kind," which makes up our own country for us, and transfer ourselves, not into the corresponding circle of the other country, for it takes years, a lifetime, several generations to locate that circle, but into the crowds who fill day-coaches and subway trains, and stand listless and inelegant at country junctions. There we sit, wide-eyed and observant, note-book in hand — French in America, Americans in France, everybody away from home anywhere — drawing graph lines that look like the trail of intoxicated serpents, and writing rapidly home about what foreign parts are really like.

Dubreuil, the philosophic French mechanic, points out that most French observers and commentators on American industrial life are singularly handicapped by a lack of the slightest acquaintance with French machine shops, that most of the French literary and academic visitors who shudder over a visit to the soulless hell of the Ford factory are in their own minds comparing it to their own pleasant studies or lecture-rooms, not at all to a French automobile (or any other) factory, because mostly they have never set foot in one, let alone never having done a lick of work on any machine, under any conditions. And those other untraveled but well-read French people, pitying us for living in a country so under the heel of tyrannical public opinion that Babbitts must conform to the pattern or perish — just let them leave their big-city, impersonal Paris life, where they can do as they please for the sole reason that they can keep people not their kind from knowing about it, move into a French small town of marked clerical tendencies, and invite the nice teacher in the public school to tea!

Ah, if we could but hold our pencils from drawing graph lines when we have no idea which way to point them, what a long step forward in international good feeling would have been made!

For it is my opinion that the longed-for breakdown of narrow, hateful nationalism, which must come if we are to escape poison-gassing one another off the globe altogether, can never come as idealists would have it, by a warm-hearted, world-wide recognition that all men are brothers. In the first place, because we are not a warm-hearted but on the whole a hateful race, and in the second place because all men are not brothers, nor anything like it. It would be impossible for us to love all humanity, and knowing more human specimens through more travel is not going to turn that trick, *rather the contrary* if we can't find a " principle " to sort out facts. For one thing, we can love only individuals, not " men " or " women " in a mass, because they do not exist as a mass. Much of our human misery comes because we fail to recognize that there is, accurately speaking, no plural to " child " or " man " or " woman." A generation of intensive study of child psychology has begun to teach us the danger of laying down rules for the correct treatment of " children." But we haven't even made a start at realizing that it is equally dangerous to try to pass judgment on " Frenchmen " or " American women." The ignominious surrender to barbarism involved in all race or national prejudice is based on this insistence of ours on treating other people in the plural, although nothing arouses more hotly one's own indignation than to be so treated himself.

I have said that we can love or be friendly only to individuals. More yet, we are so constituted as to be able to love among individuals only a few people who are " our kind." Internationalism solidly based on the realities of human nature can in my opinion only come from the knowledge that, since all nations are made up, like our own, of a jumbled lot of all kinds of specimens, " our kind " are scattered far and wide in all nations, and all races. And that the other kind, the people whose traits are so detestable that we must go to war against them once in a while, are also scattered far and wide over all nations, with a good many of them living on our street, right now. Exhortations to feel friendly toward other nations and other races cannot succeed because — there is no use talking about it — we do not " feel friendly " towards the majority of the human race anywhere. We can refrain from throwing bricks at them, perhaps from a sense of duty, perhaps from a fear that their bricks are bigger than ours; with an effort we admit theoretically that they have some right to live on the same globe with us; but we can feel friendly only with people with whom we have a good deal in common. The real barrier to international good-will is that we do not realize that there are such people in every nation and every race on earth.

Nor do we realize that the other kind are everywhere. Those hideous faults, and ridiculous flaws, and ugly vices, and bad manners, and cruelties which anybody with half an eye can discover in any country he visits, why does our race, in spite of all protests of hatred for such things, seem to make no headway against them? Isn't it because we will not look for them where we could find them, but insist on attributing them to this or that national or racial trait or custom? Of course they evade us. We could pull them out of their lairs and make at least a beginning of strangling them if we resisted with ferocity our human tendency to locate them in someone's else country, or community, or race, and would attack them where they live, in every human heart.

A Lark's Flight

Alexander Smith

Rightly or wrongly, during the last twenty or thirty years a strong feeling has grown up in the public mind against the principle, and a still stronger feeling against the practice, of capital punishments. Many people who will admit that the execution of the murderer may be, abstractly considered, just enough, sincerely doubt whether such execution be expedient, and are in their own minds perfectly certain that it cannot fail to demoralise the spectators. In consequence of this, executions have become rare; and it is quite clear that many scoundrels, well worthy of the noose, contrive to escape it. When, on the occasion of a wretch being turned off, the spectators are few, it is remarked by the newspapers that the mob is beginning to lose its proverbial cruelty, and to be stirred by humane pulses; when they are numerous, and especially when girls and women form a majority, the circumstance is noticed and deplored. It is plain enough that, if the newspaper considered such an exhibition beneficial, it would not lament over a few thousand eager witnesses: if the sermon be edifying, you cannot have too large a congregation; if you teach a moral lesson in a grand, impressive way, it is difficult to see how you can have too many pupils. Of course, neither the justice nor the expediency of capital punishments falls to be discussed here. This, however, may be said, that the popular feeling against them may not be so admirable a proof of enlightenment as many believe. It is true that the spectacle is painful, horrible; but in pain and horror there is often hidden a certain salutariness, and the repulsion of which we are conscious is as likely to arise from debilitation of public nerve, as from a higher reach of pub-

A LARK'S FLIGHT: From *Dreamthorp* (1863) by Alexander Smith.

lic feeling. To my own thinking, it is out of this pain and hatefulness that an execution becomes invested with an ideal grandeur. It is sheer horror to all concerned — sheriffs, halbertmen, chaplain, spectators, Jack Ketch,[1] and culprit; but out of all this, and towering behind the vulgar and hideous accessories of the scaffold, gleams the majesty of implacable law. When every other fine morning a dozen cut-purses were hanged at Tyburn, and when such sights did not run very strongly against the popular current, the spectacle *was* vulgar, and could be of use only to the possible cut-purses congregated around the foot of the scaffold. Now, when the law has become so far merciful; when the punishment of death is reserved for the murderer; when he can be condemned only on the clearest evidence; when, as the days draw slowly on to doom, the frightful event impending over one stricken wretch throws its shadow over the heart of every man, woman, and child in the great city; and when the official persons whose duty it is to see the letter of the law carried out perform that duty at the expense of personal pain, a public execution is not vulgar, it becomes positively sublime. It is dreadful, of course; but its dreadfulness melts into pure awfulness. The attention is taken off the criminal, and is lost in a sense of the grandeur of justice; and the spectator who beholds an execution, solely as it appears to the eye, without recognition of the idea which towers behind it, must be a very unspiritual and unimaginative spectator indeed.

It is taken for granted that the spectators of public executions — the artizans and country people who take up their stations overnight as close to the barriers as possible, and the wealthier classes who occupy hired windows and employ opera-glasses — are merely drawn together by a morbid relish for horrible sights. He is a bold man who will stand forward as the advocate of such persons — so completely is the popular mind made up as to their tastes and motives. It is not disputed that the large body of the mob, and of the occupants of windows, have been drawn together by an appetite for excitement; but it is quite possible that many come there from an impulse altogether different. Just consider the nature of the expected sight — a man in tolerable health probably, in possession of all his faculties, perfectly able to realise his position, conscious that for him this world and the next are so near that only a few seconds divide them — such a man stands in the seeing of several thousand eyes. He is so peculiarly circumstanced, so utterly lonely — hearing the tolling of his own death-bell, yet living, wearing the mourning clothes for his own funeral — that he holds the multitude together by a shuddering fascination. The sight is

---

[1] Jack Ketch (d. 1686) was a notorious executioner of the seventeenth century. His name is used allusively for any official executioner.

a peculiar one, you must admit, and every peculiarity has its attractions. Your volcano is more attractive than your ordinary mountain. Then consider the unappeasable curiosity as to death which haunts every human being, and how pathetic that curiosity is, in so far as it suggests our own ignorance and helplessness, and we see at once that people *may* flock to public executions for other purposes than the gratification of morbid tastes: that they would pluck if they could some little knowledge of what death is; that imaginatively they attempt to reach to it, to touch and handle it through an experience which is not their own. It is some obscure desire of this kind, a movement of curiosity not altogether ignoble, but in some degree pathetic; some rude attempt of the imagination to wrest from the death of the criminal information as to the great secret in which each is profoundly interested, which draws around the scaffold people from the country harvest-fields, and from the streets and alleys of the town. Nothing interests men so much as death. Age cannot wither it, nor custom stale it. " A greater crowd would come to see me hanged," Cromwell is reported to have said when the populace came forth on a public occasion. The Lord Protector was right in a sense of which, perhaps, at the moment he was not aware. Death is greater than official position. When a man has to die, he may safely dispense with stars and ribbands. He is invested with a greater dignity than is held in the gift of kings. A greater crowd *would* have gathered to see Cromwell hanged, but the compliment would have been paid to death rather than to Cromwell. Never were the motions of Charles I so scrutinised as when he stood for a few moments on the scaffold that winter morning at Whitehall. King Louis was no great orator usually, but when on January 2, 1793, he attempted to speak a few words in the Place de la Revolution, it was found necessary to drown his voice in a harsh roll of soldiers' drums. Not without a meaning do people come forth to see men die. We stand in the valley, they on the hilltop, and on their faces strikes the light of the other world, and from some sign or signal of theirs we attempt to discover or extract a hint of what it is all like.

To be publicly put to death, for whatever reason, must ever be a serious matter. It is always bitter, but there are degrees in its bitterness. It is easy to die like Stephen with an opened heaven above you, crowded with angel faces. It is easy to die like Balmerino [2] with a chivalrous sigh for the White Rose, and an audible " God bless King James." Such men die for a cause in which they glory, and are supported thereby; they are conducted to the portals of the next world by

---

[2] James Elphinstone, 1st Baron Balmerino (1553?–1612), secretary of state for Scotland under James I (then James VI of Scotland); though condemned to death, he was subsequently released.

the angels, Faith, Pity, Admiration. But it is not easy to die in expiation of a crime like murder, which engirdles you with trembling and horror even in the loneliest places, which cuts you off from the sympathies of your kind, which reduces the universe to two elements — a sense of personal identity, and a memory of guilt. In so dying, there must be inconceivable bitterness; a man can have no other support than what strength he may pluck from despair, or from the iron with which nature may have originally braced heart and nerve. Yet, taken as a whole, criminals on the scaffold comport themselves creditably. They look Death in the face when he wears his cruelest aspect, and if they flinch somewhat, they can at least bear to look. I believe that, for the criminal, execution within the prison walls, with no witnesses save some half-dozen official persons, would be infinitely more terrible than execution in the presence of a curious, glaring mob. The daylight and the publicity are alien elements, which wean the man a little from himself. He steadies his dizzy brain on the crowd beneath and around him. He has his last part to play, and his manhood rallies to play it well. Nay, so subtly is vanity intertwined with our motives, the noblest and the most ignoble, that I can fancy a poor wretch with the noose dangling at his ear, and with barely five minutes to live, soothed somewhat with the idea that his firmness and composure will earn him the approbation, perhaps the pity, of spectators. He would take with him, if he could, the good opinion of his fellows. This composure of criminals puzzles one. Have they looked at death so long and closely, that familiarity has robbed it of terror? Has life treated them so harshly, that they are tolerably well pleased to be quit of it on any terms? Or is the whole thing mere blind stupor and delirium, in which thought is paralysed, and the man an automaton? Speculation is useless. The fact remains that criminals for the most part die well and bravely. It is said that the championship of England was to be decided at some little distance from London on the morning of the day on which Thurtell was executed, and that, when he came out on the scaffold, he inquired privily of the executioner if the result had yet become known. Jack Ketch was not aware, and Thurtell expressed his regret that the ceremony in which he was chief actor should take place so inconveniently early in the day. Think of a poor Thurtell forced to take his long journey an hour, perhaps, before the arrival of intelligence so important!

More than twenty years ago I saw two men executed, and the impression then made remains fresh to this day. For this there were many reasons. The deed for which the men suffered created an immense sensation. They were hanged on the spot where the murder was committed — on a rising ground, some four miles north-east of the city; and as an attempt at rescue was apprehended, there was a considerable display of military force on the occasion. And when, in the dead silence of thousands, the criminals stood beneath the halters, an incident occurred, quite natural and slight in itself, but when taken in connexion with the business then proceeding, so unutterably tragic, so overwhelming in its pathetic suggestion of contrast, that the feeling of it has never departed, and never will. At the time, too, I speak of, I was very young; the world was like a die newly cut, whose every impression is fresh and vivid.

While the railway which connects two northern capitals was being built, two brothers from Ireland, named Doolan, were engaged upon it in the capacity of navvies. For some fault or negligence, one of the brothers was dismissed by the overseer — a Mr. Green — of that particular portion of the line on which they were employed. The dismissed brother went off in search of work, and the brother who remained — Dennis was the Christian name of him — brooded over this supposed wrong, and in his dull, twilighted brain revolved projects of vengeance. He did not absolutely mean to take Green's life, but he meant to thrash him to within an inch of it. Dennis, anxious to thrash Green, but not quite seeing his way to it, opened his mind one afternoon, when work was over, to his friends — fellow-Irishmen and navvies — Messrs. Redding and Hickie. These took up Doolan's wrong as their own, and that evening, by the dull light of a bothy [3] fire, they held a rude parliament, discussing ways and means of revenge. It was arranged that Green should be thrashed — the amount of thrashing left an open question, to be decided, unhappily, when the blood was up and the cinder of rage blown into a flame. Hickie's spirit was found not to be a mounting one, and it was arranged that the active partners in the game should be Doolan and Redding. Doolan, as the aggrieved party, was to strike the first blow, and Redding, as the aggrieved party's particular friend, asked and obtained permission to strike the second. The main conspirators, with a fine regard for the feelings of the weaker Hickie, allowed him to provide the weapons of assault — so that by some slight filament of aid he might connect himself with the good cause. The unambitious Hickie at once applied himself to his duty. He went out, and in due time returned with two sufficient iron pokers. The weapons were examined, approved of, and carefully laid aside. Doolan, Redding, and Hickie ate their suppers, and retired to their several couches to sleep, peacefully enough no doubt. About the same time, too, Green, the English overseer, threw down his weary limbs, and entered on his last sleep — little dreaming what the morning had in store for him.

---

[3] *bothy:* hut (Scot.)

Uprose the sun, and uprose Doolan and Redding, and dressed, and thrust each his sufficient iron poker up the sleeve of his blouse, and went forth. They took up their station on a temporary wooden bridge which spanned the line, and waited there. Across the bridge, as was expected, did Green ultimately come. He gave them good morning; asked, " why they were loafing about? " received no very pertinent answer, perhaps did not care to receive one; whistled — the unsuspecting man! — thrust his hands into his breeches pockets, turned his back on them, and leaned over the railing of the bridge, inspecting the progress of the works beneath. The temptation was really too great. What could wild Irish flesh and blood do? In a moment out from the sleeve of Doolan's blouse came the hidden poker, and the first blow was struck, bringing Green to the ground. The friendly Redding, who had bargained for the second, and who, naturally enough, was in fear of being cut out altogether, jumped on the prostrate man, and fulfilled his share of the bargain with a will. It was Redding it was supposed who sped the unhappy Green. They overdid their work — like young authors — giving many more blows than were sufficient, and then fled. The works, of course, were that morning in consternation. Redding and Hickie were, if I remember rightly, apprehended in the course of the day. Doolan got off, leaving no trace of his whereabouts.

These particulars were all learned subsequently. The first intimation which we schoolboys received of anything unusual having occurred, was the sight of a detachment of soldiers with fixed bayonets, trousers rolled up over muddy boots, marching past the front of the Cathedral hurriedly home to barracks. This was a circumstance somewhat unusual. We had, of course, frequently seen a couple of soldiers trudging along with sloped muskets, and that cruel glitter of steel which no one of us could look upon quite unmoved; but in such cases, the deserter walking between them in his shirt-sleeves, his pinioned hands covered from public gaze by the loose folds of his great-coat, explained everything. But from the hurried march of these mud-splashed men nothing could be gathered, and we were left to speculate upon its meaning. Gradually, however, before the evening fell, the rumour of a murder having been committed spread through the city, and with that I instinctively connected the apparition of the file of muddy soldiers. Next day, murder was in every mouth. My schoolfellows talked of it to the detriment of their lessons; it flavoured the tobacco of the fustian artizan as he smoked to work after breakfast; it walked on Change amongst the merchants. It was known that two of the persons implicated had been captured, but that the other, and guiltiest, was still at large; and in a few days out on every piece of boarding and blank wall came the " Hue and cry " — describing Doolan like a photograph, to the colour and cut of his whiskers, and offering £100 as reward for his apprehension, or for such information as would lead to his apprehension — like a silent, implacable bloodhound following close on the track of the murderer. This terrible broadsheet I read, was certain that *he* had read it also, and fancy ran riot over the ghastly fact. For him no hope, no rest, no peace, no touch of hands gentler than the hangman's; all the world is after him like a roaring prairie of flame! I thought of Doolan, weary, foot-sore, heart-sore, entering some quiet village of an evening; and to quench his thirst, going up to the public well, around which the gossips are talking, and hearing that they were talking of *him;* and seeing from the well itself, IT glaring upon him, as if conscious of his presence, with a hundred eyes of vengeance. I thought of him asleep in out-houses, and starting up in wild dreams of the policeman's hand upon his shoulder fifty times ere morning. He had committed the crime of Cain, and the weird of Cain he had to endure. But yesterday innocent, how unimportant; today bloody-handed, the whole world is talking of him, and everything he touches, the very bed he sleeps on, steals from him his secret, and is eager to betray!

Doolan was finally captured in Liverpool, and in the Spring Assize the three men were brought to trial. The jury found them guilty, but recommended Hickie to mercy on account of some supposed weakness of mind on his part. Sentence was, of course, pronounced with the usual solemnities. They were set apart to die; and when snug abed o'nights — for imagination is most mightily moved by contrast — I crept into their desolate hearts, and tasted a misery which was not my own. As already said, Hickie was recommended to mercy, and the recommendation was ultimately in the proper quarter given effect to.

The evening before the execution has arrived, and the reader has now to imagine the early May sunset falling pleasantly on the outskirts of the city. The houses looking out upon an open square or space, have little plots of garden-ground in their fronts, in which mahogany-coloured wallflowers and mealy auriculas are growing. The side of this square, along which the City Road stretches northward, is occupied by a blind asylum, a brick building, the bricks painted red and picked out with white, after the tidy English fashion, and a high white cemetery wall, over which peers the spire of the Gothic Cathedral; and beyond that, on the other side of the ravine, rising out of a populous city of the dead, a stone John Knox looks down on the Cathedral, a Bible clutched in his outstretched and menacing hand. On all this the May sunset is striking, dressing everything in its warm, pleasant pink, lingering in the tufts of foliage that nestle around the asylum, and dipping the building itself one half in light, one half in tender shade. This open space or square is an excellent place for the games of us boys, and " Prisoners' Base " is being carried out with as much earnestness as the business of life now by those of us who are left. The girls, too, have their games of a quiet kind, which we hold in huge scorn and contempt. In two files, linked arm-in-arm, they alternately dance towards each other and then retire, singing the while, in their clear, girlish treble, verses, the meaning and pertinence of which time has worn away — " The Campsie Duke's a-riding, a-riding, a-riding," being the oft-recurring " owercome " or refrain. All this is going on in the pleasant sunset light, when by the apparition of certain waggons coming up from the city, piled high with blocks and beams, and guarded by a dozen dragoons, on whose brazen helmets the sunset danced, every game is dismembered, and we are in a moment a mere mixed mob of boys and girls, flocking around to stare and wonder. Just at this place something went wrong with one of the waggon wheels, and the procession came to a stop. A crowd collected, and we heard some of the grown-up people say that the scaffold was being carried out for the ceremony of tomorrow. Then, more intensely than ever, one realised the condition of the doomed men. *We* were at our happy games in the sunset, *they* were entering on their last night on earth. After hammering and delay the wheel was put to rights, the sunset died out, waggons and dragoons got into motion and disappeared; and all the night through, whether awake or asleep, I saw the torches burning, and heard the hammers clinking, and witnessed as clearly as if I had been an onlooker, the horrid structure rising, till it stood complete, with a huge cross-beam from which two empty halters hung, in the early morning light.

Next morning the whole city was in commotion. Whether the authorities were apprehensive that a rescue would be attempted, or were anxious merely to strike terror into the hundreds of wild Irishry engaged on the railway, I cannot say; in any case, there was a display of military force quite unusual. The carriage in which the criminals — Catholics both — and their attendant priests were seated, was guarded by soldiers with fixed bayonets; indeed, the whole regiment then lying in the city was massed in front and behind, with a cold, frightful glitter of steel. Besides the foot soldiers, there were dragoons, and two pieces of cannon; a whole little army, in fact. With a slenderer force battles have been won which have made a mark in history. What did the prisoners think of their strange importance, and of the tramp and hurly-burly all around? When the procession moved out of the city, it seemed to draw with it almost the entire population; and when once the country roads were reached, the crowd spread over the fields on either side, ruthlessly treading down the tender wheat braird. I got a glimpse of the doomed, blanched faces which had haunted me so long, at the turn of the road, where, for the first time, the black cross-beam with its empty halters first became visible to them. Both turned and regarded it with a long, steady look; that done, they again bent their heads attentively to the words of the clergyman. I suppose in that long, eager, fascinated gaze they practically *died* — that for them death had no additional bitterness. When the mound was reached on which the scaffold stood, there was immense confusion. Around it a wide space was kept clear by the military; the cannon were placed in position; out flashed the swords of the dragoons; beneath and around on every side was the crowd. Between two brass helments I could see the scaffold clearly enough, and when in a little while the men, bareheaded and with their attendants, appeared upon it, the surging crowd became stiffened with fear and awe. And now it was that the incident so simple, so natural, so much in the ordinary course of things, and yet so frightful in its tragic suggestions, took place. Be it remembered that the season was early May, that the day was fine, that the wheat-fields were clothing themselves in the green of the young crop, and that around the scaffold, standing on a sunny mound, a wide space was kept clear. When the men appeared beneath the beam, each under his proper halter, there was a dead silence — every one was gazing too intently to whisper to his neighbour even. Just then, out of the grassy space at the foot of the scaffold, in the dead silence audible to all, a lark rose from the side of its nest, and went singing upward in its happy flight. O heaven! how did that song translate itself into dying ears? Did it bring in one wild burning moment father, and mother, and poor Irish cabin, and prayers said at bedtime, and the smell of turf fires, and innocent sweet-hearting, and rising and setting suns? Did it — but the dragoon's horse has become restive, and his brass helmet bobs up and down and blots everything; and there is a sharp sound, and I feel the great crowd heave and swing, and hear it torn by a sharp shiver of pity, and the men whom I saw so near but a moment ago are at immeasurable distance, and have solved the great enigma — and the lark has not yet finished his flight: you can see and hear him yonder in the fringe of a white May cloud.

This ghastly lark's flight, when the circumstances are taken into consideration, is, I am inclined to think, more terrible than anything of the same kind which I have encountered in books. The artistic uses of contrast as background and accompaniment, are well known to nature and the poets. Joy is continually worked on sorrow, sorrow on joy; riot is framed in peace, peace in riot. Lear and the Fool always go together. Trafalgar is being fought while Napoleon is sitting on horseback watching the Austrian army laying down its arms at Ulm. In Hood's poem, it is when looking on the released schoolboys at their games that Eugene Aram remembers he is a murderer. And these two poor Irish labourers could not die without hearing a lark singing in their ears. It is Nature's fashion. She never quite goes along with us. She is sombre at weddings, sunny at funerals, and she frowns on ninety-nine out of a hundred picnics.

There is a stronger element of terror in this incident of the lark than in any story of a similar kind I can remember.

A good story is told of an Irish gentleman — still known in London society — who inherited the family estates and the family banshee. The estates he lost — no uncommon circumstance in the history of Irish gentlemen — but the banshee, who expected no favours, stuck to him in his adversity, and crossed the channel with him, making herself known only on occasions of deathbeds and sharp family misfortunes. This gentleman had an ear, and, seated one night at the opera, the *keen* [4] — heard once or twice before on memorable occasions — thrilled through the din of the orchestra and the passion of the singers. He hurried home of course, found his immediate family well, but on the morrow a telegram arrived with the announcement of a brother's death. Surely of all superstitions that is the most imposing which makes the other world interested in the events which befall our mortal lot. For the mere pomp and pride of it, your ghost is worth a dozen retainers, and it is entirely inexpensive. The peculiarity and supernatural worth of this story lies in the idea of the old wail piercing through the sweet entanglement of stringed instruments and extinguishing Grisi.[5] Modern circumstances and luxury crack, as it were, and reveal for a moment misty and aboriginal time big with portent. There is a ridiculous Scotch story in which one gruesome touch lives. A clergyman's female servant was seated in the kitchen one Saturday night reading the Scriptures, when she was somewhat startled by hearing at the door the tap and voice of her sweetheart. Not expecting him, and the hour being somewhat late, she opened it in astonishment, and was still more astonished to hear him on entering abuse Scripture-reading. He behaved altogether in an unprecedented manner, and in many ways terrified the poor girl. Ultimately he knelt before her, and laid his head on her lap. You can fancy her consternation when glancing down she discovered that, *instead of hair, the head was covered with the moss of the moorland.* By a sacred name she adjured him to tell who he was, and in a moment the figure was gone. It was the Fiend, of course — diminished sadly since Milton saw him bridge chaos — fallen from worlds to kitchen-wenches. But just think how

---

[4] *keen:* lamentation or dirge for the dead.
[5] Giulia Grisi (1811–69), Italian opera singer.

in the story, in half-pity, in half-terror, the popular feeling of home-lessness, of being outcast, of being unsheltered as waste and desert places, has incarnated itself in that strange covering of the head. It is a true supernatural touch. One other story I have heard in the misty Hebrides: A Skye gentleman was riding along an empty moorland road. All at once, as if it had sprung from the ground, the empty road was crowded by a funeral procession. Instinctively he drew his horse to a side to let it pass, which it did without sound of voice, without tread of foot. Then he knew it was an apparition. Staring on it, he knew every person who either bore the corpse or who walked behind as mourners. There were the neighbouring proprietors at whose houses he dined, there were the members of his own kirk-session, there were the men to whom he was wont to give good-morning when he met them on the road or at market. Unable to discover his own image in the throng, he was inwardly marvelling whose funeral it *could* be, when the troop of spectres vanished, and the road was empty as before. Then, remembering that the coffin had an invisible occupant, he cried out, " It is my funeral! " and, with all his strength taken out of him, rode home to die. All these stories have their own touches of terror; yet I am inclined to think that my lark rising from the scaffold foot, and singing to two such auditors, is more terrible than any one of them.

What Is a University?

John Henry Newman

If I were asked to describe as briefly and popularly as I could, what a University was, I should draw my answer from its ancient designa-tion of a *Studium Generale* or " School of Universal Learning." This description implies the assemblage of strangers from all parts in one spot; — *from all parts;* else, how will you find professors and students for every department of knowledge? and *in one spot;* else, how can there be any school at all? Accordingly, in its simple and rudimental form, it is a school of knowledge of every kind, consisting of teachers and learners from every quarter. Many things are requisite to com-

WHAT IS A UNIVERSITY?: From *Rise and Progress of Universities* by John Henry Newman.

plete and satisfy the idea embodied in this description; but such as this a University seems to be in its essence, a place for the communication and circulation of thought, by means of personal intercourse, through a wide extent of country.

There is nothing far-fetched or unreasonable in the idea thus presented to us; and if this be a University, then a University does but contemplate a necessity of our nature, and is but one specimen in a particular medium, out of many which might be adduced in others, of a provision for that necessity. Mutual education, in a large sense of the word, is one of the great and incessant occupations of human society, carried on partly with set purpose, and partly not. One generation forms another; and the existing generation is ever acting and reacting upon itself in the persons of its individual members. Now, in this process, books, I need scarcely say, that is, the *litera scripta,* are one special instrument. It is true; and emphatically so in this age. Considering the prodigious powers of the press, and how they are developed at this time in the never-intermitting issue of periodicals, tracts, pamphlets, works in series, and light literature, we must allow there never was a time which promised fairer for dispensing with every other means of information and instruction. What can we want more, you will say, for the intellectual education of the whole man, and for every man, than so exuberant and diversified and persistent a promulgation of all kinds of knowledge? Why, you will ask, need we go up to knowledge, when knowledge comes down to us? The Sibyl wrote her prophecies upon the leaves of the forest, and wasted them; but here such careless profusion might be prudently indulged, for it can be afforded without loss, in consequence of the almost fabulous fecundity of the instrument which these latter ages have invented. We have sermons in stones, and books in the running brooks; works larger and more comprehensive than those which have gained for ancients an immortality, issue forth every morning, and are projected onwards to the ends of the earth at the rate of hundreds of miles a day. Our seats are strewed, our pavements are powdered, with swarms of little tracts; and the very bricks of our city walls preach wisdom, by informing us by their placards where we can at once cheaply purchase it.

I allow all this, and much more; such certainly is our popular education, and its effects are remarkable. Nevertheless, after all, even in this age, whenever men are really serious about getting what, in the language of trade, is called " a good article," when they aim at something precise, something refined, something really luminous, something really large, something choice, they go to another market; they avail themselves, in some shape or other, of the rival method, the ancient method, of oral instruction, of present communication between man and man, of teachers instead of learning, of the personal influence of a master, and the humble initiation of a disciple, and, in consequence, of great centres of pilgrimage and throng, which such a method of education necessarily involves. This, I think, will be found to hold good in all those departments or aspects of society, which possess an interest sufficient to bind men together, or to constitute what is called " a world." It holds in the political world, and in the high world, and in the religious world; and it holds also in the literary and scientific world.

If the actions of men may be taken as any test of their convictions, then we have reason for saying this, viz. — that the province and the inestimable benefit of the *litera scripta* is that of being a record of truth, and an authority of appeal, and an instrument of teaching in the hands of a teacher; but that, if we wish to become exact and fully furnished in any branch of knowledge which is diversified and complicated, we must consult the living man and listen to his living voice. I am not bound to investigate the cause of this, and anything I may say will, I am conscious, be short of its full analysis — perhaps we may suggest, that no books can get through the number of minute questions which it is possible to ask on any extended subject, or can hit upon the very difficulties which are severally felt by each reader in succession. Or again, that no book can convey the special spirit and delicate peculiarities of its subject with that rapidity and certainty which attend on the sympathy of mind with mind, through the eyes, the look, the accent, and the manner, in casual expressions thrown off at the moment, and the unstudied turns of familiar conversation. But I am already dwelling too long on what is but an incidental portion of my main subject. Whatever be the cause, the fact is undeniable. The general principles of any study you may learn by books at home; but the detail, the colour, the tone, the air, the life which makes it live in us, you must catch all these from those in whom it lives already. You must imitate the student in French or German, who is not content with his grammar, but goes to Paris or Dresden: you must take example from the young artist, who aspires to visit the great Masters in Florence and in Rome. Till we have discovered some intellectual daguerreotype, which takes off the course of thought, and the form, lineaments, and features of truth, as completely and minutely, as the optical instrument reproduces the sensible object, we must come to the teachers of wisdom to learn wisdom, we must repair to the fountain, and drink there. Portions of it may go from thence to the ends of the earth by means of books; but the fulness is in one place alone. It is in such assemblages and congregations of intellect that books themselves, the masterpieces of human genius, are written, or at least originated.

The principle on which I have been insisting is so obvious, and instances in point are so ready, that I should think it tiresome to proceed with the subject, except that one or two illustrations may serve to explain my own language about it, which may not have done justice to the doctrine which it has been intended to enforce.

For instance, the polished manners and high-bred bearing which are so difficult of attainment, and so strictly personal when attained, — which are so much admired in society, from society are acquired. All that goes to constitute a gentleman — the carriage, gait, address, gestures, voice; the ease, the self-possession, the courtesy, the power of conversing, the talent of not offending; the lofty principle, the delicacy of thought, the happiness of expression, the taste and propriety, the generosity and forbearance, the candour and consideration, the openness of hand; — these qualities, some of them come by nature, some of them may be found in any rank, some of them are a direct precept of Christianity; but the full assemblage of them, bound up in the unity of an individual character, do we expect they can be learned from books? Are they not necessarily acquired, where they are to be found, in high society? The very nature of the case leads us to say so; you cannot fence without an antagonist, nor challenge all comers in disputation before you have supported a thesis; and in like manner, it stands to reason, you cannot learn to converse till you have the world to converse with; you cannot unlearn your natural bashfulness, or awkwardness, or stiffness, or other besetting deformity, till you serve your time in some school of manners. Well, and is it not so in matter of fact? The metropolis, the court, the great houses of the land, are the centres to which at stated times the country comes up, as to shrines of refinement and good taste; and then in due time the country goes back again home, enriched with a portion of the social accomplishments, which those very visits serve to call out and heighten in the gracious dispensers of them. We are unable to conceive how the " gentlemanlike " can otherwise be maintained; and maintained in this way it is.

And now a second instance: and here too I am going to speak without personal experience of the subject I am introducing. I admit I have not been in Parliament, any more than I have figured in the *beau monde;* yet I cannot but think that statesmanship, as well as high breeding, is learned, not by books, but in certain centres of education. If it be not presumption to say so, Parliament puts a clever man *au courant* with politics and affairs of state in a way surprising to himself. A member of the Legislature, if tolerably observant, begins to see things with new eyes, even though his views undergo no change. Words have a meaning now, and ideas a reality, such as they had not before. He hears a vast deal in public speeches and private conversation, which is never put into print. The bearings of measures and events, the action of parties, and the persons of friends and enemies, are brought out to the man who is in the midst of them with a distinctness, which the most diligent perusal of newspapers will fail to impart to them. It is access to the fountain-heads of political wisdom and experience, it is daily intercourse, of one kind or another, with the multitude who go up to them, it is familiarity with business, it is access to the contributions of fact and opinion thrown together by many witnesses from many quarters, which does this for him. However, I need not account for a fact, to which it is sufficient to appeal; that the Houses of Parliament and the atmosphere around them are a sort of University of politics.

As regards the world of science, we find a remarkable instance of the principle which I am illustrating, in the periodical meetings for its advance, which have arisen in the course of the last twenty years, such as the British Association. Such gatherings would to many persons appear at first sight simply preposterous. Above all subjects of study, science is conveyed, is propagated, by books, or by private teaching; experiments and investigations are conducted in silence; discoveries are made in solitude. What have philosophers to do with festive celebrities, and panegyrical solemnities with mathematical and physical truth? Yet on a closer attention to the subject, it is found that not even scientific thought can dispense with the suggestions, the instruction, the stimulus, the sympathy, the intercourse with mankind on a large scale, which such meetings secure. A fine time of year is chosen, when days are long, skies are bright, the earth smiles, and all nature rejoices; a city or town is taken by turns, of ancient name or modern opulence, where buildings are spacious and hospitality hearty. The novelty of place and circumstance, the excitement of strange, or the refreshment of well-known faces, the majesty of rank or of genius, the amiable charities of men pleased both with themselves and with each other; the elevated spirits, the circulation of thought, the curiosity; the morning sections, the outdoor exercise, the well-furnished, well-earned board, the not ungraceful hilarity, the evening circle; the brilliant lecture, the discussions or collisions or guesses of great men one with another, the narratives of scientific processes, of hopes, disappointments, conflicts, and successes, the splendid eulogistic orations; these and the like constituents of the annual celebration, are considered to do something real and substantial for the advance of knowledge which can be done in no other way. Of course they can but be occasional; they answer to the annual Act, or Commencement, or Commemoration of a University, not to its ordinary condition; but they are of a University nature; and I can well believe in their utility. They issue in the promotion of a certain living and, as it were, bodily communication of knowledge from one to another, of a general interchange of ideas, and a comparison and adjustment of science with science, of an enlargement of mind, intellectual and social, of an ardent love of the particular study, which may be chosen by each individual, and a noble devotion to its interests.

Such meetings, I repeat, are but periodical, and only partially represent the idea of a University. The bustle and whirl which are their usual concomitants, are in ill keeping with the order and gravity of earnest intellectual education. We desiderate means of instruction which involve no interruption of our ordinary habits; nor need we seek it long, for the natural course of things brings it about, while we debate over it. In every great country, the metropolis itself becomes a sort of necessary University, whether we will or no. As the chief city is the seat of the court, of high society, of politics, and of law, so as a matter of course is it the seat of letters also; and at this time, for a long term of years, London and Paris are in fact and in operation Universities, though in Paris its famous University is no more, and in London a University scarcely exists except as a board of administration. The newspapers, magazines, reviews, journals, and periodicals of all kinds, the publishing trade, the libraries, museums, and academies there found, the learned and scientific societies, necessarily invest it with the functions of a University; and that atmosphere of intellect, which in a former age hung over Oxford or Bologna or Salamanca, has, with the change of times, moved away to the centre of civil government. Thither come up youths from all parts of the country, the students of law, medicine, and the fine arts, and the *employés* and *attachés* of literature. There they live, as chance determines; and they are satisfied with their temporary home, for they find in it all that was promised to them there. They have not come in vain, as far as their own object in coming is concerned. They have not learned any particular religion, but they have learned their own particular profession well. They have, moreover, become acquainted with the habits, manners, and opinions of their place of sojourn, and done their part in maintaining the tradition of them. We cannot then be without virtual Universities; a metropolis is such: the simple question is, whether the education sought and given should be based on principle, formed upon rule, directed to the highest ends, or left to the random succession of masters and schools, one after another, with a melancholy waste of thought and an extreme hazard of truth.

Religious teaching itself affords us an illustration of our subject to a certain point. It does not indeed seat itself merely in centres of the world; this is impossible from the nature of the case. It is intended for the many not the few; its subject matter is truth necessary for us, not truth recondite and rare; but it concurs in the principle of a University so far as this, that its great instrument, or rather organ, has ever been that which nature prescribes in all education, the personal presence of a teacher, or, in theological language, Oral Tradition. It is the living voice, the breathing form, the expressive countenance, which preaches, which catechises. Truth, a subtle, invisible, manifold spirit, is poured into the mind of the scholar by his eyes and ears, through his affections, imagination, and reason; it is poured into his mind and is sealed up there in perpetuity, by propounding and repeating it, by questioning and requestioning, by correcting and explaining, by progressing and then recurring to first principles, by all those ways which are implied in the word " catechising." In the first ages, it was a work of long time; months, sometimes years, were devoted to the arduous task of disabusing the mind of the incipient Christian of its pagan errors, and of moulding it upon the Christian faith. The Scriptures indeed were at hand for the study of those who could avail themselves of them; but St. Irenæus does not hesitate to speak of whole races, who had been converted to Christianity, without being able to read them. To be unable to read or write was in those times no evidence of want of learning: the hermits of the desert were, in this sense of the word, illiterate; yet the great St. Anthony, though he knew not letters, was a match in disputation for the learned philosophers who came to try him. Didymus again, the great Alexandrian theologian, was blind. The ancient discipline, called the *Disciplina Arcani,* involved the same principle. The more sacred doctrines of Revelation were not committed to books but passed on by successive tradition. The teaching on the Blessed Trinity and the Eucharist appears to have been so handed down for some hundred years; and when at length reduced to writing, it has filled many folios, yet has not been exhausted.

But I have said more than enough in illustration; I end as I began — a University is a place of concourse, whither students come from every quarter for every kind of knowledge. You cannot have the best of every kind everywhere; you must go to some great city or emporium for it. There you have all the choicest productions of nature and art all together, which you find each in its own separate place elsewhere. All the riches of the land, and of the earth, are carried up thither; there are the best markets, and there the best workmen. It is the centre of trade, the supreme court of fashion, the umpire of rival talents, and the standard of things rare and precious. It is the place for seeing galleries of first-rate pictures, and for hearing wonderful voices and performers of transcendent skill. It is the place for great preachers, great orators, great nobles, great statesmen. In the nature of things, greatness and unity go together; excellence implies a centre. And such, for the third or fourth time, is a University; I hope I do not weary out the reader by repeating it. It is the place to which a thousand schools make contributions; in which the intellect may safely range and speculate, sure to find its equal in some antagonist activity, and its judge in the tribunal of truth. It is a place where inquiry is pushed forward, and discoveries verified and perfected, and rashness rendered innocuous, and error exposed, by the collision of mind with mind, and knowledge with knowledge. It is the place where the professor becomes eloquent, and is a missionary and a preacher, displaying his science in its most complete and most winning form, pouring it forth with the zeal of enthusiasm, and lighting up his own love of it in the breasts of his hearers. It is the place where the catechist makes good his ground as he goes, treading in the truth day by day into the ready memory, and wedging and tightening it into the expanding reason. It is a place which wins the admiration of the young by its celebrity, kindles the affections of the middle-aged by its beauty, and rivets the fidelity of the old by its associations. It is a seat of wisdom, a light of the world, a minister of the faith, an Alma Mater of the rising generation. It is this and a great deal more, and demands a somewhat better head and hand than mine to describe it well.

Such is a University in its idea and in its purpose; such in good measure has it before now been in fact. Shall it ever be again? We are going forward in the strength of the Cross, under the patronage of the Blessed Virgin, in the name of St. Patrick, to attempt it.

True Americanism

Louis D. Brandeis

E pluribus unum was the motto adopted by the founders of the Republic when they formed a union of the thirteen States. To these we have added, from time to time, thirty-five more. The founders were convinced, as we are, that a strong nation could be built through federation. They were also convinced, as we are, that in America, under

TRUE AMERICANISM: From *Personal Growth Leaflet No. 92*, Senior Citizens of America. Reprinted by permission of the National Education Association. Originally a speech delivered in Boston in 1915.

a free government, many peoples would make one nation. Throughout all these years we have admitted to our country and to citizenship immigrants from the diverse lands of Europe. We had faith that thereby we would best serve ourselves and mankind. This faith has been justified. The United States has grown great. The immigrants and their immediate descendants have proved themselves as loyal as any citizens of the country. Liberty has knit us closely together as Americans.

Americanization

But what is Americanization? It manifests itself, in a superficial way, when the immigrant adopts the manners and the customs generally prevailing here. Far more important is the manifestation presented when he substitutes for his mother tongue the English language as the common medium of speech. But the adoption of our language, manners, and customs is only a small part of the process. To become Americanized the change wrought must be fundamental. However great his outward conformity, the immigrant is not Americanized unless his interests and affections have become deeply rooted here. And we properly demand of the immigrant even more than this. He must be brought into complete harmony with our ideals and aspirations and co-operate with us for their attainment. Only when this has been done will he possess the national consciousness of an American. I say, " He must be brought into complete harmony." But let us not forget that many a poor immigrant comes to us from distant lands, ignorant of our language and with jarring manners, who is already truly American in this most important sense; who has long shared our ideals and who, oppressed and persecuted abroad, has yearned for our land of liberty and for the opportunity of aiding in the realization of its aims.

American Ideals

What are the American ideals? They are the development of the individual for his own and the common good; the development of the individual through liberty and the attainment of the common good through democracy and social justice.

Our form of government, as well as humanity, compels us to strive for the development of the individual man. Under universal suffrage every voter is a part ruler of the State. Unless the rulers have, in the main, education and character and are free men, our great experiment in democracy must fail. It devolves upon the State, therefore, to fit its rulers for their task. It must provide not only facilities for development but the opportunity of using them. It must not only provide opportunity; it must stimulate the desire to avail of it. Thus we are compelled to insist upon the observance of what we somewhat vaguely term the American standard of living; we become necessarily our brothers' keepers.

The American Standard of Living

What does this standard imply? In substance, the exercise of those rights which our Constitution guarantees — the right to life, liberty, and the pursuit of happiness. Life, in this connection, means living, not existing; liberty, freedom in things industrial as well as political; happiness includes, among other things, that satisfaction which can come only through the full development and utilization of one's faculties. In order that men may live and not merely exist, in order that men may develop their faculties, they must have a reasonable income; they must have health and leisure. High wages will not meet the worker's need unless employment be regular. The best of wages will not compensate for excessively long working hours which undermine health. And working conditions may be so bad as to nullify the good effects of high wages and short hours. The essentials of American citizenship are not satisfied by supplying merely the material needs or even the wants of the worker.

Every citizen must have education — broad and continuous. This essential of citizenship is not met by an education which ends at the age of fourteen, or even at eighteen or twenty-two. Education must continue throughout life. A country cannot be governed well by rulers whose education and mental development are gained only from their attendance at the common school. Whether the education of the citizen in later years is to be given in classes or from the public platform, or is to be supplied through discussion in the lodges and the trade unions, or is to be gained from the reading of papers, periodicals, and books, in any case, freshness of mind is indispensable to its attainment. And to the preservation of freshness of mind a short workday is as essential as adequate food and proper conditions of working and of living. The workers must, in other words, have leisure. But leisure does not imply idleness. It means ability to work not less but more, ability to work at something besides breadwinning, ability to work harder while working at breadwinning, and ability to work more years at breadwinning. Leisure, so defined, is an essential of successful democracy.

Furthermore, the citizen in a successful democracy must not only have education; he must be free. Men are not free if dependent industrially upon the arbitrary will of another. Industrial liberty on the part of the worker cannot, therefore, exist if there be overweening industrial power. Some curb must be placed upon capitalistic combination. Nor will even this curb be effective unless the workers co-operate, as in trade unions. Control and co-operation are both essential to industrial liberty.

And if the American is to be fitted for his task as ruler, he must have besides education and industrial liberty also some degree of financial independence. Our existing industrial system is converting an ever increasing percentage of the population into wage-earners; and experience teaches us that a large part of these become at some time financial dependents, by reason of sickness, accident, invalidity, superannuation, unemployment, or premature death of the breadwinner of the family. Contingencies like these, which are generally referred to in the individual case as misfortunes, are now recognized as ordinary incidents in the life of the wage-earner. The need of providing indemnity against financial losses from such ordinary contingencies in the workingman's life has become apparent and is already being supplied in some countries. The standard worthy to be called American implies some system of social insurance.

And since the child is the father of the man, we must bear constantly in mind that the American standard of living cannot be attained or preserved unless the child is not only well fed but well born; unless he lives under conditions wholesome morally as well as physically; unless he is given education adequate both in quantity and in character to fit him for life's work.

The Distinctly American

Such are our ideals and the standard of living we have erected for ourselves. But what is there in these ideals which is peculiarly American? Many nations seek to develop the individual man for himself and for the common good. Some are as liberty-loving as we. Some pride themselves upon institutions more democratic than our own. Still others, less conspicuous for liberty or democracy, claim to be more successful in attaining social justice. And we are not the only nation which combines love of liberty with the practice of democracy and a longing for social justice. But there is one feature in our ideals and practices which is peculiarly American. It is inclusive brotherhood.

Other countries, while developing the individual man, have assumed that their common good would be attained only if the privileges of their citizenship should be limited practically to natives or to persons of a particular nationality. America, on the other hand, has always declared herself for equality of nationalities as well as for equality of individuals. It recognizes racial equality as an essential of full human liberty and true brotherhood, and that racial equality is the complement of democracy. America has, therefore, given like welcome to all the peoples of Europe.

Democracy rests upon two pillars: one, the principle that all men are equally entitled to life, liberty, and the pursuit of happiness; and the other, the conviction that such equal opportunity will most advance civilization. Aristocracy, on the other hand, denies both these postulates. It rests upon the principle of the superman. It willingly subordinates the many to the few and seeks to justify sacrificing the individual by insisting that civilization will be advanced by such sacrifices.

The struggles of the eighteenth and nineteenth centuries both in peace and in war were devoted largely to overcoming the aristocratic position as applied to individuals. In establishing the equal right of every person to development it became clear that equal opportunity for all involves this necessary limitation: each man may develop himself so far, but only so far, as his doing so will not interfere with the exercise of a like right by all others. Thus liberty came to mean the right to enjoy life, to acquire property, to pursue happiness in such manner and to such extent only as the exercise of the right in each is consistent with the exercise of a like right by every other of our fellow citizens. Liberty thus defined underlies twentieth-century democracy. Liberty thus defined exists in a part of the Western world. And even where this equal right of each individual has not yet been accepted as a political right, its ethical claim is indisputable.

America, dedicated to liberty and the brotherhood of man, rejected the aristocratic principle of the superman as applied to peoples as it rejected the principle when applied to individuals. America has believed that each race has something of peculiar value which it can contribute to the attainment of those high ideals for which it is striving. America has believed that we must not only give to the immigrant the best that we have, but must preserve for America the good that is in the immigrant and develop in him the best of which he is capable. America has believed that in differentiation, not in uniformity, lies the path of progress. It acted on this belief; it has advanced human happiness, and it has prospered.

War and Peace

On the other hand, the aristocratic theory as applied to peoples survived generally throughout Europe. It was there assumed by the stronger countries that the full development of one people necessarily involved its domination over another, and that only by such domination would civilization advance. Strong nationalities, assuming their own superiority, came to believe that they possessed the divine right to subject other peoples to their sway; and the belief in the existence of such a right ripened into a conviction that there was also a duty to exercise it.

The movements of the last century have proved that whole peoples have individuality no less marked than that of the single person; that the individuality of a people is irrepressible; and that the mis-named internationalism which seeks the obliteration of nationalities or peoples is reprehensible. The new nationalism adopted by America proclaims that each race or people, like each individual, has the right and duty to develop, and that only through such differentiated development will high civilization be attained. Not until these principles of nationalism, like those of democracy, are generally accepted will liberty be fully attained and minorities be secure in their rights. Not until then can the foundation be laid for a lasting peace among the nations.

The world turns anxiously to the United States, the one great democratic, liberal country, and bids us point the way. And may we not answer: Go the way of liberty and justice — led by democracy. Without these, international congresses and supreme courts will prove vain and peace " the Great Illusion."

And let us remember the poor parson of whom Chaucer says:

> " But Criste's loore, and his Apostles twelve,
> He taughte, but first he folwed it hymselve."

The World That Books Have Made

W. H. Auden

" Of the making of books there is no end," sighed the Preacher more than two thousand years ago. " We read many books because we cannot know enough people," said Mr. Eliot wryly only a few years ago. " They are so right," I say to myself this morning. But how is it that I am able to agree with them? Because I have bought and read their books. There is a real case to be made out against reading, but the prosecutor has to have had direct experience of what he is

THE WORLD THAT BOOKS HAVE MADE: Reprinted from the *New York Times Book Review*, December 2, 1951. Reprinted by permission of W. H. Auden and the *New York Times Book Review*.

talking about, which puts him in the paradoxical position of Carlyle, who is said to have extolled the virtues of silence in nineteen volumes.

The principal charges brought against books are two. The first is the psychologist's assertion that all imaginative literature, fiction or verse, indulges day-dreaming and makes it difficult for its devotees to adjust to the demands of reality. There is a small grain of sense in this position, but only a small one. Let us, however, swallow it whole; it still betrays a false identification of human weakness with a particular means of indulging it; like all puritanical reformers, the ascetic preacher of the Reality Principle argues that, if the means of indulgence are cut off, the desire will wither away, a doubtful proposition. I often spend time reading detective stories when I ought to be answering letters, but, if all detective stories were suppressed, I see no reason to believe that I should not find some other device for evading my duty.

The second, and more serious, objection to the printed word is that the language, sensibility and wisdom of literate persons are, in so many cases, inferior to that of the illiterate — the D. H. Lawrence pro-peasant position. How much substance is there in this? It is nonsense to talk of the " secondhand " experience gained from books in contrast to the " firsthand " experience gained from the bookless life, for human beings are not born, like the insects, fully equipped for life, but have to learn almost everything secondhand from others. If we were limited to our firsthand, that is, our sensory experience, we should still be living in trees on a diet of raw vegetables. If a literate person seems inferior to an illiterate, this means that the quality of experience he is gaining from his reading is inferior to that which a peasant gains from talking to his father or his neighbors. The remedy is not to stop him reading but to persuade him to read better books.

The pro-illiteracy position confuses symptom and cause. The real disease in our technological civilization is the ever-widening gap between the size and nature of the social organization required for the mass production of cheap consumer goods, and the size and nature of a psychologically and politically healthy community. When Aristotle asserted that a viable community is one in which everybody can recognize the faces of his neighbors, and when Plato set the population figure of the ideal community at 5,040, they based their conclusions on an estimate of man's spiritual and political nature which history has, till now, confirmed. How the problem of cheap goods versus a civilized community is to be solved, few would dare to pretend that they know; I only know that the abolition of books would solve nothing.

The what-would-happen-if game is always amusing to play. Suppose, then, our society exactly as it is except for the printed word, an industrial society without printing presses, typewriters or mimeograph machines. Two things would certainly vastly improve, our memory and our handwriting. From our earliest years we should be trained to learn great masses of material by heart, and the person whose hand was illegible would be at a grave economic disadvantage. Skilled occupations would become more and more specialized and probably hereditary. The necessity of either keeping all the knowledge requisite to one's job in one's head or of having access to rare and costly manuscripts would narrow the field in which anyone could hope to be an expert, and the personal intimacy between teacher and pupil which the oral transmission of knowledge demands would have to be so close and last so long that it would inevitably tend to become a family affair.

Mass entertainment, movies, radio, television, would not be immediately much affected, but, in the long run, the same symptoms would appear and there would grow up a caste of professional storytellers with very rigid and conservative conventions. Politically, whatever the form of state in theory, we should, in practice, be governed by a small conservative oligarchy. Indeed, every would-be dictator must dream of a world in which the means of entertainment and popular instruction are restricted to the screen and the loudspeaker. Movies require a lot of apparatus, time and money to make and exhibit, an opposition radio station can readily be jammed, a street-corner orator cannot attract a following without the knowledge of the police, but books and pamphlets are relatively cheap to produce and easy to carry and conceal. In an industrialized society, no printing press, no minority, is an axiom.

Thank God, then, for the printing press, and thank God for books, even for the publishers' free copies which keep piling up in my closet and on which I can never give an opinion because I shall never read them, just as I shall never read *Kalevala, The Anatomy of Melancholy* or *Pamela*. The annual tonnage of publications is terrifying if I think about it, but I don't have to think about it. That is one of the wonderful things about the written word; it cannot speak until it is spoken to. (Imagine the horror of life if bars had literary equivalents to Muzak and the juke-box.) In theory I may feel that there are too many books, but in practice I complain that there are not enough — when, for instance, I try to obtain the collected works of some favorite author and find that half of them are out of print, or when I try to find exactly the right book as a gift to a friend. Of course a great many of the books I do read are mediocre or dull, but life, as Henry James remarked, is, luckily for us, only capable of splendid waste, and every now and then I am rewarded by one which gives such happiness and excitement that the memory of every wasted or tedious hour is soon obliterated.

Finally, and most fervently of all, thank God for books as an alternative to conversation. People may say all they like about the plethora of books, their low quality and the damage they do, but the same charges, only ten times more strongly, can be brought against that unruly member, the human tongue. What has been said of youth applies, unfortunately, to most of us: " How wonderful we should be if we could not hear what we said." Luckily we forget 99 per cent of it immediately; otherwise we should very soon find ourselves restricted to the company of our cats and dogs. I have what I believe is an invaluable suggestion to offer to any hostess. Buy a stack of writing pads and pencils and then throw a dumb cocktail party. Even the most hardened bore who thinks nothing of trapping an unfortunate fellow guest in a corner and asking him " What do you think of Modern Poetry? " would lose his nerve, I think, if he had to commit himself on paper.

The Dog That Bit People

James Thurber

Probably no one man should have as many dogs in his life as I have had, but there was more pleasure than distress in them for me except in the case of an Airedale named Muggs. He gave me more trouble than all the other fifty-four or -five put together, although my moment of keenest embarrassment was the time a Scotch terrier named Jeannie, who had just had six puppies in the clothes closet of a fourth floor apartment in New York, had the unexpected seventh and last at the corner of Eleventh Street and Fifth Avenue during a walk she had insisted on taking. Then, too, there was the prize winning French poodle, a great big black poodle — none of your little, untroublesome white miniatures — who got sick riding in the rumble seat of a car with me on her way to the Greenwich Dog Show. She had a red rubber bib tucked around her throat and, since a rain storm came up when we were half way through the Bronx, I had to hold

THE DOG THAT BIT PEOPLE: Permission of the author; copyright 1933 James Thurber. Published in *My Life and Hard Times* by Harper & Brothers.

over her a small green umbrella, really more of a parasol. The rain beat down fearfully and suddenly the driver of the car drove into a big garage, filled with mechanics. It happened so quickly that I forgot to put the umbrella down and I will always remember, with sickening distress, the look of incredulity mixed with hatred that came over the face of the particular hardened garage man that came over to see what we wanted, when he took a look at me and the poodle. All garage men, and people of that intolerant stripe, hate poodles with their curious hair cut, especially the pom-poms that you got to leave on their hips if you expect the dogs to win a prize.

But the Airedale, as I have said, was the worst of all my dogs. He really wasn't my dog, as a matter of fact: I came home from a vacation one summer to find that my brother Roy had bought him while I was away. A big, burly, choleric dog, he always acted as if he thought I wasn't one of the family. There was a slight advantage in being one of the family, for he didn't bite the family as often as he bit strangers. Still, in the years that we had him he bit everybody but mother, and he made a pass at her once but missed. That was during the month when we suddenly had mice, and Muggs refused to do anything about them. Nobody ever had mice exactly like the mice we had that month. They acted like pet mice, almost like mice somebody had trained. They were so friendly that one night when mother entertained at dinner the Friraliras, a club she and my father had belonged to for twenty years, she put down a lot of little dishes with food in them on the pantry floor so that the mice would be satisfied with that and wouldn't come into the dining room. Muggs stayed out in the pantry with the mice, lying on the floor, growling to himself — not at the mice, but about all the people in the next room that he would have liked to get at. Mother slipped out into the pantry once to see how everything was going. Everything was going fine. It made her so mad to see Muggs lying there, oblivious of the mice — they came running up to her — that she slapped him and he slashed at her, but didn't make it. He was sorry immediately, mother said. He was always sorry, she said, after he bit someone, but we could not understand how she figured this out. He didn't act sorry.

Mother used to send a box of candy every Christmas to the people the Airedale bit. The list finally contained forty or more names. Nobody could understand why we didn't get rid of the dog. I didn't understand it very well myself, but we didn't get rid of him. I think that one or two people tried to poison Muggs — he acted poisoned once in a while — and old Major Moberly fired at him once with his service revolver near the Seneca Hotel in East Broad Street — but Muggs lived to be almost eleven years old and even when he could hardly get around he bit a Congressman who had called to see my father on business. My mother had never liked the Congressman — she said the signs of his horoscope showed he couldn't be trusted (he was Saturn with the moon in Virgo) — but she sent him a box of candy that Christmas. He sent it right back, probably because he suspected it was trick candy. Mother persuaded herself it was all for the best that the dog had bitten him, even though father lost an important business association because of it. " I wouldn't be associated with such a man," mother said. " Muggs could read him like a book."

Nobody knew exactly what
was the matter with him.

We used to take turns feeding Muggs to be on his good side, but that didn't always work. He was never in a very good humor, even after a meal. Nobody knew exactly what was the matter with him, but whatever it was it made him irascible, especially in the mornings. Roy never felt very well in the morning, either, especially before breakfast, and once when he came downstairs and found that Muggs had moodily chewed up the morning paper he hit him in the face with a grapefruit and then jumped up on the dining room table, scattering dishes and silverware and spilling the coffee. Muggs' first free leap carried him all the way across the table and into a brass fire screen in front of the gas grate but he was back on his feet in a moment and in the end he got Roy and gave him a pretty vicious bite in the leg. Then he was all over it; he never bit anyone more than once at a time. Mother always mentioned that as an argument in his favor; she said he had a quick temper but that he didn't hold a grudge. She was forever defending him. I think she liked him because he wasn't well. " He's not strong," she would say, pityingly, but that was inaccurate; he may not have been well but he was terribly strong.

One time my mother went to the Chittenden Hotel to call on a woman mental healer who was lecturing in Columbus on the subject of " Harmonious Vibrations." She wanted to find out if it was possible to get harmonious vibrations into a dog. " He's a large tan-colored Airedale," mother explained. The woman said that she had never treated a dog but she advised my mother to hold the thought that he did not bite and would not bite. Mother was holding the thought the very next morning when Muggs got the iceman but she blamed that slip-up on the iceman. " If you didn't think he would bite you, he wouldn't," mother told him. He stomped out of the house in a terrible jangle of vibrations.

One morning when Muggs bit me slightly, more or less in passing, I reached down and grabbed his short stumpy tail and hoisted him into the air. It was foolhardy thing to do and the last time I saw my mother, about six months ago, she said she didn't know what possessed me. I don't either, except that I was pretty mad. As long as I held the dog off the floor by his tail he couldn't get at me, but he twisted and jerked so, snarling all the time, that I realized I couldn't hold him that way very long. I carried him to the kitchen and flung him onto the floor and shut the door on him just as he crashed against it. But I forget about the backstairs. Muggs went up the backstairs and down the frontstairs and had me cornered in the living room. I managed to get up onto the mantelpiece above the fireplace, but it gave way and came down with a tremendous crash throwing a large marble clock, several vases, and myself heavily to the floor. Muggs was so alarmed by the racket that when I picked myself up he had disappeared. We couldn't find him anywhere, although we whistled and shouted, until old Mrs. Detweiler called after dinner that night. Muggs had bitten her once, in the leg, and she came into the living room only after we assured her that Muggs had run away. She had just seated herself when, with a great growling and scratching of claws, Muggs emerged from under a davenport where he had been quietly hiding all the time, and bit her again. Mother examined the bite and put arnica on it and told Mrs. Detweiler that it was only a bruise. " He just bumped you," she said. But Mrs. Detweiler left the house in a nasty state of mind.

Lots of people reported our Airedale to the police but my father held a municipal office at the time and was on friendly terms with the police. Even so, the cops had been out a couple of times — once when Muggs bit Mrs. Rufus Sturtevant and again when he bit Lieutenant-Governor Malloy — but mother told them that it hadn't been Muggs' fault but the fault of the people who were bitten. " When he starts for them, they scream," she explained, " and that excites him." The cops suggested that it might be a good idea to tie the dog up, but mother said that it mortified him to be tied up and that he wouldn't eat when he was tied up.

*Lots of people reported
our dog to the police.*

Muggs at his meals was an unusual sight. Because of the fact that if you reached toward the floor he would bite you, we usually put his food plate on top of an old kitchen table with a bench alongside the table. Muggs would stand on the bench and eat. I remember that my mother's Uncle Horatio, who boasted that he was the third man up Missionary Ridge, was splutteringly indignant when he found out that we fed the dog on a table because we were afraid to put his plate on the floor. He said he wasn't afraid of any dog that ever lived and that he would put the dog's plate on the floor if we would give it to him. Roy said that if Uncle Horatio had fed Muggs on the ground just before the battle he would have been the first man up Missionary Ridge. Uncle Horatio was furious. " Bring him in! Bring him in now! " he shouted. " I'll feed the —— on the floor! " Roy was all for giving him a chance, but my father wouldn't hear of it. He said that Muggs had already been fed. " I'll feed him again! " bawled Uncle Horatio. We had quite a time quieting him.

In his last year Muggs used to spend practically all of his time outdoors. He didn't like to stay in the house for some reason or other — perhaps it held too many unpleasant memories for him. Anyway, it was hard to get him to come in and as a result the garbage man, the iceman, and the laundryman wouldn't come near the house. We had to haul the garbage down to the corner, take the laundry out and bring it back, and meet the iceman a block from home. After this had gone on for some time we hit on an ingenious arrangement for getting the dog in the house so that we could lock him up while the gas meter was read, and so on. Muggs was afraid of only one thing, an electrical storm. Thunder and lightning frightened him out of his senses (I think he thought a storm had broken the day the mantelpiece fell). He would rush into the house and hide under a bed or in a clothes closet. So we fixed up a thunder machine out of a long narrow piece of sheet iron with a wooden handle on one end. Mother would shake this vigorously when she wanted to get Muggs into the house. It made an excellent imitation of thunder, but I suppose it was the most roundabout system for running a household that was ever devised. It took a lot out of mother.

A few months before Muggs died, he got to " seeing things." He would rise slowly from the floor, growling low, and stalk stiff-legged and menacing toward nothing at all. Sometimes the Thing would be just a little to the right or left of a visitor. Once a Fuller Brush salesman got hysterics. Muggs came wandering into the room like Hamlet following his father's ghost. His eyes were fixed on a spot just to the left of the Fuller Brush man, who stood it until Muggs was about three slow, creeping paces from him. Then he shouted. Muggs wavered on past him into the hallway grumbling to himself but the Fuller man went on shouting. I think mother had to throw a pan of cold water on him before he stopped. That was the way she used to stop us boys when we got into fights.

Muggs died quite suddenly one night. Mother wanted to bury him in the family lot under a marble stone with some such inscription as " Flights of angels sing thee to thy rest " but we persuaded her it was against the law. In the end we just put up a smooth board above his grave along a lonely road. On the board I wrote with an indelible pencil " Cave Canem." Mother was quite pleased with the simple classic dignity of the old Latin epitaph.

The Hour of Letdown

E. B. White

When the man came in, carrying the machine, most of us looked up from our drinks, because we had never seen anything like it before. The man set the thing down on top of the bar near the beerpulls. It took up an ungodly amount of room and you could see the bartender didn't like it any too well, having this big, ugly-looking gadget parked right there.

" Two rye-and-water," the man said.

The bartender went on puddling an Old-Fashioned that he was working on, but he was obviously turning over the request in his mind.

" You want a double? " he asked, after a bit.

" No," said the man. " Two rye-and-water, please." He stared straight at the bartender, not exactly unfriendly but on the other hand not affirmatively friendly.

Many years of catering to the kind of people that come into saloons had provided the bartender with an adjustable mind. Nevertheless, he did not adjust readily to this fellow, and he did not like the machine — that was sure. He picked up a live cigarette that was idling on the edge of the cash register, took a drag out of it, and returned it thoughtfully. Then he poured two shots of rye whiskey, drew two glasses of water, and shoved the drinks in front of the man. People were watching. When something a little out of the ordinary takes place at a bar, the sense of it spreads quickly all along the line and pulls the customers together.

The man gave no sign of being the center of attention. He laid a five-dollar bill down on the bar. Then he drank one of the ryes and chased it with water. He picked up the other rye, opened a small vent in the machine (it was like an oil cup) and poured the whiskey in, and then poured the water in.

The bartender watched grimly. " Not funny," he said in an even voice. " And furthermore, your companion takes up too much room. Why'n you put it over on that bench by the door, make more room here."

" There's plenty of room for everyone here," replied the man.

" I ain't amused," said the bartender. " Put the goddam thing over near the door like I say. Nobody will touch it."

The man smiled. " You should have seen it this afternoon," he

THE HOUR OF LETDOWN: From *The Second Tree from the Corner* by E. B. White. Copyright, 1951, by E. B. White. Reprinted by permission of Harper & Brothers.

said. " It was magnificent. Today was the third day of the tournament. Imagine it — three days of continuous brainwork! And against the top players in the country, too. Early in the game it gained an advantage; then for two hours it exploited the advantage brilliantly, ending with the opponent's king backed in a corner. The sudden capture of a knight, the neutralization of a bishop, and it was all over. You know how much money it won, all told, in three days of playing chess? "

" How much? " asked the bartender.

" Five thousand dollars," said the man. " Now it wants to let down, wants to get a little drunk."

The bartender ran his towel vaguely over some wet spots. " Take it somewheres else and get it drunk there! " he said firmly. " I got enough troubles."

The man shook his head and smiled. " No, we like it here." He pointed at the empty glasses. " Do this again, will you, please? "

The bartender slowly shook his head. He seemed dazed but dogged. " You stow the thing away," he ordered. " I'm not ladling out whiskey for jokestersmiths."

" ' Jokesmiths,' " said the machine. " The word is ' jokesmiths.' "

A few feet down the bar, a customer who was on his third highball seemed ready to participate in this conversation to which we had all been listening so attentively. He was a middle-aged man. His necktie was pulled down away from his collar, and he had eased the collar by unbuttoning it. He had pretty nearly finished his third drink, and the alcohol tended to make him throw his support in with the underprivileged and the thirsty.

" If the machine wants another drink, give it another drink," he said to the bartender. " Let's not have haggling."

The fellow with the machine turned to his new-found friend and gravely raised his hand to his temple, giving him a salute of gratitude and fellowship. He addressed his next remark to him, as though deliberately snubbing the bartender.

" You know how it is when you're all fagged out mentally, how you want a drink? "

" Certainly do," replied the friend. " Most natural thing in the world."

There was a stir all along the bar, some seeming to side with the bartender, others with the machine group. A tall, gloomy man standing next to me spoke up.

" Another whiskey sour, Bill," he said. " And go easy on the lemon juice."

" Picric acid," said the machine, sullenly. " They don't use lemon juice in these places."

" That does it! " said the bartender, smacking his hand on the bar. " Will you put that thing away or else beat it out of here. I ain't in the mood, I tell you. I got this saloon to run and I don't want lip from a mechanical brain or whatever the hell you've got there."

The man ignored this ultimatum. He addressed his friend, whose glass was now empty.

" It's not just that it's all tuckered out after three days of chess," he said amiably. " You know another reason it wants a drink? "

" No," said the friend. " Why? "

" It cheated," said the man.

At this remark, the machine chuckled. One of its arms dipped slightly, and a light glowed in a dial.

The friend frowned. He looked as though his dignity had been hurt, as though his trust had been misplaced. " Nobody can cheat at chess," he said. " Simpossible. In chess, everything is open and above the board. The nature of the game of chess is such that cheating is impossible."

" That's what I used to think, too," said the man. " But there *is* a way."

" Well, it doesn't surprise me any," put in the bartender. " The first time I laid my eyes on that crummy thing I spotted it for a crook."

" Two rye-and-water," said the man.

" You can't have the whiskey," said the bartender. He glared at the mechanical brain. " How do I know it ain't drunk already? "

" That's simple. Ask it something," said the man.

The customers shifted and stared into the mirror. We were all in this thing now, up to our necks. We waited. It was the bartender's move.

" Ask it what? Such as? " said the bartender.

" Makes no difference. Pick a couple big figures, ask it to multiply them together. You couldn't multiply big figures together if you were drunk, could you? "

The machine shook slightly, as though making internal preparations.

" Ten thousand eight hundred and sixty-two, multiply it by ninety-nine," said the bartender, viciously. We could tell that he was throwing in the two nines to make it hard.

The machine flickered. One of its tubes spat, and a hand changed position, jerkily.

" One million seventy-five thousand three hundred and thirty-eight," said the machine.

Not a glass was raised all along the bar. People just stared gloomily into the mirror; some of us studied our own faces, others took carom shots at the man and the machine.

Finally, a youngish, mathematically minded customer got out a piece of paper and a pencil and went into retirement. "It works out," he reported, after some minutes of calculating. "You can't say the machine is drunk!"

Everyone now glared at the bartender. Reluctantly he poured two shots of rye, drew two glasses of water. The man drank his drink. Then he fed the machine its drink. The machine's light grew fainter. One of its cranky little arms wilted.

For a while the saloon simmered along like a ship at sea in calm weather. Every one of us seemed to be trying to digest the situation, with the help of liquor. Quite a few glasses were refilled. Most of us sought help in the mirror — the court of last appeal.

The fellow with the unbuttoned collar settled his score. He walked stiffly over and stood between the man and the machine. He put one arm around the man, the other arm around the machine. "Let's get out of here and go to a good place," he said.

The machine glowed slightly. It seemed to be a little drunk now.

"All right," said the man. "That suits me fine. I've got my car outside."

He settled for the drinks and put down a tip. Quietly and a trifle uncertainly he tucked the machine under his arm, and he and his companion of the night walked to the door and out into the street.

The bartender stared fixedly, then resumed his light housekeeping. "So he's got his car outside," he said, with heavy sarcasm. "Now isn't that nice!"

A customer at the end of the bar near the door left his drink, stepped to the window, parted the curtains, and looked out. He watched for a moment, then returned to his place and addressed the bartender. "It's even nicer than you think," he said. "It's a Cadillac. And which one of the three of them d'ya think is doing the driving?"

The Decline of the Graces

Max Beerbohm

Have you read *The Young Lady's Book?* You have had plenty of
time to do so, for it was published in 1829. It was described by the
two anonymous Gentlewomen who compiled it as " A Manual for
Elegant Recreations, Exercises, and Pursuits." You wonder they had
nothing better to think of? You suspect them of having been triflers?
They were not, believe me. They were careful to explain, at the outset,
that the Virtues of Character were what a young lady should most
assiduously cultivate. They, in their day, laboring under the shadow
of the eighteenth century, had somehow in themselves that high moral
fervor which marks the opening of the twentieth century, and is said
to have come in with Mr. George Bernard Shaw. But, unlike us, they
were not concerned wholly with the inward and spiritual side of life.
They cared for the material surface, too. They were learned in the
frills and furbelows of things. They gave, indeed, a whole chapter to
" Embroidery." Another they gave to " Archery," another to " The
Aviary," another to " The Escrutoire." Young ladies do not now
keep birds, nor shoot with bow and arrow; but they do still, in some
measure, write letters; and so, for sake of historical comparison, let
me give you a glance at " The Escrutoire." It is not light reading.

> For careless scrawls ye boast of no pretence;
> Fair Russell wrote, as well as spoke, with sense.

Thus is the chapter headed, with a delightful little wood-engraving
of " Fair Russell," looking preeminently sensible, at her desk, to
prepare the reader for the imminent welter of rules for " decorous
composition." Not that pedantry is approved. " Ease and simplicity,
an even flow of unlabored diction, and an artless arrangement of
obvious sentiments " is the ideal to be striven for. " A metaphor may
be used with advantage " by any young lady, but only " if it occur
naturally." And " allusions are elegant," but only " when introduced
with ease, and when they are well understood by those to whom
they are addressed." " An antithesis renders a passage piquant "; but
the dire results of a too-frequent indulgence in it are relentlessly set
forth. Pages and pages are devoted to a minute survey of the pitfalls
of punctuation. But when the young lady of that period had skirted
all these, and had observed all the manifold rules of calligraphy that
were laid down for her, she was not, even then, out of the wood.

THE DECLINE OF THE GRACES: From *Yet Again* by Max Beerbohm. Reprinted by
permission of the author.

Very special stress was laid on " the use of the seal." Bitter scorn was poured on young ladies who misused the seal. " It is a habit of some to thrust the wax into the flame of the candle, and the moment a morsel of it is melted, to daub it on the paper; and when an unsightly mass is gathered together, to pass the seal over the tongue with ridiculous haste — press it with all the strength which the sealing party possesses — and the result is, an impression which raises a blush on her cheek."

Well! The young ladies of that day were ever expected to exhibit sensibility, and used to blush, just as they wept or fainted, for very slight causes. Their tears and their swoons did not necessarily betoken much grief or agitation; nor did a rush of color to the cheek mean necessarily that they were overwhelmed with shame. To exhibit various emotions in the drawing-room was one of the Elegant Exercises in which these young ladies were drilled thoroughly. And their habit of simulation was so rooted in sense of duty that it merged into sincerity. If a young lady did not swoon at the breakfast-table when her Papa read aloud from *The Times* that the Duke of Wellington was suffering from a slight chill, the chances were that she would swoon quite unaffectedly when she realized her omission. Even so, we may be sure that a young lady whose cheek burned not at sight of the letter she had sealed untidily — " unworthily " the Manual calls it — would anon be blushing for her shamelessness. Such a thing as the blurring of the family crest, or as the pollution of the profile of Pallas Athene with the smoke of the taper, was hardly, indeed, one of those " very slight causes " to which I have referred. The Georgian young lady was imbued through and through with the sense that it was her duty to be gracefully efficient in whatsoever she set her hand to. To the young lady of today, belike, she will seem accordingly ridiculous — seem poor-spirited, and a pettifogger. True, she set her hand to no grandiose tasks. She was not allowed to become a hospital nurse, for example, or an actress. The young lady of today, when she hears in herself a " vocation " for tending the sick, would willingly, without an instant's preparation, assume responsibility for the lives of a whole ward at St. Thomas's. This responsibility is not, however, thrust on her. She has to submit to a long and tedious course of training before she may do so much as smooth a pillow. The boards of the theatre are less jealously hedged in than those of the hospital. If your young lady have a wealthy father, and retain her schoolroom faculty for learning poetry by heart, there is no power on earth to prevent her from making her debut, somewhere, as Juliet — if she be so inclined; and such is usually her inclination. That her voice is untrained, that she cannot scan blank-verse, that she cannot gesticulate with grace and propriety nor move with propriety and grace across the stage, matters not a little bit — to our young lady. "Feeling," she will say, "is everything"; and, of course, she, at the age of eighteen, has more feeling than Juliet, that "flapper," could have had. All those other things — those little technical tricks — "can be picked up," or "will come." But no; I misrepresent our young lady. If she be conscious that there are such tricks to be played, she despises them. When, later, she finds the need to learn them, she still despises them. It seems to her ridiculous that one should not speak and comport oneself as artlessly on the stage as one does off it. The notion of speaking or comporting oneself with conscious art in real life would seem to her quite monstrous. It would puzzle her as much as her grandmother would have been puzzled by the contrary notion.

Personally, I range myself on the grandmother's side. I take my stand shoulder to shoulder with the Graces. On the banner that I wave is embroidered a device of prunes and prisms.

I am no blind fanatic, however. I admit that artlessness is a charming idea. I admit that it is sometimes charming as a reality. I applaud it (all the more heartily because it is rare) in children. But then, children, like the young of all animals whatsoever, have a natural grace. As a rule, they begin to show it in their third year, and to lose it in their ninth. Within that span of six years, they can be charming without intention; and their so frequent failure in charm is due to their voluntary or enforced imitation of the ways of their elders. In Georgian and Early Victorian days the imitation was always enforced. Grown-up people had good manners, and wished to see them reflected in the young. Nowadays, the imitation is always voluntary. Grown-up people have no manners at all; whereas they certainly have a very keen taste for the intrinsic charm of children. They wish children to be perfectly natural. That is (aesthetically, at least) an admirable wish. My complaint against these grown-up people is, that they themselves, whom time has robbed of their natural grace as surely as it robs the other animals, are content to be perfectly natural. This contentment I deplore, and am keen to disturb.

I except from my indictment any young lady who may read these words. I will assume that she differs from the rest of the human race, and has not, never had, anything to learn in the art of conversing prettily, of entering or leaving a room or a vehicle gracefully, of writing appropriate letters, *et patati et patata*. I will assume that all these accomplishments came naturally to her. She will now be in a mood to accept my proposition that of her contemporaries none seems to have been so lucky as herself. She will agree with me that other girls need training. She will not deny that grace in the little affairs of life

is a thing which has to be learned. Some girls have a far greater aptitude for learning it than others; but, with one exception, no girls have
it in them from the outset. It is a not less complicated thing than is
the art of acting, or of nursing the sick, and needs for the acquirement
of it a not less laborious preparation.

Is it worth the trouble? Certainly the trouble is not taken. The
" finishing school," wherein young ladies were taught to be graceful,
is a thing of the past. It must have been a dismal place; but the dismal-
ness of it — the strain of it — was the measure of its indispensability.
There I beg the question. Is grace itself indispensable? Certainly it
has been dispensed with. It isn't reckoned with. To sit perfectly mute
" in company," or to chatter on at the top of one's voice; to shriek
with laughter; to fling oneself into a room and dash oneself out of it; to
collapse on chairs or sofas; to sprawl across tables; to slam doors; to
write, without punctuation, notes that only an expert in handwriting
could read, and only an expert in misspelling could understand; to
hustle, to bounce, to go straight ahead — to be, let us say, perfectly
natural in the midst of an artificial civilization, is an ideal which the
young ladies of today are neither publicly nor privately discouraged
from cherishing. The word " cherishing " implies a softness of which
they are not guilty. I hasten to substitute " pursuing." If these young
ladies were not in the aforesaid midst of an artificial civilization, I
should be the last to discourage their pursuit. If they were Amazons,
for example, spending their lives beneath the sky, in tilth of stubborn
fields, and in armed conflict with fierce men, it would be unreasonable
to expect of them any sacrifice to the Graces. But they are exposed to
no such hardships. They have really a very comfortable sort of life.
They are not expected to be useful. (I am writing all the time, of
course, about the young ladies in the affluent classes.) And it seems
to me that they, in payment of their debt to Fate, ought to occupy the
time that is on their hands by becoming ornamental and increasing
the world's store of beauty. In a sense, certainly, they are ornamental.
It is a strange fact, and an ironic, that they spend quite five times the
annual amount that was spent by their grandmothers on personal
adornment. If they can afford it, well and good: let us have no
sumptuary law. But plenty of pretty dresses will not suffice. Pretty
manners are needed with them, and are prettier than they.

I had forgotten men. Every defect that I had noted in the modern
young woman is not less notable in the modern young man. Briefly, he
is a boor. If it is true that " manners makyth man," one doubts
whether the British race can be perpetuated. The young Englishman
of today is inferior to savages and to beasts of the field in that they are
eager to show themselves in an agreeable and seductive light to the

females of their kind, whilst he regards any such effort as beneath his dignity. Not that he cultivates dignity in demeanor. He merely slouches. Unlike his feminine counterpart, he lets his raiment match his manners. Observe him any afternoon, as he passes down Piccadilly, sullenly, with his shoulders humped, and his hat clapped to the back of his head, and his cigarette dangling almost vertically from his lips. It seems only appropriate that his hat is a billycock, and his shirt a flannel one, and that his boots are brown ones. Thus attired, he is on his way to pay a visit of ceremony to some house at which he has recently dined. No; that is the sort of visit he never pays. (I must confess I don't myself.) But one remembers the time when no self-respecting youth would have shown himself in Piccadilly without the vesture appropriate to that august highway. Nowadays there is no care for appearances. Comfort is the one aim. Any care for appearances is regarded rather as a sign of effeminacy. Yet never, in any other age of the world's history has it been regarded so. Indeed, elaborate dressing used to be deemed by philosophers an outcome of the sex-instinct. It was supposed that men dressed themselves finely in order to attract the admiration of women, just as peacocks spread their plumage with a similar purpose. Nor do I jettison the old theory. The declension of masculine attire in England began soon after the time when statistics were beginning to show the great numerical preponderance of women over men; and is it fanciful to trace the one fact to the other? Surely not. I do not say that either sex is attracted to the other by elaborate attire. But I believe that each sex, consciously or unconsciously, uses this elaboration for this very purpose. Thus the over-dressed maiden of today and the ill-dressed youth are but symbols of the balance of our population. The one is pleading, the other scorning. " Take me! " is the message borne by the furs and the pearls and the old lace. " I'll see about that when I've had a look round! " is the not pretty answer conveyed by the billycock and the flannel shirt.

I dare say that fine manners, like fine clothes, are one of the stratagems of sex. This theory squares at once with the modern young man's lack of manners. But how about the modern young woman's not less obvious lack? Well, the theory will square with that, too. The modern young woman's gracelessness may be due to her conviction that men like a girl to be thoroughly natural. She knows that they have a very high opinion of themselves; and what, thinks she, more natural than that they should esteem her in proportion to her power of reproducing the qualities that are most salient in themselves? Men, she perceives, are clumsy, and talk aloud, and have no drawing-room accomplishments, and are rude; and she proceeds to model herself on them. Let us not blame her. Let us blame rather her parents or guardians, who, though they well know that a masculine girl attracts no man, leave her to the devices of her own inexperience. Girls ought not to be allowed, as they are, to run wild. So soon as they have lost the natural grace of childhood, they should be initiated into that course of artificial training through which their grandmothers passed before them, and in virtue of which their grandmothers were pleasing. This will not, of course, ensure husbands for them all; but it will certainly tend to increase the number of marriages. Nor is it primarily for that sociological reason that I plead for a return to the old system of education. I plead for it, first and last, on aesthetic grounds. Let the Graces be cultivated for their own sweet sake.

The difficulty is, how to begin. The mothers of the rising generation were brought up in the unregenerate way. Their scraps of oral tradition will need to be supplemented by much research. I advise them to start their quest by reading *The Young Lady's Book*. Exactly the right spirit is therein enshrined, though of the substance there is much that could not be well applied to our own day. That chapter on " The Escrutoire," for example, belongs to a day that cannot be recalled. We can get rid of bad manners, but we cannot substitute the Sedan-chair for the motor-car; and the penny post, with telephones and telegrams, has, in our own beautiful phrase, " come to stay," and has elbowed the art of letter-writing irrevocably from among us. But notes are still written; and there is no reason why they should not be written well. Has the mantle of those anonymous gentlewomen who wrote *The Young Lady's Book* fallen on no one? Will no one revise that " Manual of Elegant Recreations, Exercises, and Pursuits," adapting it to present needs? . . . A few hints as to Deportment in the Motor-Car; the exact Angle whereat to hold the Receiver of a Telephone, and the exact Key wherein to pitch the Voice; the Conduct of a Cigarette. . . . I see a wide and golden vista.

Saturday's Smells

Robert Benchley

Never, even in my best form, what you would call a " drone " or " worker " at heart, I have been having a particularly tough time of it lately just sitting at my desk.

Specialists and psychoanalysts from all over the world have been working on my case, and it was only yesterday that I myself was able to give them the key to my inability to work. It is my new pipe to-bacco. It smells like Saturday, and consequently puts me in a chronic holiday mood.

This may take a little explaining. The main thesis on which I am going to build my case is that, when you were a child, certain days had their individual smells, and that these smells, when experienced today, take you back to your state of mind when you experienced them in childhood. Do I make myself clear, or must I say that all over again?

Sunday smells were, of course, the most distinctive, and, when they assail me today, I become restless and depressed and want to go to sea. In my section of the country, the first Sunday smell was of the fish-balls for breakfast. This was not so depressing, as fish-balls were good, and anyway, Sunday didn't begin to get you down until later in the day.

Then came, in slow succession, the musty draughts of the Sunday-school vestry, laden with the week's dust on the maps of Palestine and the hymnals, and freshened that morning only by the smell of black silk dresses sprinkled with lavender and the starch from little girls' petticoats and sashes. Then the return to the home, where fish-cakes had given way to fricasseeing chicken and boiling onions, which, in turn, gave way to the aroma of the paternal cigar as you started out on that Sunday afternoon walk, during which you passed all the familiar spots where you had been playing only the day before with the gang, now desolate and small-looking in the pall of Sunday.

But, sure as the smells of Sunday were, those of Saturday were none the less distinctive and a great deal more cheery. In our house we began getting whiffs of Saturday as early as Friday evening, when the bread was " set " on the kitchen table and the beans put to soak nearby. The smell of the cold bread-dough when the napkins were lifted from the pans always meant " no school tomorrow," and was a

SATURDAY'S SMELLS: From *The Benchley Round-up*, edited by Nathaniel Bench-ley. Copyright, 1934, by Robert C. Benchley. Reprinted by permission of Harper & Brothers.

preliminary to the " no school today " smells of Saturday, which are at the basis of my present trouble.

On Saturday morning early these " no school today " smells began to permeate the kitchen, and, as the kitchen was the sole port of entry and exit during the morning's play outside, they became inextricably mixed up with not only cooking, but " duck-on-the-rock," " Indian guide " and that informal scrimmaging which boys indulge in in back yards, which goes by the name of either " football " or " baseball " according to the season of the year.

In New England, of course, the *leit motif* among the Saturday smells was the one of beans baking, but the bread and pies ran it a close second. A good cake in the oven could hold its own, too. Then, along about eleven-thirty the Saturday noon dinner began to loom up, being more plebeian than the Sunday noon dinner, it usually took the combined form of cabbage, turnips, beets and corned beef, all working together in one pot, with the potatoes, to make what is known as the " New England boiled dinner." That put a stop to any other smells that thought they were something earlier in the morning.

On the outside, Saturday morning contributed the smell of burning leaves, and of shingles on the new house that was always being built in the neighborhood; and, although sounds do not come into our lecture today, there was the sound of carpenters hammering, and the re-echoing beat of rugs being dusted, which became almost smells in their affinity to them.

Now, here is the point about my pipe tobacco. A month or so ago I tried out a new blend, which, I discovered only yesterday, smells exactly like beans in an oven. So, when I settle down to a morning's work and light my pipe, I am gradually overcome with the delicious feeling that there is " no school today," and that I really ought to be outdoors playing.

So, without knowing why, I have been leaving my work and getting out my skates and yielding to the Saturday spirit. The only trouble has been that, under this subtle influence, every day has been Saturday, because every day has smelled like Saturday.

I don't suppose that the tradesmen to whom I owe money will think much of this explanation, but it satisfies me and the psychoanalysts perfectly. And, as yet, I have made no move to buy a less insidious-smelling pipe tobacco.

Love Is a Fallacy

Max Shulman

Charles Lamb, as merry and enterprising a fellow as you will meet in a month of Sundays, unfettered the informal essay with his memorable *Old China* and *Dream Children*. There follows an informal essay that ventures even beyond Lamb's frontier. Indeed, " informal " may not be quite the right word to describe this essay; " limp " or " flaccid " or possibly " spongy " are perhaps more appropriate.

Vague though its category, it is without doubt an essay. It develops an argument; it cites instances; it reaches a conclusion. Could Carlyle do more? Could Ruskin?

Read, then, the following essay which undertakes to demonstrate that logic, far from being a dry, pedantic discipline, is a living, breathing thing, full of beauty, passion, and trauma. —— AUTHOR'S NOTE

Cool was I and logical. Keen, calculating, perspicacious, acute and astute — I was all of these. My brain was as powerful as a dynamo, as precise as a chemist's scales, as penetrating as a scalpel. And — think of it! — I was only eighteen.

It is not often that one so young has such a giant intellect. Take, for example, Petey Burch, my roommate at the University of Minnesota. Same age, same background, but dumb as an ox. A nice enough fellow, you understand, but nothing upstairs. Emotional type. Unstable. Impressionable. Worst of all, a faddist. Fads, I submit, are the very negation of reason. To be swept up in every new craze that comes along, to surrender yourself to idiocy just because everybody else is doing it — this, to me, is the acme of mindlessness. Not, however, to Petey.

One afternoon I found Petey lying on his bed with an expression of such distress on his face that I immediately diagnosed appendicitis. " Don't move," I said. " Don't take a laxative. I'll get a doctor."

" Raccoon," he mumbled thickly.

" Raccoon? " I said, pausing in my flight.

" I want a raccoon coat," he wailed.

I perceived that his trouble was not physical, but mental. " Why do you want a raccoon coat? "

" I should have known it," he cried, pounding his temples. " I should have known they'd come back when the Charleston came

LOVE IS A FALLACY: From *The Many Loves of Dobie Gillis* by Max Shulman. Copyright 1951 by Max Shulman. Reprinted by permission of Doubleday & Company, Inc.

back. Like a fool I spent all my money for textbooks, and now I can't get a raccoon coat."

" Can you mean," I said incredulously, " that people are actually wearing raccoon coats again? "

" All the Big Men on Campus are wearing them. Where've you been? "

" In the library," I said, naming a place not frequented by Big Men on Campus.

He leaped from the bed and paced the room. " I've got to have a raccoon coat," he said passionately. " I've got to! "

" Petey, why? Look at it rationally. Raccoon coats are unsanitary. They shed. They smell bad. They weigh too much. They're unsightly. They — "

" You don't understand," he interrupted impatiently. " It's the thing to do. Don't you want to be in the swim? "

" No," I said truthfully.

" Well, I do," he declared. " I'd give anything for a raccoon coat. Anything! "

My brain, that precision instrument, slipped into high gear. " Anything? " I asked, looking at him narrowly.

" Anything," he affirmed in ringing tones.

I stroked my chin thoughtfully. It so happened that I knew where to get my hands on a raccoon coat. My father had had one in his undergraduate days; it lay now in a trunk in the attic back home. It also happened that Petey had something I wanted. He didn't *have* it exactly, but at least he had first rights on it. I refer to his girl, Polly Espy.

I had long coveted Polly Espy. Let me emphasize that my desire for this young woman was not emotional in nature. She was, to be sure, a girl who excited the emotions, but I was not one to let my heart rule my head. I wanted Polly for a shrewdly calculated, entirely cerebral reason.

I was a freshman in law school. In a few years I would be out in practice. I was well aware of the importance of the right kind of wife in furthering a lawyer's career. The successful lawyers I had observed were, almost without exception, married to beautiful, gracious, intelligent women. With one omission, Polly fitted these specifications perfectly.

Beautiful she was. She was not yet of pin-up proportions, but I felt sure that time would supply the lack. She already had the makings.

Gracious she was. By gracious I mean full of graces. She had an erectness of carriage, an ease of bearing, a poise that clearly indicated the best of breeding. At table her manners were exquisite. I had seen her at the Kozy Kampus Korner eating the specialty of the house — a sandwich that contained scraps of pot roast, gravy, chopped nuts, and a dipper of sauerkraut — without even getting her fingers moist.

Intelligent she was not. In fact, she veered in the opposite direction. But I believed that under my guidance she would smarten up. At any rate, it was worth a try. It is, after all, easier to make a beautiful dumb girl smart than to make an ugly smart girl beautiful.

" Petey," I said, " are you in love with Polly Espy? "

" I think she's a keen kid," he replied, " but I don't know if you'd call it love. Why? "

" Do you," I asked, " have any kind of formal arrangement with her? I mean are you going steady or anything like that? "

" No. We see each other quite a bit, but we both have other dates. Why? "

" Is there," I asked, " any other man for whom she has a particular fondness? "

" Not that I know of. Why? "

I nodded with satisfaction. " In other words, if you were out of the picture, the field would be open. Is that right? "

" I guess so. What are you getting at? "

" Nothing, nothing," I said innocently, and took my suitcase out the closet.

" Where are you going? " asked Petey.

" Home for the weekend." I threw a few things into the bag.

" Listen," he said, clutching my arm eagerly, " while you're home, you couldn't get some money from your old man, could you, and lend it to me so I can buy a raccoon coat? "

" I may do better than that," I said with a mysterious wink and closed my bag and left.

" Look," I said to Petey when I got back Monday morning. I threw open the suitcase and revealed the huge, hairy, gamy object that my father had worn in his Stutz Bearcat in 1925.

" Holy Toledo! " said Petey reverently. He plunged his hands into the raccoon coat and then his face. " Holy Toledo! " he repeated fifteen or twenty times.

" Would you like it? " I asked.

" Oh yes! " he cried, clutching the greasy pelt to him. Then a canny look came into his eyes. " What do you want for it? "

" Your girl," I said, mincing no words.

" Polly? " he said in a horrified whisper. " You want Polly? "

" That's right."

He flung the coat from him. " Never," he said stoutly.

I shrugged. " Okay. If you don't want to be in the swim, I guess it's your business."

I sat down in a chair and pretended to read a book, but out of the corner of my eye I kept watching Petey. He was a torn man. First he looked at the coat with the expression of a waif at a bakery window. Then he turned away and set his jaw resolutely. Then he looked back at the coat, with even more longing in his face. Then he turned away, but with not so much resolution this time. Back and forth his head swiveled, desire waxing, resolution waning. Finally he didn't turn away at all; he just stood and stared with mad lust at the coat.

" It isn't as though I was in love with Polly," he said thickly. " Or going steady or anything like that."

" That's right," I murmured.

" What's Polly to me, or me to Polly? "

" Not a thing," said I.

" It's just been a casual kick — just a few laughs, that's all."

" Try on the coat," said I.

He complied. The coat bunched high over his ears and dropped all the way down to his shoe tops. He looked like a mound of dead raccoons. " Fits fine," he said happily.

I rose from my chair. " Is it a deal? " I asked, extending my hand.

He swallowed. " It's a deal," he said and shook my hand.

I had my first date with Polly the following evening. This was in the nature of a survey; I wanted to find out just how much work I had to do to get her up to the standard I required. I took her first to dinner. " Gee, that was a delish dinner," she said as we left the restaurant. Then I took her to a movie. " Gee, that was a marvy movie," she said as we left the theater. And then I took her home. " Gee, I had a sensaysh time," she said as she bade me good night.

I went back to my room with a heavy heart. I had gravely underestimated the size of my task. This girl's lack of information was terrifying. Nor would it be enough merely to supply her with information. First she had to be taught to *think*. This loomed as a project of no small dimensions, and at first I was tempted to give her back to Petey. But then I got to thinking about her abundant physical charms and about the way she entered a room and the way she handled a knife and fork, and I decided to make an effort.

I went about it, as in all things, systematically. I gave her a course in logic. It happened that I, as a law student, was taking a course in logic myself, so I had all the facts at my finger tips. " Polly," I said to her when I picked her up on our next date, " tonight we are going over to the Knoll and talk."

" Oo, terrif," she replied. One thing I will say for this girl: you would go far to find another so agreeable.

We went to the Knoll, the campus trysting place, and we sat down under an old oak, and she looked at me expectantly. " What are we going to talk about? " she asked.

" Logic."

She thought this over for a minute and decided she liked it. " Magnif," she said.

" Logic," I said, clearing my throat, " is the science of thinking. Before we can think correctly, we must first learn to recognize the common fallacies of logic. These we will take up tonight."

" Wow-dow! " she cried, clapping her hands delightedly.

I winced, but went bravely on. " First let us examine the fallacy called Dicto Simpliciter."

" By all means," she urged, batting her lashes eagerly.

" Dicto Simpliciter means an argument based on an unqualified generalization. For example: Exercise is good. Therefore everybody should exercise."

" I agree," said Polly earnestly. " I mean exercise is wonderful. I mean it builds the body and everything."

" Polly," I said gently, " the argument is a fallacy. *Exercise is good* is an unqualified generalization. For instance, if you have heart disease, exercise is bad, not good. Many people are ordered by their doctors *not* to exercise. You must *qualify* the generalization. You must say exercise is *usually* good, or exercise is good *for most people.* Otherwise you have committed a Dicto Simpliciter. Do you see? "

" No," she confessed. " But this is marvy. Do more! Do more! "

" It will be better if you stop tugging at my sleeve," I told her, and when she desisted, I continued. " Next we take up a fallacy called Hasty Generalization. Listen carefully: You can't speak French. I can't speak French. Petey Burch can't speak French. I must therefore conclude that nobody at the University of Minnesota can speak French."

" Really? " said Polly, amazed. " *Nobody?* "

I hid my exasperation. " Polly, it's a fallacy. The generalization is reached too hastily. There are too few instances to support such a conclusion."

" Know any more fallacies? " she asked breathlessly. " This is more fun than dancing even."

I fought off a wave of despair. I was getting nowhere with this girl, absolutely nowhere. Still, I am nothing if not persistent. I continued. " Next comes Post Hoc. Listen to this: Let's not take Bill on our picnic. Every time we take him out with us, it rains."

" I know somebody just like that," she exclaimed. " A girl back home — Eula Becker, her name is. It never fails. Every single time we take her on a picnic — "

" Polly," I said sharply, " it's a fallacy. Eula Becker doesn't *cause* the rain. She has no connection with the rain. You are guilty of Post Hoc if you blame Eula Becker."

" I'll never do it again," she promised contritely. " Are you mad at me? "

I sighed deeply. " No, Polly, I'm not mad."

" Then tell me some more fallacies."

" All right. Let's try Contradictory Premises."

" Yes, let's," she chirped, blinking her eyes happily.

I frowned, but plunged ahead. " Here's an example of Contradictory Premises: If God can do anything, can He make a stone so heavy that He won't be able to lift it? "

" Of course," she replied promptly.

" But if He can do anything, He can lift the stone," I pointed out.

" Yeah," she said thoughtfully. " Well, then I guess He can't make the stone."

" But He can do anything," I reminded her.

She scratched her pretty, empty head. " I'm all confused," she admitted.

" Of course you are. Because when the premises of an argument contradict each other, there can be no argument. If there is an irresistible force, there can be no immovable object. If there is an immovable object, there can be no irresistible force. Get it? "

" Tell me some more of this keen stuff," she said eagerly.

I consulted my watch. " I think we'd better call it a night. I'll take you home now, and you go over all the things you've learned. We'll have another session tomorrow night."

I deposited her at the girls' dormitory, where she assured me that she had had a perfectly terrif evening, and I went glumly home to my room. Petey lay snoring in his bed, the raccoon coat huddled like a great hairy beast at his feet. For a moment I considered waking him and telling him that he could have his girl back. It seemed clear that my project was doomed to failure. The girl simply had a logic-proof head.

But then I reconsidered. I had wasted one evening; I might as well waste another. Who knew? Maybe somewhere in the extinct crater of her mind, a few embers still smoldered. Maybe somehow I could fan them into flame. Admittedly it was not a prospect fraught with hope, but I decided to give it one more try.

Seated under the oak the next evening I said, " Our first fallacy tonight is called Ad Misericordiam."

She quivered with delight.

" Listen closely," I said. " A man applies for a job. When the boss asks him what his qualifications are, he replies that he has a wife and six children at home, the wife is a helpless cripple, the children have nothing to eat, no clothes to wear, no shoes on their feet, there are no beds in the house, no coal in the cellar, and winter is coming."

A tear rolled down each of Polly's pink cheeks. " Oh, this is awful, awful," she sobbed.

" Yes, it's awful," I agreed, " but it's no argument. The man never answered the boss's question about his qualifications. Instead he appealed to the boss's sympathy. He committed the fallacy of Ad Misericordiam. Do you understand? "

" Have you got a handkerchief? " she blubbered.

I handed her a handkerchief and tried to keep from screaming while she wiped her eyes. " Next," I said in a carefully controlled tone, " we will discuss False Analogy. Here is an example: Students should be allowed to look at their textbooks during examinations. After all, surgeons have X rays to guide them during an operation, lawyers have briefs to guide them during a trial, carpenters have blueprints to guide them when they are building a house. Why, then, shouldn't students be allowed to look at their textbooks during an examination? "

" There now," she said enthusiastically, " is the most marvy idea I've heard in years."

" Polly," I said testily, " the argument is all wrong. Doctors, lawyers, and carpenters aren't taking a test to see how much they have learned, but students are. The situations are altogether different, and you can't make an analogy between them."

" I still think it's a good idea," said Polly.

" Nuts," I muttered. Doggedly I pressed on. " Next we'll try Hypothesis Contrary to Fact."

" Sounds yummy," was Polly's reaction.

" Listen: If Madame Curie had not happened to leave a photographic plate in a drawer with a chunk of pitchblende, the world today would not know about radium."

" True, true," said Polly, nodding her head. " Did you see the movie? Oh, it just knocked me out. That Walter Pidgeon is so dreamy. I mean he fractures me."

" If you can forget Mr. Pidgeon for a moment," I said coldly, " I would like to point out that the statement is a fallacy. Maybe Madame Curie would have discovered radium at some later date. Maybe somebody else would have discovered it. Maybe any number of things would have happened. You can't start with a hypothesis that is not true and then draw any supportable conclusions from it."

"They ought to put Walter Pidgeon in more pictures," said Polly. "I hardly ever see him any more."

One more chance, I decided. But just one more. There is a limit to what flesh and blood can bear. "The next fallacy is called Poisoning the Well."

"How cute!" she gurgled.

"Two men are having a debate. The first one gets up and says, 'My opponent is a notorious liar. You can't believe a word that he is going to say.' . . . Now, Polly, think. Think hard. What's wrong?"

I watched her closely as she knit her creamy brow in concentration. Suddenly a glimmer of intelligence — the first I had seen — came into her eyes. "It's not fair," she said with indignation. "It's not a bit fair. What chance has the second man got if the first man calls him a liar before he even begins talking?"

"Right!" I cried exultantly. "One hundred per cent right. It's not fair. The first man has *poisoned the well* before anybody could drink from it. He has hamstrung his opponent before he could even start. . . . Polly, I'm proud of you."

"Pshaw," she murmured, blushing with pleasure.

"You see, my dear, these things aren't so hard. All you have to do is concentrate. Think — examine — evaluate. Come now, let's review everything we have learned."

"Fire away," she said with an airy wave of her hand.

Heartened by the knowledge that Polly was not altogether a cretin, I began a long, patient review of all I had told her. Over and over and over again I cited instances, pointed out flaws, kept hammering away without letup. It was like digging a tunnel. At first everything was work, sweat, and darkness. I had no idea when I would reach the light, or even *if* I would. But I persisted. I pounded and clawed and scraped, and finally I was rewarded. I saw a chink of light. And then the chink got bigger and the sun came pouring in and all was bright.

Five grueling nights this took, but it was worth it. I had made a logician out of Polly; I had taught her to think. My job was done. She was worthy of me at last. She was a fit wife for me, a proper hostess for my many mansions, a suitable mother for my well-heeled children.

It must not be thought that I was without love for this girl. Quite the contrary. Just as Pygmalion loved the perfect woman he had fashioned, so I loved mine. I determined to acquaint her with my feelings at our very next meeting. The time had come to change our relationship from academic to romantic.

" Polly," I said when next we sat beneath our oak, " tonight we will not discuss fallacies."

" Aw, gee," she said, disappointed.

" My dear," I said, favoring her with a smile, " we have now spent five evenings together. We have gotten along splendidly. It is clear that we are well matched."

" Hasty Generalization," said Polly brightly.

" I beg your pardon," said I.

" Hasty Generalization," she repeated. " How can you say that we are well matched on the basis of only five dates? "

I chuckled with amusement. The dear child had learned her lessons well. " My dear," I said, patting her hand in a tolerant manner, " five dates is plenty. After all, you don't have to eat a whole cake to know that it's good."

" False Analogy," said Polly promptly. " I'm not a cake. I'm a girl."

I chuckled with somewhat less amusement. The dear child had learned her lessons perhaps too well. I decided to change tactics. Obviously the best approach was a simple, strong, direct declaration of love. I paused for a moment while my massive brain chose the proper words. Then I began:

" Polly, I love you. You are the whole world to me, and the moon and the stars and the constellations of outer space. Please, my darling, say that you will go steady with me, for if you will not, life will be meaningless. I will languish. I will refuse my meals. I will wander the face of the earth, a shambling, hollow-eyed hulk."

There, I thought, folding my arms, that ought to do it.

" Ad Misericordiam," said Polly.

I ground my teeth. I was not Pygmalion; I was Frankenstein, and my monster had me by the throat. Frantically I fought back the tide of panic surging through me. At all costs I had to keep cool.

" Well, Polly," I said, forcing a smile, " you certainly have learned your fallacies."

" You're darn right," she said with a vigorous nod.

" And who taught them to you, Polly? "

" You did."

" That's right. So you do owe me something, don't you, my dear? If I hadn't come along you never would have learned about fallacies."

" Hypothesis Contrary to Fact," she said instantly.

I dashed perspiration from my brow. " Polly," I croaked, " you mustn't take all these things so literally. I mean this is just classroom stuff. You know that the things you learn in school don't have anything to do with life."

"Dicto Simpliciter," she said, wagging her finger at me playfully.

That did it. I leaped to my feet, bellowing like a bull. "Will you or will you not go steady with me?"

"I will not," she replied.

"Why not?" I demanded.

"Because this afternoon I promised Petey Burch that I would go steady with him."

I reeled back, overcome with the infamy of it. After he promised, after he made a deal, after he shook my hand! "The rat!" I shrieked, kicking up great chunks of turf. "You can't go with him, Polly. He's a liar. He's a cheat. He's a rat."

"Poisoning the Well," said Polly, "and stop shouting. I think shouting must be a fallacy too."

With an immense effort of will, I modulated my voice. "All right," I said. "You're a logician. Let's look at this thing logically. How could you choose Petey Burch over me? Look at me — a brilliant student, a tremendous intellectual, a man with an assured future. Look at Petey — a knothead, a jitterbug, a guy who'll never know where his next meal is coming from. Can you give me one logical reason why you should go steady with Petey Burch?"

"I certainly can," declared Polly. "He's got a raccoon coat."

PART **5** CRITICISM

How To Write Like a Social Scientist

Samuel T. Williamson

During my years as an editor, I have seen probably hundreds of job applicants who were either just out of College or in their senior year. All wanted " to write." Many brought letters from their teachers. But I do not recall one letter announcing that its bearer could write what he wished to say with clarity and directness, with economy of words, and with pleasing variety of sentence structure.

Most of these young men and women could not write plain English. Apparently their noses had not been rubbed in the drudgery of putting one simple well-chosen word behind the other. If this was true of teachers' pets, what about the rest? What about those going into business and industry? Or those going into professions? What about those who remain at college — first for a Master of Arts degree, then an instructorship combined with work for a Ph.D., then perhaps an assistant professorship, next a full professorship and finally, as an academic crown of laurel, appointment as head of a department or as dean of a faculty.

Certainly, faculty members of a front-rank university should be better able to express themselves than those they teach. Assume that those in the English department have this ability. Can the same be said of the social scientists — economists, sociologists, and authorities on government? We need today as we never needed so urgently before all the understanding they can give us of problems of earning

HOW TO WRITE LIKE A SOCIAL SCIENTIST: Originally published in *The Saturday Review of Literature,* October 4, 1947. Reprinted by permission of *The Saturday Review.*

a living, caring for our fellows, and governing ourselves. Too many of them, I find, can't write as well as their students.

I am still convalescing from overexposure some time ago to prod ucts of the academic mind. One of the foundations engaged me to edit manuscripts of a socio-economic research report designed for the thoughtful citizen as well as for the specialist. My expectations were not high — no deathless prose, merely a sturdy, no-nonsense report of explorers into the wilderness of statistics and half-known fact. I knew from experience that economic necessity compels many a professional writer to be a cream-skimmer and a gatherer of easily obtainable material; for unless his publishers will stand the extra cost, he cannot afford the exhaustive investigation which endowed research makes possible. Although I did not expect fine writing from a trained, professional researcher, I did assume that a careful fact-finder would write carefully.

And so, anticipating no literary treat, I plunged into the forest of words of my first manuscript. My weapons were a sturdy eraser and several batteries of sharpened pencils. My armor was a thesaurus. And if I should become lost, a near-by public library was a land-mark, and the Encyclopedia of Social Sciences on its reference shelves was an ever-ready guide.

Instead of big trees, I found underbrush. Cutting through involved, lumbering sentences was bad enough, but the real chore was removal of the burdocks of excessive verbiage which clung to the manuscript. Nothing was big or large; in my author's lexicon, it was " substantial." When he meant " much," he wrote " to a substantially high degree." If some event took place in the early 1920's, he put it " in the early part of the decade of the twenties." And instead of " that depends," my author wrote, " any answer to this question must bear in mind certain peculiar characteristics of the industry."

So it went for 30,000 words. The pile of verbal burdocks grew — sometimes twelve words from a twenty-word sentence. The shortened version of 20,000 words was perhaps no more thrilling than the original report; but it was terser and crisper. It took less time to read and it could be understood quicker. That was all I could do. As S. S. McClure once said to me, " An editor can improve a manuscript, but he cannot put in what isn't there."

I did not know the author I was editing; after what I did to his copy it may be just as well that we have not met. Aside from his cat-chasing-its-own-tail verbosity, he was a competent enough workman. Apparently he is well thought of. He had his doctorate, he is a trained researcher and a pupil of an eminent professor. He has held a number of fellowships and he has performed competently several jobs of economic research. But, after this long academic preparation for what was to be his life work, it is a mystery why so little attention was given to acquiring use of simple English.

Later, when I encountered other manuscripts, I found I had been too hard on this promising Ph.D. Tone-deaf as he was to words, his report was a lighthouse of clarity among the chapters turned in by his so-called academic betters. These brethren — and sister'n — who contributed the remainder of the foundation's study were professors and assistant professors in our foremost colleges and universities. The names of one or two are occasionally in newspaper headlines. All of them had, as the professorial term has it, " published."

Anyone who edits copy, regardless of whether it is good or bad, discovers in a manuscript certain pet phrases, little quirks of style and other individual traits of its author. But in the series I edited, all twenty reports read alike. Their words would be found in any English dictionary, grammar was beyond criticism, but long passages in these reports demanded not only editing but actual translation. For hours at a time, I floundered in brier patches like this: " In eliminating wage changes due to purely transitory conditions, collective bargaining has eliminated one of the important causes of industrial conflict, for changes under such conditions are almost always followed by a reaction when normal conditions appear."

I am not picking on my little group of social scientists. They are merely members of a caste; they are so used to taking in each other's literary washing that it has become a habit for them to clothe their thoughts in the same smothering verbal garments. Nor are they any worse than most of their colleagues, for example:

In the long run, developments in transportation, housing, optimum size of plant, etc., might tend to induce an industrial and demographic pattern similar to the one that consciousness of vulnerability would dictate. Such a tendency might be advanced by public persuasion and governmental inducement, and advanced more effectively if the causes of urbanization had been carefully studied.

Such pedantic Choctaw may be all right as a sort of code language or shorthand of social science to circulate among initiates, but its perpetrators have no right to impose it on others. The tragedy is that its users appear to be under the impression that it is good English usage.

Father, forgive them; for they know not what they do! There once was a time when everyday folk spoke one language, and learned men wrote another. It was called the Dark Ages. The world is in such a state that we may return to the Dark Ages if we do not acquire wisdom. If social scientists have answers to our problems yet feel under

SAMUEL T. WILLIAMSON / 625

no obligation to make themselves understood, then we laymen must learn their language. This may take some practice, but practice should become perfect by following six simple rules of the guild of social science writers. Examples which I give are sound and well tested: they come from manuscripts I edited.

Rule 1. Never use a short word when you can think of a long one. Never say " now," but " currently." It is not " soon " but " presently." You did not have " enough " but a " sufficiency." Never do you come to the " end " but to the " termination." This rule is basic.

Rule 2. Never use one word when you can use two or more. Eschew " probably." Write, " it is probable," and raise this to " it is not improbable." Then you'll be able to parlay " probably " into " available evidence would tend to indicate that it is not unreasonable to suppose."

Rule 3. Put one-syllable thoughts into polysyllabic terms. Instead of observing that a work force might be bigger and better, write, " In addition to quantitative enlargement, it is not improbable that there is need also for qualitative improvement in the personnel of the service." If you have discovered that musicians out of practice can't hold jobs, report that " the fact of rapid deterioration of musical skill when not in use soon converts the employed into the unemployable." Resist the impulse to say that much men's clothing is machine made. Put it thus: " Nearly all operations in the industry lend themselves to performance by machine, and all grades of men's clothing sold in significant quantity involve a very substantial amount of machine work."

Rule 4. Put the obvious in terms of the unintelligible. When you write that " the product of the activity of janitors is expended in the identical locality in which that activity takes place," your lay reader is in for a time of it. After an hour's puzzlement, he may conclude that janitors' sweepings are thrown on the town dump. See what you can do with this: " Each article sent to the cleaner is handled separately." You become a member of the guild in good standing if you put it like this: " Within the cleaning plant proper the business of the industry involves several well-defined processes, which, from the economic point of view, may be characterized simply by saying that most of them require separate handling of each individual garment or piece of material to be cleaned."

Rule 5. Announce what you are going to say before you say it. This pitcher's wind-up technique before hurling towards — not at — home plate has two varieties. First is the quick wind-up: " In the following section the policies of the administration will be considered." Then you become strong enough for the contortionist wind-up: " Perhaps more important, therefore, than the question of what standards are in a particular case, there are the questions of the extent of observance of these standards and the methods of their enforcement." Also you can play with reversing Rule 5 and say *what you have said after you have said it.*

Rule 6. Defend your style as " scientific." Look down on — not up to — clear simple English. Sneer at it as " popular." Scorn it as " journalistic." Explain your failure to put more mental sweat into your writing on the ground that " the social scientists who want to be scientific believe that we can have scientific description of human behavior and trustworthy predictions in the scientific sense only as we build adequate taxonomic systems for observable phenomena and symbolic systems for the manipulation of ideal and abstract entities." . . .

It is not too much to expect that teachers should be more competent in the art of explanation than those they teach. Teachers of social sciences diligently try to acquire knowledge: too few exert themselves enough to impart it intelligently.

Too long has this been excused as " the academic mind." It should be called by what it is: intellectual laziness and grubby-mindedness.

Dickens

George Santayana

If Christendom should lose everything that is now in the melting-pot, human life would still remain amiable and quite adequately human. I draw this comforting assurance from the pages of Dickens. Who could not be happy in his world? Yet there is nothing essential to it which the most destructive revolution would be able to destroy. People would still be as different, as absurd, and as charming as are his characters; the springs of kindness and folly in their lives would not be dried up. Indeed, there is much in Dickens which communism, if it came, would only emphasize and render universal. Those schools, those poorhouses, those prisons, with those surviving shreds

DICKENS: From *Soliloquies in England and Later Soliloquies* by George Santayana. Reprinted by permission of Charles Scribner's Sons.

of family life in them, show us what in the coming age (with some sanitary improvements) would be — the nursery and home of everybody. Everybody would be a waif, like Oliver Twist, like Smike, like Pip, and like David Copperfield; and amongst the agents and underlings of social government, to whom all these waifs would be entrusted, there would surely be a goodly sprinkling of Pecksniffs, Squeerses and Fangs; whilst the Fagins would be everywhere commissioners of the people. Nor would there fail to be, in high places and in low, the occasional sparkle of some Pickwick or Cheeryble Brothers or Sam Weller or Mark Tapley; and the voluble Flora Finchings would be everywhere in evidence, and the strong-minded Betsy Trotwoods in office. There would also be, among the inefficient, many a Dora and Agnes and Little Emily — with her charm but without her tragedy, since this is one of the things which the promised social reform would happily render impossible; I mean, by removing all the disgrace of it. The only element in the world of Dickens which would become obsolete would be the setting, the atmosphere of material instrumentalities and arrangements, as travelling by coach is obsolete; but travelling by rail, by motor, or by airship will emotionally be much the same thing. It is worth noting how such instrumentalities, which absorb modern life, are admired and enjoyed by Dickens, as they were by Homer. The poets ought not to be afraid of them; they exercise the mind congenially, and can be played with joyfully. Consider the black ships and the chariots of Homer, the coaches and riverboats of Dickens, and the aeroplanes of today; to what would an unspoiled young mind turn with more interest? Dickens tells us little of English sports, but he shares the sporting nature of the Englishman, to whom the whole material world is a playing-field, the scene giving ample scope to his love of action, legality, and pleasant achievement. His art is to sport according to the rules of the game, and to do things for the sake of doing them, rather than for any ulterior motive.

It is remarkable, in spite of his ardent simplicity and openness of heart, how insensible Dickens was to the greater themes of the human imagination — religion, science, politics, art. He was a waif himself, and utterly disinherited. For example, the terrible heritage of contentious religions which fills the world seems not to exist for him. In this matter he was like a sensitive child, with a most religious disposition, but no religious ideas. Perhaps, properly speaking, he had no *ideas* on any subject; what he had was a vast sympathetic participation in the daily life of mankind; and what he saw of ancient institutions made him hate them, as needless sources of oppression, misery, selfishness, and rancour. His one political passion was philanthropy, genuine but felt only on its negative, reforming side; of positive utopias or enthusiasms we hear nothing. The political background of Christendom is only, so to speak, an old faded back-drop for his stage; a castle, a frigate, a gallows, and a large female angel with white wings standing above an orphan by an open grave — a decora tion which has to serve for all the melodramas in his theatre, intellectually so provincial and poor. Common life as it is lived was varied and lovable enough for Dickens, if only the pests and cruelties could be removed from it. Suffering wounded him, but not vulgarity; whatever pleased his senses and whatever shocked them filled his mind alike with romantic wonder, with the endless delight of observation. Vulgarity — and what can we relish, if we recoil at vulgarity? — was innocent and amusing; in fact, for the humorist, it was the spice of life. There was more piety in being human than in being pious. In reviving Christmas, Dickens transformed it from the celebration of a metaphysical mystery into a feast of overflowing simple kindness and good cheer; the church bells were still there — in the orchestra; and the angels of Bethlehem were still there — painted on the back curtain. Churches, in his novels, are vague, desolate places where one has ghastly experiences, and where only the pew-opener is human; and such religious and political conflicts as he depicts in *Barnaby Rudge* and in *A Tale of Two Cities* are street brawls and prison scenes and conspiracies in taverns, without any indication of the contrasts in mind or interests between the opposed parties. Nor had Dickens any lively sense for fine art, classical tradition, science, or even the manners and feelings of the upper classes in his own time and country: in his novels we may almost say there is no army, no navy, no church, no sport, no distant travel, no daring adventure, no feeling for the watery wastes and the motley nations of the planet, and — luckily, with his notion of them — no lords and ladies. Even love of the traditional sort is hardly in Dickens's sphere — I mean the soldierly passion in which a rather rakish gallantry was sobered by devotion, and loyalty rested on pride. In Dickens love is sentimental or benevolent or merry or sneaking or canine; in his last book he was going to describe a love that was passionate and criminal; but love for him was never chivalrous, never poetical. What he paints most tragically is a quasi-paternal devotion in the old to the young, the love of Mr. Peggotty for Little Emily, or of Solomon Gills for Walter Gay. A series of shabby little adventures, such as might absorb the interest of an average youth, were romantic enough for Dickens.

I say he was disinterested, but he inherited the most terrible negations. Religion lay on him like the weight of the atmosphere sixteen pounds to the square inch, yet never noticed nor mentioned. He lived and wrote in the shadow of the most awful prohibitions. Hearts petrified by legality and falsified by wordliness offered, indeed, a good subject for a novelist, and Dickens availed himself of it to the extent of always contrasting natural goodness and happiness with whatever is morose; and his morose people were wicked, not virtuous in their own way; so that the protest of his temperament against his environment never took a radical form nor went back to first principles. He needed to feel, in his writing, that he was carrying the sympathies of every man with him. In him conscience was single, and he could not conceive how it could ever be divided in other men. He denounced scandals without exposing shams, and conformed willingly and scrupulously to the proprieties. Lady Dedlock's secret, for instance, he treats as if it were the sin of Adam, remote, mysterious, inexpiable. Mrs. Dombey is not allowed to deceive her husband except by pretending to deceive him. The seduction of Little Emily is left out altogether, with the whole character of Steerforth, the development of which would have been so important in the moral experience of David Copperfield himself. But it is not public prejudice alone that plays the censor over Dickens's art; his own kindness and even weakness of heart act sometimes as marplots. The character of Miss Mowcher, for example, so brilliantly introduced, was evidently intended to be shady, and to play a very important part in the story; but its original in real life, which was recognized, had to be conciliated, and the sequel was omitted and patched up with an apology — itself admirable — for the poor dwarf. Such a sacrifice does honour to Dickens's heart; but artists should meditate on their works in time, and it is easy to remove any too great likeness in a portrait by a few touches making it more consistent than real people are apt to be; and in this case, if the little creature had been really guilty, how much more subtle and tragic her apology for herself might have been, like that of the bastard Edmund in *King Lear!* So, too, in *Dombey and Son,* Dickens could not bear to let Walter Gay turn out badly, as he had been meant to do, and to break his uncle's heart as well as the heroine's; he was accordingly transformed into a stage hero miraculously saved from shipwreck, and Florence was not allowed to reward the admirable Toots, as she should have done, with her trembling hand. But Dickens was no free artist; he had more genius than taste, a warm fancy not aided by a thorough understanding of complex characters. He worked under pressure for money and applause, and often had to cheapen in execution what his inspiration had so vividly conceived.

What, then, is left, if Dickens had all these limitations? In our romantic disgust we might be tempted to say, Nothing. But in fact almost everything is left, almost everything that counts in the daily life of mankind, or that by its presence or absence can determine whether life shall be worth living or not; because a simple good life is worth living, and an elaborate bad life is not. There remains in the first place eating and drinking; relished not bestially, but humanly, jovially, as the sane and exhilarating basis for everything else. This is a sound English beginning; but the immediate sequel, as the England of that day presented it to Dickens, is no less delightful. There is the ruddy glow of the hearth; the sparkle of glasses and brasses and well-scrubbed pewter; the savoury fumes of the hot punch, after the tingle of the wintry air; the coaching scenes, the motley figures and absurd incidents of travel; the changing sights and joys of the road. And then, to balance this, the traffic of ports and cities, the hubbub of crowded streets, the luxury of shop windows and of palaces not to be entered; the procession of the passers-by, shabby or ludicrously genteel; the dingy look and musty smell of their lodgings; the labyrinth of back-alleys, courts, and mews, with their crying children, and scolding old women, and listless, half-drunken loiterers. These sights, like fables, have a sort of moral in them to which Dickens was very sensitive; the important airs of nobodies on great occasions, the sadness and preoccupation of the great as they hasten by in their mourning or on their pressing affairs; the sadly comic characters of the tavern; the diligence of shop-keepers, like squirrels turning in their cages; the children peeping out everywhere like grass in an untrodden street; the charm of humble things, the nobleness of humble people, the horror of crime, the ghastliness of vice, the deft hand and shining face of virtue passing through the midst of it all; and finally a fresh wind of indifference and change blowing across our troubles and clearing the most lurid sky.

I do not know whether it was Christian charity or naturalistic insight, or a mixture of both (for they are closely akin) that attracted Dickens particularly to the deformed, the half-witted, the abandoned, or those impeded or misunderstood by virtue of some singular inner consecration. The visible moral of these things, when brutal prejudice does not blind us to it, comes very near to true philosophy; one turn of the screw, one flash of reflection, and we have understood nature and human morality and the relation between them.

In his love of roads and wayfarers, of river-ports and wharves and the idle or sinister figures that lounge about them, Dickens was like Walt Whitman; and I think a second Dickens may any day appear in America, when it is possible in that land of hurry to reach the same degree of saturation, the same unquestioning pleasure in the familiar facts. The spirit of Dickens would be better able to do justice to America than was that of Walt Whitman; because America, although it may seem nothing but a noisy nebula to the impressionist, is not a nebula but a concourse of very distinct individual bodies, natural and social, each with its definite interests and story. Walt Whitman had a sort of transcendental philosophy which swallowed the universe whole, supposing there was a universal spirit in things identical with the absolute spirit that observed them; but Dickens was innocent of any clap-trap, and remained a true spirit in his own person. Kindly and clear-sighted, but self-identical and unequivocally human, he glided through the slums like one of his own little heroes, uncontaminated by their squalor and confusion, courageous and firm in his clear allegiances amid the flux of things, a pale angel at the Carnival, his heart aflame, his voice always flute-like in its tenderness and warning. This is the true relation of spirit to existence, not the other which confuses them; for this earth (I cannot speak for the Universe at large) has no spirit of its own, but brings forth spirits only at certain points, in the hearts and brains of frail living creatures, who like insects flit through it, buzzing and gathering what sweets they can; and it is the spaces they traverse in this career, charged with their own moral burden, that they can report on or describe, not things rolling on to infinity in their vain tides. To be hypnotized by that flood would be a heathen idolatry. Accordingly Walt Whitman, in his comprehensive democratic vistas, could never see the trees for the wood, and remained incapable, for all his diffuse love of the human herd, of ever painting a character or telling a story; the very things in which Dickens was a master. It is this life of the individual, as it may be lived in a given nation, that determines the whole value of that nation to the poet, to the moralist, and to the judicious historian. But for the excellence of the typical single life, no nation deserves to be remembered more than the sands of the sea; and America will not be a success, if every American is a failure.

Dickens entered the theatre of this world by the stage door; the shabby little adventures of the actors in their private capacity replace for him the mock tragedies which they enact before a dreaming public. Mediocrity of circumstances and mediocrity of soul for ever return to the centre of his stage; a more wretched or a grander existence is sometimes broached, but the pendulum soon swings back, and we return, with the relief with which we put on our slippers after the most romantic excursion, to a golden mediocrity — to mutton and beer, and to love and babies in a suburban villa with one frowsy maid. Dickens is the poet of those acres of yellow brick streets which the traveller sees from the railway viaducts as he approaches London; they need a poet, and they deserve one, since a complete human life may very well be lived there. Their little excitements and sorrows, their hopes and humours are like those of the Wooden Midshipman in *Dombey and Son;* but the sea is not far off, and the sky — Dickens never forgets it — is above all those brief troubles. He had a sentiment in the presence of this vast flatness of human fates, in spite of their individual pungency, which I think might well be the dominant sentiment of mankind in the future; a sense of happy freedom in littleness, an open-eyed reverence and religion without words. This universal human anonymity is like a sea, an infinitive democratic desert, chock-full and yet the very image of emptiness, with nothing in it for the mind, except, as the Moslems say, the presence of Allah. Awe is the counterpart of humility — and this is perhaps religion enough. The atom in the universal vortex ought to be humble; he ought to see that, materially, he doesn't much matter, and that morally his loves are merely his own, without authority over the universe. He can admit without obloquy that he is what he is; and he can rejoice in his own being, and in that of all other things in so far as he can share it sympathetically. The apportionment of existence and of fortune is in Other Hands; his own portion is contentment, vision, love, and laughter.

Having humility, that most liberating of sentiments, having a true vision of human existence and joy in that vision, Dickens had in a superlative degree the gift of humour, of mimicry, of unrestrained farce. He was the perfect comedian. When people say Dickens exaggerates, it seems to me they can have no eyes and no ears. They probably have only *notions* of what things and people are; they accept them conventionally, at their diplomatic value. Their minds run on in the region of discourse, where there are masks only and no faces, ideas and no facts; they have little sense for those living grimaces that play from moment to moment upon the countenance of the world. The world is a perpetual caricature of itself; at every moment it is the mockery and the contradiction of what it is pretending to be. But as it nevertheless intends all the time to be something different and highly dignified, at the next moment it corrects and checks and tries to cover up the absurd thing it was; so that a conventional world, a world of masks, is superimposed on the reality, and passes in every sphere of human interest for the reality itself. Humour is the perception of this illusion, the fact allowed to pierce here and there through the convention, whilst the convention continues to be maintained, as if we had not observed its absurdity. Pure comedy is more radical, cruder, in a certain sense less human; because comedy throws the convention over altogether, revels for a moment in the fact, There take that! That's what you really are! At this the polite world pretends to laugh, not tolerantly as it does at humour, but a little angrily. It does not like to see itself by chance in the glass, without having had time to compose its features for demure self-contemplation. " What a bad mirror," it exclaims; " it must be convex or concave; for surely I never looked like that. Mere caricature, farce, and horse play. Dickens exaggerates; *I* never was so sentimental as that; *I* never saw anything so dreadful; *I* don't believe there were ever any people like Quilp, or Squeers, or Serjeant Buzfuz." But the polite world is lying; there *are* such people; we are such people ourselves in our true moments, in our veritable impulses; but we are careful to stifle and to hide those moments from ourselves and from the world; to purse and pucker ourselves into the mask of our conventional personality; and so simpering, we profess that it is very coarse and inartistic of Dickens to undo our life's work for us in an instant, and remind us of what we are. And as to other people, though we may allow that considered superficially they are often absurd, we do not wish to dwell on their eccentricities nor to mimic them. On the contrary, it is good manners to look away quickly, to suppress a smile, and to say to ourselves that the ludicrous figure in the street is not at all comic, but a dull ordinary Christian, and that it is foolish to give any importance to the fact that its hat has blown off, that it has slipped on an orange-peel and unintentionally sat on the pavement, that it has a pimple on its nose, that its one tooth projects over its lower lip, that it is angry with things in general, and that it is looking everywhere for the penny which it holds tightly in its hand. That may fairly represent the moral condition of most of us at most times; but we do not want to think of it; we do not want to see; we gloss the fact over; we console ourselves before we are grieved, and reassert our composure before we have laughed. We are afraid, ashamed, anxious to be spared. What displeases us in Dickens is that he does not spare us; he mimics things to the full; he dilates and exhausts and repeats; he wallows. He is too intent on the passing experience to look over his shoulder, and consider whether we have not already understood, and had enough. He is not thinking of us; he is obeying the impulse of the passion, the person, or the story he is enacting. This faculty, which renders him a consummate comedian, is just what alienated from him a later generation in which people of taste were aesthetes and virtuous people were higher snobs; they wanted a mincing art, and he gave them copious improvisation, they wanted analysis and development, and he gave them absolute comedy. I must confess, though the fault is mine and not his, that sometimes his absoluteness is too much for me. When I come to the death of Little Nell, or to What the Waves were always Saying, or even to the incorrigible perversities of the pretty Dora, I skip. I can't take my liquor neat in such draughts, and my inner man says to Dickens, Please don't. But then I am a coward in so many ways! There are so many things in this world that I skip, as I skip the undiluted Dickens! When I reach Dover on a rough day, I wait there until the Channel is smoother; am I not travelling for pleasure? But my prudence does not blind me to the admirable virtue of the sailors that cross in all weathers, not even to the automatic determination of the seasick ladies, who might so easily have followed my example, if they were not the slaves of their railway tickets and of their labelled luggage. They are loyal to their tour, and I to my philosophy. Yet as wrapped in my great-coat and sure of a good dinner, I pace the windy pier and soliloquize, I feel the superiority of the bluff tar, glad of breeze, stretching a firm arm to the unsteady passenger, and watching with a masterful thrill of emotion the home cliffs receding and the foreign coasts ahead. It is only courage (which Dickens had without knowing it) and universal kindness (which he knew he had) that are requisite to nerve us for a true vision of this world. And as some of us are cowards about crossing the Channel, and others about " crossing the bar," so almost everybody is a coward about his own humanity. We do not consent to be absurd, though absurd we are. We have no fundamental humility. We do not wish the moments of our lives to be caught by a quick eye in their grotesque initiative, and to be pilloried in this way before our own eyes. For that reason we don't like Dickens, and don't like comedy, and don't like the truth. Dickens could don the comic mask with innocent courage; he could wear it with a grace, ease, and irresistible vivacity seldom given to men. We must go back for anything like it to the very greatest comic poets, to Shakespeare or to Aristophanes. Who else, for instance, could have penned this:

" It was all Mrs. Bumble. She *would* do it," urged Mr. Bumble; first looking around to ascertain that his partner had left the room.

" That is no excuse," replied Mr. Brownlow. " You were present on the occasion of the destruction of these trinkets, and indeed are the more guilty of the two, in the eye of the law; for the law supposes that your wife acts under your direction."

" If the law supposes that," said Mr. Bumble, squeezing his hat emphatically in both hands, " the law is a ass, a idiot. If that's the eye of the law, the law is a bachelor; and the worst I wish the law is, that his eye may be opened by experience — by experience."

Laying great stress on the repetition of these two words, Mr. Bumble fixed his hat on very tight, and putting his hands in his pockets, followed his helpmate downstairs.

This is high comedy; the irresistible, absurd, intense dream of the old fool, personifying the law in order to convince and to punish it. I can understand that this sort of thing should not be common in

English literature, nor much relished; because pure comedy is scornful, merciless, devastating, holding no door open to anything beyond. Cultivated English feeling winces at this brutality, although the common people love it in clowns and in puppet shows; and I think they are right. Dickens, who surely was tender enough, had so irresistible a comic genius that it carried him beyond the gentle humour which most Englishmen possess to the absolute grotesque reality. Squeers, for instance, when he sips the wretched dilution which he has prepared for his starved and shivering little pupils, smacks his lips and cries: " Here's a richness! " It is savage comedy; humour would come in if we understood (what Dickens does not tell us) that the little creatures were duly impressed and thought the thin liquid truly delicious. I suspect that English sensibility prefers the humour and wit of Hamlet to the pure comedy of Falstaff; and that even in Aristophanes it seeks consolation in the lyrical poetry for the flaying of human life in the comedy itself. Tastes are free; but we should not deny that in merciless and rollicking comedy life is caught in the act. The most grotesque creatures of Dickens are not exaggerations or mockeries of something other than themselves; they arise because nature generates them, like toadstools; they exist because they can't help it, as we all do. The fact that these perfectly self-justified beings are absurd appears only by comparison, and from outside; circumstances or the expectations of other people, make them ridiculous and force them to contradict themselves; but in nature it is no crime to be exceptional. Often, but for the savagery of the average man, it would not even be a misfortune. The sleepy fat boy in *Pickwick* looks less foolish; but in himself he is no more foolish, no less solidly justified, than a pumpkin lying on the ground. Toots seems ridiculous; and we laugh heartily at his incoherence, his beautiful waistcoats, and his extreme modesty; but when did anybody more obviously grow into what he is because he couldn't grow otherwise? So with Mr. Pickwick, and Sam Weller, and Mrs. Gamp, and Micawber, and all the rest of this wonderful gallery; they are ridiculous only by accident, and in the context in which they never intended to appear. If Oedipus and Lear and Cleopatra do not seem ridiculous, it is only because tragic reflection had taken them out of the context in which, in real life, they would have figured. If we saw them as facts, and not as emanations of a poet's dream, we should laugh at them till doomsday; what grotesque presumption, what silly whims, what mad contradiction of the simplest realities! Yet we should not laugh at them without feeling how real their griefs were; as real and terrible as the griefs of children and dreams. But facts, however serious inwardly, are always absurd outwardly; and the just critic of life sees both truths at once, as Cervantes did in *Don Quixote*. A pompous idealist who does not see the ridiculous in *all things* is the dupe of his sympathy and abstraction; and a clown, who does not see that these ridiculous figures are living quite in earnest, is the dupe of his egotism. Dickens saw the absurdity, and understood the life; and I think he was a good philosopher.

It is usual to compare Dickens with Thackeray, which is like comparing the grape with the gooseberry; there are obvious points of resemblance, and the gooseberry has some superior qualities of its own; but you can't make red wine with it. The wine of Dickens is of the richest, the purest, the sweetest, the most fortifying to the blood; there is distilled in it, with the perfection of comedy, the perfection of morals. I do not mean, of course, that Dickens appreciated all the values that human life has or might have; that is beyond any man. Even the greatest philosophers, such as Aristotle, have not always much imagination to conceive forms of happiness or folly other than those which their age or their temperament reveals to them; their insight runs only to discovering the *principle* of happiness, that it is the spontaneous life of any sort harmonized with circumstances. The sympathies and imagination of Dickens, vivid in their sphere, were no less limited in range; and of course it was not his business to find philosophic formulas; nevertheless I call his the perfection of morals for two reasons: that he put the distinction between good and evil in the right place, and that he felt this distinction intensely. A moralist might have excellent judgement, he might see what sort of life is spontaneous in a given being and how far it may be harmonized with circumstances, yet his heart might remain cold, he might not suffer nor rejoice with the suffering or joy he foresaw. Humanitarians like Bentham and Mill, who talked about the greatest happiness of the greatest number, might conceivably be moral prigs in their own persons, and they might have been chilled to the bone in their theoretic love of mankind, if they had had the wit to imagine in what, as a matter of fact, the majority would place their happiness. Even if their theory had been correct (which I think it was in intention, though not in statement) they would then not have been perfect moralists, because their maxims would not have expressed their hearts. In expressing their hearts, they ought to have embraced one of those forms of " idealism " by which men fortify themselves in their bitter passions or in their helpless commitments; for they do not wish mankind to be happy in its own way, but in theirs. Dickens was not one of those moralists who summon every man to do himself the greatest violence so that he may not offend them, nor defeat their ideals. Love of the good of others is something that shines in every page of Dickens with a truly celestial splendour. How entirely limpid is his sympathy with life — a sympathy uncontaminated by dogma or pedantry or snobbery or bias of any kind! How generous is this keen, light spirit, how pure this open heart! And yet, in spite of this extreme sensibility, not the least wobbling; no deviation from a just severity of judgement, from an uncompromising distinction between white and black. And this happens as it ought to happen; sympathy is not checked by a flatly contrary prejudice or commandment, by some categorical imperative irrelevant to human nature; the check, like the cheer, comes by tracing the course of spontaneous impulse and circumstances that inexorably lead it to success or to failure. There is a bed to this stream, freely as the water may flow; when it comes to this precipice it must leap, when it runs over these pebbles it must sing, and when it spreads into that marsh it must become livid and malarial. The very sympathy with human impulse quickens in Dickens the sense of danger; his very joy in joy makes him stern to what kills it. How admirably drawn are his surly villains! No rhetorical vilification of them, as in a sermon; no exaggeration of their qualms or fears; rather a sense of how obvious and human all their courses seem from their point of view; and yet no sentimental apology for them, no romantic worship of rebels in their madness or crime. The pity of it, the waste of it all, are seen not by a second vision but by the same original vision which revealed the lure and the drift of the passion. Vice is a monster here of such sorry mien, that the longer we see it the more we deplore it; that other sort of vice which Pope found so seductive was perhaps only some innocent impulse artificially suppressed, and called a vice because it broke out inconveniently and displeased the company. True vice is human nature strangled by the suicide of attempting the impossible. Those so self-justified villains of Dickens never elude their fates. Bill Sikes is not let off, neither is Nancy; the oddly benevolent Magwitch does not escape from the net, nor does the unfortunate young Richard Carstone, victim of the Circumlocution Office. The horror and ugliness of their fall are rendered with the hand of a master; we see here, as in the world, that in spite of the romanticists it is not virtue to rush enthusiastically along any road. I think Dickens is one of the best friends mankind has ever had. He has held the mirror up to nature, and of its reflected fragments has composed a fresh world, where the men and women differ from real people only in that they live in a literary medium, so that all ages and places may know them. And they are worth knowing, just as one's neighbours are, for their picturesque characters and their pathetic fates. Their names should be in every child's mouth; they ought to be adopted members of every household. Their stories cause the merriest and the sweetest chimes to ring in the fancy, without confusing our moral judgment or alienating our interest from the motley commonplaces of daily life. In every English-speaking home, in the four quarters of the globe, parents and children will do well to read Dickens aloud of a winter's evening; they will love winter, and one another, and God the better for it. What a wreath that will be of ever-fresh holly, thick with bright berries, to hang to this poet's memory — the very crown he would have chosen!

Thomas Wolfe

James Gray

It is quite impossible to dissociate the personal history of Thomas Wolfe from his work. It was the absorbing task of his whole life to write his autobiography. He wrote it first in the two novels, *Look Homeward, Angel* and *Of Time and the River,* calling himself Eugene Gant. Then he wrote it all over again in another pair of novels, *The Web and the Rock* and *You Can't Go Home Again,* calling himself George Webber. In between these major efforts he produced volumes of short stories which read like, and probably were, shavings from the novels, which publishers dreaded to see grow out of the capacious limits of a thousand pages. He also wrote such highly personal footnotes to his own career as *The Story of a Novel,* in which he tells of his home town's bitter first reaction against his work. (One salty old lady wrote to him that " although she had never believed in lynch law, she would do nothing to prevent a mob from dragging his ' big overgrown karkus ' across the square.") When he died at thirty-seven, it was found that he had written enough letters to his mother to fill another sizable volume, and these contained still another intimate record of his spiritual and material progress.

It might be said that he spent his life crying " Wolfe! Wolfe! " and whether or not he did it once, twice, or several times too often is wholly a matter of personal opinion. For the first cry was almost exactly like the last. There was no growth and very little change in his philosophy or outlook.

THOMAS WOLFE: Copyright 1946 by the University of Minnesota. Reprinted by permission of the University of Minnesota Press.

Indeed, after the appearance of the first book, which seemed so compelling in its fresh, tireless exuberance, it became increasingly evident that Wolfe had no philosophy at all. My own interest dwindled as I found that I was expected to follow this copious writer again and again through the dark and tortuous passages of a boy's mind.

Thomas Wolfe was, as his later books forced his first admirers to admit, an egocentric monster, tenderly concerned with his own sensibilities, yet capable of blighting cruelty in his relations with others. Empathy frequently prompted him to search out the secret that moved the mind of another, but when he had found it, a characteristic adolescent impulse inspired him to expose, with gleeful spite, the pitiful weakness he had discovered. His chief requirement of experience was that it should feed his own insatiable need. His recurring cry of " Oh lost! forever lost! " was really nothing but the adolescent's characteristic incantation of wonder and self-pity and fear.

Yet in its early expression, as in *Of Time and the River,* the cry had a certain urgency and freshness that seemed impressive. . . .

It is important to remember about Thomas Wolfe that when you stand beside him he seems to be seven feet tall, to weigh two hundred pounds, and to have atop his broad shoulders a child's touching, eager face. I wonder if it is too fantastic to suggest that Thomas Wolfe has somehow come to contain within himself the genius of our time. He is still young and vigorous; he is shrewd and curious and naïve; he is a poet; he is a man whose keen eye penetrates through sham; he is a great, blundering, egocentric lout of a boy. He is all these things at once and there is no denying that anyone who can be so much is important. As Eugene Gant's great friend, Francis Starwick, says of him, " There is a great river of energy in you and it keeps bursting over and breaking loose. You could not hold it back if you tried."

I apply that to Thomas Wolfe, as he means us to understand we are entitled to do. He is a river of energy, plunging through mysterious dark caverns, rippling pleasantly under the sun, leaping from high places, recklessly spending its power, creating power — a terrific elemental force.

The narrative does not count at all. The individual scenes do, because each communicates something to Eugene Gant which Thomas Wolfe gives back to the reader. The relationship of Eugene to his strange Boston uncle is full of drama. The devastating analysis of Professor Hatcher, the elegant, shallow teacher of drama at Harvard, who actually taught boys to be only dilettantes wooing triviality, is a brilliant achievement. Eugene's bitter beginnings to many friendships, like the one with his Jewish student, Abraham Jones, are packed solid with good psychological observation. Thomas Wolfe can turn any literary trick that anyone in our time has tried. He goes in for melodrama, social satire, sentimental comedy (pretty bad and momentarily alienating). He cannot walk through the lobby of a hotel without having to overhear and record every conversation and the curious accent of every speaker.

Wolfe's virtuosity is very great. But it does not show itself merely in the power of his effects. He has his fineness too. He makes telling phrases: " the wretched kind of hatred that comes from intolerable pity without love "; a " good grotesque old empress of confusion "; " trying to suck sweetness out of paving brick." I pick these at random. But the one that seems to me most accurately to express his own mood is " ecstatic and insatiable glee." Even when he broods and yearns and feels that all is " lost, oh lost," there is in him still an ecstatic and insatiable appetite for life. . . .

And now finis is written to the career of Thomas Wolfe. Out of the brief but intense tumult of his spirit came four novels, a volume of sketches, and another volume of critical comment, which will have to be re-examined and reappraised by anyone who wishes to interpret the writing of our time.

The importance of his work lies in the fact that he made so complete and for the most part so honest a revelation of what went on in the mind and heart of one man living under the conditions of our present-day world. He was certainly not a great creative artist. Only a reader as naïve as Wolfe himself could possibly regard him as a thinker. Until he approached the writing of this last book he made scarcely any effort to generalize on his themes. He simply wanted to encompass the copiousness of himself and make permanent the record of his driving needs.

It was rather fatuous of him, in the first place, to assume that he had the right to set down at such length and with such a prophetic air his not at all remarkable observations on the education and development of a sensitive young man. But because he persisted in his task with such vehement determination, because he approached it from many angles and with an exhaustive thoroughness, the body of his work becomes a kind of heroic monument to one of the popular impulses of American writing. Thomas Wolfe was the yearning, demanding, hungry young man par excellence. . . .

So Wolfe's career ended with a question still unanswered. Who was this giant who cast his shadow over America for a decade? Was he not the attractive, unreliable — even dangerous — embodiment of all restless, assertive immaturity? I think so.

The posthumous publication of *Thomas Wolfe's Letters to His*

Mother offered the literary critic and historian a final opportunity to achieve insight into the mind of the writer.

" I know this now," Thomas Wolfe wrote to his mother when he was a young man in his teens, " I am inevitable."

It is interesting that he should have had an intuitive, anticipatory glimpse of the fact that he was to be unique among American writers of his time. But his comment does not indicate that he understood himself well then or at any later time. In 1921 he thought that a career as a playwright was inevitable for him. Actually no effort could have been more inappropriate to a man who needed nine hundred pages in which to turn around and who had no notion of compression or of economy of means.

The letters are not in themselves distinguished. They are the work of a young man who within the shell of his egotism felt pitifully vulnerable and insecure. An obsession with money runs through these pages. His tuition at Harvard has not been paid. He needs more socks. Can his mother let him have a hundred dollars a month on which to live abroad? It will be impossible for him to economize because he is traveling with some wealthy people and must live by their standards. All the while he worries about being a taker. Yet when he accepts a teaching job, he hopes fervently that something will turn up so that he can slip out of the arrangement into a more comfortable one. More comfortable ones were constantly being arranged for him.

Later the obsession turned to a flood of comments on royalties, lecture fees, hopes for magazine profits.

With schoolboy naïveté Tom tells " Dear Mama " about the " wealthy ladies " whom he has met in Paris and in New York. Despite the protestation of the editor of these letters that Wolfe did not share his mother's love of great names, it seems evident that both the wealth and the ladylikeness of these acquaintances dazzled him.

But for the most part the letters are about that glittering inevitability of fame toward which he makes his faltering but determined way. " I get lots of praise," he wrote to his mother from Chapel Hill. " There is no one like me, and I shall conquer," he chirps a few years later. " Fools will call this conceit, but let them say what they will — they are fools."

It was not at all clear to him, in those early years, what he proposed to conquer. He did not wish passionately to say something bold and free, something that would change people's minds, alter the outlook of a country's thinking. He simply had to be on a platform in a well-lighted place saying something, anything, that would make him noticeable, constantly noticeable, unique among all other exhibits of noticeable people.

Thomas Wolfe was devoted to his mother and she to him. This volume of letters addressed to "Dear Mama" explains the closeness of the bond that Wolfe felt with the past, with the village of his childhood, with the neighbors about whom his mother, who was herself a novelist *manqué,* had told her rambling stories, with the problem of whether or not you can go home again. In her talks with the editor of this volume (recorded verbatim in the introduction) Mrs. Wolfe tells such astonishing facts about the beginnings of her famous son as that she nursed him until he was three and a half years old and that every day she curled the beautiful brown hair which hung to his shoulders until he had begun to go to school. "He being the baby," she said, "I kept him a baby."

That was why he wrote the books that are his curious monument. They are the tributes of Tom Wolfe to Tom Wolfe. There he stands against the background of Asheville, scowling at fools and grasping at fame, a symbolic figure representing youthful urgency.

It is disappointing, but hardly surprising, to find that the Thomas Wolfe who revealed himself in all his unguarded innocence to his mother was such an overgrown boy. He lacked completely that selfless humility which is so touching in many of the finest creative spirits. Genius, of course, has often been petulant and demanding; it has often been bitter and dismayed. But there are a surprising number of instances in which it has shown itself to be patient and unprotesting as long as it was permitted to be the medium through which the creative impulse expressed itself. But that was not Thomas Wolfe's way.

Yet he said things about himself that were true. There was no one like him. His work stands as a monument to the adolescent as genius.

from Originals

Brendan Gill

One of the great subjects for biography is that spunky, crotchety, illiterate, and wonderfully gifted maker of things, Henry Ford. Not to bring him to life, not to have the pages of a book about him crackle and spit with his ingenuities and perversities, is a writing feat of no

From ORIGINALS: Reprinted by permission, copyright 1954 The New Yorker Magazine, Inc.

mean proportions. This feat has just been accomplished by Allan Nevins, with the collaboration of Frank Ernest Hill. They have given their mound of baggage the baggagy title of " Ford: The Times, the Man, the Company " (Scribner). In it, they accumulate the story of Ford's life from 1863, the year he was born, to 1916, a year that found him the aloof but snoopy master of thirty thousand employees and of a fortune of uncounted scores of millions. A second volume, dealing with the years to 1947, when Ford died, is presumably to follow. Since Dr. Nevins and Mr. Hill have had access to what are known as the Ford Archives (Archives! If Henry called history bunk, what would he have called archives?) this book has been looked forward to as the definitive work not only on the company but on the wiry little so-and-so who practically *was* the company. In a preface, Dr. Nevins notes that the book " is the product of an arrangement between Columbia University and the Ford Motor Company in the interests of general business history. The book has been written under the auspices of Columbia University, in its offices, and with the advice of a special University committee; the research has been done by University employees, working under ordinary academic conditions and with the usual academic salaries; all royalties on the volume are paid to the University. For the contents of the book, however, Columbia University has no responsibility whatever. It has merely guaranteed the independence and disinterestedness of those engaged on the task, and facilitated their labors. For all the faults and shortcomings of the history, the author alone is responsible." This is a modest and promising statement. One feels sure that the Ford Motor Company has been generous in its backing (less ambitious projects have been known to cost a couple of hundred thousand dollars) and that the research has been brilliantly executed. Yet what is there to show for what must have been a lavish expenditure of money and brains but a big lump of a book that is frequently padded, repetitious, and pedestrian? The reader's disappointment is heightened by incredulity. Padded, an account of that cranky barebones of a mistress, the Model T? Repetitious and pedestrian, the adventures of the tinkerer who set his fellows tearing up and down the world on wheels?

The reader ends by suspecting that Dr. Nevins, one of the most distinguished and prolific of historians, has merely supervised this book, not written it. Again and again, he has failed to remove traces of many hands doing much dusty digging. Again and again, he has failed to turn into English the jottings of hired bookworms. (Roy D. Chapin is introduced as " later Secretary of Commerce under Herbert Hoover." Some pages farther on, he is spoken of as " Roy D. Chapin, later Secretary of Commerce under Hoover." And what is to be made of a sentence beginning " House, furnishings, and landscaping and down to Thanksgiving in 1916 cost $1,032,818, while the power plant . . ." ?) Perhaps Dr. Nevins did not enjoy his task. Perhaps he found Henry Ford distasteful, though not distasteful enough to have strong feelings about. Or perhaps the sense that the Ford boys were glancing over his shoulder as he glanced over their foxy grandpa's archives led him to be dull when he intended to be lively. In any event, this book is a waste all round, and the more to be regretted because it is high time that we had not a broadside like Harry Bennett's wild and funny " We Never Called Him Henry," not a graduate thesis on transportation and the American automobile industry, but a biography worthy of the old devil who loved to play crude practical jokes on people and would never let anyone play practical jokes on him.

The Extent and Military Force of the Empire in the Age of the Antonines

Edward Gibbon

The terror of the Roman arms added weight and dignity to the moderation of the emperors. They preserved peace by a constant preparation for war; and while justice regulated their conduct, they announced to the nations on their confines that they were as little disposed to endure as to offer an injury. The military strength, which it had been sufficient for Hadrian and the elder Antoninus to display, was exerted against the Parthians and the Germans by the emperor Marcus. The hostilities of the barbarians provoked the resentment of that philosophic monarch, and, in the prosecution of a just defence, Marcus and his generals obtained many signal victories, both on the Euphrates and on the Danube. The military establishment of the Roman empire, which thus assured either its tranquillity or success, will now become the proper and important object of our attention.

In the purer ages of the commonwealth, the use of arms was reserved for those ranks of citizens who had a country to love, a property to defend, and some share in enacting those laws, which it was their interest, as well as duty, to maintain. But in proportion as the public freedom was lost in extent of conquest, war was gradually improved into an art, and degraded into a trade. The legions themselves, even at the time when they were recruited in the most distant provinces, were supposed to consist of Roman citizens. That distinction

THE EXTENT AND MILITARY FORCE OF THE EMPIRE IN THE AGE OF THE ANTONINES: From *The History of the Decline and Fall of the Roman Empire* by Edward Gibbon.

was generally considered either as a legal qualification or as a proper recompense for the soldier; but a more serious regard was paid to the essential merit of age, strength, and military stature. In all levies, a just preference was given to the climates of the North over those of the South: the race of men born to the exercise of arms was sought for in the country rather than in cities; and it was very reasonably presumed, that the hardy occupations of smiths, carpenters, and huntsmen, would supply more vigour and resolution than the sedentary trades which are employed in the service of luxury. After every qualification of property had been laid aside, the armies of the Roman emperors were still commanded, for the most part, by officers of a liberal birth and education; but the common soldiers, like the mercenary troops of modern Europe, were drawn from the meanest, and very frequently from the most profligate, of mankind.

That public virtue which among the ancients was denominated patriotism, is derived from a strong sense of our own interest in the preservation and prosperity of the free government of which we are members. Such a sentiment, which had rendered the legions of the republic almost invincible, could make but a very feeble impression on the mercenary servants of a despotic prince; and it became necessary to supply that defect by other motives, of a different, but not less forcible nature; honour and religion. The peasant, or mechanic, imbibed the useful prejudice that he was advanced to the more dignified profession of arms, in which his rank and reputation would depend on his own valour; and that, although the prowess of a private soldier must often escape the notice of fame, his own behaviour might sometimes confer glory or disgrace on the company, the legion, or even the army, to whose honours he was associated. On his first entrance into the service, an oath was administered to him, with every circumstance of solemnity. He promised never to desert his standard, to submit his own will to the commands of his leaders, and to sacrifice his life for the safety of the emperor and the empire. The attachment of the Roman troops to their standards was inspired by the united influence of religion and of honour. The golden eagle, which glittered in the front of the legion, was the object of their fondest devotion; nor was it esteemed less impious than it was ignominious, to abandon that sacred ensign in the hour of danger. These motives, which derived their strength from the imagination, were enforced by fears and hopes of a more substantial kind. Regular pay, occasional donatives, and a stated recompense, after the appointed time of service, alleviated the hardships of the military life, whilst, on the other hand, it was impossible for cowardice or disobedience to escape the severest punishment. The centurions were authorised to chastise with blows, the generals had a right to punish with death; and it was an inflexible maxim of Roman discipline, that a good soldier should dread his officers far more than the enemy. From such laudable arts did the valour of the Imperial troops receive a degree of firmness and docility, unattainable by the impetuous and irregular passions of barbarians.

And yet so sensible were the Romans of the imperfection of valour without skill and practice, that, in their language, the name of an army was borrowed from the word which signified exercise. Military exercises were the important and unremitted object of their discipline. The recruits and young soldiers were constantly trained both in the morning and in the evening, nor was age or knowledge allowed to excuse the veterans from the daily repetition of what they had completely learnt. Large sheds were erected in the winter-quarters of the troops, that their useful labours might not receive any interruption from the most tempestuous weather; and it was carefully observed, that the arms destined to this imitation of war, should be of double the weight which was required in real action. It is not the purpose of this work to enter into any minute description of the Roman exercises. We shall only remark, that they comprehended whatever could add strength to the body, activity to the limbs, or grace to the motions. The soldiers were diligently instructed to march, to run, to leap, to swim, to carry heavy burdens, to handle every species of arms that was used either for offence or for defence, either in distant engagement or in a closer onset; to form a variety of evolutions; and to move to the sound of flutes, in the Pyrrhic or martial dance. In the midst of peace, the Roman troops familiarised themselves with the practice of war; and it is prettily remarked by an ancient historian who had fought against them, that the effusion of blood was the only circumstance which distinguished a field of battle from a field of exercise. It was the policy of the ablest generals, and even of the emperors themselves, to encourage these military studies by their presence and example; and we are informed that Hadrian, as well as Trajan, frequently condescended to instruct the unexperienced soldiers, to reward the diligent, and sometimes to dispute with them the prize of superior strength or dexterity. Under the reigns of those princes, the science of tactics was cultivated with success; and as long as the empire retained any vigour, their military instructions were respected as the most perfect model of Roman discipline.

Nine centuries of war had gradually introduced into the service many alterations and improvements. The legions, as they are described by Polybius, in the time of the Punic wars, differed very materially from those which achieved the victories of Cæsar, or defended the monarchy of Hadrian and the Antonines. The constitution of the

Imperial legion may be described in a few words. The heavy-armed infantry, which composed its principal strength, was divided into ten cohorts, and fifty-five companies, under the orders of a correspondent number of tribunes and centurions. The first cohort, which always claimed the post of honour and the custody of the eagle, was formed of eleven hundred and five soldiers, the most approved for valour and fidelity. The remaining nine cohorts consisted each of five hundred and fifty-five; and the whole body of legionary infantry amounted to six thousand one hundred men. Their arms were uniform, and admirably adapted to the nature of their service: an open helmet, with a lofty crest; a breastplate, or coat of mail; greaves on their legs, and an ample buckler on their left arm. The buckler was of an oblong and concave figure, four feet in length, and two and an half in breadth, framed of a light wood, covered with a bull's hide, and strongly guarded with plates of brass. Besides a lighter spear, the legionary soldier grasped in his right hand the formidable *pilum,* a ponderous javelin, whose utmost length was about six feet, and which was terminated by a massy triangular point of steel of eighteen inches. This instrument was indeed much inferior to our modern fire-arms; since it was exhausted by a single discharge, at the distance of only ten or twelve paces. Yet when it was launched by a firm and skilful hand, there was not any cavalry that durst venture within its reach, nor any shield or corslet that could sustain the impetuosity of its weight. As soon as the Roman had darted his *pilum,* he drew his sword, and rushed forwards to close with the enemy. His sword was a short well-tempered Spanish blade, that carried a double edge, and was alike suited to the purpose of striking or of pushing; but the soldier was always instructed to prefer the latter use of his weapon, as his own body remained less exposed, whilst he inflicted a more dangerous wound on his adversary. The legion was usually drawn up eight deep; and the regular distance of three feet was left between the files as well as ranks. A body of troops, habituated to preserve this open order, in a long front and a rapid charge, found themselves prepared to execute every disposition which the circumstances of war, or the skill of their leader, might suggest. The soldier possessed a free space for his arms and motions, and sufficient intervals were allowed, through which seasonable reinforcements might be introduced to the relief of the exhausted combatants. The tactics of the Greeks and Macedonians were formed on very different principles. The strength of the phalanx depended on sixteen ranks of long pikes, wedged together in the closest array. But it was soon discovered by reflection, as well by the event, that the strength of the phalanx was unable to contend with the activity of the legion.

The cavalry, without which the force of the legion would have remained imperfect, was divided into ten troops or squadrons; the first, as the companion of the first cohort, consisted of an hundred and thirty-two men; whilst each of the other nine amounted only to sixty-six. The entire establishment formed a regiment, if we may use the modern expression, of seven hundred and twenty-six horse, naturally connected with its respective legion, but occasionally separated to act in the line, and to compose a part of the wings of the army. The cavalry of the emperors was no longer composed, like that of the ancient republic, of the noblest youth of Rome and Italy, who, by performing their military service on horseback, prepared themselves for the offices of senator and consul; and solicited, by deeds of valour, the future suffrages of their countrymen. Since the alteration of manners and government, the most wealthy of the equestrian order were engaged in the administration of justice, and of the revenue; and whenever they embraced the profession of arms, they were immediately intrusted with a troop of horse, or a cohort of foot. Trajan and Hadrian formed their cavalry from the same provinces, and the same class of their subjects, which recruited the ranks of the legion. The horses were bred, for the most part, in Spain or Cappadocia. The Roman troopers despised the complete armour with which the cavalry of the East was encumbered. *Their* more useful arms consisted in a helmet, an oblong shield, light boots, and a coat of mail. A javelin, and a long broadsword, were their principal weapons of offence. The use of lances and of iron maces they seem to have borrowed from the barbarians.

The safety and honour of the empire were principally intrusted to the legions, but the policy of Rome condescended to adopt every useful instrument of war. Considerable levies were regularly made among the provincials, who had not yet deserved the honourable distinction of Romans. Many dependant princes and communities, dispersed round the frontiers, were permitted, for a while, to hold their freedom and security by the tenure of military service. Even select troops of hostile barbarians were frequently compelled or persuaded to consume their dangerous valour in remote climates, and for the benefit of the state. All these were included under the general name of auxiliaries; and howsoever they might vary according to the difference of times and circumstances, their numbers were seldom much inferior to those of the legions themselves. Among the auxiliaries, the bravest and most faithful bands were placed under the command of præfects and centurions, and severely trained in the arts of Roman discipline; but the far greater part retained those arms, to which the nature of their country, or their early habits of life, more peculiarly adapted them. By this institution each legion, to whom a certain proportion of auxiliaries was allotted, contained within itself every species of lighter troops, and of missile weapons; and was capable of encountering every nation, with the advantages of its respective arms and discipline. Nor was the legion destitute of what, in modern language, would be styled a train of artillery. It consisted in ten military engines of the largest, and fifty-five of a smaller size; but all of which, either in an oblique or horizontal manner, discharged stones and darts with irresistible violence.

The camp of a Roman legion presented the appearance of a fortified city. As soon as the space was marked out, the pioneers carefully levelled the ground, and removed every impediment that might interrupt its perfect regularity. Its form was an exact quadrangle; and we may calculate that a square of about seven hundred yards was sufficient for the encampment of twenty thousand Romans; though a similar number of our own troops would expose to the enemy a front of more than treble that extent. In the midst of the camp, the prætorium, or general's quarters, rose above the others; the cavalry, the infantry, and the auxiliaries occupied their respective stations; the streets were broad and perfectly straight, and a vacant space of two hundred feet was left on all sides, between the tents and the rampart. The rampart itself was usually twelve feet high, armed with a line of strong and intricate palisades, and defended by a ditch of twelve feet in depth as well as in breadth. This important labour was performed by the hands of the legionaries themselves, to whom the use of the spade and the pickaxe was no less familiar than that of the sword or *pilum*. Active valour may often be the present of nature; but such patient diligence can be the fruit only of habit and discipline.

Whenever the trumpet gave the signal of departure, the camp was almost instantly broken up, and the troops fell into their ranks without delay or confusion. Besides their arms, which the legionaries scarcely considered as an encumbrance, they were laden with their kitchen furniture, the instruments of fortification, and the provision of many days. Under this weight, which would oppress the delicacy of a modern soldier, they were trained by a regular step to advance, in about six hours, near twenty miles. On the appearance of an enemy, they threw aside their baggage, and by easy and rapid evolutions converted the column of march into an order of battle. The slingers and archers skirmished in the front; the auxiliaries formed the first line, and were seconded or sustained by the strength of the legions: the cavalry covered the flanks, and the military engines were placed in the rear.

Such were the arts of war by which the Roman emperors defended their extensive conquests, and preserved a military spirit, at a time when every other virtue was oppressed by luxury and despotism. If, in the consideration of their armies, we pass from their discipline to their numbers, we shall not find it easy to define them with any tolerable accuracy. We may compute, however, that the legion, which was itself a body of six thousand eight hundred and thirty-one Romans, might, with its attendant auxiliaries, amount to about twelve thousand five hundred men. The peace establishment of Hadrian and his successors was composed of no less than thirty of these formidable brigades; and most probably formed a standing force of three hundred and seventy-five thousand men. Instead of being confined within the walls of fortified cities, which the Romans considered as the refuge of weakness or pusillanimity, the legions were encamped on the banks of the great rivers, and along the frontiers of the barbarians. As their stations, for the most part, remained fixed and permanent, we may venture to describe the distribution of the troops. Three legions were sufficient for Britain. The principal strength lay upon the Rhine and Danube, and consisted of sixteen legions, in the following proportions: two in the Lower and three in the Upper Germany; one in Rhætia, one in Noricum, four in Pannonia, three in Mæsia, and two in Dacia. The defence of the Euphrates was intrusted to eight legions, six of whom were planted in Syria, and the other two in Cappadocia. With regard to Egypt, Africa, and Spain, as they were far removed from any important scene of war, a single legion maintained the domestic tranquillity of each of those great provinces. Even Italy was not left destitute of a military force. Above twenty thousand chosen soldiers, distinguished by the titles of City Cohorts and Prætorian Guards, watched over the safety of the monarch and the capital. As the authors of almost every revolution that distracted the empire, the Prætorians will, very soon, and very loudly, demand our attention; but in their arms and institution, we cannot find any circumstance which discriminated them from the legions, unless it were a more splendid appearance, and a less rigid discipline.

The navy maintained by the emperors might seem inadequate to their greatness; but it was fully sufficient for every useful purpose of government. The ambition of the Romans was confined to the land; nor was that warlike people ever actuated by the enterprising spirit which had prompted the navigators of Tyre, of Carthage, and even of Marseilles, to enlarge the bounds of the world, and to explore the most remote coasts of the ocean. To the Romans the ocean remained an object of terror rather than of curiosity; the whole extent of the Mediterranean, after the destruction of Carthage, and the extirpation of the pirates, was included within their provinces. The policy of the emperors was directed only to preserve the peaceful dominion of that sea, and to protect the commerce of their subjects. With these moderate views, Augustus stationed two permanent fleets in the most convenient ports of Italy, the one at Ravenna, on the Adriatic, the other at Misenum, in the bay of Naples. Experience seems at length to have convinced the ancients, that as soon as their galleys exceeded two, or at the most three ranks of oars, they were suited rather for vain pomp than for real service. Augustus himself, in the victory of Actium, had seen the superiority of his own light frigates (they were called Liburnians) over the lofty but unwieldy castles of his rival. Of these Liburnians he composed the two fleets of Ravenna and Misenum, destined to command, the one the eastern, the other the western division of the Mediterranean; and to each of the squadrons he attached a body of several thousand marines. Besides these two ports, which may be considered as the principal seats of the Roman navy, a very considerable force was stationed at Frejus, on the coast of Provence, and the Euxine was guarded by forty ships, and three thousand soldiers. To all these we add the fleet which preserved the communication between Gaul and Britain, and a great number of vessels constantly maintained on the Rhine and Danube, to harass the country, or to intercept the passage of the barbarians. If we review this general state of the Imperial forces; of the cavalry as well as infantry; of the legions, the auxiliaries, the guards, and the navy; the most liberal computation will not allow us to fix the entire establishment by sea and by land at more than four hundred and fifty thousand men; a military power, which, however formidable it may seem, was equalled by a monarch of the last century, whose kingdom was confined within a single province of the Roman empire.

It Was a Stable World

Robert Graves

The world was stable — a compact world of manageable size, centrally governed — a Mediterranean world with Imperial Rome as the hub, the smoke of sacrifice reeking from a thousand altars and the

IT WAS A STABLE WORLD: From *Occupation: Writer* by Robert Graves. Reprinted by permission of the author, Farrar Straus, and Cassell & Company Ltd.

heavenly bodies circling in foreseeable fashion overhead. True, there was another world that began at the River Euphrates, the Eastern world into which Alexander the Great had freakishly broken three centuries before. But the Romans had left it alone since losing 30,000 men at Carrhae in an attempt to advance their frontiers at Parthian expense. Oriental luxury goods — jade, silk, gold, spices, vermillion, jewels — had formerly come overland by way of the Caspian Sea and now that this route had been cut by the Huns, a few daring Greek sea-captains were sailing from Red Sea ports, catching the trade winds and loading up at Ceylon. But commercial relations were chancy.

Northward, dense forests swarming with uncivilised, red-haired, beer-swilling Germans; and foggy Britain with its chariot fighters who seemed to have stepped from the pages of Homer; and the bleak steppes of Russia peopled by mare-milking nomad Scythians. Westward, the Ocean, supposedly extending to the point where it spilt over into nothingness. Nobody had thought it worth while to test the truth of the Greek legend that far out lay a chain of islands where coconuts grew on palms and life was indolent and merry. Southward, marvellous Africa, of which only the nearest regions had been explored; from beyond came rumours of burning deserts, pigmies, camel-leopards and marshes full of cranes. Though the Greek scientist Eratosthenes had calculated the distance of the sun from the earth, and the earth's circumference at the Equator, with only a small error, his theory of a global world was received with polite scorn by men of common sense: how could there be a Southern Hemisphere? An Egyptian admiral had once been sent out from Suez as a punishment for insubordination, with orders to follow the African coast as far as it went; after three years he had returned by way of Gibraltar claiming to have circumnavigated the continent. But that was centuries back, and the fellow had been put to death for an impious report that at the Southern Cape the sun had been rising in the wrong quarter of the sky. For the ordinary Roman citizen, the earth was still as flat as the palm of his hand.

"Midmost is safest," the Romans said — a dull, unadventurous, home-loving race, who hated the sea, preferred walking to riding, and thought banishment from their country scarcely preferable to death. They had become masters of the world against their real inclinations: the incentive to expand had not been patriotism or a self-imposed civilising mission, as was later alleged, but family rivalry sharpened by greed. The Republican institution of the " triumph " was to blame. While there was a Sacred King at Rome he won his title by marrying the queen's daughter or younger female relative, not by being the former king's eldest son; but in a prolonged struggle for the succession at the death of King Tullius all the royal princesses were either defiled or killed. This unfortunate accident — not " a burning love of freedom " — ended the monarchy. However, in the Republic that took its place, the Senate might decree one great privilege of the former king to honour commanders-in-chief who conquered an enemy state: to ride in triumph through Rome, with the captured gods — that is, their sacred statues — carried on carts behind him, himself impersonating and possessed by, the scarlet-faced Oak-god Mars, patron of shepherds. Republican commanders-in-chief, who were also judges of the Supreme Court, could be appointed only from the nobility, and it was rivalry between these noble families as to which could secure most triumphs that started Roman imperialism. For the commoners who did the fighting the rewards were loot, glory, decorations for valour and farm-lands in the conquered country upon their discharge.

The technique of expansion was simple. *Divide et impera:* enter into solemn treaty with a neighbouring country, foment internal disorder, intervene in support of the weaker side on the ground that Roman honour was involved, replace the legitimate ruler with a puppet, giving him the status of subject ally; later, goad him into rebellion, seize and sack the country, burn down the temples and carry off the captive gods to adorn a triumph. Conquered territories were put under the control of a provincial governor-general, an ex-commander-in-chief, who garrisoned it, levied taxes, set up courts of summary justice, and linked the new frontiers with the old by so-called Roman roads — usually built up by Greek engineers and native forced labour. Established social and religious practices were permitted so long as they did not threaten Roman administration or offend against the broad-minded Roman standards of good taste. The new province presently became a spring-board for further aggression.

Rome was now a great jackdaw's nest, with temples and mansions newly built in solid vulgar, imitation-Greek architectural style — much of it concrete with a thin marble facing — stuffed with loot from more ancient and beautiful cities. Typical scenes of " the grandeur that was Rome " at the sack of Corinth. A group of smoke-blackened Roman infantrymen squatting on a priceless old master — Aristides's *The God Dionysus* — and shooting craps for possession of sacred chalices looted from Dionysus's temple. Others hacking souvenirs from the most famous relic of antiquity, the stern of the ship *Argo* which had brought back the Golden Fleece from the Caucasus more than a thousand years before. The Army commander impressing on the transport captains detailed to convey unique works of art back to Rome — " Mind you, my men, anything you lose you'll have to replace."

The prisoners captured in these wars became slaves. The chief cause of Rome's industrial backwardness was not lack of inventiveness but the remarkable cheapness of highly skilled slave labour. A first-class smith or weaver or potter could often be bought for about the same price that a good dairy cow would fetch nowadays, and was not much more expensive to keep. (For that matter, a Greek schoolmaster or a qualified doctor could be bought for only a few pounds more.) In the Mediterranean the winter, in general, is short and mild, and the Romans could import unlimited cheap grain from Egypt, Libya and Tripoli — it was not for some centuries that overcultivation made a dust-bowl of the whole North African coast. Olive-oil, dried fish, chickpeas, wine, and fruit were also in plentiful supply. Corn-mills driven by water power had been known for some generations, yet were little used: it was a principle of industrial economy to keep one's slaves, especially women, in good physical condition by making them do their daily pull at the lever of a hand-mill. And though the carpenter had developed into a highly skilled cabinetmaker, three more centuries passed before the principle of the watermill was combined with that of the saw. Still more remarkable, the steam-engine had been invented by one Ctesibius — who also invented a water-clock and a hydraulic organ — and a working model had long been on show in the lighthouse at Alexandria where it was used as a donkey-engine. Capitalists were unimpressed: " Introduce mechanical hauling into industry and encourage laziness in the workers." In the same spirit the Emperor Tiberius, Augustus's successor, put to death an inventor who brought him a specimen of unbreakable and malleable glass: the discovery would have thrown the jewelry trade into disorder and depreciated the value of gold bullion.

On the whole, slaves were treated well and encouraged to hard work and obedience by being given occasional tips and allowed to earn money in their off hours. Eventually they could hope to buy themselves free, though still owing certain duties as freedmen to their masters; and their children would be free-born. It was dangerous to starve slaves or flog them too freely; indeed, gross cruelty to a slave was now a penal offence. This lesson had been learned in the great Slave Revolt under the gladiator Spartacus two generations before, which had all but succeeded in making the slaves their masters' masters. Slavery was now regarded by industrialists as a safeguard against the pretensions of the free-born working classes, who could not compete in price against well-organised and highly financed slave labour. Strikes of working-men were exceptional: as when the Levite bakers in the Temple at Jerusalem walked out on being refused a 100 per cent rise in pay. The High Priest tried to break the strike by importing bakers from the rival Jewish Temple at Leontopolis in Egypt, but their shewbread was not up to Jerusalem standard and the strikers gained their demands.

At the apex of the social pyramid, which was still nominally Republican, stood the Emperor Augustus. As leader of the winning side in the Civil Wars, caused by murderous rivalry between noble families, he had been invested with temporary dictatorial powers, religious as well as civil, which he often undertook to relinquish when the time should be ripe; but it never was. Under him in descending order of importance came the remains of the nobility, who formed a rubber-stamp Senate and from whom all high-ranking Army officers and Government officials were drawn; next, the Knights, merchant families eligible for less distinguished offices; next, the free-born Roman citizens with full civil rights, including that of voting at the free democratic elections which no longer took place, and exemption from the servile punishment of crucifixion. After these, free-born foreigners with more limited right; then freedmen; lastly, slaves.

In the higher income groups the birth-rate fell steadily despite bachelor taxes and personal appeals for fertility by the Emperor. Few society women could be bothered to bear children in any quantity and preferred to let their husbands amuse themselves in sporting-houses or with Greek mistresses. The society woman's day was a full one: " Madam, your warm cinnamon milk, and the bath is ready." " Madam, the masseuse, the chiropodist, the hair-dresser." " The jeweller has called to show madam the Indian emeralds." " The chief chef wishes to ask madam's advice about the wild-boar steaks. He is of opinion that they should hang a day or two longer." " Has madam decided after all to attend the wedding of her third cousin, the Lady Metalla? It is today." " Madam's pet monkey has, I regret to report, been at his tricks again in the master's study. Yes, madam, I have squared the master's secretary and, please, he has undertaken to procure madam a copy of the charming bawdy little Greek novel that she picked up at Corbulo's yesterday." " My Lady Lentula's compliments and will madam confirm last night's bet of one thousand gold pieces to three hundred against Leek Green in the second race tomorrow? "

There was constant recruitment of the nobility from the merchant class, and rich commoners went up into the merchant class and were privileged to wear a gold thumb-ring and sit in seats reserved for them at the theatre immediately behind the nobility. Morals among the less fortunately born were based largely on social ambition. Conviction for petty felonies disqualified a man from memberhip of the social clubs of his class; serious felony degraded him. There was also a vague fear that crimes, even when successfully concealed, might be punished in a shadowy Hell with perpetual tortures. Belief in the islands of Elysium, where virtue was rewarded with a life of perpetual bliss, was still vague; besides, Homer had made it clear that these abodes were reserved for royalty. Ordinary citizens became twittering ghosts and went down to Hell, and stayed there except for an annual ticket-of-leave holiday between owl-cry and cock-crow, when their pious descendants put food out for them to lick at, and themselves kept carefully indoors.

Among the governing classes superstitious fear of evil omens, ghosts, and bogeys contrasted with the fashionable scepticism about the gods. However, the majesty of Law and the sanctity of treaties depended in theory on the official Olympian cult, and so did the complicated system of national holidays and popular entertainments. Jokes at the expense of cross, lecherous old Father Jupiter, his shrewish wife Juno, and his clever unmarried daughter Minerva — the Roman trinity — were confined to intimate gatherings. But gods and goddesses, so far from being jealous guardians of family morals, permitted and even demanded periodical orgies of drunkenness and sexual promiscuity as healthy vents for popular emotion. Their images also presided at the wild-beast shows, chariot races, gladiatorial fights, dances, plays, musical entertainments and displays of juggling and contortionism, arranged in their honour by endowed priesthoods.

There was no system of public education even for the free-born except in Greek cities that still prided themselves on their high standard of culture, and among the Jews everywhere, for whom attendance at the synagogue school was now a religious obligation. Elsewhere, reading, writing, and arithmetic were luxuries reserved for the governing and mercantile classes with their stewards, secretaries, accountants, and agents. The Jews were at once a comfort and a worry to the central government. Though industrious, law-abiding and peaceful wherever they were left alone, they were not merely a nation of perhaps three and a half millions settled in Palestine under the rule of Herod the Great, a petty king appointed by the Emperor, with a tribal god, a Temple, and established festivals. They were also a huge religious fraternity, including a great many converts of non-Jewish race, whose first article of faith was that there was only one God, and the intimate contact with Goddess-worshippers was disgusting and sinful. Far more Jews lived outside Palestine than in it, spread about in small or large communities from one end of the world to another and over the edge of the world in Babylonia. They constituted a serious obstacle to the Imperial policy of encouraging provincials to pay divine honours to the Emperor, but were still allowed perfect religious freedom. The distinction between Semites and Europeans had not yet been drawn; for the Spartans who were pure Greeks, officially claimed cousinship with the Jews in virtue of a common descent from Abraham. There was, however, strong local jealousy of Jews who had broken into Greek commercial spheres, with which went resentment of them as over-righteous spoilsports.

Colour was no problem. If the question had even arisen — but it never did — whether the black races were inferior to the white the answer would immediately have been found in Homer, who was quoted as an inspired authority in all matters of general morality: " Homer relates that the blessed gods themselves used to pay complimentary visits to the Blameless Ethiopians." Colour was not popularly associated with slavery, since slaves were for the most part white, and nothing prevented coloured monarchs from owning white slaves if honestly come by. Nor was miscegenation frowned upon. Augustus rewarded his ally King Juba, a Moor, with the hand of Selene, the beautiful daughter of Cleopatra, the Greek queen of Egypt, and his own late brother-in-law Mark Antony.

The Romans were oddly backward in military development, except in the arts of entrenchment, siege warfare and infantry drill with javelin and stabbing-sword. They never practised archery even for sport, or formed their own cavalry units, but relied for flank protection of their solid, slow-moving infantry masses on allied lancers and horse-archers, including many coloured squadrons. To join the Army usually meant staying with one's regiment until the age of sixty, and campaigning was arduous, especially against active and light-armed foresters or mountaineers. The soldier's load weighed more than eighty pounds, which he had to hump for fifteen or twenty miles a day in all weathers; rations were poor, comforts few, pay irregular, floggings frequent. But peacetime garrison duty in big frontier camps was pleasant enough. A regiment kept the same station for generations, and the camp gradually developed into a city as camp-followers set up general stores under the protection of the fortifications, and soldiers married native women and built permanent huts. In remote outposts of the Empire time dragged. Last year an inscription was found on the site of a small Roman camp on the Libyan frontier to this effect " The Company commander fears that it will be a long time before their promised relief arrives from Rome; meanwhile the company have made the best of a bad job and hereby dedicate this commodious swimming-pool to the Goddess of Army Welfare."

The swimming-pool was a Greek institution. It was from the

Greeks that the Romans had learned practically all they knew: law, literary technique, public speaking, philosophy, engineering, music, medicine, mathematics, astronomy, stagecraft and acting, domestic and industrial science, sanitation, and athletics. But, with a few notable exceptions, they were all barbarians at heart, and in athletics, for example, showed no innate sense of sportsmanship or any appreciation of the finer points of play. In the public ring they abandoned the Greek style of boxing with light leather gloves in favour of Mack Sennett knuckle-dusters studded with iron points with which outsize heavy-weights slogged great chunks off one another.

No great epidemics of plague, typhus, and cholera, such as ravaged Europe in the Middle Ages, are recorded in this epoch. Well-regulated water supply and sewage system in cities, official supervision of foodstuffs and wine exposed for sale, and a general determination to enjoy life to the full while it lasted: all this increased popular resistance to disease. Medicine, too, was in a saner state than it reached again before the nineteenth century: cures were effected by tried herbal remedies, fomentations, dieting, exercise, massage, and spa waters. Greek surgeons following in the wake of Roman armies had got a better knowledge of the interior of the human body from battlefield observation than hitherto from dissection of Egyptian mummies in the Alexandrian medical school; and dentists undertook fillings and complicated bridge work as well as extractions. Mail and transport services ran smoothly throughout the Empire; the insurance rate for shipping was low, now that piracy had been suppressed, and losses by burglary and fire were infrequent. Bureaucracy had just begun rearing its anonymous head: the Emperor Augustus, grown too old and weary to undertake all the official business that falls to a dictator, allowed his ex-slave secretariat to issue minutes, demands, and routine orders under his seal.

Typical success story: M. Fullanus Atrox, grandson of a Sicilian slave, has made money in hogs, invested it in a suburban tile-factory and tenement-rents in a central block at Rome. He now sells a half interest in the factory, which is placing heavy orders in Spain and North Africa, buys a villa near Naples with central heating, baths, a picture gallery, formal gardens, stabling, twenty acres of good land and accommodation for fifty slaves — the very villa where his father once stoked the furnace. He marks the happy occasion by presenting a solid gold salver engraved with poplar leaves to the nearby temple of Hercules — it will create a good impression locally. At the same time he sends his son to the university of Athens.

It was a stable world. But the farther from the hub one went the uglier grew the scene, especially after Augustus's succession by less humane and energetic Emperors. When the poorly paid Roman armies of occupation were quartered in the provinces of Asia Minor and Syria, the rich man was bled but the poor man was skinned. Banditry, beggary, blackmail, and squalor abounded. Conditions were as bad after the death of Herod the Great in the Protectorate of Judaea, where communism was already in operation among the ascetic communities of the Dead Sea area, and in the Native State of Galilee. The cost of living in Galilee, during Jesus's Ministry, was excessively high. Everything was taxed separately: houses, land, fruit trees, cattle, carts, fishing-boats, market produce, salt. There was also a poll-tax, a road tax, and taxes on exports and imports. Worse: the collection of taxes was leased to private financiers and sub-leased by them to contractors who had to buy police protection at a high cost. The Disciples were poor working-men with dependents. When they were on the road their annual out-of-pocket account — apart even from money handed out to the distressed — can hardly have grossed less than £3,000. But out they went, two by two, deploring the instability of a world that was based on greed, lovelessness, and the power of the sword. Unexpectedly, St. Luke mentions among their financial backers the wife of a high finance officer of the rapacious Native Court.

from A Stillness at Appomattox

Bruce Catton

Federal infantry was on the road in the dark hours before dawn, with very little sleep and no breakfast at all. The men were told that if they hurried this was the day they could finish everything, and this inspired them. Yet they were no set of legendary heroes who never got tired or hungry or thought about personal discomfort. They were very human, given to griping when their stomachs were empty, and what really pulled them along this morning seems to have been the promise that at Appomattox Station rations would be issued. Most

From A STILLNESS AT APPOMATTOX: From the book *A Stillness at Appomattox* by Bruce Catton. Copyright 1953 by Bruce Catton, reprinted by permission of Doubleday & Company, Inc.

of the men who made the march that morning, one veteran admitted, did so because they figured it was the quickest way to get breakfast. Even so the straggling was abnormally heavy, and there were regiments in the column which had no more than seventy-five men with the colors.

It was Palm Sunday, with a blue cloudless sky, and the warm air had the smell of spring. The men came tramping up to the fields by the railroad station with the early morning sun over their right shoulders, and they filed off to right and left, stacked arms, and began collecting wood for the fires with which they would cook the anticipated rations. The divisions from the Army of the James were in front, Ord and John Gibbon in the lead, and the V Corps was coming up close behind. Gibbon and Ord rode to a little house near the railroad where Sheridan had his headquarters, and Sheridan came out to greet them and explain the situation.

The Lynchburg Road lay about a mile north of cavalry headquarters. It ran along a low ridge, partly concealed by timber, with a boggy little brook running along a shallow valley on the near side, and a couple of miles to the east it dipped down to a little hollow and ran through the village of Appomattox Court House. In and around and beyond this village, with its advance guard holding the breastworks half a mile west of it, was what remained of the Army of Northern Virginia. Off to the east, out of sight beyond hills and forests but not more than six or eight miles away, was Meade with the II Corps and the VI Corps, coming west on the Lynchburg Road to pound the Confederate rear. In effect, the Federals occupied three sides of a square — cavalry on the west, infantry on the south, Meade and the rest of the army on the east. The Rebel army was inside the square, and although the north side was open that did not matter because the Confederates could find neither food nor escape in that direction. Their only possible move was to fight their way west along the Lynchburg Road.

So Sheridan explained it, warning the generals that he expected the Rebels to attack at any moment and that they had better get ready to bring their troops up in support.

While he was talking the sound of musket fire came down from the ridge. It was sporadic, at first, as the skirmishers pecked away at each other, but it soon grew much heavier and there was the heavy booming of field artillery. The big push was on, and Sheridan sprang into the saddle, ordering the rest of his cavalry up into line and telling the officers to bring their infantry up as fast as they could. Then he was off, and the generals galloped back to put their men in motion.

The hopeful little breakfast fires died unnoticed, nothing ever cooked on them, and the infantry took their muskets, got into column, and went hurrying north to get astride of the Lynchburg Road. The crossroad they were on led through heavy timber and the men could see nothing, but the noise of the firing grew louder and louder as they marched. Then, for the last time in their lives, beyond the trees they heard the high, spine-tingling wail of the Rebel yell, a last great shout of defiance flung against the morning sky by a doomed army marching into the final sunset.

The Federals got across the Lynchburg Road, swung into line of battle facing east, and marched toward the firing and the shouting. As they marched, dismounted cavalry came drifting back, and the troopers waved their caps and cheered when they saw the infantry, and called out: " Give it to 'em — we've got 'em in a tight place! "

In a clearing there was Sheridan, talking with Griffin and other officers of the V Corps; Sheridan, talking rapidly, pounding a palm with his fist; and the battle line marched on and came under the fire of Rebel artillery. One brigade went across somebody's farm, just here, and as the firing grew heavier a shell blew the end out of the farmer's chicken house, and the air was abruptly full of demoralized chickens, squawking indignantly, fluttering off in frantic disorganized flight. And here was the last battle of the war, and the men were marching up to the moment of apotheosis and glory — but they were men who had not eaten for twenty-four hours and more, and they knew Virginia poultry from of old, and what had begun as an attack on a Rebel battle line turned into a hilarious chase after fugitive chickens. The battle smoke rolled down over the crest, and shells were exploding and the farm buildings were ablaze, and Federal officers were waving swords and barking orders in scandalized indignation. But the soldiers whooped and laughed and scrambled after their prey, and as the main battle line swept on most of this brigade was either continuing to hunt chickens or was building little fires and preparing to cook the ones that had been caught.

The Confederates had scattered the cavalry, and most of the troopers fled south, across the shallow valley that ran parallel with the Lynchburg Road. As the last of them left the field the way seemed to be open, and the Confederates who had driven them away raised a final shout of triumph — and then over the hill came the first lines of blue infantry, rifles tilted forward, and here was the end of everything: the Yankees had won the race and the way was closed forever and there was no going on any farther.

The blue lines grew longer and longer, and rank upon rank came into view, as if there was no end to them. A Federal officer remembered afterward that when he looked across at the Rebel lines it almost seemed as if there were more battle flags than soldiers. So small were the Southern regiments that the flags were all clustered together, and he got the strange feeling that the ground where the Army of Northern Virginia had been brought to bay had somehow blossomed out with a great row of poppies and roses.

So the two armies faced each other at long range, and the firing slackened and almost ceased.

Many times in the past these armies had paused to look at each other across empty fields, taking a final size-up before getting into the grapple. Now they were taking their last look, the Stars and Bars were about to go down forever and leave nothing behind but the stars and the memories, and it might have been a time for deep solemn thoughts. But the men who looked across the battlefield at each other were very tired and very hungry, and they did not have much room in their heads for anything except the thought of that weariness and that hunger, and the simple hope that they might live through the next half hour. One Union soldier wrote that he and his comrades reflected bitterly that they would not be here, waiting for the shooting to begin, if they had not innocently believed that tale about getting breakfast at Appomattox Station; and, he said, " we were angry with ourselves to think that for the hope of drawing rations we had been foolish enough to keep up and, by doing so, get in such a scrape." They did not mind the desultory artillery fire very much, he said, but " we dreaded the moment when the infantry should open on us."

Off toward the south Sheridan had all of his cavalry in line again, mounted now with pennons and guidons fluttering. The Federal infantry was advancing from the west and Sheridan was where he could hit the flank of the Rebels who were drawn up to oppose that infantry, and he spurred over to get some foot soldiers to stiffen his own attack. General Griffin told Chamberlain to take his brigade and use it as Sheridan might direct. Men who saw Sheridan pointing out to Chamberlain the place where his brigade should attack remembered his final passionate injunction: " Now smash 'em, I tell you, smash 'em! "

Chamberlain got his men where Sheridan wanted them, and all of Ord's and Griffin's men were in line now, coming up on higher ground where they could see the whole field.

They could see the Confederate line drawing back from in front of them, crowned with its red battle flags, and all along the open country to the right they could see the whole cavalry corps of the Army of the Potomac trotting over to take position beyond Chamberlain's brigade. The sunlight gleamed brightly off the metal and the flags, and once again, for a last haunting moment, the way men make war looked grand and caught at the throat, as if some strange value beyond values were incomprehensively mixed up in it all.

Then Sheridan's bugles sounded, the clear notes slanting all across the field, and all of his brigades wheeled and swung into line, every saber raised high, every rider tense; and in another minute infantry and cavalry would drive in on the slim Confederate lines and crumple them and destroy them in a last savage burst of firing and cutting and clubbing.

Out from the Rebel lines came a lone rider, a young officer in a gray uniform, galloping madly, a staff in his hand with a white flag fluttering from the end of it. He rode up to Chamberlain's lines and someone there took him off to see Sheridan, and the firing stopped, and the watching Federals saw the Southerners wheeling their guns back and stacking their muskets as if they expected to fight no more.

All up and down the lines the men blinked at one another, unable to realize that the hour they had waited for so long was actually at hand. There was a truce, they could see that, and presently the word was passed that Grant and Lee were going to meet in the little village that lay now between the two lines, and no one could doubt that Lee was going to surrender. It was Palm Sunday, and they would all live to see Easter, and with the guns quieted it might be easier to comprehend the mystery and the promise of that day. Yet the fact of peace and no more killing and an open road home seems to have been too big to grasp, right at the moment, and in the enormous silence that lay upon the field men remembered that they had marched far and were very tired, and they wondered when the wagon trains would come up with rations.

One of Ord's soldiers wrote that the army should have gone wild with joy, then and there; and yet, he said, somehow they did not. Later there would be frenzied cheering and crying and rejoicing, but now . . . now, for some reason, the men sat on the ground and looked across at the Confederate army and found themselves feeling as they had never dreamed that the moment of victory would make them feel.

". . . I remember how we sat there and pitied and sympathized with these courageous Southern men who had fought for four long and dreary years all so stubbornly, so bravely and so well, and now, whipped, beaten, completely used up, were fully at our mercy — it was pitiful, sad, hard, and seemed to us altogether too bad." A Pennsylvanian in the V Corps dodged past the skirmish line and strolled into the lines of the nearest Confederate regiment, and half a century after the war he recalled it with a glow: ". . . as soon as I got among these boys I felt and was treated as well as if I had been among our own boys, and a person would of thought we were of the same Army and had been Fighting under the Same Flag."

Down by the roadside near Appomattox Court House, Sheridan and Ord and other officers sat and waited while a brown-bearded little man in a mud-spattered uniform rode up. They all saluted him, and there was a quiet interchange of greetings, and then General Grant tilted his head toward the village and asked: " Is General Lee up there? "

Sheridan replied that he was, and Grant said: " Very well. Let's go up."

The little cavalcade went trotting along the road to the village, and all around them the two armies waited in silence. As the generals neared the end of their ride, a Yankee band in a field near the town struck up " Auld Lang Syne."

The American Civilization Puzzle

George F. Carter

Why, people ask, do professors like me study the things we do? Of course, they tell me, Indians are interesting — but are they important? Even if we do manage to find out when and how they developed their civilizations, is the knowledge really worth our working so hard to acquire it?

To such questions I give an emphatic Yes.

We need to know a good deal about the origin of civilization in general. We must know *how* civilization arose. And to answer the " how " we must know when and where. Did civilization arise just once, or several times? What part, if any, did climate and soil and landform and race play in its growth or growths? To give it a modern application: if we get careless with our super-bombs and wipe out civilization, what is the likelihood of a new civilization springing up? How soon? What kind? And where?

Behind these questions lies a further set of questions. Is man largely controlled or directed or influenced by his physical environment, or is he relatively independent of it? And another: Is man predominantly

THE AMERICAN CIVILIZATION PUZZLE: Reprinted by permission, from *The Johns Hopkins Magazine,* February, 1957.

inventive or retentive? There have been whole schools of thought, and still are, that take one side or another on these questions. And we still know little, with any certainty, about how civilization arose, spread, and grows.

The growth of the American Indian civilizations has come to be of crucial importance to the whole problem. For some, it is an example of the inventiveness of man. For others it is an example of the overwhelming force of the physical environment in the molding of man. For still others, it is an example of how uninventive man really is, of how extremely retentive he is, and of the complete dominance of the *spread* of ideas — or " diffusion " — over the *invention* of ideas.

Great battles — really fierce battles — have raged over such things. The current battleground, the current testing-ground, is America.

And, in these battles, I find myself in the thick of things.

In the area from southern Mexico to northern Chile, civilization apparently began rather suddenly, possibly about 1000 B.C. and probably not earlier than 2000 or 3000 B.C.

The peopling of America had been accomplished very much earlier, most probably by small bands of rather primitive people who wandered across from northeastern Asia into Alaska and then wandered slowly southward into the open, unpopulated continents that spread before them. They did not " discover " America. They simply drifted in. They did not " migrate " through the Americas. They simply multiplied and each generation moved a few miles. In such a manner it would take only a few thousand years for such people to reach all parts of North and South America. We know they had plenty of time: by the most advanced methods of measuring past time, we now know that man was here more than thirty-eight thousand years ago. If my current research is right, he was here far earlier than that.

Our present problem, however, is not with this original peopling, but with what happened once these people had settled down. They entered with simple cultures, lacking domestic animals except the dog, lacking the bow and arrow, lacking any knowledge of pottery-making. When we Europeans discovered them many thousands of years later, the Indian peoples in Middle America were practicing agriculture, making pottery, raising some domesticated animals, practicing metallurgy, using practically all the known techniques of weaving, living in organized city states and even empires, and having great capitals that would rival Rome or Athens or Thebes or Babylon.

Just how did all of this come about? Did they do all of it by themselves, with no help? Or did ideas dribble across the great watery moats of the seas? Or, perhaps, did whole floods of ideas reach them from overseas?

On the answers, scholars violently disagree. This is the Diffusion controversy, and for more than one hundred years it has rustled the ivy on academic halls. Some professors, "Diffusionists," think the evidence indicates that man crossed the oceans carrying ideas with him. Others, "Independent Inventionists," fiercely defend the doctrine that nothing of the sort ever happened. They believe that, lacking strong evidence that such transmission of knowledge took place, it is more likely that groups of men all over the world, faced with similar problems, reached similar solutions — even though these groups never had contact with one another.

Gradually, the Independent Inventionists have had to retreat. Gradually, diffusion has been demonstrated over wider and wider areas, through greater and greater time depths, and for more and more things. In the Old World, agriculture, metallurgy, architecture, and the alphabets tended to arise in one center or another and spread to the others. Each area took the basic ideas and wove them into its own particular way of life, giving them a special local flavor. But fundamentally, most of the basic ideas used in this great area of civilization's early growth had their origins in one center or the other. It has been clear for some time now that the growth of civilization in the Old World was a closely interrelated phenomenon.

The New World was the Independent Inventionist's last great stronghold. Here, he could point out, the American Indians developed *in isolation* from the culture growths of the Old World. And in this isolation they had developed nearly everything that the Old World had. They had invented agriculture, but none of the plants were like the domestic plants of the Old World. They had domesticated a few animals: ducks, turkeys, camels (llamas), guinea pigs. And while these might seem uncomfortably close to ducks, chickens, camels, and rabbits of the Old World, the Indians never domesticated any cowlike animal such as the buffalo. They never used any animal for draft purposes, never milked an animal, never made animal domestication an important part of their lives. So, said the Independent Inventionist (with obvious relief), the seeming similarities are not really significant, after all.

The Old World-New World similarities kept piling up, however. In Middle America (a convenient term to designate the area from southern Mexico to northern Chile) the Indian people built pyramids somewhat as some of the people in the Old World did. But the pyramids were built primarily as commanding locations for temples, rather than for the burial of kings as in Egypt. The Independent Inventionists tended to overlook the presence of just such pyramids in Southeast Asia, with temples on *their* truncated tops. Some of the Diffusionists were equally guilty, and played right into the Independent Inventionists' hands, by insisting that nearly all ideas came from Egypt, where of course the pyramids were royal tombs.

The list of men who have entered the debate over the separateness of the Americas from Asia and Eurafrica, and the mountains of evidence and nonsense that have been presented, could be fitted into a doctoral dissertation only with difficulty. Almost from the beginning there were rumblings of Asiatic contacts with America. The Spaniards learned from the Incas of Peru that they had legends of people coming from across the Pacific to trade. And the Incas insisted that they had sent out a great fleet of balsa-log rafts that were gone for two years and finally returned with stories of lands across the sea. This strange tale was believed by the Spaniards, and there followed a series of intrigues over who should head the expedition that would discover another source of wealth like Mexico or Peru. In the political maneuvering, the wrong man ended up in the job. He followed the wrong directions, and the Spaniards found themselves in the impoverished, Negro-populated islands of the southwest Pacific. The Incas' tale was discredited.

The sequel has been written in this decade of the twentieth century. The intrepid Thor Heyerdahl has demonstrated that the Incas could have done just what they said they did; that balsa rafts *can* be sailed across the Pacific. And Heyerdahl has since learned enough about such rafts that, should he wish to, he could now sail one to Asia and then turn around and sail back. By studies in the Galápagos Islands he has shown that the Incas used these islands, six hundred miles offshore, as a base for their fishing fleet — no mean bit of navigation for people using rafts. But it was long denied that the Indians possessed such ability.

The evidence was difficult to throttle. It was pointed out that the game of parchesi, which we got from India, was practically the national pastime in Mexico when the Spanish reached there. There was no mistaking the game. All the rules, and the shape of the board on which it was played, were as we know the game today. In addition, it had special meanings that were duplicated in India.

In America, the Indians blew on pipes of Pan. The pipes blew the identical notes, in the same scale, on both sides of the Pacific. As if this were not enough, in Peru they were played in pairs. Two people stood facing each other, connected by a string that led from one set of pipes to the other. One set of pipes was called Mama and the other Father. The same thing was done in Southeast Asia.

Surely this is stretching coincidence extremely far. Is it really reasonable that the same scale, the same notes, and the identical customs would all be reinvented? There is nothing in the climate or in the soil or in man himself that compels such detailed parallels.

Mathematical and recording systems showed similar strange parallels. In Peru, records of taxes, populations, and histories were kept by tying knots in strings. The system for numbers was a decimal one. A knot tied in one string stood for one, in the next string for ten, in the next for one hundred, and so on.

This is a remarkable invention. It involves the idea that the value of a number is established by its position, and this includes the idea of a decimal place and a zero. It leads directly into negative numbers. All of these concepts we of the Western World received from India.

But when one begins tracing the distribution of such systems as the Peruvian knots in strings, one finds them in the islands of the Pacific and, anciently, in China, Tibet, and India. The Chinese say that they recorded their history by tying knots in strings, before writing was invented.

Thus we have one of the most difficult of mathematical ideas, associated with a particular way of recording it, with a continuous distribution from the probable source, India, to the exact part of America that has a whole host of other parallels to the Southeast Asian center.

The material is formidable in extent. A partial list of further parallels appears below.

COINCIDENCE?

Here is a sampling of ideas, inventions, and legends suggesting varied contacts between America and the Old World:

MATHEMATICAL

The zero: Used in India, Peru, and Mexico.
Place numeral systems: India to China; Peru and Mexico.
Knot-in-string records: Peru, Polynesia, China (before script).
The zodiac: Asia and Mexico.

TECHNOLOGICAL

The loom: In Peru, with all its Old-World parts.
Cloth: In Peru, all known Old-World weaves.
The wheel: On toys, only, in America.

Alcoholic beverages: Close parallels in Polynesia and Peru.
Metals: Elaborate smelting, casting, and alloying techniques duplicated in Old World and Middle America.
Seamanship: Centerboards used for sailing in Peru and China.
Obsidian mirrors: Polynesia and Peru.

RACIAL

Vivid portraits in stone, clay, and paint, showing Indian, Mongolian, and bearded European types.
Legends giving emphatic, clear-cut descriptions of blond, bearded, learned visitors.
Chinese palm prints among the Maya.

Jade emphasized in Mexico, Peru, and China.

Trefoil arch: Maya and India.

Sacred tree design: Maya and India.

Tiger thrones: Maya and Southeast Asia.

Lotus staff, lotus stone, lotus panels: detailed similarities between Maya and India.

Serpent columns, balustrades: Mexico and Southeast Asia.

The diving god: Mexico and Bali.

Copper bells: Made by same technique and with same designs in Mexico and Indochina.

Featherwork cloaks: Peru and Polynesia.

LEGENDARY

Peruvian tales of an expedition across the Pacific.

Chinese document, possibly describing a Buddhist missionary effort in America about 500 A.D.

Polynesian legends of voyages to and from America.

Explicit stories of tall, bearded men who came and taught the Indians.

Serpent deities in Asia and Middle America.

Corn Mother myth (and others)

common to Southeast Asia and Middle America.

AGRICULTURAL

Sweet potato: Surely carried across seas, probably from America.

Coconut: Most probably carried to America.

Bottle gourd: Probably carried to America.

Cotton: Most probably carried to America.

Pineapple: Probably carried from America.

Terracing of mountainsides.

Specialized irrigation techniques.

A long list of possible (unconfirmed) plant transfers.

MUSICAL

Panpipe: Identical scale, notes, and ceremonial use in Middle America and Southeast Asia.

Nose flute.

Gourd whistle.

Conch-shell trumpet with similar names in both America and Polynesia. (One Polynesian shell trumpet found in Peru.)

Hollowed log with slit: Used both for music and for signaling in Africa, Middle America, and Polynesia.

One would think from all this that it would quickly be agreed that ideas were indeed carried in some quantity directly from Asia to America. But such has not been the case. Instead, it has been claimed that such transoceanic voyages were impossible, especially for such landlubbers as Chinese or Hindus. The Polynesians were discounted as people with only wooden dugouts totally incapable of such voyages. The Incas were pictured as comical fellows possessed of the world's clumsiest shipping — rafts that could not stay afloat more than a week or so before they had to be pulled out and dried in order to maintain their buoyancy.

The Inca raft, built of great logs of balsa, is now revealed as an excellent ocean-going vessel, capable of voyaging across the Pacific and back, of sailing before the wind or, by ingenious use of centerboards, of sailing into the wind, and of tacking and performing all the maneuvers of the square-rigged vessels of the days of sail. The Polynesian dugouts were often one hundred feet long, more than twice the length of Columbus's smallest ship and fully capable of making great sea voyages. The Hindus and the Chinese had large ocean-going ships when written history began in that area, and we have no evidence of how long they had had them before that.

Still, we could *prove* nothing one way or the other. I could argue that the pipes of Pan and parchesi and the system of recording things decimally by tying knots in strings are most unlikely to be independently reinvented. But the opposition could well reply that this was only my opinion. In *their* opinion there was nothing unusual about such independent invention on two sides of the vast ocean. And so there it would rest — unless there were other ways to determine which opinion was more likely right. Fortunately, there is other evidence — and evidence of such nature that opinion plays no part in it.

Man invents pottery, mathematics, pyramids, and metallurgy. And, in a very real sense, man invents agriculture.

But he does not invent plants.

Plants are natural creations. Man may modify them, and he most certainly did so in developing wild plants into the useful ones of today. But plants have definite homelands. We know for certain that oranges came from Southeast Asia, that wheat came from the Near East, and that olives came from the Mediterranean. We also know that all pumpkins and squashes, tomatoes, potatoes, and chocolate, came from America. No one, not even the Independent Inventionists, has ever claimed that men independently created identical or even similar plants in different parts of the world. Here, then, were markers that offered an opportunity to test the separateness of the two worlds.

This knowledge could not be used immediately. We did not know until rather recently just where our domestic plants came from. One of the pioneers in gathering that information was Alphonse De Candolle, who wrote his great work in 1884. At that time there was still uncertainty about such ultra-American crops as squashes and pumpkins, and their American origin was finally established as late as 1931.

About the turn of the century, O. F. Cook became interested in the coconut. He found that practically all the palms of the coconut family were American. He thought it strange indeed that only the domesticated member of this family should be non-American and concluded that it would be more natural for the domestic coconut to come *from* America.

Cook then went on to investigate a number of other plants. He found that there was considerable evidence that coconuts were not the only foreigners on the pre-Columbian American shores. Further, he found that a few American plants had strayed overseas, also. Of these, two seemed to have carried their names with them. One was the sweet potato; the other was the hibiscus. The names were the same both in parts of Middle America and in Polynesia, the island world of the mid-Pacific. On this and other evidence, Cook built the idea that agriculture had originated in America and spread across the Pacific Ocean to Southeast Asia. He was an early Diffusionist, and a pretty extreme one at that.

His ideas were attacked very sharply. Should they stand, whole schools of thought about the independent growth of civilizations, the psychic unity of mankind, the nature of the growth of culture, the nature of man, the influence of the physical environment on man, and many other beloved theories would have to be discarded. This was a grave threat to academic peace of mind. It was all the more serious because it was backed by an expert in a science.

The way out of this type of difficulty is to get another expert in the same science to counteract the first. (This is a well-known maneuver in more professions than the academic one, by the way.) The Independent Inventionists soon found a champion in the late E. D. Merrill, of Harvard. Merrill assured them that Cook was a very poor expert, indeed. The evidence of pre-Columbian coconuts was not valid. Besides, coconuts could float, so that even if they had been in America in pre-Columbian times it would not mean that men had carried them across the Pacific. The seeds of some hibiscus varities can also float and stay alive. And as for the sweet potato — well, that was just a case of poor historical research. Merrill was a devastating critic, and he demonstrated to the utter satisfaction of the Independent Inventionists, and to the considerable discomfiture of the Diffusionists, that Cook could be ignored. The botanical evidence was destined to be let alone for a few decades.

Meanwhile another champion of diffusion, a most interesting man, entered the battle. G. Elliot Smith was a physician and surgeon. He worked for many years in Egypt and, among other things, became interested in the Egyptian mummies. This is a fascinating subject, and particularly intriguing to a surgeon. In the preparation of the body for embalming, certain parts had to be removed. This was a professional problem, and Dr. Smith took a keen professional interest in the problem of the removal of the viscera and the brain, the closing of the openings so created, the problem of retaining the fingernails during the pickling process. It was enough to make an inquiring doctor wish that he could have been right there to discuss stitches and incisions, and to inquire into just why some of the operations were performed in such deucedly awkward and stylized ways. Dr. Smith was interested enough to read all that he could get his hands on concerning the funerary arts, processes, and rituals of the Egyptians.

Dr. Smith was also a great traveler. He visited the Trobriand Islanders, in the island world north of Australia. Here, to his astonishment, he found people practicing practically the identical embalming techniques: the incisions in the same awkward places, the same sort of stitches, and even some of the same rituals. His interest was aroused, and he began to trace other spreads of ideas from Egypt. Soon he was tracing everything imaginable to Egypt. Eventually he was tracing things even farther, for he had begun to look at Inca mummies. Here again he found the same improbable surgical procedures. (I hesitate to discuss the details of the preparation of a body for mummification, for it is a grisly subject to those not used to dealing rather offhandedly with cadavers. The resemblances are specific and detailed, however, and entail such singular solutions of the problem as to leave little doubt of their singular origin, if I may be allowed an apt pun.)

G. Elliot Smith marshaled vast amounts of evidence. However, he destroyed his case by insisting that *everything* came from Egypt. (It seems only fair to record that his critics have been equally extreme in discarding his evidence because of flaws in his presentation of it. This technique is known in best scientific parlance as throwing the baby out with the bathwater. It is probably the major contributor to the high infant mortality in the world of ideas, especially of those ideas that run counter to the notions held by powerful and vocal critics.)

Plant evidence was in disrepute due to the efforts of E. D. Merrill, who had overly brilliantly picked the flaws in Cook's arguments. Cook had opened the door to attack on himself by some uncritical work, and by his enthusiasm's leading him to think that the origin of agriculture, *the* origin of agriculture, was in America. Smith had made the same mistakes. He became too enthused with his Egyptian origins. The battle went to the critics. The Independent Inventionists ruled in peace. All the textbooks and all the lectures assured the rising generation that there had been no contact between America and Asia. The Pacific was a vast and impregnable moat.

But this was an uneasy peace. For facts are a bit like the fires of a volcano. They may lie dormant, but actually they are smoldering away, awaiting only the touch of an investigator's hand to spring into life, capable of destroying the most elaborate of philosophical structures.

In the world of knowledge there is utterly no way of knowing where a given piece of research will lead. The work that was to reopen the Diffusionist controversy began with an attempt by a group of botanists to untangle the relationships of the cottons of the world. Hutchinson, Silow, and Stevens teamed up on this job, using the modern techniques of genetics. They soon found that they could divide the cottons of the world into three groups: the wild and domestic cottons of the Old World, the wild cottons of the New World, and the domestic cottons of the New World. The New World domestic cottons particularly interested them. When they studied cells under high-powered microscopes they found that they contained twice as many hereditary units (chromosomes) as did the other cottons. Further, they could tell that there were two sets of chromosomes there, one the Old World type and the other the New World type. The most probable explanation they could find was that man had brought a domestic cotton from the Old World into the New, and that the two cottons had crossed, combined the full sets of chromosomes from both plants, and created this new plant.

They then did a very interesting thing. They examined the New World domestic cotton and carefully catalogued all its characteristics. Next they searched the cottons of the world to see just what two cottons, if combined, would give them these characteristics. They found the answer in an Asiatic domestic cotton and in a Peruvian wild cotton. They then succeeded in crossing these two plants and producing a near-duplicate of the American domesticated cotton.

We cannot get much nearer to proof than this. Thus the whole question of voyages to America was again wide open. Cotton seeds are not particularly tough. Plant men do not believe that they can float around the ocean and remain alive. To have got to America they must have been carried by someone. (Just how cotton got to America *and* the Old World in the first place is quite another problem of an utterly different time, and I will not try to deal with it here.)

It was at this point that I entered the controversy. Having been " properly " educated in the field of anthropology, I knew that once the American Indians entered America, they had been sealed off and had developed entirely on their own. They were of stupendous interest as the living examples of how inevitable the growth and development of cultures and civilization really were. They were the final answer to the Diffusionist. " Why just look, even the minute details are alike! Weaving, casting of metals, the shape of helmets, feathered robes for royalty. Name it and you can have it. There was almost nothing in the Old World that had not been independently reinvented in the New World. This certainly proves independent invention, doesn't it?"

Ah, yes. But *did* it prove it? Or did it prove just the opposite? Those mischievous geneticists were threatening to lift the lid of Pandora's box. If someone had brought cotton to the New World, how could we be sure that other things, such as zeros, Panpipes, metallurgy, and parchesi hadn't been brought in, also? Obviously this required looking into.

Since I had just finished a doctoral thesis in which I had used plants as tracers for determining the spread of peoples and ideas within America, it was quite natural for me to turn to the plant evidence to see just what there was to this controversy. To begin with, I knew the classical position. There were, in pre-Columbian times, no domestic plants from the Old World in the Americas, and conversely there were no American plants in the Old World. To be specific, the Indians had no wheat or rice, and the peoples of the Old World had no corn, American beans, or squash.

Work began with a review of the cotton situation. Stevens sent me a manuscript discussing the cultural implications of what he and his colleagues had done. It was a disturbing document for a man thoroughly indoctrinated with the idea of the separateness of the Old and New Worlds. I took it to a Johns Hopkins geneticist to have it read from a geneticist's point of view. (In retrospect I must secretly have been hoping that there was a gross error in the work. Otherwise there was an awful lot of reading and thinking ahead of me.) The reply was that the genetics was sound, the conclusions from the data reasonable, and the probability quite good that Hutchinson, Silow, and Stevens had drawn the right conclusion. This left me no alternative but to dive into the problem and see what more evidence there was. The results were shocking.

Cotton was not the only plant involved. The sweet potato had been investigated by a professor hostile to the idea of voyages to and from America. But he had shown that the sweet potato had been in the Pacific area before any possible European spread. Further, there was positive proof in the form of a letter written by one of Cortes's lieutenants that coconuts were in America when Cortes landed there. Still further, tests on the ability of coconuts to survive a long period of drifting in the ocean currents had raised considerable doubts that the coconut could get across the Pacific in that way. And when I applied my knowledge of ocean currents and wind directions, it seemed to me that these chances vanished. Further there were other plants. The bottle gourd was present in America in the earliest levels, and very ancient in the Old World. (I was later to prove by experiments in the Chesapeake Bay that these gourds *could* have floated to America.) But there were American weeds in the islands of the Pacific that certainly could not have blown or drifted there. There *were* American plants that had got out of America and there *were* Asiatic plants that had got into America. Someone *had* crossed the Pacific both ways. Pandora's box was open. The moat was crossed. The Independent Inventionists' vessel had sprung a leak.

This was not a leak that could be readily repaired by referring to the similarity of men's minds and claiming that the zero concept, wheels, pyramids, and games of chance are so natural to man that they prove nothing when they reappear in similar forms in distant parts of the world. Man does not invent plants. To quote O. F. Cook, " The same plant does not originate twice, and varieties dependent everywhere for their very existence on human care must also have been distributed by human agency." And again: " For the present purposes it suffices to remember that the actual introduction of plants by human agency discounts in advance all objections on the ground of distances and difficulties of communication, and justifies the fullest use of biological or other data in tracing the origin and dissemination of agricultural civilization in the tropics of both hemispheres." The plant evidence was an iceberg that in one rending crash ripped the bottom out of the isolation of pre-Columbian America.

The sequels to the plant story are of interest. The list of plants possibly carried is quite extensive, and almost nothing is now safe from question. It is suspected that Indian corn was known in Africa and in Southeast Asia before Columbus. (The reason that the Europeans first called Indian corn " Turkish wheat " is again being examined, and the old answers no longer satisfy.) Questions are being asked about the time of appearance of the American peanut in Asia, and of the Old World bananas in the Americas. The chicken from Southeast Asia is strongly suspected of being in America in pre-Columbian times, and no one claims that it could either fly or swim the Pacific.

The plant evidence is unshakable, and it is now admitted, at least in part, by its bitterest foes. They tend to retreat firing such Parthian shots as " unimportant in number," " probably a few unimportant accidental landings," " not important to the story of the growth and development of the American Indian civilizations." But I like the simile of Pandora's box. The lid has been lifted and all sorts of ideas have escaped to buzz about our heads.

Quite independently a further line of attack has been reopened. This is the investigation of art resemblances on the two sides of the Pacific. This work has been done by Professor Robert Heine-Geldern of Austria and Dr. Gordon Ekholm of the American Museum of Natural History in New York.

Comparison of the art and architecture of Southeast Asia with that of some parts of the Americas led to the discovery of some remarkable parallels. Not only were there truncated pyramids in Cambodia with temples on top of them, just as there were in Yucatán and in Peru, but they were sometimes almost identical down to small architectural details. The dragons on Chou-dynasty bronze vases were duplicated in minute detail in Mayan Indian art. And these details were multiplied. Criticism immediately centered on the fact that the similarities were picked more or less at random over a considerable range of time and space. This has since been met with a vengeance. Heine-Geldern's latest work names the individual Asiatic city states and points out their art influence in specific times and places in the Americas.

Such thoughts are met with some skepticism. If the people of Southeast Asia actually did such things, why do we have no records of all this? How could such a discovery ever be lost? My reply is to point out that the Norse discovered America about 1000 A.D. and maintained colonies in Greenland until about 1400 A.D. This is in the full light of modern European history. Yet most people are surprised to hear of this, and the effective discovery of America was left to Columbus. Further there is at least one Chinese document that probably refers to a Chinese voyage to America and return.

There are all sorts of strange bits of other evidence. The palm prints of the Maya are specifically like those of the Chinese. The Polynesian legends tell of reaching America, and the American Indian told the Spaniards that people from the Pacific came to them for trading purposes. Then there are the plants, the mathematics, the games, the arts and architecture, and all the other clues.

In capsule form, what we have learned, or are in the process of learning, is this: all the Old World civilizations were interconnected and drew on each other for ideas and inspiration. We do not know just where and how this civilization began. It seems to have started in that area we call the Near East. It is not too difficult to make a case for the single origin of civilization there. The New World civilizations seem to be to some as-yet-unknown degree dependent on the Old World growth of civilization.

Peering into the future, guessing at things to come, I would estimate that the American Indians had made some very modest advances toward agriculture and the beginnings of settled village life. The peoples of the Old World, sometime after 3000 B.C. and before 500 B.C., discovered the New World. They maintained contact over a long period of time. During this time they colonized parts of America, introduced arts, crafts, science, and governmental forms, and carried some domestic plants back and forth. It was this impact that set off the civilizations of Middle America.

We cannot say that civilization would never have been achieved by the American Indians had they been left alone. Neither do we know that they ever would have. The natives of Australia, Africa, America north of Mexico, and south and east of Peru and Bolivia certainly never did.

The interesting by-product of all this is that we are faced with the possibility that civilization has but one beginning. One could seriously argue for this view. We do not know that any particular people or any particular geography gave rise to it. Nor would we know how to start the process over again should the present civilization be extinguished. It appears to me from such studies as these that the civilization that we carry today is a unique growth.

If this is true, then man is certainly to be viewed as basically noninventive. He proves, rather, to be a splendid copyist, infinitely more able to borrow an idea than to invent a new one. To answer one of our earlier questions: man is retentive and not particularly inventive. Civilization, once the germ is implanted, can flourish in desert or jungle, on mountain plateau or lowland plain. It is not the physical environment that is all-important; it is the cultural environment.

These are important things to know, and it is the pursuit of this type of knowledge that underlies the professorial passion for study of such seemingly exotic things as the long-dead civilizations of the American Indians.

THREE VIEWS OF MARY TODD LINCOLN

from The Life of Lincoln

William Herndon and Jesse W. Weik

Before Mr. Lincoln surrenders himself completely to the public —
for it is apparent he is fast approaching the great crisis of his career —
it may not be entirely inappropriate to take a nearer and more personal view of him. A knowledge of his personal views and actions, a
glimpse through the doorway of his home, and a more thorough
acquaintance with his marked and strong points as they developed,
will aid us greatly in forming our general estimate of the man. When
Mr. Lincoln entered the domain of investigation he was a severe and
persistent thinker, and had wonderful endurance; hence he was abstracted, and for that reason at times was somewhat unsocial, reticent,
and uncommunicative. After his marriage it cannot be said that he
liked the society of ladies; in fact, it was just what he did not like,
though one of his biographers says otherwise. Lincoln had none of
the tender ways that please a woman, and he could not, it seemed, by
any positive act of his own make her happy. If his wife was happy,
she was naturally happy, or made herself so in spite of countless
drawbacks. He was, however, a good husband in his own peculiar
way, and in his own way only.

If exhausted from severe and long-continued thought, he had to
touch the earth again to renew his strength. When this weariness set

From THE LIFE OF LINCOLN: From the book *The Life of Lincoln: The True
Story of a Great Life* by William Herndon and Jesse W. Weik (1889).

in he would stop thought, and get down and play with a little dog or kitten to recover; and when the recovery came he would push it aside to play with its own tail. He treated men and women in much the same way. For fashionable society he had a marked dislike, although he appreciated its value in promoting the welfare of a man ambitious to succeed in politics. If he was invited out to dine or to mingle in some social gathering, and came in contact with the ladies, he treated them with becoming politeness; but the consciousness of his short-comings as a society man rendered him unusually diffident, and at the very first opportunity he would have the men separated from their ladies and crowded close around him in one corner of the parlor, listening to one of his characteristic stories. That a lady [1] as proud and as ambitious to exercise the rights of supremacy in society as Mary Todd should repent of her marriage to the man I have just described surely need occasion no surprise in the mind of anyone. Both she and the man whose hand she accepted acted along the lines of human conduct, and both reaped the bitter harvest of conjugal infelicity. In dealing with Mr. Lincoln's home life perhaps I am revealing an element of his character that has heretofore been kept from the world; but in doing so I feel sure I am treading on no person's toes, for all the actors in this domestic drama are dead, and the world seems ready to hear the facts. As his married life, in the opinion of all his friends, exerted a peculiar influence over Mr. Lincoln's political career there can be no impropriety, I apprehend, in throwing the light on it now. Mrs. Lincoln's disposition and nature have been dwelt upon in another chapter, and enough has been told to show that one of her greatest misfortunes was her inability to control her temper. Admit that, and everything can be explained. However cold and abstracted her husband may have appeared to others, however impressive, when aroused, may have seemed his indignation in public, he never gave vent to his feelings at home. He always meekly accepted as final the authority of his wife in all matters of domestic concern.[2] This may explain somewhat the statement of Judge Davis that, " as a general rule, when all

---

[1] " Mrs. Lincoln," said Herndon, " was decidedly pro-slavery in her views. One day she was invited to take a ride with a neighboring family, some of whose members still reside in Springfield. ' If ever my husband dies,' she ejaculated during the ride, ' his spirit will never find me living outside the limits of a slave State.' "

[2] In a footnote to the original edition Herndon wrote in illustration of this remark: " One day a man making some improvements in Lincoln's yard suggested to Mrs. Lincoln the propriety of cutting down one of the trees, to which she willingly assented. Before doing so, however, the man came down to our office and consulted Lincoln himself about it. ' What did Mrs. Lincoln say? ' inquired the latter. ' She consented to have it taken away.' ' Then, in God's name,' exclaimed Lincoln, ' cut it down to the roots! ' "

the lawyers of a Saturday evening would go home and see their families and friends, Lincoln would find some excuse and refuse to go. We said nothing, but it seemed to us all he was not domestically happy." He exercised no government of any kind over his household. His children did much as they pleased. Many of their antics he approved, and he restrained them in nothing. He never reproved them or gave them a fatherly frown. He was the most indulgent parent I have ever known. He was in the habit, when at home on Sunday, of bringing his two boys, Willie and Thomas — or " Tad " — down to the office to remain while his wife attended church. He seldom accompanied her there. The boys were absolutely unrestrained in their amusement. If they pulled down all the books from the shelves, bent the points of all the pens, overturned inkstands, scattered law-papers over the floor, or threw the pencils into the spittoon, it never disturbed the serenity of their father's good-nature. Frequently absorbed in thought, he never observed their mischievous but destructive pranks — as his unfortunate partner did, who thought much, but said nothing — and, even if brought to his attention, he virtually encouraged their repetition by declining to show any substantial evidence of parental disapproval. After church was over the boys and their father, climbing down the office stairs, ruefully turned their steps homeward. They mingled with the throngs of well-dressed people returning from church, the majority of whom might well have wondered if the trio they passed were going to a fireside where love and white-winged peace reigned supreme. A near relative of Mrs. Lincoln, in explanation of the unhappy condition of things in that lady's household, offered this suggestion:

" Mrs. Lincoln came of the best stock, and was raised like a lady. Her husband was her opposite, in origin, in education, in breeding, in everything; and it is therefore quite natural that she should complain if he answered the door-bell himself instead of sending the servant to do so; neither is she to be condemned if, as you say, she raised ' merry war ' because he persisted in using his own knife in the butter, instead of the silver-handled one intended for that purpose." Such want of social polish on the part of her husband of course gave Mrs. Lincoln great offense, and therefore in commenting on it she cared neither for time nor place. Her frequent outbursts of temper precipitated many an embarrassment from which Lincoln with great difficulty extricated himself.

A lady relative who lived for two years with the Lincolns told me that Mr. Lincoln was in the habit of lying on the floor with the back of a chair for a pillow when he read. One evening, when in this position in the hall, a knock was heard at the front door and although in his shirt-sleeves he answered the call. Two ladies were at the door whom he invited into the parlor, notifying them in his open familiar way, that he would " trot the women folks out." Mrs. Lincoln from an adjoining room witnessed the ladies' entrance and overheard her husband's jocose expression. Her indignation was so instantaneous she made the situation exceedingly interesting for him, and he was glad to retreat from the mansion. He did not return till very late at night and then slipped quietly in at a rear door.

Mrs. Lincoln, on account of her peculiar nature, could not long retain a servant in her employ. The sea was never so placid but that a breeze would ruffle its waters. She loved show and attention, and if, when she glorified her family descent or indulged in one of her strange outbreaks, the servant could simulate absolute obsequiousness or had tact enough to encourage her social pretensions, Mrs. Lincoln was for the time her firmest friend. One servant, who adjusted herself to suit the lady's capricious ways, lived with the family for several years. She told me that at the time of the debate between Douglas and Lincoln she often heard the latter's wife boast that she would yet be mistress of the White House. The secret of her ability to endure the eccentricities of her mistress came out in the admission that Mr. Lincoln gave her an extra dollar each week on condition that she would brave whatever storms might arise, and suffer whatever might befall her, without complaint. It was a rather severe condition, but she lived rigidly up to her part of the contract. The money was paid secretly and without the knowledge of Mrs. Lincoln. Frequently, after tempestuous scenes between the mistress and her servant, Lincoln at the first opportunity would place his hand encouragingly on the latter's shoulder with the admonition, " Mary, keep up your courage." It may not be without interest to add that the servant afterwards married a man who enlisted in the army. In the spring of 1865 his wife managed to reach Washington to secure her husband's release from the service. After some effort she succeeded in obtaining an interview with the President. He was glad to see her, gave her a basket of fruit, and directed her to call the next day and obtain a pass through the lines and money to buy clothes for herself and children. That night he was assassinated.

The following letter to the editor of a newspaper in Springfield will serve as a specimen of the perplexities which frequently beset Mr. Lincoln when his wife came in contact with others. What in this instance she said to the paper carrier we do not know; we can only intelligently infer. I have no personal recollection of the incident, although I knew the man to whom it was addressed quite well. The letter only recently came to light. I insert it without further comment.

[Private.]

"SPRINGFIELD, ILL., February 20, 1857.
"JOHN E. ROSETTE, ESQ.

"DEAR SIR: — Your note about the little paragraph in the Republican was received yesterday, since which time I have been too unwell to notice it. I had not supposed you wrote or approved it. The whole originated in mistake. You know by the conversation with me that I thought the establishment of the paper unfortunate, but I always expected to throw no obstacle in its way, and to patronize it to the extent of taking and paying for one copy. When the paper was brought to my house, my wife said to me, ' Now are you going to take another worthless little paper? ' I said to her *evasively,* ' I have not directed the paper to be left.' From this, in my absence, she sent the message to the carrier. This is the whole story.

"Yours truly,
"A. LINCOLN."

A man once called at the house to learn why Mrs. Lincoln had so unceremoniously discharged his niece from her employ. Mrs. Lincoln met him at the door, and being somewhat wrought up, gave vent to her feelings, resorting to such violent gestures and emphatic language that the man was glad to beat a hasty retreat. He at once started out to find Lincoln, determined to exact from him proper satisfaction for his wife's action. Lincoln was entertaining a crowd in a store at the time. The man, still laboring under some agitation, called him to the door and made the demand. Lincoln listened for a moment to his story. " My friend," he interrupted, " I regret to hear this, but let me ask you in all candor, can't you endure for a few moments what I have had as my daily portion for the last fifteen years? " These words were spoken so mournfully and with such a look of distress that the man was completely disarmed. It was a case that appealed to his feelings. Grasping the unfortunate husband's hand, he expressed in no uncertain terms his sympathy, and even apologized for having approached him. He said no more about the infuriated wife, and Lincoln afterward had no better friend in Springfield.

Mr. Lincoln never had a confidant, and therefore never unbosomed himself to others. He never spoke of his trials to me or, so far as I knew, to any of his friends. It was a great burden to carry, but he bore it sadly enough and without a murmur. I could always realize when he was in distress, without being told. He was not exactly an early riser, that is, he never usually appeared at the office till about nine o'clock in the morning. I usually preceded him an hour. Sometimes, however, he would come down as early as seven o'clock — in fact, on one occasion I remember he came down before daylight. If, on arriving at the office, I found him in, I knew instantly that a breeze had sprung up over the domestic sea, and that the waters were troubled. He would either be lying on the lounge looking skyward, or doubled up in a chair with his feet resting on the sill of a back window. He would not look up on my entering, and only answered my " Good morning " with a grunt. I at once busied myself with pen and paper, or ran through the leaves of some book; but the evidence of his melancholy and distress was so plain, and his silence so significant, that I would grow restless myself, and finding some excuse to go to the courthouse or elsewhere, would leave the room.

The door of the office opening into a narrow hallway was half glass, with a curtain on it working on brass rings strung on wire. As I passed out on these occasions I would draw the curtain across the glass, and before I reached the bottom of the stairs I could hear the key turn in the lock, and Lincoln was alone in his gloom. An hour in the clerk's office at the courthouse, an hour longer in a neighboring store having passed, I would return. By that time either a client had dropped in and Lincoln was propounding the law, or else the cloud of despondency had passed away, and he was busy in the recital of an Indiana story to whistle off the recollections of the morning's gloom. Noon having arrived I would depart homeward for my dinner. Returning within an hour, I would find him still in the office, although his house stood but a few squares away, — lunching on a slice of cheese and an handful of crackers which, in my absence, he had brought up from a store below. Separating for the day at five or six o'clock in the evening, I would still leave him behind, either sitting on a box at the foot of the stairway, entertaining a few loungers, or killing time in the same way on the courthouse steps. A light in the office after dark attested his presence there till late along in the night, when, after all the world had gone to sleep, the tall form of the man destined to be the nation's President could have been seen strolling along in the shadows of trees and buildings, and quietly slipping in through the door of a modest frame house, which it pleased the world, in a conventional way, to call his home.

Some persons may insist that this picture is too highly colored. If so, I can only answer, they do not know the facts. The majority of those who have a personal knowledge of them are persistent in their silence. If their lips could be opened and all could be known, my conclusions and statements, to say the least of them, would be found to be fair, reasonable, and true. A few words more as to Lincoln's domestic history, and I pass to a different phase of his life. One of his warmest and closest friends, who still survives, maintains the theory that, after all, Lincoln's political ascendency and final elevation to the Presidency were due more to the influence of his wife than to any other person or cause. " The fact," insists this friend, " that Mary Todd, by her turbulent nature and unfortunate manner, prevented her husband from becoming a domestic man, operated largely in his favor; for he was thereby kept out in the world of business and politics. Instead of spending his evenings at home, reading the papers and warming his toes at his own fireside, he was constantly out with the common people, was mingling with the politicians, discussing public questions with the farmers who thronged the offices in the courthouse and state house, and exchanging views with the loungers who surrounded the stove of winter evenings in the village store. The result of this continuous contact with the world was, that he was more thoroughly known than any other man in his community. His wife, therefore, was one of the unintentional means of his promotion. If, on the other hand, he had married some less ambitious but more domestic woman, some honest farmer's quiet daughter, — one who would have looked up to and worshipped him because he uplifted her, — the result might have been different. For, although it doubtless would have been her pride to see that he had clean clothes whenever he needed them; that his slippers were always in their place; that he was warmly clad and had plenty to eat; and, although the privilege of ministering to his every wish and whim might have been to her a pleasure rather than a duty; yet I fear he would have been buried in the pleasures of a loving home, and the country would never have had Abraham Lincoln for its President."

In her domestic troubles I have always sympathized with Mrs. Lincoln. The world does not know what she bore, or how ill-adapted she was to bear it. Her fearless, witty, and austere nature shrank instinctively from association with the calm, imperturbable, and simple ways of her thoughtful and absent-minded husband. Besides, who knows but she may have acted out in her conduct toward her husband the laws of human revenge? The picture of that eventful evening in 1841, when she stood at the Edwards mansion clad in her bridal robes, the feast prepared and the guests gathered, and when the bridegroom came not, may have been constantly before her, and prompted her to a course of action which kept in the background the better elements of her nature. In marrying Lincoln she did not look so far into the future as Mary Owens, who declined his proposal because " he was deficient in those little links which make up the chain of woman's happiness."

Mrs. Lincoln died at the residence of her sister Mrs. Ninian W. Edwards, in Springfield, July 16, 1882. Dr. Thomas W. Dresser, her physician during her last illness, says this of her: " In the late years of her life certain mental peculiarities were developed which finally culminated in a slight apoplexy, producing paralysis, of which she died. Among the peculiarities alluded to, one of the most singular was the habit she had during the last year or so of her life of immuring herself in a perfectly dark room and, for light, using a small candle-light, even when the sun was shining bright out-of-doors. No urging would induce her to go out into the fresh air. Another peculiarity was the accumulation of large quantities of silks and dress goods in trunks and by the cart-load, which she never used and which accumulated until it was really feared that the floor of the store-room would give way. She was bright and sparkling in conversation, and her memory remained singularly good up to the very close of her life. Her face was animated and pleasing; and to me she was always an interesting woman; and while the whole world was finding fault with her temper and disposition, it was clear to me that the trouble was really a cerebral disease."

from Mrs. Abraham Lincoln

Gamaliel Bradford

1

Kings and princes are in the habit of selecting their wives, or having them selected, with a view to the exalted station they are destined to occupy. Presidents of the United States usually marry young, like other men, and do not arrive at the White House until they are old, and sometimes they bring with them partners not wholly adapted to such a conspicuous career. The complication in Lincoln's case is peculiar. A brilliant but uncouth and almost grotesque lawyer and politician from the backwoods, with no inherited social position or distinction, marries a showy, popular belle, who considers herself an aristocrat in the limited circle which is all she knows, and feels that she is condescending vastly in accepting the husband whose only asset is an extremely nebulous future. Then the husband shows an unexampled capacity for growth and development, intellectual and spiritual, if not social, and the wife, remaining to the end the narrow rural aristocrat she was in the beginning, is decidedly left behind. The strange destiny which made the man who was to save the future of American democracy a typical American and a typical democrat was hardly equal to making him also an ideal husband, at any rate an ideal

From MRS. ABRAHAM LINCOLN: From the book *Wives* by Gamaliel Bradford. Copyright, 1925, by Harper & Brothers. Copyright, 1953, by Helen F. Bradford.

husband for such a wife. Mrs. Lincoln married Lincoln with condescension and hope that he might rise to her level, or even above it. He did, and so far as to be altogether beyond her limited power of ascent. She made a useful helpmate for a practical, aggressive lawyer in Springfield, Illinois. As the wife of the great, dreaming, smiling, creating democratic statesman of the modern world, she was just a trifle over-parted.

The difficulty of getting at the actual Mrs. Lincoln is extraordinary and exasperating. The cloud of anecdote and hearsay and gossip which envelops Lincoln himself, hangs even more impenetrably about her, because we have not the solid substance of her own words, as to a considerable extent we have his. There are but a few of her letters in print, and those few are not very significant. Many people have written about her, but they contradict one another, and misrepresent, according to their own prejudices and the strange passion for exalting Lincoln by either elevating or debasing everybody about him. How unsatisfactory the materials are may be judged from the fact that the most illuminating document, on the whole, is the record of Mrs. Keckley, the colored seamstress at the White House. Mrs. Keckley was an intelligent observer, devoted to Mrs. Lincoln, and admitted to many intimate scenes and experiences. But I suppose few women would care to have their lives filtered to posterity through such a record. In short, I cannot ask my readers to give implicit belief to anything I say about Mrs. Lincoln, for I believe very little of it myself. Yet the difficulty of investigating her adds to the fascination. One sighs at times for such superb self-presentment as one gets in the letters of Sarah Butler or Harriet Blaine. But there is a peculiar pleasure in finding little hints and threads of suggestion and following them out patiently, even when they seem to lead nowhere.

The bare, indisputable facts in the life of Mary Todd Lincoln are few and simple. She was born of a good Kentucky family, in 1818, ten years after her husband. In 1839 she came to live with her sister, Mrs. Edwards, in Springfield. After a stormy courtship Lincoln married her in 1842. Her life then led her through Illinois law and politics to the White House, and the war, and the culmination of triumphant peace. All the triumph and hope were blasted by the assassination of her husband, and her remaining years, in spite of a brief sojourn in Europe, were darkened by sorrow and misfortune till a temperament, always impulsive and intense, was unbalanced to a point of oddity approaching and at times reaching actual derangement. She died in 1882.

In studying Mrs. Lincoln, one must admit that, while it is possible to get more or less reliable accounts of her external interests and activity, her inner life is almost hopelessly obscure. She had apparently a very good education, as educations went in Southern girls' schools in the middle of the nineteenth century. Mr. Rankin tells us that " while a resident of Springfield before and after her marriage, she impressed all who were acquainted with her with the excellent and accurate literary taste she had acquired by education and general reading, especially in history, poetry, and fiction." But this was in a country town in 1840, and it must be remembered here, as elsewhere, that we are dealing with Mr. Rankin's kindly after-dinner memory. Education of a sort Mrs. Lincoln certainly had, education superior to that of many about her, and at any rate far superior to her husband's. She had also a nimble gift of words, and wrote with ease when she wished. Her natural intelligence was unquestionably shrewd, quick, and keen. Within her limits she saw into the nature of things and the motives of men, and she had a notable faculty of making observations upon them, often with a turn of wit and sarcasm which did not add to her popularity. That she had a trace of the larger humorous attitude seems unlikely, and it is still more unlikely that she ever grasped or enjoyed that attitude in the subtle, pervading, dissolving form in which it was constantly manifest in her husband. The element of Touchstone, of Charles Lamb, the instinct of remoteness, of detachment, even in the midst of vast tragic passions, perhaps most precisely in the midst of such, of illuminating them with the strange glory of laughter, which was so haunting and so fascinating in Lincoln, evidently annoyed and perplexed her, as it has many other excellent people.

If she read, we should like to know a little more definitely what she read. Mr. Rankin enlarges on her familiarity with French, as a matter of both reading and speaking, and assures us that she read the latest French literature. I wonder if Sainte-Beuve was included in the list. I doubt it. Victor Hugo she did read, which perhaps is all one could expect. She read current novels, since Lincoln writes to a friend in regard to one, " I am not much of a reader of this sort of literature; but my wife got hold of the volume I took home, read it half through last night, and is greatly interested in it." She liked to read aloud; but what I should be glad to know is whether she was one of the two or three to whom Lincoln enjoyed reading aloud in quiet evenings; yet no one tells us. And in the middle of an agitated night he used to traverse the White House corridors to read the trifles of Tom Hood to his sleepy secretaries; but I do not hear that he read them to her.

Again, we have little light as to other amusements of an intellectual order. There is no sign of any considerable aesthetic interest. Lincoln liked music, of a rather rudimentary type, but it does not appear that she played it to him. She does not seem to have cared for natural objects. Her husband enjoyed the pet goats who played about the White House. They bored her. She liked to give away the flowers from the conservatory, but I do not read that she had a passion for them, any more than had Lincoln, who complained that he had " no taste natural or acquired for such things." One pleasure they shared, that of the theatre, and in Washington they were able to indulge this till it culminated in the performance that was ruinous for both.

As to Mrs. Lincoln's religion, there is a good deal to be said on the practical side. She was generous and kindly, ready to help and to give. Stoddard's account of her hospital visitation during the war is very attractive. She made no display, sought no publicity whatever, but just went and gave and sympathized. In regard to the higher elements of spiritual life she was probably rather conventional, though she was a faithful member of the Episcopal, and then of the Presbyterian, Church, and Doctor Barton thinks that after her boy Willie's death she had some profounder religious experience. It may seem a trifling matter to note, but Mrs. Keckley's record of the ejaculation, " God, no! " as habitual seems to me singularly indicative of the woman.

I cannot think that there was much spiritual sympathy between her and her husband. We have, to be sure, Whitney's delightful sentence, " They were *en rapport* in all the higher objects of being." I do not believe that anybody was really *" en rapport "* with Lincoln in such matters, and I certainly do not believe his wife was. They both had, indeed, a superstitious turn of mind, and when the husband had dreams of horror and foreboding, the wife was ready to accept and interpret them. But, in Mr. Stephenson's admirable phrase, Mrs. Lincoln's soul " inhabited the obvious." The remote, gloomy spiritual regions haunted by him, whether he was smiling or praying, were hardly likely to be visited by her. Thousands of pages have been written about Lincoln's religion; but he still smiles and remains impenetrable. He practiced with God the same superb, shrewd opportunism by which, as contrasted with the dogmatic idealism of Jefferson Davis, he saved the American Union. With him, if ever with anyone, it seems a case for remembering Lamb's remark, which Lincoln would have thoroughly enjoyed, that he was determined his children should " be brought up in their father's religion — if they can find out what it is." Yet it is curious that, after all, the practical, unmystical wife should have given us what is perhaps the very best summary on this point (italics mine): " Mr. Lincoln had no faith and no hope in the usual acceptation of those words. He never joined a church; but still, as I believe, he was a religious man by nature. . . . But it was *a*

kind of poetry in his nature, and he was never a technical Christian.''
Excellent example of the keen common sense of the woman who understands even where she is wholly unable to appreciate. And we
come across this with Mrs. Lincoln at every turn.

2

In dealing with Mrs. Lincoln's external life we are on somewhat
surer ground, though not much, for still the cloud of intangible gossip
is likely to mislead us. Socially it is evident that she was ambitious and
eager for success. On the whole, it cannot be said that she achieved it.
Her appearance was by no means against her. Her face, in the photo-
graphs, is to me totally without charm. It is a positive, aggressive
face, without a ray of sensitiveness in it. But, even in the heaviness
of later years, she had a certain formal beauty and dignity, both of
face and figure, and could bear herself well. It would seem that she
dressed with taste, though at times too ostentatiously, and Lincoln
objected to her extreme low necks. As regards this matter of clothes
I cannot resist quoting one passage, both because it is one of the few
touches of real self-revelation that we have from her own pen and
because it is so thoroughly human. Three years after her husband's
death she writes to Mrs. Keckley: " I am positively dying with a
broken heart, and the probability is that I shall be living but a *very*
short time. May we all meet in a better world, where *such grief* is unknown. Write me all about yourself. I should like you to have about
four black widow's caps, just such as I had made in the fall in New
York, sent to me. . . . The probability is that I shall need few more
clothes; my rest, I am inclined to believe, *is near at hand."*

There are pleasant accounts of the Lincoln hospitality in Springfield. As to what happened in the White House observers differ. But
it must be remembered that few hostesses have been subjected to such
cruel criticism as Mrs. Lincoln had to meet. Those who watched her
impartially, like W. H. Russell, Bancroft, and Laugel, report in the
main favorably, though it is noticeable that they are inclined to speak
of her as better than they expected. The truth is, her ardent and impulsive temper made her tactless and uncertain. People could not
count upon her, and it is said that she changed her intimates and social advisers too frequently. The basis of her social zeal was rather
an intense ambition than a broad human sympathy, and for the widest
popularity and success the latter is indispensable. Then it must always be remembered that she had the strange, incalculable, most undomestic and unparlorable figure of Lincoln to carry with her, which
would have been a terrible handicap to any woman. His dress was
strange, his manners were strange, his talk was strange. And there

was always that flood of homely stories, reeking with the unexpected. He would not lay himself out to be agreeable to his wife's callers. Not that he was untidy. This is always justly denied. But he was magnificently inappropriate, disconcerting. One must not think of him as Dominie Sampson, but rather as if one were to attempt to introduce Charles Lamb or Shelley into a complicated conventional social life. So, if the poor lady failed, it must be admitted that she had her difficulties.

In her housekeeping and domestic arrangements she seems to have been excellent. Her table is highly spoken of and she was an exact and careful manager as to neatness and punctuality. Here again her husband was far from being a help to her. He was quite indifferent to what he ate and it was impossible to make him systematic about meals or hours generally. The remote world in which he lived was but imperfectly accessible to the tinkle of the dinner bell.

As regards the most essential element of domestic tranquillity, money, he was unsystematic also. In his legal business he could not be kept to exact accounting, had no commercial or speculative instinct whatever. Also, he was largely generous and more anxious to win his client's cause than to get his money. But he was no spender, had few needs and no costly tastes, and above all he abhorred debt, though circumstances sometimes forced him into it. How simple his financial ideas were appears in his reported remark shortly before his election as President: " I have a cottage at Springfield and about eight thousand dollars in money. . . . I hope I shall be able to increase it to twenty thousand, and that is as much as any man ought to want." As a matter of fact, his estate was much larger than this at the time of his death.

Mrs. Lincoln no doubt did her best. In the early days she made her own dresses and she had always moments of violent economy. Her first remark to Mrs. Keckley was: " We are just from the West, and are poor. . . . If you will work cheap, you shall have plenty to do." But her tastes in the matter of outlay were far different from her husband's. She liked to give, and did give. She liked the pleasant things of life, especially the kind that cost money. We have her own written words — and it is such a comfort when we do have them — on this subject: " When I saw the large steamers at the New York landing ready for the European voyage, I felt in my heart inclined to sigh that poverty was my portion. I often laugh and tell Mr. Lincoln that I am determined my next husband shall be rich." Which of course was agreeable for him. But the most pitiable exhibition in regard to Mrs. Lincoln's finances is Mrs. Keckley's story of the debts incurred from real or imagined necessities of dress to keep up the presidential dignity. The maddening pressure of these debts doubled the wife's anxiety as to the chances of her husband's second election in 1864. It must not be supposed that Mrs. Keckley's record of conversations that took place is verbally exact, but it is surely close to reality in its general tone. She says to Mrs. Lincoln, " And Mr. Lincoln does not even suspect how much you owe? " And the answer is, " ' God, no! ' This was a favorite expression of hers. ' And I would not have him suspect. If he knew that his wife was involved to the extent that she is, the knowledge would drive him mad. He is so sincere and straightforward himself, that he is shocked by the duplicity of others. He does not know a thing about my debts, and I value his happiness, not to speak of my own, too much to allow him to know anything. This is what troubles me so much. If he is re-elected, I can keep him in ignorance of my affairs; but if he is defeated, then the bills will be sent in and he will know all.' " Such are the domestic tragedies of money.

In her dealings with those about her in subordinate positions Mrs. Lincoln's uncertain temper is said to have caused her a good deal of difficulty. Herndon declares very definitely that " on account of her peculiar nature she could not long retain a servant in her employ." But it is evident that she was much attached to Mrs. Keckley, who served her faithfully for a number of years. And the testimony of the White House secretary, Stoddard, is exceedingly friendly and favorable. She was considerate, he says, and did not burden you with unreasonable demands. Probably, like many people of quick temper, she regretted her outbursts and did her best to make amends for them.

It is with her children that Mrs. Lincoln is most attractive. Both she and Lincoln were devoted to them, he in his gentle, humorous, abstracted fashion, she with no doubt erratic but effusive and genuine demonstrations of tenderness. She was interested in their education, in their health, in their mental and moral development. But fate was as cruel to her in the maternal as in the conjugal relation, and she lived to bury three of her four sons. The eldest died in the early days in Springfield. The youngest, Tad, who was her chief consolation after her husband's death, so that she wrote, " Only my darling Taddie prevents my taking my life," was snatched away in 1871. But the death of Willie, in the midst of the at once anguished and triumphant days in the White House, was the bitterest blow of all. The mother was inconsolable, and her grief led her into strange and fantastic ecstasies of passion, till the crisis came in the scene so vividly related by Mrs. Keckley, when Lincoln took his wife by the arm and led her to the window. " With a stately, solemn gesture, he pointed to the lunatic asylum, ' Mother, do you see that large white building on the hill yonder? Try to control your grief or it will drive you mad, and we may have to send you there.' "

Yet, with the curious perversity of fortune which attended so much of Mrs. Lincoln's life, even her mother's sorrow, which would seem as if it ought to have won her public respect and doubtless did so, was turned by her inborn tactlessness into an element of unpopularity. The military band had been in the habit of playing in the square near the White House. But Mrs. Lincoln's reminiscent grief could not endure the music, and she insisted upon its being stopped for months, till the people became so indignant that Lincoln was forced to overrule her. Truly, one cannot but sympathize with Mrs. Keckley's exclamation, even if it is a little exaggerated: " I never in my life saw a more peculiarly constituted woman. Search the world over, and you will not find her counterpart." And she was married to a man as strange as herself, and as strangely different.

from Women and Oxen

Ruth Painter Randall

There was nothing in her Kentucky background of ease and plenty that had given her training for housekeeping under Illinois conditions; at the same time her rearing had taught her high standards of homemaking which she lacked the means to achieve. She found her housekeeping hard to manage.

A small boy who lived near and ran errands for Lincoln in those days before telephones, remembered later that Mrs. Lincoln " was a high strung, nervous woman who frequently allowed her housekeeping or other activities to interfere with having her husband's lunch on time." The Herndon life of Lincoln, quoting Joshua Speed, says of Lincoln, " In all his habits of eating, sleeping, reading, conversation, and study he was . . . regularly irregular; that is, he had no stated time for eating, no fixed time for going to bed, none for getting up." How could she have a meal on time when she never knew when he would come home? She would not serve the meal until he came (that was her standard of respect for him) and this, when the children got hungry, created a problem, not to say a crisis.

Emilie Todd Helm recalled being at the Lincoln home for supper

From WOMEN AND OXEN: From the book *Mary Lincoln: Biography of a Marriage* by Ruth Painter Randall, by permission of Little, Brown & Company. Copyright 1953 by Ruth Painter Randall.

and the long hungry waiting for the man of the house to appear. The chickens burned and the rest of the supper got cold, and finally, at the end of two hours, " in sauntered brother Lincoln as innocent as a lamb of any infraction of domestic routine." The incident was taken lightheartedly by all. When Mary mentioned that she was afraid that the chickens were burned to a crisp, Lincoln (remembering Mammy Sally's theory about the jay bird) smiled quizzically and pointing his finger at his wife said, " Nem mine! Mr. Jay's gwine tell ole man Satan that Mary sets her hungry husband down to burned up vittals just caze he's two minutes late." He received a prompt and unanimous correction of " two minutes " to " two hours," but replied with irresistible good humor, " Nem mine, just bring on the cinders and see how quickly they will disappear."

Lovable as Lincoln was, he had traits that were very exasperating to one who had to keep house for him. Living in log cabins during the formative years, he was, through no fault of his own, ignorant of many details of refined living. He was notoriously unsystematic at the office, scattering papers about in such disorder that frequently documents were lost. Mary had enough to do at home without continually picking up after him. The office was dingy with dirt piled high in the corners, a condition that did not disturb either of those two untidy souls, Lincoln and Herndon, but Mary had a different standard.

She had been brought up to consider social conventions (including sweeping in corners) important. It rankled that her family had advised against her marrying this " mighty rough man," and this doubtless made her more determined that he should take on social polish. It annoyed her that he came to the dining table in his shirt sleeves. It was all right for him to lie on the floor reading, with the back of a turned-down chair for a pillow, but when the quaint little doorbell on the wall of the dining room tinkled, it was proper to let the maid (when they had one) answer it. Through a cousin of Lincoln's who lived at their home for about a year and a half comes the story of his going to the front door in his shirt sleeves to admit two lady callers (probably very stylish ones), ushering them into the parlor and telling them in his quaintly amiable way that he would " trot the women folks out." Mrs. Lincoln, with her usual failing for speaking her mind, scolded him sharply, which made a morsel of conversation that the visitors did not fail to circulate. When it reached the ears of Mary's relatives (who had apparently learned that Lincoln had something to offer), one of them said to her, " Mary, if I had a husband with a mind such as yours has, I wouldn't care what he did." This was consummate tact; praise of her Mr. Lincoln made Mary beam and she answered at once, " It is very foolish — it is a small thing to complain of."

An absent-minded husband whose thoughts turn inward while the fire goes out and the baby squalls, requires constant looking after, like a child. It has been said that Mary Lincoln's " soul inhabited the obvious "; it was a good thing for the welfare of the household that somebody's soul did. Records of Lincoln's appearance in early life mention his carelessness in dress; it fell to Mary to see that he did not go around with one pants leg rolled up and the other down as he had in New Salem days. She had to make sure that he took his warm shawl with him on cold days, and his umbrella on wet ones. She knew the proper dress for a rising lawyer and a gentleman and she intended that her husband should make a good appearance. Gamaliel Bradford has stated her social problem: ". . . it must always be remembered that she had the strange, incalculable, most undomestic and unparlorable figure of Lincoln to carry with her, which would have been a terrible handicap to any woman." There is no evidence that Mary, as proud as she was of Mr. Lincoln, looked at the matter quite like that, but she did give attention to his clothes and he profited by it. An old neighbor sized up the situation very neatly: " She looked her husband over carefully whenever he left the house to make sure that, in his thoughtlessness about his dress, he had not neglected some detail."

Mary Owens, when Lincoln was courting her in New Salem days, had concluded that as a husband he would not always know how to help with the babies. In her own words: " On one occasion did I say to Mr. L— that I did not believe he would make a kind husband, because he did not tender his services to Mrs. Green in helping of her carry her babe." Miss Owens continued with her accusation of thoughtlessness. " There was a company of us going to Uncle Billy Greens, Mr. L— was riding with me, and we had a very bad branch to cross, the other gentlemen were very officious in seeing that their partners got over safely; we were behind, he riding in [front] never looking back to see how I got along . . ." Piqued at his lack of courtesy, the spirited young woman rode up beside him and said tartly, ". . . you are a nice fellow; I suppose you did not care whether my neck was broken or not." Lincoln laughed and got himself out of a tight corner with a compliment that smacks of the frontier; he told the lady that he knew she was " plenty smart " to take care of herself.

Miss Owen's comment on Lincoln's ineptness as to helping with a baby recalls a well-known incident. On Sundays while Mrs. Lincoln went to church, the neighbors would see Lincoln pulling a little wagon with a baby or babies in it, up and down the street in front of his house. In one hand he would hold an open book, and, deeply absorbed, read from it as he walked. Once the baby fell out and lay squalling upon the ground while the father went on with complete unawareness of anything wrong. This was the scene which greeted Mary as she returned from her devotions at church, and many women will pardon her for shrieking at him. She did not know at that time that he would become a great statesman but it was borne in upon her forcibly that he was not a reliable baby sitter.

It is illuminating to examine the manner in which Herndon presented this incident to his collaborator Weik. He begins his letter with a statement of his theory: " Mr. & Mrs. Lincoln never lived a harmonious life "; then adds that " when she wanted to go to church or to some gathering she would go at all events and leave Lincoln to care of the babies." Herndon was an infidel and proud of it; he had no sympathy with her going to church in the first place and in the second he thought she was imposing upon her husband. " Mrs. Lincoln couldn't keep a hired girl because she was tyranical to her," he wrote, " and Lincoln per force was compelled to look after the children." Herndon's punch line is concerned with what followed the wife's return from church: ". . . you know, a hell of scolding. Poor Abe, I can see him now running and crouching." (Incidentally, he never presumed to call his partner " Abe " to his face.) And Herndon, humorless and not familiar with the Lincoln family circle, never knew that afterward the spilling of the baby was a family joke, a topic of teasing and laughter.

Herndon thought that baby-tending was woman's work and any husband who did it was henpecked, a point of view that appears also in the recollections of a very frank neighbor. She told Mr. Lincoln, apropos of his wheeling the baby, she thought that was " a pretty business " for him to be engaged in.

Herndon's biography makes the statement: " Mrs. Lincoln, on account of her peculiar nature, could not long retain a servant in her employ." This ignores the fact that other women were having the same difficulty. That young wife, Mrs. Benjamin S. Edwards, who rode into Springfield at the beginning of this story, left a record of her experience in this line: " It was almost impossible to get servants. I had brought a woman from St. Louis but found her so intemperate that in less than a year I was obliged to discharge her and my troubles in housekeeping began. I knew nothing of cooking and shed many a tear over my first attempts."

That Mary Lincoln had a difficult temperament is quite true but it is worth while to examine the testimony of servants who lived with her, some of them several years at a time, in spite of Herndon's assertion. We have the recollections of a colored woman who worked for the Lincolns when Robert, as she said, was about five. She waited on the table, washed dishes, laundered and scrubbed while Mrs. Lincoln (whom she described as " a very nice lady ") did the cooking and sewing. This included sewing for the poor when the church society met at her house, for Mary was faithfully religious and did not neglect her church attendance or duties. The limited means of the Lincolns made a deep impression on this kind Negro servant; she recalled that Mrs. Lincoln's dresses were of inexpensive material, no silks or satins, and that Robert's small pants were adorned with patches. After this servant left, Mrs. Lincoln did all the work herself.

Mary always fares well in the testimony of colored people. She was kind to them; they understood her. So did a little Portuguese girl who served her and many years later managed to say more in a few words of broken English than many could express in the same number of pages. Mrs. Lincoln, she said, " taka no sassy talk, but if you good to her, she good to you. You gotta good friend." Of the husband and father, the Portuguese woman was equally discerning: " He so kind. He choppa the wood for fire, and little Robert choppa the little wood. When he passa me, he patta my shoulder. . . . Mr. Lincoln no verra style. He just common, like some one that is poor."

All the servants were devoted to the lovable master of the house but it is rather amusing to find a former maid saying frankly that Mrs. Lincoln was " a smarter woman than he was a man." That is the way it appeared on the domestic front. This same maid remembered that the Lincolns were " very domestic in their tastes," and that Mrs. Lincoln was a " good woman," who often helped her with her work to the end that the girl might have more time to play with the children. The cream of this recollection is the account of Lincoln wholeheartedly playing blindman's buff with his little sons.

From an aged woman who once worked for the Lincolns came an understanding account of Mrs. Lincoln's quickly flaring temper. She said these outbursts lasted only a few minutes and then Mrs. Lincoln was " all sorrow " and anxious to make amends. Mary's own numerous apologies in her letters and accounts from all sides bear this out. Her lack of emotional control was a burden to her as well as to others. " She had an ungovernable temper, but after the outburst she was invariably regretful and penitent," said Harriet Hanks, who lived in the Lincoln home for many months, and Mrs. Keckley, the colored dressmaker in Washington, said the same thing. Fundamentally affectionate, all Mary needed was a little time for cooling off, a fact well understood by her husband.

The Herndon life of Lincoln tells how Lincoln once secretly paid a servant an extra dollar a week in order to have her stay on with them, which she did for " several years." It was a pleasant conspiracy on the part of a husband who knew his wife's penny-pinching complex and also her need for help in the heavy household duties. Lincoln, who had infinite tact, understood how to get around the " little woman." There is a newspaper story, given here for what it is worth, telling that a group from Springfield's volunteer fire department once called on Lincoln and asked him for a subscription for a needed new hose. With a twinkle Lincoln outlined his policy to them: he would talk it over with his wife when he went home and suggest that they contribute fifty dollars. She would immediately say that he was always too liberal; that twenty-five dollars was quite enough. Lincoln concluded with a chuckle that they could call next day for the twenty-five.

.　.　.　.　.

Mary was well centered in woman's sphere, which, as all good people of the time knew, was where any wife belonged. The mental circumference for females was as restricted as the physical. *Godey's Lady's Book* (as revealing of thought patterns as of those for dress) left no doubt on this subject; home was woman's dominion and any circumstance which drew her from that sacred sphere was to be deplored. As the author of *The Fabulous Forties* has pointed out, the ideals of that decade were all directed toward making wives " unspeakably dull."

That, however, is one of the few accusations which has not been hurled at Mary Lincoln. Her impetuosity was often lacking in wisdom, but she was always lively and interested in all that was happening. " She was fond of home," wrote her half sister; " was a cheerful woman, a delightful conversationist, and well-informed on all the subjects of the day." Mrs. Keckley spoke of her " cheery voice," and another source mentioned that voice as " soft " and " sweet." Mary went into the new-bought house to make it into a home with her usual energetic enthusiasm. She had small dainty hands and was a bit vain about them — their quick pretty gestures were a part of her personality — but those hands did not hold back from any household task. When she finally went to Washington as wife of the President-elect, her hands were hardened with toil. A gentleman who shook hands with Mrs. Lincoln on March 1, 1861, recorded: " We are pleased with her. She had no gloves on & put out her hand. It is not soft."

The little family settled into domestic routine like young married people of all generations. The Lincoln home knew drudgery, monotony, illnesses, clashes of nerves and viewpoints, scoldings, "blues," fears, disappointments, small disasters — all the elements that go into the daily exasperation of the average household. It was also a home for a man who had been homeless, who had known loneliness, a home like others down the street where the husband returned after the day's work to tell his wife all that had happened to him that day, knowing she would be more interested than anyone else and more partisan. She on her side would tell him small important news: how their little son had had an adventure with a stray kitten, or how the baby had tried to say a new word and it had come out such a dear, funny combination of sounds that they both smiled with fond parental eyes.

It is difficult to recover the inner life of a marriage. Demonstration of affection is a private matter, not for witnesses. By chance we have had a glimpse of Lincoln, during the courtship, folding Mary in his arms, kissing her and holding her on his lap. One knows well there were times when mutual affection led to such caresses. There were the binding intimacies of the night. These were two people of unusual tenderness and affection. Mary's was a demonstrative nature. Lincoln had known small demonstration of affection up to the time of his marriage; the grimness of backwoods existence had crowded it out; he was in a position to appreciate its sweetness.

There was love in the house on Eighth Street, there was fun and playfulness, there was the joy of children.

Mazie

Joseph Mitchell

A bossy, yellow-haired blonde named Mazie P. Gordon is a celebrity on the Bowery. In the nickel-a-drink saloons and in the all-night restaurants which specialize in pig snouts and cabbage at a dime a platter, she is known by her first name. She makes a round of these establishments practically every night, and drunken bums sometimes come up behind her, slap her on the back, and call her sweetheart.

MAZIE: From *McSorley's Wonderful Saloon* by Joseph Mitchell, by permission of Duell, Sloan & Pearce, Inc. Copyright 1943 by Joseph Mitchell. Originally published in *The New Yorker*.

This never annoys her. She has a wry but genuine fondness for bums and is undoubtedly acquainted with more of them than any other person in the city. Each day she gives them between five and fifteen dollars in small change, which is a lot of money on the Bowery. " In my time I been as free with my dimes as old John D. himself," she says. Mazie has presided for twenty-one years over the ticket cage of the Venice Theatre, at 209 Park Row, a few doors west of Chatham Square, where the Bowery begins.

The Venice is a small, seedy moving-picture theatre, which opens at 8 A.M. and closes at midnight. It is a dime house. For this sum a customer sees two features, a newsreel, a cartoon, a short, and a serial episode. The Venice is not a " scratch house." In fact, it is highly esteemed by its customers, because its seats get a scrubbing at least once a week. Mazie brags that it is as sanitary as the Paramount. " Nobody ever got loused up in the Venice," she says. On the Bowery, cheap movies rank just below cheap alcohol as an escape, and most bums are movie fans. In the clientele of the Venice they are numerous. The Venice is also frequented by people from the tenement neighborhoods in the vicinity of Chatham Square, such as Chinatown, the Little Italy on lower Mulberry Street, and the Spanish section on Cherry Street. Two-thirds of its customers are males. Children and most women sit in a reserved section under the eyes of a matron. Once, in an elegant mood, Mazie boasted that she never admits intoxicated persons. " When do you consider a person intoxicated? " she was asked. Mazie snickered. " When he has to get down on all fours and crawl," she said. In any case, there are drunks in practically every Venice audience. When the liquor in them dies down they become fretful and mumble to themselves, and during romantic pictures they make loud, utterly frank remarks to the actors on the screen, but by and large they are not as troublesome as a class of bums Mazie calls " the stiffs." These are the most listless of bums. They are blank-eyed and slow-moving, and they have no strong desire for anything but sleep. Some are able to doze while leaning against a wall, even in freezing weather. Many stiffs habitually go into the Venice early in the day and slumber in their seats until they are driven out at midnight. " Some days I don't know which this is, a movie-pitcher theatre or a flophouse," Mazie once remarked. " Other day I told the manager pitchers with shooting in them are bad for business. They wake up the customers."

Most Bowery movie houses employ bouncers. At the Venice, Mazie is the bouncer. She tells intimates that she feels fighting is unladylike but she considers it her duty to throw at least one customer out of the theatre every day. " If I didn't put my foot down, the customers would take the place," she says. " I don't get any fun out of fighting. I always lose my temper. When I start swinging, I taste blood, and I can't stop. Sometimes I get beside myself. Also, a lot of the bums are so weak they don't fight back, and that makes me feel like a heel." Mazie is small, but she is wiry and fearless, and she has a frightening voice. Her ticket cage is in the shadow of the tracks of the City Hall spur of the Third Avenue elevated line, and two decades of talking above the screeching of the trains have left her with a rasping bass, with which she can dominate men twice her size. Now and then, in the Venice, a stiff throws his head back and begins to snore so blatantly that he can be heard all over the place, especially during tense moments in the picture. When this happens, or when one of the drunks gets into a bellowing mood, the women and children in the reserved section stamp on the floor and chant, " Mazie! Mazie! We want Mazie! " The instant this chant goes up, the matron hastens out to the lobby and raps on the side window of Mazie's cage. Mazie locks the cash drawer, grabs a bludgeon she keeps around, made of a couple of copies of *True Romances* rolled up tightly and held together by rubber bands, and strides into the theatre. As she goes down the aisle, peering this way and that, women and children jump to their feet, point fingers in the direction of the offender, and cry, " There he is, Mazie! There he is! " Mazie gives the man a resounding whack on the head with her bludgeon and keeps on whacking until he seems willing to behave. Between blows, she threatens him with worse punishment. Her threats are fierce and not altogether coherent. " Outa here on a stretcher! " she yells. " Knock your eyeballs out! Big baboon! Every tooth in your head! Bone in your body! " The women and children enjoy this, particularly if Mazie gets the wrong man, as she sometimes does. In action, Mazie is an alarming sight. Her face becomes flushed, her hair flies every which way, and her slip begins to show. If a man defends himself or is otherwise contrary, she harries him out of his seat and drives him from the theatre. As he scampers up the aisle, with Mazie right behind him, whacking away, the women and children applaud.

Mazie's animosity toward a stiff or a drunk usually lasts until she has driven him out to the sidewalk. Then, almost invariably, she becomes contrite and apologetic. " Look, buddy, I'm sorry," she said one afternoon recently to a drunk she had chased out because he had been screaming " Sissy! Sissy! " at George Raft during the showing of a prison picture called " Each Dawn I Die." " If you didn't see the whole show," she continued, " you can go back in." " Hell, Mazie," said the drunk, " I seen it three times." " Here, then," she said, handing him a dime. " Go get yourself a drink." Although the drunk's ears were still red from Mazie's blows, he grinned. " You got a heart of gold, Mazie," he said. " You my sweetheart." " O.K., buddy," Mazie said, stepping back into the cage. " You quit acting like a god-damn jackass and I'll be your sweetheart."

The Venice is a family enterprise. It is owned by Mazie and two sisters — Rosie, the widow of a horse-race gambler, and Jeanie, an acrobatic dancer. Mazie's sisters let her run things to suit herself. She is profoundly uninterested in moving pictures and is seldom able to sit through one. " They make me sick," she says. Consequently, she employs a manager and leaves the selection and ordering of films entirely up to him. For a theatre of its class, the Venice is prosperous, and Mazie could afford to hire a ticket girl and take things easy, but she enjoys the job and will not relinquish it, as her sisters often urge her to do. From her cage she has a good view of Chatham Square, which is the favorite promenade of Bowery drunks and eccentrics. " The things I see, by God, you wouldn't believe it," she says proudly. When she catches sight of a person she knows among the passers-by, she sticks her face up to the round hole in the front window of her cage and shouts a greeting. Sometimes she discusses exceedingly personal matters with people out on the sidewalk. " Hey there, Squatty," she yelled one afternoon to a dreamy-eyed little man, " I thought you was in Bellevue." " I was, Mazie," the man said. " They turned me loose yesterday." " Where'd they put you this time — the drunk ward or the nut ward? " " I was in with the drunks this time." " How'd they treat you? " " They didn't do me no harm, I guess." " You get drunk last night, Squatty? " " Sure did." " Guess you had to celebrate." " Sure did." " Well, take care of yourself, Squatty." " Thanks, Mazie. You do the same."

Sitting majestically in her cage like a raffish queen, Mazie is one of the few pleasant sights of the Bowery. She is a short, bosomy woman in her middle forties. Some people believe she has a blurry resemblance to Mae West. Her hair is the color of sulphur. Her face is dead white, and she wears a smudge of rouge the size of a silver dollar on each cheek. Her eyes are sleepy and droopy-lidded. On duty, she often wears a green celluloid eyeshade. She almost always has a cigarette hanging from a corner of her mouth, and this makes her look haughty. Like a movie croupier, she can smoke a cigarette down to the end and not take it from her mouth once, even while talking. She has a deep cigarette cough; she smokes three and a half packs a day and says tobacco is murdering her. On her right hand she wears four diamond rings. She likes vigorous colors, and her dresses are spectacular; they come from shops on Division Street. The glass-topped Bowery and Chinatown rubberneck wagons often park in front of the Venice, and now and then a band of sightseers stand on the sidewalk and stare at Mazie. She despises sightseers and says they give the Bowery a black eye. Sometimes she thumbs her nose at them. Actually, however, she does not mind being stared at. " People walk past here just to give me the eye," she once said. " I got a public of my own, just like a god-damn movie-pitcher star."

Mazie is a talkative woman, and on most subjects she is exceedingly frank, but she rarely says anything about her private life, and some people on the Bowery consider her a mystery woman. A man who had been stopping by to chat with her several times a week for years suddenly realized recently that he did not know whether she was Miss or Mrs. Gordon. " You ever been married, Mazie? " he asked. " That's for me to know, you to find out," she said sharply. A moment later she added, " I'll ask you this. Do I look and act like a girl that never had a date? " People around Chatham Square believe, among other things, that she was a belly dancer in the Hurtig & Seamon burlesque houses when she was a young woman, which isn't true. They claim, with not much relevance, that she gives her spare money to bums because she was once disappointed in a love affair. Furthermore, they believe she was born in Chinatown. Actually, she is a native of Boston, a fact which gives her a lot of satisfaction. Every winter she takes a week off and spends it in Boston, just walking around. She believes the people of Boston are superior to the people elsewhere. One night a blind-drunk bum stumbled into an " L " pillar in front of the Venice, skinning his nose, and she rushed out and dragged him into her lobby. Then she went into a nearby saloon and yelled, " Gimme some hot water and a clean rag! " " You want to take a bath, Mazie? " asked the bartender. This remark enraged her. " Don't you talk like that to me, you yellow-bellied jerk," she said. " I come from Boston, and I'm a lady."

Mazie says her real name is Mazie Phillips, but she will not tell anything about her parents. Her intimates say that around 1903, when she was a schoolgirl in Boston, her older sister, Rosie, came to New York and married Louis Gordon, an East Side gambler and promoter. They established a home on Grand Street, and a few years later Mazie and her younger sister, Jeanie, came to live with them. The family of Belle Baker, the vaudeville singer, lived nearby on Chrystie Street. Irving Becker, Belle's brother, now the manager of a road company of " Tobacco Road," once had a job loading rifles in a shooting gallery Gordon operated at Grand Street and the Bowery. " We and the Gordons were great friends," Becker said recently. " Louie Gordon was as fine a gambler as the East Side ever produced. He was a big, stately gentleman and he gave to the poor, and the bankroll he carried a billy goat couldn't swallow it. He hung around race tracks, but he would gamble on anything. He made a lot of money on horses and invested it in Coney Island. He and his brother, Leo, helped back the original Luna Park, which opened in 1903. He was one of those silent gamblers. He never said nothing about himself. He gave everybody a fair shake, and he didn't have a thing to hide, but he just never said nothing about himself. All the Gordons were that way."

In 1914, Gordon opened a moving-picture theatre in a building he owned on Park Row, naming it the Venice, after an Italian restaurant in Coney Island whose spaghetti he liked. After operating it four years, he found that it kept him away from the tracks and he gave it to Rosie, who had been working in the ticket cage. The next year he sold his Bowery shooting gallery, in which, for several months, Mazie had been running a candy-and-root-beer concession. Rosie did not like selling tickets, so Mazie took her job. Around this time, Mazie began calling herself Mazie Gordon. She will not explain why she took her brother-in-law's name. " That's my business," she says. The Gordons left Grand Street in the early twenties, moving to a house on Surf Avenue in Coney. Mazie continued to live with them. Louis was away much of the time, following the horses. Mazie says that once, after a good season in Saratoga, he gave her a Stutz which, with accessories, cost $5,000. She used to ride down to Coney in the Stutz every night after work; one of the ushers at the Venice was her chauffeur. In October, 1932, Louis fell dead of a heart attack at the Empire City race track. Mazie and her sisters left Coney Island a few years later and returned to the East Side, eventually taking an apartment together in Knickerbocker Village, four blocks from the Venice. They live quietly. Rosie, a taciturn, sad-eyed woman, looks after property left by her husband. Besides her interest in the Venice, this property includes a number of lots along the boardwalk in Coney and an ancient red-brick tenement at 9 James Street, a block from the Venice. This tenement has sixteen cold-water flats, all occupied by unmarried Chinese men. Jeanie, a handsome young woman, boasts that she has gone to the West Coast and back ten times while working in vaudeville as an acrobatic dancer. Now and then she spells Mazie in the cage at the Venice.

Mazie's hours would kill most women. She works seven days a week, seldom taking a day off, and is usually on duty from 9:30 A.M. until 11 P.M. Her cage is not much more spacious than a telephone booth, but she long ago learned how to make herself comfortable in it. She sits on two thick pillows in a swivel chair and wears bedroom slippers. In summer she keeps an electric fan, aimed upward, on the floor, replacing it in winter with an electric heater. When the weather is especially cold she brings her dog, Fluffy, an old, wheezy Pomeranian bitch, to the theatre. She lets Fluffy sleep in her lap, and this keeps both of them warm. Mazie makes change as automatically as she breathes, and she finds time for many domestic chores while on duty. She mends clothes, puts red polish on her fingernails, reads a little, and occasionally spends half an hour or so cleaning her diamonds with a scrap of chamois skin. On rainy days she sends out for her meals, eating them right in the cage. She uses the marble change counter for a table. Once, hunched over a plate of roast-beef hash, she looked up and said to a visitor, " I do light housekeeping in here." When she gets thirsty she sends an usher across the street to the King Kong Bar & Grill for a cardboard container of beer. She used to keep a bottle of Canadian whiskey, which she calls " smoke," hidden in her cash drawer, but since an appendix operation in 1939 she has limited herself to celery tonic and beer.

There are two cluttered shelves on one wall of her cage. On the bottom shelf are a glass jar of " jawbreakers," a kind of hard candy which she passes out to children, a clamshell that serves as an ashtray, a hind leg of a rabbit, a stack of paper towels, and a box of soap. When a bum with an exceptionally grimy face steps up to buy a ticket, Mazie places a towel and a cake of soap before him and says, " Look, buddy, I'll make a bargain with you. If you'll take this and go in the gents' room and wash your face, I'll let you in free." Few bums are offended by this offer; most of them accept willingly. Occasionally she gives one fifteen cents and sends him to a barber college on Chatham Square for a shave and a haircut. If she is in a good humor, Mazie will admit a bum free without much argument. However, she says she can tell a bum by the look in his eyes, and ordinary citizens who have heard of her generosity and try to get passed in outrage her. " If you haven't got any money," she tells such people, " go steal a watch."

On Mazie's top shelf is a pile of paper-backed books, which includes " Old Gipsy Nan's Fortune Teller and Dream Book," " Prince Ali Five Star Dream Book," and " Madame Fu Futtam's Spiritual Magical Dream Book." Mazie is deeply interested in dreams, although at times she seems a little ashamed of it. " A dream just means you et something that didn't agree with you," she sometimes says, rather defiantly. Nevertheless, she makes a practice of remembering them and spends hours hunting through her books for satisfactory interpretations. Also on her top shelf are a rosary, some back numbers of a religious periodical called the *Messenger of the Sacred Heart,* and a worn copy of " Spiritual Reflections for Sisters," by the Reverend Charles J. Mullaly, S.J., which she borrowed from an Italian nun, one of the Daughters of Mary Help of Christians, who conduct a school in Chinatown. Lately Mazie has been reading a page of this book every day. She says that she understands hardly any of it but that reading it makes her feel good. Mazie is not a Catholic; she is Jewish, but she has been entranced by Roman Catholicism for many years. One of her oldest friends in the neighborhood is Monsignor William E. Cashin, rector of St. Andrews', the little church back of the Municipal Building. She frequently shows up for the Night Workers' Mass, which is said every Sunday at 2:30 A.M. in St. Andrews' by Monsignor Cashin. She sits in a middle pew with her head bowed. Surrounded by policemen, firemen, scrubwomen, telephone girls, nurses, printers, and similar night workers who regularly attend the mass, she feels at home. On the way out she always slips a dollar bill into the poor box. Now and then she calls on the Monsignor and has a long talk with him, and whenever he takes a walk on the Bowery he pauses at her cage and passes the time of day.

Mazie also knows two mothers superior quite well. The rosary she keeps in her cage is a present from the Sisters of Our Lady of Christian Doctrine, who run Madonna House, a settlement on Cherry Street. Sister Margaret, the superior there, has known Mazie for years and has made an attempt to understand her. " On the Bowery it's probably an asset to have a reputation for toughness," Sister Margaret once told a friend, " and I'm afraid Mazie tries to give people the worst possible impression of herself, just for self-protection. She isn't really tough. At heart, she's good and kind. We can always count on her for help. A few weeks ago there was a fire in an Italian tenement near here. One of the families in it had a new baby. It was late at night and we didn't know exactly how to help them. Two of the sisters went to Mazie, and she came right down and found the family a new flat and gave the mother some money." Mazie's favorite saint is St. John Bosco. There is a statue of him in a niche in the steeple of the weatherbeaten Church of the Transfiguration in Chinatown. At night the saint can be clearly seen by the light of the galaxy of neon signs on the chop-suey joints which surround the church. When she passes through Mott Street, Mazie looks up at the saint and crosses herself. " I asked a sister once if it was O.K. for me to give myself a cross, and she told me it was," Mazie says.

Mazie became interested in Catholicism in the winter of 1920. A drug addict on Mulberry Street, a prostitute with two small daughters, came to her cage one night and asked for help. The woman said her children were starving. " I knew this babe was a junky," Mazie says, " and I followed her home just to see was she lying about her kids. She had two kids all right, and they were starving in this crummy little room. I tried to get everybody to do something — the cops, the Welfare, the so-called missions on the Bowery that the Methodists run or whatever to hell they are. But all these people said the girl was a junky. That excused them from lifting a hand. So I seen two nuns on the street, and they went up there with me. Between us, we got the woman straightened out. I liked the nuns. They seemed real human. Ever since then I been interested in the Cat'lic Church."

Mazie does not spend much time at home, so she encourages people to visit her while she is working. Her visitors stand around in the lobby at the rear door of her cage. She frequently gets so interested in a caller that she swings completely around in her swivel chair and presents her back to customers, who have to shout and rap on the window before she will turn and sell them tickets. In the morning, practically all of her visitors are bums with hangovers who come to her, scratching themselves and twitching, and ask for money with which to get their first drinks of the day. She passes out dimes regularly to about twenty-five of these men. Because of this, she is disliked by many of the hard-shell evangelists who hold hymn-singings in the gutters of the Bowery every evening. One of them, a grim, elderly woman, came to the cage not long ago and shook a finger at Mazie. " We sacrifice our nights to come down here and encourage these unfortunates to turn over a new leaf," she said. " Then you give them money and they begin using intoxicants all over again." When Mazie is faced with such a situation, she makes irrelevant or vulgar remarks until the complainant leaves. On this occasion she leaned forward and said, " Par'n me, Madam, but it sounds like your guts are growling. What you need is a beer."

Few of the men to whom Mazie gives money for eye-openers are companionable. They take her dimes with quivering fingers, mutter a word of thanks, and hurry off. Two of them, however, invariably linger a while. They have become close friends of Mazie's. One is a courtly old Irishman named Pop, and the other is an addled, sardonic little man who says he is a poet and whom Mazie calls Eddie Guest. She says she likes Pop because he is so cheerful and Eddie Guest because he is so sad. " I come from a devout family of teetotallers," Pop once said. " They was thirteen in the family, and they called me the weakling because I got drunk on Saturday nights. Well, they're all under the sod. Woodrow Wilson was President when the last one died, and I'm still here drinking good liquor and winking at the pretty girls." " That's right, Pop," Mazie said. Pop works bus stops. He approaches people waiting on corners for a bus and asks for a nickel with which to get uptown or downtown, as the case may be. When he gets a nickel, he touches his hat and hurries off to the next bus stop.

At night he sings ballads in Irish gin mills on Third Avenue. Mazie thinks he has a beautiful baritone, and every morning, in return for her dime, he favors her with two or three ballads. Her favorites — she hums them — are " Whiskey, You're the Divil," " The Garden Where the Praties Grow," " Tiddly-Aye-Aye for the One-Eyed Reilly," and " The Widow McGinnis's Pig." Sometimes Pop dances a jig on the tiled floor of the lobby. " Pop's a better show than I got inside," Mazie says on these occasions.

Eddie Guest is a gloomy, defeated, ex-Greenwich Village poet who has been around the Bowery off and on for eight or nine years. He mutters poetry to himself constantly and is taken to Bellevue for observation about once a year. He carries all his possessions in a greasy beach bag and sleeps in flophouses, never staying in one two nights in succession, because, he says, he doesn't want his enemies to know where he is. During the day he wanders in and out of various downtown branches of the Public Library. At the Venice one night he saw " The River," the moving picture in which the names of the tributaries of the Mississippi were made into a poem. When he came out he stopped at Mazie's cage, spread his arms, and recited the names of many of the walk-up hotels on the Bowery. " The Alabama Hotel, the Comet, and the Uncle Sam House," he said, in a declamatory voice, " the Dandy, the Defender, the Niagara, the Owl, the Victoria House and the Grand Windsor Hotel, the Houston, the Mascot, the Palace, the Progress, the Palma House and the White House Hotel, the Newport, the Crystal, the Lion and the Marathon. All flophouses. All on the Bowery. Each and all my home, sweet home." For some reason, Mazie thought this was extraordinarily funny. Now, each morning, in order to get a dime, Eddie Guest is obliged to recite this chant for her. It always causes her to slap her right thigh, throw her head back, and guffaw. Both Eddie Guest and Mazie can be grimly and rather pointlessly amused by the signs over flophouse entrances and by the bills of fare lettered in white on the windows of pig-snout restaurants. When Mazie passes the Victoria House and sees its sign, ROOMS WITH ELECTRIC LIGHTS, 30c," or when she looks at the window of the Greek's on Chatham Square, " Snouts with French fry Pots & Coffee, T, or buttermilk, 10c," she always snickers. Mazie has considerable respect for Eddie Guest but thinks he is kidding when he calls himself a poet. Once he read to her part of a completely unintelligible poem about civilization in the United States, on which he says he has been working for twenty years and which he calls " No Rags, No Bones, No Bottles Today." " If that's a poem," Mazie said when he had finished, " I'm the Queen of Sweden."

Mazie's afternoon visitors are far more respectable than the morning ones. The people who stopped by to talk with her between noon and 6 P.M. one Saturday included Monsignor Cashin, Fannie Hurst, two detectives from the Oak Street station, a flashily dressed young Chinese gambler whom Mazie calls Fu Manchu and who is a power in Tze Far, the Chinatown version of the numbers lottery; two nuns from Madonna House, who wanted to thank her for buying a phonograph for the girl's club at their settlement; a talkative girl from Atlanta, Georgia, called Bingo, once a hostess in a Broadway taxi-dance hall and now the common-law wife of the chef of a chop-suey restaurant on Mott Street; the bartender of a Chatham Square saloon, who asked her to interpret a dream for him; and the clerk of a flophouse, who came to tell her that a bum named Tex had hanged himself in the washroom the night before. When she was told about Tex, Mazie nodded sagely and said, as she always does when she hears about the death of someone she has known, " Well, we all got to go sooner or later. You can't live forever. When your number's up, rich or poor, you got to go." Most of the visitors on that afternoon happened to be old friends of Mazie's. Miss Hurst, for example, she has known for eleven years. She calls her Fannie and likes to tell about their first meeting.

" One night," she says, " a swell-looking dame came to my cage and said she often walks on the Bowery and would like to meet me. She said her name was Fannie Hurst. ' Pleased to meet you, Fannie,' I said. ' My name is Mary Pickford.' It turned out she really was Fannie Hurst. At first I thought she was going to put me in a book, and I didn't go for her. Since she promised not to write no books about me, we been pals." Miss Hurst visits Mazie frequently. Each time she comes, Mazie looks at her dress, fingers the material, asks how much it cost, tells her she got gypped, and advises her to try one of the shops on Division Street. Miss Hurst does not mind this. " I admire Mazie," she said. " She is the most compassionate person I've ever known. No matter how filthy or drunk or evil-smelling a bum may be, she treats him as an equal." Until recently, Miss Hurst occasionally took friends down to meet Mazie. " I'm afraid they looked on her as just another Bowery curiosity," she says. " So I don't take people down any more. I used to invite Mazie to parties at my house. She always accepted but never came. I think she's still a little suspicious of me, although I've never written a line about her and never intend to. I simply look upon her as a friend."

From callers like Fu Manchu and Bingo, Mazie hears considerable gossip about the sleazy underworld of Chinatown. She says she never repeats such gossip, not even to her sisters. Detectives know that she has many Chinese friends and sometimes stop at her cage and ask apparently innocent questions about them; she shrugs her shoulders and says, " No spik English." In general, however, she coöperates with the police. Drunken tourists often come down to Bowery joints to see life, and when she notices them stumbling around Chatham Square she telephones the Oak Street station. " Such dopes are always getting rolled by bums," she says. " I got no sympathy for out-of-towners, but bums are the clumsiest thieves in the world. They always get caught, and it's best to get temptation out of their way." Although her language frequently shocks the Oak Street cops, they admire Mazie. Detective Kain, for instance, says that she has " the roughest tongue and the softest heart in the Third Precinct." " She knows this neighborhood like a farmer knows his farm," he says. " I believe she's got the second sight. If anything out of the way is happening anywhere along the Bowery, she senses it."

Detective Kain has for some time been trying to solve a mystery in which Mazie is involved. Mazie has a telephone in her booth, of course, and in June, 1929, a man whose voice she did not recognize began calling her daily at 5 P.M., asking for a date or making cryptic remarks, such as " They got the road closed, Mazie. They won't let nobody through." After three months he stopped calling. Then, around Christmas of the following year, he began again. He has been calling intermittently ever since. " I won't hear from him for maybe six months," Mazie says. " Then, one day around five, the phone will ring and this voice will say, ' All the clocks have stopped running' or ' Mazie, they cut down the big oak tree' or some other dopey remark. He never says more than a few words, and when I say something he hangs right up. One afternoon he gave me the shakes. He called up and said, ' Mazie, I got a nephew studying to be an undertaker and he needs somebody to practice on.' Then he hung up. A minute later he called again and said, ' You'll do! You'll do! ' Somehow, I get to feeling he's across the street in a booth. The worst thing is I suspect every stranger that buys a ticket. I strike up conversations with strangers just to see if I can find one who talks like him. I think he's trying to drive me crazy." Among her friends, Mazie refers to her caller as The Man. If she has visitors around five o'clock and the telephone rings, she says, " Pick up the receiver and see what The Man has to say this time." Fannie Hurst once listened. " It was macabre," she said. Detective Kain has listened often, has warned the man, and has tried vainly to trace the calls. Mazie's number has been changed repeatedly, but that does no good.

Mazie closes her cage shortly after 11 P.M., when the final show is under way, and goes to an all-night diner near Brooklyn Bridge, where she glances through the *Daily News* while having a couple of cups of coffee and a honey bun. The only things in the *News* that she regularly reads from beginning to end are the comics, the "Voice of the People," and "The Inquiring Fotographer." She says she doesn't read political or war stories because she can't understand them and because they make her blue. "The world is all bitched up," she once said. "Always was, always will be." "Do you really believe that?" she was asked. "No," she said, after a moment of deliberation, "I guess I don't." She spends half an hour in the diner. Then, practically every night, before going home to bed, she makes a Samaritan tour of the Bowery and its environs. She carries an umbrella and a large handbag, which contains a flashlight, a number of cakes of soap of the size found in hotel bathrooms, and a supply of nickels, dimes, and quarters.

If it is a cold night, she goes first to an alley near the steps leading to the footwalk of Manhattan Bridge. Bums like to keep fires going in discarded oil drums in this alley. She distributes some change. Then she inspects Columbus Park, a block west of Chatham Square, where every winter a few bums pass out on benches and die of exposure. The police say Mazie has rescued scores of men in this park. Then, passing through Chinatown, she returns to the Bowery and heads uptown, pausing whenever she recognizes a bum and giving him enough money for a meal, a drink, or a flop. Frequently, in addition to small change, she gives a bum a cake of soap. "*Please* use it, buddy," she says pleadingly. Here and there she gets out her flashlight and peers into a doorway. She pays particular attention to the drunken or exhausted bums who sleep in doorways, on loading platforms, and on sidewalks. She always tries to arouse them and stake them to flops. In warm weather, if they don't seem disposed to stir, she leaves them where they are. "A sidewalk is about as nice as a flophouse cot in the summertime," she says. "You may get up stiff, but you won't get up crummy." In the winter, however, she badgers them until they awaken. She punches them in the ribs with her umbrella and, if necessary, gets down on her knees and slaps their faces. "When a bum is sleeping off his load, you could saw off his leg and he wouldn't notice nothing," she says. Sometimes a bum who has been awakened by Mazie tries to take a poke at her. When this happens, she assumes a spraddle-legged stance, like a fencer, and jabs the air viciously with her umbrella. "Stand back," she cries, "or I'll put your eyes out." If a man is too weak, sodden, or spiritless to get up, Mazie grabs his elbows and heaves him to his feet. Holding him erect, she guides him to the nearest flophouse and pulls and pushes him up the stairs to the lobby. She pays the clerk for the man's lodging (thirty cents is the customary price) and insists on his having at least two blankets. Then, with the help of the clerk or the bouncer, she takes off the man's shoes, unbuttons his collar, loosens his belt, and puts him to bed with his clothes on. This is usually a tumultuous process, and sometimes many of the lodgers are awakened. They stick their heads out of the doors of their cubicles. " It's Mazie! " they shout. " Hello, Mazie! " Now and then an emotional bum will walk out in his underwear and insist on shaking Mazie's hand. " God bless you, Mazie, old girl! " he will cry. Mazie does not approve of such antics. " Go back to bed, you old goat," she says. If she is acquainted with the clerk and trusts him, she leaves some change with him and asks that it be given to the bum when he wakes up. Flophouses are for-men-only establishments, and Mazie is the only female who has ever crossed the threshold of many of them.

At least a couple of times a week, Mazie finds injured men lying in the street. On these occasions she telephones Police Headquarters and asks for an ambulance from Gouverneur or Beekman Street, the hospitals which take care of most Bowery cases. She knows many of the drivers from these hospitals by name and orders them around. Police say she summons more ambulances than any other private citizen in town, and she is proud of this. " I don't over-do it," she says. " Unless a man is all stove-up and bloody, I don't put in a call, but if I had my way, the wagons would be rolling all night long. There's hardly a bum on the Bowery who don't belong in a hospital."

On her walk, Mazie usually tries to steer clear of other well-known nocturnal Bowery characters. Among these are the Widow Woman and the Crybaby. The Crybaby is an old mission bum who sits on the curb for hours with his feet in the gutter, sobbing brokenly. Once Mazie nudged him on the shoulder and asked, " What's the matter with you? " " I committed the unforgivable sin," he said. Mazie asked him what the sin consisted of, and he began a theological description of it which she didn't understand and which she interrupted after a few minutes, remarking, " Hell, Crybaby, you didn't commit no sin. You just prob'ly got the stomach ulsters." The Widow Woman is a bent, whining crone who wears a mourning veil, a Queen Mary hat, and a rusty black coat, and comes hobbling down the Bowery around midnight giving bums little slips of paper on which are scribbled such statements as " God is love " and " The fires of Hell will burn forever." Mazie is afraid of her. " The Widow Woman gives me the creeps," she says. " She walks like a woman and she dresses like a woman, but when she talks I get the feeling that she's a man."

Most nights, before going home to bed, which is usually around two o'clock, Mazie makes brief stops in several saloons and all-night restaurants. She does not mind the reek of stale beer, greasy cabbage, and disinfectant in them. " After you been around the Bowery a few years, your nose gets all wore out," she says. She goes into these places not to eat or drink but to gossip with bartenders and counter-men and to listen to the conversation of drunken bums. She has found that bums do not talk much about sex, sports, politics, or busi-ness, the normal saloon topics. She says most of them are far too undernourished to have any interest in sex. They talk, instead, about what big shots they were before they hit the Bowery. Although their stories fascinate her, Mazie is generally cynical. " To hear them tell it," she says, " all the bums on the Bowery were knocking off millions down in Wall Street when they were young, else they were senators, else they were the general manager of something real big, but, poor fellers, the most of them they wasn't ever nothing but drunks."

Reveries over Childhood

W. B. Yeats

One day some one spoke to me of the voice of conscience, and as I brooded over the phrase I came to think that my soul, because I did not hear an articulate voice, was lost. I had some wretched days until being alone with one of my aunts I heard a whisper in my ear, " What a tease you are! " At first I thought my aunt must have spoken, but when I found she had not, I concluded it was the voice of my conscience and was happy again. From that day the voice has come to me at moments of crisis, but now it is a voice in my head that is sudden and startling. It does not tell me what to do, but often reproves me. It will say perhaps, " That is unjust " of some thought; and once when I complained that a prayer had not been heard, it said, " You have been helped." I had a little flagstaff in front of the house and a red flag with the Union Jack in the corner. Every night I pulled my flag down and folded it up and laid it on a shelf in my bedroom, and one morning before breakfast I found it, though I knew I had folded it up the night before, knotted round the bottom of the flag-

REVERIES OVER CHILDHOOD: From *Reveries* by W. B. Yeats. Copyright 1916 by The Macmillan Company and used with their permission.

staff so that it was touching the grass. I must have heard the servants talking of the faeries, for I concluded at once that a faery had tied those four knots and from then on believed that one had whispered in my ear. I have been told, though I do not remember it myself, that I saw, whether once or many times I do not know, a supernatural bird in the corner of the room. Once too I was driving with my grandmother a little after dark close to the Channel that runs for some five miles from Sligo to the sea, and my grandmother showed me the red light of an outward-bound steamer and told me that my grandfather was on board, and that night in my sleep I screamed out and described the steamer's wreck. The next morning my grandfather arrived on a blind horse found for him by grateful passengers. He had, as I remember the story, been asleep when the Captain aroused him to say they were going on the rocks. He said, " Have you tried sail on her? " and judging from some answer that the captain was demoralised, took over the command and, when the ship could not be saved, got the crew and passengers into the boats. His own boat was upset and he saved himself and some others by swimming; some women had drifted ashore, buoyed up by their crinolines. " I was not so much afraid of the sea as of that terrible man with his oar," was the comment of a schoolmaster who was among the survivors. Eight men were, however, drowned and my grandfather suffered from that memory at intervals all his life, and if asked to read family prayers never read anything but the shipwreck of St. Paul.

I remember the dogs more clearly than any one except my grandfather and grandmother. The black hairy one had no tail because it had been sliced off, if I was told the truth, by a railway train. I think I followed at their heels more than they did at mine, and that their journeys ended at a rabbit-warren behind the garden; and sometimes they had savage fights, the black hairy dog, being well protected by its hair, suffering least. I can remember one so savage that the white dog would not take his teeth out of the black dog's hair till the coachman hung them over the side of a water-butt, one outside and one in the water. My grandmother once told the coachman to cut the hair like a lion's hair and, after a long consultation with the stable-boy, he cut it all over the head and shoulders and left it on the lower part of the body. The dog disappeared for a few days, and I did not doubt that its heart was broken.

There was a large garden behind the house, full of apple trees, with flower-beds and grass-plots in the centre, and two figureheads of ships, one among the strawberry plants under a wall covered with fruit trees and one among the flowers. The one among the flowers was a white lady in flowing robes, while the other, a stalwart man in uniform, had been taken from a three-masted ship of my grandfather's called the *Russia,* and there was a belief among the servants that the stalwart man represented the Tsar and had been presented by the Tsar himself. The avenue, or as they say in England the drive, that went from the hall door through a clump of big trees to an insignificant gate and a road bordered by broken and dirty cottages, was but two or three hundred yards, and I often thought it should have been made to wind more, for I judged people's social importance mainly by the length of their avenues. This idea may have come from the stable-boy, for he was my principal friend. He had a book of Orange rhymes, and the days when we read them together in the hay-loft gave me the pleasure of rhyme for the first time. Later on I can remember being told, when there was a rumour of a Fenian rising, that rifles had been served out to the Orangemen; and presently, when I had begun to dream of my future life, I thought I would like to die fighting like the Fenians. I was to build a very fast and beautiful ship and to have under my command a company of young men who were always to be in training like athletes and so become as brave and handsome as the young men in the story-books, and there was to be a big battle on the sea-shore near Rosses and I was to be killed. I collected little bits of wood and piled them in the corner of the yard, and there was an old rotten log in a distant field I often went to look at because I thought it would go a long way in the making of the ship. All my dreams were of ships; and one day a sea-captain who had come to dine with my grandfather put a hand on each side of my head and lifted me up to show me Africa, and another day a sea-captain pointed to the smoke from the pern mill on the quays rising up beyond the trees of the lawn, as though it came from a mountain, and asked me if Ben Bulben was a burning mountain.

Once every few months I used to go to Rosses Point or Ballisodare to see another little boy, who had a piebald pony that had once been in a circus and sometimes forgot where it was and went round and round. He was George Middleton, son of my great-uncle William Middleton. Old Middleton had bought land, then believed a safe investment, at Ballisodare and at Rosses, and spent the winter at Ballisodare and the summer at Rosses. The Middleton and Pollexfen flour mills were at Ballisodare, and a great salmon weir, rapids and a waterfall, but it was more often at Rosses that I saw my cousin. We rowed in the river-mouth or were taken sailing in a heavy slow schooner yacht or in a big ship's boat that had been rigged and decked. There were great cellars under the house, for it had been a smuggler's house a hundred years before, and sometimes three loud raps would come upon the drawing-room window at sun-down, setting all the dogs barking: some dead smuggler giving his accustomed signal. One night I heard them very distinctly and my cousins often heard them, and later on my sister. A pilot had told me that, after dreaming three times of a treasure buried in my uncle's garden, he had climbed the wall in the middle of the night and begun to dig but grew disheartened " because there was so much earth." I told somebody what he had said and was told that it was well he did not find it, for it was guarded by a spirit that looked like a flat iron. At Ballisodare there was a cleft among the rocks that I passed with terror because I believed that a murderous monster lived there that made a buzzing sound like a bee.

It was through the Middletons perhaps that I got my interest in country stories, and certainly the first faery stories that I heard were in the cottages about their houses. The Middletons took the nearest for friends and were always in and out of the cottages of pilots and of tenants. They were practical, always doing something with their hands, making boats, feeding chickens, and without ambition. One of them had designed a steamer many years before my birth and, long after I had grown to manhood, one could hear it — it had some sort of obsolete engine — many miles off wheezing in the Channel like an asthmatic person. It had been built on the lake and dragged through the town by many horses, stopping before the windows where my mother was learning her lessons, and plunging the whole school into candle-light for five days, and was still patched and repatched mainly because it was believed to be a bringer of good luck. It had been called after the betrothed of its builder *Janet,* long corrupted into the more familiar *Jennet,* and the betrothed died in my youth, having passed her eightieth year and been her husband's plague because of the violence of her temper. Another Middleton who was but a year or two older than myself used to shock me by running after hens to know by their feel if they were on the point of dropping an egg. They let their houses decay and the glass fall from the windows of their greenhouses, but one among them at any rate had the second sight. They were liked but had not the pride and reserve, the sense of decorum and order, the instinctive playing before themselves that belongs to those who strike the popular imagination.

Sometimes my grandmother would bring me to see some old Sligo gentlewoman whose garden ran down to the river, ending there in a low wall full of wallflowers, and I would sit up upon my chair, very bored, while my elders ate their seed-cake and drank their sherry. My walks with the servants were more interesting; sometimes we would pass a little fat girl and a servant persuaded me to write her a love-letter, and the next time she passed she put her tongue out. But it was the servants' stories that interested me. At such and such a corner a man had got a shilling from a drill sergeant by standing in a barrel and had then rolled out of it and shown his crippled legs. And in such and such a house an old woman had hid herself under the bed of her guests, an officer and his wife, and on hearing them abuse her beaten them with a broomstick. All the well-known families had their grotesque or tragic or romantic legends, and I often said to myself how terrible it would be to go away and die where nobody would know my story. Years afterwards, when I was ten or twelve years old and in London, I would remember Sligo with tears, and when I began to write, it was there I hoped to find my audience. Next to Merville where I lived, was another tree-surrounded house where I sometimes went to see a little boy who stayed there occasionally with his grandmother, whose name I forget and who seemed to me kind and friendly, though when I went to see her in my thirteenth or fourteenth year I discovered that she only cared for very little boys. When the visitors called I hid in the hay-loft and lay hidden behind the great heap of hay while a servant was calling my name in the yard.

I do not know how old I was (for all these events seem at the same distance) when I was made drunk. I had been out yachting with an uncle and my cousins and it had come on very rough. I had lain on deck between the mast and the bowsprit and a wave had burst over me and I had seen green water over my head. I was very proud and very wet. When we got into Rosses again, I was dressed up in an older boy's clothes so that the trousers came down below my boots and a pilot gave me a little raw whiskey. I drove home on an outside car and was so pleased with the strange state in which I found myself that for all my uncle could do, I cried to every passer-by that I was drunk, and went on crying it through the town and everywhere until I was put to bed by my grandmother and given something to drink that tasted of black currants and so fell asleep.

Il Plœ:r dã mõ Kœ:r

Hortense Calisher

I was taught to speak French *with* tears. It was not I who wept, or the other girls in my high-school class, but the poet Verlaine — the one who wrote: " Il plœ:r dã mõ kœ:r." Inside forty slack American mouths, he wept phonetically for almost a semester. During this time, we were not taught a word of French grammar or meaning — only the International Phonetic Alphabet, the sounds the symbols stood for, and Verlaine translated into them. We could not even pick up the celebrated pen of our aunt. But by the time Verlaine and our teacher Mlle. Girard had finished with us, we were indeed ready to pick it up, and in the most classically passionate accents this side of the Comédie Française.

Mlle. Girard achieved her feat in this way. On the very first morning, she explained to us that French could never be spoken properly by us Anglo-Saxons unless we learned to reanimate those muscles of the face, throat, *poitrine* that we possessed — even as the French — but did not use. Ours, she said, was a speech almost without lilt, spoken on a dead level of intonation, " like a sobway train."

" Like this," she said, letting her jaw loll idiotically and choosing the most American subject she could find: " Ay wahnt sahm ay-iss cream." French, on the other hand, was a language *passionné* and *spirituel,* of vowels struck without pedal, of " l "s made with a sprightly tongue tip — a sound altogether unlike our " l," which we made with our tongues plopping in our mouths. By her manner, she implied that all sorts of national differences might be assumed from this, although she could not take the time to pursue them.

She placed a wiry thumb and forefinger, gray with chalk dust, on either side of her mouth. " It is these muscles 'ere I shall teach you to use," she said. (If that early we had been trained to think in phonetic symbols, we would have known that what she had actually said was " mœslz.") When she removed her hand, we saw that she had two little, active, wrinkling pouches, one on either side of her mouth. In the ensuing weeks I often wondered whether all French people had them, and we would get them, too. Perhaps only youthful body tone saved us, as, morning after morning, she went among us pinching and poking our lips into grimaces and compelling sudden ventriloquisms from our astonished sinuses.

IL PLŒ:R DÃ MÕ KŒ:R: Permission the author, © 1956 *The New Yorker* Magazine, Inc.

As a final coup, she taught us the classic " r." " Demoiselles," she said, " this is an *élégance* almost impossible for Americans, but you are a special class — I think you may do it." By this time, I think she had almost convinced herself that she had effected somatic changes in our Anglo-Saxonism. " *C'est produit*," she said, imparting the knowledge to us in a whisper, " by vibr-rating the uvula! "

During the next week, we sat there, like forty purring Renaults, vibrating our uvulas.

Enfin came Verlaine, with his tears. As a supreme exercise, we were to learn to declaim a poem by one of the famous harmonists of France, and we were to do it entirely by ear. (At this time, we knew the meaning of not one word except " *ici!*," with which, carefully admonished to chirp " œp, not down!," we had been taught to answer the roll.) Years later, when I could *read* French, I came upon the poem in its natural state. To my surprise, it looked like this:

> Il pleure dans mon cœur
> Comme il pleut sur la ville.
> Quelle est cette langueur
> Qui pénètre mon cœur?
>
> O bruit doux de la pluie
> Par terre . . .

And so on. But the way it is engraved on my heart, my ear, and my uvula is something else again. As hour after hour, palm to breast, wrist to brow, we moaned like a bevy of Ulalumes, making the exquisite distinction between " *pleure* " and " *pleut*," sounding our " r " like cat women, and dropping " l "s liquid as bulbuls, what we saw in our mind's eye was this:

> il plœːrə dã mõ kœːr
> kɔm il pl∅ syr lɑ vil
> kɛl ɛ sɛtə lãgœːr
> ki penɛtrə mõ kœːr
>
> o bryi du də lɑ plyi
> pɑr teːr . . .

And *so* on.

Late in the term, Mme. Cécile Sorel paid New York a visit, and Mlle. Girard took us to see her in " La Dame aux Camélias." Sorel's tea gowns and our own romantic sensibilities helped us to get some of her phthisic story. But what we marvelled at most was that she sounded exactly like us.

L'envoi comes somewhat late — twenty years later — but, like the tragic flaw of the Greeks, what Mlle. G. had planted so irrevocably was bound to show up in a last act somewhere. I went to France.

During the interim, I had resigned myself to the fact that although I had " had " French so intensively — for Mlle. G. had continued to be just as exacting all the way through grammar, *dictée,* and the rest of it — I still did not seem to " have " it. In college, my accent had earned me a brief eminence, but, of course, we did not spend much time *speaking* French, this being regarded as a frivolous addiction, the pursuit of which had best be left to the Berlitz people, or to tacky parlor groups presided over by stranded foreign widows in need of funds. As for vocabulary or idiom, I stood with Racine on my right hand and Rimbaud on my left — a *cordon bleu* cook who had never been taught how to boil an egg. Across the water, there was presumably a nation, *obscurcie de miasmes humains,* that used its own speech for purposes of asking the way to the bathroom, paying off porters, and going shopping, but for me the language remained the vehicle of de Vigny, Lamartine, and Hugo, and France a murmurous orchestral country where the *cieux* were full of *clarté,* the oceans sunk in *ombres profondes,* and where the most useful verbs were *souffler* and *gémir.*

On my occasional encounters with French visitors, I would apologize, in a few choicely carved phrases that always brought compliments, for being out of practice, after which I retired — into English if *they* had *it,* into the next room if they hadn't. Still, when I sailed, it was with hope — based on the famous accent — that in France I would somehow speak French. If I had only known, it would have been far better to go, as an underprivileged friend of mine did, armed with the one phrase her husband had taught her — *" Au secours! "*

Arriving at my small hotel in Paris, I was met by the owner, M. Lampacher, who addressed me in arrogantly correct English. When we had finished our arrangements in that language, I took the plunge. *" Merci! "* I said. It came out just lovely, the " r " like treacle, the " ci " not down but œp.

" Ah, Madame! " he said. " You speak French."

I gave him the visitors' routine.

" You mock, Madame. You have the accent *absolument pur."*

The next morning, I left the hotel early for a walk around Paris. I had not been able to understand the boy who brought me breakfast, but no doubt he was from the provinces. Hoping that I would not encounter too many people from the provinces, I set out. I tramped for miles, afloat upon the first beatific daze of tourism. One by one, to sounds as of northern lights popping and sunken cathedrals emerging, all the postcards were coming true, and it was not until I was returning on the bus from Chaillot that, blinking, I listened for the first time that day.

Two women opposite me were talking; from their glances, directed at my plastic rain boots, they were talking about me. I was piqued at their apparent assumption that I would not understand them. A moment later, listening with closed eyes, I was glad that they could not be aware of the very odd way in which I was not understanding them. For what I was hearing went something like this: "rəgard lamerikɛn se kautʃu sekõvnabl sa nɛspa purlãsãbl õ pøvwarlesulje"

"ɑ ɛl nəsõpavremã ʃik lezamerikɛn ʃakynrəsãblalotr"

"ɑ wi [Pause] tykonɛ mari la fijœl də mõ dəmi frɛr ãdre səlwi [or sɛl] avɛk ləbuk tylarãkõtre ʃemwa aloːr lœdi swaːr ɛl [or il] ɑ fɛt yn foskuʃ"

Hours later, in my room, with the help of the dictionary and Mlle. G's. training in *dictée,* I pieced together what they had said. It seemed to have been roughly this: " *Regarde, l'Américaine, ses caoutchoucs. C'est convenable, ça, n'est-ce-pas, pour l'ensemble. On peut voir les souliers."*

" *Ah, elles ne sont pas vraiment chics, les Américaines. Chacune ressemble à l'autre."*

" *Ah, oui. [Pause] Tu connais Marie, la filleule de mon demi-frère André — celui* [or *celle*] *avec le bouc. Tu l'as rencontré chez moi. Alors, lundi soir, elle* [or *il*] *a fait une fausse couche!* "

One of them, then, had thought my boots convenient for the ensemble, since one could see the shoes; the other had commented on the lack of real chic among American women, who all resembled one another. Digressing, they had gone on to speak of Marie, the goddaughter of a stepbrother, " the one with the *bouc.* You have met him [or her, since one could not tell from the construction] at my house." Either he or Marie had made a false couch, whatever that was.

The latter I could not find in the dictionary at all. " *Bouc* " I at first recalled as " *banc* " — either André or Marie had some kind of bench, then, or pew. I had just about decided that André had a seat in the Chamber of Deputies and had made some kind of political mistake, when it occurred to me that the word had been " *bouc* " — goatee — which almost certainly meant André. What had he done? Or Marie? What the hell did it mean " to make a false couch "?

I sat for the good part of an hour, freely associating — really, now, the goddaughter of a stepbrother! When I could bear it no longer, I rang up an American friend who had lived in Paris for some years, with whom I was to lunch the next day.

" Oh, yes, how are you? " said Ann.

"Dead tired, actually," I said, "and I've had a slight shock. Listen, it seems I can't speak French after all. Will you translate something?"

"Sure."

"What does to '*faire une fausse couche*' mean?"

"Honey!" said Ann.

"What?"

"Where are you, dear?" she said, in a low voice. "At a doctor's?"

"No, for God's sake, I'm at the hotel. What's the matter with you? You're as bad as the dictionary."

"Nothing's the matter with *me*," said Ann. "The phrase just means 'to have a miscarriage,' that's all."

"Ohhh," I said. "Then it was Marie after all. Poor Marie."

"*Are* you all right?"

"Oh, I'm fine," I said. "Just fine. And thanks. I'll see you tomorrow."

I went to bed early, assuring myself that what I had was merely disembarkation jitters (what would the psychologists call it — transliteration syndrome?), which would disappear overnight. Otherwise it was going to be very troublesome having to retire from every conversation to work it out in symbols.

A month went by, and the syndrome had not disappeared. Now and then, it was true, the more familiar nouns and verbs did make their way straight to my brain, bypassing the tangled intermediaries of my ear and the International Phonetic Alphabet. Occasionally, I was able to pick up an unpoetically useful phrase: to buy a brassière you asked for "something to hold up the gorge with;" the French said "Couci-couça" (never "*Comme ci, comme ça*") and, when they wanted to say "I don't know," turned up their palms and said "Schpuh." But meanwhile, my accent, fed by the lilt of true French, altogether outsoared the shadow of my night. When I did dare the phrases prepared carefully in my room for the eventualities of the day, they fell so superbly that any French vis-à-vis immediately dropped all thought of giving me a handicap and addressed me in the native argot, at the native rate — leaving me struck dumb.

New Year's Eve was my last night in Paris. I had planned to fly to London to start the new year with telephones, parties, the wireless, conversation, in a wild blaze of unrestricted communication. But the airport had informed me that no planes were flying the Channel, or perhaps anywhere, for the next twenty-four hours, New Year's Eve being the one night on which the pilots were traditionally "allowed" to get drunk. At least, it *seemed* to me that I had been so informed, but perhaps I libel, for by now my passion for accurately understanding what was said to me was dead. All my pockets and purses were full of paper scraps of decoding, set down in vowel-hallucinated corners while my lips moved grotesquely, and it seemed to me that, if left alone here any longer, I would end by having composed at random a phonetic variorum for France.

In a small, family-run café around the corner from my hotel, where I had often eaten alone, I ordered dinner, successive *cafés filtres,* and repeated doses of marc. Tonight, at the elegiac opening of the new year, it was " allowed " — for pilots and the warped failures of educational snobbism — to get drunk. Outside, it was raining, or weeping; in my heart, it was doing both.

Presently, I was the only customer at any of the zinc tables. Opposite, in a corner, the *grand-père* of the family of owners lit a Gauloise and regarded me with the privileged stare of the elderly. He was the only one there who seemed aware that I existed; for the others I had the invisibility of the foreigner who cannot " speak " — next door to that of a child, I mused, except for the adult password of money in the pocket. The old man's daughter, or daughter-in-law, a dark woman with a gall-bladder complexion and temperament, had served me obliquely and retired to the kitchen, from which she emerged now and then to speak sourly to her husband, a capped man, better-looking than she, who ignored her, lounging at the bar like a customer. I should have liked to know whether her sourness was in her words as well as her manner, and whether his lordliness was something personal between them or only the authority of the French male, but their harsh gutturals, so far from the sugarplum sounds I had been trained to that they did not even dissolve into phonetics, went by me like the crude blue smoke of the Gauloise. A girl of about fourteen — their daughter, I thought — was tending bar and deflecting the remarks of the customers with a petted, precocious insouciance. Now and then, her parents addressed remarks, either to her or to the men at the bar, that seemed to have the sharpness of reprimand, but I could not be sure; to my eye the gaiety of the men toward the young girl had a certain avuncular decorum that made the scene pleasant and tender to watch. In my own country, I loved to listen at bars, where the human scene was often arrested as it is in those genre paintings whose deceptively simple contours must be approached with all one's knowledge of the period, and it saddened me not to be able to savor those nuances here.

I lit a Gauloise, too, with a flourish that the old man, who nodded stiffly, must have taken for a salute. And why not? Pantomime was all that was left to me. Or money. To hell with my perfectionist urge to understand; I must resign myself to being no different from those summer thousands who jammed the ocean every June, to whom Europe was merely a montage of their own sensations, a glamorous old phoenix that rose seasonally, just for them. On impulse, I mimed an invitation to the old man to join me in a marc. On second thought, I signalled for marc for everybody in the house.

"To the new year!" I said, in French, waving my glass at the old man. Inside my brain, my monitor tapped his worried finger — did "*nouvelle*" come before or after "*année*" in such cases, and wasn't the accent a little "ice cream"? I drowned him, in another marc.

Across the room from me, the old man's smile faded in and out like the Cheshire cat's; I was not at all surprised when it spoke, in words I seemed to understand, inquiring politely as to my purpose in Paris. I was here on a scholarship, I replied. I was a writer. ("*Ecrivain? Romancier?*" asked my monitor faintly.)

"Ah," said the old man. "I am familiar with one of your writers. Père Le Buc."

"Père Le Buc?" I shook my head sadly. "I regret, but it is not known to me, the work of the Father Le Buc."

"*Pas un homme!*" he said. "*Une femme! Une femme qui s' appelle Père Le Buc!*"

My monitor raised his head for one last time. "Pɛrləbyk!" he chirped desperately. "Pɛrləbyk!"

I listened. "Oh, my God," I said then. "Of course. That is how it would be. Pearl Buck!"

"*Mais oui,*" said the old man, beaming and raising his glass. "Pɛrləbyk!"

At the bar, the loungers, thinking we were exchanging some toast, raised their own glasses in courteous imitation. "Pɛrləbyk!" they said, politely. "Pɛrləbyk!"

I raised mine. "*Il pleure,*" I began, "*il pleure dans mon cœur comme il pleut. . . .*"

Before the evening was over, I had given them quite a selection: from Verlaine, from Heredia's "Les Trophées," from Baudelaire's poem on a painting by Delacroix, from de Musset's "R-r-ra-ppelle-toi!" As a final tribute, I gave them certain stanzas from Hugo's "L'Expiation" — the ones that begin "*Waterloo! Waterloo! Waterloo! Morne plaine!*" And in between, raised or lowered by a new faith that was not all brandy, into an air freed of cuneiform at last — I spoke French.

Making my way home afterward, along the dark stretches of the Rue du Bac, I reflected that to learn a language outside its native habitat you must really believe that the other country exists — in its humdrum, its winter self. Could I remember to stay there now —

down in that lower-case world in which stairs creaked, cops yelled, in which women bought brassières and sometimes made the false couch?

The door of my hotel was locked. I rang, and M. Lampacher admitted me. He snapped on the stair light, economically timed to go out again in a matter of seconds, and watched me as I mounted the stairs with the aid of the banister.

" Off bright and early, hmm? " he said sleepily, in French. " Well, good night, Madame. Hope you had a good time here."

I turned, wanting to answer him properly, to answer them all. At that moment, the light went off, perhaps to reinforce forever my faith in the mundanity of France.

" *Ah, ça va, ça va!* " I said strongly, into the dark. " Couci-couça. Schpuh."

HANDBOOK OF GRAMMAR, PUNCTUATION, AND MECHANICS

The Parts of Speech

We normally communicate our thoughts, not through words as isolated units of meaning, but through words as elements woven together to make up a connected discourse. We can, it is true, call out a single word like " Fire! " or " Snake! " and convey meaning. The situation out of which we shout our warnings and the quality of excitement in the voice itself may go far to make our meaning quite specific: " The house is on fire " or " A snake is coiled in the path." But the use of single words to convey meaning is special, even in spoken English. Certainly in written English words function normally as *parts of speech* in a connected discourse.

There are, to be sure, words and phrases like *oh, alas, ouch,* and *good gracious* that are used independently of the sentence as *direct* expressions of emotion. We call such words **interjections,** and this name suggests the way in which they are used: thrown abruptly (interjected) into the discourse.

> *Good heavens!* You don't mean that he has already bought it?
>
> *Ouch!* That nearly took my head off.

So much for interjections. The other seven parts of speech that we conventionally recognize in English — nouns, pronouns, verbs, adjectives, adverbs, prepositions, and conjunctions — are generally used in a pattern of meaning in which they have special functions to perform.

Let us consider first the special functions performed by the words that make up this brief bit of connected discourse:

> Birds fly.

Here we have the basic unit of composition, a sentence, a thought expressed through a predication. We have something named and an assertion made about the thing that was named; i.e., a subject (*birds*) and a predicate (*fly*).

1. Substantives

(Substantive is a general term that includes not only nouns, but all words or groups of words that substitute for nouns.)

1.1 Nouns

Birds is a noun; that is, a word that names something.

1.2 Pronouns and other noun substitutes

a. Pronouns are words that stand for nouns and may be substituted for them.

> Most birds fly. *They* vary, however, in techniques of flight.
> *We* always enjoy watching *them.*

b. Adjectives (see below) are sometimes used "substantively," that is, as substitutes for nouns.

> We saw red and yellow flowers. The *red* were poppies,
> and the *yellow,* buttercups.

c. Other noun substitutes. Phrases, clauses, and certain forms of the verb may also be used as nouns. (See pages 767–68, 771.)

2. Modifiers

(Modifiers — adjectives, adverbs, and phrases or clauses that serve the same functions — describe or limit several other parts of speech.)

2.1 Adjectives

Adjectives modify (describe or limit) substantives.

> *Most* birds fly.
> *Brilliant* birds flew past.
> *Any* bird to be seen in *this* region is *migratory.*
> *A small gray* bird alighted on the bough. It was *noisy.*

2.2 Adverbs

Adverbs modify verbs and other modifiers (adjectives and other adverbs) .

> Birds fly *swiftly.*
> A *very* large bird flew toward us.
> The bird flew *most erratically.*

3. Verbs

The words *fly* and *flew* are verbs. A verb is a word that asserts action, state, or being. (A verb which asserts being often " links " its subject to a predicate adjective or noun. See page 755.)

4. Connectives

(Connectives relate one part of a sentence — a word, phrase, or clause — to another part of the sentence.) There are two kinds of connectives — prepositions and conjunctions.

4.1 Prepositions

A preposition relates a substantive to some other word in the sentence.

> The bird flew *to* the river.
> The birds flew *over* my head.
> The bird *in* the tree was gray.

4.2 Conjunctions

A conjunction links one word, or group of words, with another.

> The mockingbird *and* the butcherbird look alike.
> The bird flew off, *for* I had made a good deal of noise.
> *When* the stick broke under my foot, the bird sprang from her perch.

The words *and* and *for* are co-ordinating conjunctions. *When* is a subordinating conjunction; that is, it makes the clause it introduces subordinate to the main clause of the sentence. "When the stick broke under my foot" is an adverbial modifier which times the action of the bird. It is subordinate to "the bird sprang from her perch."

Each of these parts of speech will be treated in more detail at a later point in this Handbook. But before going further there are two general statements to be made about the parts of speech. In the first place, we should note that at different times the same words may function as different parts of speech. What part of speech we are to call a word will depend upon what it does in the sentence in question.

> On the steeple stood a large gilt *cross*. [noun]
> The child was tired and *cross*. [adjective]
> *Cross* the street here. [verb]

In the second place English has various ways of converting one part of speech into another. For example, we can make the noun *bird* function like an adjective by adding *'s*, thus:

> The *bird's* song was *beautiful*.

We call *bird's* a **possessive** and, as we shall see a little later, may regard it as a **case** of the noun; yet *bird's* functions to modify *song* quite as much as the adjective *beautiful*. Conversely, we can turn an adjective into a noun by making it the subject of the verb.

> The *great* have cause to tremble.
> The *beautiful* have nothing to fear but time.

Even the verb can be turned into a kind of noun. The gerund here is a verbal noun:

> *Flying* is delightful.

Such changes as are effected by adding *'s* to a noun or *–ing* to a verb are called **inflectional** changes. They represent only one, and this not even the most important, of the resources that give English its richness and subtlety of expression. Although English was once, like Latin or German, a highly inflected language, to-day it has lost most of its inflections. It has compensated for their loss by laying special stress upon word order. It makes all the difference in meaning whether we write:

> The ball struck the boy.
> The boy struck the ball.

The stress upon word order in English presents a real challenge to the student, for there are plenty of opportunities to trip oneself up in confused meanings. But the arrangement of the words and word groups in composition allows a good deal of scope for taste and imagination, and for the expression of the writer's personality.

---

1. Substantives

1.1 The Noun

A noun, as we have said, is the name of something: of a living creature (*man, fox*), of a thing (*tree, stone*), of a quality (*whiteness, virtue*), or of a collection (*army, mob*). These are **common** nouns. Nouns that name specific persons, places, or things are called **proper** nouns; e.g., *Judith, Montana, February*. (If you ever have trouble deciding whether or not a word is a noun, use this rule of thumb: A noun is any word that can be immediately preceded by some such word as *the, my,* or *each.*

1.1a *Number*

Nouns are either **singular** or **plural.** The rule for forming the plural of most nouns is simple: *the plural is formed by adding –s.*

EXCEPTIONS AND PROBLEMS

(1) In this first group are those nouns which add –s to form the plural but which have some further point of complication.

Nouns that end in some variety of s-like sound form the plural by adding an extra syllable, pronounced *ez.* (If the extra syllable were not added, the added –s could not be heard.)

> *house, houses   edge, edges   batch, batches   mass, masses*
> *adze, adzes   torch, torches   ash, ashes   crash, crashes*

Nouns that end in –*y* preceded by a consonant form the plural by changing *y* to *i* and adding –*es* (not pronounced as an extra syllable) :

> *fly, flies   sky, skies   body, bodies*

But note that nouns ending in –*y* preceded by a vowel form their plurals regularly:

> *survey, surveys   tray, trays   monkey, monkeys   boy, boys*

Some nouns that end in –*o* preceded by a consonant form the plural by adding –*es* (not pronounced as an extra syllable) :

> *potato, potatoes   tomato, tomatoes   hero, heroes   Negro, Negroes*
> *echo, echoes   no, noes   veto, vetoes   tornado, tornadoes*
> *torpedo, torpedoes*

Some nouns ending in –*o* preceded by a consonant have both regular plurals and plurals ending in –*es:* e.g., *cargos, cargoes. Desperado, domino, hobo,* and *motto* also have both plurals.

Other nouns ending in –*o* preceded by a consonant (*avocado, quarto*) and all those ending in –*o* preceded by a vowel (*cameo, folio, studio*) form the plural regularly by adding –*s.*

Some nouns ending in –*f* or –*fe* form the plural by changing *f* to *v* and adding *es* (*s*). Thus we have *calf, calves; half, halves; knife, knives.* Other nouns of this group are *loaf, leaf, self, shelf,* and *thief.* To this list should be added nouns that are sometimes given plurals in *–ves* but may also have regular *–s* plurals: *hoof, scarf, staff,* and *wharf.* Other nouns in *–f* have only regular plurals.

(2) In the second group of exceptions are the *–n* plurals and the vowel-change plurals, remnants of the time when English was a rather fully inflected language.

> a. *child, children   ox, oxen   brother, brethren* (though *brothers* has now ousted *brethren* from everyday use)
>
> b. *man, men   woman, women   foot, feet   tooth, teeth   mouse, mice louse, lice   goose, geese*

(3) In the third group are nouns that have the *same* form for singular and plural. Most of these forms, like those in (2), are survivors from an earlier period of English; examples are *deer* and *sheep.* Some words, such as *fish, fowl,* and *horse,* have a regular plural but the singular form can also be used as a collective plural; i.e., twenty *fish,* two dozen *waterfowl,* a troop of *horse.*

The other subdivision of this group consists of nouns ending in *–s,* many of which were once regarded as plural but which today are frequently or always regarded as singular: *news, athletics.* Note that *scissors, shears, pliers, pants,* and *trousers* are also plural in form, but we frequently testify to our realization that such words refer to one thing by writing "a pair of scissors," "a pair of trousers," and so on.

(4) In this group are those compound words (frequently hyphenated) that run counter to the usual tendency to treat a compound as one word and add the sign of the plural at the end (*penny dreadfuls*). This group instead adds the sign of the plural to some *earlier* word in the group on the assumption that it is the important element. Thus we have:

> *sons-in-law   daughters-in-law   mothers-in-law   passers-by   poets laureate attorneys general* (though *attorney generals* has now also found a place in the dictionaries, a fact that testifies to the strong tendency to normalize such forms)

(5) In this group are words that have foreign plurals. Most of these words represent borrowings from either Greek or Latin. Some such words seem at the present time on the way to becoming normalized; both their original plural and the regular English plural are used. For example,

> *curriculums, curricula   focuses, foci   formulas, formulae*

Still others (and in more formal writing, all of the class just mentioned) retain the original Greek or Latin plural. The following brief scheme may be of some help in determining these plurals, particularly to the student who has had even a smattering of Latin or Greek.

SINGULAR	PLURAL	SINGULAR	PLURAL
alumn*a*	alumn*ae*	dat*um*	data
alumn*us*	alumn*i*	oas*is*	oas*es*
vort*ex*	vort*ices*	criter*ion*	criter*ia*

A few words from French likewise can be used either with a French or an English plural:

chapeau	*chapeaux*	*chapeaus*
beau	*beaux*	*beaus*

Of course the safest thing to do when in doubt about any plural is to consult your dictionary.

1.1b *Agreement in Number*

The two rules for agreement in number are simple enough:
(1) The subject of a sentence determines the number of the verb.
(2) A pronoun agrees in number with the noun to which it refers.

EXCEPTIONS AND PROBLEMS

The chief opportunities for confusion arise from the following situations:

(1) The use of collective nouns. Words like *audience, crowd, group, majority,* and so on, may be regarded either as a unit, in which case they are treated as singular, or as a number of individuals, in which case they are treated as plural:

The jury *was* out for just one hour. The jury rendered *its* verdict.
The jury *were* sharply divided into three factions. *They* were obviously excited.

But instead of using *jury* with a plural verb, many writers would prefer as clearer and closer to current idiom:

The *members of the jury* were sharply divided into three factions.

(2) Statements of measurements and amounts. In such statements a plural subject is properly followed by a singular verb. Thus:

Seventy-five millimeters *is* about three inches.
One hundred and thirty-five pounds *is* his proper weight.
Two plus two *is* four.

In the same way, closely associated groupings of nouns may be treated as a unit, particularly in less formal English:

Ham and eggs *is* his favorite breakfast.

(3) The use of pronouns such as *each, either, another, anyone, somebody, everybody,* and so on. These words are singular, though for many people they carry powerful suggestions of a plural meaning. In speaking we are very likely to use a plural pronoun with such words:

Everybody *chooses their* favorite dessert.

But in formal English, one must say or write:

Everybody *chooses his* favorite dessert.
Each of the students *is* responsible for *his* schedule.

Standard English accepts either singular *or* plural with *none,* and the fact that a word obviously derived from *one* (*no* plus *one*) can now be considered plural graphically testifies to the strength of the present tendency to regard such words as *everybody, anyone,* and *somebody* as having plural antecedents.

(4) Other situations likely to confuse the writer as to the correct number are:

a. A singular noun as subject joined to plural nouns by a linking verb such as *to be.*

Generosity *is* the height and the depth of his character.

In a sentence such as this, one must remember that a verb agrees with its subject, not its predicate noun (see page 755). Thus one would write:

The height and the depth of his character *are* generosity.

b. The antecedent of a relative clause.

Frank is one of those students who *have* really contributed something to the school. [Not " who *has* really contributed," for the antecedent of *who* is *students.*]
Frank is the only one of our students who *has* won a state-wide rally. [In this sentence the singular form *has* is correctly used, for the antecedent of *who* is *one.*]

c. The use of more than one subject when joined by *or* or *nor*. The verb agrees with the subject nearest to it, whether singular or plural:

> Either Jim or Bob *is* to blame.
> Neither Dad nor the twins nor Mary *is* saying a word.
> Neither you nor he *knows* the answer to that.

But:

> Neither Mary nor the twins *are* saying a word.
> Neither he nor you *know* the answer to that.

1.1c *Gender*

English, unlike some other languages, has natural gender, that is, nouns designating male creatures are masculine, nouns designating female creatures are feminine, and all other nouns are neuter. The meaning of the noun thus shows its gender. Certain nouns have separate masculine and feminine forms. The feminine is sometimes formed by adding the suffix *–ess.*

shepherd	shepherdess
actor	actress
tiger	tigress

Some of these *–ess* feminine forms are falling into disuse (*poetess, Negress*). Other variant forms are derived, along with the words themselves, from foreign languages:

masseur	masseuse
alumnus	alumna

Many of the other masculine-feminine pairs are completely different in form:

king	queen
gander	goose
ram	ewe
uncle	aunt
bull	cow
horse	mare
fox	vixen

EXCEPTIONS AND PROBLEMS

A number of neuter nouns are given masculine or feminine gender through personification. Thus, the sun is usually masculine, the moon, feminine. Winter tends to be masculine; spring, feminine.

One's country and one's university are feminine. A ship is always feminine. The rule would seem to be — though there is of course no formal rule of any sort — that if the writer does personify, strong and perhaps brutal things should be referred to as *he* and graceful and fostering things as *she*.

1.1d Case

Case is the inflectional form of a noun or pronoun that shows certain syntactical relationships (nominative, objective, or possessive). Nouns have only one inflectional variant to denote case; i.e., forms ending in *'s* or *'* to indicate possession. The rules for forming the possessive are:

(1) The possessive of words not ending in an *s* (or an *s*-like) sound is formed by adding *'s:*

> *men's* clothing   *boy's* cap   *brother-in-law's* automobile
> *King of England's* son

(Note that the last phrase is treated as if it were a hyphenated word such as *brother-in-law*.)

(2) The possessive of nouns ending in an *s* (or an *s*-like) sound, including therefore all regularly formed plurals, is formed by adding an apostrophe only.

> for *conscience'* sake   *boys'* caps   *horses'* bridles   Mr. *Jones'* barn
> the *Joneses'* pretensions

EXCEPTIONS AND PROBLEMS

Proper names of one syllable ending in an *s* (or an *s*-like) sound form their possessive by adding either *'s* or the apostrophe only.

> John *Keats'* poems   *Keats's* poems
> W. B. *Yeats'* works   *Yeats's* works

It should be noted that *of*-phrases are another way of showing possession. We may write " Hamlet's problems " or " the problems of Hamlet," " a mother's pride " or " the pride of a mother." The possessive form frequently sounds awkward when any notion of active ownership is remote. Thus we ordinarily use the *of*-phrase in such expressions as

> *the noise of the machine*   instead of   *the machine's noise*
> *the management of the hotel*   instead of   *the hotel's management*

But note that often phrases of time and measure are idiomatically expressed as possessives:

a year's pay   a stone's throw   a day's journey

The possessive form of *anybody else* is *anybody else's*. (Cf. *the King of England's son.*) So also with other indefinite pronouns combined with *else*.

Nobody else's purse was found.
The schedule was clearly *someone else's*.

1.2 The Pronoun

A pronoun is a word that stands for a noun. The noun for which it substitutes is called an **antecedent**. A pronoun agrees with its antecedent in number and gender. (In this connection, see also page 776.)

The *waitress* took no notice of John's frantically wagging *fingers*. *She* managed not to see *them*.

John and *I* started out together but *we* found it harder and harder to maintain contact.

1.2a *Personal Pronouns*

The personal pronoun has special forms to signify case, gender, and person. (There are three persons: the first, the speaker; the second, the person spoken to; and the third, the person or thing spoken about.) The personal pronoun and the present tense of the verb *to be* thus represent the only elaborate inflectional systems left in English; the problems in using personal pronouns center chiefly around case.

FIRST PERSON

CASE	SINGULAR	PLURAL
Nominative	I	we
Possessive	my, mine	our, ours
Objective	me	us

SECOND PERSON

CASE	SINGULAR	PLURAL
Nominative	you	you
Possessive	your, yours	your, yours
Objective	you	you

739

THIRD PERSON

CASE		SINGULAR		PLURAL
	Masculine	*Feminine*	*Neuter*	
Nominative	he	she	it	they
Possessive	his	her, hers	its	their, theirs
Objective	him	her	it	them

The possessive pronoun can be regarded as an adjective, when it is used before a noun. Certainly it has the force of an adjective, limiting the noun with which it is associated:

my hat   *her* cape   *our* house

The double forms *my, mine*   *our, ours*   *your, yours*   *her, hers* and *their, theirs*   are used as follows: If the possessive is used immediately before a noun, the first form is used; if the possessive is used alone, the second form is used.

> *My* thanks are due to you.
> The pleasure is *mine.*
> *Yours* is a finer specimen than *hers.*

One must take note also of the use in English of a combination of an *s*-possessive with an *of*-phrase. Consider such examples as:

a friend *of ours*   a book *of his*   friends *of my mother's*

These phrases are sometimes rationalized by grammarians as meaning " a friend of that group that are our friends," " a book from among his books," and so on. But this explanation will scarcely do for such an expression as " that nose of his." Perhaps expressions of this sort are best regarded as simply idiomatic.

The problem of whether to use the nominative or the objective case arises sometimes with pronouns. It does not arise with nouns, which change in form only for the possessive. With some oversimplification one can summarize the problem in a single rule: When pronouns are the subjects of verbs, they are in the nominative case; in all other instances, they are in the objective case.

> *I* ran last in the race.   [subject of verb]
> The ball struck *me.*   [object of verb]
> John gave *her* the book.   [indirect object of *gave;* book is the direct object]
> They all come *to him* in the end.   [object of the preposition *to*]
> It is *I,* or It's *me.*

EXCEPTIONS AND PROBLEMS

(1) With this last instance, however, we get into trouble. Though, most people, including well-educated people, actually do say " It's me " rather than " It is I," still the most formal English calls for " It is I," and even more insistently calls for:

> " This is *he* " rather than " This is *him*."
> " The winner is *he* " rather than " The winner is *him*."
> " That was *she* " rather than " That was *her*."

Because the vast majority of pronouns that come *after* the verb are properly in the objective case, there is a strong tendency to put *every* pronoun coming after the verb into the objective case. But the verb *to be* is a linking verb, and logically the items should be interchangeable; that is,

> " That is she " is equivalent to " She is that (person)."

Therefore the pronoun form ought to be *she* in both positions. Our somewhat too simple rule will have to be restated, then, as follows:

Rule: Pronouns that are the subjects of verbs or that are linked to the subject by the verb *to be* are in the nominative case; otherwise pronouns are in the objective case.

Even so, most people will say and write, except in the most formal context, " It is me." If the locution offends one's sense of logic, one might remember that the logical French write " *C'est moi*," not " *C'est je*."

(2) One further problem having to do with the case of pronouns may conveniently be taken up here, the problem of *whom*. The interrogative pronoun (see **1.2b**) *who* has for its possessive form *whose,* and for its objective, *whom*. (There are no special forms to distinguish gender or number.) Problems arise largely because *who,* as an interrogative, so frequently heads the sentence, and, by preceding the verb, may trick us into taking it for a nominative. Thus, we may be tempted to write

> *Who* did you give it to?

instead of

> *Whom* did you give it to? [COMPARE: Did you give it to *him?*]

Or we may be tempted to write

> *Who* did you see?

instead of

> *Whom* did you see? [COMPARE: Did you see *him?*]

Whom is also used as a relative pronoun (see page 743), and here again the abnormal position in which *whom* frequently occurs — before rather than after the verb — tends to be confusing:

> That man *whom* I saw was the thief.
> The person *whom* she addressed was large and florid.

A recent authority on grammar counsels that the form *whom* be abandoned in all writing and *who* used instead except when the word is used directly with a preposition, thus:

> About *whom* are you talking?

We are not prepared, however, to go so far in innovation. Granting the strong tendency to substitute *who* for *whom,* we recommend that *whom* be retained in all writing that makes any pretense at formality. With a little care the student ought to be able to use *whom* (*whomever, whomsoever*) correctly and without falling into the silly overcorrection of using the *–m* form where it is not called for, like the lady of more wealth than breeding who sought to wither a rival by observing: " I don't think you know *whom* I am."

A further caution on the who-whoever *pronouns:* When *who* and *whoever* occur in indirect questions, their case depends upon their function within the indirect question. Thus:

> He asked *who should be called.*

not

> He asked *whom should be called.*

For the question does not apply merely to the one word *who* but to the whole word group " who should be called." Similarly,

> Give the message to *whoever* comes for it.

not *whomever,* for the object of the preposition *to* is the whole word group " whoever comes for it."

To sum up the matter of case, the possessive presents no special problems and can be regarded as the conversion of a noun or pronoun into an adjective. The real difficulties with case are restricted to the handling of pronouns in the objective case, specifically to the use of the following words: *me, us, him, her, them, whom,* and *whomever.*

1.2b *Kinds of Pronouns*

(1) Personal pronouns have been discussed on pages 739–41.

(2) The interrogative pronouns are *who* (*whom, whose*), *which,* and *what.* As their name indicates, these pronouns ask questions:

Who is it?
Which is your dog?
What is he doing?

Or introduce indirect questions:

We never did learn *who* did it.

(3) Relative pronouns: *who, which,* and *that.* These pronouns modify their antecedents by means of the clauses which they introduce.

Charles, *who* was limping, came on slowly.
The tree, *which* had been so beautiful the day before, was now blackened by fire.
The tree *that* died was an elm.

Who refers usually to persons; *which,* usually to animals or things; *that,* to persons or things. When the meaning cannot be mistaken, the relative pronoun is sometimes altogether omitted.

The man *I saw* was blind.
The horse *I favored* came in last.

(4) Reflexive pronouns: *myself, ourselves, yourself, yourselves, himself, herself, itself,* and *themselves.*
These pronouns are used when the subject acts upon himself.

I hurt *myself.*
They tried hard to control *themselves.*

(Since all these reflexive pronouns except *himself* and *themselves* are formed from the possessive, or at least may be so interpreted, analogy tends to push the exceptions into the same pattern, and we get people incorrectly saying *hisself* for *himself,* and even *theirselves* for *themselves.*)

(5) Intensive pronouns (same as the reflexive in form): These pronouns are used to give emphasis. Thus:

I *myself* was the real culprit.
They *themselves* suffered most by their ill-advised action.

But do not substitute intensive pronouns for simple pronouns. Do not, for example, write:

Mary and *myself* walked to the park.
It pleased Ralph and *myself.*

743

(6) Indefinite pronouns: *anybody, anyone, anything, everybody, everyone, everything, nobody, nothing, one, somebody, someone, something.*

As the name indicates, this class of pronouns has no definite antecedent. The user either cannot or does not care to specify the antecedent.

> *Anybody* knows that this story is false.
> *Somebody* told me that Mary had moved away.
> *Nobody* came to the office.

EXCEPTIONS AND PROBLEMS

Some writers include among the indefinite pronouns words like *any, few,* and *neither.* Certainly these words often do function as substantives:

> I could not see *any.*
> *Few* indeed were present.

But they function primarily as adjectives:

> We could not see *any* ships on the horizon.
> *Few* steamers ever came our way.

We have, accordingly, preferred to class them as adjectives, reminding ourselves that almost any adjective can on occasion serve as a substitute for a noun:

> None but the *brave* deserves the *fair.*

For a similar reason, we have preferred to class *this* and *that,* not as " demonstrative pronouns," but as " demonstrative adjectives." (See page 745.)

2. Modifiers

2.1 The Adjective

Adjectives are words that modify (limit or describe) nouns or pronouns. An adjective normally appears directly before the substantive that it modifies:

> *Brilliant* birds flew past.

It may in some instances also appear directly after the substantive that it modifies:

> He called her *beautiful*.

Or it may be brought into relation with the substantive it modifies by a linking verb:

> The plumage of the birds was *brilliant*.
> The child looked *unhappy*.
> He seemed *tired*.

2.1a *Number*

Only two adjectives are inflected for number: the so-called demonstrative adjectives, *this, these; that, those.*

This tree is a red oak.
These oaks are of slow growth.
That peak in the distance is a mountain; *those* masses near it are clouds.

EXCEPTIONS AND PROBLEMS

Phrases like " that kind " and " this sort " sometimes beget confusion about the proper number. Since the general notion is vaguely plural, the writer may forget that a " sort " or a " kind " is a class, and hence singular. One should not write

> *These* sort of apples are good for cooking.

but

> *This* sort of apple is good for cooking.

One should not write

> *Those* kind of automobiles are expensive.

but

> *That* kind of automobile is expensive.

If one insists upon a plural noun, he may write

> *Automobiles* of that kind are expensive.

2.1b *Comparison*

Adjectives have three degrees of comparison: **positive, comparative,** and **superlative.** As these terms suggest, the positive degree expresses the quality, e.g., *fine, good, sweet;* the comparative degree asserts a greater degree of the quality than occurs in another instance, e.g., *finer* (than), *better* (than), *sweeter* (than); and the superlative, the greatest degree of the quality, e.g., *finest, best, sweetest*.

The comparative forms of our most often used adjectives turn out to be highly irregular:

good	better	best
bad	worse	worst
much, many	more	most

But most one- and two-syllable adjectives form the comparative degree by adding *–er* and the superlative degree by adding *–est*, to the positive form. Three-syllable adjectives form the comparative by prefixing *more* and the superlative by prefixing *most* to the positive form. (This method may also be used with some two-syllable, and even one-syllable, adjectives.) Thus some typical examples of the comparison of adjectives are

big	bigger	biggest
quick	quicker	quickest
happy	happier	happiest

or

happy	more happy	most happy
beautiful	more beautiful	most beautiful
comfortable	more comfortable	most comfortable

EXCEPTIONS AND PROBLEMS

(1) The *most* forms are not always and necessarily superlative. They may be employed simply as intensives. For example, " She was most charming " means that she was very charming and does not necessarily imply that she was the most charming of any specific group.

(2) The comparative degree implies a measuring of one thing against another; i.e., there are only two items compared. But the superlative degree implies always more than two. Although this is a useful distinction, it is one that is easily lost in rapid conversation. Thus we thoughtlessly say that

Robert and Emily are actually twins, but he is the *biggest*.

But in our writing we should take time for thinking and avoid this illogical use of the superlative.

(3) Another example of blurred thinking is the ascription of comparison to certain adjectives which in strict logic cannot be com-

pared. For example, a figure is, strictly speaking, either round or it is not. Therefore we ought not to write:

> The moon is *rounder* tonight than it was last week.

or

> She has the *roundest* face of all of us.

If we are to be logical (and in more formal writing, at least, we should make the attempt), we must write:

> The moon is *more nearly round* tonight than it was last week.

and

> She has the *most nearly round* face of all of us.

Among other adjectives that logically have no comparison are *unique, full,* and *square.*

> This incident in the novel was *more nearly unique* than any other.
> This house plan is *more nearly square* than that.

(4) Another opportunity for logical blurring occurs when we attempt to say that something is " as large " (or " good " or " beautiful ") " as something else " or is perhaps " even larger " (or " better " or " more beautiful "). Thus, we may illogically write:

> The champion was as strong, if not stronger, than in his last fight.

But the construction should be completed logically:

> The champion was as strong *as,* if not stronger *than,* he was in his last fight.

(5) A similar illogicality occurs when we forget that the person or thing about which we are talking has to be included in the computation. Thus we may write

> Robin Roberts was *better* than all the pitchers in the league.

when we actually mean

> He was the *best* pitcher in the league.

or

> He was *better* than any *other* pitcher in the league.

(6) Advertising merchants are particularly addicted to the use of the incomplete comparison, which they use in place of the superlative, as in the following examples:

> Robinson's milk is *purer.*
> Smith's is the *better*-tasting cigarette.

The milk is purer *than what?* Does the cigarette taste better than truffles, chocolate parfaits, onion soup?

(7) Adjectives are sometimes mistakenly replaced by adverbs; but since the more usual fault is to employ an adjective when the construction requires an adverb, we shall defer discussion of this problem until we reach the section on the abverb, **2.2a** (5) .

2.1c *Position in Word Order*

Earlier, on pages 744–45, we touched briefly on the place of adjectives in the sentence: a single-word adjective generally (1) precedes the substantive it modifies; or if it follows the substantive, (2) is connected to it by a linking verb.

> (1) *a brave* man   *a small gray* bird   *a fine, courageous, devoted* servant of the people
> (2) He was *proud.* The scene appeared *gay.*

We manage this normal ordering of adjectives so instinctively that we may wonder that we need to be told about it. Yet the normal ordering is worth our attention for the sake of what we may learn from the exceptions.

Sometimes adjectives come immediately after the substantive they modify. For instance, there are some fossilized expressions derived from medieval legal language, such as

> body *politic*   heirs *male*   heir *apparent*

Then there are certain other conventional and idiomatic expressions such as

> John *the Baptist*   Catherine *the Great*
> chapter *ten*   comrades *all!*

To these we might add more rhetorical expressions like

> the forest *primeval*   the house *beautiful*

Is there any way of accounting for these abnormal placings of the adjective, particularly in the last two groups? (The examples in the first group are presumably to be accounted for as survivals of borrowings from the French.)

One may venture to account for them in this way: variations from the norm are always emphatic. (The man wearing spats calls attention to himself, unless everybody else is wearing spats, in which case it is the man without spats who calls attention to himself.) To place the adjective after its noun is to place it in an emphatic position. That is what we want to accomplish with " the Baptist," which deserves emphasis since it is setting this John apart from others of that name; thus putting " the Great " after Catherine distinguishes this particular queen from the other queens named Catherine. So also with " ten " in the phrase " chapter ten." The same reasoning can be invoked to justify the adjective *all* in " comrades all," where emphasis is to fall upon the unity of the comrades. So also can we justify the designation " beautiful " as a means of focusing attention upon a particular house.

One ought to add of course that such devices for securing emphasis may be abused. Overuse of a following position for adjectives destroys the effect of emphasis. The phrase " the house beautiful " was first used by John Bunyan in *The Pilgrim's Progress,* and in that particular context it was well used. But with it as an example, advertisers nowadays produce such absurdities as " the memorial park beautiful," " the body beautiful," and " the hair-do glamorous."

Variation of the normal position of the adjective, like other emphatic devices, ought to be used sparingly and with discretion. So used, the variation can be quite effective:

> An automobile, *shabby and mud-splashed,* rounded the corner.
> A small face, *dirty,* appeared at the window.

We have seen that single-word adjectives normally come before the word that they modify, but phrases and clauses that function as adjectives come after the word that they modify. Thus:

> The man *to see* is Jim. [infinitive used as adjective]
> The house *in the country* was charming. [prepositional phrase used as an adjective]
> The house *that I saw* was of red brick. [relative clause used as an adjective]
> The house *I saw* was of red brick. [relative clause, not headed by a relative pronoun, used as an adjective]

2.2 The Adverb

Adverbs are words that modify verbs, adjectives, or other adverbs.

2.2a Formation

Many adverbs are formed by adding *–ly* to an adjective:

> *quietly, happily, quickly, silently*

749

But some adverbs lack the *–ly* ending. (The corresponding adjective form, if there is one, is identical; e.g., *far, fast*.)

fast, far, then, now, here, there, very

Some adverbs have both forms:

slow and *slowly*, *loud* and *loudly*

EXCEPTIONS AND PROBLEMS

(1) The formation and use of adverbs is complicated by the fact that some adjectives have an *–ly* ending:

lonely, homely, friendly

A real problem arises with the adverbial forms of such adjectives. Although the dictionary recognizes *lonelily* and *friendlily*, many writers, in order to avoid such awkward forms, will write such phrases as

He greeted us in *friendly fashion*.

(2) Confusion in the use of the adjectival and the adverbial form is increased by the adverbs that do not have an *–ly* ending. For if the student knows he is correct in writing " The boat moved *fast*," he may be inclined to feel that he can also write " The boat moved *rapid*."

(3) The adverbs with double forms further promote confusion. The possibility of saying " The boat moved *quick* " as well as " The boat moved *quickly* " may induce the student to consider " The boat moved *powerful* " just as correct as " The boat moved *powerfully*."

Double-form adverbs, by the way, have been a long-standing problem in English. The adverb *slow*, for example, had two forms even in Old English, one of which gave rise to the modern form *slow*; the other, to the modern form *slowly*.

But if the student follows his instincts for the language and his normal speech habits, he should have little trouble with adverbs that have double forms. He will speak or write sentences like these:

Go *slow*.
I bought it *cheap*.
He held on *tight*.

And the fact that he can use these shorter adverbial forms correctly, will not keep him from using the *–ly* forms too:

The boat crept ever so *slowly* around the bend.
If it has taught you so much, the experience was purchased very *cheaply*.

He will probably use the forms without *–ly* in short sentences, commands, and so on, and the forms with *–ly* in more formal sentences.

(4) Persistent offenders in the confusion of adverbs with adjectives are the would-be intensifiers like *sure* and *real*.

> That *sure* was a good movie.
> Once you get to know her, she is *real* nice.

(It must be admitted that the substitution of *surely* and *really* will hardly restore vitality or precision to these sentences. The shift to adverbial forms makes them grammatically correct; but they remain vague and imprecise.)

Here are a few other examples of adjectives wrongly used for adverbs:

> He made the goal *easy*.

instead of

> He made the goal *easily*.
> He did pretty *good* in his first game.

The writer means to say:

> He did pretty *well* in his first game.

or, better still,

> He played *well* in his first game.

(5) Error of overcorrection. Adverbs are sometimes incorrectly used when the construction calls for an adjective. This tendency springs frequently from an overcorrection of the opposite fault. Having come to feel that any modifier without an *–ly* is in some fashion incorrect, the writer proceeds to insert *–ly* forms where they are not appropriate. Thus one of our most justly celebrated writers of fiction invariably has the characters in his stories and novels say that they " feel badly " when they are dispirited or regret some action.

(6) Linking verbs. Verbs like *feel, look, smell, sound, taste, appear, seem, become, grow,* and *be* are completed by a predicate adjective, not an adverb. Thus:

I feel *good*. [that is, " happy " or " in good spirits "]
I feel well. [*Well* here is an adjective meaning " in good health, not ill.'
It is not to be confused with *well*, the adverb, meaning " in good or ex
cellent fashion."]

She seemed *unhappy*.
Remembering what happened yesterday, he feels very *bad*.
The blossom smells *sweet*.
She looked *indignant*.

In all the instances just given, the verb is a linking verb, connecting the adjective with its subject, which the adjective modifies. It is true that we can use some of these verbs with adverbs in sentences like the following:

> The woman looked at him *indignantly*.
> He smelled the bottle *cautiously*.

But a little reflection will show that in these last two sentences, *looked* and *smelled* are not "linking" but "action" verbs. They are being used here with quite different meanings from those that they had in the earlier examples. In the present instance, *looked* means "the act of looking," not "appeared"; and *smelled* means "the act of smelling," not the "fact of giving off an odor." In these active senses these verbs properly call for an adverb to describe the way in which the action is performed.

2.2b Comparison

The comparison of adverbs follows the same rule as the comparison of adjectives: we form the comparative by adding *–er* or by prefixing *more* to the positive form, and the superlative by adding *–est* or by prefixing *most* to the positive form (see pages 745–46). (All adverbs ending in *–ly* prefix *more* or *most*.)

POSITIVE	COMPARATIVE	SUPERLATIVE
fast	faster	fastest
quietly	more quietly	most quietly
happily	more happily	most happily

2.2c Position in Word Order

Adverbs used to modify adjectives and other adverbs are usually placed next to the word they modify:

> The cup was *nearly* full.
> The horse ran *wonderfully* fast.

But adverbs used as modifiers of the verb may be disposed in various positions in the sentence. This flexibility is the more readily understandable when we remember that a frequent use of the adverb is to tell, among other things, *when,* or *where,* or *how,* or *why* the action occurred. Thus we may have such positionings as:

Then we heard, *very late* in the afternoon, the first sounds of battle.
Accordingly, the Cherokee rose is found *most usually* along hedgerows.

This relative flexibility of position in the sentence is true also of the various kinds of word groups (phrases and clauses) that have an adverbial function. They will be discussed later under the term adverbial modifiers (see page 779).

3. Verbs

Verbs are words that express action, state, or being.

> He *struck* hard.
> The leaf *was floating* lazily upon the stream.
> I *am* impatient.

3.1 Principal Parts

If in addition to the base form of the verb (the form that occurs in the dictionary), we know the forms of the past tense and of the past participle, we can make, by regular rules, all the other inflections of the verb. For this reason, these three forms are called the principal parts of the verb. In so-called " regular " verbs there are only two principal parts; for the past tense and the past participle are formed alike by adding *–ed, –d,* or *–t* to the base. Thus:

BASE	PAST TENSE	PAST PARTICIPLE
trick	tricked	tricked
bake	baked	baked
burn	burned *or* burnt	burned *or* burnt

But many of the most frequently used verbs are irregular and form the second or third principal part by changing the vowel of the stem (with or without other changes).

BASE	PAST TENSE	PAST PARTICIPLE
ride	rode	ridden
come	came	come
go	went	gone

See the Glossary, pages 809–10, for a list of the principal parts of many other verbs.

3 Verbs

3.2 Agreement

Person and **number** are two relationships of the verb which are still expressed rather fully in the inflectional system of the verb *to be*. A variety of forms, in both the present and past tenses, reflect the relationships of person and of number. But other verbs ignore these relationships except in the present tense, and here have only two forms: that with —*s* to indicate the third-person singular and that without —*s*, in which all the other person-number relationships are lumped.

> I *am* the person who broke it.
> He *is* a petty dictator.
> The horses *were* now neck and neck.
> The boy *runs* to the candy store.
> *Go.* You *are* merely in the way. [The subject of *Go* is understood to be *you*. In direct commands the *you* is not expressed.]

Present and past tenses of the verb *to be* are inflected as follows:

	PRESENT		PAST	
	SINGULAR	PLURAL	SINGULAR	PLURAL
1st person	I am	we are	I was	we were
2nd person	(thou art)	(ye are)	(thou wert)	(ye were)
	you are	you are	you were	you were
3rd person	he (she, it) is	they are	he (she, it) was	they were

If we disregard the archaic second person forms, the variations of form even in *be* are not many. It may be comforting to reflect that most of the mistakes made in getting the proper form of the verb have to do with the one —*s* form in the singular. It should not be too difficult to learn how to use properly just one form.

EXCEPTIONS AND PROBLEMS

Many of the problems with verbs have to do with nouns and pronouns that are singular in form but can be taken in a plural sense (see **1.1b**).

3.3 Transitive and Intransitive Verbs

A **transitive** verb expresses an action that affects some object.

> I *broke* the stick.   I *hit* the ball.   I *burned* the paper.

The subject is the agent; the verb expresses the action; the object is affected by the action.

Some verbs that can take a direct object, like the verb *to burn* in the foregoing example, may on some occasions be **intransitive** — that is, they may not take an object. Consider, for instance:

The house *burns*.   She *burned* with a high fever.

Or consider the intransitive and transitive uses of *sing:*

She *sang* beautifully.   She *sang* both verses.

Examination will usually reveal a difference of sense in the two uses, as between *burn* in the sense of " to be in a state of combustion " and *burn* in the sense of " to set alight, to *put* into a state of combustion." Likewise, *sing* in the first instance means to use the voice musically; in the second, to vocalize certain passages or stanzas.

Certain transitive verbs may also take indirect objects, i.e., objects that are indirectly affected by the action of the verb.

I told *him* the story.
I gave *her* the letter.

Certain verbs are invariably intransitive: *come, sit, lie, appear, seem,* and most important of all, *be.* These verbs never take objects. (One might argue that *come* does take an object in " to come a cropper " or that *sit* takes an object in " to sit a horse." But such exceptions are idiomatic.) They express intransitive actions:

The donkey *came* slowly down the path.

or states and conditions:

He *lay* at full length upon the grass.

Or they are linking verbs (see page 751) which connect a predicate adjective or noun (pronoun) with the subject:

Alice *appeared* anxious.
The day *seemed* unending.
He *has been* a dunce.

There should be no trouble in distinguishing these predicate complements from the direct objects treated above. Analysis will show that they are clearly adjectives modifying the subject (*anxious Alice, unending day*), or else are substantives meant to be equated with the subject (*he = dunce*). If we turn to our examples of direct objects, we shall find a different relationship: compare *I, stick; I, ball; I, paper.* In these instances the relationship is that of agent of the action and object of the action.

3 Verbs

3.4 Voice

There are two voices, the **active** and the **passive**. If the subject acts, the verb is in the active voice; if the subject is acted upon, the verb is in the passive voice. Consider the following contrasting sentences:

ACTIVE	PASSIVE
A rock *broke* the stick.	The stick *was broken* by a rock.
I *burned* the paper.	The paper *was burned* by me.
The waves *drove* the ship upon a lee shore and then gradually *smashed* it to pieces.	The ship *was driven* upon a lee shore and then *was* gradually *smashed* to pieces by the waves.

Passive verbs are formed by compounding parts of the verb *to be* with a past participle.* Passive verbs cannot take direct objects; indeed, what would be the direct object in the " active construction " becomes the subject in the " passive construction," and what would be the subject becomes, if it is expressed at all, the object of a preposition, e.g., " *by* me," " *by* the waves."

It should be observed that only transitive verbs can be converted to the " passive " voice, i.e., verbs that can take a direct object. (Intransitive verbs like *be, seem, become* have but one voice, and that one we can scarcely describe as " active " since these verbs express, not action, but state or condition.) It might be more accurate therefore to say that in converting to the passive voice, we do not so much " de-activate " the verb as " de-transitize " it. In any case, we shift the emphasis from what would be in normal construction the agent to the thing affected. It is the fate of the ship that we are primarily interested in when we write " The ship was driven upon a lee shore," not the agent, whether it be currents, winds, tides, or waves. It is this shift in emphasis accomplished by the " passive " construction that will be stressed on page 774. For our decision to use either an active construction or a passive construction usually turns upon the matter of what constitutes the proper emphasis. We can state the basic facts by means of either construction.

---

* Historically, the passive in English seems to have grown out of the use of a verbal adjective in the predicate:

I am hurt.   The stick is broken.

Even today, we can see that the past participle as a predicate adjective blends into the " passive " construction. Consider the following series:

The stick is broken.   The stick was broken.   The stick has been broken.
The stick will be gradually broken into splinters.

In this series, we move from what are clearly adjectival uses of the participle on to more complicated verbal compounds — though even in the last example the adjectival force of *broken* is still perceptible.

3.5 Tense

Tense is an indication of the time of action of the verb — a present action, a past action, and so on. There are six tenses in English, as the textbooks usually define them. (This scheme derives ultimately from Latin grammar.) There are, as we should expect, tenses to correspond to future, present, and past time. The tripartite division is turned into a six-part division by taking into account whether the action is complete or incomplete. Thus we have in addition to present, past, and future, the three " perfect " tenses which specify that the action is conceived of as completed in the present, the past, or future.

The conventional account of the English tense system can thus be set forth as follows:

PRESENT		PRESENT PERFECT	
I eat	we eat	I have eaten	we have eaten
you eat	you eat	you have eaten	you have eaten
he eats	they eat	he has eaten	they have eaten

PAST		PAST PERFECT	
I ate	we ate	I had eaten	we had eaten
you ate	you ate	you had eaten	you had eaten
he ate	they ate	he had eaten	they had eaten

FUTURE		FUTURE PERFECT	
I shall eat	we shall eat	I shall have eaten	we shall have eaten
you will eat	you will eat	you will have eaten	you will have eaten
he will eat	they will eat	he will have eaten	they will have eaten

But this scheme, useful as it is, does not do justice to the richness of expression and the general complexity of the English verb. To the six tenses given above we can add three more, the tenses of " continuing " action (I am eating, I was eating, I shall be eating) to match the tenses of " completed " action; for the forms of the verb *to be* plus the present participle of the verb are used to signify continuing action just as definitely as the forms of the verb *to have* plus the past participle are used to signify completed (perfect) action. And even these nine tenses, as we shall see, do not exhaust the ways we have for expressing tense relations in English.

3.5a *Present*

Complications start even with the present tense. The simple present does not merely and invariably refer to action in present time. We use the " present " to express general truths:

Certain plants *grow* toward the light.
The instructor told us that the chemical formula for water *is* H_2O.

Or to express the future:

He *goes* to the hospital tomorrow.
My plane *takes off* in the morning.

The present may even have a past reference of sorts as in the so-called " historical present " where in vivid narration past events are described as if they were presently occurring. Someone has said that the simple present in English would be more accurately named the " unpast " tense.

The most usual way of expressing present action in modern English is through the present participle, the verbal ending in *–ing* plus the present tense of the verb *be*. (This is sometimes called the progressive present.)

I am eating	we are eating
you are eating	you are eating
he is eating	they are eating

The emphatic present makes use of the auxiliary *do, does* plus the base form of the verb. Its special uses are implied by its name:

But I *do believe* you.
Does he apply himself? — Yes, he *does apply* himself, most diligently.

3.5b *Past*

The simple past refers to an indefinite past:

He *killed* and *killed* again.
The miners *struck* for higher wages.

But because we often are unwilling to let the time of the action remain so indefinitely specified — except perhaps for a calculated rhetorical effect as in the first example — we supply specific time references through modifiers:

Yesterday afternoon he fell suddenly on the pavement.

or we depend upon the context to indicate the time:

Then [the events of an afternoon are being described] he broke the stick across his knee and tossed the pieces away.

Moreover, we have devised variations of the verb to establish or emphasize the " timing " of the action. For example we may write:

He *was breaking* the stick across his knee.   [The action is in the past, but we view it as going on.]

He *did break* the stick across his knee.   [Emphatic, as if in answer to a challenging of the fact. Cf., the emphatic present, **3.5a.**]

We have seen that the simple past (and the simple present) are indefinite as to whether the action was continuing or completed. The simple past *implies* that the action has been completed: " He *broke* the stick." We have also seen that the present participle is the sign of continuing action: " He *was breaking* the stick." (The action is viewed as continuing in the past.)

3.5c Perfect Tenses

The student may be in the habit of thinking of the perfect tenses as past tenses, for it is natural to associate a completed or finished action with the past. But if we remember that one of the perfect tenses is the future perfect, we shall find it the easier to appreciate the fact that the perfect tenses are past tenses in a special way, which depends upon the point of time from which we view the action as being complete. The present perfect (*I have eaten*) views the action as now complete in the present time; the past perfect (*I had eaten*) views the action as having been completed at some time in the past; the future perfect (*I shall have eaten*) views the action as having been completed at some time in the future.

3.5d Future

English began without a genuine future tense: one used the " present " with an adverb of future reference. (See **3.5a.** We can still do so, as in " I *go* in the morning ") . Today, future tense in formal English is frequently made up of the verb base coupled with the auxiliary *shall* or *will*. (Compare these auxiliaries with the modal auxiliaries, and see page 764. The choice between *shall* forms and *will* forms will be discussed later in this section. See **3.7a.**) Since in informal and colloquial English contracted forms are ordinarily used, the distinction between *shall* and *will* often disappears: *I'll go, he'll go, they'll go,* and so on.

In informal English, another very popular form of the future tense is " I *am* (I'm) *going to* sell," " you *are going to* sell," " he *is going to* sell," and so forth. *Going to* has thus become a sign of the future tense. We also use as signs of the future tense *about to* and the simple *to:*

> I am *going to* sell the house. [future reference]
> I am *about to* sell the house. [future reference, the action imminent]
> I am *to* sell the house. [more formal and literary; the future action is indefinite, and there is even the faint suggestion of obligation, i.e., "I am expected to sell the house."]

3.5e *Summary of Tense Relationships*

It may be useful at this point to sum up some of the possibilities for expressing relationships of tense in the English verb.

	PRESENT	PAST	FUTURE
Simple	he eats	he ate	he will eat
			he is going to eat
			he is about to eat
			he is to eat
Action conceived of as continuing (progressive)	he is eating	he was eating	he will be eating
Action conceived of as completed (perfect)	he has eaten	he had eaten	he will have eaten
Emphatic	he does eat	he did eat	—

But this chart far from exhausts the possibilities of tense complication and shading of meaning. The perfect tenses in particular are capable of considerable expansion. We may need quite often to use forms like " he has been eating " or " he had been eating." By making use of *going to,* or *to,* as indications of future action, we can get even more complicated forms and more specific shadings of meaning: thus

> he *was to have been eating*
> he *will be going to eat*

To show that these last examples are not simply arbitrary fabrications to prove a point, let us put them into sentences.

> "Look," she said indignantly. "It's already eight o'clock and the child was to have been eating by seven-thirty."

" No use telephoning now. Remember the difference in time zones," he said. " In New York it is nearly seven o'clock. He will be going to eat."

The point of all this discussion is not that we should learn complicated tense structures. The point is just the opposite. As we rattle away in conversation, we frequently get into very complicated verb structures without realizing that we are doing so. As a grammarian has recently observed: " The . . . man-in-the-street can scarcely open his mouth without endowing his report of a happening with the most elaborate kind of modal and aspectual overtones. Creature of emotion, he seizes upon every grammatical occasion to express emotional reactions; and his principal emotional carrier is the system of verbal helpers. The writer has to learn to be more restrained." [1]

The writer can restrain himself by learning the simpler and more formal ways to express relationships of tense; he can acquaint himself with some of the devices by which we define and refine upon our ways of regarding an action. He can ask himself, " Is this degree of definiteness in this given case really required? " If it is, well and good; but if not, his prose will gain clarity and force from simplification. In short, the foregoing display of the complications of the time relation of the English verb has not been set forth as something to be earnestly studied and exploited. Rather, we should recognize that although we possess an elaborate tense structure, we ought to use it selectively and thoughtfully.

3.6 Mood

The concept of mood may prove difficult for the student to grasp if he has not studied a rather fully inflected language such as Latin or German. English is usually said to have three moods — the indicative, the imperative, and the subjunctive. The **indicative** mood is that of statement, declaration, and question; the **imperative,** that of command. The **subjunctive** is more difficult to define: suffice it to say that it deals with hypothetical and non-actual situations of various kinds.

The easiest way in which to approach the concept of mood is to compare a command with a statement. The difference between " Go " and " He is going " or between " Come to attention " and " He will come tomorrow " is easy to comprehend. But the fact that the imperative mood has in modern English been reduced to one form — representing one person, one tense, and one number (since

[1] Harold Whitehall, *Structural Essentials of English,* pp. 88–89.

the singular and the plural forms are the same) — tends to isolate the command from all other uses of the verb. The very simplicity of the imperative mood means that it is of little value in understanding the subjunctive mood. Moreover, since the subjunctive mood in modern English is in a state of advanced decay, its inflectional forms differing today almost not at all from those of the indicative, the student may be tempted to give up altogether the attempt to understand mood.

There is some warrant for this sense of futility, for most of the functions performed earlier by the subjunctive are handled in modern English by auxiliary verbs (the modal auxiliaries). We write:

> He *may* write to her.
> He *might* write to her.
> He *must* write to her.
> He *can* write to her.
> He *could* write to her.
> He *ought* to write to her.
> He *should* write to her.
> He *would* write to her, if you thought well of it.

The common denominator of all these expressions is that the act of writing is thought of as a non-actual (unrealized) act; i.e., an act that is viewed as possible, or necessary, or conditional, or desirable, or proper, or obligatory, but not at the present *actual*. The acts have a kind of future reference, and in English the usual way of forming the future tense (see **3.5d**) is by the use of related auxiliaries: " I *shall* write to her " and " I *will* write to her."

It will be helpful to call the attention of the student to a special feature of these otherwise familiar auxiliaries: they all lack the usual –*s* form for the third person singular. Thus, we write " he *must* write to her " not " he *musts*," " he *can* " not " he *cans*."

The rule in English, then, would seem to be that if we wish to stress the hypothetical quality of a statement (whether with the subjunctive or an auxiliary) we select a verb form without the –*s*, e.g., *be* rather than *is*, *were* rather than *was*, *call* rather than *calls*, and so on.

(1) The use of a form without –*s* is mandatory in expressing conditions contrary to fact. Thus:

> If I *were* you, I would not go.   [I obviously am not you: the condition is contrary to fact.]
> She felt as if she *were* dead.

(2) The selection of *be,* or in the case of other verbs, of forms without *–s,* is mandatory in substantive clauses after expressions such as " It is necessary," " I move," and the like. For example:

> I move that the nominations *be* closed.
> I suggest that the candidate *come* forward.
> I demand that the case *be* dismissed.
> He insisted that the name of his accuser *be* divulged.

(3) Selection of *be* or the form without the *–s* emphasizes the element of doubt and the sense of the hypothetical in any thought; but nowadays this usage occurs only in very formal writing. Thus:

> If he *be* the man I think he is, he will speak out.   [formal]
> If he *is* the man I think he is, he will speak out.   [informal]
> If he *call,* say that I am out.   [formal]
> If he *calls* (or If he *should call*), say that I am out.   [informal]
> If I *be* the one chosen, I shall have to decline.   [formal]

(4) Some traditional formulas and idiomatic expressions are frequently regarded as more or less fossilized survivals of the subjunctive:

Suffice it to say.	The devil *take* it.
Far *be* it from me.	*Would* that he could go.
God *forgive* him.	

But the student may prefer to rationalize some of these instances as imperatives or imperative-like expressions, others as expressions with a modal auxiliary implied: " *Let* it suffice "; " *May* God forgive him." But whichever way we account for their form, they should be memorized as special cases, i.e., as idioms.

To sum up the problem of mood, the student can write acceptable English prose whether or not he has a very fully developed conception of mood. Actually, most of the qualifications of meaning that we associate with the subjunctive mood are managed in English by means of the modal auxiliaries: *can, could, may, might, ought,* and so on. Formulas and idiomatic expressions such as those discussed in (4) will cause the student no trouble: he uses them automatically. The nice shadings of meaning discussed under (3) are available to him if he remembers the rule about *–s*-less forms of the verb, but they are stylistic niceties that he need not cultivate. Contrary-to-fact conditions and expressions beginning with " as if " (1) are the only constructions that are likely to give him trouble. But again if he can remember the rule-of-thumb about using *–s*-less forms of the verb, he will manage the "subjunctive" forms painlessly and perhaps without even knowing that he is doing so.

3.7 *Shall, Will,* and Other Auxiliary Verbs

3.7a Shall *and* will

In formal English a distinction is made between the use of *shall* and *will* in the future tense. Though the distinction is not much observed today, it is easily stated and easily remembered if one will take care to notice that *will* preserves a notion of volition as in the words *will power* and *willingness. Shall,* on the other hand, originally meant something like "am to, is to," and this sense still adheres to *should,* which is the past tense of *shall.* Keeping in mind these meanings, one expresses simple futurity as:

I shall [that is, *I am to*]   we shall
you will [assuming you wish
    to do what you are doing]   you will
he will [assuming he wishes
    to do what he is doing]   they will

An expression of determination or obligation, however, will just reverse this arrangement. To express determination, I want to associate the notion of *will* with my decision or our decision. And as for other people, the second or third person, I want deliberately to remove any consideration of their *willingness.* They shall (are to) whether they *will* to do so or not. Thus, we come out with this scheme:

I will   we will
you shall   you shall
he shall   they shall

The distinction is a useful one. Even speakers who think they ignore it, do not ignore it entirely. For example, in putting a question in the first person, they will ask "Shall I?" ("Am I to do this?") not "Will I?" ("Do I will to do this?").

3.7b Should *and* would

Should and *would* were originally merely the past tenses of *shall* and *will,* respectively. This force of "pastness" is evident in our use of *should* and *would* in indirect discourse after a verb in the past tense:

He said that I *should* go tomorrow. [COMPARE: He said, "You will go tomorrow."]

Mary promised that she *would* come on Wednesday. [COMPARE: Mary said, "I will come Wednesday."]

In this connection, see also section **3.8**, Sequence of Tenses.

Should and *would,* however, have developed a number of special meanings which go quite beyond their status as past tenses of *shall* and *will.*

(1) *Should* has developed the meaning of obligation — though a weaker obligation than that conveyed by *ought:*

> I *should* subscribe, I suppose.
> She *should* accept his apology.

(2) *Should* is used to convey some sense of uncertainty about a future action:

> Robert *should* be in New York by Friday. [MORE CONFIDENT: "He will be in New York by Friday."]

The sense of uncertainty may be used for the sake of politeness:

> I *should* think that you would know why I am angry. [MORE BRUSQUE: "I think that you know why I am angry."]

(3) *Should* is used in the first person to state polite requests:

> I *should* like you to tell me.

But most authorities assert no preference between *should* and *would* in such a sentence.

> I *would* like you to tell me.

(4) *Would* is used for polite requests put in the second person:

> *Would* you please let me know at your earliest convenience?
> *Would* you give me directions to Morristown? [MORE BRUSQUE: Will you give me directions to Morristown?]

(5) *Would* is used to mean " I wish fervently ":

> *Would* that the storm were over.

But this usage is archaic.

(6) *Would* is used to express habitual or customary action:

> Each time that it happened, he *would* raise his eyebrows and smile.
> We *would* go out to gather the wild grapes every autumn. [But we may

also simply write, using the past progressive tense: Each autumn, we *were* out *gathering* the wild grapes.]

3.7c Get and keep

In addition to the modal auxiliaries (see **3.6**) and the very important and constantly used auxiliaries *be* and *have,* there are two other verbs that have on occasion an auxiliary function, *get* and *keep. Get* is used frequently in informal English as a " passive " auxiliary:

> He *got* hurt.   He nearly *got* himself killed.
> Your coat *will get* mended tomorrow.
> This child *gets* spanked regularly.

As an auxiliary, it also has the force of *become* in a good many locutions:

> She *gets* tired quickly.

In addition to this usage as an auxiliary, *get* has many idiomatic uses which range from informal English to slang:

> Do you *get* me?   You couldn't *get away with* it.
> Do you think it *got* across?   Let's persuade them *to get together*

Keep as an auxiliary has come to have the meaning " continue." It can be used, therefore, to express repetitive action:

> He *keeps* talking about the high cost of living.
> She *kept* trying to find it.

3.8 Sequence of Tenses

The tense of the verb in a dependent clause is determined, according to a logical pattern, by the tense of the verb in the independent clause. If the leading verb is in the present tense, the verb following it is in the present, past, or future tense; if the leading verb is in the past tense, the following verb is in the past, past perfect, or the future tense as expressed with the auxiliary *would:*

> I *know* that our guest *is arriving.*
> I *know* that our guest *has arrived (arrived, did arrive) .*
> I *know* that our guest *will arrive.*
> I *knew* that our guest *was arriving (arrived, did arrive) .*
> I *knew* that our guest *had arrived.*
> I *knew* that our guest *would arrive.*

There is some overlapping of tenses in the second and fourth examples (*arrived, did arrive*); but the meaning of the two sentences is quite different. The second sentence indicates a present knowledge of a past act; the fourth indicates that the act of knowing and the act known are both in the past.

EXCEPTIONS AND PROBLEMS

(1) Statements of general truths: the present tense is retained in the subordinate clause in such instances as the following:

Our instructor *told* us that all organic life on this earth *depends* upon photosynthesis.
We *knew* that things equal to the same thing *are* equal to each other.

(2) Infinitives: the present tense of the infinitive is usually used even after a past tense in the main verb.

They meant *to stay* for an hour at most. [not " to have stayed "]
He had wanted *to go.* [not " to have gone "]

See also **3.9a.**

3.9 Verbals

Verbals, as the term implies, are forms derived from verbs. They function in the sentence as substantives or as modifiers. Like verbs, they can take direct objects, have tenses, may be modified by adverbs, and some can take subjects, but the prime verbal power they lack: they cannot constitute in themselves a full predicate. Only finite verbs, i.e., verbs limited as to person and number, can do this (see page 281). There are three verbals — the infinitive, the gerund, and the participle.

3.9a *The Infinitive*

The present infinitive is indicated by prefixing *to* to the base of the verb. The infinitive functions most often as a noun but also as an adjective or an adverb:

He wanted very much *to win.* [noun, direct object]
To win was his fondest hope. [noun, subject]
The man *to see* is Alfred. [adjective, modifying *man*]
He expected *to win* the match handily. [the infinitive *to win* is the direct object of *expected; match* is the direct object of the infinitive; *handily* is an adverb modifying the infinitive]
He came *to put* things in order. [adverb, modifying *came*]

After certain verbs, notably *see, let, make, hear,* and *help,* the infinitive without *to* is used.

He helped *fill* the tub.   [noun, direct object; the infinitive without *to* is called an "unmarked" infinitive]

A pronoun used as the subject of an infinitive is in the objective case:

We all expected *him* to win.

In addition to the present infinitive, there is a perfect infinitive: *to have won, to have put.*

I am happy *to have won* the match.

When we wish to refer to an action occurring at the same time as (or future to) that of the main verb, we use the present infinitive; when we wish to refer to a time previous to that of the main verb, we use the perfect infinitive. See **3.8** (2). Thus:

He is here *to ask* for money.

and

He came *to ask* for money.

but

He is not ashamed *to have asked* for money many times in the past.

3.9b *The Gerund*

The gerund is a verbal noun formed by adding *-ing* to the base of the verb.

Swimming was his greatest delight.   [subject]
The chance of his *winning* the race is remote.   [object of preposition]

Note that the proper form is "*his* winning," not "*him* winning"; for what is remote is a chance of *winning*, not a chance of *him*. The pronoun is properly put into the possessive to indicate *whose* winning. But although it is logical, the use of the possessive with the gerund sometimes leads to awkwardness, particularly with a noun. Thus, in the following sentence the possessive should not be used:

The chance of *Jack,* who is out of condition, *winning* the race is remote.

3.9c *The Participle*

The participle is a verbal adjective. The form of the present participle is identical with that of the gerund, but its function is that of an adjective, rather than a noun.

The members of the *winning* team were tired but happy.

The past participle, third of the principal parts of the verb (see page 753), is also frequently used as an adjective:

broken bones   *inflated* ego   *jammed* doors   *baked* loaves

The present perfect participle is formed by combining the present participle of *have* with the past participle of the verb:

Having won our match, we settled down to watch how our friends would fare.

4. Connectives

4.1 Prepositions

As we observed on page 731, a preposition relates a substantive to some other word in the sentence; a conjunction links one word or a group of words with another. But a few prepositions are sometimes confused with conjunctions, because some words function sometimes as one and sometimes as the other.

We were glad that he came *for* breakfast.   [preposition]
We were glad that he came, *for* he had good news.   [conjunction]

One way of discriminating between prepositions and conjunctions is to determine whether the word in question has an object. The preposition always has a substantive as its object:

for *breakfast*   of the *house*   in the *rain*   among the *farmers*   to *him* above *us*   spiked shoes good for *running*

Students sometimes mistake the conjunction *than* for a preposition, principally because the predicate is usually omitted in a subordinate clause introduced by *than*.

She is taller than I.   [i.e., than I *am*]

There may be a temptation, therefore, to write:

She is taller than *me*.

In addition to single prepositions, there are double prepositions such as *inside of, according to,* and even group prepositions such as *on top of, by way of, with respect to,* and so on. English is especially rich in its prepositional system: we can specify the relation of the noun to the rest of the sentence most minutely. Indeed, we frequently *overspecify* it, just as we tend to make overspecific the tense of the verb (see page 761). The student will probably find that he needs to simplify his prepositions rather than to complicate them; for example, he may slip into *off of* when he means *off:*

> He fell *off* the roof.   [not *off of*]

4.2 Conjunctions

Conjunctions are either co-ordinating or subordinating. **Co-ordinating** conjunctions join words or groups of words (phrases or clauses) of the same grammatical rank. They are *and, or, nor, but,* and *for.* A special use of co-ordinating conjunctions appears in what is called the **correlative** conjunction. The correlative conjunctions are *both . . . and, either . . . or, neither . . . nor, not only . . . but also.*

> *Both* Judith *and* Marie were ill.
> *Either* you sign the paper *or* we break off negotiations at once.

Subordinating conjunctions join subordinate clauses to the rest of the sentence. Typical subordinating conjunctions are *when, since, although, because, if, unless, so that,* and *that.* The clauses that they introduce have to do with *cause, purpose,* or *result,* with the *condition* under which the main clause is true, or with adverbial considerations of *place, time,* and so on. In fact, most subordinate clauses are adverbial in function. (Occasionally these clauses are elliptical; e.g., " The girl was missed, *when* gone.")

The mention of subordinate clauses leads up, quite naturally, to a discussion of the organization of the sentence and to the larger concerns of syntax.

Syntax

Syntax has to do with the organization of the sentence, with the natural divisions within sentences, and with the relationship of the parts of speech to one another within the framework of the sentence and its parts. As a matter of fact, in discussing the various parts of speech, we have already dealt with many matters of syntax. We have noted, for example, that pronouns agree with their antecedents in gender and number. In the course of our discussion of syntax, we shall repeat some of these rules. But we shall stress the whole sentence rather than the parts of speech, and the principles of relationship rather than changes in the forms of the individual words.

5. Definition of Phrase, Clause, and Sentence

A **phrase** is not simply a haphazard string of words. It is a group of words which are related to one another in a meaningful way and which function as a single part of speech. A phrase does not contain a finite verb (see page 767).* Rather, it has as its structural principle a preposition and its object: " *out of* this gloomy *cave* "; or an infinitive and its object and modifier: " *to find* the *place quickly* "; or a gerund and its object: " his *capturing* the *trophy* "; or a participle, the substantive it modifies, and the adverb, if any: " a *ship sailing homeward*." It is always dependent.

A **clause** contains a finite verb and its subject. It may be either independent (main) or dependent (subordinate). If independent, it can stand as a sentence; if dependent, it must be attached to an independent clause. The italicized words in the following examples constitute dependent (or subordinate) clauses:

> The man *that I saw* was the thief.
> *When I saw him,* I suddenly realized *that he was the thief.*

Dependent clauses may function as adjectives, adverbs, or substantives. The clause *that I saw* is adjectival, for it modifies the noun *man*. The clause *When I saw him* is adverbial, for it modifies the verb in the independent clause, *realized,* fixing the time of the act of realizing. The clause *that he was the thief* is a substantive, for the whole clause is the direct object of the verb *realized.*

A **sentence** (see page 281) must contain at least one independent clause. This means that it must have a subject and a finite verb — must name something and make a predication about it. A sentence consisting of a single independent clause is called a *simple* sentence. A sentence having more than one independent clause is called a

---

* It should be pointed out that " verb phrase " is sometimes used to refer to the string of verb elements (main verb and auxiliaries) that constitute a predicate; e.g., " He *had been writing.*" Such a verb phrase *does* contain a finite verb.

compound sentence. A sentence containing one or more dependent clauses is a **complex** sentence. A compound sentence containing one or more dependent clauses is called a **compound-complex** sentence.

6. Word Order and Emphasis

6.1 Normal Word Order

A sentence may consist of only one word:

Go!

Here we have a finite verb with a subject, i.e., *you* (as is usual with commands, the subject is not expressed but is understood). The meaning is complete and definite: you are to go — you are commanded to do so.

But the normal pattern of the English sentence gives us a subject (noun, pronoun, or noun substitute) followed by a finite verb, the verb agreeing with its subject in person and number:

Birds fly.   A bird flies.   Here I am.

If the verb requires a complement (predicate adjective, predicate noun, or direct object), the complement normally follows the verb.

He is *unhappy*.   [predicate adjective]
This is the *conqueror*.   [predicate nominative]
The guardsman struck the *boy*.   [direct object]

If there is an indirect object (see page 775), it comes *between* the verb and the direct object.

The officer gave *him* a pen.

Note that the position of the indirect object is a *fixed* position. We cannot write, " The officer gave a pen *him*." If we make use of a prepositional phrase " to him," to express the receiver of the action, we can, to be sure, place it after the complement, but then we are no longer dealing with an indirect object. The prepositional phrase can be moved even to the beginning of the sentence: " To him the officer gave a pen."

This, then, is the normal or natural word order of the English sentence:

Subject + verb + inner complement (if any) + outer complement (if any)

(In the interest of simplicity we have for the moment left out modifiers, except the articles *a* and *the,* the better to see the basic structure.)

6.2 Shifts in Word Order

Even though variety in sentence structure is desirable, the student should not strive to avoid normal order. It accords with the genius of the English language. It need not be monotonous, for changes in the modifiers and the ordering of the modifiers, not to mention changes in the length of the sentences themselves, will afford plenty of variety. Frequently the most direct way out of disorder and verbosity is to be found in returning to the word order normal to English. The truth of the matter is that any shift from normal word order ought to be questioned and made to justify itself before it is retained. A shift from the normal always calls attention to itself. The shift is thus justified only when such emphasis is justified. Consider the following instances:

How kind you have been! [The word order used here emphasizes the notion of *kindness* by altering normal order and putting the adjective before the subject and verb — an important place in the sentence.]

A bigger fool I have never seen. [*Fool* is the direct object, and the shift of position, a direct reversal of the normal pattern, is very emphatic.]

The points just made are well illustrated by the word order in questions. Questions emphasize the interrogative word by putting it first, or if they have no interrogative word, they put a special emphasis upon the verb by putting the auxiliary before the subject.

Where have you been?
What kind of person was he?
Have you heard the news?
Hear ye not what I hear? [archaic]

Sentences like the last would not be framed by any modern speaker. The only main verbs that we use in this fashion are *be* and *have.* (" *Have* you the time? " " *Are* you the delegate? ") In modern English we normally frame questions with the auxiliary verb *to do.*

Do you know the size of the Soviet Union?
Does he still subscribe?
What *do* you know about him?
Don't you hear what I hear?

773

6.3 Stress upon the Natural Complement of the Verb

In addition to the simple method of putting the complement before the subject and verb, illustrated above, we have another important device for stressing what would be in the natural word order the direct object of the verb. Thus, instead of

> The guardsman struck the boy.

we may write

> The boy was struck by the guardsman.

And if we do not know who did the striking or if, for the moment at least, we are not interested in the agent, we may write

> The boy was struck.

What we have done in essence is to reduce the verb to a predicate adjective which is linked to what was the direct object (now, the subject) by some form of the verb *to be* (see **3.3**).

What the student should note, in the first place, is that this construction, the " passive " construction, has the effect of altering the normal word order in English; and, in the second place, that though on occasion it is effective, it is not to be overused or to be used without a good reason. If one drifts into this kind of construction lazily and unthinkingly, he will exhibit the kind of woolly and flaccid writing that causes writers of grammar handbooks to warn against the " weak passive." For example, consider these " weak passives ":

> The problem of how to give people a proper sense of the perils of the atomic bomb without at the same time immobilizing them with terror *was discussed.*
>
> The matter *has been taken* under advisement and at the proper time *will be acted upon.*
>
> The whole panorama — exciting, splendid, and yet awe-inspiring — *was seen* by me.

6.4 Stress upon the Natural Subject

The subject of a sentence normally receives a good deal of emphasis from its position early in the sentence. But we can stress it further by opening the sentence with " It is (was) " or " There is (was) " and treating what would normally be the subject as a predicate nominative. Thus, instead of writing

> The girl in the green dress began screaming.

we may write

It was the girl in the green dress who began screaming.

or

There was a girl in a green dress who began screaming.

Note that in this construction the main clause of the original sentence is reduced to a relative clause modifying the noun that we want to emphasize.

It and *there* used in this fashion are called " expletives," that is, " fillers." They are mere fillers indeed if we use this construction, not for a purpose, but lazily and because we happen to drift into it. Then the special focus upon the subject will become blurred because meaningless, and we shall be turning out flabby instead of crisp and vigorous sentences.

Caution: In using the " There is, There are " construction one must exercise care to make sure that the verb agrees with the subject. Agreement in such sentences is made more difficult because the subject follows the verb.

There *are* contenders who do not deserve to win.
There *is* only one contender who seems to have no chance.

7. Adjectival Modifiers

The modifiers of the subject (and of other substantives) occupy relatively fixed positions in the word order of the sentence. If they are adjectives, they ordinarily come immediately before the substantives that they modify. If they are phrases or clauses, they usually come immediately after (see page 749) .

The *green-shuttered* house sat back in a small grove.
The house *in the country* took up more and more of his time.
The house *that he bought last year* proved to be unsatisfactory.

We must not forget to include among our modifiers of the subject predicate adjectives which follow the subject:

The house that he bought was *yellow.*

and possessives

His house is yellow.

and **appositives,** i.e., other nouns or pronouns set beside the subject in order to limit or qualify it:

Her house, a small *bungalow,* was just across the street.
His uncle *Charles* could not come.
My only companions, a *cat* and a *dog,* were even hungrier than I was.

Caution: Pronouns in apposition agree in case with the noun or pronoun with which they are in apposition:

The last guests to arrive, *he and I,* were not comfortable.
She was capable of hurting her best friends, *Ruth and me,* without any compunction.

8. Vague and Uncertain Reference of Pronouns

Clauses introduced by relative pronouns ought to be clearly associated with the antecedent of the pronoun. It is not enough that the clause modify an implied idea. Instead of writing

The batter for the third time chopped viciously but vainly, which brought a cheer from the frankly partisan crowd.

we do better to write

The batter's third strike brought a cheer from the crowd.

or we might write

The batter for the third time chopped viciously but vainly, a failure that brought cheers from the crowd.

The insertion of "an action" or "a fact" is often the easiest way to tighten up a loose sentence by giving the relative pronoun a specific word to which it can be made to refer.

She had been ill and dispirited, *a fact* which accounted for her present mood.

The student should take care that his pronouns in general, not merely the relative pronouns, be clearly related to their antecedents. One should write, not

I could not get the little gadget to work, no matter how many ways I twisted and poked it. *This* delayed us an hour.

but

This *difficulty* delayed us an hour.

Avoid also the ambiguity of reference in such sentences as

Roger told Joseph that *he* had spoken too soon.

This kind of sentence is sometimes awkwardly patched in this fashion:

Roger told Joseph that he (Roger) had spoken too soon.

It is better to recast the sentence:

Roger confessed to Joseph that he had spoken too soon.

9. Dangling Phrases

One kind of adjectival modifier that is frequently misplaced is the participial phrase. Participles are verbal adjectives (see pages 768–69) but unlike other adjectives, they are "movable modifiers." Thus, one may write:

Smoking a cigarette, James sauntered down the street.
James, *smoking a cigarette,* sauntered down the street.
James sauntered down the street, *smoking a cigarette.*

All three sentences are perfectly good English. There is no one correct position for the participial phrase, and where we place it is dictated largely by considerations of taste.

This character of movability the participle shares with adverbs and adverbial modifiers (see page 779), and this common trait makes it all the easier to confuse participles with adverbial modifiers. The confusion results in the so-called **dangling participle**, where the participle, though it is an adjective, has no substantive to modify. For example:

Walking down the street, a barber shop came into view.

What is meant is obviously

Walking down the street, I saw a barber shop.   [participle modifies *I*]

or

As I walked down the street, a barber shop came into view.   [adverbial clause substituted for the participle]

The faulty sentence originally under consideration is a mixture of, or vacillation between, the two constructions. Consider some further instances of the dangling participle:

Throwing to either side a band of hissing foam, we felt the boat shudder
under us as we turned on full power.
Based upon statistics, he should not die for some years.

Other verbals than the participle may be left dangling by the
careless writer. In this example a gerund phrase dangles:

On peering into the darkness, the shape disappeared.

Evidently the writer meant to say

On peering into the darkness, he found that the shape had disappeared.

Here an infinitive phrase dangles:

To hold it properly, the handle must be grasped.

The writer evidently meant to say

To hold it properly, one must grasp the handle.

Obviously, in order to avoid falling into absurdities we need to
consider with some care the relationship between the modifier and
the rest of the sentence; and, as the above examples indicate, verbals
call for special care. For possible exceptions and problem cases, see
section **10, Absolute Constructions.**

10. Absolute Constructions

An absolute construction is a phrase, usually consisting of a noun
or pronoun modified by a participle and having only a very general
relation to the rest of the sentence.

The mission having been carried out, the force received orders to return.
The principal danger once passed, they threw off their fears.

Such expressions tend to be formal and " literary," perhaps because
they are modeled upon the Latin ablative absolute. Such English
constructions are, in fact, sometimes called nominative absolutes.
The more normal English treatment would be to expand them into
subordinate clauses, " When the mission had been carried out," and
so forth.

Some authorities also classify as absolute constructions such
phrases as the following:

To judge from his face, he can't be very old.
Remembering the unpredictability of the weather and of human nature,
everything else portends a fine game on Saturday.
Taking all the evidence into account, the decision was a just one.

It may not be altogether easy to see just how these expressions escape being dangling modifiers. An argument sometimes urged, that they escape dangling because they designate a general truth, is not altogether convincing. Perhaps we shall do best simply to say that such expressions are idiomatic; i.e., that English simply does permit us, not altogether logically, to say

> To judge from his face, he can't be very old.

and does not require us to expand this to

> To judge from his face, I can't believe that he is very old.

11. Adverbial Modifiers

The position of adverbial modifiers is far less rigidly fixed than that of adjectival modifiers. For example, consider the variety of positions occupied by adverbial modifiers in the sentences that follow:

> *There, at ten o'clock,* I arrived *as I had been told to do.*
> *At ten o'clock,* I arrived *there, as I had been told to do.*
> *There, as I had been told to do,* I arrived *at ten o'clock.*

The first sentence tends to stress the place as the most important matter; the second sentence stresses the time of arrival. The third sentence also emphasizes the place and suggests that the instructions had been principally concerned with designating it. Control of the shadings of meaning is the mark of a skillful writer. Thus the fact that adverbial modifiers can be shifted about does not mean that we are at liberty to place them at random but, on the contrary, that if we are to write well, we must exercise great care in placing them.

11.1 Placement of Adverbs

Unless adverbs like *merely, just, only, almost* are placed immediately before the words that they modify, the meaning may become ambiguous.

> You *only* live once.
> You *just* have one bullet left.
> I *merely* asked for what was left.

Most of us fall into such sentences in daily speaking, and the inflections with which we say them can usually be counted upon to make

779

the meaning clear. But, in writing, where inflection cannot help, we should be more precise; we should make unmistakably clear that *only* modifies *once* and that *just* modifies *one*. Therefore the proper sequences are " only once " and " just one." Does *merely* indicate that I requested rather than demanded, or is the writer trying so say that he asked for nothing in excess of what was left? With this last instance, we are led to the problem of:

11.2 Squinting Constructions

In such constructions the modifier looks two ways, and it is not clear which of the two possibilities is intended. For example:

> The winner of the match tomorrow plays in the final round.

Does the sentence mean that

> The winner of the match plays in the final round tomorrow.

or does it mean

> The winner of the match to be played tomorrow goes into the final round.

In the following sentence, *often* is ambiguous:

> The pitcher that goes to the well often gets broken.

12. Miscellaneous Violations of Logic

Most of the positive observations to be made about the dispositions and arrangement of the various elements of a sentence properly fall under the heading, not of grammar, but of rhetoric; that is, they have to do with making the sentence effective rather than correct (see Chapter 9). Yet there are a number of general comments about the relationships among sentence elements that raise the question of elementary intelligibility. Some principle of logical consistency ought to preside over any piece of discourse and we can appeal to this principle against the following:

12.1 Needless Splitting Apart of Normally Closely Linked Elements

Avoid separating normally closely linked elements such as those that make up the infinitive. Instead of writing

He wished *to* fully and triumphantly *clear* his name.

write

He wished *to clear* his name fully and triumphantly.

Instead of writing

I *wish*, having made a rather careful study of this matter, *to express* my opinion on it.

write

Having made a rather careful study of this matter, *I wish to express* my opinion on it.

12.2 Mixed Constructions

Adverbial clauses should not be used as subjects or predicate nominatives. Instead of writing

Because he can't play well is the reason he dislikes baseball.

write

He dislikes baseball because he doesn't play the game well himself.

or write

The fact that he can't play baseball well makes him dislike the game.

12.3 Violations of Parallelism

Use like elements in like constructions. Instead of writing

To play tennis and swimming are his favorite amusements.

write

Playing tennis and swimming are his favorite amusements.

or write

To play tennis and to swim are his favorite amusements.

Instead of writing

Poor study habits and the fact that he had a long illness caused his failure.

write

Poor study habits and a long illness caused his failure.

781

12.4 Needless Shifts in Tense, Subject, Number

Avoid changes in the tense of the verb or in the person and number of pronouns. Instead of writing

> I think that *one* ought always to insist upon *their* rights. If *you* don't demand justice, then you will always after be at a disadvantage.

write

> I think that one ought always to insist upon his rights. If one doesn't demand justice, then he will always after be at a disadvantage.

12.5 Use of the Double Negative

Remember that two negatives make a positive. Instead of writing

> Nobody *had none* of it left.

write

> Nobody *had any* of it left.

Instead of writing

> He *can't hardly* pay his bills.

write

> He *can hardly* pay his bills.

12.6 Omission of Necessary Words

Make certain that all the terms necessary to the logic of the sentence are actually to be found in the sentence. Instead of writing

> Charles is as old, if not older, than James.

write

> Charles is as old *as,* if not older than, James.

Instead of writing (when you mean that Charles was more helpful than James)

> Charles helped me more than James.

write

> Charles helped me more than James *did.*

Punctuation

Punctuation, or "pointing" as it was once called, helps us to read. It aids us in analyzing the meaning of discourse, marking off the significant divisions. Plato, the father of philosophy, in discussing intellectual analysis in general, compared it to the work of someone cutting up a carcass of beef. It is necessary, he said, to make the cuts *at the joints,* i.e., at the natural divisions. And punctuation similarly marks the joints. The conventions that govern the marks of punctuation are rather easy to learn; it is really ignorance of where the joints are — ignorance of the anatomy of the sentence — that causes serious trouble. The ability to punctuate is a function of one's knowledge of basic grammar.

We can divide punctuation marks into four classes: (1) terminal, those that mark the end of a sentence; (2) linking, those that tie together independent clauses and other sentence elements; (3) separating, those that separate one part of a sentence from another; and (4) enclosing or parenthetical, those that work in pairs to enclose some part of the sentence. Since only separating and enclosing punctuation marks offer any considerable problems, the task of learning to punctuate is not so formidable as it may first appear.

13. Terminal Punctuation

Clearly, one cannot mark the end of a sentence unless he knows what a sentence is. This is the real problem of terminal punctuation. For unless we do know what a sentence is (i.e., a group of words containing at least one independent clause [see page 771]), we may mark off a dependent clause or a string of words that is not a sentence at all. We may claim in effect that a mere **sentence fragment** is a sentence. This act of unconscious fraud is sometimes called the "period fault." Examples:

> Knowing that the winter was fast approaching and that there was already ice on some of the pools.   [participle incorporating two dependent clauses]
>
> That he was good, provident, and of a cheery disposition.   [a dependent clause]

A sentence begins with a capital letter and ends, unless it is a question, with a period. For other uses of the period, see **Mechanics,** sections **17** and **20.**

If it asks a question, we end it with a question mark.

> When are you coming to dinner?

Or, if it is an exclamation, expressing a high degree of emotion, we may end it with an exclamation point.

> You don't mean that he's been killed!

EXCEPTIONS AND PROBLEMS

(1) Though sentences usually require a subject and predicate, in certain instances — particularly in dialogue — we do find legitimate sentences which have no subject and predicate in explicit form. For example:

> " Do you mean that you have seen him? "
> " *Yes.*" [properly punctuated as a sentence]

> " Do you really like him? Come now; tell the truth. Do you? "
> " *More or less.*" [properly punctuated as a sentence]

> *The more, the merrier. Give a dog a bad name.* [Many such proverbial and other formularized expressions are also considered sentences.]

(2) Note that indirect questions are not followed by the question mark:

> Do not ask him *what Roger has been buying.*

(3) Note that the choice of the exclamation point instead of the period is to some extent a subjective matter. There is no completely objective determination of the boiling point of excitement, when a declaration is transformed into an exclamation. Each of us will have to provide his own answer.

(4) Note also the special use of the dash as terminal punctuation. In a way it is anomalous to speak of the dash as a mark signifying the termination of a sentence, since the dash signifies an abrupt break in thought, i.e., not a proper termination but a sudden cessation. Yet we sometimes need to indicate just this state of affairs. Thus:

> " But you just said that you — "
> " I said no such thing."

14. Linking Punctuation

14.1 Independent Clauses (Comma and Semicolon)

A series of independent clauses can, of course, simply be punctuated with periods. But if the clauses are short, such treatment would give a very choppy style. If two or more independent clauses are logically related to each other and we think it desirable to include them in one sentence, we have the following options:

a. We may link them by a semicolon.

> It was late; the rain had stopped.
> I paused by the gate; I was warm and a little tired.

b. Or we may link them by means of one of the co-ordinating conjunctions, namely, *and, but, or, nor, for,* with or without the use of a comma.

> It was late and the rain had stopped.
> I paused by the gate, for I was warm and a little tired.

If we take the option under (b) we are forced to specify the relation between the clauses. For example, do we mean " It was late *and* the rain had stopped " or " It was late *but* the rain had stopped "? If we do not want to specify the relationship, or if we can gain a particular rhetorical effect by not doing so, then we may prefer to link the clauses by means of the semicolon.

If we decide to use the conjunction and the clauses are short, we probably will not use a comma except when the conjunction is *for.* (Unless we put a comma before *for,* the reader may momentarily take it for the preposition *for;* courtesy, as well as clarity, demands the use of the comma here.) If the clauses are long, we shall probably insert a comma with any one of the co-ordinating conjunctions.

> Car after car crept or rolled or whizzed down the street, but throughout the afternoon no car stopped at her door.

If the clauses have commas within them, it may be helpful to join them with a semicolon, even if they are also linked by a co-ordinating conjunction.

> Mary, sulky and petulant, kept silent throughout the ride; but Alice, though disturbed inwardly, smiled brightly and tried to chat.

EXCEPTIONS AND PROBLEMS

The so-called " comma fault " consists in using the comma instead of a semicolon to link independent clauses. For example:

> The day had been long and exciting, we were very tired.

Students who are vigilant against such obvious instances of the comma fault may, however, be tricked into it when using an " adverbial conjunction " such as *accordingly, however, nevertheless.* Thus:

I do not believe that he is the thief, however, I did not get a good look at the thief as he slipped out the window.

This sentence should be punctuated:

I do not believe that he is the thief; however, I did not, etc.

Some authorities argue that the adverbial conjunction *yet* is a genuine conjunction; but the student will be safe if he learns the conventional list of five co-ordinating conjunctions, limits his use of the comma strictly to that group, and in every other instance inserts a semicolon between two independent clauses. If he does this, no one can possibly quarrel with his punctuation.

14.2 The Colon

As a kind of linking punctuation, the colon has a far more specialized function than the semicolon. The colon is the anticipator — it signals "something to come." Like the semicolon, it is sometimes used to link two independent clauses, particularly when the first clause may be thought to look forward to the second:

After the long cold rains, the day broke warm and fair: we were grateful.

This use of the colon is a nicety for which the student will not have much practical use. But he may very well find the colon of great practical usefulness as an introducer, a signal to the reader that a list or series or an explanatory statement is to follow. Thus:

The members of the volunteer fire company represented a variety of skills and vocations: five truck gardeners, two salesmen, a plumber, an electrician, and a carpenter.

She has just three good traits: honesty, a certain candor of speech, and frugality.

The evidence all adds up to just one thing: murder!

EXCEPTIONS AND PROBLEMS

The use of the colon to anticipate a word, series, or list is somewhat formal. The student will not always want to call attention to what follows quite so emphatically. If less emphasis is desired, the colon could be changed to a comma in the second sentence given above, and perhaps also in the third. But the colon, just because it does have this clear and specific use, can be of real service in writing. The student writer should number it among his resources.

14.3 The Dash

It may seem queer to include the dash under the rubric of " linking punctuation " since the special character of the dash is to be " anti-linking." The dash, as we saw on page 784, signifies that there is an abrupt break in the thought, that rules are temporarily off.

Yet just because it does dispense with other linkage, such as that provided by conjunctions, the dash may be said to constitute a link in its own right. Consider the following sentences:

> The fact that he was scared, the fact that he was late, the fact that he was anticipating punishment — all these things account for his lie.
> A few scraps of " trap " cheese, a piece of bread, and a bag of peanuts — these were to be his food for two days.

In both sentences a line of thought is suddenly broken off in favor of a kind of summary. Such constructions are frequently clear and vigorous statements of ideas that would otherwise be complicated or pallid, or both. With the dash, the writer seems to be saying: " I could go on further with what I am saying and I could put it all tidily into one grammatical package, but I'm going to break the rules, simply drop this construction that I started in favor of a simpler and more direct one. You will know what I mean."

But just because the dash does suspend the rules, as it were, it must not be overdone. The dash is the temptation of the lazy writer. Overused, it begets lazy writing.

15. Separating Punctuation

This category has only one member, the comma — unless we also want to include the dash which, because it signifies a suspension of the rules, can be put anywhere. But for practical purposes, the only kind of separating punctuation is the comma, and specifically the single comma. (Commas arranged in pairs to set off words or phrases, we shall treat under **Enclosing Punctuation, 16.**)

15.1 The comma is used to separate the members of a series. Thus:

> A bright, merry, thoroughly freckled face greeted him.
> He placed a pot of paste, a pair of shears, and a plastic ruler on the table.

Note: Many newspapers and magazines and some books now omit the comma before *and* in such a series.

15.2 The comma is used to separate long phrases and dependent clauses that come before the main clause. Thus:

> Throughout the long and wearisome summer, she was diligent in calling on the sick man.
>
> After we saw what the situation was, we did not try to speak to him further while he sat there.

Note that the dependent clause, "while he sat there," is not here (and not usually) separated from the main clause by a comma because it comes after the main clause.

15.3 An absolute phrase beginning a sentence (including the nominative absolute; see page 778) is separated from the rest of the sentence by a comma.

> *The ford having been located,* we prepared to cross the river.

15.4 Transitional expressions such as *in fact, nevertheless, on the whole, for example,* are, if they begin the sentence, usually separated from the rest of the sentence by a comma.

> *On the whole,* I am satisfied.
> *Nevertheless,* I think you ought to go.

15.5 Vocatives used in direct address at the beginning of a sentence are separated from the rest of the sentence by a comma.

> *Charles,* what do you think?
> *My dear old friend,* how good it is to see you.

15.6 Interjections occurring at the beginning of a sentence are separated from the rest of the sentence by a comma.

> *Well,* so that's what you think.

Note: The interjection may be followed by an exclamation point rather than a comma.

> *Good grief!* You don't think I did it!

15.7 The comma is sometimes used before or after a sentence element displaced from its normal word order. For example, normal order would give us

He had books in plenty.

But, if for the sake of emphasis, we write

Books, he had in plenty.

a comma usually follows the displaced " Books." So also in such a sentence as the following:

We saw a tall man, *old and ill.* [adjectives displaced from normal position]

15.8 In addition to its use in accordance with the foregoing rules, a comma should be inserted wherever needed to prevent confusion of meaning.

Inside, the room smelled of decay and despair.

Without the comma, the reader would first take *Inside the room* as a prepositional phrase, and then be forced to go back and start the sentence over.

In waving, his hand appeared palsied and feeble.

Without the separation effected by the comma, *his hand* would seem to be the object of the gerund *waving.*

EXCEPTIONS AND PROBLEMS

Most instances of misuse of the separating comma consist in separating elements that should not be separated:

a. A subject and its verb:

A land of streams and meadow and woodland, lay smiling in the sun.

b. A verb and its object:

We realized very quickly, that the man was insane.

c. An adjective and the noun it modifies:

She is a strong, rosy-cheeked, ebullient, girl.

The comma after *ebullient* should be omitted. The other commas in the sentence, as separating the members of the series of adjectives, are necessary.

d. Elements joined by a co-ordinating conjunction:

Her antiques filled the house, and the barn.

16. Enclosing Punctuation

Under this rubric we shall discuss paired commas, and, though they are all of much less importance, paired parentheses, brackets, and dashes. These various marks of punctuation are used to enclose (that is, to segregate) parenthetical elements — elements that could be omitted without destroying the basic meanings of the sentences in which they occur.

16.1 Paired Commas

16.1a   Commas are used to enclose parenthetical words and expressions such as *nevertheless, in fact, for example, accordingly, in the first place, of course, I hope, he says* (and all other such expressions in direct discourse) when they occur within the sentence.

> It was, *in fact,* the worst automobile wreck that I had ever seen.
> He considered the match, *nevertheless,* to be a kind of moral victory.
> " We think," *he replied,* " that the fire was deliberately set."

Note that shorter parenthetical expressions such as *however, too, indeed, perhaps* may be used with or without enclosing commas.

> Mary would *also* like to go.
> This latest bulletin is *indeed* damaging to our cause.
> He knew, *indeed,* that the worst was over.

16.1b   Vocatives used in direct address are enclosed in commas.

> Do you really mean, *Vera,* that you want us to tell you that secret?
> But, *my dear fellow,* that can't be correct.

16.1c   Absolute phrases occurring within a sentence are enclosed in commas.

> He stepped, *his staff grasped firmly in his right hand,* out into the night.

16.1d   Interjections occurring in the course of a sentence are enclosed in commas.

> If you think so, *well,* you simply think so.

16.1e   Nonrestrictive phrases and clauses are set off by paired commas.

> The boat on which we were to sail, *a dismal-looking old tub,* had got up steam.

Note that " on which we were to sail " is a relative clause modifying boat and that " a dismal-looking old tub " is an appositive phrase also " modifying " boat. But the former is restrictive; the latter, nonrestrictive. For " on which we were to sail " restricts the meaning: it specifies which boat had got up steam and so is an integral part of the sentence. The phrase adds to our information about the boat, but clearly it could be omitted without changing the basic meaning of the sentence. There is no rule of thumb for distinguishing between restrictive and nonrestrictive clauses. Often one must examine the context of the sentence and the writer's intention — even when the writer is oneself — to decide on the appropriate punctuation. For example, let us look at the following sentences:

> She ladled out soup to the Boweryites, who were hungry.

This means that she fed all Boweryites, whereas

> She ladled out soup to the Boweryites who were hungry.

means that she fed only the hungry Boweryites — not necessarily all of them.

If the student has difficulty in distinguishing between restrictive and nonrestrictive phrases and clauses, he will do well to apply the " omission " test. If the phrase or clause can be omitted without altering the basic meaning of the sentence, it is nonrestrictive. Consider the following examples:

> The boy with the red tie pushed me.
> The boy who wore a red tie went first.

If the phrase " with the red tie " or the clause " who wore a red tie " is omitted, we lose the identification, and the meaning of the sentence is changed.

> John, who wore a red tie, went first.

In this sentence we can omit " who wore a red tie " without obscuring the point of the sentence, for the proper name *John* sufficiently identifies the one who went first. The dependent clause is clearly nonrestrictive.

Here are some further examples of parenthetical elements for which enclosing commas are required:

> The tall, dignified man, *who seemed a bit fidgety,* consulted his watch.
>   [relative clause nonrestrictive because the man has been identified]
> The old homestead, *newly painted white,* stood well back among its trees. [participial phrase]

791

Jim Bedloe, *the gardener,* stepped up to testify next. [appositive]
The left fielder, *not the shortstop,* caught that ball. [contrasted element, which may be regarded as a sort of " negative appositive "]

But in

The infielder who was nearest to second base caught the ball.

the relative clause, " who was nearest to second base," is clearly restrictive. To omit it would be to leave in doubt which of the infielders made the catch.

EXCEPTIONS AND PROBLEMS

Most appositives are nonrestrictive and are to be set off by commas; yet there are also restrictive appositives. Consider these:

My uncle *James* is dining with us this evening.
The novelist *Maugham* was the first modern writer to interest her.

In these examples the appositives are clearly restrictive, indicating which uncle or which novelist is meant.

16.2 Paired Parentheses, Dashes, and Brackets

The general pattern for the use of these marks of punctuation is the same as that of the enclosing commas. For the most part, commas are sufficient for enclosing punctuation, but there are occasions on which we may prefer to use the other marks.

16.2a Parentheses stress the " parenthetical " and unintegrated nature of the material they enclose.

A large majority (59 per cent to be exact) favored McKeon for the post.
The English " home counties " (which include Surrey, Middlesex, and Hertfordshire, among others) are all close to London.

16.2b Dashes here — as elsewhere — convey the sense of an abrupt interruption. We use them when the parenthetical matter seems thrown suddenly into the course of the statement.

Fred White — you've never really seen anyone like him — will be there.
This community is cool — I mean icy, glacial — to all new arrivals.

16.2c Brackets are reserved for editorial comment. If, in quoting a statement of someone else, the writer wishes to interpolate a correction or comment of his own, or if an insertion is necessary to make sense of the quotation, he encloses the interpolated matter in brackets. Thus:

> Lord Macaulay writes: "Neither John of Austria, the conqueror of Lepanto [where Turkish sea power was destroyed in 1571], nor Lord Howard of Effingham, to whose direction the marine of England was confided when the Spanish invaders were approaching our shores, had received the education of a sailor."

Brackets are also used to replace parentheses when the parentheses would otherwise occur *within* parentheses. Thus:

> On his first day he got the bag limit (five geese [brant not included] and fifteen ducks).

Mechanics

Thus far we have discussed punctuation primarily as it affects and reflects sentence structure. In this section we shall take up some of the purely conventional uses of the period and colon, the apostrophe, the hyphen, quotation marks, and also matters of mechanics such as abbreviations, capitals, and italics.

17. Abbreviations

We abbreviate words to save space, and whenever such saving is necessary or appropriate, abbreviations are properly used. Thus we address a letter to

> *Mr.* J. M. Smith [not *Mister*]

or to

> *Dr.* R. A. Ledyard [not *Doctor*]

But in ordinary writing we would *not* use these abbreviations. Thus, we would not write

> He said that he was old enough to be called "*mr.*"
> The boy kept complaining until his mother called the *dr.*

In ordinary writing we also spell out names of people, countries, states, months, days of the week, and words like *street, company, chapter,* and *page,* though in the proper place — addresses on letters or footnotes to an article — the abbreviations are quite correct and even preferable. Thus:

> The *street* he lived on rejoiced in the name of *Florida*.

but

> Mr. S. T. Boyd, 1134 Florida *St.*, Palmerston, *Fla.*

or

> I had read the first *volume* and the first three *chapters* of the second.

but, in a bibliography reference:

> Harrison, G. B., ed. *Major British Writers*. 2 vols. New York: Harcourt, Brace and Company, 1954.

There are a number of words that are rarely, if ever, spelled out: academic degrees when used after a proper name (LL.D., M.A., M.D.) ; designations of the son or father when used with a name (Jr., Sr.) ; and time designations when used with numerals: A.D. (anno Domini, in the year of our Lord) , B.C. (before Christ) , A.M., and P.M. (*ante* and *post meridiem,* before and after noon) .

For the proper form of a given abbreviation, as well as for lists of abbreviations, consult the dictionary. Most abbreviations represent a selection of letters from the word to be shortened, followed by a period or periods as a sign that the shortening has taken place. But there is a tendency today to drop the periods, especially in Great Britain. During the last thirty years, the growth of the so-called " alphabetical agencies," both on a national and international scale, has also popularized the dropping of periods, as in WPA, UNESCO, and NATO.

18. Apostrophe

The apostrophe has three main uses:

18.1 It is used to form the possessive (see page 738) .

> a man's work   men's hats   ladies' dresses   son-in-law's gift

18.2 It is used to mark the omitted letters or figures in a contraction.

> can't (cannot)   it's (it is)   couldn't (could not)   in '22 (1922)

18.3 It is used with –s to form the plural of symbolic units that ordinarily do not have plurals; for example, of a letter, numeral, symbol, or word thought of as a symbolic unit.

> He wrote three *t*'s, two *4*'s, and then two $'s.
> There are too many *so*'s in your sentence.

Caution: One must distinguish *it's* (meaning *it is*) from *its* (the possessive of *it*) and *who's* (meaning *who is*) from *whose* (the possessive of *who*). None of the possessive forms of the personal pronoun use the apostrophe: *its, his, hers, ours, yours, theirs.*

19. Capitals

19.1 We begin proper names with capital letters, whether the names are of persons, months, cities, states, countries, races, or nationalities. Ordinarily we also capitalize adjectives derived from these proper names.

> Charles   February   Atlanta   Indiana   Japanese   Indian   Polynesian

19.2 We also capitalize nouns and pronouns pertaining to the Deity.

> God   the Almighty   He   His will   Him

19.3 We also capitalize common nouns when they are used as part of a proper name or can be thought of as substitutes for a proper name.

> Old *Judge* Ralston is my neighbor.

but

> John Ralston is one of our *judges.*

> This is Andrew, *Mother,* the friend I met at camp.

but

> I introduced Andrew to my *mother*

> I live on Anderson *Avenue.*

but

> It is the longest *avenue* in our town.
> The Mississippi *River* is our mightiest *river.*

19.4 In the titles of literary works — books, stories, plays — we usually capitalize all the words after the first except articles, short prepositions, and conjunctions.

> *The Hound of the Baskervilles*
> *The Sound and the Fury*
> *Once aboard the Lugger*

or

> *Once Aboard the Lugger*

19.5 We capitalize the first word of every sentence (see page 783). If a complete sentence is a part of a larger sentence, as in dialogue, we often capitalize it even though it is preceded by a number of other words. For example:

> He told them, " We have all been betrayed."
> The problem is: How can we decently refuse to go?

19.6 Miscellaneous Use of Capitals

19.6a We always capitalize the interjection *O* (but not the interjection *oh* except at the beginning of a sentence) and the personal pronoun *I*. (In medieval manuscript writing, the personal pronoun *i* was so inconspicuous that it was easily overlooked. It was capitalized simply to make it more prominent, and then, when the age of printing began, the manuscript practice was continued.)

19.6b Personifications, especially in poetry, are frequently (though not invariably) capitalized:

> "Visit her, gentle Sleep! with wings of healing. . . ."

19.6c We usually capitalize the first word of every line of poetry, though a good deal of modern poetry has dispensed with this convention.

20. Ellipsis

Ellipsis, the omission of one or more words from a passage of quoted matter, is indicated by three spaced periods:

> "The old oaken bucket . . . that hung in the well."

Four spaced periods are used if the omitted material ends with a period.

> "Such is a University in its idea and in its purpose. . . . Shall it ever be again?"

The use of asterisks instead of periods is still occasionally to be seen, but this practice is dying out, as is also the use of the "omission dash" to conceal a proper name or take the sting out of profanity.

> Mr. M——n continued. "I don't give a d——n what the fellow says."

21. Hyphens

The function of the hyphen is to link parts of words that have been cut asunder, binding them back into one word, or to bind two or more words into one larger unit of meaning.

21.1 The hyphen is used to link parts of a word divided between two lines of written or printed matter. When we find that we do not have room enough at the end of a line of manuscript or typescript to write the whole of a word, we can divide it (taking care to do so at a "syllabic joint") and add a hyphen to signify that the reader is to look to the next line for the rest of the word. For example:

> Harry on such occasions always showed a real magna-
> nimity.

Do not divide words into unpronounceable bits, e.g., pie-ce, brou-ght, hea-dache. Consult the dictionary for proper syllabification.

21.2 The hyphen may be used to show the relationship between modifiers that precede a substantive. Thus:

> a long-discovered river

means that the river was discovered a long time ago. Remove the hyphen and the reader may, momentarily at least, take the river to be long as well as discovered.

Typical of this use of the hyphen are the following phrases:

ham-handed boorishness	fifteenth- and sixteenth-century politics
sixteenth-century lyric	devil-may-care offhandedness

Hyphenated modifiers often consist of an adverb and adjective preceding the substantive, as in the following examples:

a well-considered plan   the slow-moving procession

But when the adverb ends in *–ly* (i.e., is a clearly marked adverb) or when the adverb-adjective combination *follows* the noun, no hyphen is required. Thus:

a *gently* flowing stream   the procession, grim and slow moving

21.3   The hyphen is used in the spelling of many compound words. It is employed when the two words are felt to be connected but not simply parts of one word. Frequently the hyphenated form constitutes a transition between the stage in which the two elements of the compound are thought of as two distinct words and their final coalescence into a single word — compare *wood ibis, wood-note,* and *woodpecker.* Many single word forms must have had similar earlier stages. Thus a *blackbird* was evidently once simply a *black bird* and a *blackberry,* a *black berry.* If the *black bear* were more familiar to us and the words more often on our lips, it would by this time have become *blackbear,* or at least *black-bear.* Because authorities are not all in agreement and because the status of these compounds is steadily changing, the only safe guide to spelling them is a recent edition of a good dictionary.

21.4   Other Technical Uses of the Hyphen in Spelling

21.4a   To avoid ambiguities in pronunciation — usually in the coming together of two *e*'s or two *o*'s and the consequent interpretation of the double *e* and double *o* as one syllable rather than two. For example: *re-examine (not reexamine)*, *re-elect, co-ordinating, co-operate.*

Some printers, however, solve the problem by using a diaeresis (two dots) over the second vowel to show that it is pronounced separately *(coördinating, coöperate)*, and there is a growing tendency to spell these words without either diaeresis or hyphen.

21.4b   To distinguish words originally of the same etymology but now having different meanings: *re-creation* and *recreation; re-cover* and *recover.*

21.4c   At times with certain prefixes such as *ex–* and *all–,* which tend to be stressed: *ex-wife, all-important.*

21.4d With the prefixes just mentioned and any other prefix used with a proper name. (Here the hyphen avoids the difficulty of having a capital letter in the middle of a word.) Example: *pre-Eisenhower, anti-Fascist, pro-British.*

21.4e In compounds of *self–: self-contained, self-supporting, self-governed.*

21.4f In compound numerals from *twenty-one* to *ninety-nine.*

21.4g In such compound words as *son-in-law, mother-in-law, mayor-elect.*

22. Italics

Most fonts of type have an italic as well as a regular roman face. Italics provide an easy way to focus the reader's attention on a particular word or group of words. Words underlined in a manuscript or typescript will be set in italics by the printer.

22.1 Italics may be used to emphasize a word or group of words.

That is *not* what I meant in arguing for an increased budget.

But the use of italics is usually frowned upon as a lazy way, and if overdone, a very ineffective way, to secure emphasis. Certainly, the student will do better to try to secure his emphasis by the proper choice of words and the proper disposition of them. Indeed, the end of the whole discipline of rhetoric is to secure proper emphasis. Nevertheless, to deny all use of italics and to rely upon rhetorical skill alone is a counsel of perfection. The student may not be able to avoid an occasional underlining of the crucial word.

22.2 Titles of works of art, ships, books, magazines, newspapers, and any separately published literary or musical composition are put in italics when printed (or underlined in typing).

He sailed on the last voyage of the *Andrea Doria.*
Have you ever seen the *Venus de' Medici?*
It was a strenuous week: we were to hear *Carmen* and to read *Bleak House* and *Maud.*

A recent Roosevelt biography was reviewed in *The Yale Review* and in the New York *Times*.

EXCEPTIONS AND PROBLEMS

Titles of short literary works such as poems, stories, and essays are frequently put within quotation marks rather than italicized: Tennyson's "Ulysses," Kipling's "Phantom Rickshaw," Lamb's "Dissertation on Roast Pig." A sound rule seems to be that if the work was separately published — a book-length poem or a novel — the title is put in italics; quotation marks are reserved for the titles of compositions which appear as items within a volume.

22.3   Foreign words and phrases are put in italics.

The burning of the village was a good example of the old-fashioned *Schrecklichkeit*.
The mountain climber first drove a *piton* into a crevice of the rock face.
He gave his adversary the *coup de grâce*.

But foreign words and phrases are constantly being Anglicized — nowadays we think of words like "boudoir" and "garage" as thoroughly naturalized and would not consider putting them in italics. When in doubt about the current practice concerning a particular word, consult a late edition of a good dictionary.

22.4   Finally, words, letters, or numerals referred to as such are italicized.

The word *ecstasy* is frequently misspelled. People have trouble with the *s*'s and the *c*.
Are you familiar with the special kind of *7* that is used by Continental writers?

23. Numbers

We may either spell out numbers or represent them by means of figures. The principles that determine which procedure we will follow have to do with the length of the number and with the context in which the number appears.

23.1   In general, if the number can be expressed in one or two words, we spell it out. Thus: *fifty* dollars, *forty-seven* volunteers.

23.2 But in certain contexts we almost invariably use figures: we do so in writing dates, street addresses, statistics, page references, and lists of numbers or lists in which several numbers appear:

> The Lummus Company, 385 Madison Avenue, New York 17, New York
> 12:30 A.M.   March 10, 1944   page 33
> He owned 54 sheep, 17 cows, 3 mules, and 127 hens.

EXCEPTIONS AND PROBLEMS

It ought to be observed, however, that there are many exceptions in the application of the principles that we have suggested. One finds such forms as:

> five o'clock [though never " five A.M."]
> March 3rd   the third of March [especially when the date of the year is
>   not given]

Though almost invariably the year is given in figures, there is one exception even here: In very formal invitations the year is spelled out.

Caution:

(1) Be consistent. Do not write

> Her lot was one hundred and twenty feet wide and 75 feet across.
> He spends thirty-seven dollars a week for a room and $25.00 for food.

(2) Do not allow a numeral to begin a sentence. Instead of writing

> 147 applicants appeared at the office on the first day.

spell out *147* or recast the sentence:

> On the first day, 147 applicants appeared at the office

24. Quotation Marks

Quotation marks have three basic uses:

24.1 The first and most important use of quotation marks is to set off all direct quotations. Quotation marks may thus be regarded as a kind of " enclosing punctuation " (see page 790). Note that punctuation marks must always be " closed " at the end of the passage quoted and care must be taken to exclude all matter not actually quoted. For example:

> "You never know what such people will do," he said, gesturing vaguely; "you never know."

If a quotation occurs within a quotation, it is enclosed in single quotation marks.

> "He did not hear me enter the room," James told us, "and so he went on talking to himself. I heard him say, again and again, 'I should not have done it.'"

EXCEPTIONS AND PROBLEMS

(1) When a quotation includes more than one paragraph, the quotation marks must be used at the beginning of each new paragraph but only at the end of the final paragraph. Thus:

> "*Now!* Taking the only weed of a candle, and leaving the drinkers in the dark, he led us down a dark and stumbly earthen passage, over loose stones and an odd plank, as it would seem underground, to the stanza, the room.
>
> "The stanza! It was pitch-dark — but suddenly I saw a big fire of oak-root, a brilliant, flamy, rich fire, and my rage in that second disappeared."

(2) In written dialogue, a new paragraph begins with each change of the speaker, no matter how short the paragraphs may have to be.

> "I've got to go," Lucy said.
>
> He laughed. "They're always calling you, aren't they? Do you suppose it's because you've got such a fine name?"
>
> "I'm named after my great-grandmother," Lucy said.

(3) Very long quotations (ten lines or more) are frequently set up by the printer in smaller type to make an obvious block of related matter; in typing they are typed in single space with special indentation. If quoted material is treated in this fashion, quotation marks are omitted as unnecessary. In accordance with this same principle, lines of poetry when printed as verse do not require quotation marks.

24.2 Quotation marks are used to enclose the titles of stories, poems, short plays, and essays (see also page 800).

24.3 Quotation marks are used to warn the reader that a word or phrase is being used in a special sense.

The lecturer told us that he was going to use the word *myth* in a special way, with none of the usual implications that the "mythical" was somehow false. "Myth" was to mean any fictional construct, including constructs in which the fictional element was necessary and inevitable.

Quotation marks should not be used to indicate that a word, letter, or numeral is being referred to as such — for which use one should employ italics (see page 799).

Note on the placing of quotation marks with regard to other marks of punctuation:

It will be well to remember the following conventions of American printers:

(1) The period and comma always fall inside the quotation marks:

> "This is the time," he said, "to finish the job."

(2) The colon and the semicolon always fall outside the quotation marks:

> We were finally granted permission to see the American "conspirators and spies": two woebegone Texas hoboes and an indignant middle-aged schoolteacher from Indiana.
>
> I had just finished my first reading of "Delta Autumn"; I put the volume down.

(3) The question mark, exclamation point, and dash are placed inside or outside the quotation marks, depending upon whether they go with the quoted matter or with the whole sentence. Thus:

> The telephone operator asked, "What is your number?"

but

> How can one really know that this or any other moment is the "propitious moment"?

Index of Usage and of Grammatical Terms Used in the Handbook

A, an. The indefinite article. Use *a* before words beginning with a consonant (not merely spelled but sounded); otherwise use *an: a* tie, *an* apple, *an* hour.

Abbreviations. See **17**.

Absolute constructions. Expressions that are grammatically independent of the rest of the sentence. See **10**.

Accept, except. Sometimes confused through careless pronunciation. *To accept* is "to receive" or "to admit"; *to except* is "to exclude."

Active voice. See **3.4**.

Adjectival clause. A subordinate clause that performs the function of an adjective, i.e., modifies a substantive. See **5**.

Adjective. A part of speech that modifies a substantive. See **2.1**.

Adverb. A part of speech that modifies a verb, adjective, or other adverb. See **2.2**.

Adverbial clause. A subordinate clause that performs the function of an adverb. See **5**.

Affect, effect. Sometimes confused through careless pronunciation. *To affect* something is "to exert an influence" upon it; *to effect* something is "to bring it about, to make it happen."

Agree to, agree with. We agree *to* a proposal; *with* a person.

Agreement. Those parts of speech that vary in form to show gender, number, and case agree when they stand in certain relationships; e.g., subject and verb agree in number. See pp. 735, 739, 754, and 776.

Ain't. Since *ain't* would seem to derive in quite legitimate historical fashion from *am not (amn't)* and *are not (aren't)* and is anomalous only in being used for *isn't*, it is a pity that the schoolmarms did such a thorough job of convincing everybody (including most of those who say *ain't*) that it is hopelessly illiterate. *Ain't*, however, seems past reviving, and we are left with very awkward shifts for expressing "am not I," including the British "aren't I." (The British spelling, by the way, is not an illiterate plural but is an attempt to indicate the British broad *a* that developed parallel to the *ai* sound in the American version.)

All of. The *of* is redundant with nouns in such expressions as *"All of* the sailors perished." In formal writing use *all* alone: *"All* the bread was eaten," and *"All* the conspirators confessed." But *all of* is used with pronouns: *"All of* us enjoyed it."

All ready, all right, all together. *All ready* is to be distinguished from *already: all ready* means "all prepared"; *already* means "having occurred at some previous time." *Alright* is a misspelling of *all right. All together* means "all in unison"; *altogether* means "wholly," "fully": "Let us *all* work *together*," and "The conception is *altogether* mistaken."

Among, between. *Between* refers to two; *among*, to more than two.

And/or. Found primarily in business letters. It is awkward and even awkwardly pretentious, for the specification of both such possibilities is not often necessary.

Anyways, anywheres. These words

represent old adverbial forms in *-s* that linger on in colloquial English. Use *anyway* and *anywhere*.

Apostrophe. The sign of the possessive. See **7** and **8**.

Appositive. A substantive set beside another substantive to qualify it. For its punctuation, see **16.1e**.

Articles. The adjectives *a*, *an*, and *the*.

As. Mistakes in the use of *as* tend to occur in the following areas.

(1) **As,** *the pronoun*. *As* may be used as a relative pronoun with *same* or *such* as its antecedent: "He wears the *same* hat size *as* I," and "The spectacle was *such as* I had never seen before." But formal English does not permit *as* as a relative pronoun substituting for *who:* "I think those *as* have lied had better admit it."

(2) **As,** *the preposition*. See **Like, as,** below.

(3) **As,** *the subordinate conjunction*. In this use *as* has a number of meanings, and this vagueness, though handy for the lazy thinker who can use an *as* construction without worrying too much about its precise meaning, may defeat the purposes of the writer who wishes to be clear and forceful. Consider "*As* it was four o'clock, we chafed with impatience." If the writer means "*Since* it was four o'clock," it would be more emphatic to write *since*. The student should ask himself whether he really wants to use *as*, or whether he can think of a more accurate word like *because* or *since*. See also **Like, as,** below.

At about, at around. Double prepositions used colloquially, usually redundant in formal English. See **4.1**.

Auxiliary verb. Literally "helper" verb, used to form the precise tenses and moods of other verbs. *Be, have,* and *do* are important auxiliaries. For the modal auxiliaries, see **3.6**.

Awful. This word has departed so far from its original connection with *awe* that it can hardly be used in serious and responsible writing. *Awful*, used as a mere intensive, is colloquial or slang.

Beside, besides. *Beside* is a preposition meaning "by the side of." *Besides* is either a preposition or an adverb meaning "in addition to," "excepting."

Between, among. See **Among, between**, above.

Brackets. Enclosing punctuation. See **16.2c**.

Burst. *Bursted* and *busted* are dialectal or slang forms of the past participle of this verb. For the principal parts, see p. 809.

But what. Substandard for *but that*.

Can, may. *Can* signifies that one is *able* to perform some action; *may* signifies that one is *permitted* to perform some action.

Can't help but. Formal English requires *can but:* "I *can but* sympathize with him [i.e., "I *can only*," etc.]."

Can't seem. *Can't seem* is colloquial. In more formal writing, use "I *am unable* to do this" rather than "I *can't seem* to do this."

Capitals. See **19**.

Case. A relational aspect of nouns and pronouns as shown by inflection. See **1.1d** and **1.2a**.

Clause. A group of words containing a subject and predicate. Clauses may be independent or dependent. See **5**.

Collective noun. The name for a group of some kind; e.g., *crowd, company, army*. See **1.1b**.

Colon. Linking punctuation. See **14.2** and **23.2**.

Comma. Separating, linking, and enclosing punctuation. See **14.1, 15,** and **16.1**.

Comma fault. The attempt to link by a comma two independent clauses *not* connected by a co-ordinating conjunction. See **14.1**.

Command. The imperative form of the verb. See **3.6**.

Comparative degree. The second degree in the comparison of adjectives and adverbs. See **2.1b** and **2.2b**.

Compare to, compare with. To compare one thing *to* another is to liken it; e.g., "Because of his energy I *compared* him *to* a dynamo." To compare one thing *with* another is to set them side by side for examination of both likenesses and differences; e.g., "I patiently *compared* one essay *with* the other."

Comparison. Of adjectives, see **2.1b**; of adverbs, see **2.2b**.

Complement, compliment. A *complement* completes something or represents a completion; e.g., "The warship had her full *complement* of men." A *compliment* is an expression of courtesy or admiration.

Complement of the verb. Whatever completes the meaning of the verb: with a linking (or intransitive) verb, the predicate adjective or predicate nominative; with a transitive verb, the object. See **1.2a** and **3.3.**

Complex sentence. A sentence that contains, in addition to its independent clause, at least one dependent clause. See **Compound sentence** and **Simple sentence,** below.

Compound sentence. A sentence that contains more than one independent clause.

Conjunction. A part of speech that connects words, phrases, or clauses. See **4.2.**

Contrary-to-fact conditions. For the form of the verb in such conditional clauses, see **3.6.**

Contrasted element. A kind of negative appositive. See **16.1e.**

Co-ordinating conjunction. A conjunction that joins words, phrases, and clauses of equal rank. See **4.2** and **14.1.**

Dangling modifier. A modifier that has no specific word in the sentence to which it refers. See **9** and **10.**

Dash. Terminal, linking, and enclosing punctuation. See **13, 14.3,** and **16.2b.**

Definite article. *The* is the definite article; compare with *a, an.*

Demonstrative adjectives. *This, these,* and *that, those.* See **2.1a.**

Dependent clause. A clause that cannot stand alone; it is usually headed by a subordinating conjunction or by a relative pronoun. It functions in the sentence as a noun, an adjective, or an adverb. Also called a *subordinate clause.* See **5.**

Diaeresis. Two dots placed over the second of two consecutive vowels to show that it is pronounced as a separate vowel. See **21.4a.**

Different from. Use *different from* rather than *different than; different to* is British.

Direct address. The calling of the name of (or some equivalent term by which to refer to) the person directly addressed by the speaker.

Direct object. The noun or noun substitute which is acted upon by a transitive verb. See **3.3.**

Double negatives. In logic, one negative cancels another and formal English follows this logic. Careless writers easily slip into the double negative and may even employ it intentionally on the assumption that the second negative *emphasizes* rather than cancels the first. See **12.5.**

Due to. English still frowns upon the use of *due to* as a preposition and requires that it be treated as an adjective modifying a specific substantive. Do not write *"Due to* engine trouble, he turned back," but *"Because of* engine trouble, etc.," or "His turning back was *due to* engine trouble."

Effect, affect. See **Affect, effect,** above.

Enthuse. A verb formed from the noun *enthusiasm.* It is still regarded by careful writers as an interloper, and the student has to be advised to avoid it.

Except, accept. See **Accept, except,** above.

Expletive. Literally, a filler; applied technically to the formulas *it is (was), there is (was)* for beginning a sentence. See **6.4.**

Fewer, less. Use *fewer* when referring to items that can be numbered, and *less* when referring to amounts and quantities.

Fine. Except where its original meaning lingers in expressions like "a fine thread" or "fine workmanship," this adjective has come to express no more than vague admiration. It is too wobbly to be of much use in responsible prose.

Finite. A verb form limited as to person, tense, and number, and therefore able to constitute a predicate, as a mere verbal (infinitive, gerund, and participle) cannot. Modern English has lost so many of its inflections that the reason for calling this form of the verb "finite" has been obscured. The verb *to be,* however, can furnish illustrations: the verbal *being* is too vague, too "infinite" to peg down a thought; but the "finite" forms, *is, am, are, was, were,* can peg it down. They specify a time and the kind of subject involved. See **3.9.**

Former, latter. These terms apply to a situation in which there are only two antecedents. If there are more than two, use *first* and *last* (or *finally*).

Funny. In colloquial English this word

has established itself as meaning "odd" or "queer" as well as "amusing." But if the student, writing formal English, means "odd" or "queer," he had best use these terms.

Future tense. See **3.5d.**

Gender. Indication of sex or sexlessness in the form of a word. See **1.1c** and **1.2a.**

Gerund. The verbal noun ending in *-ing.* See **3.9b.**

Get. In addition to its original meaning "acquire," *get* has developed a great many idiomatic meanings. It has also become a linking verb (and an auxiliary verb) in certain constructions. See **3.7c.**

Going to. A sign of the future in informal English style. See **3.5d.**

Good. An adjective; *well* is the corresponding adverb. But note that *well* meaning "in good health" is an adjective. For the use of *good* with verbs like *to be, to smell, to seem,* see **2.2a(6).**

Got, gotten. The past participle of *get.* In American English, both forms are correct. Only *got,* however, is used with *have* to mean "compelled (to do something)"; e.g., "I *have got* to go." And here, it ought to be further observed, *got* is redundant. "I *have* to go" means "I *am compelled* to go." The form without *got* is preferred in formal English.

Half. One may write "half a day" or, more formally, "a half day." Avoid "a half a day."

Healthful, healthy. *Healthful* means "promoting health"; *healthy* means "possessing health": "*Healthful* food makes *healthy* bodies."

Hyphen. See **21.**

Imperative. One of the three moods of English verbs. It is the mood of command. See **3.6.**

Imply, infer. It is the speaker or writer who *implies* something in a statement; it is the hearer or reader who *infers* something from the statement.

Indefinite article. See **A, an,** above.

Independent clause. A clause that can stand alone as a sentence; it is not headed by a subordinating conjunction or by a relative pronoun. See **5.**

Indicative. One of the three moods of English verbs. It is used to make statements and to ask questions. See **3.6.**

Indirect object. A substantive that is indirectly affected by the verb. See **3.3.**

Indirect question. A question put at second hand. Direct question: "Are you all right?" Indirect question: "Someone asked *whether we were all right.*"

Infinitive. A verbal, used as a substantive or modifier, formed by prefixing *to* to the base of the verb: *to go, to see.* After some verbs, *to* is omitted and we have an "unmarked" infinitive. See **3.9a.**

Inflection. Modification in the form of a word to show certain grammatical relationships. Typical inflections are the addition of *-s* to form the plural of regular nouns and of *-ed* to form the past tense of regular verbs.

Inside of. Formal English requires *inside* rather than the double preposition *inside of.*

Intensive pronoun. See **1.2b(5).**

Interjection. One of the parts of speech. See p. 729.

Interrogation point. Terminal punctuation. See **13.**

Interrogative pronoun. The pronoun used in a question. See **1.2b(2).**

Intransitive verb. A verb that cannot take a direct object. See **3.3.**

Its, it's. *Its* is the possessive of *it; it's* is a contraction of *it is.*

Kind of, sort of. In writing do not use *kind of* or *sort of* as substitutes for *rather, somewhat, a little,* and so on. Not "I am *sort of* tired," but "I am *somewhat (a little, rather)* tired." In informal English a redundant *a* is used with such expressions as "a kind of *a* pigtail," "a sort of *a* story," where more formal English calls for "a kind of pigtail," "a sort of story."

Last, latest. *Last* refers to the final member of a series; *latest,* to the most recent member — with the implication that there may be more: "The old chief was the *last* of his tribe," or "Have you seen the *latest* fashion in coats?"

Latter, later. *Latter* is not to be confused with *later; latter* is the opposite of *former.* See **Former, latter,** above.

Lay, lie. *Lay* is the transitive verb; *lie,* the intransitive. Use *lay (laid, laid)* only where the sense is that of "placing" or "putting" something "down" or "upon." *Lie (lay, lain)* always has the sense of "repose" or "rest": "I *lie* down for a nap" (present of *lie*), but "I *lay* this plate upon the table" (present of *lay*); "The book *lay* on the table" (past of *lie*), but "I *laid* the book down" (past of *lay*).

Leave, let. Do not substitute *leave* for *let* in such expressions as "*Let* him go," "*Let* us all go."

Less. See **Fewer, less,** above. Besides *less*, we have the form *lesser*. *Lesser*, a more formal term, refers to dignity or importance; *less*, to size or quantity: "*less* petroleum," "a *lesser* poet."

Liable, likely. *Liable* means "responsible," as for damages, or "exposed" to the risk of something unpleasant or undesirable. It should therefore not be used for *likely*, which means merely "expected" or "probably occurring." "He is *likely* to win for us," but "If he climbs higher, he is *liable* to fall."

Lie, lay. See **Lay, lie,** above.

Like, as. *Like* is not yet a recognized conjunction. Therefore, in formal writing, avoid using *like* for *as* and *as if*. For example, do not write "This coffee tastes *like* good coffee should taste," or "He acts *like* he was the lord of creation." Use instead "This coffee tastes *as* good coffee should taste" (or "This tastes *like* good coffee"), and "He acts *as if* he were the lord of creation."

Linking verb. An intransitive verb that links predicate adjectives or predicate nominatives to the subject of the verb. See **2.2a(6)** and **3.3.**

Loose sentence. See **Periodic sentence,** below.

Lose, loose. *To lose* means "to be defeated" or "to miss from one's possession"; the verb *to loose* means "to untie" or "to free": "I shall *lose* my investment," and "I shall *loose* the string-entangled bird."

Lot, lots of. In formal English substitute for these expressions *much*, *many*, *a great deal*, and so on.

May. See **Can, may,** above.

Modal auxiliary. An auxiliary ("helper") verb that is used to determine the mood of the main verb. See **3.6.**

Modifier. A modifier (adjective or adverb) is a word that describes, quali-

fies, or limits another part of speech. See **2.1** and **2.2.**

Mood. How the speaker regards his expression — as a statement, as a command, as a condition contrary to fact. See **3.6.**

Most. The superlative of *many* or *much*, not a substitute for *almost*. Do not write "He *most* missed his train," when you mean "He *nearly* missed his train."

Nice. An adjective that has been worn to shreds. Avoid unless you mean to use it in its meaning of "showing delicate discrimination": "a *nice* distinction," "a *nice* sense of proportion."

No-account. As an adjective, this is a corruption of the phrase *of no account*. Write "James was *of no account*," or "James was *worthless*."

No-good. As an adjective, colloquial for *useless*.

Nominative absolute. A phrasal construction that relates only generally to the rest of the sentence. See **10.**

Nominative case. Used as a subject or a predicate nominative. See **1.2a.**

Nonrestrictive modifier. See **Restrictive modifier,** below.

Noun. A part of speech that names a person, place, thing, quality, etc. See **1.1.**

Noun clause. A clause that performs the functions of a noun. See **5.**

Number. Refers to the singular or plural aspect of nouns, pronouns, and verbs. See **1.1a** and **1.1b.**

Numbers. For the treatment of numbers in writing, see **23.**

O, oh. Distinguish between these two interjections. *O* is used in direct address, is not followed by a mark of punctuation, and is always capitalized. Examples: "*O* God, our help in ages past," "Come, *O* Conqueror." *Oh* is usually used as an exclamation, is followed by a comma or an exclamation point, and has normal capitalization.

Of. A preposition. Since *of* is frequently given a slurred pronunciation, it may be confused with the verb *have* which, when in an unstressed position, is similarly pronounced. Do not write "I could *of* gone," or "We would *of* done so if we had been able."

Parentheses. Enclosing punctuation. See **16.2c.**

Participle. Part of the progressive and perfect tenses of the verb; also a verbal with the function of an adjective. See **3.1, 3.4, 3.5,** and **3.9c.**

Passive voice. When the subject of a verb does not act but is acted upon, the verb is said to be in the *passive voice.* See **3.4.**

Past perfect tense. See **3.5.**

Past tense. See **3.5.**

Period. Terminal punctuation. See **13, 17,** and **20.**

Periodic sentence. The meaning of a *periodic sentence* is held in suspension until the end of the sentence. The *periodic sentence* contrasts with the *loose sentence.*

Person. That aspect of pronouns and verbs which has to do with the one speaking (*first person*), the one spoken to (*second person*), or the one spoken of (*third person*). See **1.2a.**

Personal pronoun. See **1.2a.**

Phrase. A group of words, without subject or verb, that functions as a grammatical unit. See **5.**

Plenty. *Plenty* is not used as an adjective or an adverb in formal writing. It is a noun. Do not write "He has *plenty* of time to think about the matter."

Possessive case. The case used to indicate possession. See **1.1d** and **1.2a.**

Predicate. The *predicate* is the finite verb, and its dependent words, which asserts, with reference to the subject, an action, condition, or state of being.

Predicate adjective. An adjective which modifies the subject through a linking verb. See **2.1c, 2.2a(6),** and **3.3.**

Predicate nominative. A substantive (noun or pronoun) in the nominative case and connected with the subject by a linking verb. See **2.2a(6)** and **3.3.**

Preposition. A part of speech which relates a substantive to some other element in the sentence. See **4.1.**

Present tense. See **3.5.**

Principal, principle. Do not confuse *principal*, meaning "head" or "chief" (the *principal* party, the *principal* of the school), with *principle*, which means "basic truths" or "rules" (*principles* of mathematics).

Principal parts of the verb. The base, the past tense, and the past participle. Knowing these forms, we can derive all the other forms of a verb. Here follows a list of the principal parts of most of the "problem" verbs in English.

Base	*Past Tense*	*Past Participle*
bear	bore	borne, born
beat	beat	beaten
begin	began	begun
bid (to buy)	bid	bid
bid (to order)	bade	bidden
bite	bit	bitten
blow	blew	blown
break	broke	broken
bring	brought	brought
burst	burst	burst
catch	caught	caught
choose	chose	chosen
come	came	come
creep	crept	crept
dig	dug	dug, digged
dive	dived	dived
do	did	done
draw	drew	drawn
drink	drank	drunk
drive	drove	driven
eat	ate	eaten
fall	fell	fallen
find	found	found
flee	fled	fled
fling	flung	flung
fly	flew	flown
forget	forgot	forgot, forgotten
freeze	froze	frozen
get	got	got, gotten
give	gave	given
go	went	gone
grow	grew	grown
hang (to execute)	hanged	hanged
hang (to suspend)	hung	hung
hear	heard	heard
hurt	hurt	hurt
know	knew	known
lay	laid	laid
lead	led	led
lend	lent	lent
let	let	let
lie	lay	lain
light	lighted, lit	lighted, lit
lose	lost	lost
pay	paid	paid

Base	Past Tense	Past Participle
prove	proved	proved, proven
ride	rode	ridden
ring	rang	rung
rise	rose	risen
run	ran	run
say	said	said
see	saw	seen
set	set	set
shine	shone	shone
show	showed	shown, showed
shrink	shrank, shrunk	shrunk, shrunken
sing	sang	sung
sink	sank	sunk
sit	sat	sat
slide	slid	slid
sow	sowed	sown, sowed
speak	spoke	spoken
spit	spat, spit	spat, spit
spring	sprang, sprung	sprung
stand	stood	stood
steal	stole	stolen
sting	stung	stung
swear	swore	sworn
swim	swam	swum
swing	swung	swung
take	took	taken
tear	tore	torn
throw	threw	thrown
wake	waked, woke	waked, woken
wear	wore	worn
weave	wove	woven, wove
win	won	won
wind	wound	wound
wring	wrung	wrung
write	wrote	written

Progressive verb form. In this form of the verb the action is conceived of as continuing. All the *progressive forms* are based upon the present participle. See **3.5a.**

Pronoun. A part of speech that substitutes for a noun. See **1.2.**

Question mark. Terminal punctuation. See **13.**

Quotation mark. See **24.**

Real. An adjective, not an adverb; must not be used as a substitute for *very*. See **2.2a.**

Reckon, guess. These words are used in colloquial English to mean "think" or "suppose." In formal English avoid using *reckon* and *guess* in these senses.

Relative clause. A clause, introduced by a relative pronoun, that has the function of an adjective. See **1.2b(3)** and **5.**

Relative pronoun. The principal relative pronouns are *which*, used for things; *who*, used for persons; and *that*, used for both persons and things. See **1.2b(3).**

Restrictive modifier. A *restrictive modifier* so limits or identifies the word to which it refers that the modifier cannot be omitted without destroying the essential meaning of the sentence. A *nonrestrictive modifier* supplies further information, but can be omitted without destroying the essential meaning of the sentence. For the punctuation of restrictive and nonrestrictive modifiers, see **16.1e.**

Right. An adjective. Avoid using *right* as an adverb to substitute for *very*. See **2.2a.**

Same. Do not use *same* as a substitute for *it* or *them*. Do not write "I have received the mittens and enclose check for *same*."

Seem. See **Can't seem,** above.

Semicolon. Linking punctuation. See **14.1.**

Sentence. A sentence is a complete thought expressed through a subject and a predicate. A sentence contains at least one independent clause. See **5** and **6.**

Sequence of tenses. See **3.8.**

Set, sit. *Set* (*set, set*) is a transitive verb meaning "to place upon"; *sit* (*sat, sat*) is an intransitive verb meaning "to occupy a seat" or "to be in a seated position": "I *set* the child down. She then *sat* there quite contentedly." Compare with **Lay, lie,** above.

Shall, will. Auxiliary verb forms. See **3.7a.**

Should, would. Auxiliary verb forms. See **3.7b.**

Simple sentence. A simple sentence contains only one independent clause. Compare with **Compound sentence,** above. See **5.**

Some. In formal writing do not use *some* as a substitute for *somewhat*.

Write "She was *somewhat* prettier than I had expected," not "She was *some* prettier than I had expected."

Sort, sort of. See **Kind of, sort of,** above.

Split infinitive. The insertion of an adverb or adverbial expression between *to* and the verb base "splits" an infinitive: "He wished *to* quietly *tell* his story." Although the splitting of an infinitive is sometimes justified and unavoidable, usually it produces an awkward construction. See **12.1.**

Subject. The subject of a sentence names the performer of the action or the subject of the condition expressed by the verb. See **1.1** and **1.2a.**

Subjunctive. One of the three moods of English verbs. It expresses wish, doubt, supposition, or some other nonactual condition. See **3.6.**

Subordinate clause. See **Dependent clause,** above.

Subordinating conjunction. A conjunction, like *although, as long as, before, in order that, since, unless, while,* that connects a subordinate clause with the rest of the sentence. See **4.2.**

Substantive. A substantive is a noun, or any other part of speech or group of words functioning as a noun. See **1** and **5.**

Such. *Such* as an intensive must not be used in formal writing. Do not write "It was *such* a bright day," but "It was *such* a bright day *that* every object wore a new look." Or write simply "It was a *very* bright day."

Sure. An adjective. Do not use as an adverb, as in "It *sure* was good." Use *surely* or *certainly* or, better still, employ another intensive. See **2.2a.**

Syntax. The proper disposition and arrangement of words and groups of words within the sentence. See p. 770.

Tense. That aspect of the verb that indicates the time of the action. See **3.5.**

Than. A subordinate conjunction, not a preposition. Do not write "James runs faster than *him*," but "John runs faster than *he*" or "John runs faster than *he does.*" See also **4.1.**

There is, there are. See **Expletive,** above, and **6.4.**

They. *They* is used colloquially as an indefinite pronoun. For example, "*They* say that there will be an eclipse

of the moon tomorrow." It will usually be better to supply a definite subject or to recast the sentence.

Transitive verb. A verb that can take direct objects. See **3.3.**

Used to. Because *d* and *t* are both dental consonants, the *d* tends to be absorbed into the following *t*, a fact that causes careless writers to misspell the expression as *use to.*

Verb. That part of speech that expresses action, condition, or state of being. See **Principal parts,** above, and **3.**

Verbal. A word that is derived from a verb and has the function of a substantive or modifier. See **3.9.**

Very. In formal writing avoid using *very* to modify past participles in such constructions as "He was *very* put out," or "The blade was *very* worn." Write "He was *very much* put out," and "The blade was *much* (or *very much*) worn."

Voice. Verbs in the *active voice* represent the subject of the verb as acting; verbs in the *passive voice* represent the subject as acted upon. See **3.4.**

Want. Avoid writing "I *want for* you to do this." Write "I *want* you to do this."

Way, ways. Write "a little *way* down the street," not "a little *ways.*" Compare with **Anyways, anywheres,** above.

Well. See **Good,** above.

While. *While* used as a subordinating conjunction means "during the time that" or "at the same time that." Example: "*While* Nero fiddled, Rome burned." In formal writing avoid using *while* to mean "although" or "whereas." Example: "*While* I do not approve of the bill, I did not vote against it."

Will, shall. See **Shall, will,** above.

Word order. See **2.1c, 2.2c,** and **6.**

Would, should. See **Should, would,** above.

You. Frequently used as an indefinite pronoun: "When *you* wake with a headache, your day is off to a bad start." Care ought to be taken not to overwork *you* in this sense and not to have it seem to refer directly to the reader. Formal English tends to make use of *one* to signify "a person," "any person."

Causal Analysis

There are four methods which are helpful when investigating a situation to determine a cause. They are called the methods of **agreement,** of **difference,** of **agreement and difference,** and of **variation.** After examining them the student may feel that he has always been acquainted with them, for they merely describe how his mind *does* work when it is working straight on problems of this kind. But studying the methods may sharpen his awareness of the processes of his own reasoning.

1. Agreement. If we have two or more situations from which we get the effect X, and find that these situations have only one constant factor, E, then that constant factor may be taken as the cause of X. Let us set this up as a chart:

CASE 1

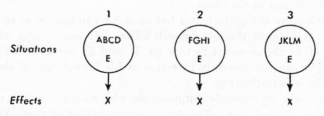

Here E is the cause of X.

The method here stated is sound in theory but in some cases is difficult to apply. Even in the laboratory, where the experimenter can create his situation with a degree of control, it is hard to be sure that only one factor, E, is constant. But it is especially difficult to apply this method to a complicated event outside of the laboratory. The investigator rarely finds a set of situations in which *only* one factor is constant. Ordinarily he will encounter a set of situations such as may be indicated by the following chart:

CASE II

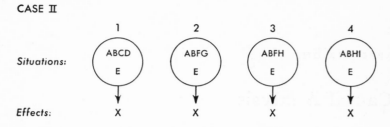

	1	2	3	4
Situations:	ABCD E	ABFG E	ABFH E	ABHI E
Effects:	X	X	X	X

We can notice two things about this set of situations.

First, several factors occur in more than one situation. For instance, factor F occurs in situations 2 and 3; factor H occurs in situations 3 and 4.

Second, three factors (A, B, and E) occur in all situations.

When the investigator sees that certain factors are repeated, as is true of F and H, he must inquire whether they are repeated in *all* situations. If they are not repeated in all situations he can discard them. So F and H can be discarded. When the investigator sees that two or more factors, as is true of A, B, and E, are repeated in all situations, there are two lines of thought open to him.

First, he may explore the possibility that A, B, and E are to be taken as components of the cause — that no one by itself would be sufficient to bring about the effect.

Second, he may explore the possibility that one or two of the factors which are present in all of his available instances might not occur in other instances when the effect does occur and therefore are not relevant to the effect.

At this point the investigator has to make a judgment as to which of the two lines of thought he will follow. He must judge whether or not all of the constant factors (A, B, and E) are relevant to the effect. He can do this only in terms of his knowledge of the field which he is investigating.

Let us take an example. Suppose we wish to learn why a certain school lost most of its football games over a period of years. We find certain things true every year. Most of the players every year are Catholic, for it is a Catholic school. Let us call this constant factor A. The same coach had been employed for a number of years (factor B). The school has very high academic standards and no one is permitted to participate in any athletic event who does not have an average grade of " fair " (factor E). The question is: Do we have a complex of factors here (A, B, and E) which are all necessary components of the cause?

Common sense and our experience with athletics at once make us rule out factor A — for we know that Catholicism bears no relation to the matter of football losses. But we cannot so readily rule out factors B and E, the matter of the coach and the matter of the high academic average required. At this point we have to make further investigation. We have to look into the coach's previous record, we have to pass a judgment on the type of instruction he gives now, and so forth. Or we must try to learn how many good players have been disqualified by the rule requiring a certain scholastic average, and so forth. We may satisfy ourselves that both of these factors (B and E) contribute to the defeats. Or we may decide that only one is the cause.

In any event, this is not a foolproof formula. Knowledge and experience are required to apply it. Even when it is applied we cannot be absolutely sure that we have determined the cause of X. We have merely indicated a certain degree of probability.

2. Difference. If we have two situations, identical save that one involves the factor E and the effect X, and the other does not involve the factor E and the effect X, then E may be taken as the cause of X or an indispensable factor in the cause. Let us put it as a chart:

CASE III

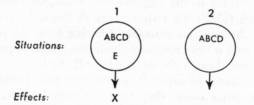

If we can be quite sure that the first situation resembles the second in all significant factors except E and X, then we may take E as the cause of X or an indispensable factor in the cause. But it is often difficult to find such clear-cut instances, and we have to draw on our judgment and experience to decide what factors are relevant.

CASE IV

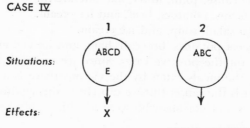

Here D as well as E is missing from the second situation. The following possibilities suggest themselves. First, D may be irrelevant, and E is the cause. Second, D may be relevant and in conjunction with E constitutes the cause. If we can control the situation, we may test the second possibility by setting up the factors ABCE. If we still get X, then we know that D is irrelevant. But if we cannot control the situation, we must consult our judgment and experience in deciding about the relevance of D.

3. **Agreement and Difference.** This is, of course, a combination of the two previous methods. Therefore the method involves both *positive* and *negative* instances. In the positive instances we apply the method of agreement, and then check the negative instances against the positive instances by the method of difference.

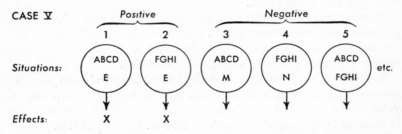

CASE Ⅴ

In situations 1 and 2 we have the ordinary method of agreement. But when we come to the negative situations, we notice that there is none which fulfills the requirement of the strict method of difference; i.e., the negative situation differing from the positive situation only in that it does not have the factor which appears to be the cause. But here, though situation 3 has all the factors of situation 1 except E, the factor of cause, it does have a new factor, M. And so on with the other cases: they would always involve, in differing combinations and sometimes with new factors, the various factors, except E, which were present when X took place.

We can set up a simple example of the method. Let us assume that in a family of five people three suffer from an attack of food poisoning. The problem is to determine what item of the restaurant meal was the cause. John, Mary, and Sue are ill.

John ate beans, potatoes, beef, and ice cream.

Mary ate a salad, soup, and ice cream.

Sue ate sweet potatoes, broccoli, ham, and ice cream.

So much for the positive cases. Since ice cream is the only item common to the meals eaten by the victims there is a strong probability that it is the cause. But we can check this against the negative cases, i.e., cases of persons who were *not* ill.

Mildred ate beans, potatoes, beef, and lemon pie.

Thomas ate a salad, sweet potatoes, and ham, with no dessert.

These negative cases include most of the dishes eaten by the victims — with the exception of ice cream. So the argument for ice cream becomes even stronger. Few situations, however, are as simple as the one given above, and in making our analysis we are often called upon to rule out many common factors which we judge to be unrelated to the effect (for instance, we might rule out the color of the plates used in all the above meals).

4. Variation. If one factor in a situation varies whenever a certain other factor varies, there is a causal connection between the factors.

CASE VI

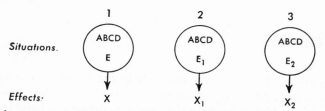

For instance, as the temperature rises, mercury expands; as the supply of a commodity increases, its price goes down; or as the amount of advertising of a product increases, its sales increase. These are illustrations of the principle, but in them are great differences in the degree of complication. In the first instance, the relation between the variation in temperature and the variation in the mercury is regular and constant. We depend on the fact, and our thermometers operate on that principle. But an economist cannot depend on the relation between supply and price with the same certainty, nor can a sales manager be sure that an increase in his advertising appropriation will pay off in the market. Here, too many unpredictable factors may be involved in the situation.

We must remember that it does not matter whether the variation is direct or inverse. For instance, we have direct variation with temperatures and mercury: as the temperature increases, the mercury increases in volume. And we have inverse variation with supply and price: as the supply increases, the price decreases.

• **Applications** •

I. Which of the methods discussed above do you find illustrated in the experiments described in "The Colors That Animals Can See" (page 478) and "The American Civilization Puzzle" (page 666)?

II. Make up incidents to illustrate two of the above methods in operation.

The Outline, Summary, and Précis

The Outline

The outline has two uses. It can help the writer to organize his own thoughts and lay a plan for his work before he begins the actual composition. And it can help the reader to define the basic meaning and structure of what he reads. The two uses have much in common, for both mean that the maker of the outline is dealing with the structure of a discourse. In fact, once an outline is completed, an observer might not be able to tell whether it was designed by a writer or a reader.

There are several common types of outlines: (1) the suggestive, or scratch outline, (2) the topic outline, (3) the sentence outline, and (4) the paragraph outline. Variations may be worked out for special purposes.

1. The Scratch Outline. The scratch outline is a set of notes and jottings which may come in handy either for writing or for understanding and remembering what one has read. It is probably not highly organized. For instance, the writer, in making a preliminary survey of his subject, may simply put down the various topics and ideas that come to him in the order in which they come. As some line of thought begins to emerge he may indicate this, too. But his primary purpose is not to define the form and order from the beginning. It is to assemble suggestive material. Some of it he may not use because, in the end, it may seem superfluous or irrelevant. The scratch outline embodies the early exploration of a subject, and may be meaningless to everybody except the maker of the outline. When such an outline is made by a reader, there is naturally some indication of the order of topics in the thing read; but even here the outline does not undertake to record the details of relations among the parts. It is merely a jog to the reader's mind, a record of the first acquaintance with the thing read.

2. The Topic Outline. The topic outline does indicate the order of treatment of individual topics and does indicate in a systematic fashion, by heads and subheads, the relation among the parts in degree of importance. But as the name indicates, it proceeds, not by sentences, but by listing topics. There is, however, one exception: the outline is to be introduced by a statement of the theme of the composition in the form of a fully rounded sentence. Let us set up a topic outline of Brandeis' "True Americanism" (page 587):

Statement: True Americanism is defined as the rights to life, liberty, and the pursuit of happiness, for both individuals and nations.

   I. Motto of United States, *E pluribus unum*
- A. Union through federation of many states
- B. Nation created through mixture of many peoples
  1. Immigration important in growth of nation
  2. Immigrants Americanized through liberty

  II. Nature of Americanization
- A. Adoption of language, manners, and customs
- B. Development of affection for and interests in United States
- C. Harmonization with American ideals

III. American ideals
- A. Development of the individual through liberty
- B. Attainment of common good through democracy and social justice
- C. Achievement of American standard of living
  1. Good working conditions
  2. Education throughout life
  3. Industrial freedom for the individual
  4. Financial security through social insurance
- D. Inclusive brotherhood
  1. Equality of individual accepted by other countries
  2. Equality of nationalities and races accepted only by United States

When you check this outline against the essay, you will see that heading I corresponds to only one paragraph, the first, but that headings II and III correspond to several paragraphs. That is, the outline is not by paragraphs but by topics. Not infrequently we find that a topic which looms very important in the outline will correspond to only part of a paragraph in the text. The outline indicates the relative importance of a topic and not the amount of space devoted to it. Sometimes, however, after we have finished an outline we may feel that the author has failed to use proper proportion or emphasis. But that is his problem, not ours. We have to face such a problem only when we are writing from our own preliminary outline.

3. The Sentence Outline. The sentence outline is the most complete and formal type. Here, every entry is in the form of a complete sentence. As with the topic outline, the entries in the sentence outline should correspond to the content and the order of arrangement in the text. The sentence outline differs from the topic outline in indicating more fully the content of each item and the relation among the items. To fulfill these requirements, the sentences should be very precise and to the point. Vague statements defeat the very purpose of the sentence outline and make such an outline look like merely an inflated topic outline. For the sentence outline should really take us deeper into the subject, defining the items more closely and indicating the structure more fully. By and large, the topic outline will serve for fairly simple material, the sentence outline for more complicated material. In setting up a sentence outline, main heads should be given Roman numerals; the subdivisions, scaling down in importance, should be marked *A, 1, a*. A dummy form will make the system clear:

I. . . . .
  A. . . . .
    1. . . . .
      a. . . . .
      b. . . . .
    2. . . . .
      a. . . . .
      b. . . . .
  B. . . . .
    1. . . . .
      a. . . . .
      b. . . . .
    2. . . . .
II. . . . .
  A. etc.

It is important to keep the indentations on the left margin consistent in each class and to be sure that a class of lower importance is more deeply indented than the class just above it. If more subdivisions are needed than are indicated here, the system can be begun over again with the key numerals and letters in parentheses. For instance, if subdivisions are needed under *a,* we can use *(I)*, *(A)*, *(1)*, and so forth. But for ordinary purposes such an extension is rarely necessary.

Here is an example of the sentence outline of the first six paragraphs of Koestler's " Seven Deadly Fallacies " (pages 551–52):

Statement: A mature foreign policy for the United States must be free of seven dangerous fallacies.

I. Neither war hysteria nor appeasement can produce a mature foreign policy.

II. There are seven fallacies which can interfere with a sound policy.
  A. The first fallacy is the confusion between East and Left.
  B. The second fallacy is that the United States is not worthy to be the leader of the free world.
    1. The United States has certain defects as a democracy and in its foreign policy.
    2. Only a perfect democracy can defend Europe.

4. The Paragraph Outline. In the paragraph outline each sentence corresponds to a paragraph in the text. In dealing with a very obviously organized piece of writing, the paragraph outline may be practically composed of the topic sentences, or adaptations of the topic sentences, of the paragraphs. (It is possible, of course, to make a paragraph outline of entries which are not complete sentences, but such a paragraph outline would have little utility. It would consist of little more than suggestive notes for paragraphs.) In dealing with other kinds of writing, however, it is necessary to summarize for each paragraph the content and intention. The paragraph outline has a very limited utility. On the one hand, in dealing with work composed by someone else, the paragraph outline often misses the real logical organization; for, as we have seen, paragraphs do not necessarily represent logical stages. On the other hand, in dealing in a preliminary way with material about which one intends to write oneself, not only may the outline fail to indicate the logical organization desired, but it may be arbitrary and misleading. It is very hard to predict the paragraph-by-paragraph development of any relatively extensive or complicated piece of work. To try to do so sometimes cramps and confuses the writer in the actual process of composition. The paragraph outline is chiefly valuable as a check on your own writing. In trying to make a paragraph outline of one of your own compositions, you may discover that some of your paragraphs have no proper center or function, and so may be led to revise.

Here is a sample of a paragraph outline designed to schematize the first three paragraphs of Skinner's " Freedom and the Control of Men " (pages 536–37) :

I. The democratic philosophy which made possible the rise of modern science has prevented the full application of scientific principles to the conduct of human affairs.

II. Science can explain human behavior by conditions outside the individual, and hence, it can produce desired behavior in men.

III. The science of behavior is similar to the optimistic eighteenth- and nineteenth-century doctrines of human perfectibility, which democracy has lately lost sight of.

Each of these three sentences sketches out the matter to be developed in the corresponding paragraph of the essay. These headings might be developed somewhat more elaborately; but for the purpose of laying out the order of the paragraphs and suggesting what is to be covered in each paragraph, they probably are developed as far as is useful. The paragraph outline, in short, is a way of outlining the sections of the sentence outline that are to be grouped together in particular paragraphs.

Summary and Précis

A **summary** summarizes. It gives in compact form the main points of a longer discourse. If it misses any fundamental points or introduces material not found in the text summarized (no matter how relevant or interesting) or gives a false notion of how the points are related to one another, it fails as a summary.

A summary is not only a digest or reduction of a longer discourse, but also a discourse itself. It is composed of complete sentences, and observes the principles of unity, coherence, emphasis, and proportion. This means that the connection among sentences must be obvious in itself or indicated by suitable transitions. If the summary is composed of more than one paragraph, the connection between paragraphs must be clear.

The general organization of a summary is a matter to be decided by reference to the purpose for which it is intended. For instance, a summary may follow the order of the original text and thereby give some notion of the approach used by its author. Or a summary may, on the other hand, be organized by a new method. Suppose, for example, an article agitating for the reform of the public school system in a certain city begins with an illustrative anecdote, then moves forward by analyzing certain particular situations, and ends by an appeal for reorganization. The summary might change this method. It might very well begin with a statement of the appeal for reform, and then proceed to give the analysis of particular situations as reasons for reform. The summary might read as follows:

The conditions in our public schools are deplorable on several accounts. It is well known that the record in college of graduates of our high schools falls below the average for graduates of schools in cities of comparable size. Local businessmen, industrialists, and editors are not satisfied with the general or vocational training of job-holders from our schools. And the schools are not doing their part in maintaining the moral health of the young, as is witnessed by the alarming and disproportionate increase in juvenile delinquency. It is time to have a general overhauling of our system.

Before we can remedy the situation, however, we must diagnose the causes. First, the school system has become a political football: members of the school board are chiefly concerned with building their political fences, and many appointments to supervisory and teaching positions are not made on merit. Second, parents have been uninterested in the schools, and many with influence have been more concerned to get special favors for their children than to raise the educational level. Third, local salaries are deplorably low, below the national average, and far below those paid in neighboring cities. No one of these causes can be taken as *the* cause, and any serious attempt to improve our schools must attempt to deal with all of them.

The organization of the original article might have provided more interesting reading and have been better adapted to catch the attention of a general audience, but the method used here is more systematic and states the logic of the case in a clearer form. Organize a summary in the way that will serve your own purpose best. At times you will wish to follow the author's organization; at other times the author's organization will be irrelevant to your purposes and your own organization will be more appropriate.

The question of the scale of a summary, like the question of organization, is to be determined by the purpose the summary is intended to serve. What do you need to have at your disposal in this capsule form? Occasionally a summary of one brief paragraph would give an adequate digest of a whole book. Or, the summary of an essay might require a number of paragraphs. In general, the important thing to remember is that a summary means a very drastic reduction.

The form of summary known as the **précis** (pronounced *pray-see*) is more standardized than the general kind of summary we have been discussing. It undertakes to retain the basic order of the original text, the same proportions of part to part, and the same tone. Like any summary, however, it is committed to presenting the fundamental points of the original and indicating the relation among them. This closer relation to the original text does not mean a dependence on quotation and paraphrase. Material should be restated for economy and emphasis. The scale of the précis, like that of any outline, may vary according to the purpose it is to serve, but since it is committed to maintaining the relative proportions of an original, it can never be as drastic in its reduction as a general summary may be.

Here is a précis of the first two paragraphs of Brandeis' "True Americanism," of which we have already given a topic outline:

The founders of the Republic, who adopted the motto *E pluribus unum,* believed that a strong nation could be developed through federation of the states and also through the mixing of many peoples. Many immigrants have entered America and it has become a great nation. Through liberty, all these people have become Americans. Americanization, superficially, is the acquiring of the language, manners, and customs of the country. Fundamentally, it is the acquisition of American ideals and aspirations.

Here the original passage contains about 360 words and the précis about 75 words. The précis itself might be reduced a little more if that seems desirable.

The Form of Footnotes and Bibliography

Variation in certain details is permissible in the form of footnotes — as we shall see in the discussion to follow — *but not* within the same paper. Learn one of the standard forms and use it consistently in all your work. Here are a few general principles:

1. The author's name appears in direct form, not with the last name first as in the bibliography.

2. The title of a book or periodical is underlined in typescript or writing. This corresponds to italics in print. Even a relatively short piece of writing which has independent publication is considered a book. Sometimes a piece of writing, a poem for instance, first appears independently as a little book and is later included in a collection of the author's work. Practice varies in treating such items, but it is permissible to treat it as a book. Thus, we would underscore the title of T. S. Eliot's Four Quartets, but we might quote " Burnt Norton " (which is one of the four poems included) or we might underscore it.

3. The title of an item in a periodical appears in quotation marks.

4. When an item is first mentioned in a footnote, full bibliographical information is given. Later references use a brief identifying form, to be described later.

Here are examples of various types of footnotes. Observe carefully the form of punctuation, the nature of the material included, and the order of the items presented.

One author:

¹ Gerald G. Walsh, *Dante Alighieri: Citizen of Christendom* (Milwaukee, 1946), p. 17.

More than one author:

¹ William Buell Meldrum and Frank Thomson Gucker, Jr., *Introduction to Theoretical Chemistry* (New York, 1936), p. 133.

Translation:

¹ Anton Chekhov, *The Party and Other Stories,* trans. Constance Garnett (London, 1919).

Work in more than one volume:

¹ Morris Bishop, ed., *A Survey of French Literature* (New York, 1955), II, 77.

FOOTNOTES FOR ITEMS FROM COLLECTIONS:

¹ Wendell L. Willkie, "Freedom and the Liberal Arts," in *The Humanities after the War,* ed. Norman Foerster (Princeton, 1944), p. 5.

[Here the abbreviation *ed.* is for editor: Norman Foerster is the editor of the collection.]

FOOTNOTES FOR ITEMS FROM PERIODICALS:

¹ Henry Albert Phillips, "The Pith of Peru," *National Geographic,* LXXXII (August, 1942), 169.

[Here the Roman numerals give the volume number of the periodical. The last number, 169, is the page reference. Notice that the abbreviation *p.* is omitted for periodicals after the volume number.]

¹ Peter F. Drucker, "The Industrial Revolution Hits the Farmer," *Harper's,* No. 1074 (November, 1939), 593.

[When, as here, the magazine carries an issue number and not a volume number, the issue number appears: "No. 1074."]

FOOTNOTES FOR ITEMS FROM THE BIBLE:

¹ Psalms 23:6–8.

[Here the first number is for chapter, the others for verses, inclusive.]

¹ II Cor. 6:9.

[Here the abbreviation *Cor.* is for Corinthians. Certain books of the Bible have such standard abbreviations. The Roman numeral indicates Second Corinthians.]

All the forms given above indicate the first reference to a work. For subsequent references, three forms may be used. When the source in a footnote is the same as that indicated in the footnote immediately preceding, the abbreviation *ibid.* (for *ibidem:* in the same place) is used, with a new page reference if that is needed. For example:

[1] Arthur Mizener, "The Desires of the Mind," *Sewanee Review*, LX, 462.
[2] *Ibid.*, 464.

When the reference to be repeated does not immediately precede, either of two basic forms may be used. If only one work by a particular author is referred to in the footnotes, his last name may be used, followed by the page reference, or his last name with the abbreviation *op. cit.* (for *opere citato:* in the work cited), with the page reference. The first practice is simpler, and is becoming more common than the other. For example:

[1] Arthur Mizener, "The Desires of the Mind," *Sewanee Review*, LX, 462.
[2] Wendell L. Willkie, "Freedom and the Liberal Arts," in *The Humanities after the War*, ed. Norman Foerster (Princeton, 1944), p. 5.
[3] Mizener, 464.

If the author has more than one work referred to in the footnotes, then his last name will not be enough, and an abbreviated title will be necessary.

[1] Mizener, "Desires," 464. *Or:* [1] Walsh, *Dante*, p. 19.
[Notice that the abbreviation *p.* is omitted in the Mizener reference, for the reference is to a periodical, while it is used in the Walsh reference, which is to a book. In other words, the short form follows the practice of the long form in this respect.]

When material is not drawn directly from its original source but from some intermediary source, acknowledgment should be made to both sources. For instance, the following note indicates that the writer has used a quotation from Stephen Spender which appeared in a book by Moody E. Prior:

[1] Stephen Spender, *The Destructive Element*, p. 11, quoted by Moody E. Prior, *The Language of Tragedy* (New York, 1947), p. 343.

We have already referred to the abbreviations *ibid.* and *op. cit.* But there are a number of other abbreviations found in notes and bibliographical forms. You will not find a use for all of them in your own writing, but you will sooner or later encounter them in works which you read. Some of the Latin abbreviations are now commonly replaced by English forms or may be omitted altogether (as with *op. cit.*). In using such abbreviations, the main thing is to be consistent. For instance, do not use *vide* (for *see*) in one place and *ff.* (for *seq.*) in another.

anon. Anonymous.

c. (*circa*)   About a certain date (to be used to indicate an approximate date, when the real date cannot be determined).

cf. (*confer*)   Compare.

ch., chap., or chaps.   Chapter(s).

col. or cols.   Column(s).

ed.   Edited by, editor, or edition.

et al. (*et alii*)   And others (when a book has several authors, the name of the first author followed by *et al.* may replace the full list).

f. or ff.   One or more pages following the page indicated.

ibid. (*ibidem*)   In the same work (referring to a work cited in a note immediately preceding).

idem   Exactly the same reference, title, and page as that given above.

infra   Below (indicating a later discussion).

l. or ll.   Line(s).

loc. cit. (*loco citato*)   In the place cited (when there is an earlier reference to the source).

MS.   Manuscript.

n.d.   No date (when publication date cannot be determined).

no.   Number (as when listing the number of the issue of a periodical or series).

n.p.   No place (when place of publication cannot be determined).

op. cit. (*opere citato*)   In the work cited (used with author's name to indicate source already referred to).

p. or pp.   Page(s).

passim   In various places (used when the topic referred to appears in several places in a work cited).

q.v. (*quod vide*)   Which see (English form: see).

rev.   Revised.

see   Used to suggest that the reader consult a certain work referred to.

seq. (*sequentia*)   Following (English form: f. or ff.).

supra   Above (when the topic referred to has already been discussed).

tr. or trans.   Translated by, translator, or translation.

vide   See (English form: see).

vol. or vols.   Volume(s) (but "vol." and "p." are not used if figures for both are given, as in listing a periodical reference; in such cases, use Roman numerals for volume and Arabic for page: II, 391).

After you have prepared a draft of your paper and established all your footnotes, you are ready to set up your final bibliography. This may differ from your working bibliography, in that it contains only items which are actually referred to in your paper, not items which have been consulted but not used.

The form for such a bibliography permits certain minor variations. For instance, the place without the publisher is sometimes given; and there may be differences in punctuation. For example, the following entry can be punctuated in two ways:

Barnes, Harry Elmer. *The Genesis of the World War.* New York: Alfred A. Knopf, 1926.

or:

Barnes, Harry Elmer, *The Genesis of the World War,* New York, Alfred A. Knopf, 1926.

But in all forms the author's name comes first, with the last name first, followed by the full title of the work, the periodical or series if any, the place of publication, the publisher (if this form is used), and the date of publication. The items may be arranged in either of two ways. First, in a straight alphabetical order, according to the last name of the author or, if there is no author, by the main word of the title. Second, alphabetically within certain groups determined by the material dealt with: " Books," " Periodicals," " Documents," and so forth. Here are some examples of entries as they might appear in the bibliography of a paper on Woodrow Wilson:

(Periodical) Baker, Ray Stannard. " Our Next President and Some Others." *American Magazine,* LXXIV (June, 1912), 131–143.

(Book) Barnes, Harry Elmer. *The Genesis of the World War.* New York: Alfred A. Knopf, 1926.

(Document) *Congressional Record,* XLIX–LI, Washington: Government Printing Office, 1913–1914.

(Book) McAdoo, Eleanor R. W. *The Woodrow Wilsons.* New York: The Macmillan Company, 1937.

(Book) Wilson, Woodrow. *The Public Papers of Woodrow Wilson.* Eds. Ray Stannard Baker and William Edward Dodd, 3 vols. New York: Harper and Bros., 1925–1927.

(Periodical) Wilson, Woodrow. " Democracy and Efficiency." *Atlantic Monthly,* LXXXVII (March, 1901), 289–299.

Notice that an over-all alphabetical order is given, by author when an author is specified, and by leading word when there is no author (" Congressional "). In this short bibliography all types of sources are grouped together — books, collections, periodicals, and documents. In a long bibliography such types might be set up as separate, each group in alphabetical order.

The Book Report

The book report is to be sharply distinguished on one hand from the research paper and on the other hand from the book review or the critical essay. It is to be distinguished from the research paper primarily because it deals with one book in its entirety, and from the review or critical essay because it merely reports on a book, presents that book, and does not compare it with other books or attempt to make judgments as to its value. But the book report may include a certain amount of background material about the author himself, his other work and his reputation, or the circumstances of the composition of the book being reported on. Such material is to be used as a means of presenting the book in question. It is not to become an end in itself, and in proportion it should be subordinated to the actual presentation of the book. Some book reports do not require this background material at all. The nature of the assignment determines its inclusion.

To write a good book report you need to answer the following questions:

1. Who is the author? (What are his nationality and origins? What is his period?)
2. What other work has he done?
3. What is his reputation?
4. Are there any important or enlightening circumstances connected with the composition of this book?
5. What kind of book is this? (Is it fiction, history, literary criticism, biography, poetry, drama, or what?)
6. What is the subject of this book?
7. What material does it treat?
8. What is the theme of the book — the author's basic interpretation of the material?

9. What method of organization does he employ?
10. What are the tone and style of the book?

You will notice that the first four questions involve background information. If your report is to present such information, you do not need to make a full-dress research paper on that part of the assignment. You can merely consult a few standard reference works to get the basic facts, or look into one or two good biographies or historical or critical works. In doing this, however, it is wise to take your notes as if for a research paper so that your material will be conveniently available and can be put into order.

The kind of book you are dealing with determines to a considerable extent the kind of treatment you can appropriately give it. For instance, if you are dealing with a biography, you should identify the character who is the subject of the work, summarize his career as given by the author (including the basic pieces of evidence which he employs to support his interpretation of the character), give some idea of his method of organization, and comment on his tone and style. This last consideration may involve such questions as these: Is he writing a scholarly treatise or a popular biography? Is his work adapted to the audience he has in mind? Does he give interesting anecdotes and colorful personal touches, or does he devote himself to facts and historical or psychological analysis? If you are dealing with a book on public policy — say on Russian influence in the Mideast or international relations — the important considerations would be somewhat different. Your primary concerns would be to present the author's picture of the situation provoking the discussion, state the policy which he recommends, and offer the arguments for that policy. You might even be led to present the philosophical or political assumptions on which he bases his policy. The kind of audience he has in mind would still be important, and you should define it; but in general in this type of book, questions of tone and style, except in so far as mere clarity is concerned, would not be important. Or if you are dealing with a novel, the emphasis in your report would again be different. It would now be important to define the kind of world your author is interested in. Does he write of drawing rooms or village parlors, of farms or battlefields? What kind of characters and issues interest him? What is the outline of his plot? How do the motivations of his characters fit the plot? What is the theme of his book? And here questions of tone and style might become very important. But in all cases, remember that the book report *presents* a book, primarily in its own terms. It does not compare, criticize, or evaluate.

Description of Feelings
and States of Mind

In the chapter on description we were concerned with the rendering of the world outside ourselves — objects, scenes, conditions, actions. But description, in some of its most subtle applications, is concerned with rendering our own inner states — or the inner states of other people as we can imagine them to be.

In our earlier discussion we saw how a description may evoke in the reader a certain mood or attitude which the writer wishes to communicate. There is some relation, then, between the physical details of the object described and human feelings. This relationship leads us to another kind of description, not of objects or persons, but of feelings or states of mind. How can such an intangible, without physical existence and with no possible appeal to our senses, be described?

Strictly speaking, the literal feeling or state of mind cannot be described because it cannot be perceived through the senses. But we have seen how a character, which is also intangible, can be indicated through description. By a kind of parallel process we can indicate a state of mind, that of the writer himself or of some person about whom he is writing.

Our common speech recognizes the principle behind this process. For instance, if a man has an evil nature we may say that he has a " black heart," or if a man is cheerful and optimistic we may say that he has a " sunny disposition." The abstract, general words *evil* and *cheerful* are replaced by the concrete words *black* and *sunny*, which properly belong to the physical world.

Here is an example of the description, not of a personality, but of a state of feeling, the feeling at the moment of passing from sleep to waking:

" I was not asleep," I answered as I awoke.
I said this in good faith. The great modification which the act of awakening effects in us is not so much that of introducing us to the clear life of consciousness, as that of making us lose all memory of that other, rather more diffused light in which our mind has been resting, as in the opaline depths of the sea. The tide of thought, half veiled from our perception, over which we were drifting still a moment ago, kept us in a state of motion perfectly sufficient to enable us to refer to it by the name of wakefulness. But then our actual awakenings produce an interruption of memory. A little later we describe these states as sleep because we no longer remember them. And when shines that bright star which at the moment of waking illuminates behind the sleeper the whole expanse of his sleep, it makes him imagine for a few moments that this was not a sleeping but a waking state; a shooting star, it must be added, which blots out with the fading of its light not only the false existence but the very appearance of our dream, and merely enables him who has awoken to say to himself: " I was asleep."
— MARCEL PROUST: *The Guermantes Way*.[1]

The same use of physical description to indicate a mental state appears in the following passage:

Sterne's discovery was made. It was repugnant to his imagination, shocking to his ideas of honesty, shocking to his conception of mankind. This enormity affected one's outlook on what was possible in this world: it was as if, for instance, the sun had turned blue, throwing a new and sinister light on men and nature. Really in the first moment he had felt sickish, as though he had got a blow below the belt: for a second the very color of the sea seemed changed — appeared queer to his wandering eye; and he had a passing, unsteady sensation in all his limbs as though the earth had started turning the other way.
— JOSEPH CONRAD: " The End of the Tether," *Youth: A Narrative*.

We notice in the above quotation how the author begins by making a general statement: the discovery is repugnant, is shocking, changes Sterne's outlook. But we notice how quickly these generalities shade over into concrete presentations which are intended to evoke in us a direct sense of Sterne's sensation: the blue sun, a blow below the belt, the sudden reversal of the earth's motion.

In the following passage we find a slightly different application of the same principle. Above we have been dealing with the description of a momentary feeling; here we shall be dealing with the description of a protracted situation, a state of being. A wife has discovered that her husband's conception of life, his " mansion," is oppressive and deadening for her:

---

[1] From *The Guermantes Way* by Marcel Proust, trans. C. K. Scott Moncrieff.

But when, as the months had elapsed, she had followed him further and he had led her into the mansion of his own habitation, then, *then* she had seen where she really was.

She could live it over again, the incredulous terror with which she had taken the measure of her dwelling. Between those four walls she had lived ever since; they were to surround her for the rest of her life. It was the house of darkness, the house of dumbness, the house of suffocation. Osmond's beautiful mind gave it neither light nor air; Osmond's beautiful mind indeed seemed to peep down from a small high window and mock at her. Of course it had not been physical suffering; for physical suffering there might have been a remedy. She could come and go; she had her liberty; her husband was perfectly polite. He took himself so seriously; it was perfectly appalling. Under all his culture, his cleverness, his amenity, under his good-nature, his facility, his knowledge of life, his egotism lay hidden like a serpent in a bank of flowers.

— HENRY JAMES: The Portrait of a Lady.

The descriptions of states of feeling just considered are direct in treatment. That is, we are introduced as fully as may be into the consciousness of the person who has the feeling or experiences the state of mind, the seaman Sterne or the disappointed wife. But there is an indirect way of using description to portray feeling or state of mind, a way which presents the symptoms but does not endeavor to describe the feeling or the state of mind itself. This way is analogous, of course, to the use of description of a person's physical appearance to indicate his character, without giving any general statements about the character.

If we describe a person as having shifty eyes and a flabby mouth, the reader is very apt to draw certain conclusions about that person's character. And by the same token, if we describe a person at the moment when his lips whiten, the blood flushes his cheeks, his eyes flash, and his respiration is rapid, the reader is apt to conclude that the person is laboring under great rage or other excitement. Such descriptions of the symptoms, as it were, of a state of feeling can be very effective in giving the reader a sense of the reality of the situation being presented. Here is an example from a student theme:

Then the policeman made us all five stand up in front of Mr. Evans, while Mr. Evans asked us some questions. He asked me first, if I had done it, and then some questions supposed to trip me up. I really didn't know a thing about how it had happened, and said so. When he stopped asking me questions, I began watching the other boys. Alex was the most nervous of the lot and he could scarcely put words together. Jack was the least nervous. When they got to him, he began answering very calmly almost before a question could be spoken. But then I began to notice a vein in his neck which gave a peculiar little jumping motion. And I noticed how the edges of his nostrils were twitching just a little bit. The nostrils, too, looked white right at the bottom. As I noticed this I wasn't following much what he was saying. Then it dawned on me. Everything he was saying was indicating in a very clever way that I was the one.

Then I saw the sweat running down under the hair back of his ears, just a drop or two coming out on the bare skin. I don't know what made me do it. I jumped in front of him, and pointed at him.

"Look," I yelled at him, "look how you're sweating! It's running down your neck, you're sweating so. Why don't you say it was you?"

He put his hands to his neck, then jerked them back to look at them. He was, all at once, white as a sheet.

• Applications •

I. Make a list of physical symptoms which you might use to indicate the following states: (1) fear, (2) rage, (3) disgust, (4) drowsiness, and (5) despair.

II. Describe briefly, say in 250 words, a person experiencing one of the above states.

Figurative Language in the Description of Feelings and States of Mind

It should be obvious from the examples given above that when a writer comes to describe a feeling or a state of mind he is often forced, to use figurative language. For instance, when Henry James wishes to describe the feeling of the wife who discovers that her husband is unsympathetic and egotistical (page 834), he resorts to figurative language: the wife feels she has been imprisoned in the "house of dumbness," the "house of suffocation," and most of the passage is an elaboration of this comparison of her condition to an imprisonment. The whole question of figurative language has been discussed at some length before in this book (Chapter 11), but the question is of so much importance for description that we must at least touch upon it here.

We may say, for the sake of convenience, that such comparisons have two functions in description, in enriching the texture. First, they may make for vividness and immediacy — the sensation of the scene unfolding before our eyes. Second, they may serve to interpret the object described or an attitude toward it.

If we write of a girl's hair that it is very black and glossy, we do little to stir the imagination of the reader to a full sense of the quality of the hair. But if we write that the girl's hair is like a raven's wing, then we have done something to set the imagination of the reader to work. The comparison just used is, unfortunately, a rather trite one; it has been used so often that its power to stir the imagination is almost gone. But when Thomas Hardy writes of the hair of one of his heroines, that " a whole winter did not contain darkness enough to form its shadow," or that it " closed over her forehead like nightfall," the imagination is stirred, and the image of the woman is evoked.

We often find that the function of a comparison is merely to increase vividness, to help the reader to grasp the object, or that the interpretative value of the comparison is very slight. For instance, in Stevenson's comparison of the atoll to a basin almost submerged in water (page 224), we have almost as pure an example as it would be possible to find of a comparison which works to aid in vividness without any interpretative force. When Faulkner describes Miss Emily (page 211): " Her eyes, lost in the fatty ridges of her face, looked like two small pieces of coal pressed into a lump of dough," the chief effect is to startle us, by this caricature of a face, into visualizing Miss Emily. But, here, if we are acquainted with the story in which the sentence appears, we realize that some interpretation may also be involved — the pallor, the pasty quality of the flesh, the unhuman quality of the comparison, are appropriate for this house of decay and death.

We can find many passages in which the interpretative value of the comparisons is more important than the value of vividness. For instance, when Melville says the vast volcanic islands " present a most Plutonian sight " (page 197), the function is primarily interpretative. By that time in the passage we already have a very strong visual impression of the islands, and we are not likely to have a clear picture of the underworld in our minds. But the comparison does strongly suggest the idea of waste and desolation — the interpretative aspect.

Let us look at the end of the following paragraph to see how the comparison there sums up the whole impression of the city described:

Except for the Marabar Caves — and they are twenty miles off — the city of Chandrapore presents nothing extraordinary. Edged rather than washed by the river Ganges, it trails for a couple of miles along the bank, scarcely distinguishable from the rubbish it deposits so freely. There are no bathing-steps on the river front, as the Ganges happens not to be holy here; indeed there is no river front, and bazaars shut out the wide and shifting panorama of the stream. The streets are mean, the temples ineffective, and though a few fine houses exist they are hidden away in gardens or down alleys whose filth deters all but the invited guest. Chandrapore was never large or beautiful, but two hundred years ago it lay on the road between Upper India, then imperial, and the sea, and the fine houses date from that period. The zest for decoration stopped in the eighteenth century, nor was it ever democratic. There is no painting and scarcely any carving in the bazaars. The very wood seems made of mud, the inhabitants of mud moving. So abased, so monotonous is everything that meets the eye, that when the Ganges comes down it might be expected to wash the excrescence back into the soil. Houses do fall, people are drowned and left rotting, but the general outline of the town persists, swelling here, shrinking there, like some low but indestructible form of life.

— E. M. FORSTER: *A Passage to India.*

Here we have an excellent example of the interpretative emphasis in a comparison: the Indian city is like " some low but indestructible form of life."

A good comparison cannot be purely arbitrary. When T. E. Lawrence describes his arrival at an Arabian port, saying, " the heat of Arabia came out like a drawn sword and struck us speechless," we have nothing which corresponds as far as shape is concerned with the sword, but we do have the metallic glitter of sea and sand, the suddenness and violence of the heat after days at sea; and then, at the level of interpretation, we have the notion of ferocity and deadliness — the pitiless heat and the drawn blade. Or when Proust uses the comparison of various depths of the sea and of various kinds of light to describe the process of waking, there is no object which corresponds to those things; but the vague shadings and confusions of dawning consciousness provide the basis for comparison.

It does not matter on what basis the comparison is established — by what senses or feelings — but there must be some primary connection if interpretation is to be established. A comparison, even if it does carry an appropriate interpretation, must not be so far-fetched that the reader cannot accept it. At the same time, the comparison which is too trite or too obvious does not stir the imagination. There is no rule for establishing these limits. The writer must simply depend on observation of the practice of others and on his own experience. For further discussion refer to Chapter 11.

• Applications •

I. From the examples of description given above and from the group at the end of Chapter 11, select ten comparisons which are effective. Try to state in your own words what each comparison implies. Try to determine what the basis of the comparison is; that is, what is common between the two things involved in the comparison.

II. Write a brief description of some feeling you have experienced — a sudden grief, shock at betrayal by a friend, the distress of a sleepless night, joy at unexpected good fortune.

Special Problems in Narration

Here we shall discuss certain special problems in narration, problems that find their greatest importance, perhaps, in formal fiction, but which are of some importance in all narration.

Scale

By **scale** we mean the degree of fullness with which an event is treated. Here we can think in terms of extremes of method — **summary rendering** and **full rendering**. The tendency in narration is to reduce the scale to that of summary in parts which are necessary only for continuity or, as it were, scaffolding, and to expand the scale in those parts which present the more significant moments. The following selection, which concludes Guy de Maupassant's story "The Diamond Necklace," illustrates the principle clearly. The main character, Mathilde Loisel, has been a vain, frivolous woman, who lived in daydreams of rich and fashionable life. When she is finally invited to a ball she borrows what she understands to be a diamond necklace from a friend, Madame Forestier. The necklace is lost at the ball, and Mathilde and her husband buy one to replace it, getting the money from usurers. At this point our selection picks up the story:

She learned the heavy cares of a household, the odious work of a kitchen. She washed the dishes, using her rosy nails upon the greasy pots and the bottoms of the stewpans. She washed the soiled linen, the chemises and dishcloths, which she hung on the line to dry; she took down the refuse to the street each morning and brought up the water, stopping at each landing to breathe. And, clothed like a woman of the people, she went to the grocer's, the butcher's, and the fruiterer's, with her basket on her arm, shopping, haggling to the last sou her miserable money.

Every month it was necessary to renew some notes, thus obtaining time, and to pay others.

The husband worked evenings, putting the accounts of some merchant in order, and at night he often copied manuscript at five sous a page.

And this life lasted ten years.

At the end of ten years, they had restored all, all, with interest of the usurers, and the compound interest besides.

Mme. Loisel looked old now. She had become a strong, hard woman, the rough woman of the poor household. Her hair tangled, her skirts awry, her hands red, she talked in loud tones, and washed the floors with a great swishing of water. But sometimes, when her husband was at the office, she would sit by the window and remember that evening of the ball, where she had been so beautiful and so happy.

What would have happened if she had not lost the necklace? Who knows? Who knows? How life is strange and changeful! How little is needed to ruin one or to save one!

One Sunday, as she was walking in the Champs Élysées, to restore herself after the work of the week, she suddenly saw a woman with a child. It was Madame Forestier, still young, still beautiful, still charming. Madame Loisel was moved. Should she speak to her? Yes, certainly. Now that she had paid, she would tell her all. Why not?

She approached her. " Good morning, Jeanne."

Her friend did not recognize her, and was surprised to be addressed by this woman of the people. She stammered: " But, Madame — I do not know — you must be mistaken — "

" No, I am Mathilde Loisel."

Her friend uttered a cry of surprise: " Oh, my poor Mathilde! How you are changed — "

" Yes, I have seen some hard days since I saw you — some miserable ones — and all because of you — "

" Because of me? How? "

" You remember the diamond necklace you loaned me to wear to the Minister's ball? "

" Yes, very well."

" Well, I lost it."

" How is that, since you returned it to me? "

" I returned one like it. And it has taken us ten years to pay for it. You can understand that it was not easy for us who have nothing. But it is finished, and I am very glad."

Madame Forestier stopped. She said: " You say that you bought a diamond necklace to replace mine? "

" Yes. You did not know it then? They were very like."

And she smiled with a joy that was proud and naïve.

Madame Forestier was touched, and seized both her hands as she said: " Oh, my poor Mathilde! My necklace was false. It was not worth over five hundred francs! "

— GUY DE MAUPASSANT: " The Diamond Necklace."

We notice here that the first half of the passage covers a time of ten years, the second half a time of three or four minutes. The ten years are summarized. The meeting in the park is rendered fully, word for word, instant by instant. We can readily see the reason why the writer summarized the ten years: they are all alike, a dreary grind of misery, and what is important is their result, Mathilde's new energy and fortitude, not the single events within them. As for the last scene, we can see that it is important in itself: it is dramatic, it is the moment when Mathilde realizes her situation, it is the result of all her past experience.

In the half of the selection rendered by summary we observe, however, that certain details do give us the impression of the quality and movement of life —Mathilde's bargaining, the coarseness of her voice, the way she scrubs the floor with great swishing sweeps of the wet mop. Narrative summary differs from the mere summary of ideas: when successful it still gives some hint of the quality and movement of life.

Dialogue

Narration often involves the use of dialogue — not only fictional narration but historical writing, biography, and other types. Dialogue sometimes seems to be an easy way to get a story told. The writer — especially an inexperienced writer — thinks that he knows how people talk. He thinks that to set down talk will be easier than to present material in the straight narrative form which he himself will have to compose. But the problem is not so simple as that. First, to compose effective dialogue is not easy, and second, to use dialogue continually is monotonous.

On the first point it can be said that dialogue which is effective on the page is rarely a direct transcript of what people would say in conversation. Conversation is often stumbling, wandering, diffuse. The real point at issue in an actual conversation frequently becomes lost in mere wordiness or in the distractions of side issues and matters of incidental interest. The writer of dialogue cannot afford to duplicate such a conversation; if he does so, the reader will not be readily able to follow the line of significance. So the writer must organize the material to permit the reader to follow the development of the issue at stake. There must be an impression of give-and-take and a forward thrust of idea.

Let us examine a piece of unsatisfactory dialogue:

Gertrude collapsed into her chair, helpless with amusement; giving herself up to her laughter, she made him feel suddenly ashamed of that remembered delight.

" Oh — oh — oh — oh! " she cried. " That is the most ridiculous thing I ever heard of. You call that girl a shy arbutus. And at your age, too. You certainly are silly."

"Well! I don't think it is so funny. You don't know the girl the way I do, and furthermore she is very modest and appealing. All sorts of people think so. For example, I have heard Mrs. Buckley say — "

" The shy arbutus! As I said, it is perfectly ridiculous. I don't want to be impolite, but she isn't exactly an arbutus, and as for Mrs. Buckley's opinion, you know what a sentimental old biddy she is, and how she gushes over everything. A shy arbutus. Forgive me, Harry, but that's too funny. How old *are* you? "

He flung his cigarette at the back-log and grinned.

"I knew it was no use," he grumbled amiably. " I can't make you see her, and it's no use trying. I know Mrs. Buckley is sentimental and does gush, but I don't think I am gushy, and I have also heard Tom Barker comment on the girl. Very favorably, too. And he is a hard-headed sort of fellow. Why, you remember, don't you, how he always brings a conversation right down to common sense. There was that time we were talking about the performance of that pianist — you know, the one who played at the Murdocks' house — last November — and everybody said how good she was, but Tom just said, ' Nuts, all she's got is ten quite ordinary fingers and a very extraordinary figure — but it is the fingers that have to play the piano! ' That's just like old Tom. But to come back to the subject, Tom may understand the girl, but I can't make you see her, and it's no use trying."

" I heard that pianist, and she was rather good, I thought. Whatever Tom Barker thought. But the trouble with you is, you're in love with this girl. It is a well-known fact that a man in love is not able to exercise his best judgment. But it's precisely when you're in love that you need to keep your wits about you. Or the wits of your friends. Now I've come to the conclusion that you *mustn't* marry her, Harry. There are very good reasons."

" Well — I don't know. I don't think that being in love has done anything to my judgment."

" *No!* It is certainly my considered opinion that to marry that girl would be ruinous for you. You must think about your career. And more important, about your happiness. Won't she bore you to death in three years. She is quite dull. Now the kind of girl you want is somebody with spirit and mischief. A girl who has got some smartness, and who could amuse your friends. Think of the dull parties with this girl in the saddle."

The trouble here is that the dialogue is loaded with irrelevant material. People do load their conversations with irrelevant material, but dialogue in narrative cannot afford that weight. It kills the forward thrust.

Let us now look at the same piece of dialogue as it actually occurs in a story, stripped to the essentials:

" Oh — oh — oh — oh! " she cried.
" Well! "
" The shy arbutus! . . . Forgive me, Harry, but that's too funny. How old *are* you? "
He flung his cigarette at the back-log and grinned.
" I knew it was no use," he grunted amiably. " I can't make you see her, and it's no use trying."
" Well — I can see this much. You *are* in love with her. Or you couldn't possibly be such a fool. But it's precisely when you're in love that you need to keep your wits about you. Or the wits of your friends. . . . You *mustn't* marry her, Harry."
" Well — I don't know."
" *No!* . . . It would be ruinous."

— CONRAD AIKEN: " Spider, Spider," *Costumes by Eros.*

In the passage above, the line of interest is clear, and the collision between Gertrude and Harry is quite definite. In the expanded version there is a blurring of the effect. This blurred effect might actually result from a conversation of a Gertrude and Harry in real life, but that fact has no final bearing on the case here. The problem of the writer of dialogue is a problem of selection and logical organization.

There is, furthermore, the problem of giving dialogue a realistic surface. There must be, in addition to the logical organization, an impression of real life, a sense of the pauses, the changes, the waverings of conversation. But this must be an *impression* and not a word-for-word recording. There is no rule for giving this impression, but there are certain considerations which may help a writer to give it.

First, we can notice, as in the example above, that the breaks and the italicized words are of some use in this respect. We get the impression of the sudden shift of idea or the hesitancy of a speaker. And from the italicized words we get the impression of Gertrude's voice, with its slightly satirical emphasis. But these are devices that would not always apply, and in any case should be used sparingly.

Second, and more important, the writer can try to indicate the fact that each speaker has his own way of phrasing and his own rhythm of voice. Expertness in giving such an impression can only come from close observation — an awareness of the little catch phrases a person tends to repeat, of the type of sentence structure he tends to use, of the mannerisms of speech.

Third, in addition to the individual qualities of speech, we can note that there are qualities dependent on cultural background, race, geographical origin, and so forth, qualities which are shared by members of a group. The commonest way to indicate these qualities is by mere dialectal peculiarities, when such exist. But mere peculiarity of spelling is a crude device, and in the end usually becomes monotonous. It is better for the writer to use such a device sparingly, and to focus his attention on the vocabulary, idiom, and rhythm of the group to which his speaking character belongs.

Here are some examples in which the language used by a speaker gives some impression of his social group and of his individuality:

A BOY WHO IS THE SON OF A JOCKEY:

I guess looking at it, now, my old man was cut out for a fat guy, one of those regular little roly fat guys you see around, but he sure never got that way, except a little toward the last, and then it wasn't his fault, he was riding over the jumps only and he could afford to carry plenty of weight then. I remember the way he'd pull on a rubber shirt over a couple of jerseys and a big sweat shirt over that, and got me to run with him in the forenoon in the hot sun.

— ERNEST HEMINGWAY: " My Old Man," *Three Stories and Ten Poems.*

A PRETENTIOUS, SERVILE WOMAN:

" Well, now, that is so like you," returned Miss Knag. " Ha! ha! ha! Of club feet! Oh very good. As I often remark to the young ladies, ' Well I must say, and I do not care who knows it, of all the ready humor — hem — I ever heard anywhere ' — and I have heard a good deal; for when my dear brother was alive (I kept house for him, Miss Nickleby) , we had to supper once a week two or three young men, highly celebrated in those days for their humor, Madame Mantalini — ' Of all the ready humor,' I say to the young ladies, ' *I* ever heard, Madame Mantalini's is the most remarkable — hem. It is so gentle, so sarcastic, and yet so good-natured (as I was observing to Miss Simmonds only this morning) , that how, or when, or by what means she acquired it, is to me a mystery indeed.' "

Here Miss Knag paused to take breath, and while she pauses it may be observed — not that she was marvellously loquacious and marvellously deferential to Madame Mantalini, since these are facts which require no comment; but that every now and then, she was accustomed, in the torrent of her discourse, to introduce a loud, shrill, clear, " hem! " the import and meaning of which was variously interpreted by her acquaintance. . . .

— CHARLES DICKENS: *Nicholas Nickleby.*

" You may be right, and then you may have a one-sided view. When I say that your prejudice is literary, I mean that you have read what universities are like and applied that reading here. You have condemned without participating. You know, there may be good things, even in this town. Why, I sometimes think you even like me a bit." Dr. Whitlock smiled. " You see, there is indifference, intellectual servility, a vague attempt at education. But to know these things is not enough. You have to go deeper, you must understand; your conviction must be intellectual as well as emotional. There are more than economic reasons at stake, and there may be greater social injustice in this small university town than in the smashing of a miners' strike by hired bullies."

— MICHAEL DE CAPITE: *No Bright Banner.*

We have said that logical organization, the development of the point at issue in a dialogue, is extremely important. But occasionally there is little or no point at issue, and then the intended significance of a passage may be the exhibition of the speaker's character, as in the speech by Miss Knag from *Nicholas Nickleby*, quoted above. There the wandering sentences, the interpolations, and the characteristic " hem! " indicate the quality of her mind, just as some of the remarks themselves indicate her mixture of vanity, pretentiousness, and servility.

In some instances, of course, a piece of dialogue may develop a point and at the same time contain elements which are irrelevant to that point but indicate the character of the speaker. Here is the famous passage between Falstaff and Mistress Quickly, who is trying to remind Falstaff that he had promised to marry her. Her talkativeness and fuzzy-mindedness appear here in the very way she presents the argument, the point, to Falstaff:

Marry, if thou wert an honest man, thyself and the money too. Thou didst swear to me upon a parcel-gilt goblet; sitting in my Dolphin Chamber, at the round table, by a sea-coal fire, upon Wednesday in Wheeson week, when the Prince broke thy head for liking his father to a singing man of Windsor — thou didst swear to me then, as I was washing thy wound, to marry me and make me my lady thy wife. Canst thou deny it? Did not goodwife Keech, the butcher's wife, come in then and call me Gossip Quickly? Coming in to borrow a mess of vinegar, telling us she had a good dish of prawns, whereby thou didst desire to eat some, whereby I told thee they were ill for a green wound? And didst thou not, when she was gone down stairs, desire me to be no more so familiarity with such poor people, saying that ere long they would call me madam? And didst thou not kiss me and bid me fetch thee thirty shillings?

—WILLIAM SHAKESPEARE: *Henry IV, Part i₁*

Characterization

Early in the discussion of narration we pointed out the relation between persons and action. Most narratives, from news stories to novels, are about people. Things happen to people and people make things happen. To understand an action we must understand the people involved, their natures, their motives, their responses, and to present an action so that it is satisfying we must present the people. This process is called **characterization**.

A news story gives a minimum of characterization. It merely identifies the persons involved — " Adam Perkins, age thirty-three, of 1217 Sunset Drive " — and then proceeds to give the bare facts of the event. If it deals with motive it does so in the barest possible way. If Adam Perkins has committed suicide, the news story may report that he had been in ill health and had, according to his wife, been worrying about financial reverses, but it will give no detail. On the other hand, a novel or biography usually gives very full characterization. It seeks to make us understand very fully the relationship between the character and the events and the effects of events on character. In between the news story and the novel or biography, there are all sorts of narratives which present more or less fully the relationship between character and event and which try to answer the fundamental questions: Why does the character do what he does to cause the event? Why does he respond as he does to the event?

To answer these questions, the writer of a narrative must characterize the person. This is as important for narratives dealing with matters of fact, such as biography or history, as it is for narratives dealing with imaginary persons, such as novels or short stories. The difference between the two types is simply this: The biographer must interpret the facts in order to understand the character and present him, and the writer of fiction must create the details in order to present the character.

Whether the details of a character are drawn from fact or from imagination, it is important to remember that a character cannot be effectively presented as a mere accumulation of details. The details must be related to one another to build up a unified impression and to convey the sense of an individual personality. As this impression of an individual personality relates to an action, we are concerned with motive or response. What is the main motive of a character or what is his main response? We must be sure that we have an answer to this question before we can give an effective characterization. Then we must be sure that we have given a clear indication of this main fact of the character.

Once the main fact of the character is established in the writer's mind, he must relate other details of the character to it. That is. the character must be consistent. We know that real people are often very complicated and therefore often do things which seem inconsistent. The same person does good things and bad things, generous things and selfish things, wise things and stupid things, but even so, we usually feel that there is an explanation for such inconsistency, that the very inconsistencies can be understood in relation to a deeper consistency of character. And the object of the writer should be to contribute to this deeper understanding of character. He may present the inconsistent details, but at the same time he wants to present them as part of a comprehensible whole. There is no formula for accomplishing this, and the only way we can learn to do it is by studying human nature as we can observe it in life and in books.

Once the conception of a character is clear, we can, however, think systematically about methods of presenting it. Generally speaking, character can be presented by means of five different methods: by appearance and mannerisms, by analysis, by speech, by reaction of other persons, or by action.

Appearance and mannerisms really involve description, considered independently or as absorbed into narration, but description as an indication of the inner nature of persons. We have already seen in Dickens' description of Chadband (page 209) how the physical oiliness of the man is taken as a lead to his " oily " personality, and how his mannerism of lifting a hand before speaking gives the suggestion of false piety and vanity, of a hypocritical preacher.

As the method of description suggests the character, that of analysis states it and explains it. This is really a kind of exposition drawn into the service of narration. It may be very obvious and systematic, as when we write:

Jack Staple's character is marked by what seems, at first inspection, to be a fundamental inconsistency: on some occasions he is kind and generous even to a fault, and at the same time he is capable of extreme cruelty. But the inconsistency disappears into a frightening consistency once we realize that the spring of his every action is a profound egotism, an egotism which can express itself as well through good as through evil. Both gratitude and fear can flatter his ego.

But in the following example, drawn from a student theme, we see a rather successful attempt to absorb the analysis into the narrative itself.

When Mr. Hinks came into the geometry class that day, there was some kind of ripple round the room. It wasn't anything you could put your finger on, and as soon as it was over you felt you had been kidding yourself. It was like when you are out in a boat on an absolutely still day, and a breath of air just ripples the water, then stops. But later on I heard some of the fellows say they had felt something funny that first minute he came in.

To look at, Mr. Hinks was not out of the ordinary. He was a sort of pudgy middle-aged man, with a round face, and a twinkle in his eye. No, it wasn't a twinkle. It was just that it was the sort of face that ought to have had a twinkle. It was the glitter of his spectacles that fooled you. When, about two months later, that day it happened — the thing I am writing about — he took his spectacles off and looked at me, it was the shock of my life. There certainly wasn't any twinkle. His eyes were the color of oysters, and looked about as cold.

Today he began his talk as pleasant as anybody. He introduced himself, and made a joke about being an old hand at squaring the circle. It wasn't much of a joke, but we all laughed, out of a sense of duty, or the way you do to an older person who is trying to be funny at your level and doesn't know how. You know how you get somewhat embarrassed and sorry for such a person, and tend to laugh too much. We were laughing, all but Jack Purvess, who was sitting way over at the end of the front row. I then saw Mr. Hinks giving Jack a sidewise look. It wasn't the sort of thing that seemed to mean much at the time, but you notice something and the fact you noticed it must be a signal. Anyway, I remembered the fact, and two days later, when he asked Jack what the study of geometry was, I remembered again. You couldn't put your finger on what Mr. Hinks did. When Jack bumbled around a little, each question that Mr. Hinks asked him, in his nicest tone of voice, seemed to be aimed at helping him. But every time Jack got in deeper. Then Jack began to flush up. He knew he was making a big fool of himself. Somebody tittered. Mr. Hinks turned very sternly, and said: " I want no one to laugh at Jack's expense. He is doing the very best he can. Aren't you, Jack? "

If Jack said yes to that he was admitting he was the biggest idiot in town. If he said no, he was admitting something else. Mr. Hinks was very patient. He kept waiting for the answer.

Under the topic of dialogue we have already discussed some of the ways by which speech indicates character: Miss Knag's habit of saying " hem " or the professor's special, somewhat stilted vocabulary and turn of phrase. But further, we must distinguish between what a person says and how he says it. The ideas or attitudes expressed should spring from the character and exhibit it, and the vocabulary, rhythm, and mannerisms (if there are mannerisms) should be significant.

It is difficult to find a brief example of the method of indicating character by the reactions of other people, for usually a fully developed scene is required to make such a point. But the principle is simple and we can observe it constantly in real life: The feelings and behavior of those around a person act as a mirror of that person's character. And we often encounter it in narratives, sometimes with some such obvious signal as, " When I first met Mr. Dobbs, I felt an uneasiness which I was at a loss to explain, for he was so civil, so fatherly . . ."; but the method may be used without the signal. The reactions may form part of the narrative itself.

The method which most concerns the writer of narrative is, of course, the exhibiting of character through action. Again it is difficult to illustrate this method by a brief extract, for we can be sure that a single act is properly expressive of character only if we test that act against the other acts in the narrative. Any good short story or novel or biography will illustrate this method. But in general terms, we must ask if the particular incident is vivid, significant in itself, and consistent with other incidents. Our final test here is human nature, and thorough observation is the best teacher.

• Applications •

I. In the Readings, study the three selections on Mary Todd Lincoln and " Mazie " by Joseph Mitchell. Do you find any effective examples of rendering character by description, by analysis, by speech, by reactions of others, or by action?

II. Write a piece of characteristic dialogue on any subject illustrating the speech of some member of a special group such as college students, lawyers, Irish laborers, ranch hands, or clergymen.

III. Take a person, real or imaginary, and write an analysis of his character, in some 150 or 200 words. Then compose a narrative of 500 words in which this person exhibits his character in action and speech.

Author—Title Index

Note: Those selections identified as Readings are complete and comprise "A Book of Readings" (Part 5); all those not so identified are excerpts and are found in Parts 1, 2, 3, 4, and the Appendixes.

Y

"Yankee School, The," George Lyman Kittredge, sample research paper, 394–426

Yeats, W. B., "Reveries over Childhood," 293–94, and Readings, 714

"You Know Me, Al," Ring Lardner, 294

Subject Index

Atmosphere: 207; as unifying mood, 222; of violence, 213; *see also* 832–38

Audience: 13 *note,* 55–56, 89, 158–59, 193, 350, 355–58, 372–75

Authority: opinion of, as evidence, 156–59

Auxiliary verbs: *shall, will,* and other, 764–66, 805

B

Begging the question, 180–81

Beginning: absence of any formula for, 19–21; of a narrative, 242–44; problem of making a, *3–22; see also* Discourse, Introduction

Bibliography: and footnotes, the form of, 825–29; research paper, 385–87; a selected, 426; specimen index card in a, 386; term paper, 430–32

Book report: 830–31

Brackets: 805; and parentheses and dashes, as enclosing punctuation, 792–93

C

Capitals: as required by mechanics of punctuation, 795–96

Caricature: 204 *note; see also* Dominant impression

Case: 805; example of a possessive, 732; how the possessive of nouns is formed, 738–39; in personal pronouns, 739–42

Causal analysis, 114–23, 813–17

Cause: in analytical exposition, 114; circumstances conditioning, 115–16; complex, 119–20; conditions controlling, 117–18; a final caution on, 120; *see also* Causal Analysis, Event

Characterization: a problem in narration, 846–49

Clarity: and rhythm, as aspects of style, 376–77

Class: deductive reasoning by, 167–76; of events, 81–85; for purpose of classification, 70–73; for purpose of illustration, 79–82; *see also* Classification, Reasoning

Classification: in deductive reasoning, 167–76; as a method of exposition, *69–78;* requirements of a scheme of, 71–72; schematized examples of, 72–77; systems, simple and complex, 70–72, 75–77; uses of, in exposition, 72–78; *see also* Class, Genus, Reasoning, Species

Clause: adjectival, 771, 804; adverbial, 771, 777, 804; linking the independent, 784–86; and the sentence and phrase defined, 771–72, 805

Clichés: 315–16; deliberate use of, for tone, 359

Coherence: distinguished from unity, 26; through over-all organization, 26–30; of paragraph, 274–76; in research paper, 427–28; through transition, 30–31

Colon: as linking punctuation, 786

Comma: as linking punctuation, 784–86; paired, as enclosing punctuation, 787, 790–92; as separating punctuation, 787–89

"Comma fault," 785–86, 805

Comparison: 805; degrees of, in adjectives, 745–48; degrees of, in adverbs, 752

Comparison and contrast: 272; interest a factor in significant, 88–89; metaphorical, 340–49; as a method of exposition, *87–96;* purpose a factor in successful, 89–90; ways of organizing material for, 90–96

Complement: effect of stress upon the natural, 774; forms, in objective case, 739–42, 754–55; inner and outer, of verb, 282; of verb, 805–06

Complication: as middle of narrative, 245, 248, 250, 254–55

Composition: organizing principles in, *23–36*

Conclusion: of a narrative, 245–46; and what to avoid in any, 21; *see also* Denouement

Concrete words: *see* Diction

Conditional: a concept in mood, 762

italic type, 799; as an organizing principle, 31; and word order, 772–75; *see also* Definition, Description, Exposition, Organization

Enclosing punctuation, 790–93

Equivocation, 180

Etymology: sample dictionary derivations, 304–08

Event: as cause, 119; as fact, 140–41; meaning of, in narration, 234–41, 257–63; movement of, in time, 232–34; nature of an, 114 *note*, 115; summary and full rendering of, 839–41; *see also* Action, Fact, Time

Evidence: in argument, 153–59; evaluating authority as, 156–59; facts as, 154–56; opinion as, 156–59

Experience: linguistic and social, 9–10; personal, as starting device, 16

Exposition: by analysis, 97–123; by classification, 69–78; by comparison and contrast, 87–96; by definition, 48–69; demands of diction in, 301–02; by extended definition, 63–69; by identification, 47–48; by illustration, 78–87; methods of, *40–123;* narrative as, 110–14, 243, 247, 249, 251, 254–55; value of tone for, 351–52

Expository narration: as distinguished from the ordinary, 110–14

Euphemisms, 313

F

Fact: analysis and propositions of, 140–41, 152; as evidence, 154–56; propositions of action or of, 131–33; *see also* Cause, Event

Fallacies: 180–84; and refutation, 183

False enthusiasm, 372–73

Feelings and states of mind: description of, 832–38

Fiction: as one type of narration, 231 *note; see also* 839–49

Figurative language, 835

Final version: writing and rewriting the, *429–53*

Finite verb: 281 and *note,* 282, 323, 771, 806; *see also* Verbals, Verbs

Footnotes: 121; and bibliography, form of, 825–29; their content and handling, 392–93, 415–17, 419–24

Frame image, 222–23

Function: as distinct from purpose, 110 *note*

G

Gender: 807; how masculine and feminine of nouns are formed, 737–38; of personal pronouns, 739–40; *see also* Agreement of parts of speech

Generalization: in description, 201; as induction, 160–62

Generalized description, 101–03; *see also* Description

Genus: defined in relation to species, 52; as device to clarify a definition, 67; illustrated diagrammatically, 53, 55; *see also* Class, Differentia, Species

Gerund: 732, 807; as a verbal, 767–68; *see also* Participle

Get and *keep:* as auxiliary verbs, 766, 807

Gobbledygook, 317–18, 376

Grammar: 280 *note;* and punctuation and mechanics, handbook of, *727–811;* and rhetoric of sentence, 280–94

H

Handbook of grammar, punctuation, and mechanics, *727–811*

Harmony: and originality, as adjuncts of style, 378–82

Historical present: use of, 258

History of the question, 133

Hyphens: 807; general and specialized uses of, 797–99

I

Identification: as a method of exposition, *47–48*

Ignoring the question, 181–82

Illustration: employed as description, 81–85; as method of exposi-

Paragraph, Cont.

of, 436, 446-48, 450-52; as a convenience to reader, 267-68; linking one with another, 277-80; the method of, 271-77; no formula for, 268; and the sentence, *267-94;* structure and organization of, 269-76; transitional, 277-79; as unit of thought, 269-70

Parallelism: as rhetorical device, 285-86; violations of, 286, 781-82

Parentheses: 808; paired, as enclosing punctuation, 792-93

Participle: 809; dangling, 777-78, 806; forms of, as verbals, 767-69; as the gerund, 732, 767-68, 807; the past, 753, 769; *see also* Modifiers, Phrases, Verbs

Parts of speech: *729-70;* agreement between, 735-37, 754-55, 804; ways of converting one to another, 731-32, 742

Passive voice, 755-56, 809

Pattern: 285; and interest, 221-22; mixing of, in description, 223-24; in narration, 242-54; and point of view, 217-20; and texture in description, *216-30*

"Period fault," 783

Periodic sentences, 289-90, 808

Person, 739, 809

Personal pronouns: case and number of, 738-42; no apostrophe in possessive of, 795; *see also* Pronouns

Personality: impress of, in originality, 379-82

Persuasion: force of, in argument, 191-95; occasion for, 193

Phrase: 809; as an absolute construction, 778-79; the dangling, 778-79; and the sentence and clause defined, 771-72; and verb phrase, 771 *note*

Plurals: how formed, in English, French, Greek, Latin, 733-35

Point of view: in description and narration, 258-63; panoramic, 260, 262-63; and pattern, 217-20

Position: of adjectives in word order, 748-49; of adverbs in word

order, 752-53; purely for emphasis, 32

Possessive case: 732; of the pronoun as adjective, 740

Précis: and outline and summary, 818-24

Predicate, 809

Predicate complement: of intransitive verbs, 755

Premise: major and minor, 273; in reasoning, 167, 169-71, 172-73, 179-80, 184, 273; *see also* Argument, Proposition, Reasoning

Preparation and note-taking, *383-93*

Principal parts: of sentence, 282, 292; of verb, 753, 809-10

Probability, 163, 167

Progressive verb form, 810

Pronouns: 300-01, 810; in apposition, 776; clauses introduced by relative, 776; demonstrative, 278; indefinite, 744; intensive, 743; interrogative, 742-43; kinds of, 742-44; no apostrophe in possessive of personal, 795; and other noun substitutes, 730, 739-43; personal, 739-42; reflexive, 743; relative, 742-43; rules for agreement of, with nouns, 735-36; vague and uncertain reference of, 776-77; *see also* Agreement, Parts of speech

Propaganda: and emotion, 523 *note*

Proportion: of parts for emphasis, 32-33; of parts in narration, 754-56

Proposition: the clear, 131-33; major and minor, 136-40; as premise, 167, 169-74, 179-80, 184; the single, 134-36; statement of, as basis for argument, 130-31, 181; two kinds of, 131; *see also* Argument, Class, Premise, Reasoning

Propositions of action: and analysis, 142-53

Propositions of fact: and analysis, 140-41, 152

Punctuation: 447; enclosing, 790-93; and grammar and mechanics, handbook of, *727-811;* linking,

Theme
Correction
Symbols

symbol	meaning	handbook or text reference
ab	abbreviations	17
ad	adjective or adverb	2.1, 2.2
agr-p	agreement of pronoun and antecedent	1.1b, 1.2, 7
agr-sv	agreement of subject and verb	1.1b, 3.2
ap	apostrophe	18
c	case of nouns or pronouns	1.1d, 1.2a
cap	capitals	19
cf	comma fault	14.1
coh	coherence	7, 9, 11, 12
emp	emphasis	6 and p. 289
frag	sentence fragment	5, 13
gl	glossary and index of terms	p. 804
ital	italics	22
MX	mechanics	17-24
mod	position of modifiers	2.1c, 2.2c, 9, 11
n	numbers	23
¶	paragraph	pp. 267-79
//	parallelism	12.3